Tradition and Innovation

Septuagint and Cognate Studies

Wolfgang Kraus, General Editor

Editorial Board:
Robert Hiebert
Karen H. Jobes
Arie van der Kooij
Siegfried Kreuzer
Philippe Le Moigne

Number 70

Tradition and Innovation
English and German Studies on the Septuagint

Martin Rösel

 **PRESS**

Atlanta

Copyright © 2018 by Martin Rösel

All rights reserved. No part of this work may be reproduced or transmitted in any form or by any means, electronic or mechanical, including photocopying and recording, or by means of any information storage or retrieval system, except as may be expressly permitted by the 1976 Copyright Act or in writing from the publisher. Requests for permission should be addressed in writing to the Rights and Permissions Office, SBL Press, 825 Houston Mill Road, Atlanta, GA 30329 USA.

Library of Congress Cataloging in Publication Control Number: 2018020289

Printed on acid-free paper.

Contents

Preface vii

Part 1. On the LXX in General

1. The Letter of Aristeas to Philocrates, the Temple in Leontopolis, and the Importance of the History of Israelite Religion in the Hellenistic Period 3

2. Schreiber, Übersetzer, Theologen. Die Septuaginta als Dokument der Schrift-, Lese-, und Übersetzungskultur des Judentums 29

3. Translators as Interpreters: Scriptural Interpretation in the Septuagint 57

Part 2. On Specific Texts

4. The Chronological System of Genesis-Septuagint (Genesis 5 and 11) 89

5. Jakob, Bileam und der Messias. Messianische Erwartungen in Gen 49 und Num 22–24 109

6. The Septuagint Version of the Book of Joshua 139

7. Salomo und die Sonne. Zur Rekonstruktion des Tempelweihspruchs 1.Kön 8,12–13 159

8. Deuteronomists in the Septuagint of the Historical Books? 179

9. Die Jungfrauengeburt des endzeitlichen Immanuel.
   Jesaja 7 in der Übersetzung der Septuaginta 197

10. Die Psalmüberschriften des Septuagintapsalters 221

Part 3. Theology and Anthropology

11. Towards a "Theology of the Septuagint" 253

12. A Theology of the Septuagint? Clarifications and Definitions..........273

13. The Reading and Translation of the Divine Name in the
    Masoretic Tradition and the Greek Pentateuch—with an
    Appendix: Frank Shaw's Book on ΙΑΩ..291

14. Der hebräische Mensch im griechischen Gewand.
    Anthropologische Akzentsetzungen in der Septuaginta...................317

15. Nomothesis: The Understanding of the Law in the Septuagint 343

16. Original Publications..365

Ancient Sources Index 369
Ancient Persons and Authors Index 377
Modern Authors Index 378

Preface

In the last two decades, the so-called Septuagint has increasingly attracted the interest of biblical scholars. No longer used solely as an important version for the textual criticism of the Hebrew Bible, it is increasingly understood as an important document that must be studied in its own right. The individual translations demonstrate how the Hellenistic period understood the writings of Israel. Changing hermeneutical conditions influenced the choice of translation equivalents in many places, to the extent that the meaning of *Vorlage* and translation differ in multiple passages.

The collection of essays presented here introduces various aspects of and challenges to Septuagint study. The first section is a collection of papers exploring the Septuagint's cultural background and its implications for the translations (chs. 1–3). The articles in the second section take as their starting point concrete problems posed by translations of individual books of the Septuagint and theorize motivations, literary or otherwise, which might have created deviations between Hebrew and Greek Bible (chs. 4–10). The final portion of the collection is devoted to the question of whether and how a "theology of the Septuagint" can be written and what its outcome might be.

The articles are the result of intense studies of the Greek Bible during the last twenty-five years, most of which occurred during the course of the project *Septuaginta.Deutsch*, the annotated translation of the Septuagint into German. Most of them were published in diverse journals, Festschriften, and proceedings of conferences. Some of them (chs. 3, 6, 11, 13) were originally published in English, while others were translated for inclusion in this collection (chs. 1, 4, 15) or emerged from papers read at Society of Biblical Literature conferences (chs. 8, 12). Some mistakes have been silently corrected, but it was not possible to update the articles by discussing results of more recent research. Occasionally, references to new publications on specific topics have been added, and one article (ch. 13) has been supplemented by an appendix in which I respond to inappropriate criticism. Bibliographical references have been harmonized, while abbreviations for biblical books follow German or American conventions, according to the article's original language.

I would like to thank Wolfgang Kraus and the editorial board for giving me the opportunity to publish these studies in the Society of Biblical Literature's Septuagint and Cognate Studies series. I am especially grateful to Wolfgang, Martin Karrer, and Siegfried Kreuzer for their encouragement and friendly collegiality during the years working on *Septuaginta.Deutsch*. Sincere thanks go to those people who have helped to improve my English: Christian Pieritz (Rostock), Jean Maurais (Montreal), and most of all Cindy Dawson (Houston). Erik Wilm (Rostock) assisted by harmonizing the bibliographies.

The title of this collection is borrowed from the motto of the University of Rostock, *traditio et innovatio*. I offer my deep gratitude for the generous scholarship provided by the "THEORIA–Kurt von Fritz Science Program" that enabled me to complete this volume and to further investigate the issue of a theology of the Septuagint.

Martin Rösel
Rostock, January 2018

Part 1
On the LXX in General

1

The Letter of Aristeas to Philocrates, the Temple in Leontopolis, and the Importance of the History of Israelite Religion in the Hellenistic Period

One of the basic distinctions to be made in the study of the history of Israel is to differentiate between at least two different meanings of the word "history." On the one hand, it can designate the events in themselves. These historical events have to be distinguished, on the other hand, from the reports about them, the *stories*. Outside of the contribution of archaeological data, the *history* of Israel and the history of its religion are only accessible via the *stories* that are preserved in the Hebrew Bible. Here again, one has to distinguish between the historical core (the substance of recollection) of the story in question and the shaping of the narrative (historiography). Thus history and its reception converge within individual stories.

It is against this background that this paper will deal with one such story and develop one of its main themes. This story is recorded in the Letter of Aristeas to Philocrates.[1] The letter is famous in great part because it tells the story about the beginnings of the translation that was to become the LXX. But there is more in the Aristeas narrative, as the following will show.

1. The Letter of Aristeas

The fictional author Aristeas, a Jew pretending to be Greek, reports that king Ptolemy II of Alexandria endowed his librarian with a large amount of money in order to attempt to collect all the books in the world (§9). This

---

1. Swete 1914, 551–606. [See now the translation and commentary by Wright 2015.] The scholarly literature on the Letter of Aristeas is abundant. It may therefore suffice to refer to the most recent studies: Honigman 2003; Wright 2006.

librarian was a philosopher named Demetrius of Phaleron.² He informs the king that the laws of the Jews should also belong in this library, but that they would first require translation into Greek. Moreover, in order to acquire this book, it would be necessary to release Judean slaves and compensate them for their work. Judeans had been enslaved not only under Ptolemy I (301 BCE), but ever since the Persian period, when Judean soldiers were in the country.

In the context of these negotiations, the first sentence with theological significance is uttered, when Aristeas tells the king (§16): τὸν γὰρ πάντων ἐπόπτην καὶ κτίστην θεὸν οὗτοι σέβονται, ὃν καὶ πάντες, ἡμεῖς δέ, βασιλεῦ, προσονομάζοντες ἑτέρως Ζῆνα καὶ Δία· "These people revere God, the overseer and creator of all things, whom all, even we, also worship, O king, using different names; Zeus and Dis."³ The king is persuaded and thus frees over one million prisoners of war (§37). A letter is then sent to Eleazar, the high priest of Jerusalem. He is asked to provide a copy and a translation of the laws of the Judeans "because this legislation is both very philosophical and uncorrupted, inasmuch as it is divine" (διὰ τὸ καὶ φιλοσοφωτέραν εἶναι καὶ ἀκέραιον τὴν νομοθεσίαν ταύτην, ὡς ἂν οὖσαν θείαν. §31).

The request is granted, and a Ptolemaic delegation travels with gifts of great value to Jerusalem. Following a detailed description of the layout and the beauty of the temple and the city, negotiations begin. On this occasion, Aristeas—being himself a Jew—enquires from the high priest Eleazar about several oddities of the Jewish religion, such as the uncleanness of animals. He states that it seems strange to differentiate between clean and unclean, since all creation is one and originates from one God. Eleazar provides fascinating allegorical and symbolic interpretations of the Jewish law (§§143 + 150). He also explains how the relationship between Jews and other peoples should be understood. In doing so he restates a traditional accusation found in Deutero-Isaiah: The Greeks foolishly worship many gods, which they themselves have made, statues of stone and wood.⁴ More stupid are the Egyptians, who not only worship animals but also their cadavers.⁵ Therefore it was necessary for the legislator (= Moses) to

---

2. Concerning the historical figure of Demetrius (who was not the head of the library of Alexandria) see besides the relevant dictionaries: Fraser 1972, 1:312–35, who assumes that Demetrius advised king Ptolemy I to build the library.

3. The translation follows Wright 2015, 122.

4. Isa 44:9–20; see also Wis 13 + 14 and Lucian, *Deor. conc.* 10–1.

5. A completely different approach to this problem can be found in Artapanus,

enclose his people with walls and ramparts (= the commandments of the torah) so that they could worship the one mighty God, free from the foolish doctrines of other nations (§§134–139).

The delegation returns to Alexandria, accompanied by seventy-two translators. Before the work begins, a splendid banquet is celebrated for seven days. The translators turn out to be very educated people, and both the king (§177) and the native philosophers (§296) are amazed by their wisdom. Then a comparatively short account of the translation of the divine law is provided. The representatives of the Jewish citizenship (πολίτευμα) accept the translation and proclaim a curse on anyone who would ever change or revise it. It also explicitly states that there were earlier but inaccurate translations. Apparently, the Letter of Aristeas wants to guard the LXX against all attempts at altering it.[6]

If we now summarize the essential themes of the Letter of Aristeas, we note the following: Obviously it presupposes that there are many Jews, some of whom have been living in Egypt for a considerable period of time. From an outsider's perspective, their religious beliefs and practices are similar to the Greek worship of Zeus. But from insider's perspective, a sharp distinction is made between their religion and the foolish practices of pagan religions. Special emphasis is laid on the temple in Jerusalem, on the one hand, and the obvious superiority of the Jewish religion, on the other. Their laws are philosophical and reasonable, and apparent oddities only confirm the superiority of the legislator. The education of the Jewish translators is at least equal to that of the Greek philosophers of the Ptolemaic court. In contrast with these major themes, the problem of the LXX—for which the letter is famous—is treated rather parenthetically.

These statements raise significant issues. Of special interest is the story's obvious deviation from historical reality, and thus the question of the author's intention. But before this can be examined, we must first address

---

frag 3:12. Here Moses is responsible for the introduction of the worship of Apis, as well as the *necropoleis*.

6. See Fernández Marcos 2000, 43–44. But see Wright 2006, for whom the Letter of Aristeas is the "foundation myth" of the Greek Pentateuch. According to him, this became necessary in the second century BCE because the translation was no longer regarded as dependent on the Hebrew Bible, but rather as an independent document. This thesis relies on the "interlinear paradigm" which has been brought forward by Albert Pietersma: Pietersma 2002. In my view this theory is hardly convincing, see Rösel 2006, for a discussion of the paradigm [ch. 5 in this volume].

the negative bias often found in Hebrew Bible/Old Testament research when it comes to Hellenistic Judaism.

2. Assessing Hellenistic Judaism in Current Research on the Hebrew Bible/Old Testament

Several areas within scholarship on the history of Israel have received more attention than others.[7] Until recently, one such area of research was the quest for the early history of Israel, and the issue of the conquest of Canaan and the emergence of kingship. In recent years, the monarchical period has received more attention. Research has focused on the development of governmental structures and the initial stages of the production and transmission of scriptural texts. Furthermore, the development of the Israelite concept of God has attracted particular interest following the archaeological finds from Kuntillet ʿAjrud, Khirbet el-Qom, and Ekron.[8] Moreover, the Persian period also grew increasingly important, an outcome of the tendency to date biblical texts to this period.[9]

The Hellenistic period is—putting it plainly—almost entirely left to New Testament scholarship or historians of antiquity. A reference to the seminal work of Martin Hengel may suffice at this point.[10]

But there are further examples: Herbert Donner states explicitly in his history of Israel that the Hellenistic period does not belong to the history of Israel.[11] He concludes his work with a brief survey of this era, dealing only with Judaism in Palestine. Rainer Albertz deals with the problem in a similar way in his history of Israelite religion. He considers the period as a time of transition and does not address topics or scriptures belonging to Hellenistic Judaism outside of biblical texts—with the unusual exception of Enoch.[12] Even Otto Kaiser, who has frequently emphasized in recent years the "importance of the Greek world for the theology of the Old Testament," only wrote a few lines on Alexandria in his most recent publication on the subject. He focused instead on the depiction of the classical

---

7. This section is mainly about German scholarship.
8. Keel and Uehlinger 1992.
9. See Koch 1995, esp. 52–53. As an example of this tendency it may suffice to refer readers to Kratz 2004.
10. Hengel 1988.
11. Donner 2001, 474.
12. Albertz 1997, 591.

topos of Athens and Jerusalem, referring to both of them as "birthplaces of theology."[13]

Furthermore, even scholars who deal with the Hellenistic period from the perspective of the Old Testament often do not take Alexandrian Judaism into account. Again, a few references to recent publications may suffice: Paolo Sacchi omitted to write even a short chapter about the diaspora in his history of the Second Temple period.[14] Ernst Haag's description of the Hellenistic age betrays a similarly narrow view, which can already be seen in the subtitle of the book: *Israel und die Bibel im 4. bis 1. Jahrhundert v.Chr.* [*Israel and the Bible from the Fourth to the First Century BCE*].[15] Although he appropriately describes Alexandria as "a center of arts and science" that could easily to be reached from Palestine (107), he devotes only four pages to the literature of Hellenistic Jewish authors, including the LXX.[16] It is obvious then that Hellenistic Judaism, especially in its Alexandrian context, is beyond the scope of Old Testament research and therefore rarely receives attention in the curriculum of the theological faculties.

There are various reasons for this reluctance. Herbert Donner argued that the movement from Israel to Judaism represented a major shift. According to him, the vivid cultic religion of Israel had become a religion of the book (German: *Buchreligion*) mainly concerned with the exposition of the torah and living in accordance with its regulations. Donner maintains that the advent of Alexander the Great must be seen as a decisive event marking the end of the Israel's history and giving way to Judaism. This position is problematic since the Judaism of this period formulates its identity based on an unbroken connection with Israel's traditions.[17] Moreover, even if mentioned briefly in the Letter of Aristeas, the importance of the Jerusalem temple is obvious. We even know of pilgrimages from the

---

13. Kaiser 2000.

14. Sacchi 2000. In Markus Sasse's *Geschichte Israels in der Zeit des Zweiten Tempels* (Sasse 2004), a total of seven pages dealing with the Egyptian diaspora can be found (pp. 107–14).

15. Haag 2003.

16. This narrow perspective is not limited to Christian researchers; see, e.g., a renowned scholar like Cecil Roth in his article on the diaspora in the *Encyclopedia Judaica* (1971, 642): "During the period of the Second Temple Jewish history was mainly concentrated in Eretz Israel."

17. Walter 1994, 155.

diaspora to the temple.[18] Thus it is far too simplistic to state that a transformation took place from a cultic religion to one focused on a book.

Robert Hanhart, Germany's most eminent scholar on the LXX and things pertaining to Hellenistic Judaism, argues differently. He also identifies a transition, which he explains *historically* as the decline of the nation of Israel and the emergence of the diaspora. From the perspective of *tradition criticism*, the change is marked by the beginnings of apocalypticism and the gradual end of sapiential and historical traditions as in the book of Chronicles. However, his analysis of the *intellectual history* (German: *Geistesgeschichte*) of the period is more significant: the Hellenistic period is seen as the era when prophecy ceased.[19] In his view, this era is therefore merely a transitional or interim period. Renewed grandeur and inspiration only came with early Christianity.[20]

The problems associated with such approaches are—in my view—mostly unresolved and require more extensive scholarly dialogue. For example, it is important to note that the phenomenon of inspired exposition of Scripture is not limited to early Christianity. There is ample evidence of such practices in the Qumran pesharim.[21]

3. The Significance of the History of Israelite Religion in the Hellenistic Period

3.1. Basic Observations

Given this state of research, I will outline the importance of the Hellenistic period for the history of Israelite religion. There are good reasons to pay more attention to this era and to abandon the narrow concept of Israel's religious history outlined above that focuses mainly on the period of Israel's monarchy on the one hand and the region of Canaan/Palestine on the other.

The first reason for doing so is based on the population count mentioned in the Letter of Aristeas. One million Jewish prisoners of war are said to live in Egypt. This number is probably exaggerated, but Philo (*Flacc.* 43) also reports that approximately one million Jews lived in Egypt

---

18. Schwartz 1996.
19. Meyer 1959; Weiss 1999.
20. Hanhart 1999c, 151.
21. Koch 2000.

during his lifetime. Josephus provides figures that are largely confirmed by modern research. According to him, about 150,000–180,000 Jews lived in Alexandria, and they accounted for about a third of its population. Papyri and inscriptions on tombstones also provide evidence of a sizeable Judeo-Aramaic diaspora outside of Alexandria, at least from the Persian period onward, as documented in the papyri from Elephantine.[22] Taking into account the Jewish population in the Seleucid territories—particularly Syria and Babylonia—one gets the distinct impression that already in the Hellenistic period more Jews lived abroad than in the territory of Palestine.[23] In my view, this fact alone challenges the scholarly focus on Palestine. Another consideration could be added: if it is true that foreign armies passed through Palestine approximately two hundred times between 323 and 63 BCE, we must abandon the idea that its Judaism was isolated.[24]

Several questions arise: How could Israel preserve its identity while living in the diaspora? How did religious practices that were developed at the periphery of the cultic center influence the traditions of the Hebrew Bible or the formation of its canon? This is a central theme of the book of Esther and the Daniel narratives.[25] Moreover, Esther even uses formal elements of the Greek novel. It is worth considering whether the adoption, reworking, and expansion of the older Daniel material during the Hellenistic period took place mainly because of its affinities with diaspora issues. These texts could provide answers to new questions arising in the pre-Maccabean era concerning the dangers of assimilation to the surrounding culture.

Another important reason for studying this era is that some texts or editorial layers of the Hebrew Bible obviously stem from the Hellenistic period. This can be safely assumed for books such as Daniel and Ecclesiastes, but remains controversial in the case of some of the Psalms or specific redactional layers in other books.[26]

---

22. See the work of Erich S. Gruen (2002), who especially emphasizes the positive aspects of living in the diaspora.

23. See Hegermann 1989; and Sterling 2001, 267–68, who estimates the Jewish population in Alexandria to be twice as large as the population of Jerusalem.

24. Smith 1987, 48, with a detailed list in n. 57 at pp. 176–77.

25. Willi-Plein 1991.

26. An often-used sample for the dating of a text from the Hebrew Bible to Hellenistic times is Ps 110; see Knauf 2000. Arguments for an earlier date are more convincing; see Koch 2002. For specific redactional layers see, e.g., the "redaction of the poor" (German: *Armenredaktion*), which is postulated by Hossfeld and Zenger for the

While one may remain unconvinced by these theories (even more so in the case of the so-called Copenhagen school and its methodology) such arguments provide ample reasons to be acquainted with the themes and intellectual issues of this era.[27] In this way, the pros and cons can be properly weighted and balanced judgments made. The importance of the Hellenistic period is further underscored by the fact that some biblical books only reached their final form in that era—final in terms of the consonantal base of the Masoretic Text—as the texts from the Judean desert make clear. This is controversial in the case of the Psalter, but commonly agreed for books such as Joshua and Jeremiah, in part because of their divergent Greek version.

3.2. The Religious Literature of the Hellenistic Period

Returning to the Letter of Aristeas, it must first be stated that we are dealing with a piece of literature belonging to a fundamentally different literary genre than that of the biblical texts. Presented as a report, the letter makes use of elements of Greek historiography, having its particular narrative intentions. The letter is generally assumed to have been written in the late second century BCE (about 120) and is considered a near-prototypical Hellenistic-Jewish work.[28] It is part of a development that began about a century earlier with Demetrius (about 200 BCE) and Eupolemus (about 155 BCE). These writings share characteristics that can be seen in the dialogue between Aristeas and the high priest Eleazar: the torah traditions are presupposed but are obviously in need of interpretation or explanation. Therefore rational or allegorical expositions are provided. This development reached its climax in the later work of Philo. We can conclude, therefore, that Hellenistic Judaism represents a step further away from the production of Scripture to its reception—at least as far as the torah is concerned. This phenomenon is one of the reasons for the alleged transformation of Judaism into a "religion of the book," as Donner theorized. This characterization is biased and unnecessarily negative, since it is through

---

book of Psalms (Hossfeld and Zenger 2000) or Christoph Levin's theory of a redaction of the book of Amos by the *anawim* (Levin 1997).

27. On the Copenhagen school, see, e.g., Kofoed 2005, but see also the harsh review by Thompson 2005, entitled "The Role of Faith in Historical Research."

28. The dating varies; see the overview by Sollamo 2001, 331–34.

such intellectual efforts of reception and actualization that Jews were able to formulate their identity within their surrounding culture.

There are two questions worth considering at this point. The first is to ask how this early Hellenistic literature sought to be understood. As pointed out above, Aristeas placed great value on the fact that the translation of the torah was authorized by both king and philosophers. This is because of its content, which is, and I quote, "both very philosophical and uncorrupted, inasmuch as it is divine" (§31).[29] Thus the Jewish legislation is set on the same level as the Greek philosophical tradition. A quote from Aristobulus, dated to the middle of the second century BCE, demonstrates how extensive this conception was: "It is clear that Plato followed the tradition of the law that we use" (frag. 3 in Eusebius). But even earlier, the LXX translation of Genesis betrayed similar tendencies when shaping Gen 1 and 2 according to the pattern of Plato's *Timaeus* dialogue.[30]

This leads me to conclude that the circumstances specific to the diaspora require us to understand this literature as apologetic in nature from its inception.[31] It was initially directed inward, presumably to assert the superiority of Judaism, in ways comparable to what we find in Dan 1–6, Esther, and Judith. The tendency from Demetrius onward to resolve inconsistencies or contradictions found in the biblical texts also fit in this picture.[32] In the LXX, such harmonizing tendencies and the desire for consistency become a feature of translation technique.

However, it remains a matter of controversy whether this literature did have an impact outside Jewish communities, whether it only served the purposes of Jewish self-affirmation, whether it was also was directed to the proselytes or God-fearers, and whether these writings were actually read by people of other religions. The literature of this period relates the various positions debated, from assimilation on the one hand to demarcation from

---

29. For a similar interpretation, see Tcherikover 1958.

30. For an exhaustive treatment of this topic, see Rösel 1994, 72–87. The theory of Platonic influence on Greek Genesis has been accepted by several scholars, e.g., Hendel 2013, 88–95. Unfortunately, Hendel provides no references and thus implies that the theory is his own.

31. With Kaiser 2000, 332.

32. See especially Artapanus (for which see Walter 1980, 125), who apparently responds to accusations by Manetho and states that Moses had been a loyal subordinate of a ruler named Chenephres and helped Egypt flourish (frag. 3.3).

the surrounding culture on the other. These negotiations must be part of the picture that is drawn of this period.

The second question is closely related to the first and is concerned with what constitutes the Bible and the question of canon. The phenomenon of rewritten Bible can be observed in the literature of this era both in Alexandria and Palestine.[33] Strictly speaking, this is nothing new since the book of Chronicles can also be understood as a reformulation of existing traditions.

However, these attempts become much more frequent in the Hellenistic period. Works such as the book of Jubilees or Qumran texts such as the Genesis Apocryphon or the Temple Scroll are well known. Greek works such as Josephus's *Antiquities* or the staging of the Exodus story by Ezekiel the Tragedian should also be mentioned. While in earlier times the biblical texts were updated via editorial layers or *Fortschreibung*, we now observe a tendency toward reformulation. Obviously, both ways of relating to older traditions were used side by side for some time: The updating by the addition of editorial layers can be found in Daniel or Esther, up to the time of the Maccabees. In Hellenistic Alexandria, however, the tendency to reformulate or to rewrite the biblical material was apparently more acceptable than updating. Various factors may have come into play such as the Greek language and the accompanying intellectual worldview. One should also mention the classical argument in favor of antiquity (*presbyteron kreitton*): In Hellenistic times, something honored by time was considered superior. We can allude once more to the citation from Aristobulus quoted above: Plato, had recognized, as a matter of course, the legislation of his predecessor Moses.[34]

As a part of this development, a revisional process began as early as the second century BCE, with the aim of adjusting the translations of the Holy Scriptures to their time-honored, authoritative originals. This is observable in the so-called kaige recension, which is known from the texts of the Judaean desert. The final outcome of this recensional process some centuries later is the standardized Masoretic Text as we have it today. Although

---

33. See especially Brooke 2000 and Fröhlich 1996, 91–104, on "The Beginnings of the 'Rewritten Bibles' "; this is the title of the fourth chapter of her book.

34. Pilhofer 1990, esp. 17–75 for the Greek and 143–220 for the Jewish Hellenistic literature.

our Bible translations are based on the Masoretic Text, this textual tradition does not always represent the original.[35]

Another dynamic within Judaism appears alongside the process of *rewriting*, whose importance can hardly be overestimated. It becomes obvious—and this might already have been obvious to the Alexandrian scholarly community—that there was no such thing as an original or single meaning for any biblical text. Instead, it became clear that the old traditions were in need of actualization. To put it more pointedly, it is only by updating texts for their new contexts that their message becomes tangible. This phenomenon can be seen, inter alia, in the exposition of Jeremiah's seventy years in Dan 9, in the Pesher Habakkuk from Qumran, or in the New Testament's use of Scripture, for example, Gen 12:3 in Gal 3:8. Thus it becomes clear that research into the reception history of biblical texts is essential in order to understand the particularities of this era.[36]

Because of this openness to new understandings of tradition, Hellenistic Judaism developed an essential means by which it could negotiate the diaspora context.[37] As Jan Assmann initially posited, one could say that monotheism had become translatable, at least to some extent. The exclusive connection between God and his people—which Assmann criticized—had been loosened.[38] Again, this was not an entirely new development, since a similar process can also be observed in the Persian period. The titles for God were modified, and formulations such as "supreme God" or "God of heaven" became more common.[39] Thus the Babylonian diaspora already felt the need to emphasize these new traits. It is precisely the issue of naming the divine that brings us back to the Letter of Aristeas.

3.3. The Supreme God and His Temples in Leontopolis and Jerusalem: A New Interpretation of the Letter of Aristeas

Such a development could become problematic. According to Robert Hanhart, the translatability of the Jewish concept of God was the greatest

---

35. An overview with further literature can be found in Rösel 2002.
36. Rösel 2005.
37. Obviously the situation in the Babylonian diaspora was quite different. Here the aspect of the Scripture's preservation was more important, see Schürer 1986, 3.1:5–10.
38. Assmann 2010.
39. As documented in Niehr 1990, 49–60.

danger in this era: it led to the *status confessionis*.⁴⁰ If the One God could be addressed by different names, monotheism would be perverted and in danger of turning into syncretism. In the first section of the Letter of Aristeas, we saw how this very argument was made in the fictional conversation between Aristeas and King Ptolemy II: The Greeks worship the same God as the Jews, only by a different name. However, the narrative continues and the high priest Eleazar later clearly rejects such ideas by mocking the statues of the Greeks and the Egyptians' zoomorphic gods. Thus the Aristeas narrative can be understood as a dialogue *within* Judaism on the issue of dealing with foreign concepts of god—and therefore about the *status confessionis*.⁴¹

When examining the Letter of Aristeas's account of the translation of the Scriptures into Greek, we find that it also relates to Hellenistic Judaism's reworking of its traditions and the accompanying dialogues and debates.

A short overview of the history of research on the Letter of Aristeas seems appropriate at this point. Scholarly literature on the letter has become vast, therefore it is necessary to limit ourselves to a few important topics. One should bear in mind that most scholars study the Letter of Aristeas primarily in order to find clues concerning the origins of the LXX. However, there are only a few lines at the beginning and in the final part of the letter that relate to the translation. Therefore two fundamental questions have to be distinguished, in accordance with the distinction made above between *history* and *story*.

The first question has to do with the historical information concerning the origins and occasion of the LXX. A strong consensus exists in recent research about the fact that Aristeas refers to the Pentateuch only, and not the entire Old Greek Bible. The second question is distinct from this one and is concerned with the intention of the author in his late second century context and whether we can infer the position against which he argues from the way he defends the LXX.

---

40. Hanhart 1999b, 171.

41. Similar Tcherikover 1958, 79; see also Honigman 2003, 146. Greek philosophers such as the Stoics could have held a position similar to Let. Aris. 16. It is questionable—so the late Nikolaus Walter in a private communication—whether there is a fundamental disagreement between "Aristeas" and "Eleazar" as supposed above. Could both positions be correct (so Walter)? Or is rather Aristeas's position in §16 only conceivable as an outward-facing statement, and not acceptable within Judaism?

1. The Letter of Aristeas to Philocrates 15

On the topic of the origins of the LXX, most scholars agree that the Letter of Aristeas is not reliable on the most important points: The translation was not carried out on behalf of the king or in order to furnish the library of Alexandria, but because of needs internal to the Jewish community.

Nevertheless, there have been repeated attempts to establish as historically reliable at minimum the basic thesis of the letter. Thus in 1956 Bruno Stricker published the theory that the translation had been imposed by the Ptolemies against the will of the Jews in order to further hellenize the population.[42] This was decisively rejected by Robert Hanhart.[43] Leonhard Rost and Dominique Barthélemy also supported the theory of a royal commissioning. According to them, this was important for constitutional reasons, in order to grant Alexandrian Jewry certain privileges.[44]

More recently two further attempts were undertaken to affirm the historical reliability of the Letter of Aristeas's core.[45] Classicist and historian Wolfgang Orth starts with the assumption that even in pseudepigraphical writings, not everything can be made up; Aristeas had to rely on what was commonly known in his community.[46] Since the ambitions of the first two Ptolemaic kings in the fields of science and culture were well known, the picture drawn by Aristeas of the circumstances is "of astonishing reality."[47] He further assumes that in the context of the Peripatetic school, there was great interest in other people's *nomoi*. This in turn exerted influence on

---

42. Stricker 1956.
43. Hanhart 1999a.
44. Rost 1970; Barthélemy 1978.
45. See also the detailed argumentation by Isserlin 1973, who tries to demonstrate that the names of the translators originate in Palestine. See also Honigman 2003, 117, who assumes connections between the king and the library on the one hand and the Jewish community in Alexandria on the other hand.
46. Orth 2001.
47. Orth 2001, 103 (in German). Both considerations are not conclusive. The fact that the Letter of Aristeas shows only little interest in issues of the translation suggests that this part of the narrative was an independent tradition (Sollamo 2001, 330 even doubts the unity of the letter), older than the letter itself. Obviously, a well-known legend (which was transmitted separately later on) had been taken up. Moreover, the interest of the first Ptolemies in matters of culture and education was not a secret, but was common knowledge in Alexandria due to the existence of the *Museion* and the library.

Demetrius of Phalerum and the Ptolemies. The translations by Manetho and Berossus should also be attributed to this movement.

The most problematic area in this line of argumentation remains that there is absolutely no evidence for the translation being done under royal patronage. Moreover, the type of documents that served as basis for the judicial system in third century Alexandria is also a matter of dispute.[48] Direct evidence of translated legal texts is sparse and emerges only in later periods (as Orth himself admits).[49] Furthermore, one finds that the Greek translation of the Torah left no traces in non-Jewish writings.[50] In my view, this is a weakness of all theories arguing for an official commissioning of the LXX.

More importantly, the translation of the book of Genesis was clearly carried out prior to and independently from the other books of the Torah.[51] Thus the need for a *nomos* cannot be the purpose of the translation. In addition, recent research indicates that the order in which the translations of the Pentateuch were produced may also differ from the usual view: it is possible that the book of Deuteronomy was translated before Leviticus and Numbers.[52] Even if this theory is still disputed, the fact remains that there was no literary unit resembling the Greek Pentateuch in the mid-third century. Thus the main argument of Orth cannot be maintained.

The reasoning of Nina Collins is different. She has expanded and reformulated her earlier thesis that the Letter of Aristeas is historically reliable in almost all details.[53] Based on a combination of various chronological figures, mostly from Christian writers, she concludes that the Pentateuch was translated in 281 BCE by seventy-one translators.[54] This took place because of Ptolemaic pressure and against the will of Alexandrian Jews. According to her, there was no Jewish need for a translation, since Alexandrian Jews spoke mostly Aramaic at that time. The fact that Philo and Josephus were using the Aristeas tradition without feeling the need

---

48. See Huss 1994, 6–9; Modrzejewski 1963; 1997, 99–119.
49. Orth 2001, 107. Recently published papyri now provide evidence that the Greek Deuteronomy was employed as *nomos* for divorces in Jewish communities; see Cowey 2004. The text of the papyri can be found in Cowey and Maresch 2001.
50. See J. Collins 2000, 6–13, and the collection by Stern 1976.
51. Rösel 1994, 142–44; 257.
52. That is the proposal of den Hertog 2004, which requires further discussion.
53. N. Collins 2000; see also N. Collins 1992.
54. N. Collins 2000, 141; on p. 178 she gives the date 291 BCE, obviously by mistake.

to correct it is in her view another element in favor of the historicity of Aristeas's report.

There are several reasons why this theory cannot be accepted.[55] One factor is the uncritical use of very late sources, such as quotations of the church fathers. Even more important is the fact that recent LXX research is almost entirely ignored. To cite one example, the research done by the so-called Finnish school (I. Soisalon-Soininen and R. Sollamo) has demonstrated that one can no longer assume that the Pentateuch was translated as a unit in one pass. Moreover, the Letter of Aristeas's apologetic character was not sufficiently acknowledged and important contributions to the research on the Letter of Aristeas (e.g., R. Hanhart, E. Tov, and S. Jellicoe) were not taken into account. The plethora of (now classical) arguments against the historicity of Aristeas's report are not addressed.[56]

In spite of these recent attempts, more convincing is the position that does not consider Letter of Aristeas as a historically accurate report concerning the beginnings of the LXX. The reasons that motivated the translation must lie elsewhere. In my view, it is more likely that Genesis was translated first, presumably for exclusively inner-Jewish discussions within the intellectual sphere of the *Museion*, and not for liturgical reasons. As such, this translation can rightly be considered part of the apologetic literature of Hellenistic Judaism, and a demonstration of the interest of Middle Platonism for protological matters, to which Manetho and Berossus attest in their own way.[57]

The second key question introduced above relates to the intention of the Letter of Aristeas in the context of the second century BCE. Again, the widely accepted opinion is based on evidence provided by the text itself; it is said that there had been earlier, less accurate attempts to translate the Hebrew Bible (§§30–31; see also the note on Theodektes the tragic poet in §316). Moreover, after its acceptance by the king and the Jewish *politeuma*,

---

55. See already Rösel 1994, 10 n. 36.

56. See the detailed review by Fernández Marcos (2002). One could put together a long list of studies missing in the book's bibliography, among them especially Schmidt 1986, which could have prevented the author from being so optimistic about the historical reliability of the Letter of Aristeas.

57. Rösel 1994, 254–60; accepted and expanded by Kreuzer 2004. Honigman 2003, 146–47 achieves similar results, but she considers the Pentateuch too much as a unit and pays no attention to the fact that the books were translated separately, each of them with characteristic intentions.

changes to the translation were expressly forbidden (§311). Such a statement is to be interpreted against the background of the early revisionary process initiated before the end of the second century BCE. The traditional version of the LXX should be safeguarded against such revisions toward the Hebrew text.[58] A variation of this argument was put forward by Sidney Jellicoe, who assumed that the Letter of Aristeas was arguing against a rival version of the Torah that had been translated in Leontopolis.[59] This theory did not receive much attention, presumably because scholarship is mostly concerned with Alexandria. But I would argue that Jellicoe's hypothesis merits further consideration, although with some modifications.

One should keep in mind that the Letter of Aristeas was written after the successful conclusion of the Maccabean revolt in Jerusalem. Surprisingly enough, nothing in the text refers to these events. But other more important topics are also omitted from the letter. Nothing is said about Jewish synagogues in Egypt, which we know existed from the third century onward, even outside of Alexandria.[60] Even in the Talmud, the Great Synagogue of Alexandria was considered a sign of Israel's greatness (y. Sukkah 5:1, 55a–b). Moreover, we have an inscription from the second century BCE commemorating the consecration of the synagogue of Athribis in the Nile Delta. This synagogue was dedicated to the supreme God *theos hypsistos* (*CIJ* 2.1443), which is astonishing since this is also a common designation of Zeus.

These observations cast doubts on one of the letter's concerns: It is hardly conceivable that there were synagogues in Egypt without Scriptures in the third or second century, or that a multitude of Jews lived without biblical texts in their common language. I would conclude that when Aristeas would imply that there was no Torah in the land, it is because he desires to favor a specific textual tradition. The emphasis on the importance of the temple and the fact that the translators and the scrolls came from Israel can be interpreted as a desire to promote the Palestinian version of the text.

---

58. See particularly Klijn 1964. Kahle 1962, 222–79 is dealing with the phenomenon of different version and their acceptance. See also above n. 6 on the deviant position by Wright 2006. Also Hacham 2005, sees the Letter of Aristeas as a foundational myth, though for the whole Hellenistic Judaism.

59. Jellicoe 1965–1966.

60. Modrzejewski 1997, 88–99 (with bibliography) and Claussen 2002, 83–112; also Kasher 1985, 106–7; and Hengel 1971.

Aristeas conceals an even more important fact: there was in this period an authentic Jewish temple in Egypt founded by the son of the high priest Onias III. Onias IV had been deposed from his priestly functions during the pre-Maccabean conflict in Jerusalem. His temple in Leontopolis was in use for about 230 years (since the 60s of the second century), until it was closed by the Romans in 73/74 CE—thus in operation even after the destruction of the Jerusalem temple.[61] This temple was so important for Ptolemaic Egypt that it was provided its own army corps. The Mishnah later concedes that its sacrifices could be considered fully valid under certain circumstances (m. Menah. 13:10).[62] Apparently, even the Deut 12 commandment calling for the centralization of worship was subject to new interpretations.[63]

Reinterpretations such as these may have been facilitated by the fact that according to Josephus, the temple was legitimized by resorting to the biblical prophecy of Isa 19:19: "In that day shall there be an altar to the LORD in the midst of the land of Egypt, and a pillar at the border thereof to the LORD" (KJV).[64] As with the synagogue of Athribis, this temple was also consecrated to the supreme God (*theos megistos*), as Josephus again relates.[65] Once more, the antique status of the Isaiah quotation obviously served as evidence for the legitimacy of the temple, which was accepted by Ptolemaic royals.

It is likely that this legitimizing exposition of Isa 19:19 can be traced back to Leontopolis traditions and that it constitutes part of the temple's foundation myth. This is supported by the research of Zacharias Frankel and Arie van der Kooij, who both found reasons to posit that the LXX version of Isaiah was translated in Leontopolis.[66] Thus, we may assume

---

61. For Leontopolis, see, e.g., Kasher 1985, 119–35, Frey 1999; Taylor 1998.
62. Schürer 1986, 3.1:145–47.
63. Gruen 1997, 61–62, who refers to rabbinic interpretations (Sifre to Deut 70) according to which it was allowed to perform rituals in places that were mentioned by the prophets, so that offerings in Leontopolis would be permissible.
64. See Josephus *B.J.* 7.426–432, also *A.J.* 13.64–68; Frey 1999, 193.
65. *A.J.* 13, 64–70. It is interesting to notice that according to Pseudo Eupolemus frag 1:5 also Mount Gerizim was connected to this title, the name "Argarizin" should be translated as "mountain of the Most High"; see Walter 1980, 142; Holladay 1983, 183 n. 21.
66. Frankel 1841, 40, n. f.; van der Kooij 1981, 60–65. The most recent study on the LXX of Isaiah, Baer 2001, 279, does not even consider the location of the translation, but assumes a "presumed situation in the Alexandrinian Diaspora."

the presence of a second Jewish intellectual center in Egypt besides Alexandria.[67] Yet, the Letter of Aristeas does not even mention it. It is therefore likely that the text is engaging in an implicit polemic against Leontopolis and its temple, by emphasizing the beauty and importance of the Jerusalem temple (§§83–99). In addition, as we reach the end of the text, we find every other translation placed under curse by the Alexandrian community (§§310–311). This aligns quite well with the observation that both Demetrius and Aristobulus made use of the Pentateuch only. Other scriptures were not deemed worthy of interpretation. Around 150 years later, Philo's community also apparently received only the Greek Torah as its canonical Bible, not the later scriptures—despite these being known.[68]

We can therefore consider whether the Letter of Aristeas could have held a similar position almost 150 years earlier. The author acknowledged the Jerusalem temple and its Torah-oriented traditions (i.e., a priestly Sadducee perspective) but not the Egyptian temple and its expanded canon of Scriptures.[69] Thus the discussion concerning the narrator's motivations outlined above is not simply about defending the Greek Pentateuch against a rival translation or a revision, but relates to the question of the expanded canon.

My investigation has thus reached its end. Although this interpretation of the Letter of Aristeas does not rest on absolute evidence, it seems a plausible basis for further discussion.[70] It addresses the diversity of themes that the letter itself addresses, as well as the diversity present within early Hellenistic Judaism. Therefore this proposal can help us move beyond some of the presuppositions of earlier Aristeas research.

4. Conclusion

The above-mentioned observations have shown that the Hellenistic period is an integrated part of the history of Israel and its religion; it should not

---

67. According to Kasher 1985, 126–27, even the organizational structure, the *politeuma*, was the same in Leontopolis and in Alexandria.
68. This is inferred from the observation that Philo makes use of passages from the Pentateuch to support his arguments, even when there were passages from the prophets that would have been more convincing. Therefore Amir (1983, 68) concludes that in Philo's view the Torah had an authority that surpasses that of the other books.
69. The Sadducees only accepted the Torah, see Weiss 1998, 592–93.
70. See Fernández Marcos 2000, 43, and his comments on earlier works.

be treated separately. The portrait of the Hellenistic age as merely a phase of transition should be abandoned. The same is true for presentations of Israel's religion in this era as a book-religion (German: *Buchreligion*), disconnected from real life. Instead, we are dealing with a formative period and its intense struggles over the appropriate ways of dealing with Israel's traditions. This led to efforts in safeguarding the wording of the biblical texts and to translate them.

In the Hellenistic period, biblical texts were reinterpreted and even reformulated. However, these new texts were not intended to replace the originals, but influenced how they came to be understood.[71] Many important traditions found in the New Testament and the early church were newly formulated on the basis of these scriptural reinterpretations. My proposal is therefore meant to promote the idea that scholars in the field of Old Testament/Hebrew Bible should do more to engage these questions and to view the Hellenistic period as an integral part of their research.

Bibliography

Albertz, Rainer. 1997. *Religionsgeschichte Israels in alttestamentlicher Zeit 2. Vom Exil bis zu den Makkabäern*. 2nd ed. ATD Ergänzungsreihe 8.2. Göttingen: Vandenhoeck & Ruprecht.

Amir, Yehoshua. 1983. *Die hellenistische Gestalt des Judentums bei Philon von Alexandrien*. FJCD 5. Neukirchen-Vluyn: Neukirchener Verlag.

Assmann, Jan. 2010. *The Price of Monotheism*. Stanford: Stanford University Press.

Baer, David A. 2001. *When We All Go Home: Translation and Theology in LXX Isaiah 56–66*. JSOTSup 318. Sheffield: Sheffield Academic.

Barthélemy, Dominique 1978. "Pourquoi la Torah a-t-elle été traduite en Grec?" Pages 322–40 in *Études d'histoire du texte de l'Ancien Testament*. Edited by Dominique Barthélemy. OBO 21. Göttingen: Vandenhoeck & Ruprecht; Fribourg: Presses Universitaires.

Brooke, George J. 2000. "Rewritten Bible." *EncDSS* 2:777–81.

Claussen, Carsten. 2002. *Versammlung, Gemeinde, Synagoge: Das hellenistisch-jüdische Umfeld der frühchristlichen Gemeinden*. SUNT 27. Göttingen: Vandenhoeck & Ruprecht.

---

71. See the important treatment of this topic by Hengel 1994.

Collins, John J. 2000. *Between Athens and Jerusalem: Jewish Identity in Hellenistic Diaspora*. 2nd ed. Biblical Resource Series. Grand Rapids: Eerdmans.

Collins, Nina L. 1992. "281 BCE: The Year of the Translation of the Pentateuch into Greek under Ptolemy II." Pages 403–503 in *Septuagint, Scrolls, and Cognate Writings: Papers Presented to the International Symposium on the Septuagint and Its Relations to the Dead Sea Scrolls and Other Writings, Manchester, 1990*. Edited by George J. Brooke and Barnabas Lindars. SCS 33. Atlanta: Scholars Press.

———. 2000. *The Library in Alexandria and the Bible in Greek*. VTSup 82. Leiden: Brill.

Cowey, James M. S. 2004. "Das ägyptische Judentum in hellenistischer Zeit." Pages 24–43 in vol. 2 of *Im Brennpunkt: Die Septuaginta; Studien zur Entstehung und Bedeutung der Griechischen Bibel*. Edited by Siegfried Kreuzer und Jürgen Peter Lesch. BWANT 161. Stuttgart: Kohlhammer.

Cowey, James M. S., and Klaus Maresch. 2001. *Urkunden des Politeuma der Juden von Herakleopolis (144/3–133/2 v. Chr) (P. Polit. Iud.)*. Abhandlungen der Nordrhein-Westfälischen Akademie der Wissenschaften, Papyrologica Coloniensia. Wiesbaden: VS Verlag für Sozialwissenschaften.

Donner, Herbert. 2001. *Geschichte des Volkes Israel und seiner Nachbarn in Grundzügen 2. Von der Königszeit bis zu Alexander dem Großen: Mit einem Ausblick auf die Geschichte des Judentums bis Bar Kochba; mit Zeittafeln*. 3rd ed. GAT Ergänzungsreihe 4.2. Göttingen: Vandenhoeck & Ruprecht.

Fernández Marcos, Natalio. 2000. *The Septuagint in Context: Introduction to the Greek Versions of the Bible*. Leiden: Brill.

———. 2002. Review of *The Library in Alexandria and the Bible in Greek*, by Nina Collins. *JSJ* 33:97–101.

Frankel, Zacharias. 1841. *Vorstudien zu der Septuaginta*. Leipzig: Vogel.

Fraser, Peter M. 1972. *Ptolemaic Alexandria I–III*. Oxford: Clarendon.

Frey, Jörg. 1999. "Temple and Rival Temple: The Cases of Elephantine, Garizim, and Leontopolis." Pages 171–203 in *Gemeinde ohne Tempel: Community without Temple; Zur Substituierung und Transformation des Jerusalemer Tempels und seines Kults im Alten Testament, antiken Judentum und frühen Christentum*. Edited by Beate Ego, Armin Lange, Kathrin Ehlers, and Peter Pilhofer. WUNT 118. Tübingen: Mohr Siebeck.

Fröhlich, Ida. 1996. *"Time and Times and Half a Time": Historical Consciousness in the Jewish Literature of the Persian and Hellenistic Eras*. JSPSup 19. Sheffield: JSOT Press.

Gruen, Erich S. 1997. "The Origins and Objectives of Onias' Temple." *Scripta Classica Israelica* 16:47–70.

———. 2002. *Diaspora: Jews Amidst Greeks and Romans*. Cambridge: Harvard University Press.

Haag, Ernst. 2003. *Das hellenistische Zeitalter: Israel und die Bibel im 4. bis 1. Jahrhundert v. Chr*. BE 9. Stuttgart: Kohlhammer.

Hacham, Noah. 2005. "The Letter of Aristeas: A New Exodus Story?" *JSJ* 36:1–20.

Hanhart, Robert. 1999a. "Fragen um die Entstehung der LXX." Pages 3–24 in *Studien zur Septuaginta und zum hellenistischen Judentum*. Edited by Reinhard G. Kratz. FAT 24. Tübingen: Mohr Siebeck.

———. 1999b. "Der status confessionis Israels in hellenistischer Zeit." Pages 165–78 in *Studien zur Septuaginta und zum hellenistischen Judentum*. Edited by Reinhard G. Kratz. FAT 24. Tübingen: Mohr Siebeck.

———. 1999c. "Zur geistesgeschichtlichen Bestimmung des Judentums." Pages 151–64 in *Studien zur Septuaginta und zum hellenistischen Judentum*. Edited by Reinhard G. Kratz. FAT 24. Tübingen: Mohr Siebeck.

Hegermann, Hans. 1989. "The Diaspora in the Hellenistic Age." *CHJ* 2:115–66.

Hendel, Ronald S. 2013. *The Book of Genesis: A Biography*. Lives of Great Religious Books. Princeton: Princeton University Press.

Hengel, Martin. 1971. "Proseuche und Synagoge: Jüdische Gemeinde, Gotteshaus und Gottesdienst in der Diaspora und in Palästina." Pages 157–84 in *Tradition und Glaube: Das frühe Christentum in seiner Umwelt; Festgabe für Karl Georg Kuhn zum 65. Geburtstag*. Edited by Gert Jeremias, Heinz-Wolfgang Kuhn, and Hartmut Stegemann. Göttingen: Vandenhoeck & Ruprecht.

———. 1988. *Judentum und Hellenismus: Studien zu ihrer Begegnung unter besonderer Berücksichtigung Palästinas bis zur Mitte des 2. Jh.s v. Chr*. 3rd ed. WUNT 10. Tübingen: Mohr Siebeck.

———. 1994. "'Schriftauslegung' und 'Schriftwerdung' in der Zeit des Zweiten Tempels." Pages 1–71 in *Schriftauslegung im antiken Judentum und im Urchristentum*. Edited by Martin Hengel. WUNT 73. Tübingen: Mohr Siebeck.

Hertog, Cornelis den. 2004. "Erwägungen zur relativen Chronologie der Bücher Levitikus und Deuteronomium innerhalb der Pentateuchübersetzung." Pages 216–28 in vol. 2 of *Im Brennpunkt: Die Septuaginta; Studien zur Entstehung und Bedeutung der Griechischen Bibel*. Edited by Siegfried Kreuzer and Jürgen Peter Lesch. BWANT 161. Stuttgart: Kohlhammer.

Holladay, Carl R. 1983. *Fragments from Hellenistic Jewish Authors: Historians*. Texts and Translations 20; Pseudepigrapha Series 10. Chico, CA: Scholars Press.

Honigman, Sylvie. 2003. *The Septuagint and Homeric Scholarship in Alexandria: A Study in the Narrative of the Letter of Aristeas*. London: Routledge.

Hossfeld, Frank-Lothar, and Erich Zenger. 2000. *Psalmen 51–100*. HThKAT. Freiburg: Herder.

Huss, Werner. 1994. "Die Juden im ptolemäischen Ägypten." Pages 1–31 in *Artibus: Kulturwissenschaft und deutsche Philologie des Mittelalters und der frühen Neuzeit; Festschrift für Dieter Wuttke zum 65. Geburtstag*. Edited by Stephan Füssel and Dieter Wuttke. Wiesbaden: Harrassowitz.

Isserlin, Benedikt. S. 1973. "The Names of 72 Translators of the Septuagint (Aristeas, 47–50)." *JANESCU* 5:190–98.

Jellicoe, Sidney. 1965–66. "The Occasion and Purpose of the Letter of Aristeas: A Re-Examination." *NTS* 13:144–50.

Kahle, Paul E. 1962. *Die Kairoer Genisa: Untersuchungen zur Geschichte des hebräischen Bibeltextes und seiner Übersetzungen*. Berlin: Akademie.

Kaiser, Otto. 2000. *Die Bedeutung der griechischen Welt für die alttestamentliche Theologie*. NGWG.PH 7. Göttingen: Vandenhoeck & Ruprecht.

Kasher, Aryeh. 1985. *The Jews in Hellenistic and Roman Egypt: The Struggle for Equal Rights*. TSAJ 7. Tübingen: Mohr Siebeck.

Keel, Othmar, and Christoph Uehlinger. 1992. *Göttinnen, Götter und Gottessymbole: Neue Erkenntnisse zur Religionsgeschichte Kanaans und Israels aufgrund bislang unerschlossener ikonographischer Quellen*. Quaestiones disputatae 134. Freiburg im Breisgau: Herder.

Klijn, A. F. J. 1964. "The Letter of Aristeas and the Greek Translation of the Pentateuch in Egypt." *NTS* 11:154–58.

Knauf, Ernst Axel. 2000. "Psalm LX und Psalm CVIII." *VT* 50:55–65.

Koch, Klaus. 1995. "Weltgeschichte und Gottesreich im Danielbuch und die iranischen Parallelen." Pages 46–65 in *Die Reiche der Welt und der kommende Menschensohn: Gesammelte Aufsätze Bd. 2*. Edited by Klaus Koch and Martin Rösel. Neukirchen-Vluyn: Neukirchener Verlag.

———. 2000. "Neutestamentliche Profetenauslegung in vorchristlicher Zeit? Der Habakuk-Peschär aus Qumran." Pages 321–34 in *Schriftauslegung in der Schrift: Festschrift für Odil Hannes Steck zu seinem 65. Geburtstag*. Edited by Reinhard G. Kratz, Thomas Krüger, and Konrad Schmid. BZAW 300. Berlin: de Gruyter.

———. 2002. "Der König als Sohn Gottes in Ägypten und Israel." Pages 1–32 in *"Mein Sohn bist du" (Ps 2,7): Studien zu den Königspsalmen*. Edited by Eckart Otto and Erich Zenger. SBS 192. Stuttgart: Katholisches Bibelwerk.

Kooij, Arie van der. 1981. *Die alten Textzeugen des Jesajabuches: Ein Beitrag zur Textgeschichte des Alten Testaments*. OBO 35. Göttingen: Vandenhoeck & Ruprecht; Fribourg: Presses Universitaires.

Kofoed, Jens B. 2005. *Text and History: Historiography and the Study of the Biblical Text*. Winona Lake, IN: Eisenbrauns.

Kratz, Reinhard G. 2004. *Das Judentum im Zeitalter des Zweiten Tempels*. FAT 42. Tübingen: Mohr Siebeck.

Kreuzer, Siegfried. 2004. "Entstehung und Publikation der Septuaginta im Horizont frühptolemäischer Bildungs- und Kulturpolitik." Pages 61–75 in vol. 2 of *Im Brennpunkt: Die Septuaginta. Studien zur Entstehung und Bedeutung der Griechischen Bibel*. Edited by Siegfried Kreuzer, and Jürgen Peter Lesch. BWANT 161. Stuttgart: Kohlhammer.

Levin, Christoph. 1997. "Das Amosbuch der Anawim." *ZTK* 94:407–36.

Meyer, Rudolf. 1959. "προφήτης κτλ. C. Prophetentum und Propheten im Judentum der hellenistisch-römischen Zeit." *ThWNT* 6:813–28.

Modrzejewski, Joseph Mélèze. 1963. "Zum Justizwesen der Ptolemäer." *ZRG* 80:42–82.

———. 1997. *The Jews of Egypt: From Rameses II to Emperor Hadrian*. Princeton: Princeton University Press.

Niehr, Herbert. 1990. *Der höchste Gott: Alttestamentlicher JHWH-Glaube im Kontext syrisch-kanaanäischer Religion des 1. Jahrtausends v. Chr.* BZAW 190. Berlin: de Gruyter.

Orth, Wolfgang. 2001. "Ptolemaios II. und die Septuaginta-Übersetzung." Pages 97–114 in vol. 1 of *Im Brennpunkt: Die Septuaginta; Studien zur Entstehung und Bedeutung der griechischen Bibel*. Edited by Heinz-Josef Fabry und Ulrich Offerhaus. BWANT 153. Stuttgart: Kohlhammer.

Pietersma, Albert. 2002. "A New Paradigm for Addressing Old Questions: The Relevance of the Interlinear Model for the Study of the Septuagint." Pages 337–64 in *Bible and Computer: The Stellenbosch AIBI-6 Conference Proceedings of the Association internationale Bible et informatique, "From Alpha to Byte."* Edited by Johann Cook. Leiden: Brill.

Pilhofer, Peter. 1990. *Presbyteron Kreitton: Der Altersbeweis der jüdischen und christlichen Apologeten und seine Vorgeschichte.* WUNT 2/39. Tübingen: Mohr Siebeck.

Rösel, Martin. 1994. *Übersetzung als Vollendung der Auslegung: Studien zur Genesis-Septuaginta.* BZAW 223. Berlin: de Gruyter.

———. 2002. "Die Septuaginta." Pages 217–49 in *Brücke zwischen den Kulturen. "Übersetzung" als Mittel und Ausdruck kulturellen Austauschs.* Edited by Hans Jürgen Wendel, Wolfgang Bernard, and Yves Bizeul. Rostocker Studien zur Kulturwissenschaft 7. Rostock: Universität Rostock.

———. 2005. "Wirkungsgeschiche/Rezeptionsgeschichte. III.1. Alttestamentliche Wissenschaft." *RGG*[4] 8:1598–600. [English version: Steinmann, Michael, Andreas Schüle, Martin Rösel, Ulrich Luz, and Ulrich Köpf, "Effective History/Reception History," in *Religion Past and Present.* http://dx.doi.org/10.1163/1877-5888_rpp_COM_224309.]

———. 2006. "Jakob, Bileam und der Messias. Messianische Erwartungen in Gen 49 und Num 22–24." Pages 151–75 in *The Septuagint and Messianism.* Edited by Michael A. Knibb. BETL 195. Leuven: Peeters. [ch. 5 in this volume.]

Rost, Leonhard. 1970. "Vermutungen über den Anlaß zur griechischen Übersetzung der Tora." Pages 39–44 in *Wort–Gebot–Glaube: Beiträge zur Theologie des Alten Testaments; Walther Eichrodt zum 80. Geburtstag.* Edited by J. J. Stamm, E. Jenni, and H. J. Stoebe. AThANT 59. Zurich: Zwingli-Verlag.

Roth, Cecil. 1971. "History. Diaspora: Second Temple Period." *EJ* 8:640–49.

Sacchi, Paolo. 2000. *The History of the Second Temple Period.* JSOTSup 285. Sheffield: Sheffield Academic.

Sasse, Markus. 2004. *Geschichte Israels in der Zeit des Zweiten Tempels: Historische Ereignisse—Archäologie—Sozialgeschichte—Religions- und Geistesgeschichte.* Neukirchen-Vluyn: Neukirchener Verlag.

Schmidt, Werner. 1986. *Untersuchung zur Fälschung historischer Dokumente bei Pseudo-Aristeas.* Habelts Dissertationsdrucke, Reihe Klass. Philologie 37. Bonn: Habelt.

Schürer, Emil. 1986. *The History of the Jewish People in the Age of Jesus Christ (175 B.C.-A.D. 135)*. Revised and edited by Geza Vermes, Fergus Millar, and Matthew Black. 3 vols. Edinburgh: T&T Clark.

Schwartz, Daniel R. 1996. "Temple or City: What Did Hellenistic Jews See in Jerusalem?" Pages 114–27 in *The Centrality of Jerusalem: Historical Perspectives*. Edited by Marcel Poorthuis. Kampen: Kok Pharos.

Smith, Morton. 1987. *Palestinian Parties and Politics That Shaped the Old Testament*. 2nd ed. London: SCM.

Sollamo, Raija. 2001. "The Letter of Aristeas and the Origin of the Septuagint." Pages 329–42 in *X Congress of the International Organization for Septuagint and Cognate Studies: Oslo, 1998*. Edited by Bernard A. Taylor. SCS 51. Atlanta: Society of Biblical Literature.

Stern, Menahem, ed. 1976. *Greek and Latin Authors on Jews and Judaism: I. from Herodotus to Plutarch*. Jerusalem: Israel Academic of Sciences and Humanities.

Sterling, Gregory E. 2001. "Judaism between Jerusalem and Alexandria." Pages 263–301 in *Hellenism in the Land of Israel*. Edited by John J. Collins. Christianity and Judaism in Antiquity 13. Notre Dame: University of Notre Dame Press.

Stricker, Bruno H. 1956. *De Brief van Aristeas: De hellenistische Codificaties der praehelleense Godsdiensten*. Verhandelingen der Koninklijke Nederlandse Akademie van Wetenschappen, Afd. Letterkunde, Nieuwe Reeks 62.4. Amsterdam: North Holland Publishing.

Swete, Henry B. 1914. *An Introduction to the Old Testament in Greek*. Revised by R.R. Ottley, with an Appendix containing the Letter of Aristeas edited by H. St. J. Thackeray. Cambridge: Cambridge University Press.

Taylor, Joan E. 1998. "A Second Temple in Egypt: The Evidence for the Zadokite Temple of Onias." *JSJ* 29:297–321.

Tcherikover, Victor. 1958. "The Ideology of the Letter of Aristeas." *HThR* 51:59–85.

Thompson, Thomas L. 2005. "The Role of Faith in Historical Research." *SJOT* 19:111–34.

Walter, Nikolaus. 1980. *Fragmente jüdisch-hellenistischer Historiker*. 2nd ed. JSHRZ 1.2. Gütersloh: Gütersloher Verlagshaus.

———. 1994. "Kann man als Jude auch Grieche sein? Erwägungen zur jüdisch-hellenistischen Pseudepigraphie." Pages 148–63 in *Pursuing the Text: Studies in Honor of Ben Zion Wacholder on the Occasion of*

His Seventieth Birthday. Edited by John C. Reeves. JSOTSup 184. Sheffield: JSOT Press.

Weiss, Hans-Friedrich. 1998. "Sadduzäer." *TRE* 29:589–94.

———. 1999. *Propheten–Weise–Schriftgelehrte: Zur Kategorie des "Prophetischen" im nachexilischen Judentum; Franz-Delitzsch-Vorlesung 1998*. Münster: Institutum Judaicum Delitzschianum.

Willi-Plein, Ina. 1991. "Daniel 6 und die persische Diaspora." *Judaica* 47:12–21.

Wright, Benjamin G. 2006. "Translation as Scripture: The Septuagint in Aristeas and Philo." Pages 47–61 in *Septuagint Research: Issues and Challenges in the Study of the Greek Jewish Scriptures*. Edited by Wolfgang Kraus and R. Glenn Wooden. SCS 53. Atlanta: Society of Biblical Literature.

———. 2015. *The Letter of Aristeas: Aristeas to Philocrates or On the translation of the Law of the Jews*. CEJL 8. Berlin: de Gruyter.

2
Schreiber, Übersetzer, Theologen. Die Septuaginta als Dokument der Schrift-, Lese-, und Übersetzungskulturen des Judentums

1. Übersetzen im AT und seiner Umwelt

Das Phänomen des Übersetzens von einer Sprache in die andere ist den Schriften der hebräisch-aramäischen Bibel so geläufig, dass kaum je darüber reflektiert wird. Zwar ist von Gen 11,1–9 her klar, dass die Sprachen der Völker verwirrt wurden,[1] doch im Verlauf der in der Bibel geschilderten Geschichte Israels spielt das Phänomen der Sprachverschiedenheit kaum mehr eine Rolle. Einige wenige Beispiele: Abraham unterhält sich problemlos mit dem Pharao Ägyptens (Gen 12,10-20), für Mose und Aaron wird Zweisprachigkeit einfach vorausgesetzt, und auch die Königin von Saba beredet mit Salomo problemlos alles, was ihr auf dem Herzen lag (1.Kön 10,2).

Andere Texte benennen jedoch das Problem, so etwa Dtn 28,49 oder Jer 5,15, wo das Nicht-Verstehen der Sprache als Zeichen negativ konnotierter Fremdheit gilt: (Deut 28,49: גוי אשר לא־תשמע לשנו; ein Volk, dessen Sprache du nicht verstehst), ähnlich Neh 13,24, vgl. auch Ez 3,5-6. Im Gegenzug gilt es nach Jes 19,18 als Zeichen der Nähe zur israelitischen Religion, wenn fünf Städte Ägyptens die Sprache Kanaans (שפת כנען) sprechen.

Nur gelegentlich wird das Phänomen des *Übersetzens* angesprochen, dann aus Gründen der Erzähltechnik. In Esra 4,7 geschieht der Sprachwechsel ins Aramäische wohl, um die Originalität des Briefes der Samaritaner zu

---

1. Das wird v. a. in den in der Diaspora angesiedelten Schriften vorausgesetzt, vgl. Est 1,22; 3,12; 8,9; Dan 3,29.

unterstreichen.² In der Rabschake-Erzählung 2.Kön 18,17-28 (par. Jes 36) wollen die judäischen Unterhändler mit dem Rabschake aramäisch (ארמית) sprechen, um die Verhandlungen vor dem nur des Hebräischen (יהודית) mächtigen Volk geheim zu halten; der Rabschake muss nach der Vorstellung des Erzählers also mindestens dreisprachig sein. In Gen 42,23 wird eher beiläufig mitgeteilt, dass Joseph sich mit seinen Brüdern durch einen מליץ „Dolmetscher" unterhalten hat; die Notiz wird nötig um zu erklären, warum sich die Brüder ungeschützt unterhalten.³ In Dan 1,4 schließlich sollen Daniel und seine Gefährten in „Schrift und Sprache der Chaldäer" ausgebildet werden (וללמדם ספר ולשון כשדים), was offenbar eine umfassende Akkulturation der judäischen Jugendlichen bis hin zu astrologischem Wissen zum Ziel hat.⁴

Strittig ist *Nehemia 8,8*. Hier wird mitgeteilt (ושום שכל ויבינו במקרא), dass zunächst die Tora verlesen wird und dann eine Erklärung des Sinnes geschieht; diese Notiz wird oft so verstanden, dass eine erklärende Übersetzung ins Aramäische geschieht, was dann mit den Targumim in Verbindung zu bringen sei.⁵ Diese Deutung hängt aber am Verständnis von מפרש als *terminus technicus* für eine *ad hoc*-Übersetzung, die nicht mehr zu vertreten ist.⁶ Vom Übersetzen wird zudem im Text nicht explizit geredet.

Andere alttestamentliche Texte setzen Übersetzungen insofern voraus, als dass sie sie verwenden oder gar erst anfertigen. Das gilt, um nur den bekanntesten Beleg zu nennen, für die Aufnahme bestimmter Passagen der Lehre des Amenemope in Prov 22-24. Bernd U. Schipper hat kürzlich auf das typisch ägyptische Lektüreverfahren des Autors hingewiesen und erschlossen, dass ihm der ägyptische Text schriftlich vorgelegen haben muss.⁷ Bei anderen Texten ist dies deutlich strittiger, erinnert sei nur an die Diskussion um die Parallelen zwischen Psalm 104 und dem Sonnenhymnus des Echnaton.⁸ Die beiden Beispiele reichen aus, um das Phäno-

---

2. Vgl. Schwiderski 2000, 346-48.

3. S. Westermann 1982, 117, der ein „intensives Nachdenken" des Erzählers über die Institution des Übersetzers vermutet; das ist bei einer so beiläufigen Notiz doch ein wenig überinterpretiert.

4. Koch 2005, 42-52.

5. Zum Problem s. van der Kooij 1991, 79-90.

6. Schunck 2003, 233-34.

7. Schipper 2005, vgl. schon Helck 1968-1969, 26-27.

8. S. etwa Köckert 2000, 259-79, der eine Beeinflussung ganz ablehnt, und Koch 2007, 21 (mit Lit.), der auch eine ältere Amun-Stufe des Hymnus für möglich hält.

men zu illustrieren; erneut findet sich in den Texten selbst keine Reflexion über die Tatsache des Übersetzens oder der Sprachverschiedenheit. Es muss aber davon ausgegangen werden, dass im antiken Israel/Juda stets das Phänomen fremder Schrift und Sprache und der Notwendigkeit zur Übersetzung vor Augen gestanden hat, dies allein wegen der umfassenden Präsenz ägyptischer Texte und Bilder im Alltagsgeschehen.[9]

Aus *Ägypten* sind eine ganze Reihe von indirekten und direkten Zeugnissen zum Problem bekannt. Allgemein lässt sich sagen, dass Ägypten eher als ethnozentrische Kultur einzustufen ist, in der man zunächst wenig Interesse an den anderen Völkern und dem Austausch mit ihnen hatte; die eigene Sprache galt als „Sprache der Menschen" schlechthin.[10] Dennoch gab es natürlich die Notwendigkeit zum Übersetzen, was sich gelegentlich in Text- oder Bildzeugnissen niederschlägt. Besonders instruktiv ist die Abbildung eines Übersetzers aus dem Grab des Haremhab (18. Dyn.). Hier ist der Übersetzer doppelt ausgeführt, auf diese Weise übermittelt er die Botschaft des Pharaos an die Gefangenen.[11] Bekannt ist auch der Titel des Gaufürsten von Elephantine—also des Gaus an der Südgrenze—, der als „Vorsteher der Dragomanen/Fremdsprachigen" gilt,[12] wobei diese Dolmetscher wohl vor allem Ausländer waren.[13] Allerdings wird hier vor allem das mündliche Übersetzen gemeint sein, also das Verstehen und Sprechen einer Fremdsprache.[14] Das Amarna-Archiv wie auch die in Hattuscha erhaltene Korrespondenz mit dem Ägypten der 19. Dynastie setzen daneben selbstverständlich die Existenz von zweisprachigen Schreibern voraus; hier haben offenbar feste Formen (Protokolle) die zweisprachige Kommunikation erleichtert,[15] daneben gab es auch ägyptisch-akkadische Wörterbücher.[16]

---

9. Instruktiv ist etwa Quack 2005.

10. Albrecht 1998, 27–28; Schenkel 1977, 314–15. Vgl. auch Herodot II. 158: „Barbaren nennen die Ägypter alle Leute, die nicht die gleiche Sprache sprechen wie sie."

11. Es handelt sich dabei nicht um das Grab des Haremhab im Tal der Könige, wie in der ursprünglichen Publikation dieses Aufsatzes irrtümlich mitgeteilt, sondern um sein Beamtengrab in Saqqara; das Relief befindet sich heute im Rijksmuseum van Oudheden in Leiden, vgl. Martin 1989, 94, pls. 113–115, scene 76.

12. Schenkel 1975, 1116.

13. Schenkel 1977, 314.

14. Rocati 1986, 834.

15. S. dazu umfassend Mekawi Ouda 2004, 135–36.

16. Rocati 1986, 835.

In der Spätzeit ergibt sich durch die zunehmende Internationalisierung von Politik und Handel (und durch die Besetzung des Niltales seit der Äthiopien-Zeit) zwangsläufig ein häufigerer und weiter gehender Kontakt mit anderen Völkern auch unterhalb der diplomatischen Ebene. So berichtet Herodot über eine ungewöhnliche Aktion des Psammetich I., der ägyptische Jungen bei seinen ionischen Siedlern in Stratopeda untergebracht habe, damit sie dort Griechisch lernen; von diesen sollen die zur Zeit Herodots aktiven Dolmetscher abstammen.[17] In persischer Zeit nehmen dann die Zeugnisse weiter zu; bekannt sind etwa die Kanalstelen des Dareios I., die nicht nur einen persischen *Text* und seine hieroglyphen-ägyptische Übersetzung bieten, sondern auch bei den *Abbildungen* die persische Flügelsonne in eine ägyptische „übersetzen": der Szene des Großkönigs vor Ahura Mazda wird mit dem klassisch-ägyptischen Motiv des Zusammenbindens der Wappenpflanzen Ober- und Unterägyptens entsprochen.[18] Die Unterwerfung Ägyptens wird auf dort eigens angefertigten und nach Susa transportierten Stelen gar viersprachig (ägyptisch elamisch, persisch, akkadisch) mitgeteilt, wobei die drei letztgenannten Versionen gleichlautend sind (TUAT I, 609–611). Auch hier ist zu erkennen, dass nicht 1:1 übersetzt wird, da der ägyptische Text deutlich umfangreicher ist. Ihm zufolge haben die Götter den Dareios als Pharao eingesetzt, er selbst nennt Atum seinen Vater; in der persischen Version wurde er aber von Ahura Mazda zum König gemacht.

Die Ausbreitung des Aramäischen in der persischen Zeit wird ein weiteres wichtiges Motiv für die Mehrsprachigkeit in breiten Bevölkerungsschichten gewesen sein. Instruktiv ist hier der demotisch-aramäische Papyrus Amherst 63, der—anders als etwa die Elephantine- oder Syene-Papyri—nicht aramäische Sprache in aramäischer Schrift verwendet, sondern aramäische Texte in demotischer Schrift enthält. Außerdem sind hier eindeutig religiöse Überlieferungen verzeichnet, neben Textelementen aus Syrien auch Vorstufen von Ps 20 und 75.[19]

Der Kulturraum *Nordsyrien-Mesopotamien* kann wegen des Nebeneinanders von Sumerischem und Akkadischem als nahezu durchgängig zweisprachig bezeichnet werden.[20] Die Problematik des Übersetzungsgeschehens wird nachhaltig durch ein weit verbreitetes Phänomen belegt:

---

17. Herodot II, 154, vgl. Franke 1992, 87–88.
18. Koch 1993, 467–68 (mit Abbildung).
19. Übersetzung in COS 1.99; vgl. Rösel 2000.
20. Vgl. Ulshöfer 2000, 163–64.

2. Schreiber, Übersetzer, Theologen   33

die Existenz ein- und mehrsprachiger Wortlisten seit der Mitte des 3. Jt.v. in Ebla. Seit Beginn des 2. Jt., als das Sumerische nicht mehr gesprochen wurde, gibt es in Mesopotamien zweisprachige Wortlisten, die ein wichtiges Hilfsmittel bei Übersetzungen in beide Richtungen waren (oft auch nach Sachgruppen der Lexeme geordnet).[21] Solche Listen sind ebenfalls—auch viersprachig—aus Ugarit belegt,[22] sie legten wohl eine Technik des wörtlichen Übersetzens nahe, was aber die Varianzbreite der Äquivalente nicht ausschließt.[23] Für die Tätigkeit von Übersetzern (*targumannu*) gibt es eine Fülle von direkten und vor allem indirekten Belegen, etwa die Amarna-Korrespondenz, die in Akkadisch und Hethitisch abgefassten Vasallenverträge zwischen Hatti und Amurru (14./13. Jh., COS 2.17) und die zweisprachigen Karatepe-Inschriften in Phönizisch und Luwisch-Hieroglyphisch (ca. 7. Jh.; COS 2.21 + 2.31). Im Bereich der Literatur-Übersetzung sei auf die hurritischen und hethitischen Versionen des Gilgamesch-Epos hingewiesen; für die alttestamentliche Exegese besonders aufschlussreich ist die akkadisch-aramäische Bilingue vom Tell Fecherije (9. Jh.), deren Texte interessanterweise nicht nur sprachlich, sondern auch inhaltlich nicht völlig deckungsgleich sind.[24]

Die Belege im Einzelnen ließen sich vermehren. Sie zeigen, dass es vor allem im Bereich der Diplomatie bzw. des Militärwesens,[25] außerdem auch im Handel,[26] schriftliche Übersetzungen gegeben hat. Über Technik oder Theorie des Dolmetschens ist allerdings wenig bekannt.[27] Außer den Wörterlisten sind aus der klassisch-alttestamentlichen Zeit keine weiteren Hilfsmittel überliefert, obwohl von offenbar geschulten Dolmetschern als Berufsgruppe die Rede ist. Eine Visualisierung findet sich auf einem Relief aus Nimrud, auf dem ein Offizieller zwei Schreibern diktiert, einer schreibt Keilschrift auf eine Tafel, der andere wohl aramäisch auf eine Rolle.[28]

---

21. Cavigneaux 1983.
22. Huehnergard 1987.
23. S. auch Veldhuis 1999, 109, der darauf hinweist, dass in späterer Zeit meist mehrere babylonische Äquivalente für ein sumerisches Wort angegeben wurden.
24. S. Schwiderski 2003.
25. Dies gilt auch für die Nachrichten griechischer Geschichtsschreiber, s. Franke 1992, bes. 92–93 zu Alexander.
26. Besonders zu nennen sind hier wohl phönizische Händler deren Alphabetschrift ja das Wiedergeben anderer Sprachen deutlich vereinfachte.
27. Ulshöfer 2000, 164–66, mit Hinweisen zu Berufsübersetzern.
28. BM 118882, Ulshöfer 2000, 170; Abbildung auch in: Reade 1983, Abb. 45 (Hier allerdings mit irreführender Beschreibung).

Auffällig ist, dass keine lexikalischen Listen mit aramäischen Äquivalenten erhalten sind, obgleich aramäisch und akkadisch seit dem 8.Jh. nebeneinander existierten und es etwa aramäische Texte in akkadischer Schrift und aramäische Beischriften zu akkadischen Texten gegeben hat.[29] Für eine ganze Reihe der erhaltenen lexikalischen Listen ist die Schulsituation als Herkunft wahrscheinlich.[30] Nicht bekannt ist allerdings, ob irgendwo theoretische Fragen des Übersetzens diskutiert wurden; die Regeln nach denen Übersetzer arbeiteten, sind nicht klar. Belegt sind sowohl sehr freie,[31] wie auch sehr wörtliche Übersetzungen, so dass keine generalisierende Aussage möglich ist.[32]

In *hellenistischer Zeit* schließlich stellt sich das Problem des Übersetzens nochmals anders dar: Nun rückt das Griechische in den Rang der allgemeinen Sprache auf, so dass mit dem Durchsetzen der Koine in offiziell-diplomatischen Kontexten kaum mehr von Dolmetschern die Rede ist.[33] Ein „Schulfach" Fremdsprachenunterricht hat es im Hellenismus nicht gegeben; entsprechende Schulen sind nicht belegbar.[34] Festzuhalten ist außerdem, dass es vor der Septuaginta offenbar keine literarischen Übersetzungen ins Griechische gegeben hat; vorher gab es nur Übersetzungen von „Fachliteratur," die nicht von Griechen, sondern von „Barbaren" angefertigt wurden.[35]

Dafür entstehen nun die Übersetzungsphänomene auf anderen Ebenen, resultierend aus den häufiger werdenden alltäglichen Kontakten von Menschen unterschiedlicher Herkunft. So gibt es im hellenistischen Ägypten Übersetzer in allen Bereichen des öffentlichen Lebens. Das gilt gewiss auch für Palästina, wie ein zweisprachiges (idumäisch?-griechisch) Ostrakon aus Khirbet el-Qom zeigt, bei dem es sich um einen Schuldschein handelt (ptolemäisch, wohl 277 v.).[36] Allgemein wird man

---

29. Vgl. auch Blasberg 1998, 18–29.
30. Dabei wird immer auf den Examenstext A verwiesen, vgl. Sjöberg 1975; s. auch Seminara 2002, 245–46; Veldhuis 1999, 102–4.
31. So etwa die anonyme Übersetzung eines Buches über Imhotep; hier beruft sich der Übersetzer auf göttliche Inspiration bei der freien Übersetzung des Ägyptischen (P. Oxy XI, 1381, dazu Brock 1979, 71. 76–77; vgl. dazu auch unten).
32. S. dazu vor allem die abgewogene Darstellung von Seminara 2002, 248–55.
33. Vgl. zur Einführung Franke 1992.
34. Dazu Werner 1992, 13.
35. Etwa eine Reisebeschreibung des Karthagers Hanno aus dem 4. Jh.; vgl. Werner 1992, 14.
36. Geraty 1975, 57.

sagen müssen, dass schon im 3. Jh. auch für Israel-Palästina mit einer Mehrsprachigkeit—hebräisch/ aramäisch einerseits, griechisch andererseits—zu rechnen ist,[37] wie allein die ständig anwachsende Verwendung von griechischen Namen belegt.[38] Dieses Faktum ist deshalb von Bedeutung, weil der Aristeas-Brief ja ausdrücklich auf die judäische Herkunft der Tora-Übersetzer abhebt, außerdem ist für manche Übersetzungen einzelner Bücher der griechischen Bibel eine Herkunft aus Israel-Palästina zu vermuten.

2. Die Milieus der griechischen Bibelübersetzungen

Damit ist der eigentliche Gegenstand der Überlegungen in den Blick genommen, die literatursoziologische Einordnung der sogenannten Septuaginta. Wie so oft, wenn soziologische Fragestellungen auf antike Problemfelder angewendet werden, wird man über eine Zusammenstellung von Wahrscheinlichkeiten kaum hinauskommen. Im Falle der LXX wird die Sachlage noch dadurch erschwert, dass wir nicht mit nur einem Milieu zu rechnen haben. Die LXX ist ein *Sammelwerk*, das in der Zeit zwischen der Mitte des 3. Jh.v. und dem 1. Jh.n.Chr. entstanden ist, wobei die Übersetzungstätigkeit sicher in Alexandrien und Palästina, vielleicht auch in Leontopolis (Jesaja) und in der östlichen Diaspora (Tob, EpJer) stattfand.[39]

Hinzu kommt das Phänomen der frühen *Rezensionen und Parallelübersetzungen*, das spätestens durch Barthélemys Studie zur Zwölfprophetenrolle aus Nahal Hever unter dem Namen *kaige* bekannt ist,[40] früher aber schon etwa durch die doppelte Überlieferung von LXX und Pseudo-Theodotion im Danielbuch präsent war. Dabei ist von Bedeutung, dass der—sich ab dem 2. Jh.v. stabilisierende—hebräische Text auf die Übersetzung zurückwirkte. Unabhängig davon, ob es sich um eine freie Übersetzung derselben Vorlage oder eine—u.U. wörtliche—Wiedergabe einer anderen Vorlage handelte, wurde in bestimmten Kreisen Wert darauf gelegt, dass

---

37. Zum Problem s. Mussies 1987, 1042–47, und Baumgarten 2002, der sich aber v.a. mit späteren Phänomenen und den rabbinischen Traditionen zur LXX beschäftigt.

38. Ilan, 2002, 9–13 und 257–324.

39. Vgl. zur Orientierung die (z.T. aktualisierungsbedürftigen) Übersichten in Harl/Dorival/Munnich 1988, 93. 106. 111. Vgl. auch Clancy 2002, der die LXX deutlich später—nach 150 v.Chr.—ansetzt.

40. Barthélemy 1963.

für verbindlich gehaltenes Original und aktuell verwendete Übersetzung übereinstimmen. Ausweislich der in Qumran gefundenen griechischen Texte wird dieser Vorgang vor allem in Palästina stattgefunden haben. Es zeigt sich zudem, dass im 2. Jh. die Neu-Übersetzung hebräischer Schriften deutlich stärker am Original orientiert wird, als das bisher der Fall war. Schriftgelehrtes hebräisches Milieu und griechisches Übersetzermilieu stehen also in einem engen Zusammenhang. Weiter erschwert wird die Lage durch neuere Arbeiten, die zeigen konnten, dass etwa im Bereich der Samuel- und Königebücher die LXX bzw. Vetus Latina die ältesten erreichbaren Texte erhalten hat; die Textform des MT ist demgegenüber sekundär.[41] Man muss also mit parallelen Rezensionsprozessen im griechischen und im hebräischen Überlieferungsstrang der Bibel rechnen. Das bedeutet letztlich, dass die Frage nach den Übersetzern nicht vom Prozess der Kanonisierung zu trennen ist, sowohl, was den Umfang der Schrift, als auch was deren Wortlaut betrifft.

Ein einheitliches Milieu oder Umfeld kann also nicht angenommen werden. Daher geschieht im Folgenden eine Beschränkung auf die Übersetzung des Pentateuch. Die späteren Bücher sind ja durch diese Pionierarbeit mitgeprägt worden, so dass vieles dessen, was hier zu sagen ist, auch auf andere Übersetzer angewendet werden kann. Hinzu kommt, dass es nur wenige aussagefähige Forschungsarbeiten zum inhaltlichen Charakter der Rezensionen gibt.

Bei der Frage, in welchem Umfeld der griechische *nomos* entstanden ist, drängt sich zunächst die Diskussion um einen möglichen *offiziellen Hintergrund* auf. Die auf den Aristeasbrief zurückgehende These, dass die Übersetzung des *nomos* der Juden auf ptolemäische Veranlassung zurückgeht, ist jüngst erneuert worden.[42] Dem ist aus verschiedenen Gründen nicht zuzustimmen,[43] auch deshalb, weil sowohl der Aristeasbrief als auch die Übersetzungen eindeutig jüdisch geprägte Interessen haben und es fast keine greifbaren außerjüdischen Wirkungsspuren der LXX gibt.[44]

---

41. Schenker 2004; Hugo 2006.
42. Orth 2001; Collins 2000.
43. S. etwa Kreuzer 2004, 61–75; Siegert 2001, 28–29, oder jüngst Honigman 2003, 94–106.
44. Ps. Longin, de sublimitate 9,9 nimmt auf Gen 1 Bezug; das ist wohl der früheste eindeutige Beleg (1. Jh.n.Chr). Unklar ist, woher das Wissen über das Judentum etwa bei Manetho stammt.

2. Schreiber, Übersetzer, Theologen

Ebensowenig ist der auf H. St. J. Thackeray zurückgehenden Überlegung zuzustimmen, die LXX sei aus *liturgischen* Gründen übersetzt worden.[45] Über den Ablauf von Proseuche- oder Synagogengottesdiensten im 3. Jh.v.Chr. ist nichts bekannt, folglich kann man nur rätseln, welche Form der Schriftlesung es in jener Zeit gegeben hat.[46] Verschiedene (allerdings spätere) Zeugnisse, etwa die Passa-Homilie des Melitto von Sardes, legen nahe, dass das hebräische Original gelesen und dann von einem Übersetzer-Dragoman ad hoc ins Griechische übertragen wurde. Dies würde dem entsprechen, was für die Targumim zu vermuten ist.[47]

Auch die Praxis einer fortlaufenden Schriftlesung, die ja erst eine vollständige Übersetzung der Tora nötig gemacht hätte, ist erst später belegbar.[48] Es ist zwar nicht ausgeschlossen, sondern sogar wahrscheinlich, dass es Übersetzungen einzelner Texte ins Griechische gegeben hat,[49] doch die Anfertigung vollständiger griechischer Bücher ist so nicht zu erklären.

Eindeutig zu sagen ist folglich nur, dass die Übersetzung offensichtlich von Juden ausgeführt wurde. Die übliche Datierung weist in die Mitte des 3. Jahrhunderts, worauf zum einen sprachliche Argumente verweisen; ein wichtiges Argument ist außerdem die relative Chronologie zu anderen Übersetzungen der LXX und jüdisch-hellenistischen Schriftstellern, die die LXX voraussetzen.[50]

Die Frage nach dem ursprünglichen Anlass zur Übersetzung ist demnach offen. Da sie nur mit inhaltlichen Argumenten aus den übersetzten Texten selbst heraus zu beantworten ist, wird sie zunächst zurückgestellt, und ich wende mich der Frage nach der Technik des Übersetzens und möglichen Hilfsmitteln zu.

---

45. Thackeray 1921; erneuert etwa durch Momigliano 1976, 91–92. Vgl. dazu die klassische Erwiderung bei Bickerman 1959, der seinerseits die These vertrat, dass die LXX ursprünglich als *nomos* dienen sollte.

46. S. Claußen 2002, 213–18, der v.a. auf spätere Zeugnisse, besonders die Theodotos-Inschrift, verweist; vgl. auch Honigman 2003, 181, Anm. 41.

47. Rabin 1968, 18, mit Anm. 62 und 63.

48. Bickerman 1959, 7–8. Die These, dass P. Fouad 266 Hinweise auf einen dreijährigen Lesezyklus erkennen lasse (Mélèze-Modrzejewski 1995), hat sich nicht durchgesetzt; vgl. Harl, Dorival und Munnich 1988, 69.

49. Bickerman 1959, 7 mit Anm. 13, denkt an Num 19,1–10 oder Lev 23,23–25.

50. Honigman 2003, 96–98; Dines 2004, 41–51; s. auch oben Anmerkung 39 zu Clancy 2002, und Collins 2000.

3. Hermeneuten und Dragomanen: Modelle und Techniken des Übersetzens

Wer waren die Septuaginta-Übersetzer? Wie und wo haben sie die Sprachen gelernt? Hatten sie Hilfsmittel? Waren sie institutionell angebunden? Wenn ja, wo?

Eine verantwortbare Antwort auf diese Fragen muss lauten: Wir wissen es nicht. Vor dem Aristeasbrief und dem Vorwort zu Jesus Sirach, das dessen angeblicher Enkel verfasst hat,[51] gibt es keine antike Nachricht zu diesem Problem. In der Genesis-LXX selbst ist an der bereits erwähnten Stelle 42,23 von einem Übersetzer die Rede. Hier wird nicht das übliche ἑρμηνεύς, sondern das sehr seltene griechische ἑρμηνευτής verwendet.[52] Möglicherweise lässt sich das so auslegen, dass der Übersetzer sich selbst so bezeichnete. Da das zum Wortfeld gehörige Nomen ἑρμηνεία und das Verbum ἑρμηνεύω in der LXX meist im Sinne von „erklären" verwendet werden,[53] ließe sich so ein Hinweis auf sein Selbstverständnis erkennen; er ist auch Erklärer der Schrift.

Wie oben bereits dargestellt, hat es im 3. Jh. Übersetzer gegeben, vor allem offenbar bei Handels- und Rechtsgeschäften. Diese Dragomanen werden in der LXX Forschung seit Rabin und Bickermann[54] gerne als mögliche Vorbilder für die LXX-Übersetzung gesehen. Deren Arbeit muss man sich als vor allem mündliche Übersetzung vorstellen, was demnach dem angenommenen Hintergrund der Targumim nahe käme. Kennzeichnend für diese Übersetzungsweise ist eine enge Orientierung am jeweiligen Original, vor allem hinsichtlich der Syntax. So ließe sich die besondere, hebraisierende Syntax der LXX erklären.

Eine weitere Differenzierung wurde durch das Einbeziehen späterer, römischer Reflexionen—vor allem Ciceros—vorgenommen,[55] wonach es zwei Haupttypen von Übersetzertätigkeiten gibt; den vor allem bei

---

51. Veltri 1994, 133–40, hat gute Gründe dafür genannt, dass der Prolog nicht in das 2. Jh.v. zu datieren ist. Dagegen hält Wright 2003b daran fest, dass der Autor des Prologs Sirachs Enkel war.

52. Nach LSJ etwa bei Plato, *Politeia* 290c, s. Harl 1986, 280. In der LXX begegnet das Wort nur an dieser Stelle. Das übliche ἑρμηνεύς begegnet in der LXX gar nicht.

53. S. etwa Sir Prologue 1,20; 47,17; Dan 5,1(Θ); Esr 4,7.

54. Rabin 1968, 21–26; Bickerman 1959, vgl. auch van der Kooij 2000, 369–72. Zum Wort „Dragoman" vgl. Albrecht 1998, 37.

55. Cicero, *De optimo genere oratorum* 5,14; vgl. dazu Wright 2003a.

Rechtstexten anzutreffenden *fidus interpres*, den wortgetreu wiedergebenden Übersetzer, und den *orator/expositor*, der v.a. bei literarischen Übersetzungen mehr dem Sinn als dem Buchstaben verpflichtet übersetzt. Die Pentateuch-Übersetzer hätten eher unreflektiert je nach zu übersetzender Textgattung die eine oder andere Übersetzungsweise adaptiert.

Das Recht dieser Position besteht darin, dass tatsächlich etwa im Buch Numeri mit seinen Wechseln zwischen narrativen und legislativen Textstücken auch eine unterschiedliche Übersetzungsweise festzustellen ist. Allerdings ist durch neuere Untersuchungen zum Problem der Übersetzungsreflexionen aus römischer Zeit deutlich geworden, dass diese Unterscheidung viel zu grob ist, dass man seinerzeit sehr viel reflektierter über die Probleme der Wirkungsäquivalenz etwa durch die Schöpfung von Neologismen nachdachte.[56] Zudem ist methodisch fraglich, ob diese Positionen in das 3. Jh.v.Chr. zurückprojiziert werden können, zumal auch das Problem der unterschiedlichen Sprachtypen und ihrer Strukturen (Hebräisch-Griechisch vs. Griechisch-Latein) zu bedenken ist.[57] Wichtiger noch ist die prinzipielle Überlegung, dass die hellenistisch-römischen Parallelen sich nicht mit dem Phänomen der Übersetzung eines religiös-kanonischen Textes beschäftigen. Schließlich zeigt das Phänomen textinterner Harmonisierungen und intertextueller Bezugnahmen zwischen einzelnen Perikopen und Büchern der LXX, dass die Übersetzer mit den Texten und bestimmten Auslegungstraditionen vertraut waren; man kann m.E. also nicht von *ad hoc*-Übersetzungen[58] wie bei den hellenistischen Dragomanen sprechen.[59]

Bei der Übersicht über das Phänomen des Übersetzens im Orient war bereits auf die Existenz der lexikographischen Listen hingewiesen worden. Für Alexandria im 4./3. Jh. sind solche Hilfsmittel m.W. nicht belegt, doch sind eine Reihe von Papyrus-Lexika aus Hibeh und Oxyrhynchus aus dem 3./2. Jh. bekannt,[60] daher lässt sich mit hoher Sicherheit vermuten, dass

---

56. Dazu v.a. Seele 1995, 5. 11. 40–45. Zu Cicero vgl. Fögen 2000, 79–91.
57. Ähnlich die Anfrage von Dines 2004, 128.
58. So etwa Wright 2003b, für die Sirach-Übersetzung.
59. Im Oxyrhynchos-Papyrus 1381 wird erzählt, dass der Übersetzer eines Buches des Heilsgottes Imhotep von jenem inspiriert wurde, um seine Aufgabe auszuführen; daran wird erkennbar, dass man dem Phänomen der Übersetzung heiliger Bücher eine besondere Aufmerksamkeit beimaß. (Leipoldt 1950) Der Text stammt aus dem 2.Jh.n.Chr. und ist daher kaum mit den Anfängen der LXX und dem Selbstverständnis der Übersetzer parallelisierbar.
60. Naoumides 1969, 181–202.

es sie gegeben haben muss. Grund für diese Annahme ist die Tatsache, dass sich bereits in der Genesis eine sehr hohe Konstanz bei der Verwendung von Standard-Äquivalenten feststellen lässt. Denkbar ist auch, dass es zumindest für Teile des Buches Vorläuferübersetzungen gegeben hat, auf die der Aristeasbrief vielleicht noch anspielt (§§314–316).[61] Auch das könnte erklären, weshalb schon die Genesis-Übersetzung ein so hohes Maß an innerer Geschlossenheit erreicht.

Im direkten Umfeld der Übersetzung ist belegt, dass es vor allem in der Bibliothek Alexandrias unter der Führung ihrer ersten Leiter zur Entwicklung lexikalischer und textkritischer Instrumentarien gekommen ist.[62] Außerdem wurden Kommentare zu Homer und Hesiod angefertigt, es gab Anthologien mit Homer-Auszügen,[63] auch Paraphrasen. Bekannt sind auch die Listen (πίνακες) des Kallimachos, die als umfassende Bibliographie und anfängliches Lexikon anzusehen sind. Aus dem 3. Jh.v.Chr. ist ein fast vollständiges Schulbuch auf einem Papyrus erhalten, das unter anderem ein Syllabar für Schreibübungen, Lektürestücke, Götter- und Wortlisten, enthielt.[64] Solche Hilfsmittel werden also den ersten Übersetzern bekannt und zugänglich gewesen sein. Spätere Übersetzer konnten dann, worauf häufig hingewiesen wurde, den übersetzten Pentateuch als Modell benutzen.[65] Möglicherweise diente er sogar als Hebräisch-Lehrbuch für hellenistische Juden,[66] erneut analog zur angenommenen Verwendung der Targumim.[67]

In späteren Papyri sind dann wieder zweisprachige Listen nachzuweisen, die ebenfalls in den Bereich der Schule gehören. Ihr ältestes Stadium sind seit dem 1. Jh.n.Chr. belegte Homer-Texte, die in Kolumnen angeordnet werden, wobei in der linken Kolumne wortweise der eigentliche Text in Hexameter-Anordnung, in der rechten die Wiedergabe des Verses

---

61. Darauf stützt sich P. Kahles Targum-Hypothese (Kahle 1959, 211–14); dagegen aber schon Gooding 1963. Vgl. ausführlich Rösel 2007a [Kapitel 1 in diesem Band].

62. Zur Bibliothek und ihrer Geschichte sind grundlegend MacLeod 2000, Fraser 1972, 1:456.

63. S. etwa Nachtergael 1971, 344–51. Zur Einführung in die philologische Methodik Alexandrias s. Pfeiffer 1978, 135–212.

64. Guéraud und Jouguet 1938. Vgl. auch die Zusammenstellung bei Cribiore 1996, zu den Wortlisten Nr. 98–128, S. 196–203.

65. So Tov 1981.

66. So van der Kooij 1999, 204–14.

67. Alexander 1999.

in zeitgenössischem Koine-Griechisch steht.[68] Aus noch späterer Zeit (ab dem 3. Jh.n.Chr.) sind dann auch zweisprachige Texte erhalten, bei denen links der lateinische Text, etwa von Vergil, Cicero oder Aesop (maximal 3-4 Worte in Folge), rechts die griechische Übersetzung der einzelnen Wörter zu finden ist.[69]

Diese inter- und juxtalineare Anordnung der Texte hat in jüngster Zeit eine besondere Aufmerksamkeit erhalten, weil Albert Pietersma aus ihrer Existenz ein neues *Paradigma der Interlinearität* zur Erklärung der meisten LXX-Schriften abgeleitet hat. Es geht davon aus, dass solche zweisprachigen Wortlisten bereits den Übersetzern des 3. Jh.v.Chr. bekannt waren. Ihre Übersetzungsweise hätte dann weitgehend diesem Vorbild entsprochen, was weitreichende Folgen hätte. So geht Pietersma davon aus, dass der Orientierungspunkt des Übersetzers vor allem die kleine Einheit *einer* Zeile gewesen ist. Übersetzung und Original hätten sich nicht nur hinsichtlich der Syntax, sondern bis in die Konnotationen der verwendeten Lexeme hinein entsprochen, auch wenn es im Griechischen andere Bedeutungsgehalte gegeben haben mag. Die Übersetzung ist folglich ohne den Referenztext nicht denkbar; sie wollte demnach nicht die hebräische Schrift ersetzen, sondern auf sie zurückweisen. Da die zweisprachigen Papyri mit dem Schulbetrieb verbunden seien, muss auch der sozio-linguistische Ursprung der LXX in der Schule gelegen haben.[70]

Das Paradigma erscheint zwar auf den ersten Blick äußerst interessant, doch bei näherer Betrachtung können die erhaltenen Papyri die Beweislast nicht tragen.[71] Zwar liegt der Sinn der zweisprachigen Papyri (die fast ausschließlich Vergil-Texte bieten), vor allem darin, Hilfen zum Lernen der *Ausgangssprache*, des Lateinischen, zu geben, also die vorbildliche Syntax des Dichters zu verstehen und manche Phrasen einzuüben. Dort, wo die griechischen Texte durchgängig erhalten sind, wird deutlich, dass nicht an das Erzeugen eines zusammenhängenden Textes gedacht war. Ein Vergleich der verschiedenen Listen zeigt überdies eine hohe Varianzbreite

---

68. Gaebel 1969–1970, 298–300.

69. Gaebel 1969–1970, 296–97; Cavenaile 1956; Kramer 2001, 28, und 100–104 zu einer Äsop-Fabel.

70. Pietersma 2002, 349. Doch man beachte Cribiore 1996, 28 (im Anschluss an Kramer 1983), die diese Wortlisten gerade nicht dem Schulbetrieb zuweist.

71. Eine ausführlichere Auseinandersetzung mit diesem Paradigma findet sich in Rösel 2006a, 152–56 [Kapitel 5 in diesem Band], vgl. auch die wichtigen Anfragen von Dines 2004, 52–54.

bei den verwendeten griechischen Äquivalenten, es wird also nicht eine verbindliche Übersetzung angestrebt.[72] Da auch alphabetisch angeordnete Homer-Wörterbücher erhalten sind, sind diese Listen wohl als reine Hilfsmittel einzuschätzen, die nicht direkt mit den LXX-Übersetzungen zu vergleichen sind. Hinzu kommt, dass der angenommene Hintergrund in der Elementarschule innerhalb der Altphilologie strittig ist.

Eine erfolgversprechendere Spur findet sich möglicherweise in den aus der Kairoer Geniza erhaltenen Fragmenten—dies aber mit aller wegen der späten Datierung gebotenen Vorsicht. Unter den Texten finden sich nämlich Fragmente eines biblischen Glossars, das Erklärungen schwieriger Worte aus Maleachi und Hiob bietet, jeweils in der Weise, dass in der rechten Spalte das hebräische Wort, links in griechischer Sprache, aber hebräischer Schrift und tiberischer Vokalisation das griechische Äquivalent geboten wird.[73] Andere erhaltene Texte bieten Glossen zum Königebuch[74] und ein Glossar schwieriger Ausdrücke aus der Mischna.[75] Diese Glossare wenden die Tradition der zweisprachigen Listen aus dem Alten Orient auf biblische Texte an. Es ist gut denkbar, dass man sich die Hilfsmittel der LXX-Übersetzer ähnlich vorzustellen hat. Doch angesichts der Tatsache, dass die Geniza-Texte nicht vollständig veröffentlicht wurden, dass die Forschung daran außerdem kaum begonnen hat, wird man gegenwärtig nicht über diese Vermutungen hinauskommen.

Schließlich sei die Frage gestellt, ob sich eine *institutionelle Anbindung* der Übersetzer erheben lässt. Oben wurde bereits gezeigt, dass der Synagogengottesdienst nicht als Anlass zur Übersetzung der LXX zu sehen ist. Das schließt natürlich nicht aus, dass sich die Übersetzer in den Kreisen der Synagogen-/Proseuche-Gemeinden bewegt haben; im Gegenteil ist es angesichts ihrer Verwurzelung im Judentum und der breiten Akzeptanz ihrer Arbeit gar nicht denkbar, dass sie nicht zu diesen Kreisen gehörten. Die von der Genesis an einheitliche Verwendung theologischer Schlüsselbegriffe wie διαθήκη für ברית, νόμος für תורה, δικαιοσύνη für צדק/צדקה[76] legen den Schluss nahe, dass es für solche Äquivalenzen nicht nur konkordante Listen, sondern auch eine vorhergegangene Prägung in der Gemeinde gab.

---

72. Diese Argumente nach Gaebel 1969–1970, 299–308.
73. de Lange 1996, 79–84.
74. A.a.O., 155–63.
75. A.a.O., 295–305.
76. Rösel 1994, 228–37.

2. Schreiber, Übersetzer, Theologen

Ein weiterer möglicher Haftpunkt der Übersetzung ist die Institution der *Schule*. Ihr kommt in dem genannten Paradigma von Pietersma eine entscheidende Rolle zu; die LXX sei nach dem Muster von Schulübungen für einen „instructional use" angefertigt worden.[77] Das Problem ist erneut, dass man nahezu nichts über jüdischen Schulbetrieb im 3. Jh.v.Chr. weiß. Die einschlägigen Studien sammeln vor allem Nachrichten aus römischer oder rabbinischer Zeit[78] und projizieren sie zurück. Aus dem hellenistischen Ägypten ist bekannt, dass die ägyptischen Schulen an den Tempeln angesiedelt waren, wo von den Priestern vor allem die Hieroglyphenschrift, Geometrie und Astronomie unterrichtet wurde,[79] dies vor allem für den Priesternachwuchs.[80] Griechische Gymnasien, gab es in den Großstädten wie Alexandria und Ptolemais, aber auch in kleineren Orten. Sie standen der griechischen Bevölkerung offen, wohl auch Juden.[81] Direkte Zeugnisse aus Ägypten für die gymnasiale Ausbildung von Juden gibt es m.W. nicht.

Später ist dann bei Philo (*Mos.* 2,215–216; *Spec.* 2,62–63) belegt, dass im Unterrichten eine vornehmliche Aufgabe der Synagogen zu sehen sei.[82] Es ist unklar, wie weit dieser Brauch zurückgeht, aber es ist denkbar, dass diese Verbindung der Funktionen schon im dritten Jahrhundert gegeben war. Aber auch dann bleibt unklar, in welcher Sprache dort unterrichtet wurde,[83] und ob der Schulbetrieb wirklich nach dem Modell der griechischen Schule ablief, oder nachbildete, was in Palästina üblich war.[84]

Festzuhalten ist aber jedenfalls, dass die Übersetzer eine gute Ausbildung genossen haben müssen. So ist bei den meisten eine hohe Kompetenz in beiden Sprachen festzustellen, auch wenn der Stil der erzeugten Texte durch die Orientierung an der Vorlage oft schwerfällig und ungriechisch wirkt.[85] Doch die Verwendung seltener Lexeme (offenbar auch zur

---

77. Pietersma 2002, 358. Es sei angemerkt, dass hier ein (unangemessenes) Verständnis von „Schule" zugrunde liegt, das eher das niedrige Niveau einer Elementarschule zu implizieren scheint.
78. Safrai 1987.
79. S. dazu die instruktive Arbeit von Cribiore 2005, 15–73.
80. Dazu Maehler 1983, 192–97.
81. Maehler 1983, 196, Anm. 18.
82. Dazu auch Bousset 1915, 8–10; Gruen 2002, 115–16.
83. In Palästina war wohl im *bet sefer* das Unterrichten von Griechisch verboten; Safrai 1987, 957.
84. Dazu etwa Davies 1998, 74–87, Crenshaw 1998, 85–113.
85. Zur Beschreibung und Einordnung der Sprache der LXX vgl. Usener 2004.

Vermeidung kultisch anders geprägter Äquivalente), die Neologismen, der auffällige Gebrauch von Kompositverben und sogar die Anwendung rhetorischer Regeln etwa in den Psalmen[86] zeigen, dass die Übersetzer auch mit wichtigen Aspekten griechisch-hellenistischer Kultur bekannt waren.[87] Hinzu kommen bereits in der Genesis eindeutige Bezugnahmen auf klassisch griechische Autoren wie Plato oder Herodot oder auf astronomisch-astrologische Vorstellungen.[88] Das Niveau dieses Wissens ist—soweit sich das heute bewerten lässt—so hoch, dass es oberhalb eines elementaren Schulbetriebs angesiedelt werden muss. Daher habe ich zumindest für die Genesis vorgeschlagen, dass sie im Umfeld der alexandrinischen Bibliothek bzw. im *Museion* entstanden sein muss.[89] Die Übersetzer lassen sich m.E. am ehesten als „Schriftgelehrte" bezeichnen,[90] weil sie eben nicht nur übersetzten, sondern die traditionellen Überlieferungen im Horizont der geänderten Sprach- und Verstehensbedingungen neu zu Gehör brachten.

Für diese Einschätzung—zumindest der Pentateuch-Übersetzung—spricht auch, dass sie sich gut in die *allgemeine kulturelle Interessenlage* der damaligen Zeit einfügt. Es genügt, an einige wenige Fakten zu erinnern, vor allem zunächst an die Entwürfe von Manetho und Berossos für die ägyptische und die babylonische Geschichte.[91] Beide Werke wollten offenbar durch Neu-Zusammenstellung der „kanonischen" Materialien und zur Selbstvergewisserung der eigenen Kultur die eigene Geschichte in griechischer Sprache zugänglich zu machen. Sie sind notwendig aus übersetzten Quellen kompiliert worden, sind aber selbst nicht als Übersetzung anzusehen. Hinweise auf ihre offizielle Beauftragung fehlen.[92]

Wenig später gibt es im jüdisch-hellenistischen Bereich Schriftsteller wie Demetrios oder Eupolemos, die aus ähnlichen Motiven heraus die eigene Geschichte neu darstellten, nun aber bereits auf der Grundlage der LXX. Dabei ist interessant, dass schon die ältesten greifbaren Autoren der hellenistisch-jüdischen Literatur Gattungen und Methoden der gelehrten

---

86. Lee 1997, 778–80.
87. Wenn Rabin 1968, 21, schreibt, Juden im 3. Jh. „had no practice in writing educated Greek", kann ich dieses Urteil nicht nachvollziehen.
88. Dazu überblicksartig Rösel 1994, 251–54.
89. A.a.O., 259; vgl. die ausdrückliche Zustimmung zu dieser Verortung bei Kreuzer 2004, 72; vgl. Dines 2004, 44.
90. Dies mit van der Kooij 2000.
91. So bereits Bickerman 1959, 10–11.
92. Dies auch gegen die These einer offiziellen Beauftragung der LXX von Orth 2001.

Umwelt aufgreifen, etwa die *aporiai kai luseis* genannte Exegese, die von offenkundigen Problemen zu meist apologetischen Lösungen führte.[93]

Im palästinischen Judentum lassen sich ähnliche Interessen etwa im Jubiläenbuch oder im Genesis-Apokryphon, aber auch in der Tempelrolle feststellen. Als eine wichtige Motivation zur Übersetzung der Genesis kann man demnach das zeitgenössische protologische und weltgeschichtliche Interesse benennen, in dem die Überlieferung der eigenen Volksgruppe ihren Ort finden sollen.[94] Die Genesis ist dazu besonders geeignet, weil sie mit einem Schöpfungsbericht beginnt, der in der griechischen Version mit Platos Weltentstehungslehre kompatibel ist. Sie endet überdies mit einer Erklärung, wie es dazu kommt, dass es in Ägypten jüdische Bevölkerungsschichten gibt—ein Problem, das auch im Anfangsteil des Aristeasbriefes begegnet—; damit passt sie bestens in die hellenistischen Diskussionen.

Interessant ist daneben die in der Zeit des Ptolemaios II. angefertigte Übersetzung bisher demotisch überlieferter Regeln und Gesetze ins Griechische, die unter dem Namen „*Demotic case book*" bekannt sind.[95] Dieser Text belegt, dass es zeitgleich einen Bedarf für eine Übersetzung von Gesetzen der verschiedenen ethnischen Gruppen im hellenistischen Ägypten gab. Wenn inzwischen als sicher gelten kann, dass die Genesis zuerst übersetzt wurde,[96] findet sich hier ein wichtiger Hinweis, warum nur wenig später die anderen Bücher des Pentateuch folgten. Ausweislich neu zugänglicher Papyri ist nun auch belegbar, dass die LXX etwa im Eherecht durchaus als Rechtsbuch verwendet wurde;[97] für Joseph Mélèze Modrzejewski ist sie gar ein *politikos nomos* gewesen.[98]

Damit fügen sich die ersten Übersetzungen problemlos in größere Strömungen der hellenistischen Kulturgeschichte ein. Sobald diese griechische Tora sich in der Gemeinde durchgesetzt hatte, bedurfte es wohl kaum der Begründung für die Übersetzung weiterer Bücher. Die Reihenfolge, in der dies geschehen ist, ist noch nicht eindeutig geklärt. Offenbar

---

93. Dazu z.B. Walter 1980, 281.

94. Die von Tilly 2005, 51–52, vorgeschlagene Deutungsvariante weicht nur marginal von diesem Vorschlag ab.

95. Mélèze-Modrzejewski 1995, vgl. Bickerman 1994, 104, der für beide Übersetzungen auf ptolemäische Veranlassung plädiert.

96. Rösel 1994, 257; Argumente hierfür sind vor allem die abweichende Chronologie in Gen 5 und die andere Prägung von Äqivalenten im Vergleich mit den Ex-Dtn-Übersetzungen.

97. P. Polit. Iud. 4, vgl. Cowey 2004, 37–38.

98. Mélèze-Modrzejewski 1995, 10.

wurden aber knapp nach der Wende zum 2. vorchristlichen Jahrhundert die Prophetenbücher übersetzt. Dabei ist das Faktum interessant, dass die Josua-LXX Spuren erkennen lässt, dass sie als allein stehendes Buch gedacht war, ohne den Kontext des Richter- und der Königebücher zu lesen und zu verstehen war.[99] Für die anderen genannten Bücher kann Ähnliches gelten, allerdings ist beim Richter- und Königebuch der textgeschichtliche Problembefund schwieriger. Doch kann auch hier als sicher gelten, dass sie als einzelne Einheiten übersetzt wurden. Die Bindekraft des dtr. Geschichtswerkes bzw. des Enneateuchs wurde damals also nicht als so hoch empfunden, wie sich das modernen Exegeten darstellt.

Elias Bickermann hat diese späteren Übersetzungen sogar als private Unternehmungen verstanden, was manche Freiheiten beim Übersetzen, aber auch beim Revidieren erklären könnte.[100] Jedenfalls ist es ein Faktum, dass es bei den späteren LXX-Büchern keine gemeinsame Linie hinsichtlich der Übersetzungstechnik gegeben hat; im Falle des Danielbuches sind z.B. zwei konkurrierende vorchristliche griechische Versionen sicher greifbar. Für das Jesajabuch wurde gar der Tempel in Leontopolis als Haftgrund wahrscheinlich gemacht.[101] Diese Übersetzergestalten und ihr Umfeld sind noch weniger greifbar als im Falle des Pentateuch. Deutlich ist aber, dass sie sich in einem Spannungsfeld mit mehreren Polen befanden: Sie wurden sowohl von ihrer hebräischen Vorlage und deren zeitgenössischem Verständnis, als auch vom griechischen Pentateuch und dessen Vorgaben beeinflusst, der zudem—wie die frühen Rezensionen und der Aristeasbrief zeigen—eine Debatte hervorgerufen hatte, wie getreu eine Übersetzung dem Original folgen muss. Wo und wie diese Diskussionen stattgefunden haben, ist bislang nicht bekannt und kaum untersucht.

4. Theologie

Abschließend soll noch die Frage nach der Theologie der Übersetzungen angeschnitten werden, obgleich sich hier ein eigenes Problemfeld auftut.[102] Einige grundsätzliche Überlegungen sind dennoch nötig. Es ist unstrittig, dass die Septuaginta in vielerlei Hinsicht andere theologische Positionen

---

99. Argumente bei Rösel 2001 [Kapitel 6 in diesem Band].
100. Bickerman 1976, 149.
101. Vgl. Frankel 1841, 40, Anm. f.; van der Kooij 1981, 60–65.
102. Zu einer eigenen Positionsbestimmung s. Rösel 2006b [Kapitel 11 in diesem Band].

2. Schreiber, Übersetzer, Theologen 47

als der hebräische Text erkennen lässt. Strittig ist, ob diese von den Übersetzern intendiert waren, wobei man wieder differenzieren kann, ob sie als Individuen gehandelt haben oder nur das in ihrer Gemeinde vorherrschende Verständnis wiedergegeben haben.[103] Doch auch falls man davon ausgeht, dass in den Übersetzungen ohne eigene Intentionen einfach der hebräische Text abgebildet werden sollte, ist dies eine implizite theologische Aussage, da man offenkundig der Schrift als Wort Gottes auch in ihrer Übersetzung eine eigene *dynamis* zumisst, die menschliche Verstehensansprüche übersteigt.[104]

Einige wenige Beispiele mögen genügen um zu zeigen, wie sich diese veränderte theologische Perspektive zeigt und auswirkt: Von der Genesis an sind eine Fülle von Harmonisierungen der Texte untereinander festzustellen. Das kann die Zufügung von Textstrukturen wie etwa in der Schöpfungs- oder der Sintflutgeschichte (1,9; 6,19–20 u.ö.) bedeuten, aber auch zur Verwendung des gleichen griechischen Lexems für unterschiedliche hebräische Wörter führen. Ähnlich sind Phänomene der Intertextualität zu verstehen, denen vor allem in der französischen Forschung zur LXX Aufmerksamkeit gewidmet wird.[105] Möglicherweise verdanken sich diese Bezugnahmen einer parallel laufenden mündlichen Auslegungstradition, was erneut auf schriftgelehrte Kreise hinweisen würde.

Hinzu kommen geprägte Übersetzungsäquivalente, wie etwa die häufige Verwendung von νόμος oder δίκαιος und Derivaten (auch mit α-*privativum*) auch an Stellen, an denen im hebräischen Text nicht von תורה oder צדקה die Rede ist. Die LXX leistet damit einem veränderten Gesamtverständnis der Bibel Vorschub, das man als *nomos*-Soteriologie bezeichnen kann. Ein instruktives Beispiel: Ps 9,21 (MT) liest: שיתה יהוה מורה להם (Lege Furcht auf sie, JHWH!). Die LXX bietet dagegen: κατάστησον κύριε νομοθέτην ἐπ' αὐτούς (Setze Herr, einen Gesetzgeber über sie).[106] Offensichtlich hat der Übersetzer unpunktiertes מורה von ירה[II] abgeleitet und mit „Lehrer" übersetzt. Die Wahl von „Gesetzgeber" ist ein weitergehendes Interpretament, das ירה zusätzlich mit תורה in Verbin-

---

103. Zur Auseinandersetzung vgl. etwa Pietersma 2006, 33–45; für den mein Ansatz als „maximalistic" gilt.
104. So Joosten 2000.
105. Vgl. besonders die Arbeit von Dorival 1995 und die Einführungen zu den Bänden der „Bible d'Alexandrie".
106. Dazu ausführlich Rösel 2007b, 140–45 [Kapitel 15 in diesem Band].

dung bringt; die Tora ist als die richtige Lehre anzusehen.[107] Diese Äquivalentwahl ist nun nicht etwa ein Einzelfall im Psalter. Wahrscheinlich wurde auf Ex 24,12 und Deut 17,10 zurückgegriffen, wo ebenfalls ירה mit νομοθετέω wiedergegeben wurde. Es wird also deutlich, wie das Thema des *nomos* in schriftgelehrter Weise buchübergreifend pointiert wird.

Schließlich wird man auch das veränderte Gottesbild nennen müssen, das sich zum einen im Wegfall des Eigennamens JHWH und der Verwendung des absoluten κύριος ausdrückt,[108] deutlicher aber noch in der späteren Übersetzung παντοκράτωρ für hb. צבאות oder שדי zu greifen ist.[109] Die jahrhundertelange Wandlung im Gottesbild Israels hat einen Höhepunkt erreicht, der als theologischer Kontrapunkt zum Hegemonialanspruch der hellenistischen Kultur zu verstehen ist.

Die Beispiele ließen sich problemlos vermehren. Auch so ist deutlich, dass die Arbeit der Übersetzer der Septuaginta nicht nur eine bedeutende sprachliche, sondern auch eine eminent wichtige theologische Leistung ist, durch die diese Version der Bibel zur γραφή und Grundlage des Christentums geworden ist.

Literatur

Albrecht, Jörn. 1998. *Literarische Übersetzung. Geschichte–Theorie–kulturelle Wirkung*. Darmstadt: Wissenschaftliche Buchgesellschaft.

Alexander, Philipp S. 1999. „How Did the Rabbis Learn Hebrew?" Seiten 71–89 in *Hebrew Study from Ezra to Ben-Yehuda*. Hrsg. von William Horbury. Edinburgh: T&T Clark.

Austermann, Frank. 2003. *Von der Tora zum Nomos. Untersuchungen zur Übersetzungsweise und Interpretation im Septuaginta-Psalter*. NAWG Phil-Hist Klasse 3, 257. MSU 27. Göttingen: Vandenhoeck & Ruprecht.

Barthélemy, Dominique. 1963. *Les Devanciers d'Aquila. Première Publication intégrale du Texte des Fragments du Dodéaprophéton*. VTSup 10. Leiden: Brill.

Baumgarten, Albert I. 2002. „Bilingual Jews and the Greek Bible." Seiten 13–30 in *Shem in the Tents of Japhet. Essays on the Encounter of Judaism and Hellenism*. Hrsg. von James L. Kugel. JSJSup 74. Leiden: Brill.

---

107. S. dazu Austermann 2003, 140–41.
108. Vgl. etwa auch Ex 8,6 LXX; s. Hanhart 1988, 76–80.
109. Dazu auch Rösel 2006b, 245–48 [Kapitel 11 in diesem Band].

Bickerman, Elias. 1959. „The Septuagint as a Translation." *PAAJR* 28:1–39.

———. 1976. „Some Notes on the Transmission of the Septuagint." Seiten 139–66 in *Studies in Jewish and Christian History*. Hrsg. von Elias Bickerman. AGJU 9. Leiden: Brill.

———. 1994. *The Jews in the Greek Age*. Cambridge: Harvard University Press.

Blasberg, Monika. 1997. „Keilschrift in aramäischer Umwelt. Untersuchungen zur spätbabylonischen Orthographie." PhD diss., Köln: Universität.

Bousset, Wilhelm. 1915. *Jüdisch-Christlicher Schulbetrieb in Alexandria und Rom*. FRLANT 6. Göttingen: Vandenhoeck & Ruprecht.

Brock, Sebastian. 1979. „Aspects of Translation Technique in Antiquity." *GRBS* 20:69–87.

Cavenaile, Robert. 1956. *Corpus papyrorum latinarum 1*. Wiesbaden: Harrassowitz.

Cavigneaux, Antoine. 1983. „Lexikalische Listen." *RLA* 6:609–41.

Clancy, Frank. 2002. „The Date of the LXX." *SJOT* 16:207–25.

Claußen, Carsten. 2002. *Versammlung, Gemeinde, Synagoge. Das hellenistisch-jüdische Umfeld der frühchristlichen Gemeinden*. SUNT 27. Göttingen: Vandenhoeck & Ruprecht.

Collins, Nina. 2000. *The Library in Alexandria and the Bible in Greek*. VTSup 82. Leiden: Brill.

Cowey, James M.S. 2004. „Das ägyptische Judentum in hellenistischer Zeit." Seiten 24–43 in Band 2 *Im Brennpunkt. Die Septuaginta. Studien zur Entstehung und Bedeutung der Griechischen Bibel*. Hrsg. von Siegfried Kreuzer und Jürgen Peter Lesch. BWANT 161. Stuttgart: Kohlhammer.

Crenshaw, James L. 1998. *Education in Ancient Israel. Across the Deadening Silence*. ABRL. New York: Doubleday.

Cribiore, Raffaella. 1996. *Writing, Teachers, and Students in Graeco-Roman Egypt*. ASP 36. Atlanta: Scholars Press.

———. 2005. *Gymnastics of the Mind. Greek Education in Hellenistic and Roman Egypt*. Princeton: Princeton University Press.

Davies, Philip R. 1998. *Scribes and Schools. The Canonization of the Hebrew Scriptures*. LAI. Louisville: Westminster John Knox Press.

Dines, Jennifer M. 2004. *The Septuagint*. Edinburgh: T&T Clark.

Dorival, Gilles. 1995. „Les phénomènes d'intertextualité dans le livre grec des Nombres." Seiten 253–85 in ΚΑΤΑ ΤΟΥΣ Ο'. *Selon Les Septante*.

En hommage à Marguerite Harl. Hrsg. von Gilles Dorival und Olivier Munnich. Paris: Cerf.

Fögen, Thorsten. 2000. *Patrii sermonis egestas. Einstellungen lateinischer Autoren zu ihrer Muttersprache. Ein Beitrag zum Sprachbewußtsein in der römischen Antike.* Beiträge zur Altertumskunde 150. München: Saur.

Franke, Peter Robert. 1992. „Dolmetschen in hellenistischer Zeit." Seiten 85-96 in *Zum Umgang mit fremden Sprachen in der griechisch-römischen Antike.* Hrsg. von Carl Werner Müller u.a. Palingenesia 36. Stuttgart: Steiner.

Frankel, Zacharias. 1841. *Vorstudien zu der Septuaginta.* Leipzig: Vogel.

Fraser, Peter M. 1972. *Ptolemaic Alexandria I-III.* Oxford: Clarendon.

Gaebel, Robert E. 1969-1970. „The Greek Word-Lists to Vergil and Cicero." *BJRL* 52:284-325.

Geraty, L.T. 1975. „The Khirbet el-Kôm Bilingual Ostracon." *BASOR* 220:55-61.

Gooding, David W. 1963. „Aristeas and Septuagint Origins. A Review of Recent Studies." *VT* 13:357-79.

Gruen, Erich S. 2002. *Diaspora. Jews amidst Greeks and Romans.* Cambridge: Harvard University Press.

Guéraud, Octave und Pierre Jouguet. 1938. *Un livre d'écolier du IIIe siècle avant J.-C.* Publications de la Societé Royale Égyptienne de Papyrologie. Textes et Documents 2. Cairo: Institut français d'Archéologie orientale.

Hanhart, Robert. 1988. „Die Bedeutung der Septuaginta für die Definition des ‚Hellenistischen Judentums.'" Seiten 67-80 in *Congress Volume Jerusalem 1986.* Hrsg. von John A. Emerton. VTS 40. Leiden: Brill.

Harl, Marguerite. 1986. *La Genèse.* BdA 1. Paris: Cerf.

Harl, Marguerite, Gilles Dorival, und Olivier Munnich. 1988. *La Bible Grecque des Septante. Du judaïsme hellénistique au christianisme ancien.* 2me éd. Paris: Cerf.

Helck, Wolfgang. 1968-1969. „Proverbia 22,17ff. und die Lehre des Amenemope." *AfO* 22:21-29.

Honigman, Sylvie. 2003. *The Septuagint and Homeric Scholarship in Alexandria.* London: Routledge.

Huehnergard, John. 1987. *Ugaritic Vocabulary in Syllabic Transcription.* HSS 32. Atlanta: Scholars Press.

Hugo, Philippe. 2006. *Les deux visages d'Elie. Texte Massorétique et Septante dans l'histoire la plus ancienne du texte de 1 Rois 17-18.* OBO

217. Göttingen: Vandenhoeck & Ruprecht; Freiburg: Universitätsverlag.

Ilan, Tal. 2002. *Lexicon of Jewish Names in Late Antiquity, Part I. Palestine 330 BCE–200 CE.* TSAJ 91. Tübingen: Mohr Siebeck.

Joosten, Jan. 2000. „Une théologie de la Septante? Réflexions méthodologique sur l'interpretation de la version greque." *RTP* 132:31–46.

Kahle, Paul E. 1959. *The Cairo Geniza.* 2me éd. Oxford: Blackwell.

Koch, Klaus. 1993. *Geschichte der ägyptischen Religion. Von den Pyramiden bis zu den Mysterien der Isis.* Stuttgart: Kohlhammer.

———. 2005. *Daniel 1–4.* BKAT 22.1. Neukirchen-Vluyn: Neukirchener Verlag.

———. 2007. „Der hebräische Gott und die Gotteserfahrung der Nachbarvölker." Seiten 9–41 in *Der Gott Israels und die Götter des Orients. Religionsgeschichtliche Studien II.* Hrsg. von Klaus Koch, Friedhelm Hartenstein, und Martin Rösel. FRLANT 216. Göttingen: Vandenhoeck & Ruprecht.

Köckert, Matthias. 2000. „Literargeschichtliche und religionsgeschichtliche Beobachtungen zu Psalm 104." Seiten 259–79 in *Schriftauslegung in der Schrift. Festschrift für Odil Hannes Steck zu seinem 65. Geburtstag.* Hrsg. von Reinhard G. Kratz und Odil H. Steck. BZAW 300. Berlin: de Gruyter.

Kooij, Arie van der. 1981. *Die alten Textzeugen des Jesajabuches. Ein Beitrag zur Textgeschichte des Alten Testaments.* OBO 35. Göttingen: Vandenhoeck & Ruprecht; Freiburg: Universitätsverlag.

———. 1991. „Nehemiah 8:8 and the Question of the Targum-Tradition." Seiten 79–90 in *Tradition of the Text. Studies offered to Dominique Barthélemy in Celebration of His Seventieth Birthday.* Hrsg. von Gerard J. Norton und Steven Pisano. OBO 109. Göttingen: Vandenhoeck & Ruprecht; Freiburg: Universitätsverlag.

———. 1999. „The Origin and Purpose of Bible Translations in Ancient Judaism. Some Comments." *AR* 1:204–14.

———. 2000. „Zur Frage der Exegese im LXX-Psalter. Ein Beitrag zur Verhältnisbestimmung zwischen Original und Übersetzung." Seiten 366–79 in *Der Septuaginta-Psalter und seine Tochterübersetzungen.* Hrsg. von Anneli Aejmelaeus und Udo Quast. NAWG Phil-Hist Klasse 3, 230. MSU 24. Göttingen: Vandenhoeck & Ruprecht.

Kramer, Johannes. 1983. *Glossaria bilinguia in papyris et membranis reperta.* PTA 30. Bonn: Habelt.

———. 2001. *Glossaria bilinguia altera. (C. Gloss. biling. II)*. APF Beiheft 8. München: Saur.

Kreuzer, Siegfried. 2004. „Entstehung und Publikation der Septuaginta im Horizont frühptolemäischer Bildungs- und Kulturpolitik." Seiten 61–75 in Band 2 *Im Brennpunkt. Die Septuaginta. Studien zur Entstehung und Bedeutung der Griechischen Bibel*. Hrsg. von Siegfried Kreuzer und Jürgen Peter Lesch. BWANT 161. Stuttgart: Kohlhammer.

Lange, Nicholas de. 1996. *Greek Jewish Texts from the Cairo Genizah*. TSAJ 51. Tübingen: Mohr Siebeck.

Lee, James A. L. 1997. „Translations of the Old Testament, I. Greek." Seiten 776–83 in *Handbook of Classical Rhetoric in the Hellenistic Period, 330 B.C.–A.D. 400*. Hrsg. von Stanley E. Porter. Leiden: Brill.

Leipoldt, Johannes. 1950. „Von Übersetzungen und Übersetzern." Seiten 54–63 in *Aus Antike und Orient. Festschrift Wilhelm Schubart zum 75. Geburtstag*. Hrsg. von Siegfried Morenz. Leipzig: Harrassowitz.

MacLeod, Roy, ed. 2000. *The Library of Alexandria. Centre of Learning in the Ancient World*. London: Tauris.

Maehler, Herwig. 1983. „Die griechische Schule im ptolemäischen Ägypten." Seiten 191–203 in *Egypt and the Hellenistic World*. Hrsg. von Edmont van't Dack. StudHell 27. Leuven: Peeters.

Martin, Geoffrey Thorndike. 1989. *The Memphite Tomb of Ḥoremḥeb, Commander-in-Chief of Tutʿankhamūn. I. The Reliefs, Inscriptions, and Commentary*. London: Egypt Exploration Society.

Mélèze-Modrzejewski, Joseph. 1995. „Law and Justice in Ptolemaic Egypt." Seiten 1–19 in *Legal Documents of the Hellenistic World*. Hrsg. von Markham J. Geller, Herwig Maehler, und A. D. E. Lewis. London: Warburg Institute.

Mekawi Ouda, Nasser. 2004. „Die Mittel der internationalen Kommunikation zwischen Ägypten und Staaten Vorderasiens in der späten Bronzezeit." Diss., Freiburg im Breisgau.

Momigliano, Arnaldo. 1976. *Alien Wisdom. The Limits of Hellenization*. Cambridge: Cambridge University Press.

Mussies, Gerard. 1987. „Greek in Palestine and the Diaspora." Seiten 1040–64 in *The Jewish People in the First Century*. Hrsg. von S. Safrai und M. Stern. CRINT 1.2. Assen: Van Gorcum.

Nachtergael, Georges. 1971. „Fragments d'anthologies homériques. (P. Strasb. inv. 2374, P. Graec. Vindob. 26740, P. Hamb. II, 136)." *CdÉ* 41:344–51.

Naoumides, Mark 1969. „Fragments of Greek Lexicography." Seiten 181–202 in *Classical Studies Presented to Ben Edwin Perry by His Students and Colleagues at the University of Illinois.* Illinois Studies in Language and Literature 58. Urbana: University of Illinois.

Orth, Wolfgang. 2001. „Ptolemaios II. und die Septuaginta-Übersetzung." Seiten 97–114 in Band 1 *Im Brennpunkt. Die Septuaginta. Studien zur Entstehung und Bedeutung der griechischen Bibel.* Hrsg. von Heinz-Josef Fabry und Ulrich Offerhaus. BWANT 153. Stuttgart: Kohlhammer.

Pfeiffer, Rudolf. 1978. *Geschichte der klassischen Philologie.* 2., durchges. Auflage. München: Beck.

Pietersma, Albert. 2002. „A New Paradigm for Addressing Old Questions. The Relevance of the Interlinear Model for the Study of the Septuagint." Seiten 337–64 in *Bible and Computer. The Stellenbosch AIBI-6 Conference Proceedings of the Association internationale Bible et informatique, „From Alpha to Byte."* Hrsg. von Johann Cook. Leiden: Brill.

———. 2006. „Exegesis in the Septuagint. Possibilities and Limits." Seiten 33–45 in *Septuagint Research. Issues and Challenges in the Study of the Greek Jewish Scriptures.* Hrsg. von Wolfgang Kraus und R. Glen Wooden. SCS 53. Atlanta: Society of Biblical Literature.

Quack, Joachim Friedrich. 2005. „Medien der Alltagskultur in Ägypten und ihre Auswirkungen auf Palästina." Seiten 237–68 in *Medien im antiken Palästina. Materielle Kommunikation und Medialität als Thema der Palästinaarchäologie.* Hrsg. von Christian Frevel. FAT 2/10. Tübingen: Mohr Siebeck.

Rabin, Chaim. 1968. „The Translation Process and the Character of the Septuagint." *Text* 6:1–26.

Reade, Julian. 1983. *Assyrian Sculpture.* London: The British Museum.

Rocati, Alessandro. 1986. „Übersetzung." *LÄ* 6:833–38.

Rösel, Martin. 1994. *Übersetzung als Vollendung der Auslegung. Studien zur Genesis-Septuaginta.* BZAW 223. Berlin: de Gruyter.

———. 2000. „Israels Psalmen in Ägypten?" *VT* 50:81–99.

———. 2001. „Die Septuaginta-Version des Josuabuches." Seiten 197–212 in Band 1 *Im Brennpunkt. Die Septuaginta. Studien zur Entstehung und Bedeutung der griechischen Bibel.* Hrsg. von Heinz-Josef Fabry und Ulrich Offerhaus. BWANT 153. Stuttgart: Kohlhammer. [englische Übersetzung Kapitel 6 in diesem Band.]

———. 2006a. „Jakob, Bileam und der Messias." Seiten 151–75 in *The Septuagint and Messianism*. Hrsg. von Michael A. Knibb. BETL 195. Leuven: Peeters. [Kapitel 5 in diesem Band.]

———. 2006b. „Towards a Theology of the Septuagint." Seiten 239–52 in *Septuagint Research. Issues and Challenges in the Study of the Greek Jewish scriptures*. Hrsg. von Wolfgang Kraus und R. Glen Wooden. SCS 53. Atlanta: Society of Biblical Literature. [Kapitel 11 in diesem Band.]

———. 2007a. „Der Brief des Aristeas an Philokrates, der Tempel in Leontopolis und die Bedeutung des Religionsgeschichte Israels in hellenistischer Zeit." Seiten 327–44 in *Sieben Augen auf einem Stein. (Sach 3,9). Studien zur Literatur des Zweiten Tempels. Festschrift für Ina Willi-Plein zum 65. Geburtstag*. Hrsg. von Friedhelm Hartenstein und Michael Pietsch. Neukirchen-Vluyn: Neukirchener Verlag. [englische Übersetzung Kapitel 1 in diesem Band.]

———. 2007b. „Nomothesie. Zum Gesetzesverständnis der Septuaginta." Seiten 132–50 in Band 3 *Im Brennpunkt. Die Septuaginta. Studien zur Theologie, Anthropologie, Ekklesiologie, Eschatologie und Liturgie der Griechischen Bibel*. Hrsg. von Heinz-Josef Fabry und Dieter Böhler. BWANT 174. Stuttgart: Kohlhammer. [englische Übersetzung Kapitel 15 in diesem Band.]

Safrai, Shmuel. 1987. „Education and the Study of Torah." Seiten 945–70 in *The Jewish People in the First Century*. Hrsg. von Shmuel Safrai und Menahem Stern. CRINT 1.2. Assen: Van Gorcum.

Schenkel, Wolfgang. 1975. „Dolmetscher." *LÄ* 1:1116.

———. 1977. „Fremdsprachen." *LÄ* 2:314–15.

Schenker, Adrian. 2004. *Älteste Textgeschichte der Königsbücher. Die hebräische Vorlage der ursprünglichen Septuaginta als älteste Textform der Königsbücher*. OBO 199. Göttingen: Vandenhoeck & Ruprecht; Freiburg: Universitätsverlag.

Schipper, Bernd U. 2005. „Die Lehre des Amenemope und Prov 22,17–24,22—eine Neubestimmung des literarischen Verhältnisses (Teil 1 + 2)." *ZAW* 117:53–72 + 232–48.

Schunck, Klaus-Dietrich. 2003. *Nehemia*. BKAT 23.2, Lfg. 3. Neukirchen-Vluyn: Neukirchener Verlag.

Schwiderski, Dirk. 2000. *Handbuch des nordwestsemitischen Briefformulars. Ein Beitrag zur Echtheitsfrage der aramäischen Briefe des Esrabuches*. BZAW 295. Berlin: de Gruyter.

———. 2003. „Studien zur Redaktionsgeschichte und Religionsgeographie der akkadisch-aramäischen Bilingue vom Tell Fecherije." Seiten 31–47 in *Religion und Region. Götter und Kulte aus dem östlichen Mittelmeerraum*. Hrsg. von Elmar Schwertheim. Asia Minor Studien 45. Bonn: Habelt.

Seele, Astrid. 1995. *Römische Übersetzer, Nöte, Freiheiten, Absichten. Verfahren des literarischen Übersetzens in der griechisch-römischen Antike*. Darmstadt: Wissenschaftliche Buchgesellschaft.

Seminara, Stefano. 2002. „The Babylonian Science of the Translation and the Ideological Adjustment of the Sumerian Text to the ‚Target Culture.'" Seiten 245–55 in *Ideologies as Intercultural Phenomena*. Hrsg. von Antonio Panaino und Giovanni Pettinato. Melammu Symposia 3. Milano: Univ. di Bologna.

Siegert, Folker. 2001. *Zwischen Hebräischer Bibel und Altem Testament. Eine Einführung in die Septuaginta*. MJS 9. Münster: LIT.

Sjöberg, Åke. 1975. „Der Examentstext A." ZA 64:137–76.

Thackeray, Henry J. St. 1921. *The Septuagint and Jewish Worship: A Study on Origins*. The Schweich Lectures of the British Academy 13. London: Milford.

Tilly, Michael. 2005. *Einführung in die Septuaginta*. Darmstadt: Wissenschaftliche Buchgesellschaft.

Tov, Emanuel. 1981. „The Impact of the LXX Translation of the Pentateuch on the Translation of the Other Books." Seiten 577–92 in *Mélanges Dominique Barthélemy. Études bibliques offertes à l'occasion de son 60e anniversaire*. Hrsg. von Pierre Casetti. OBO 38. Göttingen: Vandenhoeck & Ruprecht; Freiburg: Universitätsverlag.

Ulshöfer, Andrea M. 2000. „Sprachbarrieren und ihre Überwindung. Translatorisches Handeln im Alten Orient." Seiten 163–70 in *Landscape in Ideology, Religion, Literature and Art*. Hrsg. von Lucio Milano. HANEM 3/2. Padova: Sargon.

Usener, Knut. 2004. „Die Septuaginta im Horizont des Hellenismus." Seiten 78–118 in Band 2 *Im Brennpunkt. Die Septuaginta. Studien zur Entstehung und Bedeutung der Griechischen Bibel*. Hrsg. von Siegfried Kreuzer und Jürgen Peter Lesch. BWANT 161. Stuttgart: Kohlhammer.

Veldhuis, Niek. 1999. „Continuity and Change in the Mesopotamian Lexical Tradition." Seiten 101–18 in *Aspects of Genre and Type in Pre-modern Literary Cultures*. Hrsg. von Bert Roest und Herman Vanstiphout. COMERS Communications 1. Groningen: Styx.

Veltri, Guiseppe. 1994. *Eine Tora für den König Talmai. Untersuchungen zum Übersetzungsverständnis in der jüdisch-hellenistischen und rabbinischen Literatur.* TSAJ 41. Tübingen: Mohr Siebeck.

Walter, Nikolaus. 1980. „Fragmente jüdisch-hellenistischer Exegeten. Aristobulos, Demetrios, Aristeas." *JSHRZ* 3.2:257–99.

Werner, J. 1992. „Zur Fremdsprachenproblematik in der griechisch-römischen Antike." Seiten 1–20 in *Zum Umgang mit fremden Sprachen in der griechisch-römischen Antike.* Hrsg. von Carl Werner Müller u.a. Palingenesia 36. Stuttgart: Steiner.

Westermann, Claus. 1982. *Genesis.* BKAT 1.3. Neukirchen-Vluyn: Neukirchener Verlag.

Wright, Benjamin G. 2003a. „Access to the Source. Cicero, Ben Sira, The Septuagint and Their Audiences." *JSJ* 34:1–27.

———. 2003b. „Why a Prologue? Ben Sira's Grandson and His Translation." Seiten 633–44 in *Emanuel. Studies in Hebrew Bible, Septuagint and Dead Sea Scrolls in Honour of Emanuel Tov.* Hrsg. von Shalom M. Paul. VTSup 94. Leiden: Brill.

3
Translators as Interpreters:
Scriptural Interpretation in the Septuagint

Everyone who is taking a close look at the research on the Septuagint, the Greek translation of the Hebrew Bible, will most likely come across two sentences.[1] The first is the "truism that any translation is an interpretation."[2] The second is a quotation from the introduction to the Greek translation of the book of Jesus Sirach, written by his alleged grandson: "For what was originally expressed in Hebrew does not have exactly the same sense when translated into another language. Not only this book, but even the Law itself, the Prophecies, and the rest of the books differ not a little when read in the original" (Sir Prologue 1:21–26 NRSV).

These two statements suggest that some changes were necessarily made when the Hebrew Bible was translated into Greek and that these changes can be attributed to certain acts of interpretation that inevitably belong to the process of translation. If so, several subsequent questions arise:
1. How is it possible to trace these acts of interpretation?
2. Is it possible to make a distinction between different kinds or levels of interpretation?

---

1. In this article, the term *Septuagint* (and its abbreviation in Roman numerals: LXX) is used for the Greek Bible in general, although it was originally coined as a designation for the Greek Pentateuch only. Also, the content of the canon of the LXX can differ between the manuscripts. See Dines 2004, 1–3, for the definition; Hengel 2002; Müller 1996, for the problem of the canon.

2. See, e.g., Wevers 1996, 87. A stimulating introduction into the problems of translation is Eco 2003. It is interesting that even the translated title of Eco's book (*Mouse or Rat? Translation as Negotiation*) shows a certain degree of interpretation, because the Italian original reads "*dire quasi la stessa cosa*" ("saying almost the same"). The English title is taken from one of the examples discussed in the book.

3. Are the reasons for and strategies of scriptural interpretation in the LXX discernable?
4. Are there any differences between the translations of individual books of the Hebrew Bible, and, if so, are different attitudes toward Scripture perceptible?
5. Finally, is it possible to discern some general principles of scriptural interpretation that can be detected in all or at least in most of the books of the LXX?

These five questions will serve to outline the problem. They are kept rather general here to give an impression of the topics that are discussed in LXX research.³ Because of the limited space of this article, it will not be possible to answer them in detail; they will nevertheless prove helpful to provide the heuristic horizon for our dealing with these texts.

1. The Lawgiver in Psalm 9:21 as an Example

Following these general questions, I will begin with a textual example from the book of the Psalms in order to illustrate the complexity of LXX exegesis and to justify the differentiation just presented. Psalm 9:21 in the Hebrew Bible (MT) reads:

שיתה יהוה מורה להם ידעו גוים אנוש המה
Put fear to them, O Lord; nations shall know that they are (only) human.⁴

In the Greek version of the LXX, the verse sounds quite different:

κατάστησον κύριε νομοθέτην ἐπ' αὐτούς, γνώτωσαν ἔθνη ὅτι ἄνθρωποί εἰσιν.
Appoint, o Lord, a lawgiver over them; nations shall know that they are humans.

When comparing the texts, it is obvious that every element of the Hebrew (suffixes included) has a counterpart in the Greek version; the syntactical sequence of the words is the same. This is a characteristic of what one usually calls a "literal translation," it is one of the typical features of most

---

3. A stimulating collection of articles describing the current state of research in LXX studies is Kraus and Wooden 2006.
4. Unless otherwise noted, all translations are mine.

translations of the LXX.⁵ It should be noticed that the plural ἄνθρωποί ("humans") is used to translate the singular אנוש ("man"), but since this word can be understood as a collective ("mankind") and the plural is signaled by המה ("they") and גוים ("nations"), the translation only makes this fact explicit. This can be understood as a linguistic interpretation, but since acts like these necessarily belong to the process of reading and translation, it may be more appropriate to label it as *linguistic decoding*.⁶

The most interesting and important deviation in this verse is the translation of מורה ("fear") by νομοθέτης ("lawgiver"). When returning to the question (1) posed above (how is it possible to trace acts of interpretation?), the initial answer is quite clear: the meaning of the translated word is completely different from its *Vorlage*, and, moreover, it changes the meaning of the whole verse. The nations are able to discern their humanity not through an abstract act of fear of God but through his torah.

Who was responsible for this interpretation? Since the LXX is a translation, it is always possible that it refers back to a different *Vorlage* so that it faithfully reproduces the meaning of a different Hebrew version. This means that, after an initial comparison of the texts, we need to employ the help of textual criticism in order to determine whether the text we read in the modern *Biblia Hebraica* does in fact represent the same or at least a similar version as the one which the translator had as his *Vorlage*; and, is the modern edition of the LXX reliable, so that one can safely assume that this is the text that comes from the hand of the translator, not from any kind of later redaction?⁷

In the case of Ps 9:21, there is in fact a variant in the Hebrew textual tradition concerning מוֹרָה ("fear"), the word in question. Several manu-

---

5. It is important to notice that this use of the terms "free" and "literal" is approximate. For an exhaustive treatment of the problem, see Barr 1979, 294, for a list of six distinguishing features between literal and free translations.

6. See Siegert 2001, 121, for this distinction.

7. The problems associated with the use of the LXX for the reconstruction of its parent Hebrew text and the text-critical search for the original LXX, the history of its revisions and modern editions, cannot be discussed here. It may suffice to refer interested readers to the introductions by Jobes and Silva 2000; Tov 1997; and Fernández Marcos 2000. It should be added that several scholars hold the opinion that in cases of larger divergences between MT and LXX one has to assume the existence of a different *Vorlage* of the LXX, even if there is no witness for this text other than the translation itself. This position minimizes the possibility to attribute interpretations to the translators.

scripts read מורא, but this is only an orthographical variant that corrects the original, difficult reading to a more usual one. One can therefore conclude that the rendering "lawgiver" can be judged to be an interpretation as the result of the translation. Question (1) can thus be answered positively: Ps 9:21 is an example of scriptural interpretation.

The next question (2) concerns the kind of interpretation we can see in the current text. One should bear in mind that the translator read an unvocalized text (מורה). When decoding the verse, he has obviously derived this word as a participle *hiphil* from the root ירה III, which can mean "to instruct, to teach" (see *HALOT*). Thus the linguistic decoding would lead to the noun "instructor, teacher" (מוֹרֶה). Moreover, it is also possible that he found an etymological connection to the word תורה ("law"), which can also be derived from the root ירה.[8] Thus one can assume a combination of linguistic signals that has led the translator to amplify the meaning "instructor" to "lawgiver." This interpretation is clearly a kind of theologically motivated interpretation, because in other psalms one can find more "literal" renderings of the verb ירה ("teach, instruct").[9] Since the Lord is addressed in this verse, the new interpretation has consequences that go even further: it is not the Lord but his helpful law that brings fear to the nations.

However, question (2) can be answered in yet another way, which leads us directly to the problems that have to be discussed with respect to question (3): the reasons and strategies for interpretation. Although the word νομοθέτης ("lawgiver") in Ps 9:21 is a *hapax legomenon* in the LXX, one can find similar interpretations. According to the difficult text in Ps 84(83):7, the pious can go through a valley that has been covered by the early rain with blessings:

עברי בעמק הבכא מעין ישיתוהו גם־ברכות יעטה מורה
ἐν τῇ κοιλάδι τοῦ κλαυθμῶνος εἰς τόπον, ὃν ἔθετο· καὶ γὰρ εὐλογίας δώσει ὁ νομοθετῶν.

The MT reads מוֹרֶה ("early rain"). The translator of the LXX has chosen a similar linguistic and theological explanation of the Hebrew noun as in Ps 9:21, for we can read: "for the lawgiver [νομοθετῶν] will give blessings." Thus in Ps 84(83):7 the difficult metaphor of valley and rain has been

---

8. See Monsengwo Pasinya 1973, 131–35.
9. Pss 32(31):8; 44(43):5; 85(84):11; see Austermann 2003, 177–78.

avoided, and again the emphasis falls on the helpful, benevolent action of God and his law. Moreover, in other psalms one can also see that the verb ירה ("teach, instruct") has been translated by νομοθετήσει ("to be given the law").[10] Obviously the translator wanted to stress that the torah is the only reliable base for instruction; therefore one can assume that he followed a particular strategy of interpretation when he translated a verse that speaks about instructions and teaching.[11]

This means that question (3) can be answered in the affirmative, too: in the book of Psalms there are strategies of interpretation concerning the idea of the torah that affect individual renderings throughout the book.[12] But again, the question can be answered another way: the translation "lawgiver" in Ps 9:21 and elsewhere attests to the phenomenon of intertextuality.[13] By this I mean that a text can refer to other texts so that its meaning is enhanced. In the case of a translation, intertextuality can also mean that the translator has chosen his equivalents under the influence of other, previously translated texts. This can be due to the fact that in antiquity there was not something like a lexicon.[14] It may be that he was not sure about the exact meaning of a Hebrew word, so that another translation served as an aid for orientation.[15] It is also possible that he wanted to create a connection between texts. In this case, the translation would refer to a wider horizon of thoughts and concepts than the original.

In the case of the "lawgiver" in Ps 9:21, the translation clearly depends on Exod 24:12 and Deut 17:10, where the verb ירה ("teach, instruct") refers to the tablets of the commandments, which God has given to instruct his people. In both instances, the Greek translations were using νομοθετέω ("to give the law"), thus introducing this compound verb into the biblical language and emphasizing the special kind of divine teaching. The translator of the Psalms ties his references to the teaching of the torah back to the revelation of this law at Mount Sinai (or Horeb in Deuteronomy).

---

10. Pss 25(24):8 + 12; 27(26):11, and especially in the torah Ps 119(118):33, 102, 104.

11. It is interesting to note that in the Psalms there are other interpretative translations that advance the idea of a divine education; see Pss 2:12; 90(89):10.

12. This is the most important result of the dissertation by Austermann 2003.

13. See Dorival 1995, for an introduction to this field of research.

14. See for this problem Tov 1999b; and the critical remarks by Barr 2003.

15. Tov 1999a.

2. The Greek Bible as a Collection of Scriptures and the Question of Overall Concepts

The discussion of Ps 9:21 has served to give some exemplary answers to three of the five questions posed above. Questions (4) and (5) cannot be settled on the basis of the exegesis of one verse only but require more information. As for the individual books of the LXX and the different attitudes of their translators toward their task, it is now clear from the results of modern research that every book has to be treated as a separate entity. As a rule of thumb one can start with the assumption that each book has been translated by an individual translator (or perhaps by a group with the same working method). Only occasionally have scholars found sufficient reasons to reckon with more than one translator; the most important case is the tabernacle account in the book of Exodus.[16]

Although research on the question of the chronological setting and geographical origins of these individual translations has in most cases not led to unambiguous results, it is clear that the books of the Hebrew Bible were translated in the time from the third century BCE until the first century CE. During this period some of the existing translations were reworked or replaced by revisions or new translations. This explains why we have duplicate editions, for example, in the case of the books of Daniel, Judges, or Kingdoms. Presumably, most translations were carried out in Alexandria in Egypt, where the largest Jewish community outside of Israel flourished and where the need to possess the Holy Scriptures in Greek was urgent. But it is also possible that some of the books were translated in Israel, in Antioch, or in Leontopolis, another important Jewish settlement in Egypt, where even a second Jewish temple besides the one in Jerusalem was built.[17]

When working on the books of the LXX, it is important to bear these different chronological and geographical milieus in mind as the background for the translator's hermeneutic, because the way Scripture is interpreted always depends on theological tendencies and religious experiences (e.g., the Maccabean crisis) that are dominant at that time and in that social group.

---

16. Wade 2003.
17. For an overview, see the tables in Harl, Dorival, and Munnich 1988, 93, 107, 111.

The fact that the LXX has to be seen as a collection of Scriptures from different historical periods and geographical regions has important ramifications for our answer to question (5), the question whether or not we can detect some overall principles of scriptural interpretation in the whole of the Septuagint. The answer cannot be positive. The differences between some translations are so important—for example, between the book of Job on the one hand and Qohelet on the other, or between Exodus and Samuel—that common characteristics in scriptural interpretation that apply equally to all of them cannot be found. However, if individual translations are grouped according to their translational characteristics, then it is indeed possible to see some lines of interpretation that can be regarded as typical for these groups of books.[18]

To illustrate this approach one can refer to the enhanced importance of the concept of νόμος ("law"). This Greek word has been used very frequently, not only for Hebrew תורה ("law"), but also for other words like חקה ("ordinance") or משפט ("judgment"); moreover, the opposite ἀνομία ("lawlessness") was used to render a wide variety of Hebrew words, denoting acts of sin, lawlessness, or injustice. Therefore the idea of νόμος and the negative results of deviating from this νόμος are much more present in the Greek than in the Hebrew Bible. Thus the importance of God's law for Israel is emphasized in most of the books of the LXX. A similar process can be seen when looking at the concept of תורה in the late books of the Hebrew Bible or in Qumran.[19] It is obvious that the individual translations are influenced by an overall theological concept that was common in the Hellenistic age. This means that a positive answer for question (5) is possible, as long as we are dealing with a specific topic only and with a limited number of books.

3. A Minimalistic Objection: The Paradigm of Interlinearity

The exegesis of Ps 9:21 and the five questions to classify elements of scriptural interpretation in the LXX are based on the assumption that most of the translators wanted to produce a text that could be read and understood independently of its Hebrew *Vorlage*. Obviously they were aware that they

---

18. A fuller methodological discussion of the possibilities and limitations of such a summarizing theology of several books of the Septuagint can be found in Rösel 2006b [ch. 11 in this volume].

19. For a fuller treatment of this problem see Rösel 2007a [ch. 15 in this volume].

were translating and thereby producing a canonical text.[20] Moreover, they were also willing—although to a different extent—to correct obvious mistakes, clarify dubious passages, avoid misinterpretations, or bring the texts in line with its common interpretation in the religious community of the translator. While it is obvious that during the later *reception* history, especially in Christian communities, some new interpretations came to be associated with the texts (e.g., some messianic readings), it is also clear that already the act of *producing* the translation involved several processes, some linguistically, and others culturally and theologically motivated (questions 2, 3, and 5).[21]

The basic idea of how to approach the LXX is challenged by a new paradigm, which has been worked out by Albert Pietersma and his colleagues.[22] His concept has become very important, because the *New English Translation of the Septuagint* (NETS) is based on its principles. NETS is undoubtedly becoming very influential for the evaluation of the LXX in the English-speaking world. According to Pietersma, many of the translations in the LXX are not meant to be read independently. The Greek text was translated as a tool to understand the Hebrew, a "crib for the study of the Hebrew."[23] Only at a later stage in the history of reception were the Greek texts read independently. The paradigm is called "interlinear" because Pietersma compares the LXX with bilingual texts that were used in Hellenistic schools. These papyri originally had a Latin text (mostly by Virgil) in one column and its translation into Greek in the other.[24] The lines of these columns were very short, containing no more than one up to a few words. According to this hypothesis it can easily be explained why in the LXX the Greek translation very often follows the word order of the Hebrew slavishly, which leads to a syntax that must have sounded very strange to Greek-speaking people. The hypothesis can also answer the question of why there are inconsistencies in the translations: if the translator was mainly thinking in small units as a short line of a column, it is understandable that he was not aiming for the same translation of one Hebrew word throughout the book. Furthermore, Pietersma argues

---

20. Wevers 1996, 95.
21. For the necessary differentiation between production and reception, see Pietersma 2006b, 50–52. I disagree with his overall approach.
22. Pietersma 2002.
23. Pietersma 2002, 360.
24. See Cavenaile 1958; and Kramer 2001, 28, 100–104 for a fable by Aesop.

3. Translators as Interpreters

that the connotations of the Greek words stay in the semantic range of the Hebrew. Even if a word such as ψυχή or κόσμος has a specific significance in the Greek-speaking world, only the meaning of its Hebrew counterpart can safely be applied in the translation. Applying its usual Greek meaning would mean that the reception overrules the original meaning of the text.[25] Finally, Pietersma asserts that, like the parallel bilingual papyri, the origins of the LXX must also be seen in the educational goals of schools.[26]

This theory is the basis for one of the most significant features of the new translation of the LXX into English (NETS), which has been shaped under the editorial leadership of Albert Pietersma. It uses a translation of the Hebrew Bible, the NRSV, as the basic referential document, which is accepted also as the translation of the Greek Bible as long as its rendering can be seen as correct.[27] This means that the English translation of the LXX does not stand alone either but also refers back to the Hebrew text.[28]

Although this paradigm can in fact shed some light on obscure phenomena of the translational process, some serious problems remain. First, it should be stated that the bilingual Virgil papyri are not attested prior to the third century CE. From the first century CE we have some comparable texts with verses by Homer in two columns, one in classic Greek and one in Koine. There is no proof that these aids existed as early as in the third century BCE. Moreover, those texts were not produced to learn basic Latin, but perhaps to give students an impression of the exemplary syntactical style of the poet. The Greek translations in these papyri are at times fragmented and nearly unintelligible. They are not coherent texts but lists of words and phrases that should be used as examples.[29] Second, when comparing different papyri in which the same text from Virgil is translated, one can see a high degree of variance between the translations. The aim of these texts has obviously not been to produce something like an authoritative Greek version of Virgil or Cicero. Therefore these bilingual

---

25. See Pietersma 2006a, 38: "The primary cognitive process is thus that Greek X is deemed a good match for Hebrew Y." Earlier on this page he writes: "I am fully aware that this may sound like linguistic heresy."

26. But see Cribiore 1996, 28, who argues against the view that these bilingual papyri were written for educational purposes in schools.

27. See Pietersma and Wright 2007.

28. For the problem of how to deal with books without a Hebrew original, see Schaper 2006.

29. These arguments are based on Gaebel 1969–1970, 298–301.

papyri are not comparable to the LXX, because from the translation of Genesis legible and coherent texts were produced, even if their Hebraistic syntax may have sounded strange for Greek-speaking readers.

A third and even more important objection concerns Pietersma's focus on small translational units. According to his view, "the primary reason for a word's presence in such a translated text is to represent the Hebrew counterpart, rather than its appropriateness to the new context that is being created."[30] This does include, as mentioned earlier, the assumption that the Greek equivalents chosen by the translators have no other meaning than that of their Hebrew counterparts. Pietersma himself labels this position a kind of "linguistic heresy."[31] However, if this were a correct assumption, one could not explain why there are so many newly created Greek words (*neologisms*) in the LXX, for example, why the translators have carefully avoided words such as βωμός ("altar")—except for heathen offerings—and only used θυσιαστήριον ("place of offering") for the true cult of the God of Israel (see Num 4:11 and 23:3).

Moreover, there is an overwhelming number of examples—some of them are given in the next sections—where the translators did not only look for a quantitative equation between the Hebrew text and the Greek version but were also trying hard to produce an appropriate meaning, as we have seen in the case of the "lawgiver." Finally, it should be stated that in the translations of the LXX numerous instances can be seen where a translation goes far beyond the level of the small unit of a single line. Mention has already been made of the phenomenon of intertextual translations. One can also refer to renderings in which the Greek text is stylistically improved over the Hebrew, as well as to harmonizations between biblical texts, for example, in the account of the creation in Gen 1 or in the flood story in Gen 6–8.[32] One can add that the first known translation of the LXX, the book of Genesis, is of high quality and shows such lexical consistency as is hardly conceivable if we presume that it was produced in a school.[33] It is therefore reasonable to conclude that the hermeneutical presuppositions that lie behind the paradigm of interlinearity do not fit

---

30. Pietersma 2006a, 38.
31. Pietersma 2006a, 38.
32. See, e.g., Amos 1:13–2:6, and Gen 1:2, in Dines 2004, 54–57.
33. See van der Kooij 1998, for a more convincing theory that the translators must be seen as well-trained scribes. I for myself have proposed to see the origins of the Greek Pentateuch in an academic milieu like the *museion* in Alexandria; see

4. Examples of Interpretations in the Septuagint

Interpretations were introduced into the Greek text for different reasons. They were used inter alia because the translators wanted to clarify obscure passages, to harmonize or improve texts, or to avoid possible misunderstandings. In a number of cases they also wanted to refer to other biblical texts or to theological or cultural contexts. Moreover, one can also see that texts were applied to a new social or historical situation, mostly because of the fact that the translation was carried out in the diaspora. The remainder of this article will illustrate these phenomena by collecting some striking examples and arranging them in a systematic order. The examples will be taken mainly from the books of the Greek Pentateuch and the Psalms, because a lot of important research on these books has been carried out. It is also interesting to see how the translators were interpreting in the context of narratives or liturgical texts. In the prophetic texts and in the book of Proverbs one can find an even higher degree of scriptural interpretation, because from the start prophecies were used for different applications, and educational texts were intended to be actualized.[34]

The following examples are related to questions (2) and (3) posed at the beginning of this article. It will be demonstrated what kinds or levels of interpretation one can find in the LXX and what reasons one can assume that have led the translators to produce the renderings in question. I have chosen a rough system of classification, which begins with cases in which the translators refused to interpret their text and thus created a version that called for an interpretation on the side of the readers. I then move to instances in which the interpretations are the result of linguistic problems. Finally, we will look at texts that prove that the translators were actively attempting to improve their text, to enhance it, or to give it a specific interpretation.[35]

Rösel 1994, 254–60. This theory was accepted and expanded by Siegfried Kreuzer, see Kreuzer 2004.

34. On Proverbs, see Cook 2001; on Isaiah, see van der Kooij 1989.

35. Detailed discussions of the crucial texts can be found in Wevers's *Notes* on the individual books of the Pentateuch (e.g., Wevers 1993), and in the volumes of *La Bible d'Alexandrie* (e.g., Harl 1986).

4.1. No Interpretation Means: Interpreting Differently

First there are several instances in which the translators obviously avoided interpreting the text in order to provide their own interpretation.

> Gen 6:14:
>
> קנים תעשה את־התבה
>
> "make it an ark with compartments"
> νοσσιὰς ποιήσεις τὴν κιβωτόν
> "you shall make the ark with nests" (NETS)

Well known is the translation νοσσία ("brood, nest"; also "beehive") for קן ("nest") in Gen 6:14, where Noah is ordered to make the ark with compartments. According to James Barr, the translator was not able to understand this passage and transferred the problem to his readers by using a literal rendering.[36]

Another example of this type can be found in Gen 11:1.

> Gen 11:1:
>
> ויהי כל־הארץ שפה אחת ודברים אחדים
> "And the whole earth had one language and the same words." (NRSV)
> Καὶ ἦν πᾶσα ἡ γῆ χεῖλος ἕν, καὶ φωνὴ μία πᾶσιν.
> "And the whole earth was one lip, and there was one speech *for all*." (NETS)

According to the Hebrew text the whole earth had one language (שָׂפָה אֶחָת). In the LXX this has been translated quite literally by χεῖλος ἕν; the earth was one lip, which sounds quite strange.[37] The interesting fact is that in both contexts the translator has demonstrated his willingness to explain difficult passages by referring to other biblical texts (6:14) or by adding a word (11:1), so translating more freely.

This phenomenon occurs more often, also in other translations. In the book of Kingdoms, for example, one can find the tendency to transcribe obscure words (4 Kgdms 20:12; 23:7).[38] In an important article on Ps 29(28):6, Adrian Schenker has demonstrated that in some cases

---

36. Barr 1979, 293; see Rösel 1994, 168.

37. Perhaps the translator did not intend the meaning "lip" but "bank," referring to a primeval bank of the waters where all humans lived prior to their dispersion over the world; see Rösel 1994, 214.

38. See Siegert 2001, 284–86, for a more exhaustive discussion of these examples.

the translator obviously wanted to keep the meaning of some passages obscure. The Greek text reads: "He will beat them small," instead of "He makes Lebanon skip."[39] It is possible that even this refusal to interpret is the expression of a certain theological assumption that the words of Scripture can transfer their meaning even if they are hardly comprehensible.[40]

4.2. Linguistic Decoding and Interpretation

As argued earlier, usually the act of vocalizing the Hebrew consonantal text cannot be seen as an act of interpretation but as necessary linguistic decoding. But there are numerous instances where the boundaries between decoding and interpretation are porous. A specific decision regarding how to vocalize or to deduce the meaning of a word in its context can change the meaning of the passage in question.

Hab 3:5

לפניו ילך דבר ויצא רשף לרגליו

πρὸ προσώπου αὐτοῦ πορεύσεται λόγος, καὶ ἐξελεύσεται, ἐν πεδίλοις οἱ πόδες αὐτοῦ.

One of the most striking examples is Hab 3:5. The MT reads, "Before him went pestilence." The translator has derived the word דֶּבֶר ("pestilence") from דָּבָר ("word, speech")—perhaps because he wanted to avoid the notion of God's disease—and therefore translated: "Before his face a word will go." Since the second part of the verse now no longer fit this statement, it was changed to: "and he will go out—his feet in sandals." The Hebrew text has: "and plague followed close behind."[41]

Even today, the exact meaning of אל שדי (usually translated "God Almighty") remains unclear. Already in the oldest translations we can find this uncertainty: The translator of the Greek Genesis has used ὁ θεός σου ("your God"; Gen 17:1) or ὁ θεός μου ("my God"; 48:3), thus stressing the personal relation between God and the fathers. It is possible that this rendering is based on the linguistic derivation of שדי from Aramaic

---

39. Schenker 1994.
40. Joosten 2000, esp. 42–44.
41. The same confusion pestilence/word has happened in Ps 91(90):3, 6. For the difficulties in explaining the whole verse Hab 3:5, see Harl and Dupont-Roc 1999, 289–90.

דִּי (+ the relative particle שֶׁ or שֶׁל), a particle of relation that could be used to mark a genitive. Later translators have used a different strategy of decoding, because in the book of Ruth one can find ὁ ἱκανός ("he who is sufficient"; 1:20) for אל שדי. Here the rendering is based on the Hebrew דַּי ("sufficiency"); the theological meaning of this designation of God has completely changed. Moreover, in the translation of Job, which is generally judged to be much less literal than others, one can find a third solution of the problem: שדי was translated παντοκράτωρ ("Almighty"; 5:17), which has in other books been used for צבאות ("God of hosts"; e.g., Hab 2:13); the problem is solved by intertextuality.[42] It is reasonable that the translation παντοκράτωρ ("Almighty") reflects the attempt to accentuate God's power.

Num 24:7

יזל־מים מדליו וזרעו במים רבים וירם מאגג מלכו ותנשא מלכתו
ἐξελεύσεται ἄνθρωπος ἐκ τοῦ σπέρματος αὐτοῦ καὶ κυριεύσει ἐθνῶν πολλῶν,
καὶ ὑψωθήσεται ἢ Γωγ βασιλεία αὐτοῦ, καὶ αὐξηθήσεται ἡ βασιλεία αὐτοῦ.

Another interesting development from decoding to interpretation can be seen in Num 24:7. The Hebrew text starts with יזל־מים מדליו ("Water shall flow from his buckets"). In the Greek version the text reads: ἐξελεύσεται ἄνθρωπος ἐκ τοῦ σπέρματος αὐτοῦ ("A man shall come out of his seed"). The translator has obviously derived the verbal form יִזַּל from Aramaic אזל ("go, come").[43] This led him to parallel this verse with 24:17, where it is said that a star will come out of Jacob and a man from Israel. Therefore he translated also 24:7 in such a way that it is now the second important messianic announcement in the Balaam narrative.[44] Admittedly, one cannot say definitely whether the translator came from the Aramaic meaning of the verb to the messianic interpretation or from a preceding interpretation of the passage to this specific decoding and rendering.

Num 16,15

ויחר למשה מאד ויאמר אל־יהוה אל־תפן אל־מנחתם
לא חמור אחד מהם נשאתי ולא הרעתי את־אחד מהם

---

42. On this problem, see Olofsson 1990, 111–12; and Siegert 2001, 207–8.

43. The problem of the linguistic development from spoken Late Hebrew to Aramaic in the Hellenistic period cannot be discussed here. See Tov 1997, 105–16; Joosten 2003.

44. For a fuller discussion of Num 24, see Rösel 2006a [ch. 5 in this volume].

καὶ ἐβαρυθύμησεν Μωυσῆς σφόδρα καὶ εἶπεν πρὸς κύριον Μὴ προσσχῇς
εἰς τὴν θυσίαν αὐτῶν· οὐκ ἐπιθύμημα οὐδενὸς αὐτῶν εἴληφα οὐδὲ ἐκάκωσα
οὐδένα αὐτῶν.

The same insecurity can be observed in an interesting case of orthographical decoding. In Num 16:15 Moses states in the conflict with the group of Korah: "I have not taken one *donkey* from them!" The Greek version has: "I have not taken away the *desire* of any one of them." It is obvious that the translator has read חמוד ("desire") instead of חמור ("donkey"); the confusion of *dalet* and *resh* is quite frequent. But it is not clear whether this was mere accident or based on the translator's idea that the notion of Moses stealing things should be avoided.[45]

Ps 90(89),2b + 3a:

ומעולם עד־עולם אתה אל
תשב אנוש עד־דכא ותאמר

ἀπὸ τοῦ αἰῶνος ἕως τοῦ αἰῶνος σὺ εἶ.
μὴ ἀποστρέψῃς ἄνθρωπον εἰς ταπείνωσιν

Another phenomenon that can be discussed under the header of "decoding and interpretation" is the problem of word and verse divisions.[46] In Ps 90(89):2–3 the translator has seen the last word from verse 2, אֵל ("God") as the opening of the next verse. Moreover, he understood it as the negation אַל, which completely changed the meaning of verse 3. It now reads: "Do not turn man back to the state of humiliation." The Hebrew text has the contrary: "You return man to dust."

Deut 26:5

ארמי אבד אבי וירד מצרימה

Συρίαν ἀπέβαλεν ὁ πατήρ μου καὶ κατέβη εἰς Αἴγυπτον

A different division of two words can help to explain the deviation between LXX and MT in the confession Deut 26:5. While the MT has "A wandering Aramean was my ancestor," LXX reads "My father abandoned Syria." This can be seen as an improvement of the text because the narratives of the patriarchs do not state that the fathers, Abraham or Jacob, were Arame-

---

45. Tov 1997, 101, who calls this phenomenon "tendentious paleographical exegesis."
46. See Tov 1997, 117–21, for further examples.

ans but that they have come from Haran in Syria (Gen 11:31; 28:10). The rendering can easily be explained if one assumes that the translator has not read ארמי אבד ("a wandering Aramean") but ארם יאבד ("Aram, he left"), then modernizing "Aram" to "Syria" and taking it as an accusative. Again, it is hard to decide whether this was an accidental misreading or an intended act of interpretation on the side of the translator. But since in later rabbinic sources this method of enhancing the meaning of a text by using new divisions of words (*notarikon*) is used frequently, one can assume that it was a deliberate exegesis carried out by the translator.[47]

From these few examples it has become clear that interpretation can often be induced by linguistic or orthographical peculiarities in the Hebrew text, which then leads the translator to find a less ambiguous rendering. In this process, his own religious or theological convictions can easily guide the process of translating the word in question adequately.[48] This means that there has not been a uniform and overall strategy of interpretation, but an openness on the side of the translator to update the text where it has seemed suitable or necessary.

4.3. Improvements of the Text

As we have seen earlier, there is sometimes a tendency to keep literal translations, even if the text thus produced is hard to understand. On the other hand, in some cases we notice an effort to improve the text. One of the most striking phenomena of this kind is the frequently occurring harmonization. As an example, in Gen 1 the translator has not only added several sentences that seem to be missing in the clearly structured Hebrew text, moreover, he has tried to smooth out the problem that there are two conflicting accounts of the creation. Thus he has translated 2:3: "God ceased from all his works which he *began to do*," instead of: "God rested from all the work that he had done in creation" (NRSV). In 2:9, 19 he added ἔτι ("*further* God made") over against his parent text, thus emphasizing that there is only one act of creation. It should be added that

---

47. See Kreuzer 2007, 49. The observation that some predecessors of the rabbinic rules stand behind some of the LXX translations goes back to the pioneering work of Frankel 1851, where still a wealth of interesting examples can be found.

48. See also the different strategies to deal with unknown words, which Tov has systematized: contextual guesses and manipulations; reliance of parallelisms; employments of general words; or etymological renderings (Tov 1999a).

3. Translators as Interpreters 73

the translator has not only harmonized the texts of Gen 1 and 2; from his choice of equivalents it is also clear that he has used the Platonic idea of a twofold creation of the immaterial and material world as a paradigm to understand the sequence of Gen 1 and 2.[49]

Harmonizations can be found throughout the LXX. In some cases, as in Gen 1 or in the account of the flood (e.g., Gen 7:3), texts were added so that different passages match each other. In Num 1 the list of tribes has been standardized by additions and omissions. Moreover, it has been rearranged to match the order of the sons of Jacob in Gen 35 and 49. In other instances it was sufficient to use only one Greek equivalent for different Hebrew words, or to change the number of verbs or nouns. There are also cases in which one translator harmonized his text with passages from other books.[50] For example, Num 24:7, which we discussed above, obviously has been brought in line with Gen 49:10.

Another way to improve a text was to translate some of the stylistic features of the Hebrew into better Greek. The Hebrew narratives are characterized by the use of a paratactic syntax: the sentences are mostly connected by "and," which led to a rather clumsy style. The easiest way was to translate the conjunctive *waw* not only by καί ("and") but also by other particles like the adversative δέ ("but"). This can be easily seen in Gen 3. In Gen 3:1 δέ is used to signal the new topic. In Gen 3:3 δέ stands to emphasize the central commandment, and in 3:17 one can find δέ in the final condemnation of Adam (this is also a harmonization with v. 11). The same attempt to bring a clearer structure into the narrative can be seen in Gen 4:1. Here the use of "but" marks the beginning of the story, and in 4:5 emphasis is laid on the main problem: *but* God did not accept Cain's offering.

The account of the flood begins in its Greek version (Gen 6:5–6) with another stylistic improvement. Here the paratactical structure of the sentence ("and ... and ... and") was rendered into a hypotactical, subordinate one, using a participle: "When Lord-God saw."[51] This rendering is

---

49. For a detailed argumentation, see Rösel 1994, 28–87.
50. See the instructive list in Dorival 1994, 42–43, and the discussions of the texts in his commentary. It should be added that it is not always easy to distinguish harmonizations from intertextual translations.
51. There are also cases in which the use of participles to avoid the paratactical structure of the Hebrew cannot be seen as an improvement; see the striking example in Gen 22:9–10, where a chain of seven *waw*-consecutive clauses has been used in the

quite frequent in the Balaam narrative in Num 22–24 (but not in the surrounding passages); the Greek version of this account gives a much more dynamic impression. In other cases sentences have been changed from a prospective to a retrospective view by using the future tense in the Greek text for an imperfect in the Hebrew (Gen 22:14). In Num 14:3 one can see that a question in the Hebrew has been changed to an affirmative sentence in the Greek version.

Num 8:9

והקהלת את־כל־עדת בני ישראל

καὶ συνάξεις πᾶσαν συναγωγὴν υἱῶν Ισραηλ

Although some of the improvements have the effect that the translated text sounds more like a Greek text, it is also possible to find the contrary. In Num 8:9 the Hebrew "assemble the whole congregation" is translated as "you shall assemble all the assembly." The LXX version has a *figura etymologica*, which is not very common in Greek literature.[52] But there are also instances where this figure has not been translated, for example, in Gen 2:16 or in Gen 11:3.

Gen 11:3

הבה נלבנה לבנים ונשרפה לשרפה

Δεῦτε πλινθεύσωμεν πλίνθους καὶ ὀπτήσωμεν αὐτὰς πυρί

Here the first *figura etymologica* has been translated "let us brick-makingly make bricks," the second not: "let us burn them in fire" (the translator also added αὐτάς ["them"] for the sake of clarification). There is no strategy discernable why the translators sometimes kept this Hebraism, sometimes skipped it, and occasionally imitated it.

Another characteristic feature of the Hebrew texts, especially from the prophetic or the wisdom literature, is the use of the *parallelismus membrorum*. Here the same multiplicity of approaches can be seen. Sometimes it is rendered quite literally, as in Gen 27:29: "accursed is who curses you, and blessed is who blesses you."

Hebrew to intensify the drama of the story. The LXX has used three participles and sounds much less dramatic. Beck 2000, 30, offers a lot of interesting examples for the stylistic intentions of the translators.

52. See, e.g., Tov 1999c; and Sollamo 1985.

Num 27:17

אשר־יצא לפניהם ואשר יבא לפניהם ואשר יוציאם ואשר יביאם
ולא תהיה עדת יהוה כצאן אשר אין־להם רעה

ὅστις ἐξελεύσεται πρὸ προσώπου αὐτῶν καὶ ὅστις εἰσελεύσεται πρὸ προσώπου
αὐτῶν καὶ ὅστις ἐξάξει αὐτοὺς καὶ ὅστις εἰσάξει αὐτούς,
καὶ οὐκ ἔσται ἡ συναγωγὴ κυρίου ὡσεὶ πρόβατα, οἷς οὐκ ἔστιν
ποιμήν.

In other cases it is changed as if the translator wanted to play with words. See, for example, Num 27:17, where the Hebrew text has the verbs בוא ("come") and יצא ("go out"). In both parts of the parallelism, the translator has used ἔρχομαι ("go") in the first stichos, and ἄγω ("go, lead") in the second, differentiating them by two different prefixes. Finally, sometimes one can find texts in which the translator is constructing a new parallelism; this phenomenon is frequent in the Psalms and in the book of Proverbs, and it can already be found in the book of Deuteronomy (32:23).[53]

There can be no doubt that in most cases there is no possibility to explain those improvements of the text with the assumption of a diverging *Vorlage*. Therefore these phenomena prove that some of the translators, especially those of the books which were translated first, wanted to produce a text that could stand on its own and does not refer back to the Hebrew original in any detail. Obviously they thought that some corrections or alterations might be in order, if these served to improve the persuasiveness of the Scriptures.

4.4. Identifications and Actualizations

Another possibility to improve a translation and to bring it closer to the reader is to modernize the text. As we have already seen in Deut 26:5, the ancient "Aramean" has been rendered by "Syria," which was easily recognizable as the territory of the Seleucids. For Padan-Aram, where Jacob's relative Laban dwelled, Mesopotamia was used (Gen 28:5). Other actualized names include Idumea for Edom (Gen 37:16) and Heliopolis for On (Gen 41:45). And even the third river of paradise in Gen 2:14 has been explicitly identified with a well-known stream, the Euphrates.

---

53. See Tauberschmidt 2004, for an extensive discussion of this phenomenon in the book of Proverbs.

Especially in the Joseph story one can find a lot of Hellenistic designations for professions. Most striking is the fact that in Gen 50:2 the word הרפאים ("doctors") was translated ἐνταφιαστής, which means the "embalmer," well known in Egypt. According to the Greek book of Numbers, the tribes of Israel are not segmented into *clans* (משפחות) but into *demous* (δήμους, 1:20), the usual designation for ethnic groups in Hellenistic Egypt. In the account of the wandering through the desert the Israelites' way of life has been accommodated to modern times. In the Hebrew text of Num 19:14 the Israelites live in tents, but according to the LXX they live in houses. The officials of the Israelites are now called σύγκλητοι βουλῆς ("councilors"); according to the Hebrew text they were only chosen from the assembly (קראי מועד, Num 16:2). It is obvious that outdated or unknown elements of the Scripture were identified with more modern terms. This is also true for God's blessing after the flood (Gen 8:22). In the Hebrew text God promises that "seedtime and harvest, summer and winter" shall not cease. The LXX has "summer and spring," which at first is quite astonishing. But in the Egyptian agricultural year there were only three seasons, the folding of the Nile in the winter, the heat of the summer, and sowing and harvesting in the spring. It is therefore easy to understand why the translator chose "spring" to designate the third season of the Egyptian year.

There are many other modernizations or actualizations like these.[54] Well known is the example of the ibis in the list of unclean animals in the book of Leviticus, who replaces the owl (Lev 11:17). Because the ibis was the holy bird of the Egyptian god Thot, it is clear that a pious Jewish translator wished to have the bird of this pagan god in the official list of detestable animals and therefore skipped the owl. On the other hand, the hare is missing in the Greek lists of unclean animals (Lev 11:6; Deut 14:7), because the usual Greek translation Λαγώς sounded too similar to the byname "Lagos" of the Ptolemaic king Ptolemy I.

One final example in this category will demonstrate that even a kind of demythologization could take place. In the account of the flood in Gen 6–9, the Hebrew word מבול ("flood") has been translated by the Greek κατακλυσμός ("deluge"; e.g., Gen 7:6). Upon closer examination one can see that this word has a special meaning. According to a theory by the

---

54. See, e.g., the path-breaking article by the Egyptologist Siegfried Morenz (1964); or Schmitt 1974. See most recently Görg 2001.

philosopher Eudoxos from Knidos, the term designates regular catastrophes when all the planets are properly aligned. This theory had also been accepted by Plato (*Tim.* 22a–g; 39d). The Greek text brings the biblical tradition in accord with the philosophical knowledge of its time. Moreover, the flood is now a kind of a natural phenomenon rather than a punishment by an angry God.[55]

Besides this rendering there are many others that prove that the translators had a good knowledge of the philosophical and religious discussions in the cultures around them.[56] They are not hesitant to adopt those concepts. It is also interesting to see that the translator of Genesis corrected the whole chronology in Gen 5 and 11, presumably to bring the biblical chronology in line with the Egyptian reckoning of dynasties.[57] But there are also limitations to this approach. One important line that is never crossed is the idea of God. This will be illustrated in the next section.

4.5. Corrections, Expansions, and Explanations: Theological Exegesis

The last example has already shown that the Greek version reveals aspects of a specific theology. Recent research has brought up numerous examples in which the Greek version shows distinctive deviations when it comes to anthropological, messianic, cultic, or theological topics.[58] Only a small selection of these can be given here, but they suffice to demonstrate that the translators were also theological thinkers.

Gen 2:2, 3

ויכל אלהים ביום השביעי מלאכתו אשר עשה ...
ויברך אלהים את־יום השביעי ויקדש אתו
כי בו שבת מכל־מלאכתו אשר־ברא אלהים לעשות

καὶ συνετέλεσεν ὁ θεὸς ἐν τῇ ἡμέρᾳ τῇ ἕκτῃ τὰ ἔργα αὐτοῦ, ἃ ἐποίησεν ...
καὶ ηὐλόγησεν ὁ θεὸς τὴν ἡμέραν τὴν ἑβδόμην καὶ ἡγίασεν αὐτήν,
ὅτι ἐν αὐτῇ κατέπαυσεν ἀπὸ πάντων τῶν ἔργων αὐτοῦ, ὧν ἤρξατο ὁ θεὸς ποιῆσαι.

---

55. See Rösel 1994, 169–70, for a fuller discussion of this topic.
56. See for the book of Proverbs, Cook 2001.
57. Genesis has a "long" chronology that shows that the Second Temple was built in the year 5000 *anno mundi*; see Rösel 1994, 129–44 [English version ch. 4 in this volume].
58. See Tov 1999d; and, for my own approach, Rösel 2006a [ch. 5 in this volume].

Genesis 2:2–3 shows how translators were at the same time theologians. The Hebrew text reads: "And on the seventh day God ended his work which he had made.... And God blessed the seventh day, and sanctified it: because on it he had rested from all his work which God created and made." The Greek text is rather different. "And God finished on the *sixth* day his works which he made.... And God blessed the seventh day and sanctified it, because in it he ceased from all his works which God began to do." Verse 3 has already been cited to demonstrate that the translator wanted to bring the two accounts of the creation into line with one another. Moreover, it was also important for him that God did not perform any kind of work on the Sabbath, which is why he had God finish work already on the sixth day.[59]

Gen 4:7

הלוא אם־תיטיב שׂאת ואם לא תיטיב
לפתח חטאת רבץ ואליך תשׁוקתו ואתה תמשׁל־בו
οὐκ, ἐὰν ὀρθῶς προσενέγκῃς, ὀρθῶς δὲ μὴ διέλῃς, ἥμαρτες;
ἡσύχασον· πρὸς σὲ ἡ ἀποστροφὴ αὐτοῦ, καὶ σὺ ἄρξεις αὐτοῦ.

Another important deviation can be seen in the crucial story of Cain and Abel in Gen 4. The Hebrew text of verse 7 is very difficult to understand, perhaps because it is damaged. "If you do well, will you not be accepted? And if you do not do well, sin is lurking at the door; its desire is for you, but you must master it" (NRSV). The translator tried to make sense out of his difficult *Vorlage* and was also driven by "a desire to understand why God should be upset with Cain for bringing an offering that is approved in the Mosaic legislation."[60] Thus his rendering reads: "Have you sinned if you have [in fact] brought it [the offering] rightly, but not rightly divided it? Calm down, to you shall be its [the sin's] return, and you shall rule over it."[61] Although this version, too, is not easy to understand, the problem is solved: Cain has not divided the offering in a ritually correct way (the verb

---

59. This variant is also present in the Samaritan Pentateuch, in the Peshitta, and in Jub. 2.16, 25. Therefore the possibility cannot be ruled out that this deviation has already been in the *Vorlage*, but most scholars now opt for an interpretation of the translator; see Jobes and Silva 2000, 98; Brayford 2007, 225.

60. Jobes and Silva 2000, 213.

61. For the translation, see Wevers 1993, 104–7.

διαιρέω, "divide," is the same as in Gen 15:10); therefore God is not guilty of not accepting his offering without a reason.

The Greek version of Gen 4 is revealing in yet another aspect. The Hebrew text is using the Tetragrammaton YHWH to refer to God's actions throughout this section. The Septuagint distinguishes between two designations for God: It is ὁ θεός ("God") who is not looking upon Abel and his offering; in verse 6 κύριος ὁ θεός ("Lord God") is speaking to Cain, and in verses 9–10 ὁ θεός ("God") is accusing the murderer, who in verse 16 is going forth from the presence of God (τοῦ θεοῦ; MT: יהוה "Lord"/YHWH). It is interesting to see that in this section there are two verses, 3 and 13, in which the regular use of κύριος ("Lord") for the Tetragrammaton can be seen. These texts speak about Cain's offering (v. 3) and Cain's prayer to the Lord (v. 13). Thus one has to conclude that κύριος is avoided when it is about the punishing or judging aspects of God. This view is confirmed by several other texts from the book of Genesis, so that the translator of Genesis must have seen a theological differentiation between the two most used designations for God—YHWH/Lord on the one hand and *elohim*/God on the other.[62] Moreover, he has made use of this differentiation to correct the text or to avoid a possible misunderstanding that God acts unjustly (see esp. the translations in Gen 38:7, 10). Again, this phenomenon can also be seen in other translations of the LXX.

Exod 15:3

יהוה איש מלחמה יהוה שמו
κύριος συντρίβων πολέμους, κύριος ὄνομα αὐτῷ.

According to Exod 15:3 the Lord is not a warrior, as the Hebrew text suggests, but someone who is breaking wars; the meaning has been reverted.[63] In Num 16:5, 11 and Deut 2:14 one can detect the same hesitation to say that the Lord has killed someone; therefore *elohim*/God is used although the *Vorlage* has had the Tetragrammaton.[64] Moreover, there are other texts where one can see that several aspects of the picture of God have been changed: it is no longer possible to see God, but only the *place* where God

---

62. See Rösel 2007b, for details [ch. 13 in this volume].
63. See also Ps 9:21; God brings his law, not fear, to the people.
64. One could add that there is also a hesitation to use *kyrios*—the translation of the *name* of the God of Israel—together with foreigners, which can easily be seen in the Balaam story in Num 22–24; see Wevers 1999.

stood (Exod 24:10); not only blaspheming the name of the Lord carries the death penalty but already *naming* his name (Lev 24:16). Some of the translators seemed also to avoid anthropomorphic renderings.[65] Others avoided metaphorical designations, like God as a rock, as in Ps 78(77):35, where צוּר ("rock") has been translated by βοηθός ("helper"), or in Ps 84(83):12, where God is no longer sun or shield (MT), but he loves mercy and truth.[66]

5. Conclusion

Many more examples could be given to demonstrate different phenomena of interpretation in the Scriptures collected under the label "Septuagint," and many more topics like messianism or cultic terminology or the depiction of biblical persons like Moses could be treated.[67] One should also bear in mind that in this article I have separated the text examples from their contexts and arranged them in a systematic way. Usually one should clarify the specific profile of an individual translation as the first methodological step. But in spite of these—in the present context justifiable—shortcomings, it has become clear that the Greek translation of the Bible reflects the earliest stages of the history of interpretation of the Jewish Scriptures. Therefore it is good to see that in recent years the focus of scholarship has moved from text-critical to exegetical questions. Only after the different levels of linguistic and theological interpretation of a Greek translation have been described can it be used also for purposes of textual criticism.[68]

When comparing the individual profiles of scriptural interpretation in the books of the LXX with the targumim or with contemporary literature like the Hellenistic-Jewish texts or the texts from Qumran, it becomes clear that the approach of the Greek translators was different.[69] Their aim was not to rewrite the Bible or to comment on it, but to produce an authoritative Greek version that was suitable for the needs of Jewish groups in

---

65. See, e.g., the classic study by Charles T. Fritsch (1943).
66. See Olofsson 1990 for Ps 78(77):35.
67. Moreover, much more secondary literature could have been cited. Instead, the readers are referred to reference works like Jobes and Silva 2000; Fernández Marcos 2000; Dines 2004; or the systematically arranged bibliography by Dogniez 1995.
68. Rösel 1998; van der Louw 2007, 368–73.
69. For the targumim, see Le Déaut 1984; for Qumran, see the fine introduction by VanderKam 2006.

the Hellenistic world.[70] Because they were aware that they were translating and producing not an ordinary text but Scripture, they obviously felt restricted in how they could treat this text. It is interesting to see that those translations that were done first are less literal than later ones. One can assume that the circulation of the Greek Pentateuch caused discussions about the question of the extent to which deviations from the original are acceptable. But even a more literal translation like the Greek Psalms shows a dynamic understanding of how to render these highly important texts. Even if cast in a new language, they will still be able to speak directly into the new situation and provide confidence in the God of Israel and his just government of the whole world. Thus scriptural interpretation in the LXX is not an end in and of itself or an academic exegetical game. Instead, it manifests the ways in which the translators and their community understood Scripture and how they thought it should be understood. Therefore, the Greek translation is a pivotal part of the earliest reception history of the Hebrew Bible.

Bibliography

Austermann, Frank. 2003. *Von der Tora zum Nomos: Untersuchungen zur Übersetzungsweise und Interpretation im Septuaginta-Psalter*. NAWG Phil-Hist Klasse 3, 257; MSU 27. Göttingen: Vandenhoeck & Ruprecht.

Barr, James. 1979. *The Typology of Literalism in Ancient Biblical Translations*. NAWG Phil-Hist Klasse 11; MSU 15. Göttingen: Vandenhoeck & Ruprecht.

———. 2003. "Did the Greek Pentateuch Really Serve as a Dictionary for the Translation of the Later Books?" Pages 523–43 in *Hamlet on a Hill: Semitic and Greek Studies Presented to Professor T. Muraoka on the Occasion of His Sixty-Fifth Birthday*. Edited by Martin F. J. Basten and W. Th. van Peursen. OLA 118. Leuven: Peeters.

Beck, John A. 2000. *Translators as Storytellers: A Study in Septuagint Translation Technique*. StBibLit 25. New York: Lang.

Brayford, Susan. 2007. *Genesis*. Septuagint Commentary Series 4. Leiden: Brill.

---

70. The LXX of Job can be seen as an exception to not rewriting the Bible; see Cox 2006.

Cavenaile, Robert. 1958. *Corpus papyrorum latinarum 1.* Wiesbaden: Harrassowitz.

Cook, Johann. 2001. "The Ideology of Septuagint Proverbs." Pages 463–79 in *X. Congress of the International Organization for Septuagint and Cognate Studies. Oslo 1998.* Edited by Bernard A. Taylor. SCS 51. Atlanta: Society of Biblical Literature.

———. 2004. "Exegesis in the Septuagint." *JNSL* 30:1–19.

Cox, Claude E. 2006. "The Historical, Social, and Literary Context of Old Greek Job." Pages 105–16 in *XII Congress of the International Organization for Septuagint and Cognate Studies, Leiden, 2004.* Edited by Melvin K. H. Peters. SCS 54. Atlanta: Society of Biblical Literature.

Cribiore, Raffaella. 1996. *Writing, Teachers, and Students in Graeco-Roman Egypt.* ASP 36. Atlanta: Scholars Press.

Dines, Jennifer M. 2004. *The Septuagint.* London: T&T Clark.

Dogniez, Cécile. 1995. *Bibliography of the Septuagint: Bibliographie de la Septante (1970–1993).* VTSup 60. Leiden: Brill.

Dorival, Gilles. 1994. *Les Nombres.* BdA 4. Paris: Cerf.

———. 1995. "Les phénomènes d´intertextualité dans le livre grec des Nombres." Pages 261–85 in ΚΑΤΑ ΤΟΥΣ Ο´: *Selon Les Septante; Festschrift Marguerite Harl.* Edited by Gilles Dorival and Olivier Munnich. Paris: Cerf.

Eco, Umberto. 2003. *Mouse or Rat? Translation as Negotiation.* London: Weidenfeld & Nicolson.

Fernández Marcos, Natalio. 2000. *The Septuagint in Context: Introduction to the Greek Versions of the Bible.* Translated by W. G. E. Watson. Leiden: Brill.

Frankel, Zacharias. 1851. *Ueber den Einfluss der palästinischen Exegese auf die alexandrinische Hermeneutik.* Leipzig: Barth.

Fritsch, Charles T. 1943. *The Anti-Anthropomorphisms of the Greek Pentateuch.* POT 10. Princeton: University Press.

Gaebel, Robert E. 1969–1970. "The Greek Word-Lists to Vergil and Cicero." *BJRL* 52:284–325.

Görg, Manfred. 2001. "Die Septuaginta im Kontext spätägyptischer Kultur." Pages 115–30 in vol. 1 of *Im Brennpunkt: Die Septuaginta; Studien zur Entstehung und Bedeutung der griechischen Bibel.* Edited by Heinz-Josef Fabry and Ulrich Offerhaus. BWANT 153. Stuttgart: Kohlhammer.

Harl, Marguerite. 1986. *La Genèse.* BdA 1. Paris: Cerf.

Harl, Marguerite, Gilles Dorival, and Olivier Munnich. 1988. *La Bible Grecque des Septante: Du judaïsme hellénistique au christianisme ancien.* Paris: Cerf.

Harl, Marguerite, and Roselyne Dupont-Roc. 1999. *Les douze prophètes: Joël, Abdiou, Jonas, Naoum, Ambakoum, Sophonie.* BdA 23.4–9. Paris: Cerf.

Hengel, Martin. 2002. *The Septuagint as Christian Scripture: Its Prehistory and the Problem of Its Canon.* London: T&T Clark.

Jobes, Karen H., and Moises Silva 2000. *Invitation to the Septuagint.* Grand Rapids: Baker Academic.

Joosten, Jan. 2000. "Une théologie de la Septante? Réflexions méthodologique sur l'interpretation de la version greque." *RTPh* 132:31–46.

——. 2003. "On Aramaising Renderings in the Septuagint." Pages 587–600 in *Hamlet on a Hill: Semitic and Greek Studies Presented to Professor T. Muraoka on the Occasion of His Sixty-Fifth Birthday.* Edited by Martin F. J. Basten and W. Th. van Peursen. OLA 118. Leuven: Peeters.

Kooij, Arie van der. 1989. "The Septuagint of Isaiah: Translation and Interpretation." Pages 127–33 in *The Book of Isaiah–Le Livre d'Isaïe: Les Oracles et leurs Relectures; Unité et complexité de l'ouvrage.* Edited by Jaques Vermeylen. BETL 81. Leuven: Peeters.

——. 1998. "Perspectives on the Study of the Septuagint. Who are the Translators?" Pages 214–29 in *Perspectives in the Study of the Old Testament and Early Judaism: A Symposium in Honour of Adam S. van der Woude on the Occasion of His Seventieth Birthday.* Edited by Florentino García Martínez and Edwart Noort. VTSup 73. Leiden: Brill.

Kramer, Johannes. 2001. *Glossaria bilinguia altera (C. Gloss. biling. II).* Archiv für Papyrusforschung und verwandte Gebiete: Beiheft 8. Munich: Saur.

Kraus, Wolfgang, and R. Glenn Wooden, eds. 2006. *Septuagint Research: Issues and Challenges in the Study of the Greek Jewish Scriptures.* SCS 53. Atlanta: Society of Biblical Literature.

Kreuzer, Siegfried. 2004. "Entstehung und Publikation der Septuaginta im Horizont frühptolemäischer Bildungs- und Kulturpolitik." Pages 61–75 in vol 2 of *Im Brennpunkt: Die Septuaginta; Studien zur Entstehung und Bedeutung der Griechischen Bibel.* Edited by Siegfried Kreuzer and Jürgen Peter Lesch. BWANT 161. Stuttgart: Kohlhammer.

——. 2007. "Die Septuaginta im Kontext alexandrinischer Kultur und Bildung." Pages 28–56 in vol. 3 of *Im Brennpunkt: Die Septuaginta;*

Studien zur Theologie, Anthropologie, Ekklesiologie, Eschatologie und Liturgie der Griechischen Bibel. Edited by Heinz-Josef Fabry and Dieter Böhler. BWANT 174. Stuttgart: Kohlhammer.

Le Déaut, Roger. 1984. "La Septante, un Targum?" Pages 147–95 in *Études sur le Judaïsme Hellénistique (Congrès de Strasbourg 1983)*. Edited by Raymond Kuntzmann and Jacques Schlosser. Lectio Divina 119. Paris: Cerf.

Louw, Theo A. W. van der. 2007. *Transformations in the Septuagint: Towards an Interaction of Septuagint Studies and Translation Studies*. CBET 47. Leuven: Peeters.

Monsengwo Pasinya, Laurent. 1973. *La notion de Nomos dans le Pentateuque grec*. AnBib 52. Rome: Biblical Institute Press.

Morenz, Siegfried. 1964. "Ägyptische Spuren in den Septuaginta." Pages 250–58 in *Mullus: Festschrift Theodor Klauser*. Edited by Alfred Stuiber. JAC.E 1. Münster: Aschendorff.

Müller, Mogens. 1996. *The First Bible of the Church: A Plea for the Septuagint*. JSOTSup 206. Copenhagen International Seminar 1. Sheffield: Sheffield Academic.

Olofsson, Staffan. 1990. *God is My Rock: A Study of Translation Technique and Theological Exegesis in the Septuagint*. ConBOT 31. Stockholm: Almqvist & Wicksell.

Pietersma, Albert. 2002. "A New Paradigm for Addressing Old Questions: The Relevance of the Interlinear Model for the Study of the Septuagint." Pages 337–64 in *Bible and Computer: The Stellenbosch AIBI-6 Conference proceedings of the Association internationale Bible et informatique, "From Alpha to Byte."* Edited by Johann Cook. Leiden: Brill.

———. 2006a. "Exegesis in the Septuagint: Possibilities and Limits (The Psalter as a Case in Point)." Pages 33–45 in *Septuagint Research: Issues and Challenges in the Study of the Greek Jewish Scriptures*. Edited by Wolfgang Kraus and R. Glen Wooden. SCS 53. Atlanta: Society of Biblical Literature.

———. 2006b. "Messianism and the Greek Psalter: In Search of the Messiah." Pages 49–75 in *The Septuagint and Messianism*. Edited by Michael A. Knibb. BETL 195. Leuven: Peeters.

Pietersma, Albert, and Benjamin G. Wright, eds. 2007. *A New English Translation of the Septuagint and the Other Greek Translations Traditionally Included under That Title*. New York: Oxford University Press.

Rösel, Martin. 1994. *Übersetzung als Vollendung der Auslegung: Studien zur Genesis-Septuaginta*. BZAW 223. Berlin: de Gruyter.

———. 1998. "The Text-Critical Value of the Genesis-Septuagint." *BIOSCS* 34:62–70.

———. 2006a. "Jakob, Bileam und der Messias. Messianische Erwartungen in Gen 49 und Num 22–24." Pages 151–75 in *The Septuagint and Messianism*. Edited by Michael A. Knibb. BETL 195. Leuven: Peeters. [ch. 5 in this volume.]

———. 2006b. "Towards a 'Theology of the Septuagint.'" Pages 239–52 in *Septuagint Research: Issues and Challenges in the Study of the Greek Jewish Scriptures*. Edited by Wolfgang Kraus and R. Glenn Wooden. SCS 53. Atlanta: Society of Biblical Literature. [ch. 11 in this volume.]

———. 2007a. "Nomothesie: Zum Gesetzesverständnis der Septuaginta." Pages 132–50 in vol. 3 of *Im Brennpunkt: Die Septuaginta; Studien zur Theologie, Anthropologie, Ekklesiologie, Eschatologie und Liturgie der Griechischen Bibel*. Edited by Heinz-Josef Fabry and Dieter Böhler. BWANT 174. Stuttgart: Kohlhammer. [English version ch. 15 in this volume.]

———. 2007b. "The Reading and Translation of the Divine Name in the Masoretic Tradition and the Greek Pentateuch." *JSOT* 31:411–28. [ch. 13 in this volume.]

Schaper, Joachim. 2006. "Translating 2 Maccabees for NETS." Pages 225–32 in *XII Congress of the International Organization for Septuagint and Cognate Studies. Leiden, 2004*. Edited by Melvin K. H. Peters. SCS 54; Atlanta: Society of Biblical Literature.

Schenker, Adrian. 1994. "Gewollt dunkle Wiedergaben in LXX? Am Beispiel von Ps 28 (29)." *Bib* 75:546–55.

Schmitt, Armin. 1974. "Interpretation der Genesis aus hellenistischem Geist." *ZAW* 86:137–63.

Siegert, Folkert. 2001. *Zwischen Hebräischer Bibel und Altem Testament: Eine Einführung in die Septuaginta*. MJS 9. Münster: LIT.

Sollamo, Raija. 1985. "The LXX Renderings of the Infinitive Absolute Used with a Paronymous Finite Verb in the Pentateuch." Pages 101–13 in *La Septuaginta en la Investigación Contemporánea (V. Congreso de la IOSCS)*. Edited by Natalio Fernández Marcos. Textos y estudios "Cardenal Cisneros" 34. Madrid: Inst. "Arias Montano."

Tauberschmidt, Gerhard. 2004. *Secondary Parallelism: A Study of Translation Technique in LXX Proverbs*. AcBib 15. Atlanta: Society of Biblical Literature.

Tov, Emanuel. 1997. *The Text-Critical Use of the Septuagint in Biblical Research*. 2nd ed., revised and enlarged. JBS 8. Jerusalem: Simor.

———. 1999a. "Did the Septuagint Translators Always Understand their Hebrew Text." Pages 203–18 in *The Greek and Hebrew Bible: Collected Essays on the Septuagint*. VTSup 72. Leiden: Brill, 1999.

———. 1999b. "The Impact of the LXX Translation of the Pentateuch on the Translation of the Other Books." Pages 183–94 *The Greek and Hebrew Bible: Collected Essays on the Septuagint*. VTSup 72. Leiden: Brill, 1999.

———. 1999c. "Renderings of Combinations of the Infinitive Absolute and Finite Verbs in the Septuagint: Their Nature and Distribution." Pages 247–56 in *The Greek and Hebrew Bible: Collected Essays on the Septuagint*. VTSup 72. Leiden: Brill, 1999.

———. 1999d. "Theologically Motivated Exegesis Embedded in the Septuagint." Pages 257–69 *The Greek and Hebrew Bible: Collected Essays on the Septuagint*. VTSup 72. Leiden: Brill, 1999.

VanderKam, James C. 2006. "To What End? Functions of Scriptural Interpretation in Qumran Texts." Pages 302–20 in *Studies in the Hebrew Bible, Qumran, and the Septuagint Presented to Eugene Ulrich*. Edited by Peter W. Flint. VTSup 101. Leiden: Brill.

Wade, Martha L. 2003. *Consistency of Translation Techniques in the Tabernacle Accounts of Exodus in the Old Greek*. SCS 49. Atlanta: Society of Biblical Literature.

Wevers, John W. 1993. *Notes on the Greek Text of Genesis*. SCS 35. Atlanta: Scholars Press.

———. 1996. "The Interpretative Character and Significance of the Septuagint Version." Pages 84–107 in *Hebrew Bible/Old Testament: The History of Its Interpretation, Vol. I, 1 Antiquity*. Edited by Magne Sæbø. Göttingen: Vandenhoeck & Ruprecht.

———. 1999. "The Balaam Narrative According to the Septuagint." Pages 133–44 in *Lectures et Relectures de la Bible: Festschrift P.-M. Bogaert*. Edited by Jean-Marie Auwers, and André Wénin. BETL 144. Leuven: Peeters.

Part 2
On Specific Texts

4
The Chronological System of Genesis-Septuagint (Genesis 5 and 11)

The genealogies in Gen 5 and 11 give information for each patriarch about his lifespan and the age at which he begot his first son. Since the line begins with Adam, it is possible to come to an absolute, full chronology by adding the number of years leading up to the birth of each firstborn. One example (Gen 5:3–6): since Seth, who was begotten by Adam in his 130th year, fathers Enosh in his 105th year, the year of Enosh's begetting is the year 235 *anno mundi* in the overall chronology according to the Masoretic Text (see the chart below). Any date connected to information about the age of one of the patriarchs can therefore be converted into the absolute chronology. For example, in Gen 7:6, Noah was six hundred years old when the flood came; this is year 1656 *anno mundi* according to the Masoretic Text (MT). The information about the remaining lifetime of the respective patriarch is not relevant for the absolute chronology.[1]

This simple procedure is hampered because the numbers that are given in the MT of Gen 5 show traces of revision. Moreover, all important textual witnesses (MT, Samaritan Pentateuch [SP], and LXX) differ considerably from each other. Therefore the problems posed by the chronology of the Greek Genesis have attracted attention early on, from the church fathers to modern exegetes.[2] In the following I will discuss the question of the chronological system that led to the deviating figures in

---

This paper was part of my dissertation (Rösel 1994, 129–44 [in German]). It has been slightly revised for inclusion in this collection; there was no attempt to include a full discussion of recently published articles on the topic.

1. But see Northcote 2007, who sums together the lifespan figures for the generations from Adam to Moses and ends up with a total of 12600.

2. Basic literature in chronological order: Preuss 1859; Bousset 1900; Bosse 1908; Skinner 1910, 127–39, 231–39; Jepsen 1929, 1968; Murtonen 1954; de Vries 1962;

the Greek version. The deviations in the MT and the SP cannot be discussed extensively, and the different systems of Josephus and the book of Jubilees remain out of consideration because they offer no help for clarifying the data in the LXX. In the first section I will present the material of Gen 5 and 11; in the second, I discuss earlier attempts at solving the problem; and finally, I will present my own solution.

1. Chronological Differences in Genesis 5

In Gen 5 the Greek version has the following differences when compared with the MT: From verse 3 on we can see the phenomenon that the LXX raises the age in which a patriarch begets his first son by one hundred years in comparison with the MT and the SP. The same period of one hundred years is subtracted when the remaining lifetime is specified, so that the total of the lifetime of a patriarch is the same in the Greek and the Hebrew versions. This schematic increase can be seen in the generations from Adam to Enoch (Gen 5:23), with the exception of Jared.

In the case of Jared (5:18), both LXX and MT give the date of him fathering Enoch as year 162. This fits to the usual figures in LXX but is too high for the MT. Since the SP gives the number 62, which corresponds to the regular numbers in MT, one can assume that this is the original date for Jared.

In the case of Methuselah (5:25–27), all versions differ from each other. SP gives the year 67 for Methuselah begetting Lamech. LXX raises this number as usual by 100 to 167, while the MT raises it by 120 to 187.[3] In the MT and the SP, Methuselah dies in the year of the flood or in the flood: 1656 *anno mundi* according to the MT and 1307 *anno mundi* according to the SP. Surprisingly, in the LXX Enoch survives the flood, which is in the year 2242 *anno mundi*, and lives on until the year 2256 *anno mundi*.[4]

Johnson 1969; Larsson 1973, 1983; Klein 1974; Koch 1978, 1983; Fraenkel 1984; Hughes 1990; Etz 1993.

3. Some Greek witnesses also attest to 187 years for Methuselah (see the apparatus of the Göttingen edition of the LXX), also Demetrius (see below) calculates with this number. But this reading must be regarded as harmonization with the MT and is therefore secondary.

4. See Harl 1986, 123–24 for solutions to solve this problem by early church fathers.

4. The Chronological System of Genesis-Septuagint

The situation is even more complicated in the case of Lamech (5:28–31), because the common basis of the calculation is no longer recognizable: MT gives the year 182 for fathering Noah, SP has the year 53 and LXX has 188. The numbers for the remaining lifetime and the total of the age of the patriarch also differ from each other. In the MT, Lamech dies before the flood in 1651 *anno mundi*, while in the SP he dies like his father in the year of the flood, 1307 *anno mundi*. One can assume that this was the reason for changing the dates of his life.[5] Moreover, it is noteworthy that the total length of Lamech's life according to the MT (777 years) is obviously connected with the notion about seven times vengeance by Kain and seventy times seven vengeance by Lamech in Gen 4:24.[6]

If one now turns to the synopsis on the chronological data in Gen 5:3–32 and 7:6 (dating of the flood), the following observations can be noted:[7]

- MT and SP are in accordance until Mahalalel.
- From Jared on, the ages of begetting seem to be altered in the MT. The age of Enoch shows that begetting prior to the age of one hundred seems to be original. Moreover, in the SP the ages of begetting decrease continually.
- LXX is in accordance with MT and SP until Mahalalel but raises the ages of begetting by one hundred and subtracts the same figure from the remaining lifetime.
- With the exception of Methuselah and Lamech, the numbers in the three versions seem to stem from a common basis. In the case of Methuselah, LXX obviously had a *Vorlage* of the SP-type (see above), while in the case of Lamech there is no accordance at all.
- In the SP the patriarchs Jared, Methuselah, and Lamech die in the year of the flood, but in the MT, only Methuselah perishes. According to the LXX, Methuselah survives the flood. While the other versions pay attention to the inner consistency of the chronology, LXX is more concerned with raising the figures of the absolute chronology than with the details.

---

5. Wevers, 1993, 72–73; Hendel 2012, 9–10; he assumes an error of a scribe for the year 53 in SP.
6. Hughes 1990, 14.
7. The following list is based on Jepsen 1929, and Hughes 1990, 5–43.

Synopsis on the Chronology of Genesis 5

The synopsis contains the genealogical data of MT, Samaritan Pentateuch (SP), and LXX on the chronology in Gen 5. Dates in regular characters are taken directly from the text of the respective version. Dates in *italics* were calculated. Underlined figures indicate the death of the respective patriarch in the year of the flood or after the flood.

The first column (a.m. = *anno mundi*, year after creation) shows the dates according to the absolute chronology of this specific version. The date of death in the last column is also related to the absolute chronology. One example for clarification: according to the LXX, Kenan fathered Mahalalel in year 795 a.m. at the age of 170 years. He then lived on for 740 years and died at the age of 910 in year 1535 after creation. Compare similar charts in Klein 1974, 259–60; de Vries 1962, 581.

	MT					SP					LXX				
	a.m.	beget	rest	total	death	a.m.	beget	rest	total	death	a.m.	beget	rest	total	death
Adam	130	130	800	930	930	130	130	800	930	930	230	230	700	930	930
Seth	235	105	807	912	1042	235	105	807	912	1042	435	205	707	912	1142
Enosh	325	90	815	905	1140	325	90	815	905	1140	625	190	715	905	*1340*
Kenan	395	70	840	910	1235	395	70	840	910	1235	795	170	740	910	*1535*
Mahalalel	460	65	830	895	1290	460	65	830	895	1290	960	165	730	895	*1690*
Jared	622	162	800	962	*1422*	522	62	785	847	<u>*1307*</u>	1122	162	800	962	*1922*
Enoch	687	65	300	365	*(987)*	587	65	300	365	887	1287	165	200	365	*1487*
Methuselah	874	187	782	969	<u>*1656*</u>	654	67	653	720	<u>*1307*</u>	1454	167	802	969	<u>*2256*</u>
Lamech	1056	182	595	777	*1651*	707	53	600	653	<u>*1307*</u>	1642	188	565	753	*2207*
Noah	1556	500				*1207*	500				*2142*	500			
flood	*1656*					*1307*					*2242*				

4. The Chronological System of Genesis-Septuagint

- According to the MT, the flood took place in the year 1656 *anno mundi*, according to the SP in 1307 *anno mundi*, and according to the LXX in the year 2242.

2. Chronological Differences in Genesis 11

When turning to the chronological data in Gen 11:10–32, an inconsistency within the text requires consideration: According to Gen 5:32, Noah begets his three sons, Shem, Ham, and Japheth, in his five hundredth year, and according to Gen 7:6 + 11 Noah was six hundred years old when the flood came on the earth. This means that Noah's sons were one hundred years old in the year of the flood. Therefore it is surprising to read in Gen 11:10 that Shem begot Arpachshad in his one hundredth year, *the second year after the flood*. The source of this note is unclear, but since it is the first date that is given in Gen 11, one must take this date into account when calculating the dates of the absolute chronology of Gen 11.[8]

As in Gen 5, the Greek version of Gen 11 also displays the tendency to raise the ages in comparison with the MT: From Arpachshad (11:12) to Serug (11:22), the age at which a patriarch fathers his first son is raised schematically by one hundred. In the case of Nahor (11:24), it is raised by fifty years only. These differences are shared by the SP, indicating a common textual tradition, which differs from the MT. For Terah, Abraham's father, all witnesses give the same age of seventy years for begetting his son.

Even more interesting is the fact that in the Greek version another patriarch is inserted. By the addition of Kainan in 11:13, LXX arrives at a total of ten patriarchs fathered after the flood, from Arpachshad to Abram.[9] In the other versions, there are ten patriarchs fathering after the flood. This is the more original scheme. In LXX the name Καιναν is obvi-

---

8. See Westermann 1983, 745, and Hughes 1990, 18–23, for a discussion of the problem of source.

9. Wevers 1993, 154, therefore in his view the insertion is "systematically determined." He also offers the explanation that Kainan was included to come to a total of one thousand years between the birth of Shem's son and Abram's father. Also in the book of Jub. 8:1–9 Kainan appears as Arpachshad's son; according to Berger 1981, 369, this is taken from Gen 11:13 in the Greek version.

ously taken from Gen 5:9, and the details of his life are copied from Shelah, the next patriarch in the list, who has now become Kainan's son.[10]

The following can be inferred from the synopsis of the three versions in Gen 11:

- The MT preserves low ages of begetting, which fit the original dates in Gen 5. SP and LXX raise these figures by one hundred and in the case of Nahor, by fifty. If according to Gen 17:17 Abraham thinks that it is impossible that a child can be born to a man who is hundred years old, this statement only makes sense with the chronology of the MT. In the SP and the LXX, an age of one hundred or more would be completely normal.
- As stated earlier, LXX has inserted over against the MT and the SP an additional patriarch, Kainan II. This addition can also be found in Gen 10:22 + 24, again in the Greek version only, indicating that the patriarch Kainan II is a secondary addition. Once more it seems as if the LXX is concerned with raising the dates of the absolute chronology.
- In Gen 11, several stages of the development of the chronology are discernable: One version of the MT-type was reworked by raising the ages of begetting by one hundred or fifty. This intermediate type can be seen in the SP. Traces of later, independent editing are evident: in the SP, for each patriarch a calculation of the total of his lifespan was added, together with a recalculation of the remaining years (which is not included in the synopsis); furthermore, the LXX inserts Kainan II.

3. In Search for a System behind the Numbers

The discussion about the problem caused by the numbers in Gen 5 and 11 has mainly centered on the question of whether there are different periodicities or systems behind these differing ages or whether they are targeting historic dates. Moreover, since each of the three versions shows traces of redactional activity, attempts have been made to reconstruct the original chronological framework that lies behind the texts. The results of prior research can be summarized as follows:

---

10. Rösel 1994, 223; Hughes 1990, 15–18.

Synopsis on the Chronology of Genesis 11

The synopsis contains the genealogical data of the MT, Samaritan Pentateuch (SP), and LXX on the chronology in Gen 11. Dates in regular characters are taken directly from the text of the respective version. Dates in italics were calculated.

The first column (a.m. = *anno mundi*, year after creation) shows the dates according to the absolute chronology of this specific version. The second column (p.d. for *post diluvium*, after the flood) gives the calculated figure of the year after the flood according to the chronology of the respective version. The calculations of the absolute chronology are based on Gen 11:10: Shem fathered Arpachshad *two years after the flood*. Compare similar charts in Klein 1974, 256–57; de Vries 1962, 581.

	MT				SP				LXX			
	a.m.	p.d.	beget	rest	a.m.	p.d.	beget	rest	a.m.	p.d.	beget	rest
Flood	1656				1307				2242			
Shem	1658	2	100	500	1309	2	100	500	2244	2	100	500
Arpachshad	1693	37	35	403	1444	137	135	303	2379	137	135	430
Kainan									2509	267	130	330
Shelah	1723	67	30	403	1574	267	130	303	2639	397	130	330
Eber	1757	101	34	430	1708	401	134	270	2773	531	134	370
Peleg	1787	131	30	209	1838	531	130	109	2903	661	130	209
Reu	1819	163	32	207	1970	663	132	107	3035	793	132	207
Serug	1849	193	30	200	2100	793	130	100	3165	923	130	200
Nahor	1878	222	29	119	2179	872	79	69	3244	1002	79	129
Terah	1948	292	70	135	2249	942	70	75	3314	1072	70	135
Abram	2048	392	100		2349	1042	100		3414	1172	100	

All solutions display a basic commonality: the figures of Gen 5 and 11 must be combined with other chronological data from the books of Genesis, Exodus, Kings, and Ezra. The relevant texts are:

- Gen 21:5: Isaac is born in Abraham's 100th year (= 2048 *anno mundi*: MT).
- Gen 25:26: Jacob is born in Isaac's 60th year (= 2108 *anno mundi*: MT).
- Gen 47:9: Jacob goes to Egypt in his 130th year (= 2238 *anno mundi*: MT).
- Exod 12:40: The Israelites live 430 years in Egypt (= 2668 *anno mundi*: MT). According to the SP and the LXX, the Israelites live 430 years *in Canaan* and Egypt = 215 years in Egypt.
- 1 Kgs 6:1: The beginning of the construction of the Solomonic temple takes place in the 480th year after the Exodus (= 3148 *anno mundi*: MT). Again, LXX records a different number: 440 years.
- The information in the book of Kings about the regnal years allows the reconstruction of 430 years after the beginning of the construction of the temple until its destruction (= 3578 *anno mundi*: MT).[11]
- Ezra 3:8 dates the beginning of the construction of the second temple to the year after the return to Jerusalem. Thus the reconstruction has begun 50 years after the destruction of the first temple, leading to the year 3628 *anno mundi* in the MT (537 BCE).[12]

If these figures are combined with the date from the different versions of Gen 5 and 11, the following results can be obtained:[13]

- The chronological system of the MT has its reference point in the rededication of the second temple by the Maccabees in 164 BCE. If the chronological data of the MT are combined, they point to the year 4000 *anno mundi* for this event.[14] This theory fits the observation that the figures in the MT were obviously reworked

---

11. See, e.g., Jepsen 1929, 254; or Koch 1978, 435. Even Hendel 2012, 12 accepts this calculation.

12. See Hughes, 1990, 39, and de Vries 1962, 597, table 6, on the method of calculating and Hughes 1990, 53, for the question whether Ezra 3:8–9 is historically reliable.

13. For a survey of earlier attempts to solve the problem, see Northcote 2004, 3–7.

14. Thus, e.g., Murtonen 1954, 133–37; Koch 1983, 423; Hughes 1990, 233–37, with a different way of calculation. But see Hendel 2012, who rejects this theory

4. The Chronological System of Genesis-Septuagint

after the translation of the LXX and the separation of the text type of the SP.

- The chronology of the SP obviously has its reference point in the dedication of the sanctuary on Mount Gerizim in the year 2800 *anno mundi*.[15] This year seems plausible as a multiple of the numbers forty and seven.[16]
- Jeremy Hughes's attempt to reconstruct the original priestly chronology calculates the year 1600 *anno mundi* as the first year of Abraham; 1200 years later, the temple was built according to the figures of the MT (pretemple age).[17] A second epoch of 1200 years (temple age) has to be assumed for the existence of both temples so that the post-Abrahamic age sums up to 2400 years. For the age of the first temple, he calculates 480 years (including destruction), in parallelism to 480 years from the exodus to the construction of the temple. For the second temple he assumes a duration of 720 years in parallelism to 720 years from Abraham to the Exodus. This reconstructed chronology is based on the idea of a world era of 4000 years; again, this multiple of 40 seems plausible as a symbolic age of an epoch.[18]

All these calculations presuppose that the year of begetting the firstborn is the same year as his birth. The biblical texts give no indication whether this assumption is correct. An alternative would be to add one year for each patriarch to the absolute chronology for the time between conception and birth. This can be inferred from a combination of Gen 17:1 (Abraham is ninety-nine years, when the Lord appears to him) and 17:17 ("Can a

---

because he sees no convincing evidence for the existence of an overall chronological system (see below).

15. See, e.g., Jepsen 1929, 253; or Koch 1983, 424; Hughes 1990, 237–38.

16. See Koch 1983, 425–29, for the evidence of the multiple of seven, he speaks of "Sabbatstruktur" (sabbatical structure).

17. Hughes 1990, 21–54. The theory by Etz 1993, has very speculative assumptions of different steps of additions and multiplications, therefore I am not discussing it. Another explanation is offered by Ziemer 2009, who includes the theory of a divine day that lasts a thousand years, which in my view is not supported by the text of Gen 5 and 11. Moreover, Ziemer adds for each patriarch one year between fathering and birth (p. 3), therefore he reckons with different figures than scholars usually do.

18. This reconstruction matches the theory of Jepsen 1929, 253, who also comes to the year 2800 as the first year of Solomon's temple. But for him year 2800 is the target point of the chronology.

child be born to a man who is a hundred years old?").[19] But because this text also uses round numbers such as one hundred for Abraham or ninety for Sarah, it is more plausible to calculate with round numbers in the chronologies of Gen 5 and 11 as well.

Until now, no plausible pattern behind the chronology of the Greek version has been detected[20]. Most scholars are content with the explanation that the LXX did not have a specific chronological system, but rather the intent of bringing the ages of begetting into a better relation to the overall lifespan. Therefore, these figures were raised and the corresponding numbers of the remaining lifetime lowered.[21] The weak point of this argument is the fact that LXX has no simple schematic. In the case of Nahor in 11:24, the age is raised by 50, not by 100 as in most other cases, and in 5:28 the age of Lamech is raised by 135 in comparison with the SP. Moreover, the insertion of the patriarch Kainan II cannot be rationally explained if one is not content with the explanation that the LXX wanted to create "greater formal symmetry between antedeluvian and postdeluvian sections of the genealogy."[22]

Thus it stands to reason that the deviating figures in the Greek version attest to a specific chronological model. But again, the proposals brought forward in the exegetical discussion are not convincing. Alfred Bosse has considered that the Greek dating of the foundation of the temple to the year 4260 *anno mundi* is the result from a calculation of 12 x 355, pointing to the idea of a great year consisting of great months with 355 days of a lunar year (*großes Jahr mit einem großen Monat von 355 Tagen* [*Mondjahr*]).[23] According to his theory, the chronology of the MT is based on the idea of a great solar year, and the LXX would have converted this scheme to a great lunar year. There are two weak points in Bosse's proposal. One, he has to add one year to the duration of the flood, a calculation not attested in the text. Two, besides the reconstructed length of the 355 days of the flood (Gen 7:11), there is no indication in the LXX pointing to a high esteem of the number 355. His theory was therefore not supported by later research.[24]

---

19. Ziemer 2009, 3.
20. See Koch 1983, 425.
21. E.g., Preuss, 1859, 37; de Vries 1962, 581; Murtonen 1954, 136; Klein 1974, 263; Larsson 1973, 407.
22. Hughes 1990, 9–10, who himself admits that the argument is not very strong.
23. Bosse 1908, 31–36, citation from p. 33.
24. As to my knowledge only Skinner 1910, 234–35, has reluctantly signaled

Like Bosse, Hughes calculates the year 4260 *anno mundi* as the first year of the temple.[25] He assumes that the LXX has used a system of post-dating that intentionally focuses on the year 4260 as the first full year.[26] He therefore does not need to insert an additional year for the flood as required by Bosse. He then adds 430 years until the destruction, thus dating the first year of the destructed temple as 4690 *anno mundi*. From Zech 1:12, he adds 70 years to the rebuilding of the second temple (first year: 4760 *anno mundi*), leaving 240 years to the year 5000. He then switches to a modern chronology of the era and arrives in 280 BCE, based on the year 520 BCE as the date of the foundation of the second temple.[27] While the figure 5000 presented by Hughes is reasonable for the idea of a world era, he is not able to explain why this world age should be related to this specific historical situation in the third century BCE. He assumes that the system was adopted from the underlying Hebrew *Vorlage* that had an eschatological expectation for the year 5000 *anno mundi*, an expectation no longer known to us. Since he cannot give a sound explanation for purpose and intent of this chronology, this theory seems inconclusive to me.[28]

4. A New Proposal

Up to now it is not clear whether the figures in the Greek version point to a specific historical date, whether an unknown period scheme lies behind them, or whether they serve to establish synchronisms with other chronological systems of the Hellenistic environment. For the sake of clarification I will start with an overview of the absolute chronology, according to the LXX:

---

approval of Bosse's theses.

25. Hughes 1990, 238–41.

26. See Hughes 1990, 20–21; 180–81.

27. See also Northcote 2004, 12–17, who corrects the chronology of the LXX with numbers from different sources, including later codices and reckons with the year 5000 *anno mundi* in 292 BCE, "a few years after Palestine came under the control of Ptolemaic Egypt in 301 BCE and just a few years prior to the accession of Ptolemy II Philadelphus in 285 BCE" (16).

28. This also applies for his attempt to reconstruct the chronology of the Hebrew text underlying the LXX, which reckons with the year 4000 *anno mundi* for the exodus (Hughes 1990, 240–41), because he has to combine figures from several textual witnesses to arrive at this date.

2242	flood
3314	birth of Abraham
3389	Abraham departs from Haran (Gen 12:4: 75th year)
3414	birth of Isaac (Gen 21:5: Abraham's 100th year)
3474	birth of Jacob (Gen 25:26: Isaac's 60th year)
3604	Jacob in Egypt (Gen 47:9: Jacob's 130th year)
3819	exodus (Exod 12:40: The Israelites were dwelling 430 years in Canaan and Egypt = 215 years in Egypt. [MT: 430 years in Egypt])
4259	foundation of the temple (3 Kgdms 6:1: 440 years after the exodus [MT 1 Kgs 6:1: 480 years])
4689	destruction of the temple (3–4 Kgdms/1–2 Kgs: 430 years, calculated from the regnal years)
4739	rebuilding of the temple (Ezra 3:8: second year after the return = 50 years after destruction)

It is obvious that the ages imply a system of postdating: from Abraham's birth forward, the year in focus is the *following* year. This is similar to regnal years, in which the beginning of a king's reign is dated from the new year after his ascension.[29] This leads to round numbers like "five" and "ten." Besides this observation, there is no indication of a specific scheme or periodicity centered on multiples of characteristic numbers such as seven, twelve, forty, or a Jubilee-scheme. Moreover, none of the important events of the history of Israel can be dated to a symbolic figure like 2800, 3500, or 4000. It should be noticed, however, that the figures taken from the LXX are lower than those of the MT, beginning with the duration of the stay in Egypt until the foundation of the temple. This contradicts the tendency of LXX Genesis to raise the figures and to expand the chronology by inserting another patriarch.

Another explanation of the dates is that specific events of the history of Israel are synchronized with well-known chronological systems in the translator's own environment. This would fit into a special effort in the scientific discussions of that time to obtain reliable chronological data and to formulate a framework for mythological and historical data.[30] It may suffice to mention the *Babyloniaka* by Berossos, Manetho's *Aigyptiaka*, or

---

29. For this system, see Hughes 1990, 20.

30. For what follows, see Kubitschek 1928; Bickermann 1980; Wacholder 1968; Hermann, Schmidtke, and Koep 1956.

4. The Chronological System of Genesis-Septuagint 101

the Greek chronology by Eratosthenes from Cyrene, all of them from the third century BCE.[31]

It is clear that Jewish Hellenistic writers of this time period were interested in matters of chronology. Thus the fragments by Demetrios from Alexandria display the attempt to synchronize biblical dates from the time of Israel's monarchy with the regnal years of Ptolemy IV (frag. 6.1–2). Moreover, fragment 2 reveals Demetrios's interest in Israel's sojourn in Egypt, which is dated according to the numbers of the LXX (frag. 2.18–19).[32] Shortly after, Pseudo-Eupolemus draws connections between extrabiblical traditions (probably Berossos, Hesiod, and Ktesias) and biblical texts; in his emphasis on deriving identifications, chronological considerations are not preserved. About fifty years later (around 158/157 BCE), Eupolemus attempts to prove the antiquity of the biblical history. According to his calculations, Adam dates to the year 5149 before his days and the exodus to 2580 years before (frag. 5).[33]

It is therefore evident that beginning in the third century, there was vivid interest in establishing a common historical and chronological framework.[34] In the beginning, this was primarily directed at the history of the calculators' own people, as in Berossos's or Manetho's work. Jewish writers then attempted to combine events and characters known from biblical and foreign sources and to calculate synchronisms. By about 250 BCE, then, when LXX Genesis presumably was translated, there was already a great interest in chronology. However, obviously no synchronism existed that could also account for the primeval dates of the flood story. This coincides with the observation that none of the dates in the LXX can be related to known extrabiblical dates of contemporary historians.

In light of this background, it is possible to go one step further and to come to a solution regarding the chronology of the Greek Genesis: As stated earlier, the Greek version has lower figures than the MT from Exod 12 on, while in Genesis the figures were raised. But if one remembers that Genesis was translated first, one can consider that the translator was calculating with figures still unchanged by later writers/translators. If this alternative is taken into account, the following picture emerges:

---

31. See Adler 1989, 15–30.
32. Holladay 1983, 87; see also Walter 1980, 281, 289.
33. For the reading 2580, see Holladay 1983, 155.
34. See Fraser 1972, 1:457, 510.

Until the year 3604 (the beginning of Jacob's stay in Egypt), I follow the chronology of Genesis. Then I add 430 years until the Exodus (MT-figure from Exod 12:40) and 480 years until the temple is built (MT-figure from 1 Kgs 6:1). The statement in Exod 12:40 in the MT is obviously more original, because it has to be judged as *lectio brevior et difficilior*.[35] SP and LXX (or their antecessor) have tried to solve the problem of the long duration of the stay in Egypt by inserting *and Canaan*. In 1 Kgs 6:1, LXX has changed the original MT figure of 480 to 440, probably to attain a period of 40 years for each of the priestly generations from Aaron to Zadok according to 1 Chr 5:27–34 (6:1–8).[36]

The question of the calculation of the time for existence of the first temple is more difficult to answer. In the MT, the regnal years of the kings of Judah after the foundation of the temple total 430 years.[37] However, the Lucianic/Antiochene version of the Greek text records different figures for Abijam (3 Kgdms 15:2: six years instead of three in the MT) and Joram (4 Kgdms 8:17: ten instead of eight years). Thus the chronology of the Lucianic version is five years longer than that of the MT; moreover, the number 435 is atypical and could therefore be a remnant of a more original, unreworked chronology.[38] In the books of the Kings, the Lucianic version has in many instances more original readings, especially in texts related to chronological problems.[39] Moreover, it can be safely considered that Josephus has used a text of the (proto-)Lucianic type in his rewriting of the narrative material from Samuel and Kings.[40] Thus there is ample reason to assume that the figure 435 for the time from the foundation of the temple until the exile goes back to an old tradition that could have been known by the translator. The last step is then to add fifty years from the beginning of the exile until the foundation of the second temple, a figure computed from Ezra 3:8. The calculation utilizing these alternative figures arrives at a surprising result for the chronology of the Septuagint:

---

35. Kreuzer 1991. The figure 430 which is attested to in LXX and SP has also been used by Paul in Gal 3:17, see Lührmann 1988.
36. Thus Montgomery and Gehman 1951, 143.
37. See the chart in Koch 1978, 435, and tables 4–6 in de Vries 1962.
38. Hughes 1990, 38.
39. On the reliability of the Lucianic version's reliability, see Swete 1914, 237–41; Kreuzer 2015. Shenkel 1968, 110 concludes that the Lucianic text did preserve the original chronology of the Hebrew *Vorlage* of the first translation of the books of Kings into Greek. See also Larsson 2002, 511–14 with a similar result.
40. Harl, Dorival, and Munnich 1988, 170.

4. The Chronological System of Genesis-Septuagint 103

2242 flood
3604 Jacob in Egypt
4034 exodus (MT: Exod 12:40: The Israelites were dwelling 430 years in Egypt)
4514 foundation of the temple (MT: 1 Kgs 6:1: 480 years after the exodus)
4949 destruction of the temple (LXX^L: 435 years of Judean kings from the foundation of the first temple until its destruction)
4999 rebuilding of the temple (Ezra 3:8: second year after the return = 50 years after destruction)

According to this reconstruction, the translator of the Greek Genesis has dated the first year of the second temple to the year 5000 *anno mundi*. The beginning of the existence of the new temple is obviously seen as the beginning of a new era, comparable to the rededication of the temple in the year 4000 *anno mundi*, if this reconstruction of the chronology of the MT is correct.

Against this proposal, Ronald Hendel has objected that I have commingled chronological data from LXX, MT, and modern calculations.[41] Unfortunately, Hendel does not cite my work correctly, because I have not tried to yield the modern date of 515 BCE. As stated above, I am not working with modern data but with the chronology of Ezra 3:8, which refers to the start of the construction of the temple under Sheshbazzar in the second year after the return to Jerusalem, which is year 50 after the destruction of the temple (537 BCE). This period of 50 years is generally accepted as representing the priestly chronology which prefers a schematic pattern of 2 x 480 years (1 Kgs 6:1): 480 years from the exodus to the foundation of the first temple, 430 years of the first temple's existence, plus 50 years until the foundation of the second temple.[42]

Hendel's own suggestion that the chronologies in Genesis and Kings are more easily explained as "responses to local exegetical problems" is not convincing because he does not attempt to explain why in the Greek version the numbers in Gen 11 are raised and the patriarch Kainan is inserted. This obvious interest in raising the numbers is contrary to the fact that in the books translated *after* Genesis, the numbers are lowered. Therefore, in my view it is permissible to calculate with the oldest extant dates that

---
41. Hendel 2012, 15.
42. Hughes, 1990, 39.

could have been known to the translator. Moreover, one must take a systematic reworking of the numbers into account, because in my view the differences between the versions or their respective *Vorlage* cannot be explained by scribal errors.

The question remains why the translator—or the tradition he mirrors—has chosen this date, resulting in the calculation of such a long chronology. One can easily imagine that the figure 5000, a multiple of fifty, relates this chronology with the idea of the Jubilees: every fiftieth year must be hallowed according to Lev 25:10.[43] Thus a new cycle of sabbath-years would have begun with the new temple.

One can also consider influence by the work of Manetho or the Egyptian tradition on which his work is based. According to the *Aigyptiaca*, the historical pharaohs reigned for approximately 3000 years. This figure would contradict a short and medium chronology of the biblical history, because according to Gen 10:6, Mizraim, the son of Ham, founded Egypt only after the flood. According to the chronology of the LXX as it is reconstructed above, the flood happened 2857 years prior to the foundation of the second temple. If the translator's date of authorship was about 280 years after the foundation of the temple, this assumption would place his lifetime approximately 3135–3140 years after the flood, thus avoiding any contradiction between Egyptian and biblical traditions. This explanation might fit the early attempts to synchronize chronological data in Hellenistic times I have outlined above. Thus the combination of the figures taken from the LXX of Genesis and older Hebrew sources makes it possible to solve the problem of the chronology underlying Gen 5 and 11.[44]

Bibliography

Adler, William. 1989. *Time Immemorial: Archaic History and Its Sources in Christian Chronography from Julius Africanus to George Syncellus*. Dumbarton Oaks Studies 26. Washington: Dumbarton Oaks.

Berger, Klaus. 1981. *Das Buch der Jubiläen*. JSHRZ 2.3. Gütersloh: Gütersloher Verlagshaus.

---

43. Ringe 2008, 418.

44. If later Byzantine theologians date the birth of the redeemer to the year 5500 *anno mundi*, their calculations must have been quite similar to the theory advanced here; see Petkov 2016, 145.

Bickerman, Elias J. 1980. *Chronology of the Ancient World*. Rev. ed. Aspects of Greek and Roman Life. London: Thames & Hudson.
Bosse, Alfred. 1908. *Die chronologischen Systeme im Alten Testament und bei Josephus*. MVG 13.2. Berlin: Peiser.
Bousset, Wilhelm. 1900. "Das chronologische System der biblischen Geschichtsbücher." *ZAW* 20:136–47.
Etz, Donald V. 1993. "The Numbers of Genesis V 3–31: A Suggested Conversion and Its Implications." *VT* 43:171–89.
Fraenkel, Detlev. 1984. "Die Überlieferungen der Genealogien Gen 5,3–28 und Gen 11,10–26 in den 'Antiquitates Judaicae' des Flavius Josephus." Pages 175–200 in *De Septuaginta: Studies in Honour of John William Wevers On His Sixty-Fifth Birthday*. Edited by Albert Pietersma and Claude E. Cox. Mississauga: Benben.
Fraser, Peter M. 1972. *Ptolemaic Alexandria I–III*. Oxford: Clarendon.
Harl, Marguerite. 1986. *La Genèse*. BdA 1. Paris: Cerf.
Harl, Marguerite, Gilles Dorival, and Olivier Munnich. 1988. *La Bible Grecque des Septante: Du judaïsme hellénistique au christianisme ancien*. Paris: Cerf.
Hendel, Ronald S. 2012. "A Hasmonean Edition of MT Genesis? The Implications of the Editions of the Chronology in Genesis 5." *HBAI* 1:1–17.
Hermann, A., F. Schmidtke, and L. Koep. 1957. "Chronologie." *RAC* 11:30–60.
Holladay, Carl R. 1983. *Fragments from Hellenistic Jewish Authors*. Pseudepigrapha Series 10. Chico, CA: Scholars Press.
Hughes, Jeremy. 1990. *Secrets of the Times: Myth and History in Biblical Chronology*. JSOTSup 66. Sheffield: JSOT Press.
Jepsen, Alfred. 1929. "Zur Chronologie des Priesterkodex." *ZAW* 47:251–55.
———. 1968. "Noch einmal zur israelitisch-jüdischen Chronologie." *VT* 18:31–46.
Johnson, Marshall D. 1969. *The Purpose of the Biblical Genealogies: With Special Reference to the Setting of the Genealogies of Jesus*. SNTSMS 8. London: Cambridge University Press.
Klein, Ralph W. 1974. "Archaic Chronologies and the Textual History of the Old Testament." *HTR* 67:255–63.
Koch, Klaus. 1978. "Die mysteriösen Zahlen der judäischen Könige und die apokalyptischen Jahrwochen." *VT* 28:433–41.
———. 1983. "Sabbatstruktur der Geschichte: Die sogenannte Zehn-Wochen-Apokalypse (I Hen 93,1–10; 91,11–17) und das Ringen um

die alttestamentlichen Chronologien im späten Israelitentum." *ZAW* 95:403–30.

Kreuzer, Siegfried. 1991. "Zur Priorität und Auslegungsgeschichte von Exodus 12,40 MT: Die chronologische Interpretation des Ägyptenaufenthaltes in der judäischen, samaritanischen und alexandrinischen Exegese." *ZAW* 103:252–58.

———. 2015. "Translation and Recensions: Old Greek, Kaige, and Antiochene Text in Samuel and Reigns." Pages 154–75 in *The Bible in Greek: Translation, Transmission, and Theology of the Septuagint*. Edited by Siegfried Kreuzer. SCS 63. Atlanta: SBL Press.

Kubitschek, Wilhelm. 1928. *Grundriss der antiken Zeitrechnung*. Handbuch der Altertumswissenschaft 1.7. Munich: Beck.

Larsson, Gerhard. 1973. *The Secret System: A Study in the Chronology of the Old Testament*. Leiden: Brill.

———. 1983. "The Chronology of the Pentateuch: A Comparison of the MT and the LXX." *JBL* 102:401–9.

———. 2002. "Septuagint versus Massoretic Chronology." *ZAW* 114:511–21.

Lührmann, Dieter. 1988. "Die 430 Jahre zwischen den Verheißungen und dem Gesetz (Gal 3,17)." *ZAW* 100:420–23.

Montgomery, James A., and Henry S. Gehman. 1951. *A Critical and Exegetical Commentary on the Books of Kings*. ICC. Edinburgh: T&T Clark.

Murtonen, A. 1954. "On the Chronology of the Old Testament." *ST* 8:133–37.

Northcote, Jeremy. 2004. "The Schematic Development of Old Testament Chronography: Towards an Integrated Model." *JSOT* 29:3–36.

———. 2007. "The Lifespans of the Patriarchs: Schematic Orderings in the Chrono-genealogy." *VT* 57:243–57.

Petkov, Julian. 2016. *Altslavische Eschatologie: Texte und Studien zur apokalyptischen Literatur in kirchenslavischer Überlieferung*. TANZ 59. Tübingen: Attempto.

Preuss, Eduard. 1859. *Die Zeitrechnung der Septuaginta vor dem vierten Jahr Salomo's*. Berlin: Oehmigke.

Ringe, Sharon H. 2008. "Jubilee, Year of." *NIDB* 3:418–19

Rösel, Martin. 1994. *Übersetzung als Vollendung der Auslegung: Studien zur Genesis-Septuaginta*. BZAW 223. Berlin: de Gruyter.

Shenkel, James D. 1968. *Chronology and Recensional Development in the Greek Text of Kings*. HSM 1. Cambridge: Harvard University Press.

Skinner, John. 1910. *A Critical and Exegetical Commentary on Genesis*. ICC 1. Edinburgh: T&T Clark.
Swete, Henry B. 1914. *An Introduction to the Old Testament in Greek*. Rev. by R. R. Ottley. With an Appendix containing the Letter of Aristeas edited by H. St. J. Thackeray. Cambridge: Cambridge University Press.
Vries, Simon J de. 1962. "Chronology of the OT." *IDB* 1:580–99
Wacholder, Ben Z. 1968. "Biblical Chronology in the Hellenistic World Chronicles." *HTR* 61:451–81.
Walter, Nikolaus. 1980. *Fragmente jüdisch-hellenistischer Exegeten: Aristobulos, Demetrios, Aristeas*. JSHRZ 3.2. 2nd ed. Gütersloh: Gütersloher Verlagshaus
Westermann, Claus. 1983. *Genesis: Teilband 1; Genesis 1–11*. 3rd ed. BKAT 1.1. Neukirchen-Vluyn: Neukirchener Verlag.
Wevers, John W. 1993. *Notes on the Greek Text of Genesis*. SCS 35. Atlanta: Scholars Press.
Ziemer, Benjamin. 2009. "Erklärung der Zahlen von Gen 5 aus ihrem kompositionellen Zusammenhang." *ZAW* 121:1–18.

5
Jakob, Bileam und der Messias.
Messianische Erwartungen in Gen 49 und Num 22–24

Zu den Basistexten messianischer Erwartungen gehören neben klassischen Prophezeiungen wie Jes 11 vor allem zwei Texte aus dem Pentateuch: Jakobs Segen in Gen 49 (besonders V. 10) und die Bileam-Orakel in Num 23–24 (hier besonders 24,7 + 17).[1] Auch wenn die Frage verhandelt wird, ob sich schon in der griechischen Übersetzung des Pentateuch messianische Vorstellungen finden lassen, wird in der Regel auf diese Texte verwiesen, weil sich hier eine eindeutig interpretierende Übersetzungsweise der jeweiligen Übersetzer erkennen lasse.[2]

Diese Einschätzung ist allerdings von Johan Lust vehement in Frage gestellt worden, der bei beiden Stellen zu dem Ergebnis kommt, dass die LXX-Übersetzer keineswegs eine individuelle messianische Erwartung pointieren würden.[3]

Wenn über die Frage gesprochen werden soll, ob es im LXX-Pentateuch messianische Erwartungen gibt, muss eine gründliche Untersuchung der beiden Texte erfolgen. Dies wird so geschehen, dass zunächst Gen 49 und danach Num 24 im Mittelpunkt stehen sollen. Dabei sollen nicht nur—wie sonst weithin üblich—die klassischen Belegstellen in den Blick genommen werden, da m.E. auch der weitere Textzusammenhang von entscheidender Bedeutung ist.

---

1. Dieser Aufsatz beruht auf den einleitenden Referaten für die beiden Sitzungen des deutschsprachigen Seminars im Rahmen des 53. Colloquium Biblicum Lovaniense 2004, das zu leiten ich die Ehre hatte.

2. Vgl. u.a. Siegert 2001, 294 (zu Num 24,7.17) und 297–301; vgl. Harl, Dorival und Munnich 1994, 219–22. 284.

3. Lust 1995, 1997.

Hier ist auf ein prinzipielles methodisches Problem hinzuweisen, das gegenwärtig die Gemeinde der LXX-Forscher/innen entzweit: In der Regel handelt es sich ja bei der LXX-Übersetzung des Pentateuch um die älteste greifbare Auslegung der Texte. Daher ist oft strittig, ob bestimmte Übersetzungsphänomene, etwa der „Mensch" in Num 24,7. 17 oder der „Führer" aus Gen 49,10 schon Hinweis auf eine veränderte inhaltliche Vorstellung haben oder nicht. Denn selbst wenn etwa Texte aus Qumran, die Targumim oder andere jüdisch-hellenistische Autoren belegen, dass der Text später messianisch verstanden wurde, ist das zwar ein Indiz, *allein* aber kein hinreichender Beleg dafür, dass dies schon für die Übersetzung der LXX gilt.[4] M.E. lässt sich dieses Problem nicht isoliert auf der Ebene einzelner Lexeme lösen, sondern nur unter Berücksichtigung des näheren Kontextes der fraglichen Übersetzung. Das betrifft aber nicht nur den Textzusammenhang, sondern auch die religionsgeschichtliche Situation, in der die Übersetzung angefertigt wurde.[5]

Ein weiteres Problemfeld ist die Frage nach der übersetzten Textgattung. Hier stehen ausführliche Vergleiche noch aus, dennoch möchte ich als Arbeitshypothese formulieren, dass die poetischen Partien in den erzählenden Büchern die Übersetzer einerseits vor besondere Schwierigkeiten stellten, ihnen aber andererseits auch einen größeren Gestaltungsspielraum eröffneten. Zum einen stellen die verwendeten Bilder mit ihrem oft ausgefallenen Vokabular eine besondere Herausforderung dar, zum anderen eröffnet die Struktur des *parallelismus membrorum* die Möglichkeit, Aussageinhalte zu variieren bzw. zu pointieren.

1. Das Interlinearitäts-Paradigma

Mein Zugang unterscheidet sich nach dem eben Gesagten deutlich vom Paradigma der Interlinearität, das Albert Pietersma vorgetragen hat, und dem im Verlauf des Kongresses in Leuven gelegentlich explizit oder implizit zugestimmt wurde.[6] Pietersma rechnet für die meisten Bücher der LXX damit, dass sie *nicht* als selbständige Texte gelten können. Sie seien

---

4. Dies wäre als prinzipieller Vorbehalt gegen die Arbeitsweise von Vermes 1961, 49–63 zu äußern, dessen Argumentation zu Gen 49,10 oder Num 24,7. 17 weithin Zustimmung gefunden hat.

5. Vgl. dazu meinen Versuch zu Jes 7,14: Rösel 1991 [Kapitel 9 in diesem Band].

6. Pietersma 2002. Die folgende Auseinandersetzung muss notwendig thetisch bleiben, soll sie nicht den Rahmen dieses Beitrages sprengen.

vielmehr so zu verstehen, dass sie immer auch auf ihre Vorlage zurückverweisen. Nur so ließen sich s.E. Fälle erklären, in denen offenbar unverständliches Griechisch produziert wurde; das Modell erklärt folgerichtig den hebraisierenden Charakter von Syntax und Semantik der Übersetzung. Hintergrund dieses Paradigmas sind erhaltene Schülerübungen, die das Phänomen der interlinearen Übersetzung für Homer-Wiedergaben in aktuelles Griechisch oder spätere Übersetzungen ins Lateinische belegen. Dem entsprechend rechnet Pietersma auch mit dem Schulbetrieb als Sitz im Leben der griechischen Bibelübersetzungen.

Dieses Modell hat weitreichende Konsequenzen, da Pietersma es auch als Grundlage für die Lexikographie der LXX verwenden möchte; der semantische Wert des fraglichen hebräischen Wortes hat dann auch für das verwendete griechische Äquivalent zu gelten. Im Griechischen belegte, abweichende Konnotationen hätten danach keine oder nur untergeordnete Bedeutung für die Interpretation der Übersetzungstexte.[7] Außerdem wird angenommen, dass die Übersetzer in kleinen Übersetzungseinheiten im Umfang von nur wenigen Wörtern vorgegangen sind; kontextuelle Exegese lasse sich also im Regelfall auch nur in diesem engen Kontext feststellen. Nur wenige Bücher der LXX-Schriftensammlung seien nicht mit diesem Modell einer *verbum e verbo*-Übersetzungsweise erklärbar; als einzige Ausnahme, in der *sensus de sensu* übersetzt wurde, nennt Pietersma das Hiobbuch.[8]

Die Vorteile dieses vorgeschlagenen Paradigmas sind unübersehbar: Es wird leicht verstehbar, wie es in Einzelfällen zu seltsamen Übertragungen oder einfachen Transkriptionen gekommen ist, ebenso ist die oft sklavisch an der Vorlage orientierte Syntax einiger Übersetzungen erklärbar. Genauso deutlich sind aber die Grenzen des Modells: So lassen sich schon von der Genesis-Übersetzung an eine Fülle von Phänomenen feststellen, die eher zum Bereich der *sensus de sensu*-Übersetzungsweise zuzurechnen sind. Gemeint sind Fälle von Harmonisierungen von Texten untereinander, die offenbar eine größere Widerspruchsfreiheit der Schrift erzielen sollen. Als Beispiele mögen die verschiedenen Umstellungen in Gen

---

7. Damit wird ein alter Streit erneuert, der sich an der Kritik von James Barr am ThWNT entzündet hatte; A. Pietersma stellt sich auf die Seite Barrs. Die Problematik habe ich ausführlicher in meiner Dissertation diskutiert (Rösel 1994, 22–24); dies soll hier nicht wiederholt werden.

8. Zum Hintergrund dieser auf Hieronymus (epist. 57,5) zurückgehenden Bestimmungen vgl. die wichtige Arbeit von Seele, 1995.

1 oder die Zufügung von ἔτι in Gen 2,9 + 19 genügen, das den zweiten Schöpfungsbericht leichter an den ersten anschließen lässt; der Übersetzer hatte demnach eindeutig den größeren Kontext Gen 1+2 im Blick. Ferner hat besonders Gilles Dorival auf das Phänomen der Intertextualität hingewiesen,[9] was etwa dazu geführt hat, dass in Num 1 LXX die Stämme Israels nach dem Modell von Gen 35 und 49 neu angeordnet wurden. Dies widerspricht der Annahme, dass sich im weitesten Sinne exegetische Eingriffe der Übersetzer nur im Nahkontext des Problems feststellen lassen.

Natürlich ist unbestritten, dass die LXX-Übersetzungen stets auf die hebräische Bibel zurückverweisen. Die Frage ist aber, ob dies wirklich in der engen Weise geschieht, die Pietersma annimmt. Die Harmonisierungen und Intertextualitäten belegen ja, dass es so etwas wie Auslegungs- oder Verstehenstraditionen neben der eigentlichen Schrift gegeben hat. Diese sind leider nur in Ausnahmefällen zeitnah—etwa bei Schriftstellern wie Demetrius oder Aristobulos—schriftlich erhalten. Doch man muss notwendig mit mündlichen wie schriftlichen Paralleltraditionen rechnen, die nebeneinander existieren; im Falle der Chronologie der Urgeschichte (Gen 5 + 11)[10] sind etwa drei verschiedene Traditionen in MT, LXX und Samaritanus eindeutig greifbar. Die Übersetzung verweist also nicht einfach nur auf die geschriebene Schrift als ihre Vorlage, sondern auch auf die tradierte und in charakteristischer Weise verstandene Schrift einer genau zu definierenden religiösen Gemeinschaft. Wie dies in das eher starre, bipolare Interlinearitätsparadigma zu integrieren ist, wird nicht deutlich.

Methodisch erschwerend kommt hinzu, dass solche parallelen Verstehenstraditionen oft in späteren Schriften Niederschlag gefunden haben. Es ist also den Texten nicht angemessen, wenn man die Einbeziehung später belegter Auslegungen von vornherein für die Bestimmung des Sinngehaltes der Übersetzung ausschließt. Eine Fülle von Beispielen dafür, dass etwa rabbinisch belegte Deutungen schon den Übersetzern bekannt gewesen sein mussten, finden sich bereits in den Arbeiten von Zacharias Frankel und Leo Prijs.[11]

Daneben gibt es weitere Problemfelder: So ist nicht ausgemacht, dass die Übersetzer tatsächlich ein solches in den Schulen verankertes Interlinearitätsmodell nutzten. Die von Pietersma angeführten Belege für die Existenz solcher Interlinearübersetzungen sind allesamt jünger als etwa

---

9. Dorival 1995.
10. Dazu Rösel 1994, 129–44 [englische Übersetzung Kapitel 4 in diesem Band].
11. Prijs 1948; Frankel 1851.

die Pentateuch-LXX. Hinzu kommt das prinzipielle Problem der zwischen Hebräisch und Griechisch unterschiedlichen Schreibrichtungen, die bei nur durchschnittlich langen Schreibzeilen, wie sie etwa in Qumran belegt sind, schnell zu großer Unübersichtlichkeit führt; hebräisches Ausgangswort und griechisches Äquivalent stehen eben nicht direkt untereinander.[12]

Meine eigenen Forschungen an der Genesis-LXX, wie auch die (von Pietersma kurz angeführten) Überlegungen von Arie van der Kooij[13] weisen eher auf den Umkreis von Akademie oder Museion in Alexandria als auf Schulen hin; für die Jesaja-LXX ist gar mit dem Tempel von Leontopolis als Entstehungsort zu rechnen.[14] Die Aufgabe der vollständigen Übersetzung eines biblischen Buches ist m.E. auch zu komplex, als dass man sie auf den vergleichsweise niedrigen Niveau einer Schule ansiedeln sollte; die hohe Konkordanz schon der ersten greifbaren Übersetzung weist eher auf akademische Kreise hin. Natürlich ist damit nicht ausgeschlossen, dass die übersetzten Bücher später dann in den Schulen verwendet wurden; nach einer ansprechenden Vermutung von Holger Gzella wurden sie sogar zum Lernen und Lehren des Hebräischen eingesetzt.[15] Doch leider fehlen hier genauere Kenntnisse über die das alexandrinische Judentum des 3. Jh.v.Chr.

Schließlich ist innerhalb der einzelnen Bücher zu beobachten, dass die gleichen Übersetzer unterschiedliche Texte auf unterschiedliche Weise übersetzen. So bleiben etwa im Numeribuch die Übersetzungen von gesetzlichen Partien deutlich enger an der Vorlage als Erzählungen; auf die besondere Weise der Übersetzung der Bileam-Perikope wird unten noch einzugehen sein. In der Genesis ist das gleiche Phänomen beim Vergleich von Erzählungen und poetischen Stücken wie Gen 49 zu beobachten. Im Buch Exodus stehen offenbar sogar die sehr unterschiedlichen Erzeugnisse von zwei Übersetzern hintereinander.[16] Offenbar sind die Phänomene also sehr viel komplexer, als es das Modell voraussetzt. Interessanterweise weisen ausgerechnet die Bücher des Pentateuch größere Abweichungen

---

12. Dieses Problem lässt sich wohl nur umgehen, wenn man mit der Existenz einer Transkription des hebräischen Textes ähnlich der zweiten Kolumne der Hexapla rechnet; dagegen spricht aber die Fülle von Fällen, in denen die Übersetzer eindeutig einen hebräischen Text vor sich gehabt haben müssen.
13. Van der Kooij 1998.
14. So schon Frankel 1841, 40, Anm. f.; van der Kooij 1981, 60–65.
15. Gzella 2002, 33.
16. Dazu jetzt Wade 2003.

von ihrer Vorlage auf, als die später übersetzten Geschichtsbücher. Das ist aber schwer erklärbar, wenn die Übersetzung nur ein „tool" zum Verständnis des hebräischen Originals sein soll;[17] hier wäre gerade bei der Tora mit größerer Vorbildtreue zu rechnen. Damit scheint mir weiterhin wahrscheinlicher zu sein, dass die meisten Übersetzer eigenständige Schriften erzeugen wollten, in die—absichtlich oder nicht—ihr eigenes Verständnis der biblischen Stoffe einfloss. Dass die Frage des Verhältnisses zur hebräischen Vorlage spätestens im 2. Jahrhundert v.Chr. im hellenistischen Judentum virulent wurde, belegen die Diskussionen im Aristeasbrief, aber auch die deutlich wörtlicher werdenden Übersetzungen dieser Zeit und die nun einsetzenden Revisionen zum hebräischen Text hin. Dies aber sind Phänomene, die auf ein in manchen Kreisen verändertes Schriftverständnis hinweisen.[18] Folglich scheint mir das Interlinearitäts-Paradigma ein heuristisch interessantes Verstehensmodell zu sein; für die Beschreibung der Komplexität der vielen unterschiedlichen Übersetzungsphänomene der LXX reicht es aber m.E. nicht aus.

2. Genesis 49

Im Mittelpunkt des Interesses soll zunächst der Spruch über Juda in Gen 49,8–12 stehen.[19] Es sei aber zumindest kurz darauf hingewiesen, dass sich in den anderen Stammessprüchen eine Fülle von Differenzen zwischen Vorlage und Übersetzung feststellen lassen, die ein eindeutiges interpretatives Interesse des Übersetzers belegen. So werden etwa die negativen Bewertungen über Ruben, Simeon und Levi verstärkt; Issachar wird dagegen positiver dargestellt als im hebräischen Text. Zudem sei an 49,1 erinnert, wo im hebräischen Text zu lesen ist, dass Jakob verkünden werde, was in künftigen Zeiten (באחרית הימים) geschehen wird. LXX hat dies mit ἐπ' ἐσχάτων τῶν ἡμερῶν übersetzt, was eine eschatologische Leserichtung des folgenden Textes zumindest ermöglicht, wenn nicht impliziert.[20]

---

17. Pietersma 2002, 360.
18. Dies nach Joosten 2000.
19. Die hier vorgetragenen Überlegungen zu Gen 49 LXX basieren im wesentlichen auf Rösel 1995. Durchgängig verwendet wurden Harl 1986 und Wevers 1993. Die Literatur zum hebräischen Text ist nahezu unübersehbar. Es möge daher genügen, wenn ich auf die Studie von Macchi 1999, hinweise, die auch die ältere Literatur bespricht.
20. Ähnlich Collins 2006, 138: "This phrase ... definitely has eschatological over-

5. Jakob, Bileam und der Messias

Im ersten Vers des Juda-Spruches (49,8) lassen sich nur kleinere Differenzen zwischen den Textformen markieren, die kaum weiter aussagekräftig sind.

49,9

גור אריה יהודה	σκύμνος λέοντος Ιουδα
מטרף בני עלית	ἐκ βλαστοῦ υἱέ μου ἀνέβης
כרע רבץ כאריה	ἀναπεσὼν ἐκοιμήθης ὡς λέων
וכלביא מי יקימנו	καὶ ὡς σκύμνος τίς ἐγερεῖ αὐτόν

| Juda ist ein junger Löwe; vom Raub, mein Sohn, bist du hochgekommen. Er kauert, er lagert sich wie ein Löwe und wie eine Löwin. Wer will ihn aufreizen? | Ein Junglöwe ist Juda! Aus einem Spross, mein Sohn, wuchsest du hoch. Als du dich niederlegtest, schliefst du wie ein Löwe und wie ein Junglöwe: Wer wird ihn wecken? |

Doch bereits im ersten Stichos von V. 9 ist ein gravierender Unterschied zu greifen: Der hebräische Text liest מטרף בני עלית „vom Raub, mein Sohn, bist du hochgekommen." Demgegenüber hat LXX ἐκ βλαστοῦ υἱέ μου ἀνέβης; טרף wurde als „frischer Zweig, Spross" (טָרָף) verstanden, nicht als „Raub, Beute" (טֶרֶף). Da der Übersetzer beide Wörter bzw. Derivate an anderen Stellen aber angemessen übersetzen konnte—vgl. nur יִטְרָף im Spruch über Benjamin 49,27[21]—ist nicht mit einer einfachen Vokalisationsvariante zu rechnen. So denkt Wevers dem Kontext entsprechend an ein Löwenjunges;[22] dagegen spricht aber, dass βλαστός eindeutig in den Bereich der Botanik gehört (LSJ). Daher ist zu überlegen, ob nicht der Spross aus Jes 11,1 oder der sprießende Weinstock in Ez 17 im Hintergrund der Übersetzung stehen.[23] In der späteren Ezechiel-Übersetzung steht jedenfalls in Ez 17,8. 23; 19,10 βλαστός bei der Erwartung des kommenden Heilskönigs. Da auch in Gen 49,11 vom Weinstock die Rede ist,

---

tones." Zum Problem vgl. vor allem Steudel 1993, 231 (Hinweis von H.-J. Fabry). Frau Steudel weist auf, dass der Terminus in Qumran fast ausschließlich in auslegenden Texten verwendet wird und sich auf eine abgegrenzte Zeitperiode bezieht, die als die letzte, entscheidende Periode der Geschichte anzusehen ist.

21. Weitere Belege bei Rösel 1995, 61.
22. Wevers 1993, 825.
23. So auch Horbury 1998, 50.

kann diese intertextuelle Bezugnahme leicht erklärt werden.[24] Auch im *Genesis-Päschär* aus Qumran (4Q252) ist in Frg. 6, Col. V die in Gen 49 gelesene Messiasgestalt eindeutig von Texten wie Jes 11; Jer 23,5; 33,15 her beeinflusst, in denen die Erwartung eines Sprosses/(צדיק) צמח ausgedrückt wird.[25] Das im Futur formulierte „Aufwecken" am Versende ist schließlich als Hinweis auf ein künftiges Geschehen zu verstehen, bei dem die Juda-Gestalt eingreifen wird.

Der wirkungsgeschichtlich wichtigste Vers des Abschnitts ist gewiss V. 10, der allerdings auch große textliche Schwierigkeiten bietet. Ich stelle die Texte zunächst gegenüber:

49,10

לא־יסור שבט מיהודה	οὐκ ἐκλείψει ἄρχων ἐξ Iουδα
ומחקק מבין רגליו	καὶ ἡγούμενος ἐκ τῶν μηρῶν αὐτοῦ
עד כי־יבא שילה [שילו]	ἕως ἂν ἔλθῃ τὰ ἀποκείμενα αὐτῷ
ולו יקהת עמים	καὶ αὐτὸς προσδοκία ἐθνῶν
Nicht weicht das Zepter von Juda, noch der Herrscherstab zwischen seinen Füßen,	Nicht wird weichen aus Juda ein Fürst und von seinen Lenden ein Herrscher,
bis dass „Schilo" kommt,	bis das kommt, was für ihn aufbewahrt ist,
dem gehört der Gehorsam der Völker.	und er selbst ist die Erwartung der Völker.

Im Parallelismus des ersten Stichos hat LXX שבט und מחקק personalisiert übersetzt; sie redet nicht von Herrschaftsinsignien, sondern von Führerpersönlichkeiten. Dabei ist zunächst von Bedeutung, dass im Kontext von Gen 49 das Lexem שבט an drei Stellen vorkommt, wobei es jeweils anders übersetzt wurde; in V. 16 mit φυλή und in V. 28 mit υἱός: Jakob segnete nicht die Stämme, sondern seine Söhne; dies harmonisiert den letzten Vers mit der Überschrift.

Aus dem seltenen מחקק hat der Übersetzer ein Partizip herausgelesen und die Wortbedeutung offenbar im Parallelismus aus dem Vor-

---

24. Wenn die obige Interpretation richtig ist, handelt es sich hier in Gen 49,9 um die erste Zusammenstellung des Löwenbildes mit der Messiaserwartung, die später für die christliche Vorstellung von David bedeutsam wurde. Vgl. dazu Karrer 2003, 333.

25. Dazu etwa García Martínez, 1993, 174–77.

hergehenden erschlossen. Dabei fällt auf, dass das in Gen 36 für fremde Herrscher gebrauchte Nomen ἡγεμών nicht verwendet wurde; offenbar sollte zwischen unterschiedlichen Formen von Herrschaft differenziert werden. Johan Lust ist darin zuzustimmen, dass der Ersatz des Symbols durch das Symbolisierte (hier der Herrscherinsignien durch die Nennung der Herrscher selbst) eine häufiger zu beobachtende Übersetzungsweise ist, die folglich allein nicht aussagefähig ist.²⁶ Allerdings geht er nicht auf folgende weitere Auffälligkeit ein: Die Übersetzung des מבין רגליו durch ἐκ τῶν μηρῶν αὐτοῦ ist nämlich im Zusammenhang anderer Stellen der Genesis-LXX (46,26; 50,23) als Hinweis auf den Geburtsvorgang zu verstehen.²⁷ Demnach wird hier auf die dynastische Vorstellung angespielt, dass ein Führer aus der Nachkommenschaft Judas nicht vergehen wird.²⁸

In der zweiten Vershälfte ist die Übersetzung des שילה (Qᵉre: שילו) durch τὰ ἀποκείμενα αὐτῷ auffällig und rätselhaft zugleich.²⁹ Die LXX-Übersetzung beruht offenbar auf der Lesart שֶׁ לוֹ (Relativpartikel und suffigiertes *lamed*), sie bestätigt also das Qᵉre zumindest teilweise. Die Interpretation der Aussage ist schwierig, vielleicht ist sie bewusst uneindeutig formuliert³⁰. Offenbar geht es darum, dass die Herrschaft der erwarteten Herrschergestalt bis zu einem bestimmten, für sie vorgesehenen Ereignis begrenzt wird.³¹ Möglicherweise wird hier an den Anbruch der Gottesherrschaft ähnlich wie in Dan 7 gedacht; dort erhält zunächst der Menschenähnliche die Herrschaft, dann erst das Reich der Heiligen Höchsten.³² Anders ist dagegen die in Targum Neofiti und 4Q252 formulierte Erwartung: Hier wird das schwierige *Schilo* auf eine Person gedeutet: In Juda wird kein Herrscher vergehen, bis der König Messias/der Messias der Gerechtigkeit kommt.³³ Deutlich ist jedenfalls die messianische Deutung der Stelle, die sich m.W. in der Sekundärliteratur durchgesetzt hat.³⁴

---

26. Lust 1997, 40.
27. רגל wird sonst mit πούς übersetzt, vgl. nur Gen 49,33.
28. So schon Frankel 1851, 49–51; anders Harl 1986, 308–9.
29. Zur Diskussion um den hebräischen Text und seine Bedeutung vgl. zusammenfassend Seebass 2000, 167 + 174–76; der die Form letztlich für unerklärbar hält.
30. So Collins 2006, 138.
31. Prijs 1948, 67, bezieht τὰ ἀποκείμενα αὐτῷ ohne weitere Problematisierung direkt auf den Messias, dies wegen des parallelen Verständnisses in jüdischen Midraschim.
32. Dazu Koch 1995.
33. Vgl. Harl 1986, 309, auch zur altkirchlichen Wirkungsgeschichte.
34. So auch Wevers 1993, 826; Monsengwo-Pasinya 1980, 364, der allerdings

Dieses Verständnis der LXX wird noch unterstützt durch den letzten Stichos. Hier wurde das seltene Nomen יקהה „Gehorsam" offenbar von der Wurzel קוה „hoffen" her verstanden; der Nominalsatz wurde beibehalten. Anders als im vorhergehenden Stichos wird לו nun als Subjekt gefasst, da der Übersetzer offenbar jeden Teilsatz als sinntragende Einheit verstand: Der Herrscher aus Juda ist die Hoffnung/Erwartung der Völker;[35] damit ist ein universales Heilsverständnis angesprochen, das sich u.a. in den Gottesknechtsliedern des Jesajabuches (42,6; 52,15), aber auch in Jes 11,10 findet.

Überblickt man den Vers im Ganzen, so ist m.E. eindeutig, dass er von der Erwartung einer Herrschergestalt aus der Dynastie Juda handelt. Diese wird bis zu einem nicht näher spezifizierten Ereignis zeitweise die Herrschaft ausüben, worauf die Hoffnung der Völker abzielt. Damit scheint mir das allein auf das Problem der Übersetzung von שבט und מחקק gestützte Urteil Johan Lusts nicht aufrechtzuerhalten sein, dass sich in Gen 49,10 keine messianische Erwartung finde.[36]

In der Diskussion des deutschsprachigen Seminars wurde als Alternative überlegt, dass der Vers rein innergeschichtlich zu verstehen sei: Es werde beständig einen Herrscher aus Juda geben; erwartet würde demnach die fortwährende Existenz der Davidsdynastie. Dem widerspricht m.E. zum einen das αὐτός in V. 10; das eindeutig auf eine Einzelperson zu beziehen ist; das „aufwecken" aus V. 9 und das „kommen" dessen, was aufbewahrt ist, sind ebenfalls besser auf ein Einzelereignis, als auf eine durchgängige Herrschaft zu beziehen. Eine eindeutige Lösung wird dadurch erschwert, dass der Bezug des αὐτῷ unklar ist: bezieht es sich, wie hier vorgeschlagen, auf den Fürst/Herrscher, oder (unwahrscheinlicher) auf Juda?[37]

---

auch für die LXX die Erwartung einer Person annimmt; der Text spiele an den מושׁל aus Mi 5,1 an. Dann aber ist nicht verständlich, weshalb das Neutrum τὰ ἀποκείμενα als Übersetzung gewählt wurde.

35. Monsengwo-Pasinya 1980, 367, nimmt allerdings an, dass nur die Stämme Israels gemeint seien; universale Aussagen würden immer mit πᾶς (ἔθνη) formuliert; das aber kann schon von Gen 10,24; 14,5 her nicht stimmen.

36. Es sei angefügt, dass schon der Grundtext Gen 49 MT als Ansage einer eschatologischen Herrschaft des Stammes Juda verstanden werden kann, so Schmitt 1999.

37. So Collins 2006, 139, Anm. 47, mit dem Hinweis darauf, dass ἄρχων und ἡγούμενος unbestimmt seien, sich das αὐτῷ also nicht auf sie beziehen könne. Das aber ist gerade auch wegen des folgenden αὐτός nicht sicher.

49,11

אסרי לגפן עירה [עירו]
ולשרקה בני אתנו
כבס ביין לבשו
ובדם־ענבים סותה [סותו]

δεσμεύων πρὸς ἄμπελον τὸν πῶλον αὐτοῦ
καὶ τῇ ἕλικι τὸν πῶλον τῆς ὄνου αὐτοῦ
πλυνεῖ ἐν οἴνῳ τὴν στολὴν αὐτοῦ
καὶ ἐν αἵματι σταφυλῆς τὴν περιβολὴν αὐτοῦ

An den Weinstock bindet er sein Eselsfüllen,
an die Edelrebe das Junge seiner Eselin;
er wäscht im Wein sein Kleid
und im Blut der Trauben sein Gewand;

der sein Füllen an einen Weinstock bindet
und das Füllen seiner Eselin an eine Weinranke.
Im Wein wird er sein Kleid waschen,
und im Blut der Traube seinen Umhang.

In den Versen 11 und 12 sind keine so gravierenden Abweichungen mehr zu erkennen. In V. 11 war dem Übersetzer offenbar עירה unbekannt; er leitete es wie in 32,16 von עיר „Hengst (vom Esel)" (HAL) ab; dies war möglicherweise auch von בן־אתון im folgenden Halbvers mit beeinflusst, da dort ebenfalls πῶλος verwendet wurde. Es zeigt sich also, dass unbekannte Wörter aus dem Kontext heraus erklärt wurden. Zu notieren ist noch die futurische Wiedergabe des כבס mit πλυνεῖ, die sich wohl dem Ansagecharakter von V. 10 verdankt.

Der Vers ist aufgrund seiner bildhaften Ausdrucksweise nicht eindeutig verstehbar, es erscheint aber am sinnvollsten, ihn als Hinweis auf den Überfluss der Heilszeit zu werten; dann ist der Reichtum so groß, dass man Tiere an Weinreben festbinden und den Wein wie Wasser zum Waschen nutzen kann. Der den Juda-Spruch abschließende Vers 12 weist ebenfalls nur geringe Differenzen auf, die für die hier behandelte Fragestellung nichts austragen.

Der vorläufige Ertrag der Beobachtungen zum Juda-Spruch ist damit m.E. eindeutig: Anders als der hebräische Text gibt die griechische Version der Hoffnung auf eine kommende Heilsgestalt Ausdruck, die aus dem Stamme Juda kommt. Sie wird mit der Erwartung eines paradiesischen Friedensreiches konnotiert (V. 11 + 12).

49,20

מאשר שמנה לחמו	Ασηρ πίων αὐτοῦ ὁ ἄρτος
והוא יתן מעדני־מלך	καὶ αὐτὸς δώσει τρυφὴν ἄρχουσιν
Von Asser: Fettes ist sein Brot; und er, königliche Leckerbissen gibt er.	Ascher: Fett ist sein Brot, und er selbst wird den Fürsten Üppigkeit geben.

Interessanterweise geschieht im weiteren Verlauf der griechischen Stammessprüche offenbar ein intertextueller Verweis auf diese erwartete Heilszeit: Im Spruch über Ascher wird als Kennzeichen dieses Stammes mitgeteilt, dass er ein üppiges Leben führen wird. Nur hier in der Genesis-LXX steht ἄρχων für מלך, so dass diese Übersetzung kaum zufällig sein wird. Die Verwendung von τρυφή weist außerdem auf Gen 3,23–4 (עדן) zurück, denn nur hier wurde das Lexem sonst verwendet. So lässt sich auch dieser Text als Verweis auf eine paradiesische Zukunft lesen. Deutlich wird zudem, dass der Übersetzer eben nicht nur kleinteilig am unmittelbaren Kontext interessiert ist, wie es das Interlinearitätsmodell nahelegt.

3. Numeri 22–24

Die Erzählung um den Propheten Bileam gehört sicher zu den meistkommentierten Kapiteln der hebräischen Bibel.[38] Die Forschung an der LXX-Übersetzung hat sich vor allem auf die Verse 24,7 + 17 konzentriert, da man hier eindeutige messianische Referenzen gesehen hat.[39] Bevor diese Texte in den Blick genommen werden, sei aber im Sinne der oben erhobenen methodischen Anforderung, den Kontext mit einzubeziehen, wenigstens überblicksweise auf folgende Phänomene hingewiesen:

Es ist eindeutig erkennbar, dass der Übersetzer sich bei der Wahl der Äquivalente auch von theologischen Überlegungen hat leiten lassen, die klare Bewertungen der Personen und Vorgänge ausdrücken. Die eindeutigsten seien kurz genannt:[40] Nach Num 23,1 verlangt Bileam von Balak, dem König der Moabiter, dass er sieben Altäre (מזבחת) bauen lassen soll.

---

[38]. Vgl. die immense Literaturmenge, die Seebass 2007, zusammengestellt hat. Rezeptionsgeschichtlich orientiert ist ein eigener Versuch zum Thema: Rösel 1999.

[39]. Zur Auslegungsgeschichte in der alten Kirche s. v.a. Dorival 1996. Vgl. auch Hayward 1999.

[40]. S. dazu auch Rösel 2001.

5. Jakob, Bileam und der Messias   121

Die LXX übersetzt dies mit βωμούς,[41] und kennzeichnet so bereits durch die Wortwahl die Opfer des Bileam als nicht rechtmäßig, da nämlich βωμός anders als θυσιαστήριον nicht für einen *rite* errichteten und gebrauchten Altar stehen kann.[42]

Ebenfalls mit fremden Kulten bzw. Göttern konnotiert ist die Übersetzung des Ortsnamens Bamoth Ba'al in 22,41, wohin Balak den Bileam bringt. LXX sah hier offenbar במה „Kulthöhe", daher die Übersetzung ἀνεβίβασεν αὐτὸν ἐπὶ τὴν στήλην τοῦ Βααλ; στήλη war in Lev 26,1 (dort für מצבה) und 26,30 (für במתיכם) eindeutig mit fremden Göttern verbunden worden.[43]

Vor diesem Hintergrund wundert es dann nicht, dass das Bileam-Bild der LXX fast durchgängig negativ ist.[44] Dies wird auf unterschiedliche Weise erreicht; am auffälligsten ist aber das Insistieren darauf, dass Bileam kein Verehrer des Gottes Israels sein kann. So wird in 22,18 die Aussage, dass Bileam nur weitergeben könne, was JHWH, mein Gott (יהוה אלהי) ihm sage, nicht ganz wörtlich, sondern nur mit κυρίου τοῦ θεοῦ übersetzt. In der Eselin-Perikope—aber auch in Kap. 23–24—wird gar konsequent das Tetragramm (bei der Rede vom „Engel des Herrn") mit θεός wiedergegeben; der Gott Israels ist nicht der Gott Bileams. Interessanterweise ist eine einzige Ausnahme von dieser Übersetzungskonvention festzustellen: In 22,34, wo Bileam Gott in einem Schuldbekenntnis direkt anspricht, wird יהוה mit dem üblichen κύριος übersetzt.[45]

Diese Beobachtungen, die durch eine genaue Untersuchung der Gesamtperikope Num 22–24 leicht vermehrt werden können, zeigen, dass

---

41. Ebenso an allen anderen Stellen: V. 2; 4; 14; 29; 30.

42. In Num 3,10 steht ebenfalls βωμός, allerdings ohne Pendant in der Vorlage. Da es hier um den Kult der Priester geht, ist die Verwendung von βωμός auffällig. Mit van der Kooij 2003, ist hier wohl an eine nachträgliche Glosse zu rechnen, die in den Text der LXX eingedrungen ist; dies in Anschluss an Daniel 1966, 27–28.

43. Anders noch in der Genesis, vgl. 19,26; 28,18.22 u.ö. Diese Interpretation findet sich jetzt auch bei Seebass 2007, 18, der allerdings den Bezug zu Lev 26 ablehnt und damit verkennt, wie eng sich der Übersetzer in vergleichbaren Fällen an Vorgaben aus den früher übersetzten Büchern gehalten hat.

44. Vgl. dazu Wevers 1999, der sich auf die Bearbeitung der narrativen Teile von Num 22–24 LXX beschränkt. Vgl. zum Textkomplex im Ganzen Wevers 1998, und Dorival 1994.

45. Zu dieser Deutung s. auch Wevers 1998, 373; Dorival 1994, 104; dazu auch Rösel 2001, 38–39; anders Seebass 2007, 17, der diese Überlegungen ohne eigene Erklärung für „unglaubwürdig" hält.

der Übersetzer ein besonderes interpretatives Interesse an diesem Text hatte; das geht so weit, dass sich nur hier stilistische Verbesserungen wie hypotaktische Partizipien feststellen lassen, die in anderen narrativen Texten der Übersetzung nur selten angewendet wurden. Vor diesem Hintergrund seien nun einige Phänomene der vier Orakel in den Blick genommen.

23,10

Zu Abschluss des ersten Orakels Bileams über Israel findet sich in 23,10 ein Vers, dessen Differenzen zum Hebräischen Text nur schwer erklärbar sind:

מי מנה עפר יעקב	τίς ἐξηκριβάσατο τὸ σπέρμα Ιακωβ
ומספר את־רבע ישראל	καὶ τίς ἐξαριθμήσεται δήμους Ισραηλ
תמת נפשי מות ישרים	ἀποθάνοι ἡ ψυχή μου ἐν ψυχαῖς δικαίων
ותהי אחריתי כמהו	καὶ γένοιτο τὸ σπέρμα μου ὡς τὸ σπέρμα τούτων
Wer könnte zählen den Staub Jakobs	Wer hat die Nachkommenschaft Jakobs
und der Zahl nach den vierten Teil[46] Israels?	genau geschätzt und wer wird die Volksgruppen Israels zählen?
Meine Seele sterbe den Tod der Aufrichtigen,	Meine Seele sterbe unter den Seelen der Gerechten,
und mein Ende sei gleich dem ihren!	und möge meine Nachkommenschaft werden wie deren Nachkommenschaft.

Im ersten Stichos findet sich offenbar eine intertextuelle Bezugnahme auf die Verheißung an Abraham in Gen 13,16 („Und ich will deine Nachkommen machen wie den Staub der Erde"; vgl. Gen 28,14); anders ist die Übersetzung von עפר mit σπέρμα nicht erklärbar.[47] Im zweiten Stichos hatte der Übersetzer offenbar größere Verständnisschwierigkeiten. Daher scheint er sich am ersten orientiert zu haben. Wie der Smr las er statt des ומספר die zwei Wörter מי ספר, wobei kaum zu entscheiden ist, ob diese Trennung schon in der Vorlage gegeben war. Das schwierige את־רבע wurde wohl im Kontext-Parallelismus durch δήμους vermutend

---

46. Oder: Die Wohnstätten, nach Smr^MSS. Vgl. die Übersicht über die Deutungen bei Seebass, 2007, 19.

47. So auch Wevers 1998, 390; Dorival 1994, 70.

übersetzt⁴⁸. Damit entstand ein stärker entwickelter, besser verständlicher Parallelismus als im hebräischen Text.⁴⁹

Die zweite Vershälfte konnte bisher nicht zufrieden stellend erklärt werden. Nach Gilles Dorival handelt es sich um eine intertextuelle Bezugnahme auf Num 31,1–8.⁵⁰ Dort wird Bileam durch die Israeliten getötet, daher sei die LXX-Version so zu erklären, dass er nicht den Tod der Aufrechten stirbt, sondern unter den Seelen der Gerechten, weil er durch die Gerechten = Israel getötet werde. Im letzten Stichos erwartet Bileam nach der griechischen Version nicht für sich selbst das gleiche Schicksal wie Israel, sondern nur für seine Nachkommenschaft. Auch dies kann—so Dorival—auf den gewaltsamen Tod Bileams hindeuten. Auffällig ist, dass nun אחרית mit σπέρμα übersetzt wurde, was die beiden Vershälften zusammenschließt. Bileam erwartet also wenn schon nicht für sich, so doch für seine Nachkommenschaft eine großartige Zukunft, wie sie Jakob/Israel gewährt sein wird. Der Akzent liegt einmal mehr auf der positiven Perspektive für Israel; Bileam aber hat eine solche keinesfalls.

23,19

Auch im zweiten Orakel lassen sich auffällige Abweichungen feststellen: Eine interessante Perspektive auf das Gottesbild des Übersetzers ist in 23,19 zu gewinnen:

לא איש אל ויכזב	οὐχ ὡς ἄνθρωπος ὁ θεὸς διαρτηθῆναι
ובן־אדם ויתנחם	οὐδὲ ὡς υἱὸς ἀνθρώπου ἀπειληθῆναι
ההוא אמר ולא יעשה	αὐτὸς εἴπας οὐχὶ ποιήσει
ודבר ולא יקימנה	λαλήσει καὶ οὐχὶ ἐμμενεῖ

Nicht ein Mensch ist Gott, dass er lüge,

noch der Sohn eines Menschen, dass er bereue.

Nicht wie ein Mensch ist Gott, dass er (von seinem Vorhaben) abgehalten werden könnte,

und nicht wie ein Menschenkind, dass er sich zwingen ließe;

---

48. Ähnlich Wevers 1998, 390; anders Dorival 1994, 159, der „sans doute" eine andere hebräische Vorlage annimmt. Die Verwendung des seltenen Verbums ἐξαριθμέω weist m.E. eindeutig auf Gen 13,16 zurück, wo dasselbe Verbum verwendet wurde.

49. Hinweis von Eberhard Bons, dem ich für seine kritische Lektüre des Artikels danken möchte.

50. Dorival 1994, 130.

Sollte er gesprochen haben und es nicht tun und geredet haben und es nicht aufrecht halten?	hat er etwas gesagt und wird es nicht tun? Wird er sprechen und nicht dabei bleiben?

Auffällig ist zunächst die doppelte Einfügung des ὡς, die jeglichen direkten Vergleich zwischen Gott und Mensch ausschließen soll; dies entspricht der Neigung des Übersetzers, Anthropomorphismen zu vermeiden.[51] Das Verbum כזב (sonst nicht mehr in Num) wurde offenbar als Ni. oder Pu. aufgefasst, und mit dem seltenen διαρτάω im Passiv wiedergegeben (nur hier in LXX). Allerdings wird der Akzent nicht auf das von der Wurzel כזב her nahe liegende Wortfeld „täuschen/lügen" gelegt,[52] sondern eine einlinige Aussage des gesamten Verses angestrebt: Gott kann in seinen Vorhaben nicht von Menschen abgehalten werden. Das passt perfekt zur Logik der Bileam-Erzählung. Die Wiedergabe von איש und אדם mit ἄνθρωπος ist vor allem deshalb bemerkenswert, weil der Übersetzer im Parallelismus *nicht* differenziert.[53] Alles scheint ihm also am Gegenüber von Gott und Mensch zu liegen.

23,21

לא־הביט און ביעקב ולא־ראה עמל בישראל יהוה אלהיו עמו ותרועת מלך בו	οὐκ ἔσται μόχθος ἐν Ιακωβ οὐδὲ ὀφθήσεται πόνος ἐν Ισραηλ κύριος ὁ θεὸς αὐτοῦ μετ' αὐτοῦ τὰ ἔνδοξα ἀρχόντων ἐν αὐτῷ
Man erblickt kein Unrecht in Jakob	Es wird keine harte Arbeit geben in Jakob,
und sieht kein Verderben in Israel;	und es wird keine Mühe gesehen werden in Israel;
der Herr, sein Gott, ist mit ihm, und Königsjubel ist in ihm.	der Herr, sein Gott ist mit ihm, die glanzvollen Taten der Fürsten sind in ihm.

---

51. S. die Übersicht bei Dorival 1994, 156–56.

52. So noch in Lust, Eynickel und Hauspie 1992, 108 (nach LSJ): „to deceive, to mislead"; auch Wevers 1998, 394; Dorival 1994, 438: „être trompé"; S. 439 auch: „pour être inconsequent". Anders Muraoka 2002, 119 „so as to be deterred", dies entspricht eher der in LSJ s.v. gegebenen Grundbedeutung „to suspend".

53. Im Numeribuch werden sowohl איש als auch אדם mit ἄνθρωπος übersetzt, so dass die Wahl der Äquivalente an sich nicht auffällig ist (anders Wevers 1998, 394).

5. Jakob, Bileam und der Messias

Ab V. 21 ist eine weitere wichtige Differenz zwischen hebräischem und griechischem Text festzustellen, da von diesem Vers an der griechische Text als Prophezeiung im Futur gestaltet ist—Ausnahme ist nur der rückblickende Vers 22 mit der Aussage, dass Gott Israel aus Ägypten geführt hat. V. 21 sagt dabei eine paradiesische Zukunft für Jakob und Israel an, in der es keine harten Arbeiten (μόχθος, noch Num 20,14) noch Mühen (πόνος, nicht mehr in Num) gibt. Dies spielt auf Ex 18,8 bzw. 2,11 an, wo die beiden Lexeme für die Bedrückungen durch die Ägypter verwendet wurden;[54] der hebräische Text redet davon, dass man *zur Zeit* kein Unrecht (און) und Verderben/Unheil (עמל) in Israel sieht.

Im letzten Stichos ist eine weitere Auffälligkeit festzuhalten: LXX vermeidet hier wie auch sonst die wörtliche Wiedergabe von מלך, wohl deshalb, weil nur Gott selbst König ist.[55] Daher wird ἄρχων als Äquivalent gewählt, dies aber im Plural stehend.[56] Die ebenfalls ungewöhnliche Wiedergabe von תרועה mit τὰ ἔνδοξα bezieht sich wohl auf die an Mose gegebene Bundesverheißung in Ex 34,10 (dort für נפלאת) zurück, da das Lexem an anderen, vor dem Numeribuch übersetzten Stellen sonst nicht mehr begegnet.[57] Die Interpretation dieses Stichos ist nicht unmittelbar einsichtig; offenbar wird eine besondere Zukunft Israels erwartet, in der es wieder glanzvolle, rühmenswerte Taten seiner Anführer gibt. Im Horizont der Bileam-Erzählung kann damit die verklärte Königszeit gemeint sein, die ja aus der Perspektive der erzählten Zeit in der Zukunft liegt, genauso aber auch eine unbestimmt-ferne Endzeit.[58]

Im folgenden Vers 23,22 fällt vor allem die Übersetzung von כתועפת ראם durch ὡς δόξα μονοκέρωτος auf: Gott hat nicht Hörner wie ein Wildstier (HAL), sondern sein Glanz/seine Ehre ist wie der eines Einhorns. Fast immer steht in der LXX μονόκερως als Normalübersetzung für ראם,[59]

---

54. Mit Dorival 1994, 70. 137.

55. Mit Wevers 1998, 396. So auch Lust 1991, 203, allerdings eher fragend; es könne sich auch um eine Bezugnahme auf die Landnahmezeit handeln, in der es keinen König gab.

56. Seebass 2007, 21 rechnet damit, dass LXX den Plural מלכים gelesen habe.

57. Mit Dorival 1994, 137–38. BHS überlegt eine Verlesung von ותרועת aus der Wurzel ירע, dies ist aber sonst nicht belegt.

58. Dorival 1994, 138 deutet den Vers auf die Siege über die Kanaanäer in der Landnahmezeit.

59. Ausnahme ist Jes 34,7 und Hi 39,10 (hier aber im Kontext erklärbar). Interessant ist Dtn 33,17, weil hier in der Übersetzung trotz des μονόκερως von *zwei* Hörnern die Rede ist (dazu Wevers 1995, 549); das Äquivalent wurde offenbar ohne größeres

wobei der Text in Num 23,21 und der parallele in 24,8 als älteste Belege zu sehen sind. Joachim Schaper hat in einer gründlichen Studie gezeigt, dass dies als interpretierende Wiedergabe gesehen werden muss,[60] bei der das altorientalisch-mythologische Motiv der „Hörner" als Zeichen der Macht nun durch ein äquivalentes griechisch-hellenistisches Motiv abgelöst wird.[61] Dabei wird dem Einhorn-Motiv insbesondere von 24,7–8 her ein spezifisch messianischer Sinn zugeschrieben. Dieser ist allerdings in 23,22 m.E. nicht feststellbar; hier steht μονόκερως als Zeichen einer besonderen Macht Gottes. 24,8 für sich alleine genommen ist in seiner Aussage 23,22 unmittelbar vergleichbar, auch hier wird die Macht Gottes gepriesen, die sich im Exodusgeschehen zeigt. Die Verwendung von μονόκερως taugt also nicht zum Nachweis eines messianischen Verständnisses, das sich in diesen Versen spiegelt. Allerdings werden über die Stichworte τὰ ἔνδοξα und δόξα die Verse 23,21+22 zusammengebunden, so dass verständlich ist, dass spätere Leser das Einhorn mit der Heilszeit konnotierten.

23,24

הן־עם כלביא יקום	ἰδοὺ λαὸς ὡς σκύμνος ἀναστήσεται
וכארי יתנשא	καὶ ὡς λέων γαυριωθήσεται
לא ישכב עד־יאכל טרף	οὐ κοιμηθήσεται ἕως φάγῃ θήραν
ודם־חללים ישתה	καὶ αἷμα τραυματιῶν πίεται

Siehe, ein Volk: wie eine Löwin steht es auf,
und wie ein Löwe erhebt es sich.

Es legt sich nicht nieder, bis es Beute verzehrt
und das Blut der Erschlagenen getrunken hat!

Siehe, ein Volk wird aufstehen wie ein Löwenjunges,
und wie ein Löwe wird es sich stolz zeigen;
es wird nicht schlafen, bis es die Beute gegessen hat
und wird das Blut der Verwundeten trinken.

Der Vers weist einige Berührungen mit Gen 49,9 (und Num 24,9) auf, und es ist anzunehmen, dass der Übersetzer diesen Bezug gesehen hat,

---

Problematisieren aus dem griechischen Numeribuch oder einer Vokabelliste übernommen.

60. So auch Dorival 1994, 138 mit Hinweisen auf parallele Deutungen in den Targumim; auf S. 440 finden sich Hinweise zur jüdisch-christlichen Wirkungsgeschichte des Motivs.

61. Schaper 1994; vgl. auch Schaper 2001, und im Anschluss an den erstgenannten Aufsatz Gzella 2001, ibs. 283.

zumal σκύμνος „Löwenjunges" nur selten verwendet wurde.⁶² Als starkes Argument zur Unterstützung dessen kann gesehen werden, dass sich in 4QNumᵇ zu 24,9 eine wichtige Variante findet: Hier hat der MT כרע שכב כארי „er ist geduckt, liegt wie ein Löwe;" im Qumrantext liest man dagegen: בער רבץ כא]ריה. Das erste Wort ist offenbar ein Schreibfehler. Die Variante רבץ muss aus Gen 49,9 stammen; ein Beleg für eine offenbar gängige intertextuelle Lektüre dieser beiden durch die Löwenthematik verbundenen messianischen Weissagungen. Im Unterschied zu Gen 49,9 ist v.a. zu notieren, dass טרף hier angemessener mit θήρα übersetzt wurde; dies liegt aber gewiss auch am Kontext, in dem ja das Verbum אכל den Sinn vorgibt. Inhaltlich ist anzumerken, dass der Vers die Erwartung einer kommenden, machterfüllten Heilszeit für das ganze Volk weiterführt.⁶³

24,7

יזל־מים מדליו	ἐξελεύσεται ἄνθρωπος ἐκ τοῦ σπέρματος αὐτοῦ
וזרעו במים רבים	καὶ κυριεύσει ἐθνῶν πολλῶν
וירם מאגג מלכו	καὶ ὑψωθήσεται ἢ Γωγ βασιλεία αὐτοῦ
ותנשא מלכתו	καὶ αὐξηθήσεται ἡ βασιλεία αὐτοῦ

Von seinen Schöpfeimern rinnt Wasser,
reichlich Wasser hat seine Saat.
Sein König ist Agag überlegen,

seine Königsherrschaft erstarkt.

Ein Mensch wird herauskommen aus seiner Nachkommenschaft
und über viele Völker herrschen,
und seine Herrschaft wird erhöht werden über Gog,
und seine Herrschaft wird wachsen.

Die wichtigsten Abweichungen seien kurz genannt: Es geht nicht darum, dass Wasser aus Eimern rinnt und die Saaten Israels tränkt, sondern es wird ein Mensch erwartet, der aus seiner = Israels (V. 5) Nachkommenschaft kommt und über viele Völker herrschen wird. Nicht Israels König wird Agag überlegen sein und erstarken (vgl. 1.Sam 15), sondern die Königsherrschaft jenes Menschen wird die des endzeitlichen Herrschers Gog (Ez 38) noch überragen. Nach V. 8 hat Gott ihn aus Ägypten heraufge-

---

62. So auch Hayward 1999, 25–26. (auch zu 24,19).
63. Nach Dorival 1994, 441, kann der Sieg über die Midianiter in 31,8 gemeint sein, dies wegen des Stichwortes τραυματίας in beiden Texten; allerdings scheint mir diese Verbindung eher schwach zu sein.

führt, sein Glanz—unklar ob der Gottes oder des Menschen—ist der eines Einhornes, vgl. 23,22, und er wird die feindlichen Völker besiegen.

Die Differenzen der LXX zum hebräischen Text weisen erstaunliche Parallelen zu einem Vers im vierten Orakel Bileams, 24,17, auf. Daher sollen sie zusammen besprochen werden.

24,17

אראנו ולא עתה	δείξω αὐτῷ καὶ οὐχὶ νῦν
אשורנו ולא קרוב	μακαρίζω καὶ οὐκ ἐγγίζει
דרך כוכב מיעקב	ἀνατελεῖ ἄστρον ἐξ Ιακωβ
וקם שבט מישראל	καὶ ἀναστήσεται ἄνθρωπος ἐξ Ισραηλ
ומחץ פאתי מואב	καὶ θραύσει τοὺς ἀρχηγοὺς Μωαβ
וקרקר כל־בני־שת	καὶ προνομεύσει πάντας υἱοὺς Σηθ

Ich sehe ihn, aber nicht jetzt,	Ich werde (es) ihm zeigen, und nicht jetzt,
ich schaue ihn, aber nicht nahe.	ich preise glücklich, und es ist nicht nahe.
Es tritt hervor ein Stern aus Jakob,	Ein Stern wird aufgehen aus Jakob
und ein Zepter erhebt sich aus Israel	und ein Mensch wird aufstehen aus Israel;
und zerschlägt die Schläfen Moabs	er wird die Oberhäupter Moabs zerschmettern
und zerschmettert alle Söhne Sets.	und alle Söhne Seths als Beute nehmen.[64]

Zunächst ist zu notieren, dass der Inhalt der Vision Bileams (ab dem 3. Stichos) in der griechischen Version im Futur formuliert ist; der hebräische Text hat die Verben durchgängig in der Afformativkonjugation. Der Inhalt der LXX weicht nicht so stark wie in V. 7 vom hebräischen Text ab. Umso mehr fällt auf, dass das sonst immer angemessen übersetzte שבט nun mit ἄνθρωπος wiedergegeben wird. Es ist m.E. eindeutig, dass es sich in der Perspektive der Übersetzung um den gleichen „Menschen" wie in V. 7 handeln muss. Im Parallelismus des Textes kann dann auch der „Stern" personal verstanden werden.[65] Deutlich ist zudem, dass der eindeutige

---

64. LXX hat offenbar das seltene קור Pilp. nicht verstanden und daher eine dem Kontext angemessene Übersetzung gesucht, die von der Kampf- und Feindthematik beeinflusst wurde; das gewählte Verbum προνομεύω ist in Num 31 mehrfach belegt—für unterschiedliche hebräische Verben.

65. So Wevers 1998, 413.

Bezug auf eine *königliche* Person durch die Vermeidung der Wiedergabe des Zepters (שבט) in der griechischen Version nicht mehr gegeben ist.

Jener Mensch wird nach dem folgenden Teilvers nicht die „Schläfen" Moabs, sondern seine Befehlshaber zerschlagen. Da das Lexem פאה „Schläfe, Kante" in 34,3+35,5 mehrfach wörtlich übersetzt wurde, ist erneut mit einer interpretativen Übersetzung zu rechnen, die die Erwartung eines Kampfgeschehens ausdrückt.

Die Interpretation für und wider ein messianisches Verständnis dieser Verse läuft entlang folgender Linien—wobei ich die Argumente nicht im Einzelnen wiederholen möchte. Die Verfechter einer messianischen Deutung weisen v.a. darauf hin, dass die ungewöhnliche Übersetzung „Mensch" auf die Erwartung eines Menschen(-sohnes) als Heilsgestalt anspiele, die ausgehend von 2.Sam 23,1; Sach 13,7; Dan 7,13 im zeitgenössischen Judentum üblich gewesen sei und in einer Reihe von Texten aus Qumran belegt ist.[66] Auch andere Äquivalente der beiden Verse und ihres näheren Kontextes verweisen auf klassische messianische Stellen, so etwa das ἐξελεύσεται aus 24,7 auf Jes 11,1 (LXX); das im hebräischen Text von 24,7 genannte Wasser habe an Jes 45,8 erinnert und damit den Kontext einer Heilszeit evoziert. Ein wesentliches Argument ist auch die Erwähnung von Gog als endzeitlichem Gegner in der LXX gegenüber Agag im MT; dabei wird aber oft nicht erwähnt, dass auch der Samaritanus diese Textvariante bietet.[67]

Demgegenüber hat sich Johan Lust um den Nachweis bemüht, dass die Verwendung von ἄνθρωπος ganz unspezifisch sei; nicht ein Messias, nicht einmal eine königliche Gestalt würden erwartet. Hinzu komme, dass diese Lesart erst von Philo an für die LXX gesichert sei; ihre Ursprünglichkeit sei also zweifelhaft. Schließlich ist die abweichende Übersetzung in 24,7 durch eine Reihe von Konjekturen zu erklären, so dass anzunehmen ist, dass der Übersetzer zumindest teilweise eine andere Vorlage vor sich hatte, die er zudem sprachlich anders interpretierte.[68] Allerdings stimmt Lust darin mit den Vertretern der anderen Position überein, dass die Erwähnung von Gog nicht anders denn als eschatologischer Hinweis zu verstehen ist.[69]

---

66. So etwa Vermès 1961, 56–60; besonders auch Horbury 1985, 48–50, und Schaper 1994, 127–28; die Belege ließen sich leicht vermehren.

67. So etwa Horbury 1985, 49.

68. Die ausführliche Interpretation findet sich bei Lust 1995.

69. Dorival 1994, 139–40, hat sich im Wesentlichen der Interpretation J. Lusts angeschlossen.

Beide Lösungsansätze des Problems haben m.E. je für sich grundsätzliche Aporien. Die bisher referierten Argumente für ein messianisches Verständnis kommen nicht darüber hinweg, dass alle Belegstellen[70] jünger sind als die Numeri-LXX, man also in methodischer Hinsicht nicht sicher sein kann, dass der Übersetzer und seine Gemeinde das entsprechende Verständnis hatten.[71] Die Erklärung der Abweichungen in Num 24,7 durch Johan Lust hat demgegenüber das Problem, dass seine Rekonstruktionen zwar je für sich möglich sind, keine von ihnen ist aber textlich belegt, noch dazu ist die Fülle solcher Verlesungen innerhalb eines Verses sehr unwahrscheinlich. Hinzu kommt, dass seine Bestreitung des messianischen Verständnisses auch—dies hat Arie van der Kooij m.E. überzeugend gezeigt—den methodischen Nachteil, dass sie in beinahe atomistischer Weise nur Verlesungen und Verstehensmöglichkeiten der einzelnen Wörter einbezieht, nicht aber nach dem umfassenden Verständnis des Übersetzers auf Satz- und Versebene fragt.[72] Dies wiederum ist genau die Stärke der „messianischen" Mehrheitsmeinung.

Dennoch scheint es mir möglich, auf der Basis der bisher gemachten Textbeobachtungen über diese Aporie hinauszukommen. Dabei sei zunächst daran erinnert, dass sich in der Bileam-Perikope tatsächlich eine ganze Reihe von Interpretationen seitens des Übersetzers feststellen ließen. Es gibt also keinen Grund dafür, bei dem schwierigen Text 24,7 davon auszugehen, dass er sich ausgerechnet hier nicht solcher Freiheiten bedient habe. Hinzu kommt, dass bei der Übersetzung der früheren Orakel gesehen werden konnte, dass sie als Zukunftsweissagungen verstanden wurden, die eine heilvolle, nahezu paradiesische Perspektive für Israel erwarten lassen. Erneut wird diese eschatologische Leserichtung schon durch den hebräischen Text in 24,14 mit באחרית הימים deutlich signalisiert; es geht um das, was das *Volk* in den letzten Tagen zu erwarten hat.[73] Weiterhin konnte in 23,24, aber auch in 24,9 beobachtet werden,

---

70. Ausnahmen sind nur 2.Sam 23,1; Sach 13,7, die allerdings das messianische Verständnis von Num 24 gar nicht belegen können. Dabei wird so argumentiert, dass das in diesen beiden Versen vorkommende גבר in Num 24,3 + 15 auch mit ἄνθρωπος übersetzt worden sei; es sich also um einen Vorstellungszusammenhang handele.

71. Hinzu kommt das Problem der unklaren Vorstellung, welche Vorstellung eigentlich zu welcher Zeit in welcher Gruppe Israels mit dem „Menschensohn" in Dan 7 verbunden ist; vgl. überblicksartig Collins 1995, 173–94; vgl. auch Koch 1993, 80–82.

72. Van der Kooij 1998.

73. S. oben Anm. 20.

dass sich der Übersetzer besonders beim „Löwen"-Vokabular an Gen 49 orientierte. Die wiederkehrende Verwendung von ἄνθρωπος in 24,7 + 17 und von ὡς δόξα μονοκέρωτος in 23,22 und 24,8 schließlich belegen, dass der Übersetzer den Gesamtzusammenhang der Orakel im Auge hatte.

Folgende Erklärung des Textes leuchtet mir am ehesten ein: In 24,5 + 6 wird der dritte Spruch Bileams mit der Darstellung der paradiesischen Lebensverhältnisse eröffnet. An sie schließt sich die Aussage über das Kommen des „Menschen" an. Für die Interpretation grundlegend scheint mir hier die offenbar in der Vorlage vom Smr-Typ vorgegebene Erwähnung von Gog statt Agag zu sein, der ausgehend von Ez 38–39 als endzeitlicher Gewaltherrscher gilt.[74] Damit ist, worauf auch Johan Lust hinweist, ein eindeutige Veränderung des Verses in eine eschatologische Verheißung gegeben.[75] So ist zugleich ein interpretativer Referenzrahmen gegeben, der die Deutung des Orakels auf die Situation der Landnahmezeit nicht mehr zulässt.[76]

Der Anfang des hebräischen Verses 24,7 ist kaum verständlich. Möglicherweise hat der Übersetzer tatsächlich יזל vom aramäischen Vb. אזל „gehen, kommen" abgeleitet. Dies kann ihn an das in 24,17 doppelt erwähnte „Herauskommen … aus Jakob/Israel" erinnert haben, was dann die Übersetzung in 24,7 beeinflusste. In 24,17 ist jedenfalls das gleiche Phänomen wie in 49,10 zu beobachten, dass das Symbol der Herrschaft (שבט) durch die Erwähnung des Herrschers selbst übersetzt wurde, hier „Mensch", dort „Führer". Die Übersetzung in 24,7 mag zusätzlich dadurch erleichtert worden sein, dass man מים als „Same" verstanden hat—dies unterstützt durch das Verb im Sg.—so dass die Wiedergabe mit „Mensch" näher lag.[77] Die Thematik des Herrschens über andere Völker war sowohl durch die Erwähnung von Gog, als auch durch den Paralleltext 24,17 vorgegeben. So war es dann nur ein kleiner interpretativer Schritt, aus במים רבים „viele Völker" (עמים רבים) herauszulesen—das entsprechende Bild begegnet auch in Jes 17,12—; dies umso mehr, wenn מים bereits auf einen Menschen gedeutet war.

---

74. S. dazu Lust 1999.
75. Lust 1995, 238.
76. So mit Recht Wevers 1998, 405–6, dessen Interpretation ich im Wesentlichen folge.
77. Dies parallel zu Jes 48,1, für dessen „Wasser" im Targum und bei Hieronymus das Verständnis „Familie, Nachkommenschaft" belegt ist, van der Kooij 1998, 224–25.

Auffällig ist schließlich ein Element am Ende des Verses, das Johan Lust als „less relevant"[78] bezeichnet hat. LXX übersetzt nämlich sowohl מלכו, als auch מלכתו mit βασιλεία αὐτοῦ. In der Numeri- und Deuteronomium-LXX wird nämlich „König/βασιλεύς" nur für fremde, nicht für Israels Herrscher verwendet, da offenbar nur Gott selbst König Israels ist.[79] Umso auffälliger ist in Num 24,7 die doppelte Verwendung von „Königreich" für zwei unterschiedliche hebräische Lexeme, dies auch noch verbunden mit dem für Num-LXX ungebräuchlichen Verbum κυριεύω.[80] Möglicherweise wurde die wörtliche Übersetzung „sein König/Führer" für מלך nicht gewählt, da es sich notwendig auf den „Menschen" zurückbezogen hätte. Damit wäre dieser aber zum Herrn eines Königs geworden, was offenbar nicht in das Bild des Übersetzers passte. So wurde stattdessen von der Herrschaft dieses Menschen gesprochen.[81]

Bedenkt man zudem, wie eifersüchtig der Übersetzer die Verwendung von κύριος mit Bezug auf Bileam vermieden hat, ist m.E. deutlich, dass es sich in 24,7 um die Ansage einer eschatologischen Herrschergestalt in göttlicher Vollmacht handeln muss. Zugleich—und darin ist m.E. Johan Lust und Gilles Dorival zuzustimmen—hat die Darstellung dieser erwarteten Menschengestalt keine spezifischen Bezüge zum David-Messias; dies ist in Gen 49 schon durch den Kontext anders gewesen. Da aber andererseits so eindeutig von der Erwartung der Königsherrschaft die Rede ist, stellt sich die Frage, wie anders als auf einen Messias weisend man diese Texte verstanden haben soll.[82]

Als begleitendes Argument sei angefügt, dass die Vorstellung von der Königsherrschaft (aram. מלכותא) im etwa zeitgleich kompilierten Danielbuch von großer Bedeutung ist, vgl. Dan 7,18. 23. Die Thematik der Überwindung der Herrschaft irdischer Herrscher ist jedenfalls sowohl in Num 24,8 wie in Num 24,17–8 präsent. Der Hinweis auf die besondere Vorstellung, die sich in der Numeri-LXX mit dem Königtum verbindet, erklärt

---

78. Lust 1995, 238.
79. So Wevers 1998, 405; Schaper 1994, 129.
80. Nur noch im „Brunnenlied" 21,18, dort ebenfalls mit βασιλεία zusammenstehend.
81. In seiner Untersuchung zur König-Archon-Problematik geht Freund 1990 auf Num 24,17 leider gar nicht ein; er begnügt sich mit dem unbefriedigenden Hinweis, „the Aramaic translation of this passage and 24,17 all use ‚kingly' language" (S. 65, Anm. 14), als bestünde nicht genau darin das Problem.
82. Schüle 2001, 278, versteht schon die hebräischen Orakel 3 und 4 als messianische Texte und verweist auf das nicht-davidische Messiasbild, das hier belegt sei.

zugleich auch, weshalb das unspezifische ἄνθρωπος verwendet wurde. Der Akzent liegt in den Bileam-Orakeln auf der heilvollen Zukunft Israels, die erst nach Kämpfen mit endzeitlichen Gewaltherrschern wie Gog, Moab oder Seth verwirklichen wird. Zur Durchsetzung der Gottesherrschaft wird das Kommen einer menschlichen Führergestalt erwartet; die aber nicht mit den klassischen Attributen eines königlich-davididischen Messias beschrieben wird.[83] Damit steht der Text den Vorstellungen von Dan 7 tatsächlich sehr nahe—ähnlich wie auch Gen 49, wo die Herrschaft des ἄρχων ἐξ Ιουδα vergleichbar zu Dan 7 nur eine Durchgangsphase bis zur eigentlichen Königsherrschaft Gottes ist.

Hinzuweisen ist schließlich auf einen Text, der m.E. eine sehr ähnliche Endzeiterwartung formuliert. Es handelt sich um die aramäische Apokalypse 4Q246, die als „Sohn Gottes Text" bekannt geworden ist. Mir scheint folgendes Verständnis des schwierigen Textes am nächsten zu liegen: Auch hier steht die Erwartung des ewigen Königtums Israels (מלכותה) im Mittelpunkt, das sich gegen die Feinde durchsetzen wird.[84] Das Volk Israel hat dabei die Rolle des königlichen Messias eingenommen; die gesamte Darstellung der Taten des Volkes geschieht in personalisierender Weise, als handele es sich um ein Individuum. Der Text belegt also, dass es im 2. Jh. eine Endzeiterwartung in Israel gab, die ohne die geprägten Bilder des Messias aus dem Stamm Davids auskommen konnte; dies passt perfekt zum Bild, das Num 24 in der griechischen Version vermittelt.[85]

---

83. Im Unterschied zu Auslegungen wie die von Géza Vermès oder William H. Brownlee kann ich nicht sehen, dass „*Man* (ἄνθρωπος) clearly refers to the Messiah;" so Vermès 1961, 59 mit Bezug auf Brownlee 1954, 33–38.

84. Vorausgesetzt ist dabei, dass das „Sohn Gottes/Sohn des Höchsten" in Col II, Z. 1, auf die Ansprüche des Antiochus IV. Epiphanes hinweist, also nicht den Messias benennt. Text und Anmerkungen bei Steudel 2001, 167–73. Eine ähnliche Deutung findet sich bei Fabry 1999.

Die besondere Rolle des Volkes ist aber unabhängig von der Beantwortung dieser strittigen Frage, wie der „Sohn Gottes/Sohn des Höchsten" zu deuten ist, ob auf Antiochus IV. Epiphanes, einen individuellen oder angelischen Messias oder ein Kollektiv; vgl. die abwägende Darstellung bei Collins 1995, 154–72 oder Knibb 1999, 379–402; beide befürworten letztlich eine messianische Deutung.

85. Vgl. auch Zimmermann 1998, der S. 129–70 eine außerordentlich detaillierte Analyse des Textes vorlegt. Auch er deutet den „Sohn Gottes" letztlich messianisch, bestätigt aber die besondere Rolle der Herrschaft des Volkes; der Sohn Gottes wird als inklusiver Repräsentant des Volkes gesehen (S. 169).

4. Ergebnis

Angesichts der Komplexität des Textbefundes lassen sich in diesem kurzen Beitrag nicht alle anstehenden Fragen lösen; dies wird einem ausführlicheren Kommentar der griechischen Bileamperikope vorbehalten bleiben. In der Abwägung der Argumente ist aber bei beiden besprochenen Textkomplexen—Gen 49 und Num 22–24—die Interpretation die wahrscheinlichere, die damit rechnet, dass schon die Übersetzer und nicht erst spätere Ausleger die Weissagungen als auf die Endzeit und eschatologische Herrschergestalten zielend verstanden haben. Die Bildhaftigkeit der in den Sprüchen verwendeten Sprache und die Unbestimmtheit der verwendeten mythologischen Bilder, auch die oftmals schwer verständlichen Teilverse der Orakel haben die Eintragung dieses Verständnisses noch erleichtert.[86] Dabei ist von Bedeutung, dass die Erwartungen der beiden Texte nicht deckungsgleich sind; während in Gen 49 die Bezüge zur David-Tradition unübersehbar sind, fehlen diese in Num 24. Die besonders in Num 24 verwendete unspezifische Terminologie passt gut zu dem allgemeinen Befund, dass es im zeitgenössischen Judentum verschiedene messianische Konzepte gegeben hat. Gerade diese Unbestimmtheit hat dann spätere Rezeptionen erleichtert, und so verwundert es nicht, dass diese beiden Texte zu Zentralstücken der Messiaserwartung werden konnten.

Literatur

Brownlee, William H. 1954. „The Servant of the Lord in the Qumran Scrolls II." *BASOR* 135:33–38.

Collins, John J. 1995. *The Scepter and the Star: The Messiahs of the Dead Sea Scrolls and other Ancient Literature.* ABRL. New York: Doubleday.

———. 2006. „Messianism and Exegetical Tradition. The Evidence of the LXX Pentateuch." Seiten 129–49 in *The Septuagint and Messianism.* Hrsg. von M. A. Knibb. BETL 195. Leuven: Peeters.

Daniel, Suzanne. 1966. *Recherches sur le Vocabulaire du Culte dans la Septante.* EeC 61. Paris: Klincksieck.

Dorival, Gilles. 1994. *Les Nombres.* BdA 4. Paris: Cerf.

---

86. Vgl. etwa Schüle 2001, 287, der davon ausgeht, dass die Symbolik schon im hebräischen Text „gezielt vielschichtig angelegt" war, so dass „ihre Deutung mehrere semantische Ebenen erfasst".

―――. 1995. „Les phénomènes d'intertextualité dans le livre grec des Nombres." Seiten 253–85 in ΚΑΤΑ ΤΟΥΣ Ο'. Selon Les Septante. En hommage à Marguerite Harl. Hrsg. von Gilles Dorival und Olivier Munnich. Paris: Cerf.

―――. 1996. „,'Un astre se lèvera de Jacob'. L'interprétation ancienne de Nombres 24,17." ASE 13:295–352.

Fabry, Heinz-Josef. 1999. „Die frühjüdische Apokalyptik als Reaktion auf Fremdherrschaft. zur Funktion von 4Q246." Seiten 84–98 in Antikes Judentum und frühes Christentum. Festschrift für Hartmut Stegemann zum 65. Geburtstag. Hrsg. von Bernd Kollmann. BZNW 97. Berlin: de Gruyter.

Frankel, Zacharias. 1841. Vorstudien zu der Septuaginta. Leipzig: Vogel

―――. 1851 Ueber den Einfluss der palästinischen Exegese auf die alexandrinische Hermeneutik. Leipzig: Barth.

Freund, Richard A. 1990. "From Kings to Archons. Jewish Political Ethics and Kingship Passages in the LXX." SJOT 4:58–72.

García Martínez, Florentino. 1993. „Messianische Erwartungen in den Qumranschriften." JBTh 8:171–208.

Gzella, Holger. 2001. „Das Kalb und das Einhorn, Endzeittheophanie und Messianismus in der Septuaginta-Fassung von Ps 29(28)." Seiten 257–90 in Der Septuaginta-Psalter. Sprachliche und theologische Aspekte. Hrsg. von Erich Zenger. HBS 32. Freiburg: Herder.

―――. 2002. Lebenszeit und Ewigkeit. Studien zur Eschatologie und Anthropologie des Septuaginta-Psalters. BBB 134. Berlin: Philo.

Harl, Marguerite. 1986. La Genèse. BdA 1. Paris: Cerf.

Harl, Marguerite, Gilles Dorival, und Olivier Munnich. 1994. La Bible Grecque des Septante. Du judaïsme hellénistique au christianisme ancien. 2me édition. Paris: Cerf.

Hayward, Robert C. T. 1999. „Balaam's Prophecies as Interpreted by Philo and the Aramaic Targums of the Pentateuch." Seiten 19–36 in New Heaven and New Earth. Prophecy and the Millennium. Essays in Honour of Anthony Gelston. Hrsg. von Peter J. Harland und Robert Hayward. VTSup 77. Leiden: Brill.

Horbury, William. 1985. „,The Messianic Associations of ,the Son of Man.'" JTS 36:34–55.

―――. 1998. Jewish Messianism and the Cult of Christ. London: SCM Press.

Joosten, Jan. 2000. „Une théologie de la Septante? Réflexions méthodologiques sur l'interpretation de la version greque." RTP 132:31–46.

Karrer, Martin. 2003. „Von David zu Christus." Seiten 327–65 in *König David—biblische Schlüsselfigur und europäische Leitgestalt*. Hrsg. von Walter Dietrich und Hubert Herkommer. Stuttgart: Kohlhammer.

Knibb, Michael A. 1999. "Eschatology and Messianism in the Dead Sea Scrolls." Seiten 379–402 in *The Dead Sea Scrolls after Fifty Years. A Comprehensive Assessment*. Hrsg. von Peter W. Flint und James C. VanderKam. Leiden: Brill.

Koch, Klaus. 1993. „Messias und Menschensohn. Die zweistufige Messianologie der jüngeren Apokalyptik." *JBTh* 8:73–102.

———. 1995. „Das Reich der Heiligen und des Menschensohnes. Ein Kapitel politischer Theologie." Seiten 140–72 in *Die Reiche der Welt und der kommende Menschensohn. Studien zum Danielbuch*. Hrsg. von Martin Rösel. Neukirchen-Vluyn: Neukirchener Verlag.

Kooij, Arie van der. 1981. *Die alten Textzeugen des Jesajabuches. Ein Beitrag zur Textgeschichte des Alten Testaments*. OBO 35. Göttingen: Vandenhoeck & Ruprecht; Freiburg: Universitätsverlag.

———. 1998. „Perspectives on the Study of the Septuagint. Who are the Translators?" Seiten 214–29 in *Perspectives in the Study of the Old Testament and Early Judaism*. Hrsg. von Florentino García Martínez und Edwart Noort. VTSup 73. Leiden: Brill.

———. 2003. "On the Use of Βωμός in the Septuagint." Seiten 601–7 in *Hamlet on a Hill. Semitic and Greek Studies Presented to Professor T. Muraoka on the Occasion of His Sixty-Fifth Birthday*. Hrsg. von Martin F. J. Basten und Th. van Peursen. OLA 118. Leuven: Peeters.

Lust, Johan. 1991. „Molek and ΑΡΧΩΝ." Seiten 193–208 in *Phoenicia and the Bible. Proceedings of the Conference Held at the University of Leuven on the 15th and 16th of March 1990*. Hrsg. von Edward Lipiński. OLA 44. Leuven: Peeters.

———. 1995. „The Greek Version of Balaam's Third and Fourth Oracles. The ἄνθρωπος in Num 24:7 and 17. Messianism and Lexicography." Seiten 233–57 in *VIII Congress of the International Organization for Septuagint and Cognate Studies. Paris 1992*. Hrsg. von Leonard Greenspoon und Olivier Munnich. SCS 41. Atlanta: Scholars Press.

———. 1997. „Septuagint and Messianism, with a Special Emphasis on the Pentateuch." Seiten 26–45 in *Theologische Probleme der Septuaginta und der hellenistischen Hermeneutik*. Hrsg. von Henning Graf Reventlow. VWGT 11. Gütersloh: Gütersloher Verlagshaus.

———. 1999. „Gog." *DDD*[2] 373–75.

Lust, Johan, Erik Eynikel, und Katrin Hauspie. 1992. *A Greek-English Lexicon of the Septuagint. Part I.* Stuttgart: Deutsche Bibelgesellschaft.
Macchi, Jean-Daniel. 1999. *Israël et ses tribus selon Genèse 49.* OBO 171. Göttingen: Vandenhoeck & Ruprecht; Freiburg: Universitätsverlag.
Monsengwo-Pasinya, Laurent. 1980. „Deux textes messianiques dans la Septante. Gn 49,10 et Ez 31,32." *Bib* 61:357–76.
Muraoka, Takamitsu. 2002. *A Greek-English Lexicon of the Septuagint. Chiefly of the Pentateuch and Twelve Prophets.* Leuven: Peeters.
Pietersma, Albert. 2002. „A New Paradigm for Addressing Old Questions. The Relevance of the Interlinear Model for the Study of the Septuagint." Seiten 337–64 in *Bible and Computer. The Stellenbosch AIBI-6 Conference Proceedings of the Association internationale Bible et informatique, „From Alpha to Byte".* Hrsg. von Johann Cook. Leiden: Brill.
Prijs, Leo. 1948. *Jüdische Tradition in der Septuaginta.* Leiden: Brill.
Rösel, Martin. 1991. „Die Jungfrauengeburt des endzeitlichen Immanuel. Jesaja 7 in der Übersetzung der Septuaginta." *JBTh* 6:135–51. [Kapitel 9 in diesem Band.]
———. 1994. *Übersetzung als Vollendung der Auslegung. Studien zur Genesis-Septuaginta.* BZAW 223. Berlin: de Gruyter. [englische Übersetzung Kapitel 4 in diesem Band.]
———. 1995. „Die Interpretation von Genesis 49 in der Septuaginta." *BN* 79:54–69.
———. 1999. „Wie einer vom Propheten zum Verführer wird. Tradition und Rezeption der Bileamgestalt." *Bib* 80:506–24.
———. 2001. „Die Septuaginta und der Kult. Interpretationen und Aktualisierungen im Buch Numeri." Seiten 25–40 in *La double transmission du texte biblique. Études d'histoire du texte offertes en hommage à Adrian Schenker.* Hrsg. von Christoph Uehlinger und Yohanan Goldman. OBO 179. Göttingen: Vandenhoeck & Ruprecht; Freiburg: Universitätsverlag.
Schaper, Joachim L.W. 1994. „The Unicorn in the Messianic Imagery of the Greek Bible." *JTS* 45:117–36.
———. 2001. „Die Renaissance der Mythologie im hellenistischen Judentum und der Septuaginta-Psalter." Seiten 171–83 in *Der Septuaginta-Psalter. Sprachliche und theologische Aspekte.* Hrsg. von Erich Zenger. HBS 32. Freiburg: Herder.
Schmitt, Hans-Christoph. 1999. „Eschatologische Stammesgeschichte im Pentateuch. Zum Judaspruch von Gen 49,8–12." Seiten 1–11 in *Antikes Judentum und Frühes Christentum. FS H. Stegemann.* Hrsg.

von Bernd Kollmann, Wolfgang Reinbold, und Annette Steudel. BZNW 97. Berlin: de Gruyter.

Schüle, Andreas. 2001. Israels Sohn – Jahwes Prophet: Ein Versuch zum Verhältnis von kanonischer Theologie und Religionsgeschichte anhand der Bileam-Perikope (Num 22–24). Altes Testament und Moderne 17. Münster: LIT.

Seebass, Horst. 2000. *Genesis III. Josephsgeschichte (37,1–50,26)*. Neukirchen-Vluyn: Neukirchener Verlag.

———. 2007. *Numeri 22,2–36,13*. BKAT 4.3. Neukirchen-Vluyn: Neukirchener Verlag.

Seele, Astrid. 1995. *Römische Übersetzer. Nöte, Freiheiten, Absichten*. Darmstadt: Wissenschaftliche Buchgesellschaft.

Siegert, Folkert. 2001. *Zwischen Hebräischer Bibel und Altem Testament. Eine Einführung in die Septuaginta*. MJS 9. Münster: LIT.

Steudel, Annette. 1993. „אחרית הימים in the Texts from Qumran." *RevQ* 16, 62:225–46.

———, Hrsg. 2001. *Die Texte aus Qumran II*. Darmstadt: Wissenschaftliche Buchgesellschaft.

Vermès, Géza. 1961. *Scripture and Tradition in Judaism. Haggadic Studies*. StPB 4. Leiden: Brill.

Wade, Martha L. 2003. *Consistency of Translation Techniques in the Tabernacle Accounts of Exodus in the Old Greek*. SCS 49. Atlanta: Society of Biblical Literature.

Wevers, John William. 1993. *Notes on the Greek Text of Genesis*. SCS 35. Atlanta: Scholars Press.

———. 1995. *Notes on the Greek Text of Deuteronomy*. SCS 39. Atlanta: Scholars Press.

———. 1998. *Notes on the Greek Text of Numbers*. SCS 46. Atlanta: Scholars Press.

———. 1999. „The Balaam Narrative According to the Septuagint." Seiten 133–44 in *Lectures et relectures de la Bible. Festschrift P.-M. Bogaert*. Hrsg. von Jean-Marie Auwers und André Wénin. BETL 144. Leuven: Peeters.

Zimmermann, Johannes. 1998. *Messianische Texte aus Qumran. Königliche, Priesterliche und prophetische Messiasvorstellungen in den Schriftfunden von Qumran*. WUNT 2/104. Tübingen: Mohr Siebeck.

6
The Septuagint Version of the Book of Joshua

The Septuagint translation of the book of Joshua is for many reasons one of the most interesting books of the Greek Bible. Starting from the assumption that in the Alexandrinian-Jewish milieu the Pentateuch has been translated first as a *nomos*-giving identity, the following questions can be raised: Has a different kind of translation-technique been used in this presumed first translation after the Pentateuch? Are there hints for another canonical dignity compared to the five books of the Greek Torah? Are the theological guidelines, which could be seen as characteristics of the LXX Pentateuch, still valid in this book?[1] But prior to the discussion of these questions, one has to deal with some peculiarities of the translation of the book of Joshua, to which previous research has drawn attention.

1. Text-Critical Problems of the Book of Joshua

First it has to be stated that the Greek manuscripts of the book of Joshua show a great amount of variety. Even uninitiated users of the LXX edition by Alfred Rahlfs can see this fact easily in chapters 15 and 19, where the text of the important manuscripts B and A is presented in a synopsis because the deviations of the witnesses cannot be harmonized toward one text. When preparing his critical edition of LXX Joshua, Max Margolis has distinguished two main groups of witnesses, each with three subdivisions. However, later he came to the conclusion that the witnesses are to be divided into five groups. Unfortunately, Margolis could not finish his critical edition.[2] A fifth fascicle, which was based on Margolis's own preparations, has been published posthumously by Emanuel Tov, the final

---
1. See M. Rösel 1998a.
2. Margolis 1931–1938.

sixth part, in preparation by Leonard Greenspoon and Seppo Sipilä, is still to come.[3] To make the situation even more difficult, in the first fascicles of the edition are some mistakes and conjectures that can hardly be justified today, so that the text cannot be used without supplemental scholarly literature.[4] Since the Göttingen-edition of LXX Joshua is also still in preparation, the text of the Rahlfs edition will be usually used here, although its provisional character has to be recognized.[5]

Broadening the horizon beyond the text history of the Greek Joshua, the much disputed question of the relationship between the Greek translation and the Masoretic Text (MT) appears as the next problem. First one has to state the fact that there are a lot of partly serious deviations between LXX and the MT. Among them are often discussed verses where LXX has considerably more text than the MT. This phenomenon appears, inter alia, in 6:26; 15:59; 16:10; 21:35, 42; 24:33, but also in other verses, for example, 22:33–34; 23:5; 24:4.[6] The opposite phenomenon, the MT having more text than the Greek version, can also be detected; important examples are 8:12–13; 20:4–6.[7] This leads to the fact that the Greek text is considerably shorter than the MT. Moreover, there are instances where differences concerning the arrangement of pericopes have to be noted. Thus the account of the building of an altar on Mount Ebal can be found in the MT in 8:30–35, concluding the report of the conquest of Ai; in the LXX it is to be read after 9:2, before the story of the trickery of the Gibeonites. There are more alterations like these, for example, the different order of 19:47–48 and the position of 24:31 after verse 28.

These differences in extent and sequence have led to the assumption that the Greek version of the book of Joshua can be traced back to a different Hebrew *Vorlage*. Already in his book from 1914 Samuel Holmes formulated this position.[8] Moreover, he came to the judgment that this presumed text underlying the LXX should be preferred to the MT. The

---

3. Margolis 1992. Information concerning the history of research can be found in Bieberstein 1994, 9–14, and den Hertog 1996.

4. See the lists of suggestions for improvements by Bieberstein 1994, 22–27; and den Hertog 1996, 70–81; 1995. See also Sipilä 1993.

5. For a characterization of this edition see Moatti-Fine 1996, 41–42, she also follows Rahlfs.

6. A good survey concerning these differences can be found in Mazor 1994, and Moatti-Fine 1996, 33–38.

7. See the clear description by Tov 1992, 327–30.

8. Holmes 1914.

opposite standpoint can be seen in the research of Margolis, who has come to the position that in nearly every questionable instance the MT has to be seen as the superior text.[9] Furthermore he refused the opinion that the LXX is based on a different *Vorlage*; in his view the differences could be explained as results of the process of translation. The following history of research has supported the position of Samuel Holmes, and further support has come from A. Graeme Auld and Harry M. Orlinsky.[10] Now scholars generally are of the opinion that the Hebrew and the Greek texts give witness to two different stages in the literary development of the book of Joshua.

This thesis gained further support by the Joshua-fragments from Qumran, though they became accessible only very late.[11] Interesting enough, the fragments of the two scrolls 4Q47 and 4Q48 (4QJosh^{a+b}) show the same characteristics as the LXX, because there are differences in comparison to the text handed down by the Masoretes both in arrangement and quantity. Possibly even citations and allusions in nonbiblical texts like 4Q175 (Testimonia); 4Q378+379 (Joshua apocryphon^{a+b}) and CD (Damascus Document) can be seen as witnessing to a different textual tradition.[12] Again, there are some instances that lead to the conclusion that here the MT displays the younger, the fragments from Qumran the more original readings, for example, in 8:10–14.[13] The most important theological difference can be seen in the already mentioned account of the building of the altar in Josh 8:30–35, which again has been transposed: following 4Q47 it stands between chapters 4 and 5; in accordance with Deut 27:2–5 the altar is built directly after crossing the Jordan and going into the land.[14]

For a judgment about the Greek version it is important to notice that the fragments from Qumran show the same literary phenomena, but that they cannot be seen as the *Vorlage* of LXX Joshua. So one has to assume three different stages in the development of the text of the book of Joshua,

---

9. Margolis 1931–1938.
10. Auld 1979; Orlinsky 1969.
11. Now in Ulrich 1995, 143–60. The fragments are dated to the second/first century BCE and to the middle of the first century BCE. See also Greenspoon 1992.
12. Mazor 1994, 33.
13. See Greenspoon 1992, 170–71.
14. See Ulrich 1995, 145–46, and Noort 1998, who already before the Qumran fragments were available has assumed that this position of the narrative is theologically more appropriate (see Noort 1993).

attested by the Q-fragments, LXX, and the MT. Often the MT can be seen as the youngest of these witnesses, but it seems more appropriate to think of the three textual traditions in a juxtaposition rather than in a succession; they can be seen as independent expositions of a common base text. Therefore it seems to be methodologically inadequate when literary-critical studies of the book of Joshua neglect this problem caused by the history of the text.[15]

2. The Septuagint Version of the Book of Joshua

Returning back to the Septuagint and the questions raised above, one can see already after this short survey over the history of the text that in the time of the translation there obviously must have been different canonical dignities of the different texts. While the Hebrew text of the Torah has been transmitted in a comparatively standardized shape, in the book of Joshua one can detect clearly recognizable differences between the textual traditions. Thus one can infer from these observations that the text has not been established and fixed in a way that can be compared to the Torah.

When working on the Greek Joshua, this leads to the methodological consequence that the assumption of a different *Vorlage*, which can be responsible for differences regarding the contents of the book, has a higher priority than in books like Genesis.[16] But if we see in the fragments from Qumran that a relatively free way of transmitting biblical texts was possible at that time, one cannot rule out the possibility that also a translator could take liberties with regard to his parent text. Thus a high degree of uncertainty remains when judging about the problems of the text, whether differences have occurred in the process of the transmission of the text or whether they are a result of the rendering from one language into the other.[17] Before this problem is presented by discuss-

---

15. As an example see Fritz 1994, who on p. 2 dismisses the problem of the LXX and assigns it to special studies. But his judgment that the MT can be seen as the oldest accessible text of the book of Joshua (2) has to be regarded as falsified. See Tov 1986, and Rofé 1994.

16. This methodological problem is highly disputed. To avoid repetitions it may suffice to refer to my positioning in M. Rösel 1998b. But see also the reactions by Hendel 1999 and Brown 1999.

17. See Tov 1978, esp. 51–52 (although without the evidence from Qumran).

ing some examples from the texts, the available information about LXX Joshua will be collected.

In his dissertation from 1996 Cornelis den Hertog has tried to come to a relative chronology of the Greek version of Joshua by carefully comparing some of the oldest translations. This has led him to a confirmation of the natural assumption that Joshua was translated shortly after the Pentateuch. Moreover, he has been able to show that in some instances the Joshua-translator obviously has made use of the earlier translations into Greek.[18] Concerning the book of Judges he has come to the thesis that apparently the translator of this book has "known and used" the Greek Joshua.[19] Unfortunately, there are hardly hints to establish an absolute chronology; den Hertog argues for a *terminus ad quem* "not long after 198 BCE."[20] Marguerite Harl, Gilles Dorival, and Olivier Munnich have voted for a time about 170, and Tov has opted for the late third or the early second century BCE.[21] The book has obviously been translated outside Israel.[22] This does not necessarily lead to the conclusion of a translation in Alexandria, but this assumption seems reasonable because of our knowledge about the learned Jewish-Hellenistic society in this Egyptian city.[23]

In the following some of the characteristics of LXX Joshua shall be presented. In the first section some of the major additions of the Greek version are discussed. After that some phenomena of theological exposition are shown.

2.1. The Additions of the Septuagint of Joshua

6:26

וישבע יהושע בעת ההיא לאמר   καὶ ὥρκισεν Ἰησοῦς ἐν τῇ ἡμέρᾳ ἐκείνῃ
לפני יהוה ארור האיש   ἐναντίον κυρίου λέγων ἐπικατάρατος ὁ
אשר יקום ובנה את־העיר הזאת את־   ἄνθρωπος ὃς οἰκοδομήσει τὴν πόλιν
יריחו   ἐκείνην ἐν

---

18. Den Hertog 1996, 110–25.
19. Den Hertog 1996, 134.
20. Den Hertog 1996, 142.
21. Harl, Dorival, and Munnich 1994, 93–111; Tov 1986, 338.
22. Den Hertog 1996, 144. Harl, Dorival, and Munnich 1994, 106, are arguing for Alexandria, although even in their view questions are remaining.
23. See Tov 1986, 339. See now van der Kooij 1999.

בבכרו ייסדנה ובצעירו יציב דלתיה	τῷ πρωτοτόκῳ αὐτοῦ θεμελιώσει αὐτὴν καὶ ἐν τῷ ἐλαχίστῳ αὐτοῦ ἐπιστήσει τὰς πύλας αὐτῆς καὶ οὕτως ἐποίησεν Οζαν ὁ ἐκ Βαιθηλ ἐν τῷ Αβιρων τῷ πρωτοτόκῳ ἐθεμελίωσεν αὐτὴν καὶ ἐν τῷ ἐλαχίστῳ διασωθέντι ἐπέστησεν τὰς πύλας αὐτῆς

When comparing Josh 6:26 in its Hebrew and Greek version, it is noticeable that only in the Greek text Joshua's adjuration is happening ἐναντίον κυρίου. This can be caused by the fact that in the Hebrew text one can read לפני יהוה as a part of the curse. But in the wider horizon of the account of Jericho's fall, the Greek version refers back to other texts, because following 6:7 + 8 +13 the armed men and priests passed on before the Lord (ἐναντίον κυρίου). Here an interesting fact can be detected which has already been mentioned above: The MT reads in all these verses לפני ארון יהוה, while in the LXX the references to the ark are missing.[24] It is interesting to notice that now the MT shows a feature that can usually be seen in the Greek translations of the Pentateuch, namely that very explicit references to God and his presence were avoided. This leads to the impression that the MT has to be judged as secondary in this respect.[25] But one can also think about the opposite standpoint that LXX wanted to emphasize the power of God and therefore has deleted the references to the ark. A definitive answer to this problem depends on the diachronic relationship between the two versions, which cannot be clarified sufficiently at the moment.

More interesting than this question is the long addition that can be found in the Greek version after the curse upon the one who rebuilds Jericho. The English translation of the text reads "And so did Hozan of Bethel; in Abiron his first-born he laid the foundation, and in his youngest surviv-

---

24. There is an exception in 6:8b, where LXX and MT agree in this point; the explicit mentioning of the ark in this verse is perhaps the reason for the expansions in the MT.

25. The addition of the ark has happened in the MT also in 4:5 and 7:6, of which in 4:5 the references are not completely clear, because LXX here has a kind of "deuteronomistic" text, so Moatti-Fine 1996, 110; see also Tov 1986, 335, who speaks about a "theological correction" of the MT. One may also assume that in 3:14, 17 the ark has been added too, because here הארון has an own article and is also determined by its position in the *status constructus* (personal communication with den Hertog). But it has to be stated that in both instances there is no deviation between MT and LXX.

ing son he set up the gates of it."²⁶ The text alludes to 1 Kgs 16:34, which again refers to Josh 6.²⁷ The Greek text of Josh 6:26 is parallel with the LXX version of 3 Kgdms 16:34, although it is noticeable that the proper names do not correspond and that the younger son now has a name.²⁸

In the context of 1 Kgs 16, verse 34 appears like an addition, moreover, the text is missing in the Lucianic recension.²⁹ Thus there are good reasons that both texts in question are secondary supplements with the aim of emphasizing the "Deuteronomistic" scheme of prophetical foretelling and historical fulfillment. Whether 1 Kgs 16:34 does depend on Josh 6:26 in the version of the LXX and its *Vorlage* cannot be reliably verified nor falsified.³⁰ Anyway, one has to state that the phenomenon of these expansions marked as Deuteronomistic took place in a time in which scholars generally assume the transmission of the text, no longer its production.

15:59

ומערת ובית־ענות ואלתקן	καὶ Μαγαρωθ καὶ Βαιθαναμ καὶ Θεκουμ
ערים שש וחצריהן	πόλεις ἓξ καὶ αἱ κῶμαι αὐτῶν
	Θεκω καὶ Εφραθα αὕτη ἐστὶν Βαιθλεεμ
	καὶ Φαγωρ καὶ Αιταν καὶ Κουλον καὶ
	Ταταμ καὶ Εωβης καὶ Καρεμ καὶ Γαλεμ
	καὶ Θεθηρ καὶ Μανοχω πόλεις ἕνδεκα
	καὶ αἱ κῶμαι αὐτῶν

The second addition of the LXX has no such far-reaching consequences. It is a list of eleven places that will belong to the tribe of Judah. It seems certain that the list preserved in the LXX has been part of the original text and was lost by *homoioteleuton*, caused by overlooking וחצריהן, that can be read in 15:59a; b* and 60. In the LXX it has always been translated by καὶ αἱ κῶμαι αὐτῶν.³¹

---

26. All translations are mine unless otherwise noted.
27. For the problem see Mazor 1988.
28. 4Q379 22 also alludes to the rebuilding of the city, although here the form of a prophecy is used.
29. See, e.g., Würthwein 1977, 203–4. It is characteristic that again every reference to LXX Joshua is missing.
30. See the arguments of Mazor 1988, 23–24. See also Butler 1983, 66, who seems to be sure that the LXX addition is "taken from 1 Kgs 16:34, another example of scribal interpretation of the text to show explicit fulfillment."
31. With Barthélemy 1982, 44; also Butler 1983, 181.

16:10

ולא הורישו את־הכנעני היושב בגזר	καὶ οὐκ ἀπώλεσεν Εφραιμ τὸν Χαναναῖον
וישב הכנעני בקרב אפרים	τὸν κατοικοῦντα ἐν Γαζερ καὶ κατῴκει ὁ
עד־היום הזה ויהי למס־עבד	Χαναναῖος ἐν τῷ Εφραιμ ἕως τῆς ἡμέρας

καὶ οὐκ ἀπώλεσεν Εφραιμ τὸν Χαναναῖον
τὸν κατοικοῦντα ἐν Γαζερ καὶ κατῴκει ὁ
Χαναναῖος ἐν τῷ Εφραιμ ἕως τῆς ἡμέρας
ταύτης ἕως ἀνέβη Φαραω βασιλεὺς
Αἰγύπτου καὶ ἔλαβεν αὐτὴν καὶ ἐνέπρησεν
αὐτὴν ἐν πυρί καὶ τοὺς Χαναναίους καὶ τοὺς
Φερεζαίους καὶ τοὺς κατοικοῦντας ἐν Γαζερ
ἐξεκέντησαν καὶ ἔδωκεν αὐτὴν Φαραω ἐν
φερνῇ τῇ θυγατρὶ αὐτοῦ

ולא הורישו את־הכנעני היושב בגזר
וישב הכנעני בקרב אפרים
עד־היום הזה ויהי למס־עבד

The next text under discussion causes some problems: The note that the Canaanites were dwelling in Gezer "until this day" has been expanded in the Greek version by a new theme: "until Pharao the king of Egypt went up and took it, and burnt it with fire; and the Canaanites, and Pherezites, and the dwellers in Gaza they destroyed, and Pharao gave them for a dowry to his daughter." A comparable text is found in 1 Kgs 9:16–7 // 3 Kgdms 5:14b. The version of LXX Joshua shows important deviations from the Greek book of Kings; it seems to be an independent translation of the extant Hebrew text with the naming of the Pherezites as a new element in the Joshua text.[32] Once again, the phenomenon of a tendency towards harmonization despite the borders of the books can be seen, which is not preserved in the Masoretic version of the book of Joshua.

21:42

תהיינה הערים האלה עיר
עיר ומגרשיה סביבתיה
כן לכל־הערים האלה

κύκλῳ τῶν πόλεων τούτων, πόλις καὶ τὰ
περισπόρια κύκλῳ τῆς πόλεως πάσαις ταῖς
πόλεσιν ταύταις.
[1] καὶ συνετέλεσεν Ἰησοῦς διαμερίσας τὴν γῆν ἐν τοῖς
ὁρίοις αὐτῶν [2] καὶ ἔδωκαν οἱ υἱοὶ Ισραηλ μερίδα τῷ
Ἰησοῖ κατὰ πρόσταγμα κυρίου ἔδωκαν αὐτῷ τὴν πόλιν
ἣν ᾐτήσατο τὴν Θαμνασαραχ ἔδωκαν αὐτῷ ἐν τῷ ὄρει
Εφραιμ [3] καὶ ᾠκοδόμησεν Ἰησοῦς τὴν πόλιν καὶ
ᾤκησεν ἐν αὐτῇ [4] καὶ ἔλαβεν Ἰησοῦς τὰς μαχαίρας
τὰς πετρίνας ἐν αἷς περιέτεμεν τοὺς υἱοὺς Ισραηλ τοὺς
γενομένους ἐν τῇ ὁδῷ ἐν τῇ ἐρήμῳ καὶ ἔθηκεν αὐτὰς ἐν
Θαμνασαραχ

---

32. See Niemann 1993, for the problem of the Pherezites, although a reference to the text in question is missing.

An extensive addition can be noticed at this point, when the account of the division of the land comes to its end. The text reads in translation as follows: (1) "And Joshua ceased dividing the land in their borders.[33] (2) And the Israelites gave a portion to Joshua because of the commandment of the Lord, they gave him the city that he asked for: they gave him Thamnasarach in Mount Ephraim; (3) and Joshua built the city, and dwelt in it. (4) And Joshua took the knives of stone, wherewith he circumcised the children of Israel that were born in the desert by the way, and put them in Thamnasarach."

The note takes up the text of Josh 19:49–50; the differences between the two Greek texts are only very limited. Again, one can assume that LXX is not an independent formulation, but can be traced back to an otherwise lost *Vorlage*. In the context of the Greek book of Joshua a more adequate outcome of the account of the division of the land has been achieved, although it is not clear why the redactor who was responsible for this addition has kept the text in 19:49–50 and thus allowed the existence of a doublet.

The interesting fact is that there is a relation between this plus and two other texts that show far-reaching differences between the Greek and the Hebrew tradition of Joshua. The first text is another expansion of the LXX:

24:31 (MT 24:30)

ויקברו אתו בגבול נחלתו בתמנת־סרח	καὶ ἔθαψαν αὐτὸν πρὸς τοῖς ὁρίοις τοῦ κλήρου αὐτοῦ ἐν Θαμναθασαχαρα
אשר בהר־אפרים מצפון להר־געש	ἐν τῷ ὄρει τῷ Εφραιμ ἀπὸ βορρᾶ τοῦ ὄρους Γαας [1] ἐκεῖ ἔθηκαν μετ' αὐτοῦ εἰς τὸ μνῆμα εἰς ὃ ἔθαψαν αὐτὸν ἐκεῖ τὰς μαχαίρας τὰς πετρίνας ἐν αἷς περιέτεμεν τοὺς υἱοὺς Ισραηλ ἐν Γαλγαλοις ὅτε ἐξήγαγεν αὐτοὺς ἐξ Αἰγύπτου καθὰ συνέταξεν αὐτοῖς κύριος καὶ ἐκεῖ εἰσιν ἕως τῆς σήμερον ἡμέρας

First the burial of Joshua is told, then the text reads: "there they put with him into the tomb in which they buried him, the knives of stone with which he circumcised the Israelites in Gilgal, when he brought them

---

33. Sg. with MS A against the pl. in MS B; see also Moatti-Fine 1996, 219; Rofé 1982, 34.

out of Egypt, as the Lord appointed them; and there they are to this day." The Greek version gives the strange impression that Joshua has been the responsible leader of the exodus. On the other side the text seems to refer to a kind of reliquary cult with the knives of stone. These two statements, which surely were offensive for Jewish ears in later times, may have been the reason why the text has been excluded or was transmitted only in parts of the tradition.[34] Interesting enough, there is a parallel in the historical retrospective in Josh 24:5. Here the LXX does not contradict the MT's indication that Moses and Aaron were responsible for the exodus; the text in question has been deleted. Thus, following the picture LXX Joshua is drawing, it is Joshua who has been the real hero of the exodus.[35] Furthermore, the text in Josh 24 is stating that Joshua has circumcised the Israelites, which is referring to the well-known story in Josh 5, telling that the desert generation of the Israelites had to be circumcised.

5:4–5

וזה הדבר אשר־מל יהושע כל־העם היצא ממצרים
הזכרים כל אנשי המלחמה מתו במדבר בדרך בצאתם ממצרים

ὃν δὲ τρόπον περιεκάθαρεν Ἰησοῦς τοὺς υἱοὺς Ἰσραηλ
ὅσοι ποτὲ ἐγένοντο ἐν τῇ ὁδῷ

5:5

כי־מלים היו כל־העם היצאים וכל־העם הילדים במדבר בדרך בצאתם ממצרים לא־מלו

καὶ ὅσοι ποτὲ ἀπερίτμητοι ἦσαν τῶν ἐξεληλυθότων ἐξ Αἰγύπτου

Joshua 5 again shows a distinctively different point of view than the Hebrew tradition: Following the Hebrew text, which is considerably longer, Joshua has to circumcise all men because those who were circumcised before the exodus died in the wilderness, but all the men that were born in the wilderness had not been circumcised until that day. Following the LXX, "Joshua purified the Israelites; as many as were born in the way, and as many as were uncircumcised of them that came out of Egypt, all

---

34. With Rofé 1982, 23–24, although his judgment that the text "was excised from MT" seems to be too definite in consideration of the complicated text history of the book. Therefore the comment of Butler 1983, 281 is still valid: "The question certainly deserves more comment than it normally receives."

35. With Moatti-Fine 1996, 27–28.

these Joshua circumcised." The most important differences are obvious.[36] First, the act of the circumcision is understood as purification of the Israelites; second there is a notion that some (uncircumcised!) Israelites have survived the way through the wilderness. Last, according to 5:6 (LXX), the whole wandering took forty-two years, not forty, as one can read in the MT.

Once more it can be assumed that the Greek translator was working with a different *Vorlage* from which some of the peculiarities stem, most of all the brevity. But in my view all the proposed retroversions of the LXX and reconstructions that were built on them, are so speculative that I refrain from working with them.[37] Especially noteworthy is the exceptional rendering of מול with περικαθαίρω, which can be postulated as an interpretation of the translator. It may derive from the idea of circumcising the heart in Deut 30:6. Here the LXX has used περικαθαρίζω to translate מול; the heart shall be purged, not circumcised. While the translation in Deuteronomy can be seen as a unique, but adequate, rendering, one has to state an obvious difference between the two versions of the book of Joshua.[38] Since those who are already circumcised cannot be circumcised again (LXX omits also the שנית in 5:2!), a first ceremonial act of a moral purification is needed and only then the actual circumcision takes place. It is possible that an actualization on the part of the translator has happened; thus those who have come from Egypt uncircumcised can be seen as uncircumcised Jews in temporary Hellenistic Alexandria. Following a convincing theory by den Hertog this can be seen as a statement in an urgent discussion in Hellenistic times: He who is not circumcised, has not removed the reproach of Egypt (v. 9: τὸν ὀνειδισμὸν Αἰγύπτου).[39] Although it has to be admitted that this interpretation is hypothetical, I do not see another possibility to explain the obvious contradiction to the tradition of the Pentateuch, according to which only Joshua and Caleb have survived the wandering through the desert (Num 26:65).

Likewise unique is the difference between the forty and forty-two years in 5:6a. It can be explained if the duration of the stay at the Sinai—two years

---

36. See also the careful exegesis by den Hertog 1996, 145–49; 1998; also Auld 1979, 8–9; and the notes by Moatti-Fine 1996, 117–18.

37. Anyhow, interesting is the assumption of den Hertog 1996, 146, who thinks of a homoioarkton עם/העם, being responsible for the shorter text in 5:4–5.

38. So Wevers 1995, 480–81.

39. See the question of Moatti-Fine 1996, 117–18.

according to Num 10:11—is counted with the forty years of the punishment.[40] Thus this discrepancy can be understood in the same way as the additions that serve to clarify the connections with the book of Kings.

24:33

ואלעזר בן־אהרן מת	καὶ ἐγένετο μετὰ ταῦτα καὶ Ελεαζαρ υἱὸς
ויקברו אתו בגבעת פינחס בנו	Ααρων ὁ ἀρχιερεὺς ἐτελεύτησεν καὶ ἐτάφη ἐν
אשר נתן־לו בהר אפרים	Γαβααθ Φινεες τοῦ υἱοῦ αὐτοῦ ἣν ἔδωκεν αὐτῷ ἐν
	τῷ ὄρει τῷ Εφραιμ
	[1] ἐν ἐκείνῃ τῇ ἡμέρᾳ λαβόντες οἱ υἱοὶ Ισραηλ
	τὴν κιβωτὸν τοῦ θεοῦ περιεφέροσαν ἐν ἑαυτοῖς καὶ
	Φινεες ἱεράτευσεν ἀντὶ Ελεαζαρ τοῦ πατρὸς αὐτοῦ
	ἕως ἀπέθανεν καὶ κατωρύγη ἐν Γαβααθ τῇ ἑαυτοῦ
	[2] οἱ δὲ υἱοὶ Ισραηλ ἀπήλθοσαν ἕκαστος εἰς τὸν
	τόπον αὐτῶν καὶ εἰς τὴν ἑαυτῶν πόλιν καὶ ἐσέβοντο
	οἱ υἱοὶ Ισραηλ τὴν Ἀστάρτην καὶ Ασταρωθ καὶ τοὺς
	θεοὺς τῶν ἐθνῶν τῶν κύκλῳ αὐτῶν καὶ παρέδωκεν
	αὐτοὺς κύριος εἰς χεῖρας Εγλωμ τῷ βασιλεῖ Μωαβ
	καὶ ἐκυρίευσεν αὐτῶν ἔτη δέκα ὀκτώ

At the end of the book of Joshua the LXX version again has an important addition. More precisely, the plus consists of two separate notes. The first informs the readers about the Israelites taking the ark of God and carrying it among them, and about Phinehas, who officiates in the place of Eleazar his father until he dies and is buried in Gabaath. The second ending records that the Israelites were worshiping the gods "Astarte and Astaroth and the gods of the people around them." That is why God has given them over in the hands of Eglon, the king of Moab.

Especially in this second note Alexander Rofé has seen an old, more original, connection between the books Joshua and Judges. In his view this assumed older version has left out the first two chapters of the book of Judges together with the Othniel story; it therefore testifies to a very late redactional form of the book of Judges as we have it today.[41] This far-reaching theory has been questioned with good reasons, because the additions only allude to the themes of these chapters rather than to take them up.[42] Anyway, the phenomenon of a late, quasi-deuteronomistic

---

40. Moatti-Fine 1996, 118.
41. Rofé 1982, 28–29, accepted by Tov 1997, 274–45.
42. See H. Rösel 1980, now with more restraint in H. Rösel 1999, 51 n. 102.

expansion, whose origin is not fully clear, has to be stated anew.[43] It is interesting that the ending of the Greek version of the book of Joshua refers to a point beyond itself, to the stories of the judges. The reason for that can be seen in another intention of the narrative as a whole: the history of deterioration is already present in the legend of the very beginnings of Israel.

To sum up what can be concluded from the expansions of the LXX in comparison to the MT, it is obvious that the translator/redactor has tied his book of Joshua closer to the other historical books; this was especially clear when looking at the references to the books of Judges or Kings. It seems as if the distance between the book and the Pentateuch and its traditions has been widened.[44] This became obvious when looking at the two most remarkable differences: Joshua has become the leader of the exodus and not all members of the desert generation have died on their way. With all due caution this should be seen as a unique accent of the translator, a hint to his own exposition of the book of Joshua that leads to a higher unity of the book. Assuming that the book has been translated as the first of the historical books and that it existed at least a short time without the company of other Greek versions, the inclusion of themes from the other historical books becomes clear. In the Hebrew text there was no need to make these references explicit, because the readers would come to them in the course of their reading. In a Greek book of Joshua that was standing alone, one could compensate for the still missing translations.[45]

2.2. Theological Peculiarities of the Greek Joshua

Again in Josh 24, one can see the interesting phenomenon that the LXX has transferred the gathering of the tribes from Shechem to Shiloh, which can easily be explained as a proof for an anti-Samaritan tendency of the

---

43. The assembly of Ἀστάρτη καὶ Ασταρωθ is interesting, because usually both words are used to translate עשתרות, only in 2 Chr 15:16 one can find Ἀστάρτη for אשרה. Rofé 1982, 21, offers as an attempt to retrovert the text into Hebrew ואת העשתרות העשתרת, but these names of gods never occur together in the Old Testament.

44. Thus also Moatti-Fine 1996, 239, in respect to Josh 24:33.

45. This idea stems from Cornelis den Hertog, whom I would like to thank for his willingness to discuss this article with me.

translator.⁴⁶ The assembly of the Israelites now takes place where the σκηνὴ τοῦ θεοῦ Ισραηλ stands, this according to 24:25 LXX; in the MT this notion is lacking. This can be seen as a reference to the book of Samuel, because here the legitimate place of the ark until its transfer to Jerusalem is in the city of Shiloh.

The fact that the Greek version of Joshua has a special interest in the question of the legitimate cult can very clearly be seen in the well-known account of the building of an altar by the tribes from the east in Josh 22. The Hebrew text tells that the tribes Reuben, Gad, and the half tribe of Manasseh are building an altar (מזבח) by the Jordan (22:10), which should be seen as a תבנית, a pattern of the one true altar (22:28). The Greek version emphasizes this event in using a distinction that can be traced back to the earliest books of the LXX.⁴⁷ Ever since the first offering of Noah in Gen 8:20 the Hebrew word מזבח for the altar has been translated by the neologism θυσιαστήριον. The usual Greek rendering βωμός has in contrast to this only been used for foreign מזבחת. It is with this distinction that the words are used in Josh 22: the two and one-half tribes are building a βωμός (22:10–34), but it is meant to be a ὁμοίωμα τοῦ θυσιαστηρίου κυρίου 22:28:

22:34

ויקראו בני־ראובן ובני־גד	καὶ ἐπωνόμασεν Ἰησοῦς τὸν βωμὸν τῶν
למזבח כי עד הוא	Ρουβην καὶ τῶν Γαδ καὶ τοῦ ἡμίσους φυλῆς
בינתינו כי יהוה האלהים	Μανασση καὶ εἶπεν ὅτι μαρτύριόν ἐστιν ἀνὰ μέσον
	αὐτῶν ὅτι κύριος ὁ θεὸς αὐτῶν ἐστιν

The closing verse again makes explicitly clear that it is a βωμός that is named by Joshua (i.e., called a pagan altar?) and is declared to be a witness that the Lord is their God. In comparison with this the Hebrew text tells that the tribes are naming the altar; no mention of Joshua is made.

A stone serving as a witness can be found also in 24:27:

ויאמר יהושע אל־כל־העם	καὶ εἶπεν Ἰησοῦς πρὸς τὸν λαόν
הנה האבן הזאת תהיה־בנו	ἰδοὺ ὁ λίθος οὗτος ἔσται ἐν ὑμῖν εἰς μαρτύριον
לעדה כי־היא שמעה את כל־	ὅτι αὐτὸς ἀκήκοεν πάντα τὰ λεχθέντα αὐτῷ ὑπὸ
אמרי יהוה	κυρίου

---

46. So Barthélemy 1982, 42.
47. See Daniel 1966, 26–32.

אשר דבר עמנו והיתה בכם	ὅ τι ἐλάλησεν πρὸς ἡμᾶς σήμερον καὶ ἔσται
לעדה	οὗτος ἐν ὑμῖν εἰς μαρτύριον
פן־תכחשון באלהיכם	ἐπ' ἐσχάτων τῶν ἡμερῶν ἡνίκα ἐὰν ψεύσησθε
	κυρίῳ τῷ θεῷ μου

The stone set up by Joshua should be a witness for the Israelites not to deny their God. The LXX expands this text with ἐπ' ἐσχάτων τῶν ἡμερῶν and adds another accent in having Joshua speak about *my* God, in contrast the MT reads באלהיכם. If one remembers the end of the book with its allusion to a future fall from God, it seems obvious to me that the translator is speaking about an eschatological judgment. This interpretation can be transferred to the βωμός of the tribes from the east Jordanian area: It will always stand as a witness to their sins.[48]

Further hints to an exegetically motivated translation can be seen in cases where Israel is called λαός, even if there is גוי in the Hebrew text. This is the case in 3:17, when Israel is crossing the Jordan, and in 4:1 as well. In 4:10–1 one can find the usual equation λαός–עם. In the same chapter (4:24) the foreign nations are called ἔθνη, even if the MT has עם (pl.).[49] Like other translations before it, the Greek Joshua also emphasizes the distinction between Israel and the other peoples.

The gods of these foreign nations have also been the target of the translator's will to present a nuanced rendering. In 23:7 MT one can read that the Israelites are not allowed to swear by the names of the gods of the nations that remain among them (ובשם אלהיהם לא־תזכירו). This is intensified in the LXX, because even the mentioning of their names is prohibited καὶ τὰ ὀνόματα τῶν θεῶν αὐτῶν οὐκ ὀνομασθήσεται ἐν ὑμῖν. In 24:14 they were named clearly as τοὺς θεοὺς τοὺς ἀλλοτρίους, the MT here only reads אלהים.[50] In the next verse the God of Israel is honored by a special designation that makes him alone worthy to be worshiped. In a plus over the MT LXX reads ὅτι ἅγιός ἐστιν as a summarizing ending of the speech, which has obviously been taken from 24:19. Although it is possible to retranslate this formula to כי קדוש הוא, this is not very likely because there is nowhere

---

48. Den Hertog 1996, 181, is interpreting v. 34 as a positive ending of the story, but this seems problematic since a βωμός cannot have positive connotations.

49. See also den Hertog 1996, 182–83.

50. But compare 24:23, where אלהי הנכר has been rendered by τοὺς θεοὺς τοὺς ἀλλοτρίους.

an attestation to such a designation in the Hebrew Bible, which is why I am assuming a free exposition of the translator.

Two last examples: When discussing 6:26 it has already been noted that LXX tried to emphasize God's power. This impression is certainly true for 1:14. While in the MT Moses is explicitly labeled as having given the land, the LXX leaves משה בעבר הירדן out, God alone is the giver of the land.[51]

1:7–8

רק חזק ואמץ מאד לשמר לעשות	ἴσχυε οὖν καὶ ἀνδρίζου φυλάσσεσθαι καὶ ποιεῖν
ככל־התורה אשר צוך משה עבדי	καθότι ἐνετείλατό σοι Μωυσῆς ὁ παῖς μου
אל־תסור ממנו ימין ושמאול	καὶ οὐκ ἐκκλινεῖς ἀπ' αὐτῶν εἰς δεξιὰ οὐδὲ εἰς ἀριστερά
למען תשכיל בכל אשר תלך	ἵνα συνῇς ἐν πᾶσιν οἷς ἐὰν πράσσῃς

1:8

לא־ימוש ספר התורה הזה מפיך	καὶ οὐκ ἀποστήσεται ἡ βίβλος τοῦ νόμου τούτου ἐκ τοῦ στόματος
והגית בו יומם ולילה	σου καὶ μελετήσεις ἐν αὐτῷ ἡμέρας καὶ νυκτός
למען תשמר לעשות ככל־הכתוב בו	ἵνα συνῇς ποιεῖν πάντα τὰ γεγραμμένα
כי־אז תצליח את־דרכך ואז תשכיל:	τότε εὐοδωθήσῃ καὶ εὐοδώσεις τὰς ὁδούς σου καὶ τότε συνήσεις

In Josh 1 one can also learn about a differentiated conception of the Torah: Following 1:7 MT, he who observes the torah will prosper where ever he goes (שכל hiphil), and according to 1:8 one should observe (שמר) to do according to the torah. The LXX has translated both verbs by only one Greek equivalent and has chosen συνίημι "have insight into." This rendering is based on a special understanding of שכל, which in the *hiphil*-stem can mean "to instruct, make wise." In this sense, naming an instructor of the community, it is used in the book of Daniel (12:3) and in Qumran (e.g., 1QS III, 13). The translation of שמר by συνίημι occurs nowhere else in the Bible. Thus one has to conclude that here in Josh 1:7–8 a special insight is seen as a precondition for rightly observing the torah. Day and night one shall meditate in the book of the law, to have insight how to do all the things that are written in it; in the end one will really be wise, καὶ τότε συνήσεις (1:8). The salvation of people depends on real

---

51. With Butler 1983, 19. In the next verse 1:15 the reference to Moses is not omitted, possibly because the theme is not the giving of the land but the inheritance (τὴν κληρονομίαν αὐτοῦ ἣν δέδωκεν ὑμῖν Μωυσῆς).

insight into the torah; this conception is comparable to the one that has led to the well-known sentence "if you do not believe, you will not at all understand" (Isa 7:9).[52]

These examples may suffice. They could easily be increased and used to draw a more detailed picture, for instance with respect to special Greek terms or to the toponyms. But it has already become clear that the Greek version of the book of Joshua together with its presumable *Vorlage* have to be seen as independent witnesses of the text, each with its own characteristic meaning and ways of interpreting the tradition. Admittedly, it has not been clear in any instance which deviation has to be ascribed to which stage in the development of the texts; here further studies are required. But it is evident that neither the Greek version nor the texts from Qumran can be left out of consideration in the future discussion about the book of Joshua.

Bibliography

Auld, A. Graeme. 1979. "Joshua: The Hebrew and Greek Texts." Pages 1–14 in *Studies in the Historical Books of the Old Testament*. Edited by John A. Emerton. VTSup 30. Leiden: Brill.

Barthélemy, Dominique. 1982. *Critique textuelle de l'Ancien Testament: Josué, Juges, Ruth, Samuel, Rois, Chronique, Esdras, Néhémie, Esther*. OBO 50.1. Göttingen: Vandenhoeck & Ruprecht; Fribourg: Presses Universitaires.

Bieberstein, Klaus. 1994. *Lukian und Theodotion im Josuabuch: Mit einem Beitrag zu den Josuarollen von Ḥirbet Qumrān*. BN.B 7. Munich: Institut für Biblische Exegese.

Brown, William P. 1999. "Reassessing the Text-Critical Value of Septuagint-Genesis 1: A Response to Rösel." *BIOSCS* 32:35–39.

Butler, Trent C. 1983. *Joshua*. WBC 7. Waco, TX: Word Books.

Daniel, Suzanne. 1966. *Recherches sur le Vocabulaire du Culte dans la Septante*. EeC 61. Paris: Klincksieck.

Fritz, Volkmar. 1994. *Das Buch Josua*. HAT 1.7. Tübingen: Mohr Siebeck.

Greenspoon, Leonard. 1992. "The Qumran Fragments of Joshua: Which Puzzle are They Part of and Where Do They Fit?" Pages 159–94 in *Septuagint, Scrolls and Cognate Writings: Papers Presented to the Inter-*

---

52. See M. Rösel 1991, 139–40 [ch. 9 in this volume].

national *Symposium on the Septuagint and its Relations to the Dead Sea Scrolls and other Writings, Manchester, 1990*. Edited by George J. Brooke and Barnabas Lindars. SCS 33. Atlanta: Scholars Press.

Harl, Marguerite, Gilles Dorival, and Olivier Munnich. 1994. *La Bible Grecque des Septante. Du judaïsme hellénistique au christianisme ancien*. 2nd ed. Paris: Cerf.

Hendel, Ronald S. 1999. "On the Text Critical Value of Septuagint Genesis: A Reply to Rösel." *BIOSCS* 32:31–34.

Hertog, Cornelis den. 1995. "Anmerkungen zu Margolis' The Book of Joshua in Greek." *BIOSCS* 28: 51–56.

———. 1996. "Studien zur griechischen Übersetzung des Buches Josua." ThD diss., University of Giessen.

———. 1998. "Jos 5,4–6 in der griechischen Übersetzung." *ZAW* 110:601–6.

Holmes, Samuel. 1914. *Joshua: The Hebrew and Greek Texts*. Cambridge: Cambridge University Press.

Kooij, Arie van der. 1999. "The Origin and Purpose of Bible Translations in Ancient Judaism: Some Comments." *AR* 1:204–14.

Margolis, Max L., ed. 1931–1938. *The Book of Joshua in Greek according to the Critically Restored Text, with an Apparatus Containing the Variants of the Principal Recensions and of the Individual Witnesses: Parts I–IV*. Paris: Geuthner.

———, ed. 1992. *The Book of Joshua in Greek: According to the Critically Restored Text with an Apparatus Containing the Variants of the Principal Recensions and of the Individual Witnesses; Part V*. Preface by Emanuel Tov. Monograph Series/Annenberg Research Institute. Philadelphia: Annenberg Research Institute.

Mazor, Lea. 1988. "The Origin and Evolution of the Curse upon the Rebuilder of Jericho." *Text* 14:1–26.

———. 1994. "The Septuagint Translation of the Book of Joshua." *BIOSCS* 27:29–38.

Moatti-Fine, Jacqueline. 1996. *Jésus (Josué)*. BdA 6. Paris: Cerf.

Niemann, Hermann Michael. 1993. "Das Ende des Volkes der Perizziter: Über soziale Wandlungen Israels im Spiegel einer Begriffsgruppe." *ZAW* 105:233–57.

Noort, Edward. 1993. *Een Pleek om te Zijn: Over de theologie van het land aan de hand van Jozua 8:30–35*. Kampen: University Press.

———. 1998. "4QJosh[a] and the History of Tradition in the Book of Joshua." *JNSL* 24:127–44.

Orlinsky, Harry M. 1969. "The Hebrew Vorlage of the Septuagint of the Book of Joshua." Pages 187–95 in *Congress Volume: Rome 1968*. Edited by Theodorus Christiaan Vriezen. VTSup 17. Leiden: Brill.

Rofé, Alexander. 1982. "The End of the Book of Joshua according to the Septuagint." *Hen* 4:17–36.

———. 1994. "The Edition of the Book of Joshua in the Light of 4QJosh[a]." Pages 73–80 in *New Qumran Texts and Studies*. Edited by George J. Brooke. STDJ 15. Leiden: Brill.

Rösel, Hartmut N. 1980. "Die Überleitungen vom Josua- ins Richterbuch." *VT* 30:342–50.

———. 1999. *Von Josua bis Jojachin: Untersuchungen zu den deuteronomistischen Geschichtsbüchern des Alten Testaments*. VTSup 75. Leiden: Brill.

Rösel, Martin. 1991. "Die Jungfrauengeburt des endzeitlichen Immanuel: Jesaja 7 in der Version der Septuaginta." *JBTh* 6:135–51. [ch. 9 in this volume.]

———. 1998a. "Theo-Logie der griechischen Bibel." *VT* 48:49–62.

———. 1998b. "The Text-Critical Value of the Genesis-Septuagint." *BIOSCS* 34:62–70.

Sipilä, Seppo. 1993. "A Note to the Users of Margolis' Joshua-Edition." *BIOSCS* 26:17–21.

Tov, Emanuel. 1978. "Midrash-Type Exegesis in the LXX of Joshua." *RB* 85:50–61.

———. 1986. "The Growth of the Book of Joshua in the Light of the Evidence of the LXX Translation." Pages 321–39 in *Studies in Bible*. Edited by Sara Japhet. ScrHier 31. Jerusalem: Magnes.

———. 1992. *Textual Criticism of the Hebrew Bible*. Minneapolis: Fortress.

Ulrich, Eugene, et al. 1995. *Qumran Cave 4.IX: Deuteronomy to Kings*. DJD XIV. Oxford: Clarendon.

Wevers, John W. 1995. *Notes on the Greek Text of Deuteronomy*. SCS 39. Atlanta: Scholars Press.

Würthwein, Ernst. 1977. *Das erste Buch der Könige: Kapitel 1–16*. ATD 11.1. Göttingen: Vandenhoeck & Ruprecht.

7
Salomo und die Sonne. Zur Rekonstruktion des Tempelweihspruchs 1.Kön 8,12–13

Der Tempelweihspruch Salomos gehört zu den Texten, die die Exegese immer wieder beschäftigen, obgleich sich die zur Verfügung stehenden Informationen nicht verändern. Dies liegt daran, dass man seit langem vermutet, über eine zu rekonstruierende ältere Textform Einblick in die Tempeltheologie Salomos und damit in die Früh- oder gar Vorgeschichte israelitischer Heiligtumsvorstellungen zu erhalten.

Von Bedeutung ist dabei die griechische Version, weil sie den Spruch in einer anderen Form und an anderer Stelle (V. 53-4) überliefert. Das hat seit J. Wellhausen[1] dazu geführt, dass die durch Rückübersetzung erschlossene Vorlage der LXX als die ältere Variante des Spruches angesehen wird. Je nach Rekonstruktion ist in der Vorform davon die Rede, dass JHWH die Sonne an den Himmel stellt oder sie dort bekannt macht. Spätere Redaktoren hätten dies durch Entfernung der Sonnenaussage dogmatisch abgemildert und den Text durch Umstellung an den Anfang des Tempelweihgebetes besser in den Kontext eingebettet. Diese Überlegungen sind in jüngster Zeit von A. Schenker aufgegriffen worden, der 3 Regn 8,53-4 als weiteres Indiz dafür sieht, dass die griechische Version der Königebücher auf eine ältere Vorlage als den Konsonantentext des MT verweist.[2]

Prominenz hat der Text durch O. Keels großes Werk über Jerusalem erfahren, da er auf eine neue Rekonstruktion zurückgegriffen hat, um seine These zu belegen, dass der Tempel in Jerusalem ursprünglich ein Sonnenheiligtum gewesen sei.[3] Noch weiter gehen F. Stolz und E.A. Knauf,

---

1. Wellhausen 1889, 271.
2. Schenker 2000, 130–35. Anders jetzt van Keulen 2005, der an der Priorität des MT festhält.
3. Keel 2007, 267–86; vgl. Keel 2002, 9–23.

die den Verweis auf eine El-Gottheit hinter dem griechischen Text vermuten.[4] Die hellenistische LXX erhält so ein enormes Gewicht bei der religionsgeschichtlichen Rekonstruktion der frühisraelitischen Tempelvorstellung. Daher verwundert nicht, dass es einen vehementen Einspruch von F. Hartenstein gegeben hat, der ebenfalls durch die Rekonstruktion einer hebräischen Vorlage von 3.Regn 8,53–54 zu dem Ergebnis kommt, dass die LXX sekundär gegenüber dem MT sei und eine typisch hellenistische Schöpfungsvorstellung (analog etwa zu Sir 42,15) in den Text eintrage.[5]

Angesichts dieser Diskussion scheint es angemessen, die Plausibilität der vorgeschlagenen Rekonstruktionen zu überprüfen. Dabei fällt auf, dass der nähere Kontext der LXX-Übersetzung nur selten mitbedacht wird. Dieser ist aber zur Erhebung von Arbeitstechnik und Aussageabsicht einer Übersetzung oft von entscheidender Bedeutung, wie auch für diesen schwierigen Text demonstriert werden kann.

1. Die Problemlage

Im heutigen MT steht der fragliche Passus nach der erzählenden Einleitung V. 1–11 und vor dem eigentlichen dtr. Tempelweihgebet V. 22–53, das seinerseits durch eine Bezugnahme auf 2.Sam 7 eingeleitet wird (V. 14–21). Der Text lautet: Damals hat Salomo gesprochen: „JHWH hat gesagt, im Wolkendunkel zu wohnen. (13) Ich habe gewisslich ein fürstliches/erhabenes Haus für dich gebaut, ein feste Gründung für dein Wohnen/Thronen in Ewigkeiten."

Die Vorstellung vom Wohnen Gottes im Wolkendunkel (ערפל) knüpft an die Erwähnung der Wolke (ענן) in V. 10 + 11 an; dies mag einer der Gründe für die jetzige Position des Spruches sein.[6] Der Tempel gilt als fest gegründetes Fundament für die ewige Präsenz Gottes in Jerusalem, daneben steht kaum untereinander vermittelt die Vorstellung von JHWHs Wohnen im Wolkendunkel.[7] Allgemein akzeptiert ist, dass der Spruch eine inhaltliche Einheit darstellt. Nach vorne ist er nur sehr lose

---

4. Knauf 1997; darauf basiert die Rekonstruktion von Bösenecker, 2000. Stolz 1970, 168: im Tempelweihspruch sei „El durch Jahwe ersetzt" worden.

5. Hartenstein 2007, 53–69.

6. Nach Hartenstein 2007, 55, wurden umgekehrt V. 10-1 nachträglich durch eine priesterliche Bearbeitung eingefügt (Anm. 8); vgl. Noth 1968, 180–81.

7. Hartenstein 2007 versteht dies analog zu Jes 6; Ps 18,10–13* als komplementäre Vorstellung; der Tempel repräsentiert den kosmischen Wohnsitz eines Wettergottes.

7. Salomo und die Sonne. 161

mit אז verbunden.[8] Eine Verknüpfung mit V. 14 fehlt,[9] damit ergibt sich ein inhaltliches Problem insofern, als Salomo den Spruch in Richtung auf den Tempel und den dort erschienenen כבוד־יהוה gesprochen haben müsste und sich erst danach zum Volk wendet.[10] Literarkritisch spricht also viel dafür, dass der Spruch nicht ursprünglich zwischen die V. 11 und 14 gehört. Damit ist aber nicht zugleich sicher, dass die Position in der LXX die ältere ist. Dort nämlich steht der Spruch in deutlich erweiterter Version an V. 53 angefügt, also nach dem mit dem Gebetsanruf אדני יהוה „mein Herr JHWH" abgeschlossenen Gebet. Diese Position wäre nach internen Hinweisen des hebräischen Textes die eigentlich zu erwartende. V. 54 spricht nämlich davon, dass Salomo כל־התפלה והתחנה הזאת „dieses ganze Gebet und Flehen" vollendet habe, wobei nach V. 28+29 eindeutig תפלה das Tempelweihgebet meint. In der vom griechischen Text bezeugten Position wäre dann der Tempelweihspruch התחנה, diese Version stimmt also mit der Reihung in V. 54 überein. Dies kann sowohl der Platz der ursprünglichen Komposition als auch sekundäre Erleichterung sein.

Wichtiger sind aber die quantitativen und inhaltlichen Differenzen, die sich am besten in einer Synopse erschließen:

1.Kön 8,12–13 (MT)	3.Regn 8,53a (LXX)
אז אמר שלמה	τότε ἐλάλησεν Σαλωμων
	ὑπὲρ τοῦ οἴκου ὡς συνετέλεσεν τοῦ οἰκοδομῆσαι αὐτόν
	ἥλιον ἐγνώρισεν ἐν οὐρανῷ κύριος
יהוה אמר לשכן בערפל	εἶπεν τοῦ κατοικεῖν ἐν γνόφῳ
בנה בניתי בית זבל לך	οἰκοδόμησον οἶκόν μου οἶκον ἐκπρεπῆ σαυτω
מכון לשבתך עולמים	τοῦ κατοικεῖν ἐπὶ καινότητος οὐκ ἰδοὺ αὕτη γέγραπται
	ἐν βιβλίῳ τῆς ᾠδῆς

Die Differenzen seien kurz zusammengefasst: LXX hat zunächst ein Plus „über das Haus, als er es zu bauen vollendet hatte,"[11] das sich u.U. an 2,36; 8,1. 54 orientiert. Es ergibt sich eine Abfolge vom Infinitiv in 8,1

---

8. Vgl. Burney 1903, 35, zur Verwendung von אז als unspezifischer Überleitung. Bündig Würthwein 1977, 88: „ist als Anhängsel zu betrachten".

9. So auch Görg 1974, 55. Sein eigener Versuch, den Spruch von ägyptischen Parallelen her zu verstehen, hat m.W. keine Nachfolger gefunden.

10. Dies spricht nach Gooding 1969, 24, als *lectio difficilior* dafür, dass LXX eine erleichternde Position des Textes gewählt habe. Aufgegriffen wurde dies durch Peterca 1987, und van Keulen 2005, 179.

11. Übersetzung nach Septuaginta.Deutsch (J. Bösenecker).

zum Aorist in V. 53, jetzt erst ist nach der griechischen Version der eigentliche Abschluss des Baus erreicht. Der Text kann innergriechisch bei der Einfügung des Spruches in diesen konkreten Kontext entstanden sein,[12] genauso gut ist er aber auch als enge Übersetzung einer hebräischen Vorlage denkbar.[13]

Entscheidend für die gesamte bisherige Diskussion ist der folgende Stichos: „Die Sonne hat am Himmel bekannt gemacht der Herr." Zunächst fällt die im Griechischen der Könige-LXX ungewöhnliche Voranstellung des Akk. ἥλιον auf. Damit entsteht eine betonte, eindeutige Aussage: Der Gott Israels ist für den Lauf der Sonne verantwortlich. Da Gott selbst, so der nächste Halbvers, unsichtbar im Dunkel wohnt, ist zugleich an der Sonne Gottes Macht und Größe abzulesen.[14] V. 8,12b ist im Griechischen eine sehr enge Wiedergabe des im MT erhaltenen Textes.

Im folgenden Stichos gibt es kleinere Differenzen: Statt des Inf. abs. „Ich habe gewisslich gebaut" findet sich der Imperativ „baue mein Haus," was auf den nahezu gleichen Konsonantenbestand zurückverweisen kann: בנה ביתי statt MT בנה בניתי. Die folgenden drei Worte haben je ein Äquivalent im Griechischen, allerdings steht ἐκπρεπής (Variante in G^L: εὐπρεπής) sonst eher für נוה (Hiob 18,15), נעים (2.Sam 1,23) oder הוד (Sach 10,3),[15] wobei zudem auffällt, dass beide Lexeme (ἐκπρεπής und εὐπρεπής) besonders in späten Schriften ohne hebräisches Original verwendet wurden. Das erschwert die Möglichkeit der Rückübersetzung. Differenzen gibt es auch in der letzten Zeile, die im Griechischen „um auf eine neue Art und Weise zu wohnen" lautet. Hier fehlt eine Wiedergabe von מכון; עולמים wird andernorts nicht mit καινότης wiedergegeben, dieses steht in Ez 47,12 für חדשים.[16] Die Wendung מכון לשבתך begegnet in 1.Kön 8 noch an drei weiteren Stellen (V. 39+43+49) und wird dort durchgängig mit ἐξ ἑτοίμου κατοικητηρίου σου übersetzt; damit ist deutlich, dass der Übersetzer in V. 53 eine andere Vorlage gehabt oder frei übersetzt haben muss.

Abschließend findet sich über den MT hinaus die Notiz „Siehe, ist dies nicht aufgeschrieben im Buch des Liedes," die an die Frage „Ist das nicht aufgeschrieben im Buch des Aufrechten?" (Jos 10,13; vgl. 2.Sam 1,18) erinnert. Daher wird oft vermutet, τῆς ᾠδῆς sei aus der Verlesung

---

12. So Bösenecker 2000, 169.
13. Schenker 2000, 131; van Keulen 2005, 167.
14. Schenker 2000, 132; ähnlich Hartenstein 2007, 58.
15. Vgl. Schenker 2000, 131.
16. Schenker 2000, 131.

7. Salomo und die Sonne.

von הישר in השיר entstanden.[17] Davon unabhängig ist zu fragen, was der Übersetzer mit dem „Buch des Liedes" gemeint hat.

2. Die Rekonstruktionen

Eben war bereits auf Möglichkeiten und Grenzen der Rekonstruktion einer Vorlage der LXX-Version hingewiesen worden. An solchen Versuchen, einen älteren hebräischen Text zu gewinnen, hängt für den religionsgeschichtlichen Umgang mit diesem Text alles, da nur so behauptet werden kann, hier ließen sich Informationen aus der Frühzeit des Tempels erlangen. Die Zuversicht, mit der solche Rekonstruktionen vorgetragen werden, steht allerdings im Widerspruch zur neueren Septuaginta-Forschung, die die Möglichkeit von durchgängigen Rückübersetzungen sehr skeptisch beurteilt.[18] Es ist symptomatisch, dass A. Schenker auf eine Rekonstruktion der Vorlage verzichtet und nur mögliche Äquivalenzen für einige Worte vorschlägt[19]. Im Folgenden werden zunächst die wichtigsten Vorschläge für die hebräische Vorlage dargestellt, dann daraus Konsequenzen gezogen.

F. Hartenstein[20]	O. Keel[21]
שמש הודיע בשמים יהוה	שמש הודיע בשמים
[ו]אמר	יהוה אמר לשכן בערפל
לשכן בערפל	בנה ביתי בית זבל לך
בנה ביתי	לשבת לחדשיו
בית זבל לך	
לשבת לחדשות	

Diese jüngsten Vorschläge stimmen in der rekonstruierten Textgrundlage weitgehend überein, unterscheiden sich aber durch die Segmentierung der Sätze. Zunächst zum Text: שמש ist unstrittig; auch הודיע als Übersetzung von ἐγνώρισεν ist in der jüngsten Forschung akzeptiert, da γνωρίζω im Samuel- und Königebuch an allen Stellen für eine Form von ידע steht.[22]

---

17. Seit Wellhausen 1889, 271.
18. S. v.a. Tov 1997, 57–99.
19. Schenker 2000, 130–32.
20. Hartenstein 2007, 58–59.
21. Keel 2007, 269–71, vgl. ders. 2002, 16–17.
22. Vgl. nur 1.Kön 1,27; 8,12, auch 1.Sam 6,2; 10,8 u.ö. Dieses Faktum wurde in der älteren Forschung meist ignoriert, bis van den Born 1965, 239–40 darauf hinge-

Die Form לחדשיו hat O. Keel direkt aus Ez 47,12 übernommen, obwohl LXX kein Suffix repräsentiert; F. Hartenstein ist daher näher am griechischen Ausgangstext.

Die entscheidende Differenz liegt in der syntaktischen Zuordnung. F. Hartenstein übernimmt die Satzstruktur der LXX mit dem betont voranstehenden Objekt; danach bleibt die Sonne JHWH untergeordnet. Zu konstatieren ist aber, dass dieser hebräische Text eine ganz ungewöhnliche Syntax hätte. Ein so betont vorangestelltes Objekt kommt m.W. nur dann vor, wenn die Struktur im Nachsatz eines chiastischen Parallelismus eindeutig ist, oder wenn durch Kontext oder Semantik klar wird, dass das voranstehende Nomen nicht Subjekt des Verbs sein kann.[23] Im vergleichbaren Ps 19,5 steht folglich auch präfigiertes לשמש als vorangestelltes Objekt. In der nach vorne kontextlosen Fassung, wie Hartenstein sie rekonstruiert, wird man m.E. שמש nicht anders denn als Subjekt begreifen können; die Sonne tut JHWH (Objekt) am Himmel kund. Wenn LXX tatsächlich eine solche Vorlage hatte, konnte sie die bedenkliche Aussage durch die so nur im Griechischen mögliche Verwendung des Akkusativs umgehen. LXX hätte dann eine inhaltliche Korrektur der ihr vorgegebenen Aussage unternommen.

Aufgrund dieser Problematik ist *prima vista* die Erklärung O. Keels näher am Text, der שמש als Subjekt der Aussage fasst: „Die Sonne hat vom Himmel her bekannt gemacht."[24] Der Gottesname wird dann als Subjekt der zweiten Aussage verstanden: „JHWH hat gesagt, er wolle im Dunkeln thronen."[25] Allerdings ist das Verständnis von בשמים als „vom Himmel

---

wiesen hat. Allerdings hat er sein Argument dadurch entwertet, dass er wenig plausibel הודיע als Verlesung für הויעד erklärt hat. Auch Thackeray 1921, 78, hatte הודיע als Vorlage der LXX angesehen, doch als Verlesung für הופיע „scheinen" vermutet. Van Keulen 2005, 175, schlägt ein *nif.* נודיע vor; die Sonne habe sich selbst kundgetan.

23. Dazu s. Muraoka 1985, 37–41; Joüon/Muraoka 1996, §155. Zur generellen Syntax vgl. auch Keel 2007, 268: „Die Folge Objekt (‚Sonne'), Verb, Subjekt (‚JHWH') ist nicht üblich". Irsigler 2004, 31–32 hält die Syntax zwar für „keineswegs unmöglich", gibt aber keinen genau passenden Beleg.

24. Ungewöhnlich ist zudem der vor dem Subjekt stehende Lokativ. Zwar verweist Keel 2007, 268, für die vorangestellte adverbiale Näherbestimmung mit Bezug auf D. Michel und A. Schenker auf eine Parallele in Ps 65,6, doch kann diese die Beweislast nicht tragen, da das vorangestellte Objekt נוראות aus inhaltlichen Gründen gar nicht Subjekt des Prädikats תעננו sein kann und die Näherbestimmung „in Gerechtigkeit" בצדק vor dem Verb steht.

25. Ähnlich Dus 1960.

her" kaum zu rechtfertigen.²⁶ Ebensowenig ist einzusehen, warum die erste Zeile zu lang sein sollte (Keel, ebd.), wenn der Gottesname nicht Subjekt der zweiten Aussage ist, sondern, wie sprachlich zu erwarten ist, Objekt der ersten.²⁷ Hier wird deutlich, dass der religionsgeschichtliche Wunsch der Vater des rekonstruierenden Gedankens ist.

Damit komme ich zu Rekonstruktionsversuchen, die sich noch weiter vom griechischen Ausgangstext entfernen.

Knauf²⁸	Bösenecker²⁹
שמש הכין בשמים אל	שמש העמד בשמים אל
יהוה אמר לשכן בערפל	יהוה אמר לשכן בערפל
בניתי בית זבל לך	בנה בניתי בית זבל לך
מכון לשבתך עלמים	מכון לשבתך עולמים

Ich kommentiere nur die wichtigsten Differenzen zu den jüngeren Versuchen: In der ersten Zeile bleibt Knauf bei der überholten, auf Wellhausen zurückgehenden Überlegung (s.u.), ursprüngliches הכין wäre zu הבין verlesen, was im Griechischen mit γνωρίζω übersetzt wurde.³⁰ Bösenecker dagegen kommt auf העמד, weil er eine mehrstufige Verlesung annimmt. Jos 10,13 (ebenfalls aus dem ספר ישר) sei die Idee vom Stehen der Sonne (עמד) zu entnehmen und daher auch für 3.Regn 8,53a anzunehmen. Das *mem* sei zu *waw* und *jod* verlesen worden, was—nach Buchstabenvertauschung—zu הודיע geführt habe (S. 171). Tragfähig ist diese Spekulation nicht.

Dieses Urteil gilt erst recht für E.A. Knaufs Zufügung von אל.³¹ Sie reagiert auf die problematische Syntax, ohne dabei jedoch das Problem zu lösen. Denn Knauf nimmt weiterhin שמש als voranstehendes Objekt der ersten und יהוה als Subjekt der zweiten Aussage. Damit bedarf es eines Subjekts im ersten Stichos, wofür aus religionsgeschichtlichen Gründen nur der Gott 'el in Frage komme. Eine solche Konjektur ist, selbst wenn

---

26. Mit Recht Hartenstein 2007, 60, mit Hinweis auf Jenni 1992, 27.

27. Eine Mischform dieser Argumentationen findet sich bei Taylor 1993, 137, der zwar JHWH an die erste Position der zweiten Zeile setzt, ihn aber als Subjekt der ersten Zeile versteht.

28. Knauf 1997, 84.

29. Bösenecker 2000, 169–72.

30. Vgl. Knauf 1997, Anm. 6 auf S. 82–83.

31. Diese wurde von Bösenecker 2000 (so S. 172, Anm. 418) von Knauf 1997, 84–85, übernommen.

man sie als „within the limits of reasonable speculation" sieht[32], nicht geeignet, belastbare Aussagen zur Unterordnung JHWHs unter El in salomonischer Zeit zu begründen.

Auch am Ende des Spruches gibt es eine problematische Rekonstruktion: Bei beiden steht מכון לשבתך, obgleich man von diesem Text nicht zur LXX-Lesung τοῦ κατοικεῖν kommt und obwohl sonst in 3.Regn 8 ἐξ ἑτοίμου κατοικητηρίου σου als Äquivalent für diese Wendung steht. Zu notieren ist aber die Überlegung Knaufs, dass dem ursprünglichen Spruch einige Zeilen vorausgegangen sein müssen, etwa ein Lobpreis für den Schöpfergott (S. 84). Auch O. Loretz hatte vermutet, dass es sich bei unserem Text um einen „Torso eines kanaanäischen Tempelweihspruchs" handelt[33]. Auch das ist nicht erweisbar, doch ließe sich so die Syntax des ersten Verses als Resultat einer Bruchstelle erklären.

Schließlich sei die Rekonstruktion J. Wellhausens und deren Variation durch M. Noth mitgeteilt, die die Diskussion letztlich generiert hat.

Wellhausen[34]	Noth[35]
שמש הכין בשמים יהוה	שמש הכין בשמים יהוה
אמר לשכן ערפל	אמר לשכן בערפל
בנה ביתי בית נוה לי	בנה בניתי בית זבל לך
לשבת עולמים	מכון שבתך עולמים
הלא היא כתובה על ספר הישר	הלא היא כתובה על ספר הישר

Die Differenzen zwischen den beiden Versionen sind recht gering. Während Wellhausen נוה als Hintergrund von εὐπρεπής vermutet (s.o.), bevorzugt Noth das vom MT her angebotene זבל. Auch sonst blieb Noth näher am MT, was sich in seiner Wahl der Inf. abs.-Konstruktion בנה בניתי und der Beibehaltung von מכון (vgl. Knauf) zeigt. Weit durchgesetzt hat sich die bereits dargestellte Vermutung, הכין sei—verlesen zu הבין—als Grundlage von ἐγνώρισεν anzusehen. Da im Zusammenhang der Schöpfungs- und der Tempelthematik, zudem auch in 1.Kön 8, die Wurzel כון häufig verwendet wird, ließ sich dies rechtfertigen.[36] So kam es zu einer ganzen Reihe von

---

32. Knauf 1997, 86.
33. Loretz 1974, 478–80.
34. Wellhausen 1889, 271, weitestgehend übernommen und masoretisch punktiert von Burney 1903, 111.
35. Noth 1968, 168. 172–73; allerdings gab Noth selbst keine vollständige Rückübersetzung.
36. Zumal die lukianische Rezension statt ἐγνώρισεν ἔστησεν las, s. Rehm 1937,

Diskussionen über הכין im Zusammenhang mit 1.Kön 8,13, obgleich dieses Lexem dort nicht belegbar noch wahrscheinlich ist.[37] Schließlich stimmen Wellhausen und Noth darin überein, dass sie ein ursprüngliches ספר הישר als Quelle des Spruches ansehen (das Noth aber nicht textkritisch für MT rekonstruiert); auch dies wurde weitgehend akzeptiert.[38]

Die Divergenz der bisherigen Rekonstruktionsversuche zeigt, dass die Zurückhaltung der modernen LXX-Forschung gegenüber solchen Unternehmungen berechtigt ist. Unsicher sind die Vorlagen für ἐγνώρισεν, für nahezu alle Elemente in den beiden Stichoi οἰκοδόμησον οἶκόν μου οἶκον ἐκπρεπῆ σαυτω und τοῦ κατοικεῖν ἐπὶ καινότητος, außerdem für βιβλίῳ τῆς ᾠδῆς. Hinzu kommt die ungewöhnliche Syntax des ersten Satzes mit dem vorangestellten Objekt, die möglicherweise den Wegfall vorhergehender Textteile nahelegt.[39] Folglich lässt sich die Aussage der ursprünglichen Dichtung nicht eindeutig erheben. Sicher ist offenbar nur, dass der Text JHWH und die Sonne aufeinander bezogen hatte, doch die Frage nach Subjekt und Objekt der Beziehung ist nur im griechischen Text eindeutig.

Immerhin scheint mir deutlich zu sein, dass die LXX eine andere Vorlage als den Text hatte, den wir im heutigen MT sehen. Doch wie die Analyse von J. Bösenecker gezeigt hat, ist die Vorlage der LXX oft von schlechter Qualität gewesen, was zu Lesefehlern und eigenen Korrekturen führte.[40] Im fraglichen Text 8,53a weist die Übersetzung eine Reihe ungewöhnlicher Formulierungen auf (ἐγνώρισεν, ἐκπρεπῆ/εὐπρεπής, ἐπὶ καινότητος), die vielleicht als freie Übersetzungen oder Fehlerkorrekturen zu sehen sind, jedenfalls aber nicht sicher ins Hebräische zurückübersetzt werden können. Hinzu kommt, dass die LXX eine eigene Intention hinsichtlich der Tempelvorstellung hat, was die Rekonstruktion weiter erschwert. Diese theologische Absicht der LXX soll im folgenden Abschnitt erhoben werden.

3. Die griechische Version 3.Regn 8

Die griechische Version der 4 Königebücher gehört zu den problematischsten Büchern der LXX. Sicher—wegen der in Qumran gefundenen

---

89; Burney 1903, 111. Dies ist aber späte Angleichung an Vorstellungen des MT; Keel 2002, 15, vermutet Einfluss von Ps 74,16 oder Jes 40,20 her.
37. So Koch 1984, 107. Ähnlich Janowski 1995, 226.
38. S. z.B. Taylor 1993, 139; Dietrich 1997, 231, Anm. 9; anders aber S. 257!
39. Ähnlich Barthélemy 1982, 350–51.
40. Bösenecker 2000, z.B. 98. 167–87.

hebräischen Fragmente—ist, dass die Vorlage oft von dem abwich, was im heutigen MT geboten wird. Die Diskussion darüber, ob die LXX-Version oder der MT die ältere Textform bietet, die v.a. A. Schenker angestoßen hat, ist nicht entschieden.[41] Hinzu kommt, dass die griechische Textüberlieferung uneinheitlich ist. Codex Vaticanus weist in 2.Regn 10–3.Regn 2,11 und 3.Regn 22–4.Regn 25 deutliche Zeichen der am MT orientierten sog. *kaige*-Redaktion auf, so dass diese Abschnitte nicht als älteste Übersetzung gelten.[42] Stattdessen ist wohl der sog. antiochenische Text ursprünglicher.[43] Zum gegenwärtigen Zeitpunkt ist zudem nicht einmal klar, ob die vier Bücher ursprünglich von einem oder mehreren Übersetzern stammen, auch über Zeit und Ort der Übersetzung können nur Vermutungen angestellt werden.

Für das dritte Buch ist als Charakteristikum festzuhalten, dass es im Vergleich zum MT eine ganze Reihe von Textumstellungen gibt, die sowohl intentional, als auch von einer anderen Vorlage her erklärt werden können.[44] Dies ließ sich bei der Position des Weihspruches in 8,53 sehen, außerdem gibt es in Kap. 8 gegenüber dem MT sowohl Zufügungen als auch Auslassungen (V. 49 + 50), ebenso Erleichterungen wie einen besseren syntaktischen Abschluss (V. 52).[45] Offenbar spiegeln sich in beiden Versionen unabhängige redaktionelle Bearbeitungen, wobei im Fall des griechischen Textes nicht immer klar ist, auf welcher Ebene—Vorlage oder Übersetzung—diese stattgefunden hat.[46]

Zu den wichtigsten Unterschieden gehört, dass die LXX durchgängig die Differenz zwischen Himmel und Erde betont. So wird in V. 32 + 34 + 39 + 45 + 49 jeweils die Präposition ἐκ hinzugefügt; Gott erhört die Gebete nicht im Himmel, sondern „aus" dem Himmel. Parallel dazu steht in V. 39+43+49 ἐξ ἑτοίμου κατοικητηρίου σου, wo die hebräische Vorlage ebenfalls keine Präposition bietet. Das erleichtert den syntaktischen Anschluss und verstärkt zugleich die Distanz zu Gott und dem

---

41. Schenker 2000, passim; ders. 2004; kritisch dazu z.B. Pietsch 2007, und van Keulen 2005.

42. Zur mutmaßlichen Buchteilung in 3.Regn 2,11, vgl. Bösenecker 2000, 86–87.

43. Fernández Marcos 2004; ders. 1994.

44. S. z.B. Rehm 1937, 24–8; Burney 1903, xx–xxxi und die Einzelbeobachtungen bei Bösenecker 2000, passim. Zu den Ergänzungen in Kap 2 s. Tov 1999.

45. Bösenecker 2000, 184.

46. Dazu Bösenecker 2000, 98 + 177, der aber meist eine Redaktion der hebräischen Vorlage vermutet.

himmlischen Heiligtum. Durch ἕτοιμον κατοικητήριον wird überdies eine intertextuelle Verbindung zu Ex 15,17 geknüpft. Dort war מכון לשבתך mit ἕτοιμον κατοικητήριον übersetzt worden, was—im Zusammenspiel mit Ex 25,9+40—in der Exodus-LXX die Vorstellung eines präexistenten Heiligtums evoziert. In der Königtümer-LXX wird diese freie Wiedergabe offenbar zustimmend aufgenommen, wie die dreimalige Wiederholung zeigt. Die Orientierung an der Exodus-LXX zeigt sich überdies an der Verwendung von γνόφος für ערפל „(Wolken-)Dunkel" in V. 53, vgl. Ex 20,21.

Zu weiteren Differenzen zählt, dass V. 23 durch die Verwendung des Singulars δοῦλος auf (den in V. 24 genannten) David zielt, dem Gottes Aufmerksamkeit gilt, nicht dem ganzen Volk. Da auch das abhängige Partizip ההלכים im Sg. wiedergegeben wurde, kann dies kein einfacher Übersetzungsfehler sein.[47] In 8,38 hat die LXX eine universalistischere Position „jedes Gebet, jede Bitte, die von irgend einem Menschen ergeht," während diese im MT durch לכל עמך ישראל eingeschränkt ist. Auch die Differenz von V. 42 lässt sich aus der Diaspora heraus verstehen: Nach LXX beten die Ausländer „zu diesem Ort" hin (εἰς τὸν τόπον τοῦτον), nicht zu diesem Haus, wie das hebräische בית nahe legen würde. Da sonst in 3.Regn 8 immer οἶκος zur Wiedergabe von בית steht, kann dies kein Zufall sein. Überdies soll sich Gott in V. 50 nicht über „dein Volk" (לעמך), sondern über „ihre Sünden" (ταῖς ἀδικίαις αὐτῶν) erbarmen; auch diese Änderung ist gut vor dem Hintergrund einer Existenz in der Diaspora verstehen. In V. 41 sind im MT erneut die Zusagen durch „Israel" einschränkt, in der LXX werden sie mit „welcher (s.c. der Ausländer) um deines Namens willen aus fernem Land kommt" inhaltlich weiter differenziert. Nach der LXX können also alle Fremden direkt zum Ort des Tempels beten (V. 41+42). Interesse am Tempel findet sich überdies in der Zufügung in V. 65, wonach das von Salomo gefeierte Fest ausdrücklich „in dem Haus, das er gebaut hat" stattfand.

Beim eingangs skizzierten Problembestand der Königtümer-LXX ist nicht eindeutig zu sagen, welche Differenz auf eine andere Vorlage oder auf den Gestaltungswillen des Übersetzers zurückgeht, auch ist nicht immer klar, ob der MT die frühere oder spätere Version ist. Wahrscheinlich muss man tatsächlich von parallel laufenden Bearbeitungsprozessen

---

47. Bösenecker 2000, 174, spricht diese Diskrepanz ohne weitere Begründung der Vorlage zu.

ausgehen. Immerhin ist deutlich, dass die LXX eine andere, eher in die Diaspora-Situation passende Aussage hat.

Kehrt man zum griechischen Weihspruch in V. 53a zurück, so ist zunächst die Frage nach Alter und Position im Vergleich zum MT zu klären. Es scheint mir eindeutig zu sein, dass die griechische Version sich auf eine andere hebräische Vorlage stützt. Dies wird auch durch eine Reihe von Stellen nahe gelegt, an denen LXX parallel zu Lesarten in 4QKgs geht (s. oben zu 8,16). Für die Annahme eines höheren Alters im Vergleich zum MT ergibt sich ein Argument aus dem Vergleich mit den entsprechenden Stellen in der Chronik. Hier fällt auf, dass im MT 1.Kön 8,12–3 bis in die Einzelheiten parallel zu 2.Chr 6,1–2 geht.[48] Demgegenüber weicht die Chronik-LXX in 6,2 aber so weit vom MT ab, dass man um die Annahme einer anderen Vorlage kaum herumkommt; hier ist vom „Wohnen deines heiligen Namens," nicht vom „erhabenen Haus" die Rede. Das spricht dafür, dass im MT 1.Kön 8,12–3 und 2.Chr 6,1–2 parallel überarbeitet wurden, wohingegen die LXX jeweils eine ältere Version hat.[49]

Als Argument hinsichtlich der Position des Spruches war bereits genannt worden, dass die späte Stellung und damit veränderte Abfolge von Gebet und Weihspruch in der LXX besser zu der Notiz in 8,54 passt, wonach Salomo „dieses ganze Gebet und Flehen" vollendet habe, was als Erleichterung der LXX anzusehen ist. Ein weiterer Hinweis ergibt sich aus dem Vergleich mit 2.Sam 7. J. Bösenecker konnte zeigen, dass die griechische Version von 3.Regn 8 exakt der Struktur von 2.Regn 6 + 7 entspricht: Beide weisen die Abfolge (1) Überführung der Lade, (2) Gebet Davids, (3) Hinweis auf den Exodus, (4) Dynastie-Spruch, (5) Segen auf; 3.Regn 8 folgt demnach dem Muster der Nathansweissagung. Das spricht für die sekundäre Stellung in 3.Regn.[50]

Die Beobachtung wird dadurch unterstützt, dass die Königtümer-LXX ein eigenes tempeltheologisches Interesse hat. Dieses konnte bereits in den Differenzen in 3.Regn 8 gesehen werden, es ist aber auch in 2.Regn 7 (2.Sam 7) deutlich. Hier wird die Dynastieverheißung (οἶκος) auf den Bau des Tempels (οἶκος) hin gelesen bzw. gedeutet.[51] 2.Sam 7 LXX zielt

---

48. Die einzige Differenz ist die Lesung von ואני statt בנה in 2.Chr 6,2.

49. Gegen Hognesius 2003, 102 der die LXX ohne Diskussion als „Greek corruption" erklärt und dafür auf Allen 1974 verweist. Dort aber wird gar nicht auf die Frage einer anderen Vorlage eingegangen (Bd. 1, S. 122; Bd. 2, S. 36).

50. Bösenecker 2000, 186–87.

51. So Rehm 1937, 23; ausführlich jetzt Pietsch 2003, 176–85: „die Dynastiever-

demnach auf Salomo,[52] diese Verheißung wird in 1.Kön 8 eingelöst. Auch von daher ist die andere Anordnung des Weihspruches in der griechischen Version als theologisch motiviert plausibel: Im Gebet Salomos wird zunächst der vollzogene Bau des Tempels (οἶκος) gefeiert. Der Weihspruch bezieht sich dann wieder neu auf die Dynastie (οἶκος), wenn Salomo Gott bittet: Baue mir nun ein Haus, um *von neuem* darin zu wohnen. Insofern ist auch verständlich, warum Salomo in der LXX *nach* dem Bau des Tempels Gott um den Bau des Hauses bittet; ein messianischer Unterton ist überdies kaum verkennbar. Für die griechische Version müsste man folglich eher von einem *Dynastieweihspruch* als von einem Tempelweihspruch reden.[53]

Die Parallelisierung mit 2.Sam 7 ist auch in einer weiteren Hinsicht aufschlussreich. W.M. Schniedewind hat darauf hingewiesen, dass in 4Q174 (Florilegien) III,1–3 die Verse 2.Sam 7,10 und Ex 15,17 nebeneinander zitiert werden. Offenbar gab es einen festen Traditionszusammenhang dieser Texte, so dass leicht verständlich ist, warum auch die griechische Übersetzung intertextuelle Bezüge zu Ex 15 erkennen lässt. In Aufnahme einer alten These von H.St. J. Thackeray[54] kann man überlegen, ob nicht der Hinweis am Ende von 3.Regn 8,53a: οὐκ ἰδοὺ αὕτη γέγραπται ἐν βιβλίῳ τῆς ᾠδῆς auf genau diese ᾠδή (Ex 15,1) verweisen soll.[55] Auch dann, wenn tatsächlich eine Verlesung von ישר zu שיר im Hintergrund dieser Notiz stehen sollte (s.o.), wird sich der Übersetzer etwas bei der Erwähnung des Liederbuches gedacht haben.[56]

Damit ist deutlich, dass sich die griechische Version von 1.Kön 8 in einem Bezugsgeflecht mit anderen Texten befindet, in dem sie eigene Aussageakzente setzt: Sie knüpft zum einen an die Vorstellung des präexistenten Heiligtums an (Ex 15,17), zum anderen an die des Wohnens Gottes im Dunkel (Ex 20,21; 2.Sam 22,10: ערפל/γνόφος). Die vom hebräischen Text

---

heißung (wurde) in der Septuaginta unter der Leitfrage nach dem Bau des Tempels (V1–7) gelesen" (S. 185).

52. So Schniedewind 1994, 113.
53. Ähnlich Schenker 2000, 134–35, Argument (e).
54. Thackeray 1927, 46–51.
55. Bösenecker 2000, 186, denkt an den Psalter oder einzelne Pss wie 45; 89 oder 132.
56. Ein Kandidat für das „Lied" ist auch Davids Danklied 2.Sam 22 par. Ps 18(17), da dort mit der Erwähnung des Dunkels (ערפל) unter Gottes Füßen (V. 10), ein vergleichbarer Vorstellungszusammenhang gegeben ist. Beide werden im Titel ᾠδή genannt.

her vorgegebene Aussage vom Wohnen Gottes wird also aufgenommen, aber auf das himmlisch-unanschauliche Wohnen gemünzt; dies erneut in Übereinstimmung mit der Exodus und Deuteronomium-LXX, wo durchgängig die Rede vom Wohnen Gottes vermieden wird.[57]

Dazu gehört auch, dass Gott dennoch für die Schaffung der Sonne zuständig ist; er hat sie bekannt gemacht. Dies ist eine schöpfungstheologische Aussage über die Sonne, die sowohl in hellenistischer Zeit (so Sirach 42,15-6) als auch früher (so Ps 19,2-7) möglich ist. Von daher ist also kein Argument für die Datierung des Textes zu finden.

Möglich ist aber, dass die Aussage über die Abhängigkeit der Sonne mit einem polemischen Unterton verstanden werden konnte. Im ptolemäischen Ägypten war die Legitimität der Könige als „Sohn des Re" (υἱὸς τοῦ Ἡλίου, so die Übersetzung des Thronnamens) grundlegend; durch die Installation von Geburtshäusern (Mammisi) mit entsprechenden Zeremonien, z.B. in Edfu, wurde diese Tradition trotz des neu eingeführten Sarapis-Kultes wach gehalten.[58] Seit Ptolemaios I. stellte sich die Dynastie in die Traditionslinie der Göttlichkeit Alexanders und übernahm daher z.B. auf Münzen Kennzeichnungen von Ammon-Re oder Helios; offizielle Denkmäler tragen zuoberst die geflügelte Sonnenscheibe.[59] Auch in den nicht unmittelbar mit der Königsideologie verbundenen Kulten breiten sich solare Elemente aus; für die Götter wird jährlich das Fest einer Vereinigung mit der Sonnenscheibe als nötig gesehen.[60] Zwar verliert der direkte Kult des Gottes Re deutlich an Einfluss, doch die solare Dimension ist über diese Kombination mit anderen Göttern und vor allem über Horus, der den Sonnenlauf symbolisiert, allgegenwärtig. Insofern ist die Aussage des griechischen Weihspruchs, dass der Gott Israels die Sonne bekannt gemacht hat, ein unerhörter Anspruch.

Eine weitere Dimension ergibt sich, wenn es im jüdischen Tempel in Leontopolis tatsächlich keine Menora, sondern eine goldene Lampe als Symbol der Sonne gab (JosAnt VII, 429).[61] Das würde bedeuten, dass die Aussage des griechischen Tempelweihspruches sogar Einfluss auf die Symbolik dieses Tempels hatte.

---

57. S. z.B. Joosten 2000, 39–40.
58. S. dazu z.B. Koenen 1983, 143–90; Hölbl 2004, 11; 229–37.
59. Hölbl 2004, 86; Koch 1993, 497–500.
60. Koch 1993, 506–7.
61. So vermutend Hayward 1982, 434–37, der auf Ps 84,11f. als möglicher biblischer Belegstelle hinweist.

4. Fazit: Salomos Tempel und die Sonne

Aus dem oben gesagten wird deutlich, dass der LXX-Übersetzer offenbar eine vom MT abweichende Vorlage hatte. Diese ist im konkreten Wortlaut nicht mehr sicher zu rekonstruieren, auch, weil in die Übersetzung diasporatypische Aussagen und ein eigenes tempeltheologisches Interesse geflossen sind: Zum einen wird eine Beziehung zu Tempelvorstellungen der Pentateuch-Septuaginta hergestellt, zum anderen knüpft an die tempelorientierte LXX-Interpretation der Nathansweissagung angeknüpft. Letzteres ist wohl auch für die neue Position des Spruchs nach dem Gebet verantwortlich.

Die Vorlage enthielt sicher den intensiv diskutierten Bezug zwischen Sonne und JHWH. In der LXX wurde daraus eine Aussage der Unterordnung der Sonne unter die Macht des Gottes Israels, die sich vielleicht polemisch mit der ptolemäischen Umwelt auseinandersetzt. Die ungewöhnliche Syntax des mutmaßlichen hebräischen Textes der Vorlage lässt nicht sicher entscheiden, ob der ursprüngliche Anfang des Spruches erhalten ist; dann müsste die Sonne als Subjekt einer Aussage über JHWH gesehen werden. Wahrscheinlicher ist, dass der Beginn nicht mehr erhalten ist, wir es also mit dem zweiten Teil einer chiastisch formulierten Aussage zu tun haben. Diese konnte der Übersetzer durch die im Griechischen mögliche Verwendung des betonten Akkusativs am Satzanfang abgetrennt haben, zumal so eine klarere Struktur entstand.[62]

Wegen der textgeschichtlichen Situation der Königebücher ist kein sicheres Urteil möglich, ob die Textfassung, die dem heutigen MT zugrunde liegt, den fraglichen Passus enthielt und aus inhaltlichen Gründen ausgeschieden hat, oder ob der Spruch nur im von der LXX repräsentierten Stratum der Textgeschichte zu finden war. Die jüngere textkritische Forschung an den Königebüchern ist daher über diese einfache Alternative hinaus und rechnet mit einer Phase von „intensive earlier editorial activity."[63]

Für die eingangs skizzierte Verwendung der LXX-Version des Weihspruches hat das Ergebnis Konsequenzen: Zum einen muss künftig klarer getrennt werden, ob Aussagen über die hebräische oder griechische Textform gemacht werden; das bisherige Vermischen von LXX-Lesarten, ver-

---

62. Dies mit Schenker 2000, 134, Argument (a).
63. So Trebolle Barrera 1991, 299.

muteten Vorlagen und Redaktionsstufen des MT sollte unterbleiben. Aus methodischen Gründen ist es m.E. nicht haltbar, die kaum zu sichernde Rückübersetzung von 3.Regn 8,53 zur Grundlage einer Aussage über alte Vorstellungen über den Tempel zu machen. Für die Frage nach der Gottheit, die vor JHWH in Jerusalem verehrt wurde, sollte die Septuaginta künftig nicht mehr herangezogen werden.

Literatur

Allen, Leslie C. 1974. *The Greek Chronicles. The Relation of the Septuagint of I and II Chronicles to the Masoretic Text; Part 1. The Translator's Craft; Part 2. Textual Criticism.* VTSup 25, 27. Leiden: Brill.

Barthélemy, Dominique. 1982. *Critique textuelle de l'Ancien Testament.* OBO 50.1. Göttingen: Vandenhoeck & Ruprecht; Freiburg: Universitätsverlag.

Born, A. van den. 1965. „Zum Tempelweihspruch. (1 Kg viii 12f)." *OTS* 14:235–44.

Bösenecker, Jobst. 2000. „Text und Redaktion. Untersuchungen zum hebräischen und griechischen Text von 1 Könige 1–11." ThD diss., Rostock.

Burney, Charles F. 1903. *Notes on the Hebrew Text of Kings.* Oxford: Clarendon.

Dietrich, Walter. 1997. *Die frühe Königszeit in Israel. 10. Jahrhundert v. Chr.* Biblische Enzyklopädie 3. Stuttgart: Kohlhammer.

Dus, Jan. 1960. „Gibeon–Eine Kultstätte des ŠMŠ und die Stadt des benjaminitischen Schicksals." *VT* 10:353–74.

Fernández Marcos, Natalio. 1994. *Scribes and Translators. Septuagint and Old Latin in the Books of Kings.* VTSup 54. Leiden: Brill.

———. 2004. „Der antiochenische Text der griechischen Bibel in den Samuel- und Königsbüchern." Seiten 177–213 in Band 2 *Im Brennpunkt. Die Septuaginta. Studien zur Entstehung und Bedeutung der Griechischen Bibel.* Hrsg. von Siegfried Kreuzer und Jürgen Peter Lesch. BWANT 161. Stuttgart: Kohlhammer.

Gooding, David W. 1969. "Problems of Text and Midrash in the Third Book of Reigns." *Text* 7:1–29.

Görg, Manfred. 1974. „Die Gattung des sogenannten Tempelweihspruchs. (1 Kg 8,12f.)." *UF* 6:55–63.

Hartenstein, Friedhelm. 2007. „Sonnengott und Wettergott." Seiten 53–69 in *Mein Haus wird ein Bethaus für alle Völker genannt werden (Jes*

56,7). *Judentum seit der Zeit des Zweiten Tempels in Geschichte, Literatur und Kult. FS Thomas Willi.* Hrsg. von Julia Männchen und Torsten Reiprich. Neukirchen-Vluyn: Neukirchener Verlag.

Hayward, Robert. 1982. "The Jewish Temple at Leontopolis." *JJS* 33:429–443.

Hognesius, Kjell. 2003. *The Text of 2 Chronicles 1–16. A Critical Edition with Textual Commentary.* ConBOT 51. Stockholm: Almqvist & Wiksell.

Hölbl, Günther. 2004. *Geschichte des Ptolemäerreiches. Politik, Ideologie und religiöse Kultur von Alexander dem Großen bis zur römischen Eroberung.* Darmstadt: Wissenschaftliche Buchgesellschaft.

Irsigler, Hubert. 2004. „Vom Mythos zur Bildsprache. Eine Einführung am Beispiel der ‚Solarisierung' JHWHs." Seiten 9–42 in *Mythisches in biblischer Bildsprache. Gestalt und Verwandlung in Prophetie und Psalmen.* Hrsg. von Hubert Irsigler und Eberhard Bons. QD 209. Freiburg: Herder.

Janowski, Bernd. 1995. „JHWH und der Sonnengott. Aspekte der Solarisierung JHWHs in vorexilischer Zeit." Seiten 214–41 in *Pluralismus und Identität.* Hrsg. von Joachim Mehlhausen. VWGTh 8. Gütersloh: Gütersloher Verlag.

Jenni, Ernst. 1992. *Die hebräischen Präpositionen I. Die Präposition Beth.* Stuttgart: Kohlhammer.

Joosten, Jan. 2000. „Une théologie de la Septante? Réflexions méthodologique sur l'interpretation de la version greque." *RTP* 132:31–46.

Joüon, Paul, und Takamitsu Muraoka. 1996. *A Grammar of Biblical Hebrew. Part 1. Orthography and Phonetics. Part 2. Morphology.* SubBi 14. Rome: Pontifical Biblical Institute.

Keel, Othmar. 2002. „Der salomonische Tempelweihspruch. Beobachtungen zum religionsgeschichtlichen Kontext des ersten Jerusalemer Tempels." Seiten 9–23 in *Gottesstadt und Gottesgarten. Zur Geschichte und Theologie des Jerusalemer Tempels.* Hrsg. von Othmar Keel und Erich Zenger. QD 191. Freiburg: Herder.

———. 2007. *Die Geschichte Jerusalems und die Entstehung des Monotheismus.* OLB 4.1. Göttingen: Vandenhoeck & Ruprecht.

Keulen, Percy S. F. van. 2005. *Two Versions of the Solomon Narrative. An Inquiry into the Relationship between MT 1 Kgs. 2–11 and LXX 3 Reg. 2–11.* VTSup 104. Leiden: Brill.

Knauf, Ernst Axel. 1997. „Le roi est mort, vive le roi! A Biblical Argument for the Historicity of Solomon." Seiten 81–95 in *The Age of Solomon. Scholarship at the Turn of the Millennium.* Hrsg. von Lowell K. Handy. SHCANE 11. Leiden: Brill.

Koch, Klaus. 1984. „בון." *ThWAT* 4:95–107.

——. 1993. *Geschichte der ägyptischen Religion. Von den Pyramiden bis zu den Mysterien der Isis.* Stuttgart: Kohlhammer.

Koenen, Ludwig. 1983. „Die Adaptation ägyptischer Königsideologie am Ptolemäerhof." Seiten 143–90 in *Egypt and the Hellenistic World.* Hrsg. von Edmond van't Dack. StudHell 27. Leuven: Katholieke Universiteit Leuven.

Loretz, Oswald. 1974. „Der Torso eines kanaanäischen Tempelweihspruchs." *UF* 6:478–80.

Muraoka, Takamitsu. 1985. *Emphatic Words and Structures in Biblical Hebrew.* Jerusalem: Magnes.

Noth, Martin. 1968. *Könige Buch 1, Kapitel 1–16.* BKAT 9,1. Neukirchen-Vluyn: Neukirchener Verlag.

Peterca, Vladimir. 1987. „Ein midraschartiges Auslegungsbeispiel zugunsten Salomos." *BZ* 31:270–75.

Pietsch, Michael. 2003. *„Dieser ist der Sproß Davids…". Studien zur Rezeptionsgeschichte der Nathanverheißung im alttestamentlichen, zwischentestamentlichen und neutestamentlichen Schrifttum.* WMANT 100. Neukirchen-Vluyn: Neukirchener Verlag.

——. 2007. „Von Königen und Königtümern. Eine Untersuchung zur Textgeschichte der Königsbücher." *ZAW* 119:39–58.

Rehm, Martin. 1937. *Textkritische Untersuchungen zu den Parallelstellen der Samuel- und Königsbücher und der Chronik.* ATA 13.3. Münster: Aschendorff.

Schenker, Adrian. 2000. *Septante et texte massorétique dans l'histoire la plus ancienne du texte de 1 Rois 2–14.* CRB 48. Paris: Gabalda.

——. 2004. *Älteste Textgeschichte der Königsbücher. Die hebräische Vorlage der ursprünglichen Septuaginta als älteste Textform der Königsbücher.* OBO 199. Göttingen: Vandenhoeck & Ruprecht; Freiburg: Universitätsverlag.

Schniedewind, William M. 1994. "Textual Criticism and Theological Interpretation. The Pro-Temple Tendenz in the Greek Text of Samuel-Kings." *HTR* 87:107–16.

Stolz, Fritz. 1970. *Strukturen und Figuren im Kult von Jerusalem. Studien zur altorientalischen, vor- und frühisraelitischen Religion.* BZAW 118. Berlin: de Gruyter.

Taylor, J. Glen. 1993. *Yahweh and the Sun. Biblical and Archaeological Evidence for Sun Worship in Ancient Israel.* JSOTSup 111. Sheffield: JSOT Press.

Thackeray, Henry Saint John. 1921. *The Septuagint and Jewish Worship. A Study on Origins.* London: Milford.

———. 1927. *Some Aspects of the Greek Old Testament.* London: Allen & Unwin.

Tov, Emanuel. 1997. *The Text-Critical Use of the Septuagint in Biblical Research.* 2nd ed. revised and enlarged. JBS 8. Jerusalem: Simor.

———. 1999. „The Septuagint Additions (‚Miscellanies') in 1 Kings 2 (3 Reigns 2)." Seiten 549–70 in *The Greek and Hebrew Bible. Collected Essays on the Septuagint.* VTSup 72. Leiden: Brill.

Trebolle Barrera, Julio. 1991. „The Text-Critical Use of the Septuagint in the Books of Kings." Seiten 285–99 in *VII Congress of the International Organization for Septuagint and Cognate Studies, Leuven, 1989.* Hrsg. von Claude E. Cox. SCS 31. Atlanta: Scholars Press.

Wellhausen, Julius. 1889. *Die Composition des Hexateuchs und der historischen Bücher des Alten Testaments.* 2. Druck mit Nachträgen. Berlin: Reimer.

Würthwein, Ernst. 1977. *Die Bücher der Könige. 1.Könige 1–16.* ATD 11.1. Göttingen: Vandenhoeck & Ruprecht.

8
Deuteronomists in the Septuagint of the Historical Books?

1. The Problem

In 1943, Martin Noth formulated his influential theory about an author and redactor of the books of Joshua–Kings he called "the Deuteronomist," a theory that has since triggered lively discussions on how to determine the range and amount of this Deuteronomistic activity.[1] Frank Moore Cross, Rudolf Smend, and their subsequent successors provided the next important steps in developing these theories, showing that there was not one single Deuteronomist but several redactors at work, each with his own specific intentions.[2]

Beginning in the 1960s on, the search for Deuteronomistic elements expanded into writings outside the corpus of the historical books. Werner H. Schmidt located them in the book of Amos; Ernest W. Nicholson and Winfried Thiel singled out a Deuteronomistic redaction in Jeremiah; and scholars successfully detected Deuteronomistic influence even in books as late as Second Zechariah.[3] This trend was met by a tendency—especially in German scholarship—to assume a very complex history of redaction of most biblical books with only a very thin stratum of old material and several successive acts of expanding and reworking these texts. To give but one example: a recently published dissertation on the book of Hosea ascribes only six sayings to the oldest stratum of the book, which then in the next five hundred years grew into the version as now represented in

---

1. See M. Rösel 2010 for an expanded German version of this sketch. For overviews of the history of research, see Thiel 2007, 63–81; and Römer and de Pury 2000.
2. Cross 1980; Smend 1971.
3. Schmidt 1965; Nicholson 1970; Thiel 1973; 1981; Person 1993.

the MT.[4] This means that on the level of the Hebrew text, scholars assume redactional activities inspired by ideas from the book of Deuteronomy as late as Hellenistic times. For example, Odil Hannes Steck assumed "wandering Levites" as the kernel of a Deuteronomistic movement around 200 BCE.[5] The prevailing impression has been of a school of Deuteronomists working with the texts from late preexilic times well into the Maccabean era.[6] Some scholars are so trained in detecting traces of this work that they are able to distinguish up to ten layers even in short texts.[7]

The criteria for determining Deuteronomistic strata are based on observations in the texts themselves, which led to lists of typical Deuteronomistic formulae or expressions. In Germany, most influential has been Winfried Thiel's work and in the English-speaking world, the book written by Moshe Weinfeld, containing forty-five pages of Deuteronomistic phraseology.[8] The work of these scholars led to the impression that every occurrence of a specific phrase implied that this text necessarily stemmed from a Deuteronomistic pen, even if such a conclusion is not appropriate given the context of the verse in question.[9] Other scholars have voiced important objections against this kind of redactional criticism; the German scholar Norbert Lohfink, for example, warned against a "pandeuteronomistic" view.[10] David Carr's stress on the importance of oral transmission

---

4. Rudnig-Zelt 2006, but see the principle criticism of an approach like hers by Scherer 2005.

5. Steck 1967.

6. See Schwienhorst 1986, 137–46, who finds in Josh 6 extensions by several hands in the tradition of the Temple Scroll from Qumran. He does not consider that these extensions are also witnessed in the LXX, although this translation is usually dated to earlier times. A similar result concerning late Deuteronomists can be found in Knauf 2000, 393.

7. See Achenbach 1991, who sees so many layers in Deut 5–11 that it is not possible to count or assign them: "Wir haben es nicht mit einem 'DtrD' zu tun, sondern mit einer Vielzahl von Schülern" (288).

8. See the summary in Thiel 1981, 91–115, entitled "The Character of the Deuteronomistic Redaction" with a collection of criteria. Weinfeld 1992, appendix A, 320–65.

9. See, e.g., Carasik 2009, on the Joseph story, who finds traces of Deuteronomistic work even in formulas which are not typical Deuteronomistic according to Weinfeld. For a criticism of such an approach see Knauf 2000, 389, who points, e.g., to "Dtr theology in Priestly style" in Num 25:6–18; 31:1–54, or "Priestly theology in Dtr style" in Gen 15 or Deut 9:4–6. However, he does not consider whether it is still meaningful to use those labels like "Priestly" or "Dtr."

10. Lohfink 1995, 317; see also the studies collected in Schearing and McKenzie

of biblical texts causes a necessary hesitation in the confident detection of different layers of Deuteronomistic work.[11]

After the publication of the texts found near Qumran and new insights from research on the LXX—especially concerning the so-called Antiochene text—the problem has become even more complex.[12] Important developments to note:

1. There have been different editions of several books. The examples of Samuel and Jeremiah are well known and the subjects of lively debate, as are the Greek versions of Exodus, Kings, or Job.
2. Ancient authors tended to rewrite biblical texts, as evident in books such as the Temple Scroll, the Genesis Apocryphon, or the Reworked Pentateuch 4Q158+364–367.[13]
3. Finally, these texts reveal a developing interest in revising texts to bring different texts in line with a kind of "master copy." This process eventually led to proto-Masoretic texts and was moreover extended to translations into Greek, as is evident in the so-called kaige-texts.[14]

Thus, there are two overlapping developments, one internal and the other external. On the one hand is the detection of Deuteronomistic redactions of the text, which works with internal data from the texts themselves. On the other hand is the emerging insight, based on newly found texts or from synoptic comparisons and which is therefore comparative—that is, external—that those reworkings of the texts are in fact attested until the second century BCE. This leads to the question whether some of the redactional activities in the third or second century can be traced back to late branches of a Deuteronomistic "movement" or "school." This question is not as absurd as it may sound if one remembers that there are in fact hints pointing in this direction. Daniel 9 is an apt example, a chapter that deals with the problem of the seventy years of Jer 25; despite its late date, this text

---

1999, with L. S. Schearing's statement: "the growing epidemic of pan-Deuteronomism that has infected scholarship" (13). Lohfink's German article can be found in this collection in a shortened translation into English. For a similar argumentation, see Ausloos 1997.

11. Carr 2006.

12. For the Antiochene text see Fernández Marcos 2004.

13. See Tov 2008a, on the Reworked Pentateuch, who sees the text as a "biblical manuscript" with "exegetical additions" (21).

14. Lange 2009.

is saturated with Deuteronomistic thoughts and terminology.[15] Another important factor is the chronology of the Pentateuch and its alteration in the middle of the second century, a fact evident in the Masoretic text's dating of the reconsecration of the temple in 164 BCE.[16] Because Deuteronomistic and Maccabean or Hasmonean interests converged at this point, it is not impossible to think of Deuteronomists in Hellenistic times.[17]

2. Examples from the Book of Joshua

As an initial offering, I would like to discuss some examples from the Septuagint that seem to fit into the scheme of typical Deuteronomistic activity. Here the book of Joshua is of special interest. On the one hand, this text has been a mainstay in Deuteronomistic studies; scholars have seen at work in this text reworkings of older texts by Dtr H, Dtr N, and final Priestly redactions.[18] Moreover, it is still debated whether Joshua was once intended to be the ending of a Hexateuch narrating the history of Israel from the creation to the conquest of the land.[19]

Besides these questions of redactional and compositional activity, there are problems on the text-critical level because the LXX and fragments found in Qumran show important deviations from the Hebrew text as found in the MT.[20] The latest extensive study on this book by the Dutch scholar Michael van der Meer concluded that these deviations can be explained as secondary compared with the MT version.[21] He claims that text-critical and literary-critical hypotheses must be kept separate as long

---

15. Lohfink 1995, 371, speaks of an imitation of the "Deueronomistic prose of Jeremiah," because he assumes that in the library of the temple in Jerusalem the whole canon of Deuteronomistic writings was present and served for educational purposes.

16. See my paper "The Chronological System of Genesis-Septuagint (Genesis 5 and 11)," ch. 4 in this volume.

17. See Römer and de Pury 2000, 140, who were asking for criteria for differentiating between "the 'real' editors of DH and the epigones."

18. See Schwienhorst 1986; Cf. also more recently van der Meer 2004, who assumes only three redactional layers.

19. Becker 2006, 155–56, in his view Joshua was part of a Hexateuch (but without Genesis and Deuteronomy), which later became the Enneateuch. See Schmid 2008, 158–59, for a concise introduction into the discussion.

20. See, e.g., Tov 1999a; M. Rösel 2001 [ch. 6 in this volume]; for the problem of rewriting material from the book of Joshua see Tov 1999b.

21. van der Meer 2004.

as possible and therefore postulates that the LXX and the Qumran texts are witnesses to the later stages of the reception of the Hebrew text. Others (e.g., A. Graeme Auld, Kristin De Troyer) have judged that the differences between the versions are explained best by assuming different editions of the text; hence the LXX would also be a witness for redactional activity.[22] A few examples shall serve to illustrate the problems.

2.1. LXX Has a Longer Text

In some instances, the Greek text includes additions that sound typically Deuteronomistic. Thus in Josh 9:27 the MT includes the formula אל־המקום אשר יבחר ("in the place that he should choose") while the Septuagint has the longer text εἰς τὸν τόπον ὃν ἐὰν ἐκλέξηται κύριος, thus adding the reference to the Lord.[23] This fuller text is known from Deut 12:5, 11, 14, but it is important to notice that in the book of Deuteronomy the Hebrew formula usually has אלהיכם (your God) added after the Tetragram. This is also reflected in LXX Deuteronomy: in Deut 12:14, 26 LXX the translator has even added ὁ θεός σου, even though his source text does not read it. This means that the addition in Josh 9:27 cannot be a mere harmonization with the text of Deuteronomy.

Joshua 24:4 includes an even longer addition in the LXX: καὶ ἐγένοντο ἐκεῖ εἰς ἔθνος μέγα καὶ πολὺ καὶ κραταιόν ("and they became there a great and populous and mighty nation") is added, which reflects the creed from Deut 26:5–6. Again, it is not a direct citation from LXX Deuteronomy because there are some differences in the texts.[24]

The same phenomenon can be found in the section on Joshua's altar in 8:30–35 that, in the LXX, has been transferred to a new location following 9:2a. The translation in several instances refers to Deut 27:5–6 and furthermore explicitly mentions the τὸ δευτερονόμιον νόμον Μωυσῆ ("*deuteronomion*, a law of Moses") from Deut 17:18 (note the double translation of תורה in משנה תורת משה).[25]

---

22. De Troyer 2005; Auld 2005, who assumes that the *Vorlage* of the LXX did differ from the MT text type in many instances.
23. With Tov 2008b, 405. Unless otherwise noted, all translations are mine.
24. Similar Auld 2005, 222, who only notes the differences and sees the text as "substantial LXX plus" without further explanation.
25. With Auld, 2005, 152; den Hertog 1996, 124–25.

Most interesting is an addition in the Greek text of chapter 6 after the curse upon Jericho's rebuilder (v. 26). The English translation of this addendum reads, "and so (building Jericho) did Hozan of Bethel; in Abiron his first-born he laid the foundation, and in his youngest surviving son he set up the gates of it."[26] The text alludes to 1 Kgs 16:34, which itself refers explicitly back to Josh 6.[27] The Greek text of Josh 6:26 is congruent with the LXX version of 3 Kgdms 16:34, although it is noticeable that the proper names do not correspond and that the younger son in 3 Kingdoms receives a name (Segoub).[28]

In the context of 1 Kgs 16, verse 34 appears like an addition; moreover, the text is missing in the Lucianic/Antiochene text.[29] Thus there are good reasons to conclude that *both* texts in question are secondary supplements with the aim of emphasizing the Deuteronomistic scheme of prophetical foretelling and historical fulfillment. It is not possible to reliably verify or falsify whether 1 Kgs 16:34 depends on Josh 6:26 in the version of the LXX or its *Vorlage*.[30] It is obvious, however, that there has been a redactional connection beyond the borders of a single book.[31] In addition, it is worth noting that in Josh 6 there are several important differences between LXX and MT, some of which seem to imply that the MT is the younger version. While the LXX speaks of God's immediate presence, the MT includes in several instances the addition that the Israelites are followed by the ark of the Lord (e.g., 6:7 + 13), thus avoiding the impression that God himself was present.

There is another expansion in LXX Joshua that establishes an interesting link between this book and the book of Judges. Again, content and style resemble Deuteronomistic features: the last verses of the Greek Joshua (24:33) inform the readers that the Israelites have taken the ark of God and carried it among them and that Phinehas was serving in the

---

26. Auld 2005, 139, and Tov 1978.

27. See Mazor 1988.

28. In Josh 6:26 it is possibly represented by διασωθέντι. Also 4Q175 (Testimonia) and 4Q379 22 (Joshua Apocryphon) refer to the rebuilding of the city, but in the form of a prophecy.

29. See the commentaries, Würthwein 1997, 203–4; Noth 1983, 355.

30. See the discussion in Mazor 1988, 23–24. According to Butler 1983, 66, it is obvious that the addition of the LXX in Josh 6:26 is "taken from 1 Kgs 16:34, another example of scribal interpretation of the text to show explicit fulfillment."

31. This phenomenon can also be seen in Josh 16:10, where a plus in the LXX alludes to 3 Kgdms 5:14b; see M. Rösel 2001, 203.

place of Eleazar his father until he died.³² A second note records that the Israelites were worshiping the gods Astarte and Astaroth and the gods of the people around them, which is why God has given them over in the hands of Eglon, the king of Moab. Especially this last verse clearly reflects the Deuteronomistic scheme of a history of deterioration in the time of the Judges. It refers to the story of Eglon, King of Moab in Judg 3:12–30, who has been killed by the judge Ehud. The mention of the Israelites serving the goddess Astaroth and other gods reflects Judg 10:6 or 1 Sam 7:4. But neither text is quoted verbatim, therefore the version in Josh 24:33 cannot be a mere harmonization but is a newly formulated text.

2.2. Characteristics of the Translation Technique of LXX Joshua

The examples mentioned until now are comparable because they are additions in comparison with the MT in Deuteronomistic style. But there are also cases in which the parent Hebrew text has been translated without longer additions yet still bears resemblance to the ideas of Deuteronomy. One characteristic feature of LXX Joshua is the differentiation between the people of Israel—λαός—and foreign people—ἔθνος—even if the *Vorlage* does not make this distinction (uses גוי for Israel).³³ The gods of these foreign nations have also been the target of the translator's desire for a nuanced rendering. In 23:7 MT, the Israelites are not allowed to remember or to swear by the names of the gods of the nations that remain among them (ובשם אלהיהם לא־תזכירו ולא תשביעו). The prohibition is even more pronounced in the LXX, where even the mentioning of their names is prohibited and therefore swearing by their names is not mentioned: καὶ τὰ ὀνόματα τῶν θεῶν αὐτῶν οὐκ ὀνομασθήσεται ἐν ὑμῖν. In 24:14, they are named clearly as τοὺς θεοὺς τοὺς ἀλλοτρίους, while the MT here only reads אלהים. The spirit of Deut 7 and its repulsion of foreign nations have guided the pen or brush of the translator.

Moreover, he has also emphasized the importance of the true altar chosen by the Lord via use of the word βωμός with its negative connotations in Josh 22:10–34: The Reubenites and the Gadites and the half-tribe

---

32. See Rofé 1982, for this text.
33. Thus in 3:17 or in 4:1. In 4:10–11 one can find the usual equation λαός-עם. In the same chapter the foreign peoples are called ἔθνη, even if they are עמים according to the MT (4:24). See also den Hertog 1996, 182.

of Manasseh are building an illegitimate altar—βωμός—by the river Jordan, not a lawful θυσιαστήριον, as the Hebrew מזבח is usually translated.[34]

2.3. MT Has a Longer Text

These examples may suffice to show that in the LXX of Joshua, it is possible to detect variant readings that show a specific resemblance to Deuteronomistic thinking. Even more interesting is the fact that, according to Emanuel Tov and others, some typical Deuteronomistic phrases are missing in LXX yet present in the MT.[35] Some examples may be in order. There are four instances where LXX has no counterpart for עבד יהוה in describing Moses (1:1; 1:15; 12:6; 22:4), while in fourteen cases it has been translated by παῖς κυρίου (22:2) (cf. θεράπων [1:2; 9:2]). This phenomenon has been explained by van der Meer as a stylistic improvement of the translator, but it is hard to understand why this should have happened in these four cases only and not in others.[36] It therefore seems more likely that the phrase was lacking in the *Vorlage* of LXX and has been inserted later in the MT as we have received it.[37]

Joshua 1:7 is one of the cases where both MT and LXX have עבד יהוה (or its equivalent). But in this verse LXX lacks the reference to the torah ככל־התורה, and since the Hebrew text has a masculine suffix, it is clear that the reference to the torah must be a later addition.[38]

The Hebrew text often includes longer insertions, for example, in 1:15, where the LXX reads "then you shall depart each one to his inheritance," while the MT reads, "then you shall return to the land of your possession and you shall possess it." In 24:17, the Hebrew has the clear Deuteronomistic formula referring to Egypt: מבית עבדים ואשר עשה לעינינו את־האתות הגדלות האלה "the house of bondage, and who made those wondrous signs before our very eyes," which again is not present in the LXX.[39] Finally, in

---

34. See van der Kooij 2003 on the problem of βωμός, and Schenker 2008 on this pericope.
35. See Tov 2008b, 402–4, for examples mentioned above.
36. Van der Meer 2004, 178–93.
37. See Josh 22:2, here Μωυσῆς ὁ παῖς κυρίου stands for משה עבד יהוה, with 22:4, where עבד יהוה is not represented.
38. Following Tov 2008b, 402. Already Smend 1971, n. 3, has judged that ככל־התורה must be a later insertion, but without commenting on its origin. Differently van der Meer 2004, 210–22, but he cannot solve the problem of the suffix (222).
39. Auld 2005, 224, explains the plus as a "midrashic expansion of MT."

23:16 the MT includes a partial quotation from Deut 11:17, while in the LXX the text is shorter and missing the second half of verse 16.

Finally, one of the main arguments for a late reworking of the Hebrew text comes from chapter 20, a description of the cities of refuge. Here the MT has in verses 4–6 an addition referring to Deut 4 and 19, while the shorter LXX is closer to the regulations of the Priestly code (Num 35). According to the results of the study by Alexander Rofé, it is clear that LXX represents the older version that has been expanded in the MT to align it with the laws of Deuteronomy.[40]

To sum up the observations from the book of Joshua: The different editions of the book, detected in both the Greek and Hebrew versions, obviously show traces of separate redactional activities that can be labeled as Deuteronomistic. It should be noted that scholars do not agree on the question of whether the Deuteronomistic elements represent the translator´s activity or reflect a different *Vorlage*.[41] But this is not of importance for the problem of late Deuteronomistic reworkings of the text. Even if one could attribute every single deviation to the Hebrew *Vorlage* (which I doubt), it would not change the result that there have been changes by different hands as late as in the third or early second century BCE. This means that a model of Deuteronomistic history working with three layers of Dtr H, N and RP only does not suffice to explain the difficult textual situation.

3. Examples from the Book of Kings

It would be easy to collect many more instances of presumed Deuteronomisms in the historical books of the LXX. But it may suffice to cite some interesting phenomena in the book of Kings (3 and 4 Kingdoms in the LXX): In 1 Kgs 6:11–14, the MT has a long addition when compared to the LXX.[42] Its phraseology is typically Deuteronomistic: "If you follow my laws and observe my rules and faithfully keep my commandments,

---

40. Rofé 1982.

41. One can question the position of De Troyer 2005, 80, why she detects recensional or editorial changes only on the level of the transmission of the Hebrew text, but assumes that the Greek translator clung slavishly to his *Vorlage*.

42. See Tov 2008b, 406–7. Noth 1983, 118, remarks that the passage is a "late addition," but does not even mention that it is missing in the LXX. Bösenecker 2000, 135, assumes that the text of the LXX evinces an "older redactional layer," while the

I will fulfill for you the promise that I gave to your father David" (NJPS). Because this text interrupts the technical report of the building of the temple, it is clearly identified as a later insertion that makes explicit reference to Nathan's oracle in 2 Sam 7. On the other hand—and similar to evidence from the book of Joshua—LXX includes more material than the MT in 1 Kgs 9:9, where the reference to Egypt is enhanced by the typical ἐξ οἴκου δουλείας "from the house of slavery."[43]

The narration about the dedication of the temple is found in 1 Kgs 8. Here again the MT includes additions which sound typically Deuteronomistic; thus verse 42 has the phrase, "For they shall hear of your great name and your mighty hand and your outstretched arm," which is clearly an addition because of the verb in the plural while the context has the singular, related to the foreigner in verse 41. On the other hand, the LXX includes in 8:16 the addition καὶ ἐξελεξάμην ἐν Ιερουσαλημ εἶναι τὸ ὄνομά μου ἐκει "but I chose Jerusalem that my name should be there."[44] In verse 52 LXX adds καὶ τὰ ὦτά σου "and your ears," presumably to align the text with Deut 29:3; 31:11, 28.[45]

A final example can be found in 2 Kgs 17, the account of Israel's fall. According to Norbert Lohfink, this is one of the texts in which Deuteronomistic influence is visible beyond any doubt.[46] Here the Antiochene Greek text, which should be regarded as older than the LXX, shows interesting differences when compared to the MT: verse 7 speaks about the ὀργὴ κυρίου ἐπὶ τὸν Ισραηλ yet has no counterpart in the MT, moreover adding a typical reference to the exodus "from the day on that he has brought them up and until this day."[47] Verse 15 adds that the fathers have rejected

---

version of the MT was "independent redactional formulation." It is not said who this redactor might have been.

43. Again Noth 1983, 195, 198, does not mention the deviating reading of the LXX. Bösenecker 2000, 197, assumes independent reworkings in both MT and LXX.

44. See 2 Chr 6:5–6: ואבחר בירושלם להיות שמי שם, this text may be the *Vorlage* of the addition in the LXX. See also 4Q54 (4QKgs) 7; obviously LXX had a different *Vorlage*. However, in the Greek version the passage is missing "has God not chosen a *nagid* over Israel" (v. 5b); there is no equivalent for ולא־בחרתי באיש להיות נגיד על־עמי ישראל. It cannot be decided whether the translator himself has shortened the text or whether already his *Vorlage* had a shorter version.

45. Bösenecker 2000, 185, assumes influence from 2 Chr 6:40.

46. Lohfink 1995, 318. But see also H. N. Rösel 2009, who doubts that this is a text of reflection that is typical for DtrG.

47. See Fernández Marcos 2004; or Kreuzer 2008.The Greek texts are quoted from

his covenant and his ordinances ἀπώσαντο τὴν διαθήκην καὶ τὰ δικαιώματα, which he has given to their fathers. In verse 17 ephod and teraphim are added to prove the idolatry of Israel, which refers back to Judg 17:5 and 18:14–20. And finally, verse 19 states explicitly that Israel has rejected the Lord (here supported by LXX). All these additions fit into the ideology that the fall of the kingdom of Israel is a just punishment because of their transgressions. Again it is evident that the Greek version of the text shows traces of Deuteronomistic influence not present in the Hebrew text.

4. Further Arguments

I am only touching upon some supporting insights of previous research: Hans Ausloos has convincingly shown that some readings in LXX Exodus and LXX Numbers can best be explained as a type of Deuteronomistic harmonization.[48] He then goes on to ask, if these harmonizations exist in the LXX or its *Vorlage*, why do scholars exclude the possibility that late Deuteronomistic intrusions of this kind have also happened on the level of the Hebrew text?

As for the book of Kings, Adrian Schenker has developed the highly disputed theory that the oldest version of this book can be found in the LXX and the Vetus Latina, while the MT is a later edition.[49] Interestingly, according to his exegesis, many typical Deuteronomisms are attested in the younger MT-parts only. Schenker even asserts that the LXX, not the MT, should be the subject of redactional-critical studies on the book of Kings.[50] For the book of Samuel, Steven Pisano has shown that it is often not possible to determine whether a reading in the Hebrew text of the MT is really Deuteronomistic or a late alteration.[51] And finally, it is worth remembering that in the book of Jeremiah, both the MT and LXX include

---

Fernández Marcos and Busto Saiz, 1992.

48. Ausloos, 1996, 2001.

49. Besides a wealth of articles he has written on textual phenomena; cf. Schenker 2000, 2004. Hugo 2006 has come to similar conclusions for 1 Kgs 17–18. Schenker's theory is based on a plethora of minute individual observations, which cannot bear the burden of proof alone, but convince in sum. For criticism of this theory cf. van Keulen 2005; Pietsch 2007; and Turkanik 2008.

50. Schenker 2004, 171–94.

51. Pisano 2000. This impression is supported by Hugo 2008, although he does not explicitly discusses the question of Deuteronomism.

typically Deuteronomistic phrases in texts that have no counterpart in the other version.[52]

5. Outlook

The outcome of these observations can now be determined: Phrases and thoughts usually identified as "Deuteronomistic" can be detected in Greek versions, in their *Vorlage*, and in late expansions of the MT as well. This means that the label "Deuteronomistic" is not a category of redactional layers of the Hebrew text only, but is rather an overall theological concept—with many subconcepts—based on the fifth book of the Torah and which attracted some portions of Jewish society well into the second century BCE.

It is obvious that at the assumed time of translation, the text of the historical books was not fixed at all. This means that the questions of redactional criticism and textual criticism cannot be separated and that methodologically speaking, it is no longer sound to work, as many commentators have done in the past, with the MT only. The Old Greek version must be taken into account. Moreover, the typical method of an isolated textual criticism addressing single variants only should be abandoned. It is necessary to determine the characteristics of the whole text of the version and to decide whether it could be a variant edition with older elements. Finally, this overview challenges scholars who too confidently wield this outdated methodology to detect and single out traces of individual Deuteronomistic thinkers.

Bibliography

Achenbach, Reinhard 1991. *Israel zwischen Verheißung und Gebot: Literarkritische Untersuchungen zu Deuteronomium 5–11*. EHS.T 422. Frankfurt am Main: Lang

Auld, A. Graeme. 2005. *Joshua: Jesus son of Nauē in Codex Vaticanus*. Septuagint Commentary Series. Leiden: Brill

Ausloos, Hans. 1996. "The Septuagint Version of Exod 23:20–33. A 'Deuteronomist' at Work?" *JNSL* 22:89–106.

---

52. Stipp 1994, 60–65; see also Tov 2008b, 410–16.

———. 1997. "Les extrêmes se touchent ... Proto-Deuteronomic and Simili-Deuteronomistic Elements in Genesis–Numbers." Pages 341–66 in *Deuteronomy and Deuteronomic Literature: Festschrift C. H. W. Brekelmans*. Edited by Marc Vervenne and Johan Lust. BETL 133. Leuven: Peeters.

———. 2001. "LXX Num 14:23. Once More a 'Deuteronomist' at Work?" Pages 415–27 in *X. Congress of the International Organization for Septuagint and Cognate Studies. Oslo 1998*. Edited by Bernard A. Taylor. SCS 51. Atlanta: Society of Biblical Literature.

Becker, Uwe. 2006. "Endredaktionelle Kontextvernetzungen des Josua-Buches." Pages 139–61 in *Die deuteronomistischen Geschichtswerke: Redaktions- und religionsgeschichtliche Perspektiven zur "Deuteronomismus"-Diskussion in Tora und Vorderen Propheten*. Edited by Markus Witte and Johannes F. Diehl. BZAW 365. Berlin: de Gruyter.

Bösenecker, Jobst. 2000. "Text und Redaktion: Untersuchungen zum hebräischen und griechischen Text von 1 Könige 1–11." ThD diss., University of Rostock.

Butler, Trent C. 1983. *Joshua*. WBC 7. Waco, TX: Word Books.

Carasik, Michael. 2009. "A Deuteronomistic Voice in the Joseph Story." Pages 3–14 in *Mishneh Todah: Studies in Deuteronomy and Its Cultural Environment in Honor of Jeffrey H. Tigay*. Edited by Nili S. Fox, David A. Glatt-Gilad, and Michael J. Williams. Winona Lake, IN: Eisenbrauns.

Carr, David. 2006. "Empirische Perspektiven auf das Deuteronomistische Geschichtswerk." Pages 1–17 in *Die deuteronomistischen Geschichtswerke: Redaktions- und religionsgeschichtliche Perspektiven zur "Deuteronomismus"-Diskussion in Tora und Vorderen Propheten*. Edited by Markus Witte and Johannes F. Diehl. BZAW 365. Berlin: de Gruyter.

Cross, Frank M. 1980. "The Themes of the Book of Kings and the Structure of the Deuteronomistic History." Pages 274–89 in *Canaanite Myth and Hebrew Epic: Essays in the History of the Religion of Israel*. Harvard: Harvard University Press.

De Troyer, Kristin. 2005. *Die Septuaginta und die Endgestalt des Alten Testaments: Untersuchungen zur Entstehungsgeschichte alttestamentlicher Texte*. UTB 2599. Göttingen: Vandenhoeck & Ruprecht.

Fernández Marcos, Natalio. 2004. "Der antiochenische Text der griechischen Bibel in den Samuel- und Königsbüchern (1–4 Kön

LXX)." Pages 177–213 in Band 2 *Im Brennpunkt: Die Septuaginta; Studien zur Entstehung und Bedeutung der Griechischen Bibel*. Edited by Siegfried Kreuzer and Jürgen Peter Lesch. BWANT 161. Stuttgart: Kohlhammer.

Fernández Marcos, Natalio, and Jose Ramon Busto Saiz. 1992. *El texto antioqueno de la Biblia griega II, 1–2 reyes*. Textos y estudios Cardenal Cisneros 53. Madrid: Instituto de Filología, Consejo Superior de Investigaciones Cientificas.

Hertog, Cornelis den. 1996. "Studien zur griechischen Übersetzung des Buches Josua." ThD diss., University of Giessen.

Hugo, Philippe. 2006. *Les deux visages d'Élie: Texte massorétique et Septante dans l'histoire la plus ancienne du texte de 1 Rois 17–18*. OBO 217. Göttingen: Vandenhoeck & Ruprecht; Fribourg: Presses Universitaires.

———. 2008. "Die Septuaginta in der Textgeschichte der Samuelbücher: Methodologische Prinzipien am Beispiel von 2Sam 6,1–3." Pages 336–52 in *Die Septuaginta: Texte, Kontexte, Lebenswelten*. Edited by Martin Karrer and Wolfgang Kraus. WUNT 1/219. Tübingen: Mohr Siebeck.

Keulen, Percy S. F. van. 2005. *Two Versions of the Solomon Narrative: An Inquiry into the Relationship between MT 1 Kgs. 2–11 and LXX 3 Reg. 2–11*. VTSup 104. Leiden: Brill.

Knauf, Ernst Axel. 2000. "Does 'Deuteronomistic Historiography' (DtrH) Exist?" Pages 388–98 in *Israel Constructs Its History: Deuteronomistic Historiography in Recent Research*. Edited by Albert de Pury, Thomas Römer, and Jean-Daniel Macchi. JSOTSup 306. Sheffield: Sheffield Academic.

Kooij, Arie van der. 2003. "On the Use of βωμός in the Septuagint." Pages 601–7 in *Hamlet on a Hill: Semitic and Greek Studies Presented to Professor T. Muraoka on the Occasion of His Sixty-Fifth Birthday*. Edited by M. F. J. Baasten and W. Th. van Peursen. OLA 118. Leuven: Peeters.

Kreuzer, Siegfried. 2008. "Towards the Old Greek: New Criteria for the Evaluation of the Recensions of the Septuagint (Especially the Antiochene/Lucianic Text and the Kaige-Recension)." Pages 239–53 in *XIII Congress of the International Organization for Septuagint and Cognate Studies, Ljubljana, 2007*. Edited by Melvin K. H. Peters. SCS 55. Atlanta: Society of Biblical Literature.

Lange, Armin. 2009. "'They Confirmed the Reading' (y. Taʿan. 4.68a): The Textual Standardization of Jewish Scriptures in the Second Temple

Period." Pages 29–80 in *From Qumran to Aleppo: A Discussion with Emanuel Tov About the Textual History of Jewish Scriptures in Honor of His Sixty-Fifth Birthday*. Edited by Armin Lange. FRLANT 230. Göttingen: Vandenhoeck & Ruprecht.

Lohfink, Norbert. 1995. "Gab es eine deuteronomistische Bewegung?" Pages 313–82 in *Jeremia und die "deuteronomistische Bewegung."* Edited by Walter Groß and Dieter Böhler. BBB 98. Weinheim: Beltz Athenäum.

Mazor, Lea. 1988. "The Origin and Evolution of the Curse upon the Rebuilder of Jericho." *Text* 14:1–26.

Meer, Michael N. van der. 2004. *Formulation and Reformulation: The Redaction of the Book of Joshua in the Light of the Oldest Textual Witnesses*. VTSup 102. Leiden: Brill.

Nicholson, Ernest W. 1970. *Preaching to the Exiles: A Study of the Prose Tradition in the Book of Jeremiah*. Oxford: Blackwell.

Noth, Martin. 1983. *Könige I,1–16*. BKAT 9.1. Neukirchen-Vluyn: Neukirchener Verlag.

Person, Raymond F. 1993. *Second Zechariah and the Deuteronomic School*. JSOTSup 167. Sheffield: JSOT Press.

Pietsch, Michael. 2007. "Von Königen und Königtümern: Eine Untersuchung zur Textgeschichte der Königsbücher." *ZAW* 119:39–58.

Pisano, Stephen. 2000. "2 Samuel 5–8 and the Deuteronomist: Textual Criticism or Literary Criticism?" Pages 258–83 in *Israel Constructs Its History: Deuteronomistic Historiography in Recent Research*. Edited by Albert de Pury, Thomas Römer, and Jean-Daniel Macchi. JSOTSup 306. Sheffield: Sheffield Academic.

Rofé, Alexander. 1982. "The End of the Book of Joshua according to the Septuagint." *Hen* 4:17–36.

Römer, Thomas, and Albert de Pury. 2000. "Deuteronomistic Historiography (DH): History of Research and Debated Issues." Pages 24–141 in *Israel Constructs Its History: Deuteronomistic Historiography in Recent Research*. Edited by Albert de Pury, Thomas Römer, and Jean-Daniel Macchi. JSOTSup 306. Sheffield: Sheffield Academic.

Rösel, Hartmut N. 2009. "Why 2 Kings 17 Does Not Constitute a Chapter of Reflection in the 'Deuteronomistic History.'" *JBL* 128:85–90.

Rösel, Martin. 1994. *Übersetzung als Vollendung der Auslegung: Studien zur Genesis-Septuaginta*. BZAW 223. Berlin: de Gruyter.

———. 2001. "Die Septuaginta-Version des Josuabuches." Pages 197–211 in vol. 1 of *Im Brennpunkt: Die Septuaginta; Studien zur Entstehung und Bedeutung der griechischen Bibel*. Edited by Heinz-Josef Fabry und Ulrich Offerhaus. BWANT 153. Stuttgart: Kohlhammer. [English translation ch. 6 in this volume.]

———. 2010. "Deuteronomisten in der Septuaginta? Text- und Redaktionsgeschichte der historischen Bücher." Pages 192–210 in: *Geschichte Israels und deuteronomistisches Geschichtsdenken: Festschrift zum 70. Geburtstag von Winfried Thiel*. Edited by Peter Mommer and Andreas Scherer. AOAT 380. Münster: Ugarit Verlag.

Rudnig-Zelt, Susanne. 2006. *Hoseastudien: Redaktionskritische Untersuchungen zur Genese des Hoseabuches*. FRLANT 213. Göttingen: Vandenhoeck & Ruprecht.

Schearing, Linda, ed. 1999. *Those Elusive Deuteronomists: The Phenomenon of Pan-Deuteronomism*. JSOTSup 268. Sheffield: Sheffield Academic.

Schenker, Adrian. 2000. *Septante et texte massorétique dans l'histoire la plus ancienne du texte de 1 Rois 2–14*. Cahiers de la Revue biblique 48. Paris: Gabalda.

———. 2004. *Älteste Textgeschichte der Königsbücher: Die hebräische Vorlage der ursprünglichen Septuaginta als älteste Textform der Königsbücher*. OBO 199. Göttingen: Vandenhoeck & Ruprecht; Fribourg: Presses Universitaires.

———. 2008. "Altar oder Altarmodell? Textgeschichte von Jos 22,9–34." Pages 417–25 in *Florilegium Lovaniense: Studies in Septuagint and Textual Criticism in Honour of Florentino García Martínez*. Edited by Hans Ausloos, Benedicte Lemmelijn, and Marc Vervenne. BETL 224. Leuven: Peeters.

Scherer, Andreas. 2005. "Vom Sinn prophetischer Gerichtsverkündung bei Amos und Hosea." *Bib* 86:1–19.

Schmid, Konrad. 2008. *Literaturgeschichte des Alten Testaments: Eine Einführung*. Darmstadt: Wissenschaftliche Buchgesellschaft.

Schmidt, Werner H. 1965. "Die deuteronomistische Redaktion des Amosbuches: Zu den theologischen Unterschieden zwischen dem Prophetenwort und seinem Sammler." *ZAW* 77:168–93.

Schwienhorst, Ludger. 1986. *Die Eroberung Jerichos: Exegetische Untersuchungen zu Josua 6*. SBS 122. Stuttgart: Katholisches Bibelwerk.

Smend, Rudolf. 1971. "Das Gesetz und die Völker. Ein Beitrag zur deuteronomistischen Redaktionsgeschichte." Pages 494–509 in *Probleme biblischer Theologie: Gerhard von Rad zum 70. Geburtstag*. Edited by Hans Walter Wolff. Munich: Kaiser.

Steck, Odil Hannes. 1967. *Israel und das gewaltsame Geschick der Propheten: Untersuchungen zur Überlieferung des deuteronomistischen Geschichtsbildes im Alten Testament, Spätjudentum und Urchristentum.* WMANT 23. Neukirchen-Vluyn: Neukirchener Verlag.

Stipp, Hermann-Josef. 1994. *Das masoretische und das alexandrinische Sondergut des Jeremiabuches.* OBO 136. Göttingen: Vandenhoeck & Ruprecht; Fribourg: Presses Universitaires.

Thiel, Winfried. 1973. *Die deuteronomistische Redaktion von Jeremia 1–25.* WMANT 41. Neukirchen-Vluyn: Neukirchener Verlag.

———. 1981. *Die deuteronomistische Redaktion von Jeremia 26–45: Mit einer Gesamtbeurteilung der deuteronomistischen Redaktion des Buches Jeremia.* WMANT 52. Neukirchen-Vluyn: Neukirchener Verlag.

———. 2007. *Unabgeschlossene Rückschau: Aspekte alttestamentlicher Wissenschaft im 20. Jahrhundert. Mit einem Anhang: Grundlinien der Erforschung des "Deuteronomistischen Geschichtswerkes."* BThSt 80. Neukirchen-Vluyn: Neukirchener Verlag.

Tov, Emanuel. 1978. "Midrash-Type Exegesis in the LXX of Joshua." *RB* 85:50–61.

———. 1999a. "The Growth of the Book of Joshua in Light of the Evidence of the Septuagint." Pages 385–96 in *The Greek and Hebrew Bible: Collected Essays on the Septuagint.* Edited by Emanuel Tov. VTSup 72. Leiden: Brill.

———. 1999b. "The Rewritten Book of Joshua as Found at Qumran and Masada." Pages 233–561 in *Biblical Perspectives: Early Use and Interpretation of the Bible in Light of the Dead Sea Scrolls; Proceedings of the First International Symposium of the Orion Center for the Study of the Dead Sea Scrolls and Associated Literature, 12–14 May 1996.* STDJ 28. Leiden: Brill.

———. 2008a. "4QReworked Pentateuch: A Synopsis of Its Contents." Pages 21–26 in *Hebrew Bible, Greek Bible, and Qumran.* TSAJ 121. Tübingen: Mohr Siebeck.

———. 2008b. "The LXX and the Deuteronomists." Pages 398–417 in *Hebrew Bible, Greek Bible, and Qumran.* TSAJ 121. Tübingen: Mohr Siebeck.

Turkanik, Andrzej S. 2008. *Of Kings and Reigns: A Study of Translation Technique in the Gamma/Gamma Section of 3 Reigns (1 Kings).* FAT 2/30. Tübingen: Mohr Siebeck.

Weinfeld, Moshe. 1992. *Deuteronomy and the Deuteronomic School.* Winona Lake, IN: Eisenbrauns.

Würthwein, Ernst. 1977. *Das erste Buch der Könige: Kapitel 1–16*. ATD 11.1. Göttingen: Vandenhoeck & Ruprecht.

9
Die Jungfrauengeburt des endzeitlichen Immanuel.
Jesaja 7 in der Übersetzung der Septuaginta

Die Verheißung des Immanuel in Jes 7,14 mag zwar der meistkommentierte Vers des Alten Testamentes sein.[1] Doch die weitreichenden exegetischen Bemühungen um diese für das Neue Testament und die christliche Kirche so folgenreiche Weissagung stehen in einem merkwürdigen Kontrast zu der eher geringen Aufmerksamkeit, die der Septuaginta-Version von Jes 7 entgegengebracht wird, obgleich sie doch in diesem Falle als das Bindeglied zwischen Altem und Neuern Testament zu sehen ist. So wird zwar die Frage gestellt, ob die Übersetzung παρθένος für עלמה „schon die Vorstellung einer jungfräulichen Messiasgeburt voraussetzt."[2] Doch man gibt sich damit zufrieden, dass die Frage unbeantwortbar bleibt.[3] Dieses unbefriedigende Ergebnis liegt m.E. darin begründet, dass man

---

1. So Wildberger 1972, 288. Dieser Aufsatz verdankt seine Entstehung einer Anregung von Klaus Koch, dem ich für alle Hinweise und Hilfestellungen danken möchte.

2. Gese 1974, 145.

3. So Gese 1974, 145; Delling 1954, 831; Dibelius 1953, 40. Auch die bisher gründlichste Untersuchung zur Jesaja-Septuaginta von I. L. Seeligmann (Seeligmann 1948) begnügt sich S. 120 damit, die Frage offenzulassen und eine fehlerhafte Übersetzung nicht auszuschließen. In J. Zieglers Untersuchungen zur Septuaginta des Buches Jesaja (Ziegler 1934) wird das Problem erst gar nicht verhandelt Eine Ausnahme bilden Grundmann 1961, 60–61, der für die Eintragung der Idee der Jungfrauengeburt auf der Ebene der Septuaginta votiert, dies allerdings ohne eigene Bearbeitung des Problems, und Kilian 1970, der die Septuaginta-Übersetzung παρθένος als von dem ägyptischen Mythos von Pharaos wunderbarer Zeugung und Geburt abhängig erklärt (s. dazu unten Anm. 56). Einzig van der Kooij 1977 widmet dem Kapitel Jes 7 LXX besondere Aufmerksamkeit, sein Lösungsvorschlag wird unten Anm. 44 diskutiert werden. Zu anderen als den hier vorzutragenden Lösungsvorschlägen s. zudem unten Anm. 44 und 66.

sich letztlich auf das eine Übersetzungsproblem עלמה-παρθένος konzentriert, ohne den größeren Zusammenhang des Kapitels Jes 7 in seiner Septuaginta-Fassung zur Kenntnis zu nehmen.

Im Folgenden soll es darum gehen, in ähnlicher Weise, wie es R. Hanhart zu Jes 9,1–7(8,23–9,6) vorgeführt hat,[4] die eigene Aussageabsicht der ältesten greifbaren griechischen Übersetzung von Jes 7 über den hebräischen Text hinaus zu erhellen, um so einer Antwort auf die Frage nach der Übersetzung „Jungfrau" näher zu kommen. Diese eigene Sehweise des Übersetzers soll dadurch rekonstruiert werden, dass die Differenzen zwischen hebräischem und griechischem Text exegetisch bearbeitet werden.[5] Dabei wird der Interpretation des hebräischen Textes nur soweit Bedeutung zugemessen, als sie für das Verständnis der Septuaginta-Version von Belang ist. Der eigentlich zur Debatte stehende Vers 7,14 wird sinnvollerweise anfangs ausgeklammert werden, um so ein Bild von der Grundtendenz des Kapitels entwerfen zu können, in dem dann die Interpretation dieser Stelle verankert werden kann.

1. Jes 7 LXX als Heilsansage

Zunächst ist zu erkennen, dass der Übersetzer Jes 7 offenbar als Heilsweissagung verstanden hat. Dies zeigt sich an solchen Wiedergaben, die vom Sinn der Vorlage deutlich abweichen: Nach V. 2 und V. 6 hat sich Aram nicht in Ephraim niedergelassen (נחה),[6] sondern nur mit ihm verbündet (συμφωνέω). Darauf ziehen sie nach Jerusalem, nicht, um gegen Judäa zu kämpfen und es zu erobern, sondern um es zu überreden und so auf eine gemeinsame Linie einzuschwören (καὶ συλλαλήσαντες αὐτοῖς ἀποστρέψομεν αὐτοὺς πρὸς ἡμᾶς für ונקיצנה ונבקענה אלינו). Dazu passt allerdings der vom hebräischen Text aufgenötigte Nachsatz, den Sohn des Tabeel zum König Judäas machen zu wollen, nicht mehr. Auffällig ist, in welcher Nähe diese Interpretationen und die modernen Erkenntnisse über die Gründe des syrisch-ephraimitischen Krieges zueinander stehen.[7] Rechnet man damit, dass der hebräische Text von Jes 7 typologisch ver-

---

4. Hanhart 1983.
5. Vgl. zur Methodik Seeligmann 1948, 3–5. 76. 95 und Tov 1987.
6. Zum Problem des נָחָה in V. 2 vgl. Wildberger 1972, 265; Kaiser 1981, 135; HAL s.v.; am wahrscheinlichsten bleibt wohl doch die Ableitung von נוח. S. dazu auch Anm. 11.
7. Vgl. Seeligmann 1948, 50. Bickert 1987 bestreitet allerdings ganz, dass es einen

standen wurde, dass also der Übersetzer geschichtliche Fakten des Textes in seiner Gegenwart wiederfand,[8] sind diese Abweichungen erklärlich. So kann ארם in Jes 9,12(11) und 17,3 mit Συρία übersetzt werden, womit das Reich der Seleukiden gemeint ist,[9] unter Εφραιμ kann man nach Ausweis von 9,21(20); 17,3; 28,1. 3 die von Israel abtrünnigen Verbündeten der Seleukiden verstehen, für diese Interpretation finden sich auch in Qumran Parallelen.[10] Dann wird das ἀποστρέφειν in V. 6 im Sinne einer Verführung zum Abfall zu deuten sein (vgl. 30,11; 36,9). Der Übersetzer hat demnach den vom hebräischen Text vorgegebenen Bericht als seine eigene Situation betreffend verstanden. Die auf ihn zurückgehenden Abweichungen haben m.E. die Funktion, diese Überzeugung anderen mitzuteilen und zugleich die bevorstehende Bedrohung Judäas, die wohl allen vor Augen stand, abzuschwächen.[11]

Eine der zentralen Erwartungen, nicht nur Jesajas, sondern auch des Übersetzers, wird in V. 3 (und 22bβ) angesprochen, die des Restes. In der Jesaja-Septuaginta wird mit τὸ κατάλειμμα bzw. Partizipialformen von καταλείπω durchgängig der für das Heil bestimmte Rest bezeichnet (4,3; 10,21; 11,11; 60,19),[12] unter dem der Übersetzer nicht nur Israel, sondern offensichtlich auch die Juden in der Diaspora verstand (14,2; 24,14). Die Erwartung des Heils wird in 4,2 unter Uminterpretation des hebräischen Textes ausgeführt: An jenem Tag wird Gott aufstrahlen τοῦ ὑψῶσαι καὶ δοξάσαι τὸ καταλειφθὲν τοῦ Ισραηλ (für לגאון ולתפארת לפליטת ישראל). Wenn demnach ὁ καταλειφθείς (V. 22bβ) als geprägter Begriff für die Zukunftserwartung des Übersetzers angesehen werden kann, wird die

---

solchen Plan zu einer großen antiassyrischen Koalition und überhaupt einen syrisch-ephraimitischen Krieg gegeben habe.

8. Zu solchen Aktualisierungen und Erfüllungsinterpretationen vgl. Seeligmann 1948, 81–91 und van der Kooij 1981, 33–65.

9. So Seeligmann 1948, 81; Hengel 1969, 61 und van der Kooij 1981, 35–39 (mit weiterem Material).

10. Vgl. 4QpNah I,12; II,2.8; III,8; 4QpPs 37 II,18; CD VII,13. Diesen Hinweis verdanke ich M. Hengel.

11. Auch Ziegler 1934, 109 stellt die Abweichungen in V. 2 und 6 fest und konstatiert ihren „politischen Sinn", der dem Thema von 7,1–9 entspreche: Das συμφωνέω in V. 2 übersetze ein ursprüngliches נאחה statt des נחה, das συλλαλέω in V.6 gilt ihm als freie Übersetzung. Unerwähnt bleibt die niemals sonst in der Septuaginta begegnende Übersetzung von בקע hif. mit ἀποστρέφω, wie auch eine Interpretation dieser Abweichungen unterbleibt.

12. Vgl. Seeligmann 1948, 115–17.

Bedeutung der Wiedergabe des Namens שאר ישוב des Sohnes Jesajas in 7,3 durch ὁ καταλειφθεὶς Ιασουβ deutlich:[13] Wird der Rest Israels bei Jesaja selbst noch als klein und „armselig" gesehen,[14] so verweist das „der übriggebliebene Jasub, dein Sohn" auf die neu verstandene, auf alle Juden erweiterte Vorstellung vom für die Rettung bestimmten Rest.[15] Geht man zudem von einem typologischen Verstehen des Übersetzers aus, mag auch eine Naherwartung mitschwingen: Das Heil ist nicht ferner als die Zeit einer Generationsstufe.

Ein weiterer Hinweis auf die Tendenz des Übersetzers, Jesaja 7 als Heilsansage zu verstehen, zeigt sich in 7,4b. Die Erklärung, dass mit den beiden Feuerbrandstummeln der Zorn Rezins, Arams und des Sohnes Remaljahus gemeint ist, fehlt in der Septuaginta-Version völlig. Grund dafür dürfte sein, dass sich V. 4b durch die Verwendung der Präposition בְּ im Gegensatz zu vorhergehendem מִן schwer in den Kontext fügt,[16] zumal V. 4a gut in sich verständlich ist. Die letzten Worte von V. 4b (ארם־ובן־רמליהו) wurden offenbar als zum folgenden Vers gehörig verstanden, weshalb dann ארם, אפרים und ובן־רמליהו in V. 5 als Doppelung entbehrlich waren. So blieb ein Satzfragment mit einer Bedingung durch ב übrig, das zur Interpretation nötigte: ὅταν γὰρ ὀργὴ τοῦ θυμοῦ μου γένηται πάλιν ἰάσομαι.[17] Damit wird die dem hebräischen Text innewohnende Spannung, dass nämlich erst in V. 9b etwas über Judas Geschick ausgesagt wird, bereits an früher Stelle gelöst: Gottes Zorn währt nur kurz, danach wird er sein Volk wieder heilen.[18] In der Jesaja-Septuaginta wird ἰάομαι

---

13. Diese Übersetzung mag noch dadurch veranlasst worden sein, dass שאר ישוב als Name sonst nicht bekannt ist, während Ιασουβ in der Septuaginta geläufig ist (Gen 46,13; Num 26,20; 1.Chr 7,1).

14. So Wildberger 1972, 278.

15. Interessanterweise bleibt in 10,21, wo erneut שאר ישוב zu übersetzen gewesen wäre, der Ausdruck unübersetzt. An beiden Stellen, 7,3 und 10,21, liegt der Ton einzig auf der Heilszukunft des Rests.

16. Vgl. Wildberger 1972, 265–66; Kaiser 1981, 135, liest in 4b mit Syr מן statt ב.

17. Die Doppelung ὀργὴ τοῦ θυμοῦ μου „Zorn meines Eifers" belegt, dass der Übersetzer den heute erhaltenen Text בחרי־אף „bei der Glut des Zornes" voraussetzte. Anders Seeligmann 1948, 56, der vermutet, der Übersetzer hätte hier אך gelesen, dieses Missverständnis habe ihn zu einer freien Erklärung veranlasst.

18. Ziegler 1934, 62, stellt fest: „Der Übersetzer hat sich hier nach 6,10 einen Satz zurechtgelegt." Er vermutet mit Ottley 1906, 140, dass der Übersetzer aus אפרים das Verbum רפא herausgelesen habe—eine wenig überzeugende Erklärung dieses Problems.

9. Die Jungfrauengeburt des endzeitlichen Immanuel 201

(als Übersetzung von רפא und חבש) beinahe zum *terminus technicus* für das wiederherstellende Handeln Gottes zum Heil (19,22; 30,26; 61,1 u.ö.); dies schließt auch die Umkehr der Verstockten (6,10) oder von Fremdvölkern (19,22) mit ein.

Ein besonderes exegetisches Problem bietet die überraschende Übersetzung von 7,9b. Dieser Halbvers bildet den Abschluss des in V. 7 begonnenen Unheilsorakels an die Feinde, dessen Sinn noch heute ohne Ergänzungen unvollständig bleibt.[19] Der Übersetzer hat offenkundig V. 8 mit ἀλλά so an V. 7 angeschlossen, dass V. 8–9 nicht mehr die Begründung gibt, weshalb das Vorhaben keinen Bestand hat, sondern die Folge des Scheiterns zeigt: Das Haupt Arams ist Damaskus, das Königreich Ephraim wird entvölkert werden. Da dem Übersetzer die Namen vorgegeben waren, ist eine genaue Erklärung problematisch. Deutlich ist m.E. soviel, dass V. 8–9a auf Zukünftiges weisen und daran der (im hebräischen Text unverbunden stehende) V. 9b durch καί angeschlossen wurde. Möglicherweise verstand der Übersetzer die V. 8–9a als rätselhaft im Sinne eines eschatologischen Geheimnisses. So wäre die Motivation seiner Übersetzung von V. 9b verständlich. Ausgebend von אם לא תאמינו כי לא תאמנו „Glaubt ihr nicht, so bleibt ihr nicht", kommt er nämlich zu „Glaubt ihr nicht, so versteht ihr nicht" (ἐὰν μὴ πιστεύσητε οὐδὲ μὴ συνῆτε).[20] Im Jesajabuch wird sonst das Verbum אמן *nif./hif.* durchgängig durch Ableitungen von πιστεύω wiedergegeben,[21] wobei πιστός durchaus auch im in V. 9 geforderten Sinn „beständig" verwendet wurde (33,16; 49,7; 55,3). Doch offenkundig wurde ein mögliches „wenn ihr nicht πιστός seid, werdet ihr nicht πιστός bleiben" nicht als überzeugende Lösung des durch die beiden Formen von אמן gegebenen Übersetzungsproblems angesehen, die im Hebräischen ja Bedingung und Folge angeben konnten. Möglicherweise in

---

Van der Kooij 1977, 94–95, nimmt an, dass die hebräische Vorlage in V. 4b רצון statt רציץ in M geboten hatte. Dies habe der Übersetzer wie in 60,10 im Sinne von „Erbarmen" aufgefasst (dort ἔλεος) und nach 6,10 mit ἰάομαι übersetzt. Wenn auch diese Erklärung etwas konstruiert erscheint, gleicht sie doch in der Konsequenz der hier vorgetragenen: Bereits zu Beginn des Kapitels wird Gottes Erbarmen angesagt.

19. Vgl. Wildberger 1972, 272–73; 282–83; Kaiser 1981, 135–36. 138–39.

20. Wildberger 1972, 266, vermutet hier eine einfache Textverderbnis von תאמינו zu תבינו; van der Kooij 1977, 95–96, begnügt sich mit der Vermutung, die Wiedergabe des תאמינו sei von 6,9–10 her beeinflusst, ohne dies jedoch befriedigend zu erläutern.

21. Die einzige Ausnahme begegnet in 60,4, dort aber ist der Sinn von תאמנה „tragen;" dies wird richtig mit ἀρθήσονται übersetzt.

Erinnerung an אמת wählte der Übersetzer „verstehen" zur Wiedergabe,[22] wodurch der Sinn des Verses gravierend verändert wurde. Das hier verwendete Verbum συνίημι steht in der Jesaja-Septuaginta an insgesamt acht Stellen,[23] im Regelfall zur Übersetzung von בין. Allerdings wird בין nicht prinzipiell mit συνίημι wiedergegeben,[24] so dass nach den Bedeutungsdifferenzen zu fragen ist.

Der Übersetzer scheint συνίημι nur an Stellen verwendet zu haben, wo es um das Verstehen in Bezug auf Gott geht, welches über Heil und Unheil entscheidet. So wird Israel zum Vorwurf gemacht, dass es nicht versteht (1,3; 6,9. 10; 59,15), oder es geht um das Verstehen des Gottesknechts (52,13) bzw. um die durch ihn vermittelte Einsicht (52,15). Besonders auffällig ist die Zusammenstellung in 43,10:

אתם עדי נאם־יהוה	γένεσθέ μοι μάρτυρες κἀγὼ μάρτυς λέγει κύριος ὁ θεός
ועבדי אשר בחרתי	καὶ ὁ παῖς ὃν ἐξελεξάμην
למען תדעו ותאמינו לי ותבינו	ἵνα γνῶτε καὶ πιστεύσητε καὶ συνῆτε
כי־אני הוא	ὅτι ἐγώ εἰμι

Der Sinn des hebräischen Textes wird durch die Übersetzung deutlich modifiziert. Israel wird zur Zeugenschaft nach dem Vorbild Gottes und seines Knechts aufgerufen, um das Gottsein Gottes zu erkennen, zu glauben und so zu verstehen. Dieser Gebrauch von συνίημι unterscheidet sich auffällig von der Verwendung der Wortgruppe im außerbiblischen Griechisch.[25] Sie bezeichnet dort eine Fähigkeit zum Urteil, doch werden weder Verbum noch Substantiv in den Rang philosophischer Begriffe erhoben. Erst bei Josephus erhält das Wort eine moralische Färbung.[26] Eine überraschende Parallele ergibt sich aber, wenn man den zeitgleichen Gebrauch von בין beachtet. Diese Wurzel wird auffällig oft im Danielbuch für die Bezeichnung der apokalyptischen Einsicht verwendet (vgl. z.B. 9,2; 10,14; 12,10), in Qumran bezeichnet sie später die erlösende Einsicht, die auf Offenbarung gegründet ist (vgl. 1QM X,16; 1QS IV,3 u.ö.).[27]

---

22. „Wahrheit" und „verstehen" begegnen aufeinander bezogen in Jes 59,15 LXX.
23. 1,3; 6,9. 10; 7,9; 43,10; 52,13. 15; 59,15.
24. Es wird noch übersetzt mit γινώσκω, κατανοέω, συλλογίζομαι.
25. Ähnliches gilt, wenngleich in abgeschwächter Weise, für den Gebrauch von σύνεσις, vgl. z.B. 33,19; 47,10; 53,11.
26. Vgl. Conzelmann 1966, 886–88.
27. Vgl. Ringgren 1973, 629.

Nun haben schon I. L. Seeligmann[28] und R. Hanhart[29] gute Gründe dafür genannt, dass die Septuaginta-Übersetzung des Jesajabuches Ereignisse der Makkabäerzeit widerspiegelt, bzw. Weissagungen des hebräischen Textes auf diese Bedrängungssituation bezogen hat. Zwar ist das allein kein hinreichender Beleg dafür, dass sich der Übersetzer hier geprägter apokalyptischer Sprache seiner Zeit bediente, doch wird dies eindeutiger, wenn man den Gebrauch von συνίημι in apokalyptischen Schriften beachtet. Dazu bieten sich die beiden griechischen Übersetzungen des Danielbuches an. Auffällig sind hier die Unterschiede im Gebrauch: Während die Theodotion zugeschriebene Übersetzung sowohl בין als auch שכל bis auf wenige Ausnahmen unter Verwendung der Wortgruppe συνίημι übersetzt, schränkt die ältere Septuaginta-Übersetzung, die etwa zeitgleich mit der Jesaja-Septuaginta entstanden ist,[30] den Gebrauch in derselben Weise ein, wie es oben bei der Jesaja-Septuaginta beobachtet werden konnte. So wird συνίημι in Dan 11,33. 35; 12,3 für die Einsichtigen verwendet, denen das endzeitliche Heil gilt. Gott ist der, der diese apokalyptische Einsicht in den Geschichtslauf vermittelt (2,21), mit der in besonderer Weise Daniel ausgestattet ist (1,20; 8,16; 6,4, hier ohne Veranlassung durch den aramäischen Text). Besonders auffällig ist 1,17: Hier wird מדע mit σύνεσις übersetzt, obwohl dies sonst nie im Danielbuch, weder bei Theodotion noch in der Septuaginta, vorgenommen wird und obwohl das eigentliche Äquivalent שכל direkt anschließend folgt. Dies geschah m.E., weil שכל hier auf בכל־ספר וחכמה bezogen ist. Eine solche Verbindung von σύνεσις und weltlicher Weisheit musste offensichtlich vermieden werden, da sie nicht zum dargestellten Bedeutungsfeld des Wortes gehörte. Der Übersetzer setzte folglich an dieser Stelle φρόνησις für שכל ein, was in der gesamten Septuaginta nur dreimal geschieht.[31]

So lässt sich festhalten, dass συνίημι in der Zeit der Übersetzung des Jesajabuches mit einiger Sicherheit ein für das Heil notwendiges apokalyptisches Verstehen meinte. Diese Einsicht ist, so Jes 7,9 LXX, vom Glauben

---

28. Vgl. Seeligmann 1948, 82–90; vgl. auch van der Kooij 1981, 33–65; s. noch oben zu V. 2 und 6.

29. Vgl. Hanhart 1983, 338–44.

30. Charles 1929, LI und Grelot 1974, 23, Anm. 18 nehmen eine Entstehungszeit der Daniel-Septuaginta um 145 v.Chr. an, Seeligmann 1948, 87, und van der Kooij 1981, 72–73 datieren die Jesaja-Septuaginta um ca. 140 v.Chr.

31. Vgl. Ps 93(94),8; Hi 17,4; Dan 1,17 θ.

abhängig.³² Unklar ist nun noch, wie diese Feststellung im Zusammenhang des Kapitels 7 zu verstehen ist. Im hebräischen Text ist der Vers noch als Mahnung, angesichts der Bedrohung beim Glauben zu bleiben, zu verstehen. Der Septuaginta-Übersetzer aber ist am Verstehen interessiert. So erhält V. 7,9b eine Scharnierfunktion für das gesamte Kapitel. In der gegenwärtigen Bedrängungssituation (1–6) wird Gott nicht nur kurzfristig die Gefahr abwenden (7–9a), sondern auch eine vollständige Wendung zum Heil herbeiführen (10–17). Diese Heilsabsicht gilt es zu verstehen, und das kann nur der, der glaubt und nicht zweifelt.

So verstanden, fügt sich das Kapitel gut ein in eine typisch apokalyptische Geschichtsschau, wie sie z.B. in Dan 7 und 10–12 begegnet. Der Übersetzer hat sich demnach in einer vergleichbaren historischen Situation desselben Materials wie die frühe israelitische Apokalyptik bedient, um Traditionen der Heiligen Schrift auf die Gegenwart zu deuten. Auch dieses Verfahren begegnet schon im Danielbuch (vgl. Dan 9).

Ein weiterer Hinweis darauf, dass der Übersetzer Jes 7 durchgängig positiv interpretierte, findet sich in V. 13. Aus der abgelehnten Zeichenforderung, die Ahas angeboten war, resultiert im hebräischen Text der Vorwurf Jesajas an das Haus Davids, dass es nicht nur Menschen, sondern auch Gott ermüde. Offensichtlich hat der Übersetzer diesen Vorwurf zurücknehmen wollen (zumal sich Ahas ja korrekt gemäß Dtn 6,16 verhalten hatte). So bietet er μὴ μικρὸν ὑμῖν ἀγῶνα παρέχειν ἀνθρώποις καὶ πῶς κυρίῳ παρέχετε ἀγῶνα; („Ist es etwas Geringes für euch, dass ihr einen Kampf mit Menschen führt? Und wie ist es möglich, dass ihr mit dem Herrn einen Kampf führt?") für המעט מכם הלאות אנשים כי תלאו גם את־ אלהי. Das Wort ἀγών, auf dessen Deutung es hier vor allem ankommt, wird in der Septuaginta nur selten verwendet (Est 4,17, Sap 4,2; 10,12, 6mal 2Makk, 5mal 4Makk). Es hat die Grundbedeutung des edlen Wettstreits im Stadion oder im Wortgefecht.³³ Später bezeichnet es, vor allem in der hellenistisch-jüdischen Literatur, die Übung in der Tugend, den sittlichen Kampf des Frommen im Leben der Welt. Die Wortgruppe ἀγών κτλ. weist demnach durchweg positive Konnotationen auf. Dass sich der Überset-

---

32. Seeligmann 1948, 108, der leider Jes 7,9b LXX nicht verhandelt hat, kommt auf Grund von Jes 26,9; 11,2; 53,10–11 und Hos 10,12–13 sogar dazu, die Septuaginta als Vorläuferin gnostischer Systeme zu bezeichnen. Für die Wirkungsgeschichte dieses Verses ist die Beobachtung interessant, dass Anselms *fides quaerens intellectum* auf Jes 7,9 LXX zurückgeführt werden muss, so Hanhart 1962, 151.

33. Vgl. Stauffer 1933.

9. Die Jungfrauengeburt des endzeitlichen Immanuel 205

zer dessen bewusst bediente, zeigt die Tatsache, dass er das Verb לאה, zu dessen Wiedergabe er hier ἀγῶνα παρέχω benutzte, in anderen Zusammenhängen durchaus im Sinne seiner eigentlichen Bedeutung übersetzen konnte, vgl. 1,14; 16,12; 47,13 (dort jeweils nif. „sich abmühen").

Beachtet man die Verwendung von ἀγών in den Makkabäerbüchern, fällt auch hier dessen uneingeschränkt positive Wertung auf. In 2Makk werden die von Judas und seinen Leuten bestandenen Auseinandersetzungen als περὶ τῆς πατρίδος ἀγῶσιν bezeichnet (14,18, vgl. 10,28; 15,9). In 4Makk steht das Wort ausschließlich für das Martyrium der Mutter und ihrer Söhne, das als θεῖος ἀγών gilt (17,11, vgl. 11,20; 13,14; 15,29; 16,16), als Kampf für die wahre Religion.[34]

Nun wurde oben bereits genannt, dass die Jesaja-Septuaginta vor dem Hintergrund der Ereignisse der Makkabäerzeit verstanden werden muss. So ist zu fragen, ob nicht auch Jes 7,13 in ähnlicher Weise typologisch verstanden wurde. Der erste Teil der Anrede an das Haus Davids meint das im Kampf mit den Seleukiden stehende Volk, der zweite Teil bezieht sich auf die abgelehnte Zeichenforderung: Indem er mit Gottes Wort gegen Gott argumentiert, ist Ahas in ein verdienstvolles Ringen mit Gott eingetreten.[35] Darauf reagiert nun Gott seinerseits damit, dass er selbst das Zeichen gibt: Die Jungfrau gebiert einen Heilsbringer (V. 14–17). Damit ist deutlich, dass das Angebot zur Zeichenforderung V. 11 nicht als Tat zur Bewährung des Glaubens, sondern als Versuchung gewertet wurde, ähnlich Mt 4,1–11, besonders V. 7 mit seiner Nähe zu Jes 7,12 LXX.

Wie unten gezeigt wird, ist die Weissagung 7,14–17 eindeutig als Heilsansage zu verstehen. Von dort her erhält die positive Wertung von ἀγών eine zusätzliche Stütze. Der erhaltene hebräische Text ist seiner Grundstruktur nach als ein Unheilszeichen zu verstehen, das an Ahas auf seine Weigerung hin ergeht.[36] Dies wird an V. 17 deutlich, der eine Katastrophe ansagt, die der des Abfalls des Nordreiches gleichkommt. Daneben stehen aber in

---

34. Vgl. Dehandschutter 1989.
35. Auffällig ist auch, dass der Übersetzer die Konfrontation von „dein Gott" V. 11 und „mein Gott" V. 13, die im hebräischen Text die Kritik am Haus Davids ausdrückte (vgl. Wildberger 1972, 288), nicht aufrechterhält: In V. 13 fehlt ein entsprechendes Personalpronomen. Auch dies ist ein Zeichen dafür, dass der Text als durchgängig Heil ansagend zu verstehen ist.
36. Vgl. zur Interpretation Wildberger 1972, 288. 294. 297; Kaiser 1981, 165, allerdings unter Ausgliederung von 14b–16, und Clements 1990, sowie zusammenfassend Höffken 1989, 27–29.

V. 15–16 auch Elemente, die eine Heilszeit ansagen.[37] In der Septuaginta-Version gibt es diese Ambivalenz nicht mehr. Hier werden eindeutig die wundersame Gestalt eines Erlösers und in V. 17 eine messianische Heilszeit angekündigt. Diese Interpretation von V. 17 stützt sich darauf, dass der Text mit einem zu V. 16b adversativem ἀλλά einsetzt; das folgende soll gegen die Furcht vor den zwei Königen gesagt sein. Erwartet wird eine Heilszeit, die der des davidischen Großreiches vor der Reichsspaltung gleicht.[38] Folglich kann der Umstand, auf den dieses Zeichen folgt, nicht negativ als Verschulden gewertet worden sein. Deshalb wohl hat der Übersetzer aus dem Vorwurf Jesajas ein Lob gemacht, Ahas zum Streiter mit Menschen und Gott umgedeutet und ihn so zur positiven Identifikationsfigur gestaltet—in Zeiten der Not hilft Gott bei korrektem Verhalten weiter.

Auch der Schluss des Kapitels zeigt ein eigenes Verständnis des hebräischen Textes: Die als Erläuterung des in V. 17 Angekündigten zu verstehenden Weissagungen 7,18–25, die zwar auch Heil (V. 21–22), aber doch überwiegend Unheil ansagen, wurden vom Übersetzer ganz offensichtlich als Heil weissagend gesehen, beinahe als Szenario eines vor der Heilszukunft ablaufenden Dramas. V. 18 schildert das Versammeln der beiden Großmächte Ägypten und Assyrien, wobei durch die Einfügung von κυριεύει deutlich die Ebene des Politischen angesprochen wird. Die Feinde lassen sich im Land nieder (V. 19), bis dann aber der Herr das Schermesser von jenseits des Flusses der Assyrer holt (V. 20). Durch die Wiedergabe des במלך אשור mit einem an ποταμός angeschlossenen Genitiv wird ausgedrückt, dass an eine andere Macht als die der Assyrer gedacht ist, die dann, so ist V. 20b wohl zu verstehen, die beiden im Lande befindlichen Gegner vernichtend schlägt. Dadurch wird der Weg zum Heil (V. 21) frei.

---

37. Diese Interpretation setzt voraus, dass Dickmilch/Rahm und Honig nicht als Speisen einer Nomaden- oder Notzeit, sondern wie in 7,22 als Zeichen für die Fülle der Heilszeit zu verstehen sind. Vgl. zur Diskussion darüber Wildberger 1972, 295–96 und Kaiser 1981, 159. 173.

38. Problematisch ist die Übersetzung von V. 17b, weil der Kasus des Eigennamens Εφραιμ nicht erkennbar ist. Entweder ist (1) noch ὁ θεός das Subjekt; Gott hätte dann Ephraim von Juda weggenommen. Problematisch ist in diesem Falle der Anschluss von τὸν βασιλέα τῶν Ἀσσυρίων, das entweder (durch zu ergänzendes καί?) parallel zu Ephraim geordnet werden müsste, woraus sich zwei Heilstaten Gottes ergeben würden (vgl. 2.Kön 18), oder mit dem Rest des Verses, wie im hebräischen Text, nicht zu verbinden ist. Oder (2) Ephraim ist Subjekt, welches den König der Assyrer von Juda weggenommen hätte. Diese Lösung ist allerdings historisch schwierig; die erstgenannte Deutung scheint letztlich am wahrscheinlichsten.

9. Die Jungfrauengeburt des endzeitlichen Immanuel 207

Auch dieser Passus ist gut vor dem Hintergrund der Auseinandersetzungen der 1. Hälfte des 2. Jh.v.Chr. zu verstehen, wenn man sich die Gebietsansprüche der Seleukiden und Ptolemäer auf Israel und die daraus resultierenden Auseinandersetzungen vergegenwärtigt.

Ebenfalls als Heilsweissagung ist der neu verstandene V. 25 zu sehen:

וכל ההרים אשר במעדר יעדרון	καὶ πᾶν ὄρος ἀροτριώμενον ἀροτριαθήσεται
לא־תבוא שמה יראת שמיר ושית	καὶ οὐ μὴ ἐπέλθῃ ἐκεῖ φόβος
והיה למשלח שור ולמרמס שה	ἔσται γὰρ ἀπὸ τῆς χέρσου καὶ ἀκάνθης
	εἰς βόσκημα προβάτου καὶ εἰς καταπάτημα βοός

Statt dass man die Berge aus Furcht vor Dornen und Disteln nicht mehr betritt und nur noch Rinder und Schafe dort weiden können, werden die Berge wieder gepflügt werden. Furcht wird nicht mehr dorthin kommen, weil es vom unfruchtbaren und dornigen Land zum Weideland der Schafe und Rinder geworden sein wird.[39] Auffällig ist dabei, dass hier πρόβατον und βοῦς für die Wiedergabe von שׁוֹר und שֶׂה verwendet wurden. Damit soll an die Heilsverheißung in V. 21 erinnert werden, wo eben diese Worte (als Übersetzung von בקר und צאן) gebraucht wurden. So interpretieren sich die Verse gegenseitig: Das unfruchtbare, dornige Land wird wieder verwendbar werden, und die Menschen können dort die ihnen verheißenen Haustiere weiden lassen und so die angekündigte Menge von Milch, Butter und Honig (V. 22) erzeugen.

Als Zwischenergebnis ist festzuhalten, dass Jes 7 LXX als einlinige Heilsansage zu verstehen ist, die auf die Situation der späteren Makkabäerzeit zielt und in ihr konkrete Hoffnung schenkt. In diesem Rahmen ist nun auch der strittige Vers 7,14 zu sehen.

2. Die Jungfrauengeburt des kommenden Heilbringers

Zunächst ist zu beachten, dass der hebräische Text von Jes 7,14 Unklarheiten birgt, die bei einer Übersetzung zu berücksichtigen waren bzw. Anlass

---

39. Diese Übersetzung kann dadurch veranlasst worden sein, dass לא־תבוא als 3. Pers. fem. Sg. aufgefasst und auf יראת bezogen wurde (Fischer 1930, 20 nimmt zusätzlich eine irrtümliche Verlesung von יראת in יראה an). שמיר ושית sah der Übersetzer dann als Beginn des zweiten Halbsatzes an. Auch bei einer solchen Erklärung der Übersetzung als nicht absichtliche Veränderung des Sinnes bleibt das Ergebnis, dass schon der Übersetzer das Kapitel 7 als mit einer Heilsansage endend verstand.

zur Interpretation boten. Dazu gehört das Verständnis von עלמה, einem Wort, das in der Hebräischen Bibel nur neunmal verwendet wurde und in den Septuaginta-Schriften, die dem Jesaja-Übersetzer wohl vorlagen,[40] mit νεᾶνις (Ex 2,8; Ps 68[67],25) und παρθένος (Gen 24,43) übersetzt wurde. Weiterhin gehören dazu (1) die Offenheit der Zeitstufe des Adjektivs הרה und des Partizips [41]ילדת und (2) die Frage, ob וקראת als 2. Pers. fem./mask. oder als Nebenform zur 3. Pers. fem.[42] oder als Part. fem. anzusehen ist. Der Übersetzer hat in allen Fällen eindeutig entschieden: ἰδοὺ ἡ παρθένος ἐν γαστρὶ ἕξει καὶ τέξεται υἱόν καὶ καλέσεις τὸ ὄνομα αὐτοῦ Εμμανουηλ.[43] Er verstand (1) den Vers als auf die Zukunft gerichtete Weissagung. Die Jungfrau wird erst noch schwanger werden. Dem Kind wird (2) Ahas den Namen geben, denn dieser ist ja noch angesprochen. Damit ist erneut auf die Nähe des kommenden Heils, wieder innerhalb einer Generation, hingewiesen. Bestätigt wird dadurch auch, dass Ahas vom Übersetzer positiv verstanden wurde, denn er wird am Heilsgeschehen beteiligt.

Weniger eindeutig ist der Sinngehalt von παρθένος. Das griechische Wort konnte, ähnlich wie das hebräische עלמה, einfach die junge, kinderlose Frau bezeichnen, dann aber auch die tatsächlich unberührte Jungfrau, ohne dass eine Bedeutung die andere abgelöst hätte. Vom lexikalischen Befund her ist das Problem also nicht zu lösen.[44] Im nächsten Schritt ist

---

40. Seeligmann 1948, 71–73.
41. Vgl. Wildberger 1972, 267.
42. So Gesenius/Kautzsch[28], §74g.
43. Es lässt sich fragen, ob der Name Εμμανουηλ bereits geprägt den Ehrennamen des kommenden Heilsbringers meinte. Dafür spricht m.E., dass er ohne deutende Änderungen bzw. Übersetzung (vgl. 7,3; 8,4; 9,6[5]) einfach transkribiert wird. Doch da der Name sonst nicht mehr begegnet (in 8,8. 10 wird עמנו אל nicht als Name aufgefasst), lässt sich kein sicheres Urteil fällen.
44. Vgl. Delling 1954, 825–26. 831 und Liddell/Scott, s.v. Syrén 1989, 54–55, kommt in einer kurzen Diskussion von Jes 7,14 LXX zu dem Ergebnis, dass die Bedeutung von griech. παρθένος im Rahmen von hebr. עלמה bleibt. Das leitet er daraus ab, dass in Gen 34,3 παρθένος für die vergewaltigte Dina verwendet werden konnte. Doch ist m.E. an dieser Stelle eher damit zu rechnen, dass Sicherns Liebe zu (der Jungfrau) Dina, von der in V. 3 die Rede ist, den Beweggrund für die Vergewaltigung (V. 2) darstellt, so dass παρθένος letztlich nicht für die vergewaltigte Frau verwendet wurde. Da außerdem die Genesis-Septuaginta aus anderer Zeit und von anderer Hand stammt, ist diese Parallele wenig wert, zumal bei Syren über die Konkordanzarbeit hinausgehende Überlegungen zum Problem fehlen.

Zu demselben Ergebnis, dass παρθένος in Jes 7,14 LXX nicht „Jungfrau" bedeutet, kommen Haag 1969, ebenfalls mit Bezug auf Gen 34,3 LXX, und Ford 1965–1966.

9. Die Jungfrauengeburt des endzeitlichen Immanuel 209

nun danach zu fragen, ob es zur Zeit der Übersetzung eine geprägte Verwendung von παρθένος im Zusammenhang mit Heilserwartungen und der Geburt von Erlösergestalten gegeben hat.

Im griechischen Bereich sind seit dem 5. Jh. verschiedene als Παρθένος bezeichnete Göttinnen nicht nur auf der Krim und in Thrakien, sondern auch in Griechenland selbst belegt.[45] Sie sollten zu Gesundheit, Fruchtbarkeit und Reichtum verhelfen und Feinde abwehren. Zusammengefasst wurden solche Erwartungen an lokale Gottheiten dann in der Verehrung von Athene und Artemis als Δύο θεαὶ παρθένοι.[46]

Bekannt und im Zusammenhang mit Jes 7 bzw. Mt 1 häufig zitiert ist die Schilderung der Zeremonien aus dem alexandrinischen Koreion, die bei Epiphanius (haer LI 22,8) erhalten ist.[47] Danach wurde im Tempel der Κόρη[48] in der Nacht vom 5. zum 6. Januar die Geburt des Αἰών durch den Umzug eines Gottesbildes gefeiert. Als Sinn der Feier galt: ταύτῃ τῇ ὥρᾳ σήμερον ἡ Κόρη ἐγέννησε τὸν Αἰῶνα, wobei ἡ Κόρη durch τουτέστιν ἡ παρθένος erläutert wurde. Ebenfalls als Ruf beim Geburtsfest Aions wird

---

Zu einer anderen Lösung kommen Brown 1977, 145–49. 523–24 und Davies 1981, 214. Beide verstehen παρθένος so, dass an eine Frau gedacht sei, die zur Zeit Jungfrau ist, dann aber in natürlicher Weise empfangen werde. An ein Wunder sei nicht gedacht, sondern es solle nur herausgestellt werden, dass das erwartete Kind eine Erstgeburt sei.

Van der Kooij 1997, 97–99 interpretiert παρθένος in 7,14 von 37,22 und 62,5 her, wo παρθένος auf Zion-Jerusalem zu beziehen sei. Die Jungfrau Zion werde, so seine Deutung von 7,14, einen Sohn gebären, der mit dem Rest zu identifizieren ist (7,7). Methodisch liegt dem der Versuch zugrunde, „dass gewisse freie Übersetzungen mittels anderer Texte in LXX-Jes verständlicher werden" (S. 99).

Exegetisch ist anzumerken, dass bei den vier Belegstellen von παρθένος in der Jesaja-Septuaginta neben 7,14 (23,4; 37,22; 47,1; 62,5) nur in 37,22 von einer direkten Identifikation von Jungfrau und Zion zu reden ist, und diese ist von M vorgegeben. Eine Bearbeitung der παρθένος-Belege aus der Umwelt fehlt leider völlig. So ist m.E. van der Kooijs Deutungsversuch als nicht überzeugend abzulehnen, selbst wenn sein Gesamtverständnis von Jes 7 (LXX) als aktualisierende Heilsansage dem hier vorgetragenen nahe steht.

45. Vgl. Fehrle 1910, 162–67.
46. Ebd., 197–204: 204.
47. Vgl. Norden 1931, 28; Dibelius 1953, 41, Anm. 66.
48. Παρθένος und Κόρη sind weitgehend bedeutungsgleich, vgl. Delling 1954, 827, und Fehrle 1910, 164.

von Hippolyt aus Eleusis überliefert: ἡ παρθένος ἡ ἐν γαστὴρ ἔχουσα καὶ συλλαμβάνουσα καὶ τίκτουσα υἱόν.[49]

Wiederum in Alexandria wurde in der Nacht zum 25. Dezember das Geburtsfest des Aion-Helios gefeiert,[50] bei dem die ersten Lichtstrahlen des neuen Tages mit dem Ruf ἡ παρθένος τέτοκεν, αὔξει φῶς begrüßt wurden (Epiphanius, Pan. LI 22,5). Dasselbe Fest ist auch bei den Nabatäern und in Elusa belegt.[51] Obwohl die erhaltenen Berichte über die Aion-Feiern erst aus später Zeit stammen, ist doch der Name des Festes (Κικήλλια) bereits im Kanopusdekret von 239/8 v.Chr. zu finden, so dass auch mit der Durchführung der Zeremonien in ptolemäischer Zeit zu rechnen ist,[52] zumal Aion schon im ptolemäischen Alexandria als Weltgott verehrt wurde, der den ewigen Bestand der Stadt verbürgt.[53] Neben dieser Vorstellung steht die vom sich ständig erneuernden Aion als Gott der Zeitperioden und des Weltverlaufs,[54] im hermetischen Schrifttum tritt dann noch die Vorstellung hinzu, dass Aion als Kraft Gottes die Welt durchdringt und belebt.[55]

Die Feier der Geburt des Aion muss vor dem Hintergrund ägyptischer Königs- und Göttervorstellungen gesehen werden.[56] Seit dem 2. Jt. ist nämlich die auf ältere Vorstellungen zurückgehende Legende belegt, dass der Gott Amun sich in Gestalt des regierenden Königs der jungfräulichen Königin nähert und mit ihr einen neuen Gottkönig erzeugt. Für das erste Jahrtausend lässt sich eine Veränderung dieser Vorstellung deutlich machen. Gefeiert wurde nun die übernatürliche Zeugung von jungen Göttern, nicht mehr nur der Könige. So wurden die Tempel der letzten Jahrhunderte vor der Zeitenwende mit eigenen Geburtshäusern (Mammisi) ausgestattet, in denen die wunderhafte Geburt der Götter nicht nur im Mythos vergegenwärtigt, sondern wohl auch im Ritual nachvollzogen wurde.[57] In hellenistischer Zeit wurde dieses Geburtsritual in die Isis- und Osirismythen einbezogen. So begegnen nun Aussagen über die jung-

---

49. Seeligmann 1948, 120, mit Hinweis auf Kittel 1924, 14. 23–24.
50. Vgl. Norden 1931, 24–25, und Dibelius 1953, 41, Anm. 66.
51. Vgl. Greßmann 1929, 361–62, und Norden 1931, 27, Anm. 2.
52. Ebd., 25, Anm. 5; 30.
53. Vgl. Weinreich 1919, 189. Zur Diskussion um den Aionkult zu ptolemäischer Zeit in Alexandria und Eleusis vgl. ebenso Fraser 1972, I, 199–200; II, 336–37, Anm. 79.
54. Vgl. Fauth 1964, 185–88 und Nilsson 1950, 480–83.
55. Vgl. Zepf 1927, 231.
56. Vgl. zum folgenden Brunner 1986, 29. 191 und Brunner-Traut 1960.
57. Vgl. dazu Daumas 1977.

fräuliche Geburt des Sonnengottes Re durch Neith und des Horus durch Isis.[58] Schon in der 19. Dyn. begegnet im Tempel Sethos' I. in Abydos eine Selbstprädikation der Isis „ich bin die große Jungfrau" gemeinsam mit der Aussage, dass sie Mutter des Horus sei. Diese Selbstbezeichnung leitet sich aus der Königslegende ab.[59] Neith und Isis konnten miteinander identifiziert und als Kore bezeichnet werden, Horus wurde in ptolemäischer Zeit zur Aionsfigur.[60] Wie oben bereits deutlich wurde, konnte Aion zudem als Aion-Helios in die Nähe des Sonnengottes gerückt werden. Auf diese Weise ist die Traditionskette von der Geburt des Gottkönigs bis hin zur Geburt Aions geschlossen. Wenn nun in Alexandrien die jungfräuliche Geburt Aions in der dargestellten Weise gefeiert wurde, lässt sich vermuten, dass diese Feste der Erwartung auf eine Horusgeburt, also auf einen Heilskönig, Ausdruck gaben, welche gewiss eine eschatologische Dimension beinhaltete.

Belegt ist außerdem die Sage, dass die Sternbild-Göttin Παρθένος zu Zeiten des goldenen und silbernen Geschlechts auf der Erde lebte, sich dann aber wegen der Schlechtigkeit der Menschen in den Himmel zurückzog, weshalb sie dort als Sternbild zu sehen ist. In Aratus' Phainomena (96–146) wurde sie als Dike besungen, die ihren ewigen Platz am Himmel als leuchtende Garantin für Recht und Gerechtigkeit hat. Mit Beginn des neuen goldenen Zeitalters werde sie zur Erde zurückkehren.[61] In der Astrologie gilt die Jungfrau als universale Herrscherin in Zeit und Raum. Zudem findet sich auch die Identifikation der Sternbild-Παρθένος mit Kore.[62]

---

58. Vgl. Pettazoni 1954, 174.
59. Vgl. Bergmann 1968, 219–26.
60. So Merkelbach 1963, 48–50.
61. Diese Erwartung fand ihren wohl bekanntesten Ausdruck im letzten vorchristlichen Jahrhundert in Vergils vierter Ekloge. Dort wurde sie verbunden mit der Vorstellung, dass ein Kind die neue Heilszeit heraufführen werde, wobei sich bei der Beschreibung des goldenen Zeitalters deutlich Motive aus Jes 7; 9 und 11 feststellen lassen. Unklar bleibt allerdings das Verhältnis zwischen der Jungfrau und dem Knaben, namentlich, ob sie ihn gebiert. Zur fast unübersehbaren Literatur zu Vergil vgl. Briggs 1981; zur Interpretation Kraus 1980. Zur Diskussion um die Frage nach der Abhängigkeit Vergils von alttestamentlichen oder jüdischen Vorstellungen, die über Alexandrien, insbesondere die Sibyllinischen Orakel, vermittelt wurden, vgl. Norden 1931, 53–58; Groß 1956, 53–57 und Gatz 1967, 87–103.
62. Vgl. Gundel 1949, 1945–46. 1953–54.

Über diese direkten Verbindungen einer Παρθένος-Gestalt mit Heilserwartungen hinaus ist bei Plutarch (Numa 4,6 [1,62c]) belegt, dass es in Ägypten die Vorstellung einer übernatürlichen Zeugung gab.[63] Der Alexandriner Philo führt zu Sara, Lea, Rebekka und Zippora aus, dass sie übernatürlich durch Gott schwanger wurden (de Cherub 45–47);[64] Heilsgestalten der Geschichte Israels wurden demnach ohne direkten Anhalt im Bibeltext in Zusammenhang mit Gedanken einer von Gott gewirkten Zeugung gebracht. Diese Vorstellung begegnet auch im griechischen Bereich, z.B. für Platon und Alexander den Großen.[65]

Festzuhalten bleibt nach der Beleuchtung dieser ganz unterschiedlichen Stoffe, dass es offenbar eine feste gedankliche Verbindung von Παρθένος bzw. übernatürlicher Zeugung und der Erwartung von Heilsgestalten oder -zeiten gab, die gerade im ägyptischen Alexandria eine lange Tradition hatte und gefeiert wurde.[66] Dass es auch in der Jesaja-Septuaginta, die ja in Alexandria übersetzt wurde, um eine ganz besondere Heilsgestalt geht, zeigt der Kontext. Denn die V. 15–16 werden deutlich anders aufgefasst als im hebräischen Text. Dort hat V. 16 die Funktion einer Zeitangabe: Ehe der Knabe versteht, das Böse zu verwerfen und das Gute zu wählen, wird die Gefahr vergangen sein. V. 15 ist weniger eindeutig, er meint entweder eine Bedingung des Heils[67] oder eine Illustration der

---

63. Vgl. Delling 1954, 828.
64. Vgl. Dibelius 1953, 31.
65. Vgl. Fehrle 1910, 3–4.
66. Dieses Ergebnis und die daraus abzuleitende Interpretation von Jes 7,14 LXX widerspricht in allen Punkten der Arbeit von Guthknecht 1952, 68, der die These vertritt, dass sich nirgends in den altorientalischen Religionen und in der hellenistisch-römischen Welt vor der Zeitenwende die Vorstellung der Geburt eines heilbringenden Herrschers von einer jungfräulichen Göttin nachweisen lasse. Das παρθένος in Jes 7,14 sei somit im Bedeutungsrahmen des hebr. עלמה zu verstehen (S. 31–34. 108). Auf eine eingehende Exegese von Jes 7 LXX hat Guthknecht jedoch verzichtet. Diese abweichende Anschauung resultiert vor allem aus einer anderen Interpretation der Belege aus Äypten (S. 46–52) und einer Datierung der Geburtsfeiern Aions in nachchristliche Zeit (S. 69–73). Doch die Schwäche der Argumentation zeigt sich besonders bei der Verhandlung der philonischen Belege (S. 74. 97–98). Um nicht für das Judentum die Vorstellung der Jungfrauengeburt annehmen zu müssen, erklärt Guthknecht Philos Anschauung als aus hellenistischem Gedankengut resultierend, obgleich es diese Erwartung dort aber, seinen eigenen Ergebnissen zufolge, noch gar nicht gab. Letztlich kann er nicht erklären, wie es überhaupt zu der Vorstellung von der Jungfrauengeburt gekommen ist—ein wenig befriedigendes Ergebnis.
67. So Kaiser 1981, 158–59.

9. Die Jungfrauengeburt des endzeitlichen Immanuel 213

übernatürlichen Erkenntnis des Immanuel.[68] In der Septuaginta-Fassung haben die beiden Verse eine identische Aussage: πρὶν ἢ γνῶναι αὐτὸν ἢ προελέσθαι πονηρὰ ἐκλέξεται τὸ ἀγαθόν (V. 15b), bevor das Kind zwischen gut und böse unterscheiden kann, hat es schon das Böse verworfen, das Gute gewählt.[69] Was im hebräischen Text als Zeitangabe der Heilsankündigung untergeordnet ist, wird in der Septuaginta folglich zum eigentlichen Hauptsatz.

Alles Gewicht dieser Verse liegt also darauf, die besondere, übernatürliche Begabung des Kindes herauszustreichen, die seiner wunderhaften Zeugung entsprechen würde: Dem Kind wird so etwas wie ein Unvermögen zum Bösen anhaften, eine Vorstellung, die nach Jer 31,31–34 und Ez 11,19–20 zu Israels Erwartungen an die Heilszeit gehört. Es lässt sich fragen, ob sich nicht diese Beschreibung des Jungfrauensohns und der Name des in 9,6(5) angekündigten Kindes μεγάλης βουλῆς ἄγγελος[70] gegenseitig erläutern, der Übersetzer also von einer einheitlichen Heilserwartung aus beide Weissagungen gestaltet hat: Der Messias wird stets rechtes Verhalten vor Gott üben, und so wird es ewigen Frieden geben. Dabei wird die Messiaserwartung gegenüber der Jesajas bzw. der hebräischen Bibel modifiziert. Der Messias wird als übernatürliches, sündloses Wesen gesehen—dem dann verständlicherweise auch eine besondere Herkunft eignen muss.

Es bleibt der mögliche Einwand, dass der Übersetzer παρθένος unreflektiert verwendete. Doch dagegen sprechen Beobachtungen über die Aufnahme religiöser Sprache Alexandriens, die I. L. Seeligmann zu Jes 65,11 gemacht hat.[71] Danach hat der Übersetzer bewusst den (sonst in der Septuaginta vermiedenen) Namen des alexandrinischen Stadtgottes δαίμων und den der Göttin Τύχη verwendet, um das im hebräischen Text angeführte Götterpaar גד und מני aktualisierend wiederzugeben. In 14,12 wird הילל בן־שחר mit ὁ ἑωσφόρος übersetzt, der in Alexandria als Schutzgott der Stadt verehrt wurde.[72] Wenn also der Übersetzer offensichtlich

---

68. So Wildberger 1972, 296.
69. Mit dieser Interpretation erübrigt sich Seeligmanns Annahme (1948, 34), 7,16 sei aus zwei ursprünglich getrennten Übersetzungen zusammengesetzt worden. M.E. ist die erhaltene Fassung von V. 16 unter Zugrundelegung des vom hebräischen Text gebotenen Materials parallel zu V. 15 gestaltet worden.
70. Vgl. dazu Hanhart 1983, 335. 345–46.
71. Seeligmann 1948, 99–100. Vgl. auch Morenz 1964, 251.
72. Vgl. Seeligmann 1948, 100, und Fraser 1972, 219–20. In Jes 13,21 (für hebr.

mit den Kulten Alexandrias vertraut war, wäre es dann erklärbar, dass er den geprägten Begriff der im griechischen und ägyptischen Bereich bekannten Vorstellung von der παρθένος-Geburt eines Heilskönigs bzw. neuen Zeitalters irrtümlich oder unbewusst verwendet? Dagegen spricht nicht die Tatsache, dass sich der Übersetzer in 65,11 und 14,12 polemisch gegen die hellenistischen Gottheiten richtet. Denn wenn die hier vorgetragene Interpretation von παρθένος richtig ist, ging es ja nicht um eine Identifizierung der Jungfrau, die den Immanuel gebiert, mit hellenistischen Göttinnenvorstellungen, sondern um ein Anknüpfen der aus der hebräischen Bibel gelesenen Heilsbotschaft an die Verstehensmuster der hellenistischen Umgebung im ägyptischen Alexandria. παρθένος ist demnach nicht als Eigenname oder als feststehendes Epitheton für eine konkrete Göttin verwendet worden, sondern als Zeichen für die besondere Bedeutung des kommenden Heilsbringers. Wie im griechischen Bereich jungfräuliche Priesterinnen oder Prophetinnen eine besondere Nähe und Mittlerschaft zu Gott hatten,[73] gab es später im orientalischen Raum das Ideal eines heiligen Lebens, getrennt von der unreinen Welt (vgl. Dan 9,3; 10,2-3).[74] Da dieser alte Äon der Sünde zugrunde gehen muss (4.Esr 4,27-32), darf man sich nicht an ihm beflecken (syrBar 44,9; Offb 3,4). Vor diesem Hintergrund wird klar, dass eine Abkunft der messianischen Gestalt von der sündhaften Welt ausgeschlossen sein muss. Daher steigt der Messias in 4.Esr 13 aus dem Wasser heraus, kommt der Menschensohn in Dan 7,13-14 auf Wolken heran (vielleicht ist so auch das כ in כבר אנש erklärlich—es soll die nötige Distanz zum Irdischen ausdrücken).[75] Nach Philo (de Cherub 49-50) verbürgte Jungfräulichkeit die Freiheit von Unreinheit, weshalb Gott Sara nachträglich wieder zur Jungfrau machte. Die Aussage von der Jungfrauengeburt will also zum Ausdruck bringen, dass der kommende Heilsbringer von Beginn an dem normalen sündigen Lauf von Zeugung und Geburt enthoben ist, demnach einer neuen Zeit angehört und gerade deshalb die Möglichkeit zum Heil verbürgt.

יענה „Strauß" und 34,13; 43,20 (für hebr. תן „Schakal") werden außerdem noch σειρῆνες erwähnt, vgl. Hengel 1976, 132.

73. Vgl. Fehrle 1910, 93.

74. Vgl. Hengel 1969, 387.

75. Erste christliche Ausleger deuteten gar den Stein in Dan 2,34 als Prophezeiung der Jungfrauengeburt Christi, weil er ohne Zutun von Menschenhand vom Berg losgerissen wurde. Auch dies belegt die Vorstellung, dass der Messias von Geburt an der Menschenwelt enthoben sein muss. Vgl. dazu Rowley 1935, 61 mit Anm. 1; 76.

3. Zusammenfassung

Damit ist der Schluss der Untersuchung erreicht. Die Septuaginta-Version von Jes 7 erscheint als theologisch durchdachtes Zeugnis für das Bestreben, die alten Prophezeiungen an Israel in eine neue Situation hinein sprechen zu lassen, um so der bedrängten Gemeinde konkrete Hoffnung zu vermitteln. Gleichzeitig wurden Traditionen der nichtjüdischen Umwelt aufgenommen. Um die erwartete Heilszeit als tatsächlich neue, alles übertreffende Weltzeit kenntlich zu machen, griff man die Vorstellung von der Jungfrauengeburt des Weltaltergottes Aion auf.[76] Damit wurde den von ihrer Umwelt geprägten Lesern die besondere Bedeutung des Immanuel-Kindes als kommende Heilsgestalt schon vor der Beschreibung seiner wunderhaften Fähigkeiten signalisiert und gleichzeitig der Gegenwartsbezug der alten Weissagung betont.

Ein solches Verständnis von Jes 7 muss auch die urchristliche Gemeinde gehabt haben, die dieses Kapitel zur Interpretation des Christusgeschehens heranzog (Mt 1,21–23; Lk 1,31). Dabei ist offensichtlich, dass die Septuaginta-Version des Jesajabuches nicht nur die Messiaserwartung der Gemeinde prägte und so zur Übertragung der Vorstellung von der Jungfrauengeburt auf Jesus führte, sondern zumindest Matthäus auch tatsächlich als Heilige Schrift vorlag.[77] Denn er entnahm ihr nicht nur in 1,23 das Reflexionszitat Jes 7,14, sondern er übernahm außerdem noch das τέξεται (δὲ) υἱὸν καὶ καλέσεις τὸ ὄνομα αὐτοῦ aus der Jesaja-Septuaginta, durch das Joseph die Geburt Jesu angekündigt wird. Interessant ist, dass Matthäus in 1,21 den Septuaginta-Text original zitiert, in 1,23 dann jedoch charakteristisch ändert: καὶ καλέσουσιν τὸ ὄνομα αὐτοῦ Ἐμμανουήλ—ein Zeichen dafür, dass man in seiner Gemeinde im Bekenntnis Jesus mit dem aus Jesaja entnommenen Ehrennamen Immanuel belegte. Dies wurde als Erfüllung der Heilsansage gesehen, und daher musste der Text der Weissagung angepasst werden. Damit ist exemplarisch deutlich geworden, dass die Septuaginta nicht nur als ein eigenständiges Dokument der frühen Wirkungsgeschichte alttestamentlicher Texte zu sehen ist, sondern auch

---

76. Zwar wird in der Jesaja-Septuaginta αἰών verwendet, doch da dies zumeist zur Wiedergabe von hebr. עולם geschieht (vgl. z.B. 9,7[6]; 14,20; 30,8; 51,6.8), lässt sich m.E. nicht entscheiden; ob hier eine dualistische Anschauung von gegenwärtigem und zukünftigem Aion zugrunde liegt—so sehr dies bei dem festgestellten apokalyptischen Gedankengut zu erwarten wäre.

77. Vgl. Luz 1989, 100.

als Station im Prozess der Entwicklung von der Hebräischen Bibel hin zum Neuen Testament, eine Station, die ihrerseits selbständig traditionsbildend wirkte.[78]

Literatur

Bergmann, Jan. 1968. *Ich bin Isis. Studien zum memphitischen Hintergrund der griechischen Isisaretalogien.* Acta Universitatis Upsaliensis. Historia religionum 3. Uppsala: Uppsala University Press.

Bickert, Rainer. 1987. „König Ahas und der Prophet Jesaja. Ein Beitrag zum Problem des syrisch-ephraimitischen Krieges." *ZAW* 99:361–384.

Briggs, Ward W. 1981. „A Bibliography of Virgil's ‚Eclogues.'" *ANRW* 31.2:1267–1357.

Brown, Raymond E. 1977. *The Birth of the Messiah. A Commentary on the Infancy Narratives in Matthew and Luke.* ABRL. Garden City, NY: Doubleday.

Brunner, Hellmut. 1986. *Die Geburt des Gottkönigs. Studien zur Überlieferung eines altägyptischen Mythos.* ÄgAbh10. 2. erw. Auflage. Wiesbaden: Harrassowitz.

Brunner-Traut, Emma. 1960. „Die Geburtsgeschichte der Evangelien im Lichte ägyptologischer Forschungen." *ZRGG* 12:97–111.

Charles, Robert H. 1929. *A Critical and Exegetical Commentary on the Book of Daniel.* Oxford: Clarendon.

Clements, Ronald E. 1990. "The Immanuel Prophecy of Isa. 7:10–17 and Its Messianic Interpretation." Seiten 225–40 in *Die Hebräische Bibel und ihre zweifache Nachgeschichte. Festschrift für Rolf Rendtorff zum*

---

78. Damit wird gegen Gese 1974, 145, behauptet, dass die Vorstellung der jungfräulichen Messiasgeburt vor der neutestamentlichen Traditionsbildung nachweisbar ist. Sie wird zwar im Rahmen biblischer Traditionen, doch unter deutlicher Aufnahme außerbiblischer Motive formuliert. So scheint mir Geses Erklärung einer einlinigen Entstehung dieser Tradition „vom Ganzen der biblischen Traditionsbildung her" (131) nicht möglich. Das gilt um so mehr, als er die Herkunft des besonderen Motivs der Jungfräulichkeit gerade nicht erläutert; über den Satz „Der Davidismus wird dazu geführt haben, dass dieses Erscheinen nur als jungfräuliche Geburt vorgestellt werden konnte" (133) kommt er an dieser Stelle nicht hinaus. Trotz dieser Kritik bleibt natürlich die Frage bestehen, weshalb diese Tradition in den Gemeinden von Matthäus und Lukas übernommen werden konnte, welche Anknüpfungspunkte es im palästinischen Judentum für eine solche Vorstellung gegeben hat. Zur Diskussion zwischen Juden und Christen um Jes 7,14 in der Zeit der Alten Kirche vgl. Kamesar 1990.

65. Geburtstag. Hrsg. von Erhard Blum. Neukirchen-Vluyn: Neukirchener Verlag.

Conzelmann, Hans. 1966. „συνίημι κτλ." *ThWNT* 7:886–88.

Daumas, François. 1977. „Geburtshaus." *LÄ* 2:462–75.

Davies, William D. 1981. *Matthew 1–7. A Critical and Exegetical Commentary on the Gospel according to St. Matthew.* ICC 1. Edinburgh: T&T Clark.

Dehandschutter, Boudewijn. 1989. „Martyrium und Agon. Über die Wurzeln der Vorstellung vom ΑΓΩΝ im Vierten Makkabäerbuch." Seiten 215–19 in *Die Entstehung der jüdischen Martyrologie.* Hrsg. von Jan W. van Henten. StPB 38. Leiden: Brill.

Delling, Gerhard. 1954. „παρθένος." *ThWNT* 5:824–35.

Dibelius, Martin. 1953. „Jungfrauensohn und Krippenkind. Untersuchungen zur Geburtsgeschichte Jesu im Lukas-Evangelium." Seiten 1–78 in *Botschaft und Geschichte I. Zur Evangelienforschung.* Hrsg. von Günther Bornkamm. Tübingen: Mohr Siebeck.

Fauth, Wolfgang. 1964. „Aion." *KP* 1:185–88.

Fehrle, Eugen. 1910. *Die kultische Keuschheit im Altertum.* RVV 6. Gießen: Töpelmann.

Fischer, Johannes. 1930. *In welcher Schrift lag das Buch Jesaja den LXX vor? Eine textkritische Studie.* BZAW 56. Gießen: Töpelmann.

Ford, J. Massingberd. 1965–1966. „The Meaning of Virgin." *NTS* 12:293–99.

Fraser, Peter M. 1972. *Ptolemaic Alexandria.* Oxford: Clarendon.

Gatz, Bodo. 1967. *Weltalter, goldene Zeit und sinnverwandte Vorstellungen.* Spudasmata 16. Hildesheim: Olms.

Gese, Hartmut. 1974. „Natus ex virgine." Seiten 130–46 in *Vom Sinai zum Zion. Alttestamentliche Beiträge zur biblischen Theologie.* BEvTh 64. München: Kaiser.

Grelot, Pierre. 1974. „La Septante de Daniel IV et son substrat sémitique." *RB* 81:5–23.

Greßmann, Hugo. 1929. *Der Messias.* FRLANT 43 = NF 26. Göttingen: Vandenhoeck & Ruprecht.

Groß, Heinrich. 1956. *Die Idee des ewigen und allgemeinen Weltfriedens im Alten Orient und im Alten Testament.* TThS 7. Trier: Paulinus.

Grundmann, Walter. 1961. *Das Evangelium nach Lukas.* ThHK 3. 2. neubearb. Aufl. Berlin: Evangelische Verlagsanstalt.

Gundel, Wilhelm. 1949. „Παρθένος I." *PRE* 18.4:1936–49.

Guthknecht, Gottfried. 1952. „Das Motiv der Jungfrauengeburt in religionsgeschichtlicher Beleuchtung." Diss. masch., Greifswald.
Haag, Herbert. 1969. „Is 7,14 als alttestamentliche Grundstelle der Lehre von der Virginitas Mariae." Seiten 137–44 in *Jungfrauengeburt gestern und heute*. Hrsg. von Hermann Josef Brosch und Josef Hasenfuß. MSt 4. Essen: Driewer.
Hanhart, Robert. 1962. „Fragen um die Entstehung der LXX." *VT* 12:139–63.
———. 1983. „Die Septuaginta als Interpretation und Aktualisierung. Jes 9,1 (8,23)–7(6)." Seiten 331–46 in *Isaac Leo Seeligmann Volume*. Vol. 3. Hrsg. von Alexander Rofé und Yair Zakovitch. Jerusalem: Rubinstein.
Hengel, Martin. 1969. *Judentum und Hellenismus. Studien zu ihrer Begegnung unter besonderer Berücksichtigung Palästinas bis zur Mitte des 2. Jh. v. Chr.* WUNT 10. Tübingen: Mohr Siebeck.
———. 1976. *Juden, Griechen und Barbaren. Aspekte der Hellenisierung des Judentums in vorchristlicher Zeit*. SBS 76. Stuttgart: Katholisches Bibelwerk.
Höffken, Peter. 1989. „Grundfragen von Jesaja 7,1–17 im Spiegel neuerer Literatur." *BZ* 33:25–42.
Kaiser, Otto. 1981. *Das Buch des Propheten Jesaja. Kapitel 1–12*. ATD 17. 5. Aufl. Göttingen: Vandenhoeck & Ruprecht.
Kamesar, Adam. 1990. "The Virgin of Isaiah 7:14. The Philological Argument from the Second to the Fifth Century." *JTS* 41:51–75.
Kilian, Rudolf. 1970. „Die Geburt des Immanuel aus der Jungfrau." Seiten 9–35 in *Zum Thema Jungfrauengeburt*. Hrsg. von Karl Suso. Stuttgart: Katholisches Bibelwerk.
Kittel, Gerhard. 1924. *Die hellenistischen Mysterienreligionen und das Alte Testament*. BWAT 32. Stuttgart: Kohlhammer.
Kooij, Arie van der. 1977. „Die Septuaginta Jesajas als Dokument jüdischer Exegese. Einige Notizen zu LXX-Jes. 7." Seiten 91–102 in *Übersetzung und Deutung. Studien zu dem Alten Testament und seiner Umwelt. Alexander Reinard Hulst gewidmet von Freunden und Kollegen*. Nijkerk: Callenbach.
———. 1981. *Die alten Textzeugen des Jesajabuches*. OBO 35. Göttingen: Vandenhoeck & Ruprecht; Freiburg: Universitätsverlag.
Kraus, Walther. 1980. „Vergils vierte Ekloge. Ein kritisches Hypomnema." *ANRW* 31.1:604–45.

Luz, Ulrich. 1989. *Das Evangelium nach Matthäus, Bd I. Mt 1,1–7,29.* EKK 1.2. Aufl. Neukirchen-Vluyn: Neukirchener Verlag.
Merkelbach, Reinhold. 1963. *Isisfeste in griechisch-römischer Zeit.* Beiträge zur Klassischen Philologie 5. Meisenheim: Hain.
Morenz, Siegfried. 1964. „Ägyptische Spuren in der Septuaginta." Seiten 250–58 in *Mullus. Festschrift für Theodor Klausner.* Hrsg. von Alfred Stuiber. JAC 1. Münster: Aschendorff.
Nilsson, Martin P. 1950. *Geschichte der griechischen Religion II. 2, Die hellenistische und römische Zeit.* HAW V,2(2). München: Beck.
Norden, Eduard. 1931. *Die Geburt des Kindes. Geschichte einer religiösen Idee.* SBW 3. 2. Aufl. Leipzig: Teubner.
Ottley, Richard Rusden. 1906. *The Book of Isaiah According to the Septuagint (Codex Alexandrinus). II, Text and Notes.* Cambridge: Cambridge University Press.
Pettazoni, Raffaele. 1954. "Aion-(Kronos)Chronos in Egypt." Seiten 171–79 in *Essays on the History of Religions.* Leiden: Brill.
Ringgren, Helmer. 1973. „בִּין." *ThWAT* 1:621–29.
Rowley, Harold H. 1935. *Darius the Mede and the Four World Empires in the Book of Daniel.* Cardiff: University of Wales Press.
Seeligmann, Isaac Leo. 1948. *The Septuagint Version of Isaiah. A Discussion of its Problems.* MEOL 9. Leiden: Brill.
Stauffer, Ethelbert. 1933. „ἀγών κτλ." *ThWNT* 1:134–40.
Syrén, Roger. 1989. „The Isaiah-Targum and Christian Interpretation." *SJOT* 1:46–65.
Tov, Emanuel. 1987. „Die Septuaginta in ihrem theologischen und traditionsgeschichtlichen Verhältnis zur hebräischen Bibel." Seiten 237–68 in *Mitte der Schrift? Ein jüdisch-christliches Gespräch.* Hrsg. von Martin Klopfenstein u.a. Judaica et Christiana 11. Bern: Lang.
Weinreich, Otto. 1919. „Aion in Eleusis." *ARW* 19:174–90.
Wildberger, Hans. 1972. *Jesaja 1–12.* BKAT 10,1. Neukirchen-Vluyn: Neukirchener Verlag.
Zepf, Max. 1927. „Der Gott AIΩN in der hellenistischen Theologie." *ARW* 25:225–44.
Ziegler, Joseph. 1934. *Untersuchungen zur Septuaginta des Buches Jesaja.* ATA 12.3. Münster: Aschendorff.

10
Die Psalmüberschriften des Septuagintapsalters

1. Problemanzeige

Der Kreis derer, die sich intensiver mit der LXX beschäftigen, ist noch vergleichsweise überschaubar, und die einzelnen Arbeitsfelder sind meist so deutlich voneinander absetzbar, dass man in der Regel die Ergebnisse der Kolleginnen und Kollegen zwar zur Kenntnis nimmt, es aber kaum je wirkliche Debatten um den rechten Umgang und die angemessene Interpretation spezifischer Septuaginta-Probleme gibt. In der jüngsten Zeit hat es jedoch (verglichen mit der bisherigen Beschaulichkeit) intensivere Auseinandersetzungen um die LXX-Übersetzung zweier biblischer Bücher gegeben, die sich letztlich auf die Frage zuspitzen lassen, mit welchem Kriterienkatalog man bestimmte Abweichungen zwischen der LXX und dem MT oder früheren hebräischen Texten als theologische Interpretation des jeweiligen Übersetzers kennzeichnen kann. Die Frage wird in verschiedenen Variationen gestellt, je nachdem, ob der Erkenntnishorizont derjenige der hebräischen Textkritik ist, man also die LXX als Zeugen für die Rekonstruktion vormasoretischer Lesarten befragt, oder ob man die LXX eigenständiger interpretieren möchte als Hinweis auf frühe Rezeptionsformen biblischer Texte und Traditionen. Es ist unmittelbar einsichtig, dass sich die beiden Fragehinsichten nicht voneinander trennen lassen, sondern nur unterschiedlich akzentuiert werden.

Die beiden Debatten, auf die ich angespielt habe, beschäftigen sich mit den Büchern Genesis und Psalmen. Die erste wurde mit der Veröffentlichung eines Vortrags vom SBL-Kongress in Orlando angestoßen, als ich für die Genesis-LXX folgendes methodisches Postulat formuliert habe: Danach kann eine LXX-Variante, die nicht von einem unabhängigen weiteren Zeugen unterstützt wird, nur dann textkritische Relevanz haben, wenn sie nicht als (1) Harmonisierung, (2) sprachlich oder (3) exegetisch motivierte Abweichung erklärbar ist.¹ Damit soll der Eigenwert der griechischen Übersetzung gegen oftmals naive Textkritik stärker pointiert werden; im Gefolge J. W. Wevers wird die Gen-LXX als „humanistic document of interest by and for itself"² verstanden, dem eigenständige theologische Konzeptionen zu entnehmen sind.³ Die Reaktionen auf diesen Vortrag in BIOSCS 32 (1999) durch R. S. Hendel und W. P. Brown waren harsch und eindeutig ablehnend, haben sich aber leider nur mit Details und nicht mit der methodischen Leitthese beschäftigt, so dass es für eine Revision dieser Position keine wesentlichen Argumente gibt.

Die Debatte um die Psalmen-LXX wurde mit der Veröffentlichung der Dissertation von Joachim Schaper eingeleitet,⁴ die von manchen Rezensenten ungewöhnlich kritisch beurteilt wurde,⁵ anders als die Arbeit von Staffan Olofsson,⁶ die von ähnlichen Fragestellungen geleitet ist und von vergleichbaren methodischen Voraussetzungen ausgeht. Auch hier ist der hermeneutische Ausgangspunkt der, dass bei der Erklärung der Äquivalente, die der Übersetzer gewählt hat (das gilt auf Lexem- wie auf Satzebene), das jeweilige kulturelle und religiöse Milieu zu bedenken sei. Ein allein linguistisch fragender Zugang zum Problem sei nicht angemessen. Im Rahmen des Göttinger Symposions zum Septuaginta-Psalter hat sich Arie van der Kooij ausdrücklich auf die Seite dieses Ansatzes gestellt, er sieht hier sein am Jesajabuch entwickeltes (und an der Genesis bestätigtes) Modell vom Übersetzer als einem auch interpretierenden Schriftgelehrten bestätigt.⁷

Die Gegenposition zu diesem Zugang hat in vorbildlicher Deutlichkeit Frank Austermann ebenfalls im Rahmen des Göttinger Symposions vorgetragen.⁸ So formuliert er etwa in These 8,

---

1. Dazu Rösel 1998a.
2. Wevers 1996, 95.
3. Vgl. dazu die umfassenderen Ausführungen in Rösel 1998b.
4. Schaper 1995.
5. Vgl. Pietersma 1997; Peters 1997; Bons 1997. Doch vgl. die positive Bewertung durch Siegert 1997; van der Horst 1997.
6. Olofsson 1990. Doch vgl. die kritischen Anfragen von Aejmelaeus 1992.
7. Van der Kooij 2000, 372–76. Als ältere Versuche sind zu nennen: Fritsch 1973; Soffer 1957. Zu einer sehr ausgewogenen Stellungnahme zu Möglichkeiten und Grenzen der theologischen Interpretation der LXX s. auch Joosten 2000. Als extreme Position lässt sich jetzt außerdem Beck 2000 nennen, der die LXX ganz mit erzähltechnischen Fragestellungen zu erfassen sucht.
8. Austermann 2000, 381–85.

10. Die Psalmüberschriften des Septuagintapsalters 223

über die morphologische, syntaktische und semantische Analyse hinaus müssen keine notwendigen Schritte der Interpretation der Vorlage durch den Übersetzer vorausgesetzt werden.

In pointierter Überspitzung könnte man diese und die folgende These so zusammenfassen, dass die Annahme einer eigenen Aussageabsicht des Übersetzers nur so etwas wie die *ultima ratio* des modernen Auslegers sein darf. Dies rührt davon her, dass Austermann in These 5 eine Unterscheidung zwischen Übersetzungen und auslegenden Texten einführt,[9] in These 4 wird sogar formuliert,

> Eine Übersetzung ist keine Interpretation, Übersetzung und Interpretation sind nicht gleichzusetzen. Vielmehr schließt die Tätigkeit des Übersetzens die Tätigkeit des Interpretierens ein.[10]

Das Problem liegt hierbei in einer sehr spezifischen Füllung des Begriffs „interpretieren," der vor allem auf sprachliche Interpretation abzielt. Dies ist These 7 zu entnehmen, wo es heißt,

> Übersetzen umfasst (mindestens) zwei Tätigkeiten: Die Interpretation einer ausgangssprachlichen Vorlage und ihre zielsprachliche Wiedergabe.[11]

Später geschieht dann eine implizite Auseinandersetzung mit der Arbeit von J. Schaper, der ja versucht hatte, exegetische Regeln der frühen rabbinischen Exegese für die LXX-Interpretation fruchtbar zu machen. In These 10 heißt es:

---

9. Austermann 2000, 383. Diese Unterscheidung ist m. E. nicht haltbar, zumindest nicht in der verkürzten Form der veröffentlichten Thesen. Zum einen ist in Rechnung zu stellen, wie unterschiedlich schon die in der LXX erhaltenen Einzelübersetzungen hinsichtlich der von Austermann vorgetragenen Kriterien für diese Unterscheidung zu beurteilen sind (Bezug auslegender Texte auf außertextliche Gegebenheiten, Zurückverweisung übersetzender Texte auf den Inhalt der Vorlage). Hinzu kommt, dass sein Postulat, dass übersetzende Texte ihre Vorlage in Hinblick auf die zielsprachlichen Rezipienten ersetzen sollten, vom Wissen um die antike Übersetzungspraxis her nicht haltbar ist, zumindestens aber keinen Anspruch auf Allgemeingültigkeit haben kann, vgl. dazu Seele 1995, 13 u.ö., ebenso die Überlegungen von Flashar 1912, 90-91.
10. Austermann 2000, 382-83.
11. Austermann 2000, 383.

Spätere Interpretationen der Vorlage und Übersetzung und spätere Methoden der Interpretation können nicht ohne weiteres zur Erklärung der Deutung der Vorlage durch den Übersetzer herangezogen werden.[12]

Es ist einsichtig, dass das Problem dieser These in dem „nicht ohne weiteres" liegt; eine genauere Bestimmung dieser Einschränkung geschieht leider nicht.

Ein eigener Beitrag zur Psalmen-LXX im Rahmen dieser knapp umrissenen Diskussionslage geschieht unter folgenden Voraussetzungen: Zunächst beschränke ich mich bei dem Zugang zum Problemfeld auf einen Teilaspekt, nämlich den der Psalmenüberschriften. Dies hat den methodischen Vorteil, dass das gesamte Material präsentiert werden kann und es nicht zu einer eklektischen und damit fragwürdigen Auswahl kommt. Die Besonderheit der Textüberlieferung der LXX an diesem Punkt ist zudem schon seit der alten Kirche klar gewesen,[13] ohne dass es jedoch m.W. eine eigene Untersuchung des Phänomens gegeben hätte. In den Psalmüberschriften bündeln sich die Probleme insofern, als hier zum einen die Frage einer abweichenden Vorlage zu erörtern ist und zum anderen die Wahl der Äquivalente und damit die Frage nach der impliziten Hermeneutik des Übersetzers zu kommentieren ist. Ich arbeite dabei mit der Annahme, dass die Psalmen-LXX auf einen Übersetzer zurückgeht,[14] der seine Arbeit im 2. Jh. ausgeführt hat. Die viel diskutierte Frage, wo dies geschehen ist, ob in hellenistischen Ägypten oder Palästina, blende ich aus, weil sie mir für diesen Zugang nicht relevant scheint.[15]

2. Überblick über die Standardäquivalente in den LXX-Psalmüberschriften

Zunächst soll das Material katalogartig dargeboten werden, dabei wird auf die musikalischen Fachtermini in einem eigenen Abschnitt eingegangen. Folgende Normal- oder Standardäquivalente können festgestellt werden, wobei bereits hier eine sehr weitgehende Konkordanz als Kennzeichen der spezifischen Übersetzungsweise in der Psalmen-LXX konstatiert werden

---

12. Austermann 2000, 385.
13. Visser 1963.
14. Dies als ein Ergebnis der Studie von Soffer 1957, 88.
15. Als Einführung in die Einleitungsfragen der Psalmen-LXX eignet sich vor allem Harl, Dorival und Munnich 1994, 86–111 (mit weiterführender Literatur).

kann.¹⁶ Daher ist bei Abweichungen von Normalübersetzungen besondere Aufmerksamkeit geboten. Weiterhin sei schon jetzt mitgeteilt, dass es bei der Fülle der in Qumran belegten Psalmenmanuskripte nur zwei Fälle gibt, in denen eine abweichende Lesung der LXX durch eine hebräische Handschrift unterstützt wird; von diesen ist nur ein Fall als eine wirklich übereinstimmende Lesart zwischen Q und LXX zu sehen.¹⁷ Bei Ps 151, der hier außer Betracht bleiben soll, weichen hebräische und griechische Textüberlieferung im Bereich der Überschrift stark voneinander ab.

2.1. Psalmbezeichnungen

Für מזמור לדוד steht nahezu immer (insgesamt 29x) ψαλμὸς τῷ Δαυιδ.¹⁸ Ohne Parallele im MT findet es sich noch in Ps 43(42) und 99(98); im ersten Fall wird LXX von verschiedenen hebräischen Manuskripten,¹⁹ im zweiten Fall wird der MT von 4QPsᵏ unterstützt. Ebenso steht achtmal für מזמור לאסף ψαλμὸς τῷ Ασαφ²⁰ und für לבני־קרח מזמור steht viermal entsprechend τοῖς υἱοῖς Κορε ψαλμός.²¹ Alleinstehendes מזמור findet sich an drei Stellen ebenfalls mit ψαλμός übersetzt,²² gleichermaßen das nur in Ps 7 begegnende שגיון; offenbar konnte der Übersetzer dem Wort keinen anderen Sinn abgewinnen. An insgesamt vier Stellen hat LXX über den MT hinaus ψαλμός,²³ wobei die erhaltenen Fragmente aus der judäischen Wüste in drei Fällen den Text des MT unterstützen—sofern darüber

---

16. Dazu auch Flashar 1912, 101-2.
17. Ps 104(103) stimmt das לדוד mit τῷ Δαυιδ überein, in Ps 33(32) hat 4QPsᵃ einen gegenüber LXX umfangreicheren Text, der nur hinsichtlich des τῷ Δαυιδ übereinstimmt. Eine übersichtliche Auflistung der Differenzen findet sich bei Flint 1997, 118–34. Der strittigen Frage nach der Bewertung des Befundes der Vielfalt der hebräischen Texte kann hier nicht nachgegangen werden, man vergleiche dazu die Kritik von Fabry 1998, an dem Entwurf von P. Flint.
18. Vgl. Ps 3; 5; 6; 8; 9; 12(11); 15(14); 19(18); 20(19); 21(20); 22(21); 23(22); 31(30); 38(37); 41(40); 51(50); 62(61); 63(61); 64(63); 65(64); 108(107); 140(139); 141(140); 143(142); ebenso trotz Umkehrung der Reihenfolge zu לדוד מזמור in 24(23); 139(138); in den Psalmen 68(67); 101(100); 109(108) wird der veränderten Reihenfolge auch im Griechischen mit τῷ Δαυιδ ψαλμός entsprochen.
19. Diese lesen jedoch nur לדוד, nicht auch das von LXX her zu erwartende מזמור.
20. Ps 50(49); 73(72); 75(74); 76(75); 77(76); 79(78); 82(81); 83(82).
21. Ps 49(48); 84(83); 85(84); 87(86); variiert Ps 47(46); 48(47) und 88(87).
22. Ps 66(65); 67(66); 92(91).
23. Ps 11(10); 14(13); 25(24); 81(80).

Urteile möglich sind. Da hier aber im unmittelbaren Kontext entweder David oder Asaf steht, kann es sich dabei um Harmonisierungen handeln, die die übliche Überschrift herstellen sollen. In gleicher Weise wird in Ps 98(97) τῷ Δαυιδ nachgetragen, wo MT ein alleinstehendes מזמור hat.

Im Griechischen bedeutet das vom Verbum ψάλλω abgeleitete ψαλμός ursprünglich das Zupfen an Saiten, wobei auch die eines Bogens gemeint sein konnten (LSJ s.v.), der Bezug auf ein Saiteninstrument (ψαλτήριον)[24] und die Entwicklung zu einer auf Harfe oder Kithara gespielten Weise und dann zu einem Lied sind wohl spätere Erscheinungen.

An zwei Stellen steht für מזמור לדוד abweichend vom sonstigen Befund ᾠδὴ τῷ Δαυιδ, dies in Ps 4 und 39(38). Im Falle von Ps 4 lässt sich das als bewusste Variation erklären, denn hier ist das voranstehende בנגינות mit ἐν ψαλμοῖς übersetzt worden; offenbar sollte die Wiederholung von ψαλμός vermieden werden. Für בנגינות steht an allen anderen Stellen allerdings als Normalübersetzung ἐν ὕμνοις,[25] so dass in Ps 4 eine doppelte Abweichung festzustellen ist. In Ps 39(38) ist mir die Verwendung von ᾠδή nicht erklärlich.

Für שיר wurde beinahe durchgehend (29x) ᾠδή verwendet,[26] nur an einer Stelle findet sich ψαλμός.[27] Interessant ist das Faktum, dass an insgesamt fünf Stellen (drei in Überschriften) das vergleichsweise seltene (vgl. LSJ s.v.) ᾆσμα zur Wiedergabe von שיר steht.[28] Hier fällt auf, dass es an den fraglichen Stellen im hebräischen Text jeweils um ein שיר חדש geht. Der Übersetzer hat demnach offenbar in ᾆσμα die Konnotation eines neuen Liedes im Unterschied zu einer ehrwürdigeren, künstlerisch gestalteten „Ode" gesehen.[29] Diese Differenzierung zeigt, dass der Übersetzer trotz

---

24. Cod. Alexandrinus benennt mit diesem Begriff die gesamte Sammlung der Psalmen (ebenso Cod. R^s), wovon sich die übliche Bezeichnung „Psalter" abgeleitet hat.

25. Ps 6; 54(53); 55(54); 61(60), hier für על-נגינת, das von LXX als Plural gelesen wurde; 67(66); 76(75). Interessanterweise wurde hier mit ἐν ὕμνοις ein Äquivalent gewählt, das von der sonstigen Wiedergabe der Wurzel נגן abweicht. Das Verbum begegnet in Ps 33(32),3; 68(67),26 und wird dort mit ψάλλω übersetzt, offenbar sollte zwischen מזמור und נגינה auch bei der Übersetzung begrifflich unterschieden werden, selbst wenn der Bezug auf ein Saiteninstrument verloren ging.

26. Ps 30(31); 45(44); 65(64)–68(67); 75(74); 76(75); 83(82); 87(86); 88(87); 92(91); 108(107); 120(119)–134(133). In Ps 48(47) ist offenbar die Reihenfolge der Äquivalente für מזמור und שיר vertauscht.

27. Ps 46(45). Zu Ps 48(47) vgl. die voranstehende Anmerkung.

28. Ps 33(32),3; 40(39),4; 96(95); 98(97); 149.

29. So einleuchtend Pietersma 2000a, xxiv. Der übliche griechische Sprachge-

seines Bemühens um konkordante Übersetzungsweise auf inhaltliche Akzentuierungen bedacht war.

Die kurze Notiz לדוד wird selten (viermal) mit dem Genitiv τοῦ Δαυιδ im Sinne einer Autorenschaft wiedergegeben,[30] deutlich häufiger ist die (im strengen Sinne wörtlichere) Formulierung mit dem Dativ τῷ Δαυιδ,[31] die sich an drei Stellen auch über den MT hinaus findet, zwei dieser Zusätze sind auch in Qumran belegt.[32]

Die weiteren Psalmbezeichnungen werden konkordant wiedergegeben. Für מכתם לדוד steht durchgängig στηλογραφία τῷ Δαυιδ „Pfeilerinschrift."[33] Das hebräische Lexem ist nicht sicher erklärbar, es wird dabei an akk. *katāmu* „bedecken, sühnen" gedacht (vgl. Jer 2,22), so dass man es (auch unter Einfluss der LXX) als Sühne- oder Weihinschrift gedeutet hat.[34] Es ist unklar, ob LXX eine solche Ableitung kannte oder, möglicherweise veranlasst von den Psalmen 57–59(56–58) wo es heißt „zerstöre nicht," das Äquivalent erschlossen hat. Festzuhalten ist, dass στηλογραφία außerhalb der Psalmen-LXX nicht mehr belegt ist, es sich damit offenbar um eine Prägung des Psalmen-Übersetzers handelt, die sich am häufiger verwendeten Verbum στηλογραφέω orientiert.

Für תפלה steht durchgängig προσευχή, das sowohl mit dem Genitiv (Gebet des David 17(16),1; des Mose 90(89),1), als auch mit dem Dativ (Ps 86(85),1); konstruiert werden kann.[35] In drei Überschriften findet sich תהלה, das mit αἴνεσις „Loblied" übersetzt wurde.[36] Mit beiden Äquivalenten hat der Übersetzer die Konnotationen der wiederzugebenden Lexeme durchaus angemessen getroffen, wobei im Falle von αἴνεσις als sicher gelten kann und im Fall von προσευχή nicht auszuschließen ist, dass es sich um

---

brauch, wonach ᾠδή im Unterschied zu ᾆσμα eher ein künstlerisch ausgestaltetes Lied (etwa in Tragödien, vgl. LSJ s.v.) bezeichnet, passt zu dieser Überlegung.

30. Ps 26(25); 27(26); 28(27); 37(36). Pietersma 2000a korrigiert dies in der NETS an allen Stellen zum Dativ, vgl. auch Pietersma 1980, 225.

31. Ps 32(31); 34(33); 35(34); 36(35); 40(39); 60(59); 61(60); 68(67); 69(68); 70(69); 144(143).

32. Ps 33(32), vgl. 4QPs^q: לדויד שיר מזמור; 104(103), vgl. 11QPs^a: לדויד; 137(136).

33. Ps 16(15); 56(55); 57(56); 58(57); 59(58); 60(59).

34. S. dazu Seybold 1996, 71; vgl. Hossfeld und Zenger 1993, 110; 2000, 107.

35. Die verbleibenden Stellen sind 102(101),1; 142(141),1. Auch im Kontext des Psalms wird in der Regel προσευχή oder ein Derivat verwendet, vgl. etwa 42(41),9; 109(108),4; Ausnahme ist 102(101),18, wo δέησις verwendet wird.

36. Ps 33(32); 145(144); 147(146).

eigene Wortbildungen des hellenistischen Judentums handelt.³⁷ Die Wortbildung orientiert sich dabei an den entsprechenden Verbalwurzeln (פלל, הלל) und ihren Übersetzungen.

Zu notieren bleibt noch משכיל „Weisheitslied/Unterweisung," für das stets σύνεσις steht.³⁸ Zur Klärung des genauen Bedeutungsgehalts dieser Übersetzung sind weitergehende Überlegungen nötig, dies wird daher in einem eigenen Abschnitt zu geschehen haben.

Der letzte in diesem Paragraphen zu notierende Psalmtitel ist למנצח, das an allen 56 Stellen mit εἰς τὸ τέλος wiedergegeben wird.³⁹ An einer einzigen Stelle bietet LXX εἰς τὸ τέλος über den hebräischen Text hinaus, dies in Ps 30(29); hier ist leider keine Qumran-Variante erhalten. Da der genaue Sinn dieser Übersetzung strittig ist, soll auch dieser Frage in einem eigenen Abschnitt nachgegangen werden.

2.2. Musikalische Fachtermini

Eine ganze Reihe der in den hebräischen Psalmüberschriften verwendeten Ausdrücke sind heute nicht mehr zweifelsfrei verständlich, was beispielsweise für das eben erwähnte למנצח genauso gilt wie für das oben angesprochene מכתם. In der Regel ist davon auszugehen, dass es sich bei ihnen um Termini handelt, die im weitesten Sinne einen musikalischen oder aufführungstechnisch-liturgischen Hintergrund haben. Diese Einschätzung stützt sich häufig auf den Befund der Septuaginta-Übersetzung. Als älteste erreichbare Interpretation der Termini stellt sie eine unverzichtbare Hilfe dar, dies besonders in den Fällen, in denen mittels der Etymologie des fraglichen Begriffs keine Klärung erreicht werden kann. Die folgende Übersicht hat die Funktion, das gesicherte Wissen über die griechische Wiedergabe der musikalischen Fachtermini mitzuteilen.

---

37. So fragend im entsprechenden Eintrag bei Lust, Eynikel, und Hauspie 1996, 401, vgl. Lee 1983, 46.

38. Ps 32(31); 42(41); 44(43); 45(44); 52(51); 53(52); 54(53); 74(73); 78(77); 89(88); 142(141).

39. Dies gilt in folgenden Psalmen: 4; 5; 6; 8; 9; 11(10); 12(11); 13(12); 14(13); 18(17); 19(18); 20(19); 21(20); 22(21); 31(30); 36(35); 39(38); 40(39); 41(40); 42(41); 44(43); 45(44); 46(45); 47(46); 49(48); 51(50); 52(51); 53(52); 54(53); 55(54); 56(55); 57(56); 58(57); 59(58); 60(59); 61(60); 62(61); 64(63); 65(64); 66(65); 67(66); 68(67); 69(68); 70(69); 75(74); 76(75); 77(76); 80(79); 81(80); 84(83); 85(84); 88(87); 109(108); 110(109); 139(138); 140(139).

10. Die Psalmüberschriften des Septuagintapsalters

In der Reihenfolge der Psalmen ist zunächst die Wendung אל־הנחילות aus Ps 5,1 anzusprechen, die mit ὑπὲρ τῆς κληρονομούσης (ψαλμός) „Ein Psalm über die, die erbt" übersetzt wurde. Es ist offensichtlich, dass der Übersetzer sich von נחלה „Erbe/Erbbesitz" hat leiten lassen, die feminine Pluralendung wurde aber nur insoweit aufgenommen, als die Wiedergabe nun auf ein weibliches Individuum verweist. Damit lässt sich der gesamte Psalm als Lied einer Frau verstehen, die in ihrer Not zu Gott ruft und auf seine Hilfe am Morgen hofft (V. 4). Das Verbum κληρονομέω ist in der Regel mit dem Landbesitz verbunden (37(36),11 u.ö.), dies als gute Gabe Gottes für die, die auf ihn trauen. Der hebräische Text meint mit אל־הנחילות offenbar einen Hinweis auf eine Flöte.[40]

In Ps 6,1 begegnet der nächste unklare Terminus, על־השמינית, der in Ps 12(11),1 ein weiteres Mal Verwendung fand. Er wird mit einem achtsaitigen Instrument[41] oder der achten, tiefen Saite als Angabe einer Tonhöhe[42] in Verbindung gebracht, doch sind diese Erklärungen nicht gesichert. Auch der LXX-Übersetzer hat den Bezug zur Zahl שמנה gesehen und an beiden Stellen entsprechend mit ὑπὲρ τῆς ὀγδόης „über die achte" übersetzt. Welchen Sinn er damit verband, ist heute jedoch unklar.

Dem Übersetzer sicherlich unbekannt war שגיון,[43] das nur in Ps 7,1 begegnet; er hat es mit ψαλμός wiedergegeben.

In Ps 8,1 steht erstmals die Anweisung על־הגתית, die LXX ebenso wie an den anderen beiden Stellen (81(80),1; 84(83),1) mit ὑπὲρ τῶν ληνῶν „über die Keltern" übersetzt hat. Der Terminus ist heute nicht mehr verständlich, man rechnet entweder mit einem Musikinstrument „aus Gath,"[44] einer bestimmten Weise oder mit einem bestimmten Fest.[45] Der griechische Übersetzer hat offensichtlich an גת „Kelter" gedacht, das an einigen Stellen ληνός übersetzt wurde.[46] Was er aber mit dieser Wiedergabe inhaltlich verbunden haben mag, ist unklar; der Gebrauch des Wortes in den

---

40. So Kraus 1989, 22 und spätere Kommentare.
41. Kraus, 1989, 27.
42. Hossfeld und Zenger 1993, 69.
43. Die genaue Bedeutung des שגיון ist auch heute nicht geklärt, zu den Deutungsversuchen vgl. HAL s.v. Hossfeld und Zenger 1993, 75, und Seybold 1996, 46, votieren für „Klagelied".
44. Seybold 1996, 49.
45. Vgl. die Übersicht über die vorgeschlagenen Deutungen bei Tate 1990, 318.
46. Ri 6,11, Neh 13,15; Jo 4,13, Jes 63,2, Klgl 1,15.

prophetischen Schriften legt immerhin die Konnotation eines Machterweises Gottes nahe, was zu den Hymnen 8, 81 und 84 passen könnte.

Ebenfalls unbekannt ist der Sinn von עלמות, das in Psalm 9,1 in der Verbindung עלמות לבן steht; in Ps 46(45),1 findet sich על־עלמות. LXX hat beide Stellen mit ὑπὲρ τῶν κρυφίων „Über die Geheimnisse (des Sohnes, Ps 9)" übersetzt und damit offensichtlich eine Ableitung von der Wurzel עלם vollzogen. Die ebenfalls mögliche Segmentierung zu על מות wurde vom Übersetzer nicht vorgenommen.⁴⁷ Interessanterweise findet sich der gleiche Konsonantenbestand על מות in Ps 48(47),15, m. E. muss er ursprünglich zur Überschrift des folgenden Psalms gehören. Die LXX fand die Konsonanten offensichtlich schon am Ende von Ps 48 vor, sie hat sie als ein Wort gelesen und mit εἰς τοὺς αἰῶνας wiedergeben; dies ist angesichts der femininen Plural-Endung eine bemerkenswerte Interpretation.⁴⁸

Der nächste Terminus in der kanonischen Reihenfolge ist in Ps 22(21),1 die berühmte „Hinde der Morgenröte," על־אילת השחר. Dieser Melodietitel wurde in der LXX mit ὑπὲρ τῆς ἀντιλήμψεως τῆς ἑωθινῆς „über die Hilfe am Morgen" übersetzt, wobei sie sich offenkundig von אילות in V. 20 hat leiten lassen, denn dort steht ebenfalls ἀντίλημψις. Die Überlegung, hier sei eine Verschreibung aus ἀντιλάμψεως „Widerschein, Leuchten" anzunehmen,⁴⁹ ist nicht durch Manuskripte begründet und daher unnötig. Das Beispiel belegt, dass sich der Übersetzer bei der Bestimmung schwieriger Worte um eine kontextangemessene Wiedergabe bemüht hat.

In zwei Psalmen, 38(37),1 und 70(69),1, findet sich der Hinweis להזכיר, der mit dem Nomen εἰς ἀνάμνησιν übersetzt wurde; in 38(37),1 mit dem zugefügten Hinweis περὶ σαββάτου (dazu s. u.). Es ist überlegt worden, dass diese Wiedergaben „zusätzliche Präzisierungen" seien, „die dem Psalm eine reale oder übertragene kultische Dimension" geben.⁵⁰ Dies ist insofern denkbar, als ἀνάμνησις in Lev 24,7 und Num 10,10 (ebenso schon bei Lysias, vgl. LSJ) tatsächlich in kultischen Zusammenhängen verwendet wurde; dafür spricht auch die Tatsache, dass zur Wiedergabe ein Nomen verwendet wurde, nicht aber der zu erwartende Infinitiv.⁵¹

---

47. Vgl. BHS und die Einheitsübersetzung, aufgenommen bei Hossfeld und Zenger 1993, 83: „Stirb für den Sohn."

48. Hossfeld und Zenger 1993, 296, erwägen hier die LXX-Lesung als ursprünglich, was kaum überzeugt.

49. Gegen Seybold 1996, 96. Zur Schreibweise vgl. Rahlfs 1979, Einleitung §7.11.

50. Hossfeld und Zenger 2000, 286.

51. Vgl. 1.Kön 17,18: ἀναμνῆσαι; Am 6,10 ὀνομάσαι für להזכיר.

10. Die Psalmüberschriften des Septuagintapsalters 231

Zu nennen sind nun die Überschriften, in denen es ידותון zu übersetzen galt, das in Ps 39(38),1 mit vorangestelltem ל, in 62(61),1; 77(76),1 mit על steht. In der Forschung ist strittig, ob es sich hierbei um einen Namen (vgl. 2.Chr 5,12) oder einen musiktechnischen Begriff handelt.[52] Der Übersetzer hat *Jedutun* offenbar als Namen aufgefasst und durchgängig als Transkription mit τῷ/ὑπὲρ Ιδιθουν wiedergegeben, so dass der Eindruck entsteht, dass der jeweilige Psalm von David oder Asaph für jenen Menschen gedichtet wurde.

Das Prinzip der kontextsensitiven Übersetzung wird auch bei der Übersetzung von שיר ידידת (Ps 45(44),1) gegolten haben, das mit ᾠδὴ ὑπὲρ τοῦ ἀγαπητοῦ „Lied über den Geliebten" übersetzt wurde. Hierbei fällt die Wiedergabe im Singular auf, die vermuten lässt, dass der Übersetzer eine konkretere Identifizierung für möglich hielt. Zur Erklärung wird man Ps 68(67),13 heranziehen können, die einzige Stelle in der Pss-LXX, an der ἀγαπητός noch im Singular begegnet. Hier ist das Wort eindeutig auf Gott zu beziehen, es geht um die Könige der Heerscharen des Geliebten.[53] Daher wird man auch für Ps 45(44) annehmen können, dass es um den Gottkönig geht, wobei allerdings von V. 2 her der Bezug auf den König nicht völlig ausgeschlossen werden kann.

In der gleichen Überschrift findet sich außerdem die Melodieangabe על־ששנים, die noch in Ps 69(68),1 zu finden ist, vgl. noch אל־ששנים עדות in Ps 80(79),1. In der LXX wurde durchgehend ὑπὲρ τῶν ἀλλοιωθησομένων „über die, die verändert werden" zur Wiedergabe verwendet, in Ps 60(59),1 steht für על־שושן עדות τοῖς ἀλλοιωθησομένοις ἔτι. Dies lässt erschließen, dass der Übersetzer eine Ableitung von der Wurzel שנה vorgenommen hat, die Partizipialform lässt außerdem vermuten, dass ein vorangestelltes, relativisches ש erschlossen wurde.[54] Die Identifikation mit שושנה „Lilie," die in 1.Kön 7,19 und mehrfach im Hohenlied von den jeweiligen Übersetzern vorgenommen wurde, hat der Psalmen-Übersetzer nicht geleistet.

Die Interpretation dieser griechischen Überschriften ist problematisch. Da aber, dies im Vorgriff auf den nächsten Abschnitt der Untersuchung, das jeweils voranstehende εἰς τὸ τέλος gewiss eschatologisch zu verstehen ist, kann ein solcher Unterton auch hier vermutet werden. Es geht dann um diejenigen, die am Ende verändert, also gerettet werden. Diese

---

52. Dazu Hossfeld und Zenger 2000, 182.
53. Der Vers und sein näherer Kontext hätte eine ausführlichere Exegese verdient, denn hier wird der hebräische Text eindeutig eschatologisch interpretiert.
54. Mit Seybold 1996, 185.

Interpretation passt sowohl zu dem in der griechischen Version deutlich eschatologisierten Ps 45(44)—man beachte nur die Wiedergabe von V. 18—als auch zu den anderen Psalmen, in denen es jeweils um Bitten angesichts von Notlagen der Gerechten geht.

In Ps 53(52),1 und 88(87),1 griff der Übersetzer bei der Wiedergabe von על־מחלת erneut zum Mittel der Transkription, so dass sich ὑπὲρ μαελεθ in der griechischen Version findet. Wegen des in 88(87),1 folgenden τοῦ ἀποκριθῆναι wird man erneut damit rechnen können, dass Maëleth als Name aufgefasst wurde, so dass der Titel zu übersetzen wäre: „über Maëleth, dass ihm geantwortet werde."[55]

Ps 56(55),1 bietet mit על־יונת אלם רחקים „nach: Taube der Stummheit unter Fernen" eine ausgeführte Melodieangabe.[56] Ihr wird in der LXX entsprochen durch ὑπὲρ τοῦ λαοῦ τοῦ ἀπὸ τῶν ἁγίων μεμακρυμμένου „Über das Volk, das weit von den heiligen Dingen entfernt wurde." Unter den vorgetragenen Lösungsansätzen scheint die Überlegung sinnvoll, dass der Übersetzer ein Partizip מרחקים gelesen hat, so dass dann אל יונת übrigblieb. Das Bild von der Taube Gottes wäre dann, ähnlich wie im Targum, auf das Volk Gottes bezogen worden, das, so die zusätzliche Interpretation durch Zusatz von ἀπὸ τῶν ἁγίων, von seinem Heiligtum entfernt wurde.[57]

Die Psalmüberschriften 57–59(56–58) sind bereits oben im Zusammenhang mit στηλογραφία besprochen worden. Es ist noch zu erwähnen, dass die Wendung אל־תשחת noch einmal in Ps 75(74),1 begegnet und dort ebenfalls mit μὴ διαφθείρῃς übersetzt wurde. Während sich die verbale Aussage in den erstgenannten Psalmen leicht auf die Pfeilerinschrift deuten lässt, ist der Bezug in Ps 75(74) unklar.

Eine wörtliche Wiedergabe findet sich auch in Ps 60(59),1, wo ללמד mit εἰς διδαχήν übersetzt wurde. Die Struktur der hebräischen Überschrift, die den Psalm als autorisierte Lehre Davids vorstellt, wird damit genau nachvollzogen.[58] Interessanterweise wird das Nomen διδαχή nur an dieser Stelle in der gesamten LXX verwendet,[59] dies mag auch damit zusammen-

---

55. Vgl. Pietersma 2000a, 86: „Over Maeleth, in order that he be answered."
56. Zur Interpretation s. Hossfeld und Zenger 2000, 106.
57. So Mozley 1905, 93, anders Tate 1990, 65, und Hossfeld und Zenger 2000, 117, nach denen אלם als „Götter" verstanden und auf „Heiliges" bezogen wurde. Das aber ist m.W. nirgendwo belegt.
58. Dazu Hossfeld und Zenger 2000, 161.
59. Für ללמד stehen sonst Infinitivformen wie διδάξαι (Dtn 4,14 u.ö.) oder διδάσκειν (2.Chr 17,7).

hängen, dass der Begriff im 2.Jh. offensichtlich militärische Konnotationen hatte (LSJ). Im Zusammenhang von Ps 60(59) passt dies ausgesprochen gut, so dass man dem Übersetzer erneut eine gelungene Wiedergabe bescheinigen kann.

Als letzte Überschrift ist noch das שיר המעלות der Wallfahrtspsalmen 120–134(119–133) zu nennen, das durchgehend mit ᾠδὴ τῶν ἀναβαθμῶν wiedergegeben wurde. Während der Sinn der hebräischen Angabe nicht eindeutig geklärt ist,[60] sind in der LXX die Bezüge klarer, denn das Nomen ἀναβαθμός ist von den anderen Vorkommen in der LXX wie der griechischsprachigen Umwelt her[61] eindeutig als architektonischer Fachbegriff für „Stufen/Treppe" zu begreifen. Damit unterstützt die Psalmenseptuaginta die im Mischna-Traktat Middot gegebene Erklärung, wonach es sich um Lieder handelt, die auf den Stufen des Nikanortores gesungen worden sind.

Zusammenfassend wird sich sagen lassen, dass die Übersetzungsweise hinsichtlich der musikalischen Fachtermini kein besonderes Interesse an dieser Thematik oder einer etwaigen Aufführungspraxis erkennen lässt; in der religiösen Gemeinschaft des Übersetzers wurden offensichtlich unbekannte Begriffe nicht durch aktuell verständliche musikalische oder liturgische Termini ersetzt. Das kann—bei aller Problematik eines solchen Urteils—gegen eine kultische Verwendung dieser griechischen Texte sprechen.

Im nächsten Schritt sind nun die noch ausstehenden Klärungen des Sinngehalts von σύνεσις und εἰς τὸ τέλος vorzunehmen.

3. Sinnverschiebungen bei den gewählten Standardäquivalenten

3.1. σύνεσις

Zunächst ist auf die Übersetzung σύνεσις für משכיל „Weisheitslied/Unterweisung" zurückzukommen. Dabei ist festzuhalten, dass die griechische Version den kausativen Aspekt nicht wiedergibt, denn σύνεσις bezeichnet stets das eigene Verstehen bzw. die eigene Intelligenz (s. Bauer[6]). Auffällig ist auch, dass die Übersetzung σύνεσις nur in den Psalmüberschriften

---

60. Zu den Erklärungsmöglichkeiten vgl. Kraus 1989, 17-18.
61. S. etwa 1.Kön 10,20; 2.Kön 9,13; Ez 40,49; vgl. auch LSJ s.v.

verwendet wurde. Wenn im fortlaufenden Text משכיל zu übersetzen war, steht die eigentlich zu erwartende Partizipform.[62]

Das fragliche Nomen ist nun mitsamt dem zugehörigen Verbum συνίημι in der Jesaja-LXX wie in der Dan-LXX eindeutig im Sinne eines eschatologisch-apokalyptischen Verstehens der Wege Gottes konnotiert; man erinnere sich nur an die berühmte Übersetzung von Jes 7,9 mit „glaubt ihr nicht, so versteht ihr nicht."[63] Auch andere Vorkommen von σύνεσις im Psalter fügen sich gut in dieses Bild, so ist etwa Ps 147(146),5 zu notieren. Dort findet sich für גדול אדונינו ורב־כח לתבונתו אין מספר „Groß ist unser Herr und reich an Macht. Seine Einsicht ist ohne Maß" die Übersetzung μέγας ὁ κύριος ἡμῶν καὶ μεγάλη ἡ ἰσχὺς αὐτοῦ καὶ τῆς συνέσεως αὐτοῦ οὐκ ἔστιν ἀριθμός, die ebenfalls als eschatologisch-apokalyptisches Verstehen gedeutet werden kann, ähnlich auch Ps 111(110),10. Beide Male wird σύνεσις zur Wiedergabe der Wurzel בין verwendet, nicht für שכל.[64] Zu vergleichen ist auch Ps 78(77),72, wo es von Gott heißt ἐν ταῖς συνέσεσι τῶν χειρῶν αὐτοῦ ὡδήγησεν αὐτούς, „in den Einsichten seiner Hände hat er sie geleitet;" dies zur Übersetzung von ובתבונות כפיו ינחם „mit der Geschicklichkeit seiner Hände leitete er sie." Der Übersetzer hat also σύνεσις nicht allein zur Wiedergabe der Wurzel שכל eingesetzt, wie es von den Überschriften her zu erwarten wäre, sondern verbindet mit diesem Nomen eine konkrete Vorstellung.

Das gilt wohl auch für das zugehörige Verbum, wie ein stichprobenartiger Blick auf wenige Stellen belegt. So findet sich in Ps 16(15),7 die überraschende Formulierung εὐλογήσω τὸν κύριον τὸν συνετίσαντά με „Ich lobe den Herrn, der mich verständig gemacht hat" für אברך את־יהוה אשר יעצני „Ich segne JHWH, der mir einen Rat gegeben (*HAL*) hat;" der griechische Psalm schließt in V. 11 mit einer nur eschatologisch verstehbaren Heilsperspektive εἰς τέλος. Im berühmten Kehrvers in Ps 49(48),13. 21[65]

---

62. So in 14(13),2; 41(40),2; 47(46),8, hier das Adverb συνετῶς; 53(52),3. Diese Übersetzungsweise steht im Einklang mit den Konventionen, die in anderen Büchern (ohne Proverbien) festzustellen sind.

63. Ein ausführlicher Nachweis findet sich bei Rösel 1991, 139-40 [§9 in diesem Band].

64. Aufschlussreich ist auch die Wiedergabe von שכל in 36(35),4, wo aus dem hebräischen Text חדל להשכיל להיטיב „er hat es aufgegeben, verständig zu handeln, Gutes zu tun" in der griechischen Version οὐκ ἐβουλήθη συνιέναι τοῦ ἀγαθῦναι, „er wollte nicht verstehen, Gutes zu tun". Einzig Ps 32(31),9 fügt sich nicht in das Bild, weil es dort um unverständige Tiere geht.

65. Während der MT in V. 21 בין liest, steht in V. 13 das schwierige לין. M. E.

10. Die Psalmüberschriften des Septuagintapsalters 235

wurde συνίημι für den unverständigen, dem Todesschicksal ausgesetzten Menschen verwendet; im Umkehrschluss ist zu formulieren, dass wahres Verstehen Kennzeichen des Geretteten ist. So wage ich zusammenfassend die Behauptung, dass auch die mit σύνεσις gebildeten Überschriften die in Jesaja und Daniel deutlich gemachte Konnotation eines auf die Endzeit gerichteten Verstehens haben können.[66]

3.2. εἰς τὸ τέλος

Die eben vorgetragene Interpretation erhält Unterstützung durch die Übersetzung des למנצח mit εἰς τὸ τέλος. Der genaue Bedeutungsgehalt des למנצח ist heute unklar; es wird sich in irgendeiner Weise um einen aufführungs- oder musiktechnischen Terminus handeln.[67] Die griechische Übersetzung weist keinerlei dazu vergleichbare Konnotationen auf, sie gibt den Begriff demnach nicht im Sinne einer liturgischen Deutung wieder. Dies spricht gegen eine Art Aufführungspraxis im Umfeld der Übersetzung, was damit auch gegen Palästina, zumindest gegen ein tempelnahes Milieu sprechen kann. Das Zustandekommen der Übersetzung εἰς τὸ τέλος ist leicht zu klären. LXX hat nämlich den Ausdruck לנצח beinahe durchgängig entsprechend wiedergegeben; das bedeutet, dass sie למנצח gleichermaßen vom Nomen נצח „Dauer" (s. HAL s.v.) her verstanden hat. Allerdings ist eine entscheidende Variation festzustellen, denn immer in den Überschriften wird εἰς τὸ τέλος mit Artikel verwendet, die Übersetzung von לנצח im fortlaufenden Text ist demgegenüber immer artikellos. Die Artikelsetzung soll damit wohl dem unterschiedlichen Konsonantenbestand Rechnung tragen; für die Annahme, LXX habe durchgängig לנצח gelesen, spricht daher nichts.[68] Allein dieses Faktum, das zu dem der besonderen

---

ist wahrscheinlich, dass LXX an beiden Stellen בין gelesen hat, wenn auch nicht ausgeschlossen werden kann, dass die Verlesung älter ist und schon LXX ihrerseits die Verse harmonisiert hat.

66. Auch an anderen Stellen gibt es Parallelen zwischen der Psalmen-LXX und der Jesaja-LXX, etwa bei der Wiedergabe des Gottesepithetons אביר mit θεός in Jes 60,16 und Ps 132,2.5, vgl. dazu Olofsson 1990, 87–92. Ähnliche Berührungen gibt es bei der sonst nicht üblichen Wiedergabe von פשע mit ἄνομος κτλ., vgl. Ps 51,15 mit Jes 1,28. S. dazu Olofsson 2001.

67. Dazu Hossfeld und Zenger 1993, 60; ausführlicher Kraus 1989, 25, und Delekat 1964, 287–90.

68. Gegen Delekat 1964, 288.

Übersetzung von משכיל in den Psalmüberschriften passt, spricht für eine überlegte, differenzierende Arbeitsweise des Übersetzers.[69]

Der exakte Bedeutungsgehalt von εἰς τὸ τέλος ist strittig, dies auch wegen der neutestamentlichen Diskussion um 1.Thess 2,16, wonach der Zorn Gottes εἰς τέλος über die Juden gekommen ist. Methodisch angemessen scheint mir, die semantische Näherbestimmung durch Parallelen innerhalb der Psalmen-LXX durchzuführen. Dabei ist vor allem zu beachten, dass εἰς τέλος auch mit εἰς τὸν αἰῶνα in Parallele stehen kann;[70] τέλος beinhaltet demnach eine zeitliche Dimension. Das schließt aus, τὸ τέλος im Sinne eines Tributs zu verstehen, wie sich von Lev 27,23; Num 31,37–40 her anbieten würde. Sinnvoller ist die Übersetzung mit „Ende," die man wohl auf die Endzeit beziehen muss;[71] die entsprechenden Lieder zielen demnach auf die Endzeit. Diese Überlegung wird durch die auffällige Verwendung des Artikels unterstützt, die ja m. E. eindeutig auf ein bestimmtes Ende zielt.

Interessanterweise hat Aquila die εἰς τὸ τέλος-Wiedergabe nicht übernommen, was vielleicht auch aus inhaltlichen Gründen geschehen sein kann. Seine Übersetzung mit τῷ νικοποιῷ[72] orientiert sich ebenfalls an נצח, das besonders im Aramäischen die Konnotation „Sieg" haben kann (HAL); inhaltlich gemeint ist wohl Gott. Immerhin ist auch diese Übersetzung eschatologisch verstehbar.

Ein weiteres Argument für die Annahme, dass die *eis to telos*-Übersetzung auf die Endzeit zielt, lässt sich wohl Ps 30(29) entnehmen. Dies ist der einzige Psalm, in dem sich diese Überschrift über den MT hinaus findet. Dies ist m. E. kein Zufall, denn die auch im hebräischen Text erhaltene weitere Überschrift bezeichnet den Psalm als מזמור שיר־חנכת הבית, was mit εἰς τὸ τέλος ψαλμὸς ᾠδῆς τοῦ ἐγκαινισμοῦ τοῦ οἴκου wiedergegeben

---

69. Schaper 1995, 31–32, sieht die Wiedergabe des למנצח als Zeichen für unzureichende Sprachkompetenz des Übersetzers an. Zum einen ist m. E. sehr fraglich, ob man damals bereits eine lexikographische Differenzierung von נצח I und II durchgeführt hat, zum anderen dient gerade die Verwendung des Artikels dazu, das gegenüber לנצח zusätzliche *mem* in למנצח anzuzeigen. So zeigt gerade dieses Beispiel die überlegte Arbeitsweise des Übersetzers, deren Ergebnisse deshalb anders sind, weil seine Verstehensvoraussetzungen andere waren als die heutiger Exegeten.

70. Ps 9,19; 77(76),8–9; 103(102),9.

71. S. Ez 15,5; 20,40; 36,10; Dan 3,34 (LXX und Th), wo τέλος eindeutig die Endzeit meint.

72. Symmachus hat ἐπινίκιος, Theodotion εἰς τὸ νῖκος (vgl. Ps 3; 6 u.ö.).

wurde.⁷³ Diese Notiz wird im späten 2. Jahrhundert, der mutmaßlichen Entstehungszeit der Psalmen-LXX, kaum anders denn als Bezug auf die Wiedereinweihung des Tempels nach der seleukidischen Entweihung verstanden worden sein.⁷⁴ Dass die Ereignisse dieser Auseinandersetzung als endzeitliches Geschehen verstanden wurden, bezeugt das Danielbuch in aller Klarheit. Will man nicht von bloßer Zufälligkeit ausgehen, scheint mir eindeutig zu sein, dass die einmalige Einfügung der *eis to telos*-Überschrift ausgerechnet an dieser Stelle ein weiteres Indiz dafür ist, dass alle diese Überschriften als Hinweise auf ein eschatologisches Verständnis des Psalters zu deuten sind.

Die Sachgemäßheit dieser Überlegungen wird sich im nächsten Abschnitt durch weitere Beobachtungen an den Psalmüberschriften zu bewähren haben.

4. Zusätze der Psalmen-Septuaginta im Vergleich mit hebräischen Textzeugen

Eines der länger bekannten Phänomene der griechischen Psalmtitel ist das Faktum, dass sich an verschiedenen Stellen mehr Text als im gegenüberzustellenden hebräischen Psalm findet. Oben war bereits auf einige dieser Phänomene hingewiesen worden, namentlich auf die Zufügung von ψαλμός oder Δαυιδ, bei denen mit Harmonisierungstendenzen gerechnet wurde, oder der eben erwähnte Zusatz von εἰς τὸ τέλος.

Allerdings ist hier mit besonderer Aufmerksamkeit die Textüberlieferung zu bedenken, denn bei einer Reihe von Überschüssen des griechischen Textes ist gewiss, bei anderen nicht sicher zu entscheiden, ob sie bei der Übersetzung oder im Gefolge der späteren Rezeptionsgeschichte der Psalmen zugefügt wurde. Dies erkennt man bereits an den eckigen Klammern, die A. Rahlfs in seiner Ausgabe der Psalmen-LXX verwendete, um solche sekundären Elemente zu kennzeichnen.⁷⁵ Offenbar hatten die

---

73. חנכה wird seit Num 7,10–11. 84 mit ἐγκαινισμός wiedergegeben; LXX benutzt hier das geprägte Äquivalent. Vgl. dazu Dorival 1994, 126–27.

74. Das gilt auch für den erweiterten Titel von Ps 96(95): ὅτε ὁ οἶκος ᾠκοδομεῖτο μετὰ τὴν αἰχμαλωσίαν, das in Dan 8,11 (LXX + Th) eindeutig mit Bezug auf die Makkabäerzeit steht. Zu Ps 96(95) und seinen eschatologischen Pointen vgl. Seiler 2001.

75. Bereits die ausführliche Rezension von Hedley 1933, 65, wies darauf hin, dass im Bereich der Psalmüberschriften Verbesserungen des Rahlfsschen Textes nötig seien. Durch die Veröffentlichung von zwei Handschriften aus der Chester Beatty Lib-

Psalmtitel eine besondere Rolle, so dass Zufügungen leichter als im eigentlichen Psalmtext möglich waren. Die sprachlichen Besonderheiten bei der Formulierung weisen in der Regel auf eine freie Formulierung ohne hebräische Vorlage hin,[76] doch sagt diese Beobachtung allein nichts über ihre Herkunft aus. Da dieser Aufsatz keinen eigenen Beitrag zur Textgeschichte leisten kann, sollen hier die Textüberschüsse vorgestellt und nach Phänomenen geordnet werden. Abschließende Urteile über deren Ursprung können nicht gefällt werden.

In mehreren Psalmüberschriften finden sich überraschende Hinweise auf Prophetengestalten. So steht in Ps 65(64) die ausführliche Notiz ᾠδὴ Ιερεμιου καὶ Ιεζεκιηλ ἐκ τοῦ λόγου τῆς παροικίας ὅτε ἔμελλον ἐκπορεύεσθαι („eine Ode Jeremias und Ezechiels aus dem Wort der [in der Fremde wohnenden?] Gemeinde als sie dabei waren, hinauszugehen"), für die es im hebräischen Text nur Anhalt gibt, als hier allein das שיר belegt ist.[77] Worauf dieser Zusatz anspielt, ist nicht deutlich, möglicherweise werden Ezechiel und Jeremia daher zusammengestellt, weil beide Israel verlassen mussten. Ob es um ihren Aufbruch aus Israel oder aus dem Exil geht, kann nicht sicher entschieden werden; wegen der Konnotation der Fremdheit scheint aber eher an die Gemeinde im Exil gedacht zu sein. Inhaltlich geht es in dem Psalm um Gottes Zuwendung zum Zion, so dass man spekulieren kann, dass die beiden Propheten Zion und Jerusalem im Exil nicht vergessen haben und dorthin zurückkehren. Das ausschlaggebende Faktum ist jedenfalls, dass hier über die beiden Namen die prophetische Dimension ausdrücklich im Titel des Psalms zu finden ist.

Dies ist kein singulärer Fall, denn in den Psalmen 146(145)–48 findet sich jeweils der Zusatz Αγγαιου καὶ Ζαχαριου.[78] Die Formulierung im Genitiv zeigt, dass die beiden Propheten als Sänger der Halleluja-Lieder gesehen wurden. Wieder ist nicht recht einsichtig, weshalb ausgerechnet diese beiden Propheten mit diesen Psalmen in Verbindung gebracht werden.

---

rary durch Pietersma 1978 sind die Probleme dieser Textausgabe noch offenkundiger geworden.

76. Dazu Pietersma 1978, 53.

77. Pietersma 2000a, 60, streicht diese Notiz ohne Angabe von Gründen; aus seinen Ausführungen in Pietersma 1978, 53, ist zu erschließen, dass die Verwendung von ὅτε das Ausschlusskriterium war, vgl. ders. 1980, 225. Vgl. zum Problem auch §7.5, S. 64 in der Einleitung der Göttinger Pss-LXX-Ausgabe von A. Rahlfs.

78. Pietersma 2000a, 144–46 streicht erneut die Erwähnung der Propheten, dies wohl aus Analogiegründen.

Inhaltlich sind sie alle Hymnen auf Gottes Macht, und da in Ps 147(146),2 ausdrücklich der Wiederaufbau Jerusalems erwähnt wird, ist dies möglicherweise als Grund für die Nennung der beiden Propheten anzusehen, die sich besonders für den Neubau des zweiten Tempels eingesetzt haben. Sicher ist jedenfalls, dass Psalmen mit Propheten in Verbindung gebracht werden, was m. E. die oben gegebene Interpretation von σύνεσις und εἰς τὸ τέλος stützt und zeigt, dass der griechische Psalter als prophetische Schrift verstanden wurde.

Zwei weitere interessante Zusätze sind zu notieren. So liest man in Psalm 76(75),1 πρὸς τὸν Ἀσσύριον „für den Assyrer" und in 80(79),1 ὑπὲρ τοῦ Ἀσσυρίου „wegen des Assyrers." Nur an diesen beiden Stellen wird im griechischen Psalter auf die Assyrer Bezug genommen. In Ps 83(82),9, wo von אשור die Rede ist, wird dagegen der Name zu Ασσουρ transkribiert, was Grund für die Überlegung war, dass die beiden Assyrer-Belege sekundär gegenüber der ursprünglichen Übersetzung sind.[79]

Inhaltlich ist festzustellen, dass Ps 80(79) eine Anrufung Gottes ist, damit er Israel helfe, das zum Spielball der Nachbarn geworden ist. Ps 76(75) ist ebenfalls von kämpferischer Thematik geprägt, nach V. 4 hat Gott am Zion die Kriegswaffen zerschlagen, laut V. 3 in der LXX-Version dem Ort zum Frieden verholfen. Nun ist zu bedenken, dass im 2. Jahrhundert Syrer und Assyrer nahezu durchgängig als Chiffre für die Seleukiden galten, so dass auch bei diesen beiden Psalmen zu erwägen ist, ob nicht der Psalmtext durch den Hinweis auf die Geschehnisse der Makkabäerzeit aktualisiert wird. Für diesen Vorgang der Aktualisierung gäbe es ja mit der von J. Schaper deutlich gemachten Übersetzung des יהודה מחקקי durch Ιουδας βασιλεύς μου eine deutliche Parallele. Zu den Tendenzen dieser Zeit könnte auch passen, dass in Ps 88(87) und 89(88) Ethan und Heman nicht Esrachiter wie im MT sind, sondern zu Israeliten wurden.[80]

Fasst man die einzelnen Beobachtungen trotz der Unsicherheiten bei einzelnen Stellen im Sinne einer kumulativen Evidenz zusammen, so scheint mir der Eindruck kaum abwendbar zu sein, dass auch die Psalmen-LXX Zeichen einer theologischen Tendenz hat, die man als aktualisierend-eschatologisierend beschreiben könnte. Auch außerhalb der Psalmüberschriften lassen sich ja völlig unstrittige Eschatologisierungen

---

79. So Pietersma 1978, 52–53. Allerdings bietet der Pap. Chester Beatty XIII das πρὸς τὸν Ἀσσύριον in 76(75),1; das ὑπὲρ τοῦ Ἀσσυρίου in 80(79),1 fehlt dagegen, ein Faktum, das Pietersmas These nicht eindeutig unterstützt.

80. Die MT-Lesung in Ps 89,1 wird von 4QPs^e gestützt.

feststellen, so etwa in 49(48),10[81] + 16[82] und, besonders prominent, in Ps 1,5, wo es heißt, dass die Gottlosen nicht im Gericht auferstehen werden (διὰ τοῦτο οὐκ ἀναστήσονται ἀσεβεῖς ἐν κρίσει); MT hat hier nur קום.[83]

Von diesem Text her ist auch die sicher spätere, vielleicht christliche Zufügung in der Überschrift von Ps 66(65) verstehbar. Dort wird ἀναστάσεως ergänzt; es sei ein Psalm der Auferstehung. Diese Charakterisierung des Psalms kann von V. 9 abgeleitet sein, wo es im Hebräischen heißt: השם נפשנו בחיים; „der unsere Seele zum Leben bringt"; LXX weist hier mit der Übersetzung τοῦ θεμένου τὴν ψυχήν μου εἰς ζωὴν „der meine Seele ins Leben stellt" ebenfalls auf eine individualisierende Auferstehungshoffnung hin. Es zeigt sich also, dass die Zufügungen Aussagen der Psalmen pointiert voranstellen, was gewiss auch für das ἐκστάσεως in 31(30),1 gilt, das ein Motiv aus V. 23 aufnimmt und zur Überschrift macht. Daher sind diese Titel als wichtiges Element der Rezeptionsgeschichte jener Texte zu begreifen, selbst wenn sie nicht auf den Übersetzer selbst zurückgehen.

An dieser Stelle sei an ein Argument Frank Austermanns erinnert, das oben bereits kurz angesprochen wurde. In seiner These 10 hieß es, dass

> spätere Interpretationen der Vorlage und Übersetzung und spätere Methoden der Interpretation ... nicht ohne weiteres zur Erklärung der Deutung der Vorlage durch den Übersetzer herangezogen werden (können).[84]

Dies erscheint mir im Licht der bisherigen Beobachtungen fraglich, denn die Vermutung, dass sich in der Pss-LXX eine eschatologisierende Tendenz bereits an den Überschriften erkennen lässt, wird durch weitere Fakten unterstützt, die nach dem obigen Zitat als „spätere Interpretationen" zu gelten haben. So gibt es im NT eine Reihe von Texten, an denen Psalmstellen eindeutig als Prophezeiung verstanden werden; vgl. die Aufnahme von Ps 110(109),1 in Mt 22,44 oder die von Ps 8,3 in Mt 21,16; vgl. auch Ps 44(43),23 in Röm 8,36 oder Ps 19(18),5 in Röm 10,18. In Röm 11,9

---

81. ὅτι οὐκ ὄψεται καταφθοράν ὅταν ἴδῃ σοφοὺς ἀποθνῄσκοντας „denn er wird den Tod nicht sehen, wenn er Weise sterben sieht."

82. πλὴν ὁ θεὸς λυτρώσεται τὴν ψυχήν μου ἐκ χειρὸς ᾅδου ὅταν λαμβάνῃ με „doch Gott wird meine Seele befreien aus der Macht des Hades, wenn er mich annimmt."

83. Dazu Schaper 1995, 46–48 und schon Flashar 1912, 115, mit einem weiteren Hinweis auf eine parallele Übersetzung in der Jesaja-LXX (26,19).

84. Austermann 2000, 385.

erscheint sogar David selbst mit dem Zitat von Ps 68(67),23 als Prophet. Der gleiche Vorgang ist ebenso in Schriften aus Qumran belegt, wie in 11QPs^a 27,11 ausdrücklich formuliert wird: „alle diese sprach er durch Prophetie, die ihm vor dem Höchsten gegeben war." Folgerichtig wurden daher auch Psalmen wie andere prophetische Schriften in eigenen *pescharim* ausgelegt, vgl. 4Q171 + 173.[85] Die Übereinstimmungen zwischen dem Befund zur Psalmen-LXX und den externen, späteren Belegen sind eindeutig. Der LXX-Psalter ist damit als eine wesentliche Etappe auf dem Weg zu einem prophetischen Verständnis der Psalmen zu sehen. Sein Übersetzer hat dabei zumindest bei den εἰς τὸ τέλος und σύνεσις-Übersetzungen, die ja keinesfalls auf abweichende Vorlagen zurückgeführt werden können, eigene Pointen hinterlassen, die von späteren Tradenten aufgegriffen werden konnten.

Dieses Urteil gilt wohl auch für einen verwandten Themenkomplex, den der Davidisierung des Psalters. An verschiedenen Stellen ist nämlich zu beobachten, dass über den hebräischen Text hinaus Psalmüberschriften auf David verweisen, die zu den historisierenden Überschriften des hebräischen Psalters passen. Zu erwähnen ist hier zunächst Ps 71(70): τῷ Δαυιδ υἱῶν Ιωναδαβ καὶ τῶν πρώτων αἰχμαλωτισθέντων „ein für David von den Söhnen Jonadabs, und den ersten der Gefangenen (gesungener Psalm)."[86] Hier ist nicht ganz sicher, auf welchen Jonadab sich die Notiz bezieht. Wenn das τῷ Δαυιδ und der Rest der Überschrift zusammengehören, ist an den in 2.Sam 13 erwähnten Jonadab zu denken, der David im Bezug auf die Königssöhne Rat gibt; das könnte auch zur Erwähnung der Gefangenen passen. Als „Söhne Jonadabs" werden dagegen in Jer 35(42) die Rechabiter bezeichnet, die vor Nebukadnezzar nach Jerusalem geflohen sein sollen; dann würde diese Notiz einmal mehr einen Bezug zur prophetischen Überlieferung herstellen. Doch dazu passt der Bezug zu David schlecht, und da die meisten der historisierenden Davidstitel aus dem 1. und 2. Davidspsalter auf den Komplex der Davidsgeschichten anspielen, liegt dieser Bezug wohl auch hier näher. Eindeutiger mit David in Verbindung zu bringen ist Ps 97(96): τῷ Δαυιδ ὅτε ἡ γῆ αὐτοῦ καθίσταται „für David, wenn sein Land bestellt wird." Die singuläre, aber eindeutige Formulierung im futurischen Passiv scheint mir den Schluss unausweich-

---

85. Brooke 2000, 694–700.
86. Nach Pietersma 1980, 224, gehört diese Überschrift nicht zum ursprünglichen Bestand der griechischen Übersetzung.

lich werden zu lassen, dass hier auf eine messianische Davidserwartung angespielt wird.[87]

Näher an den „kanonischen" Davidsüberschriften stehen die aus Ps 143(142) und 144(143). Der erste Psalm, ein Klagelied, wird auf die Situation bezogen ὅτε αὐτὸν ὁ υἱὸς καταδιώκει, was gewiss an den Absalomaufstand 2.Sam 15 anspielt. Der zweite Psalm, der Gottes Hilfe im Krieg preist, wird über πρὸς τὸν Γολιαδ mit 1.Sam 17 in Verbindung gebracht, gleiches geschieht in Ps 151,1. Überdies sind an einer ganzen Reihe von Stellen weitere Zufügungen unspezifischer Hinweise auf David zu notieren.[88] Trotz der Unsicherheiten in der Textüberlieferung zeigt damit der LXX-Psalter—zumindest seine frühesten Rezeptionsstufen—eine auch im Sirachbuch wie in Qumran[89] belegte Tendenz: Das Bild Davids als Psalmbeter wird weiter ausgebaut, eine Tendenz die im Dienst der messianischen Erwartung eines neuen David steht.[90]

5. Die Sabbat-Problematik

Zum Schluss sei noch an ein Problem erinnert, das andernorts gut dokumentiert ist und daher keiner so umfassenden Erörterung bedarf.[91] Es geht um die fünf Überschriften, an denen die LXX einen Psalm einem bestimmten Tag der Woche zuordnet; im MT ist dies nur bei Ps 92 der Fall. Die Texte sind—in der Reihenfolge der Wochentage:

Ps 24(23):   ψαλμὸς τῷ Δαυιδ τῆς μιᾶς σαββάτων
Ps 48(47):   ψαλμὸς ᾠδῆς τοῖς υἱοῖς Κορε δευτέρᾳ σαββάτου
Ps 94(93):   ψαλμὸς τῷ Δαυιδ τετράδι σαββάτων
Ps 93(92):   εἰς τὴν ἡμέραν τοῦ προσαββάτου ὅτε κατῴκισται ἡ γῆ αἶνος ᾠδῆς τῷ Δαυιδ
Ps 92(91):   ψαλμὸς ᾠδῆς εἰς τὴν ἡμέραν τοῦ σαββάτου

---

87. Erneut sieht Pietersma 1980, 225, die Überschrift als sekundär an.
88. Ps 33(32), vgl. 4QPs^q: מזמור שיר לדויד; 43(42); 91(90); 93(92); 94(93); 95(94); 104(103), vgl. 11QPs^a: לדויד; 137(136). Allerdings fehlt in der LXX der Hinweis auf David in den Wallfahrtsliedern 122(121); 124(123) gegen MT. Zum Problem vgl. ausführlich Pietersma 1980.
89. Vgl. etwa zu Ps 89/4Q236 Rüsen-Weinhold 2001.
90. So die Leitthese von Kleer 1996; vgl. etwa S. 320-21; leider wird der LXX-Befund hier nicht wahrgenommen.
91. Dazu Schaper 1998, 177–79; van der Kooij 1983, 71–74 und zuletzt, mit sehr differenzierter Argumentation, Pietersma, 2000b, 29–30.

10. Die Psalmüberschriften des Septuagintapsalters 243

Die Zuordnung der Psalmen zu Sabbaten stimmt bekanntermaßen mit einer in der Mischna mTamid 7,4 erhaltenen Liste überein, die zusätzlich Ps 82 für den dritten und Ps 81 für den fünften Tag vorsieht. In der LXX gibt es in der textlichen Überlieferung nur zu Ps 81(80) einen Anhalt auf diese Zuordnung, als dort Vetus Latina und noch jüngere Übersetzungen ebenfalls auf den 5. Tag verweisen.

Interessanterweise ist in der bisherigen Diskussion kaum auf Ps 38(37),1 hingewiesen worden, wo sich—ebenfalls über den MT hinaus—der Hinweis περὶ σαββάτου findet; offenbar soll auch dieser Psalm zum Sabbat gehören. Zu erwähnen ist außerdem noch Ps 29(28),1, wo LXX gegen MT den Psalm ἐξοδίου σκηνῆς zuordnet. Der Text ist insofern schwierig, als m.W. ἐξόδιον sonst nicht mit σκηνή verbunden wird, der Bezug zum Laubhüttenfest ist damit nicht eindeutig. Im Pentateuch wird demgegenüber σκηνή sehr oft auf die Stiftshütte bezogen (vgl. Ex 26,6 u.ö.; Num 1,1 u.ö.), dies passt eher zum Text des Psalms als Bezug auf die Laubhütte. Deutlich ist jedenfalls, dass die Überschrift der rabbinischen Tradition (Soferim 18,3) widerspricht, die jenen Psalm mit dem Wochenfest verbindet.[92] Man wird also auch bei den Sabbat-Titeln nicht so ohne weiteres von einer vollständigen Identität der Zuordnungen in LXX und Mischna ausgehen können.

Nun weiß man, wie Johann Maier eindrücklich gezeigt hat,[93] nahezu nichts Sicheres über die Verwendung der Psalmen im frühen Synagogengottesdienst. Der Gebrauch in Qumran und im NT legt zudem eine messianisch-prophetische und weniger eine kultische Verwendung der Psalmen nahe, und auch die εἰς τὸ τέλος-Überschriften lassen keinen Bezug zu Lied- oder Aufführungspraxis erkennen. Außerdem sollte man erwarten, dass ein griechischer Psalter, der als Liederbuch für den Synagogengottesdienst verwendet wurde, wenigstens eine vollständige und eindeutige Zuordnung von Liedern und Wochentagen erkennen lässt. So scheint es mir wenig wahrscheinlich zu sein, dass sich im LXX-Psalter tatsächlich Hinweise auf eine liturgische Verwendung im Synagogengottesdienst finden lassen.[94] Hinzu kommt die Überschrift in Ps 27(26),1 τοῦ Δαυιδ

---

92. S. Schaper 1998, 179, der daher von „abweichenden Traditionen" spricht und es für am wahrscheinlichsten hält, dass die Überschrift in Ps 29(28) „eine alte, (möglicherweise) palästinische, im Umfeld der Synagoge angesiedelte Tradition wiedergibt."
93. Maier 1983.
94. Gegen Schaper 1998, 179. Als weiteres Argument führt Pietersma 2000b an, dass die Überschriften von Ps 92 + 93(91 + 92), die mit εἰς τὴν ἡμέραν formuliert

πρὸ τοῦ χρισθῆναι, die sich entweder auf die Salbung des Hohepriesters bezieht,[95] oder, was wahrscheinlicher ist, erneut eine Referenz auf David herstellt: „bevor (er) gesalbt wurde."[96] Beide Lösungsvorschläge weisen nicht auf den Synagogengottesdienst, sondern passen besser zur Hochschätzung des Tempels, die sich auch sonst in der Pss-LXX zeigt,[97] oder zum bereits angesprochenen Phänomen der Davidisierung des Psalters.

6. Schluss

Die Untersuchung hat damit ihr Ziel erreicht, eine Übersicht über die Besonderheiten der griechischen Psalmtitel zu geben, um auf dieser Basis Urteile über die theologische Interpretation zu geben, die sich hier greifen lässt. Es ist zwar theoretisch möglich, alle Textüberschüsse der LXX auf eine uns nicht mehr zugängliche, abweichende Vorlage zurückzuführen oder als innergriechische Zuwächse zu erklären. Doch spricht gegen ersteres die Tatsache, dass sich nur an zwei inhaltlich unwichtigen Stellen Parallelen zur LXX in Qumran finden ließen. Dies ist umso bedeutsamer, als die Psalmen dasjenige Buch sind, von dem in Qumran die meisten Exemplare gefunden wurden. Die Überlegung eines innergriechischen Textwachstums ist zwar wahrscheinlicher als die einer abweichenden Vorlage, doch scheint es kaum möglich zu sein, auf der Basis der vorhandenen Handschriften in allen fraglichen Fällen zu sicheren Urteilen pro oder contra zu gelangen.

Doch selbst wenn man solchen theoretischen Positionen zustimmt, ist m. E. von den εἰς τὸ τέλος und den σύνεσις-Titeln her deutlich, dass schon der Übersetzer selbst seine eigenen Intentionen eingetragen hat. Einmal mehr ist damit deutlich—dies als Stellungnahme zur eingangs skizzierten Methodendiskussion—dass eine LXX-Übersetzung zugleich Übersetzung und Auslegung ist. Man sollte hier folglich keine künstliche

---

sind, sich nicht auf liturgischen Gebrauch, sondern auf den Gegenstand des Psalms beziehen lassen sollen; für ihn sind die Tagesnennungen wahrscheinlich christliche Ergänzungen.

95. Rahlfs 1979, 72.

96. So Pietersma 2000b, 31-32. Die Herkunft dieser Notiz wird nicht abschließend geklärt, für Pietersma ist allerdings in Einklang mit seinen sonstigen Urteilen eine Entstehung nach der Übersetzung wahrscheinlicher als eine abweichende hebräische Vorlage.

97. Vgl. dazu Seiler 2001, 214-15 zu Ps 96(95),8.

Trennung einführen, die zudem im Widerspruch zu den Erkenntnissen der modernen Rezeptionsforschung wie dem Wissen über Übersetzungen in der Antike steht. Damit scheint mir auch bei den griechischen Psalmen das Denkmodell eines Übersetzers als eines *auch interpretierenden* Schriftgelehrten bestätigt.[98]

Literatur

Aejmelaeus, Anneli. 1992. Review of *God Is My Rock*, by Staffan Olofsson. *TLZ* 117:508–10.

Austermann, Frank. 2000. „Thesen zur Septuaginta-Exegese am Beispiel der Untersuchung des Septuaginta-Psalters." Seiten 380–86 in *Der Septuaginta-Psalter und seine Tochterübersetzungen*. Hrsg. von Anneli Aejmelaeus und Udo Quast. NAWG Phil-Hist Klasse 3, 230. MSU 24. Göttingen: Vandenhoeck & Ruprecht.

Beck, John A. 2000. *Translators as Storytellers. A Study in Septuagint Translation Technique*. StBibLit 25. New York: Lang.

Bons, Eberhard. 1997. Review of *Eschatology in the Greek Psalter*, by Joachim Schaper. *RevSR* 71:257–58.

Brooke, George J. 2000. "Prophecy." *EDSS*:694-700.

Delekat, Ludwig. 1964. „Probleme der Psalmenüberschriften." *ZAW* 76:280–97.

Dorival, Gilles. 1994. *Les Nombres*. BdA 4. Paris: Cerf.

Fabry, Heinz-Josef. 1998. „Der Psalter in Qumran." Seiten 137–63 in *Der Psalter in Judentum und Christentum. (Norbert Lohfink zum 70. Geburtstag)*. Hrsg. von Erich Zenger. HBS 18. Freiburg: Herder.

Flashar, Martin. 1912. „Exegetische Studien zum Septuagintapsalter." *ZAW* 32:81–116; 161–89; 241–68.

---

98. Nachtrag: Die in diesem Aufsatz vorgetragenen Thesen wurden von Albert Pietersma (2005, 456-71) und Staffan Olofsson (2014) mit unterschiedlichen Argumenten in Frage gestellt, vor allem die Überlegung der eschatologischen Ausrichtung der εἰς τὸ τέλος-Überschriften. Olofsson 2014, 182, muss aber zugestehen, dass er nicht sagen kann, wie der Übersetzer diese Formulierung verstanden hat, wenn τέλος eher im Sinne von „Vollständigkeit/Erfüllung" zu verstehen ist, wie er es vorschlägt. Beide Autoren sind sehr zurückhaltend bei der Frage, welche theologische Exegeseleistungen den Übersetzern zuzutrauen sind, sie sehen das Phänomen der eschatologischen Interpretation der Psalmen eher als Element der Rezeptionsgeschichte der griechischen Texte, vgl. etwa die Definition bei Olofsson 2001, 291.

Flint, Peter W. 1997. *The Dead Sea Psalms Scrolls and the Book of Psalms*. STDJ 17. Leiden: Brill.

Fritsch, Charles T. 1973. "Studies in the Theology of the Greek Psalter." Seiten 729–41 in *Zer Li´gevurot. The Zalman Shazar Jubilee Volume*. Hrsg. von Ben Zion Luria. Jerusalem: Qiryat Sēfer.

Harl, Marguerite, Gilles Dorival, und Olivier Munnich. 1994. *La Bible Grecque des Septante. Du judaïsme hellénistique au christianisme ancien*. 2me édition. Paris: Cerf.

Hedley, P. L. 1933. "The Göttingen Investigation and Edition of the Septuagint." *HTR* 26:57–72.

Horst, Pieter van der. 1997. Review of *Eschatology in the Greek Psalter*, by Joachim Schaper. *JSJ* 28:123–24.

Hossfeld, Frank Lothar, und Erich Zenger. 1993. *Die Psalmen I. Psalm 1–50*. NEB 29. Würzburg: Echter.

———. 2000. *Psalmen 51–100*. HThKAT. Freiburg: Herder.

Joosten, Jan. 2000. „Une théologie de la Septante? Réflexions méthodologique sur l´interpretation de la version greque." *RTP* 132:31–46.

Kleer, Martin. 1996. „*Der liebliche Sänger der Psalmen Israels." Untersuchungen zu David als Dichter und Beter der Psalmen*. BBB 108. Bodenheim: Philo.

Kooij, Arie van der. 1983. "On the Place of Origin of the Old Greek of Psalms." *VT* 33:67–74.

———. 2000. „Zur Frage der Exegese im LXX-Psalter. Ein Beitrag zur Verhältnisbestimmung zwischen Original und Übersetzung." Seiten 366–79 in *Der Septuaginta-Psalter und seine Tochterübersetzungen*. Hrsg. von Anneli Aejmelaeus und Udo Quast. NAWG Phil-Hist Klasse 3, 230. MSU 24. Göttingen: Vandenhoeck & Ruprecht.

Kraus, Hans Joachim. 1989. *Psalmen. Psalmen 1–59*. 6. Auflage. BKAT 15,1. Neukirchen-Vluyn: Neukirchener Verlag.

Lee, John A.L. 1983. *A Lexical Study of the Septuagint Version of the Pentateuch*. SCS 14. Chico, CA: Scholars Press.

Lust, Johan, Erik Eynikel, und Katrin Hauspie. 1996. *A Greek-English Lexicon of the Septuagint, Part II. K–Omega*. Stuttgart: Deutsche Bibelgesellschaft.

Maier, Johann. 1983. „Zur Verwendung der Psalmen in der synagogalen Liturgie (Wochentag und Sabbat)." Seiten 55–90 in *Liturgie und Dichtung. Ein interdisziplinäres Kompendium*. Hrsg. von Hansjakob Becker. Pietatis Liturgica 1. Sankt Ottilien: EOS Verlag.

Mozley, Francis W. 1905. *The Psalter of the Church. The Septuagint Psalms Compared with the Hebrew, with Various Notes*. Cambridge: Cambridge University Press.

Olofsson, Staffan. 1990. *God Is My Rock. A Study of Translation Technique and Theological Exegesis in the Septuagint*. ConBOT 31. Stockholm: Almqvist & Wiksell.

———. 2001. „Law and Lawbreaking in the LXX Psalms. A Case of Theological Exegesis." Seiten 291–330 in *Der Septuaginta-Psalter. Sprachliche und theologische Aspekte*. Hrsg. von Erich Zenger. HBS 32. Freiburg im Breisgau: Herder.

———. 2014. „Does the Septuagint Translator Speak about the End of Times? A Study of εἰς τὸ τέλος, σύνεσις and συνίημι." Seiten 173–93 in *In the Footsteps of Sherlock Holmes. Studies in the Biblical Text in Honour of Anneli Aejmelaeus*. Hrsg. von Kristin De Troyer, Timothy M. Law, und Marketta Liljeström. CBET 72. Leuven: Peeters.

Peters, Melvin K. 1997. Review of *Eschatology in the Greek Psalter*, by Joachim Schaper. *JBL* 116:350–52. Online: https://tinyurl.com/SBL0468a.

Pietersma, Albert. 1978. *Two Manuscripts of the Greek Psalter in the Chester Beatty Library Dublin. Edited with Textual-critical Analysis and with Full Facsimile*. AnBib 77. Rom: Biblical Institute Press.

———. 1980. „David in the Greek Psalms." *VT* 30:213–16.

———. 1997. Review of *Eschatology in the Greek Psalms*, by Joachim Schaper. *BO* 54:185–90.

———. 2000a. *A New English Translation of the Septuagint. And the Other Greek Translations Traditionally Included under That Title. The Psalms*. Oxford: Oxford University Press.

———. 2000b. „The Present State of the Critical Text of the Greek Psalter." Seiten 12–32 in *Der Septuaginta-Psalter und seine Tochterübersetzungen*. Hrsg. von Anneli Aejmelaeus und Udo Quast. NAWG Phil-Hist Klasse 3, 230. MSU 24. Göttingen: Vandenhoeck & Ruprecht.

———. 2005. „Septuagintal Exegesis and the Superscriptions of the Greek Psalter." Seiten 443–75 in *The Book of Psalms. Composition and Reception*. Hrsg. von Peter W. Flint und Patrick D. Miller. VTSup 99. Leiden: Brill.

Rahlfs, Alfred. 1979. *Septuaginta. Vetus Testamentum Graece. Psalmi cum Odis*. SVTG 10. 3. unveränderte Aufl. Göttingen: Vandenhoeck & Ruprecht.

Rösel, Martin. 1991. „Die Jungfrauengeburt des endzeitlichen Immanuel. Jesaja 7 in der Übersetzung der Septuaginta." *JBTh* 6:135–51. [Kapitel 9 in diesem Band.]

———. 1998a. „The Text-critical Value of Septuagint-Genesis." *BIOSCS* 31:62–70.

———. 1998b. „Theo-Logie der griechischen Bibel. Zur Wiedergabe der Gottesaussagen im LXX-Pentateuch." *VT* 48:49–62.

———. 2015. „A Theology of the Septuagint? Clarifications and Definitions." Paper presented at the Annual Meeting of the Society of Biblical Literature. Atlanta. 23 November 2015.

Rüsen-Weinhold, Ulrich. 2001. „Der Septuaginta-Psalter in seinen verschiedenen Textformen zur Zeit des Neuen Testamentes." Seiten 61–87 in *Der Septuaginta-Psalter. Sprachliche und Theologische Aspekte*. Hrsg. von Erich Zenger. HBS 32. Freiburg im Breisgau: Herder.

Schaper, Joachim. 1995. *Eschatology in the Greek Psalter*. WUNT 2/76. Tübingen: Mohr Siebeck.

———. 1998. „Der Septuaginta-Psalter. Interpretation, Aktualisierung und liturgische Verwendung der biblischen Psalmen im hellenistischen Judentum." Seiten 165–83 in *Der Psalter in Judentum und Christentum. (Norbert Lohfink zum 70. Geburtstag)*. Hrsg. von Erich Zenger. HBS 18. Freiburg im Breisgau: Herder.

Schildenberger, Johannes. 1972. „Einige beachtliche Septuaginta-Lesarten in den Psalmen." Seiten 145–59 in *Wort, Lied und Gottesspruch. Beiträge zur Septuaginta. Festschrift für Joseph Ziegler*. Hrsg. von Josef Schreiner. Würzburg: Echter.

Seele, Astrid. 1995. *Römische Übersetzer. Nöte, Freiheiten, Absichten. Verfahren des literarischen Übersetzens in der griechisch-römischen Antike*. Darmstadt: Wissenschaftliche Buchgesellschaft.

Seiler, Stefan. 2001. „Theologische Konzepte in der Septuaginta. Das theologische Profil von 1 Chr 16,8ff. LXX im Vergleich mit Ps 104; 95; 105 LXX." Seiten 197–225 in *Der Septuaginta-Psalter. Sprachliche und theologische Aspekte*. Hrsg. von Erich Zenger. HBS 32. Freiburg am Breisgau: Herder.

Seybold, Klaus. 1996. *Die Psalmen*. HAT 15. Tübingen: Mohr Siebeck.

Siegert, Folker. 1997. Review of *Eschatology in the Greek Psalter*, by Joachim Schaper. *TLZ* 122:39–41.

Soffer, Arthur. 1957. „The Treatment of Anthropomorphisms and Anthropopathisms in the Septuagint of Psalms." *HUCA* 28:85–107.

Tate, Marvin A. 1990. *Psalms 51–100*. WBC 20. Waco, TX: Word.

Wevers, John William. 1996. „The Interpretative Character and Significance of the Septuagint Version." Seiten 84–107 in vol. 1, part 1 von *Hebrew Bible/Old Testament. The History of Its Interpretation*. Hrsg. von Magne Sæbø. Göttingen: Vandenhoeck & Ruprecht.

Visser, A. J. 1963. „De Geheimenissen van de griekse Opschriften der Psalmen ontsluierd. Gregorius van Nyssa's ‚in inscriptiones psalmorum'." *NedTT* 18:14–29.

Part 3
Theology and Anthropology

11
Towards a "Theology of the Septuagint"

This paper is intended to ask just one very basic question: Can a book be written on the theology of the Septuagint?[1] The answer will be as simple as the question: yes, it can be written. But since I am fully aware of the scholarly debates concerning this and related questions, I will try to clarify things in the following way: first, I will ask what "theology of the Septuagint" can mean; second, I will discuss some texts and topics that show characteristic theological and anthropological distinctions between the Hebrew and the Greek Scriptures; and finally, I will briefly outline *how* in my view such a work can be written. It should be added that the topics can only be sketched very roughly to give a preliminary, overall impression.

1. What Does Theology of the Septuagint Mean?

Beginning with the work of Zacharias Frankel in 1841 and culminating in Adolf Deissmann's *Hellenisierung des semitischen Monotheismus* there have been several attempts to determine the content and range of specific ideas in the LXX.[2] Some of the observations of these early scholars are still very valuable because of their vast knowledge of both Greek authors and Jewish traditions. Especially in Germany this kind of research has been burdened by the work of Georg Bertram, who was very close to the national-socialistic party and to the theology of the "German Christians/ *Deutsche Christen*." He tried to demonstrate that there was a characteristic Septuagint-piety ("*Septuaginta-Frömmigkeit*" in German).[3] This theology

---

1. Throughout this article, "theology of the Septuagint" will refer to a book devoted to theology in the LXX.
2. Frankel 1841, 1851; Deissmann 1903, 162–77.
3. See, inter alia, Bertram 1961,1957, 1972. See also the remarks by Walter 2001, 83–84.

of the Septuagint should be seen, according to him, as *praeparatio evangelica*, by which he meant that the foundation of the New Testament is to be found not in the Jewish-Semitic Hebrew Bible but in the more enlightened Greek Bible. One should add that the famous Paul de Lagarde held similar views.[4]

It should be stated that the work of Bertram is still very influential, because he contributed thirty-seven articles to Kittel's *Theologisches Wörterbuch zum Neuen Testament*, which has also been translated into English.[5] In these articles he tried to show how the meaning of keywords used in the New Testament was shaped by the LXX. Unfortunately scholars who are not familiar with LXX matters still use these articles under the impression that through them they gain access to the LXX and its theology.

There are serious methodological problems with these earlier attempts to determine a theology of the Septuagint. The most significant is that usually the LXX was viewed as a unity without considering that the individual books have been translated by different people at different times not only in Alexandria but also elsewhere.[6] So a first conclusion can be drawn: a theology of the Septuagint cannot be based on the leveling of differences among the individual books or the specific profiles of the translators for the sake of a common edifice of ideas.

In recent years there has been a growing interest in clarifying the theological positions of individual translations of the Jewish Greek Scriptures by going beyond the level of text criticism or text history. Many important details can be found, for example, in the *Notes* of John Wevers on the books of the Pentateuch, in Arie van der Kooij's significant contributions to the understanding of the Greek Isaiah, and in Johann Cook's work on the Greek Proverbs.[7]

Currently the translation generating the most debate is that of the book of Psalms, which in recent years has seen the publication of three volumes of collected essays, Joachim Schaper's published dissertation and the reactions to it, and most recently the fine study of Holger Gzella, again

---

4. See Hanhart 1999a, 248–80.

5. See, e.g., Bertram 1979a, 1979b, 1979c, 1979d.

6. Here the pioneering book by Seeligmann 1948 should be mentioned. See also Seeligmann 1990. Very helpful summaries and charts concerning the date and localization of the individual books of the LXX can be found in Harl, Dorival, and Munnich 1994, 92–111.

7. Wevers 1990, 1993, 1995, 1997, 1998; van der Kooij 1981, 1998; Cook 1997, 2001.

on eschatology and anthropology in Psalms.⁸ A much greater number of scholars could be named, but the studies mentioned suffice for the following statement: the search for theological concepts is now at the level of the individual book. This is good news after the long time of concentration on text-critical questions; nevertheless it is regrettable, because only occasionally are there comparisons of the exegetical or hermeneutical concepts of the individual books.⁹ The need for a synthesis seems not to be very high, although it could strengthen the results for one book if one could find similar ideas in others. So I come to my next conclusion: a treatise on the theology of the Septuagint should be more than a collection of unrelated studies on some or all of the books; it needs unifying elements such as theological topics. One reason for this requirement is that even the earliest readers understood "the Scripture" (ἡ γραφή) as a unity not as a mere collection of separate books.

Third, something obvious should be stated: a theology of the Septuagint should not simply repeat what is usually dealt with in a theology of the Hebrew Bible. The characteristic feature of such a project would be a comparative approach. It would highlight the differences between the versions or the theological developments from one to the other.¹⁰ Thus a theology of the Septuagint would be a substantial enhancement of our understanding of the theology of the Old Testament/Hebrew Bible. This has some important implications:

(1) A theology of the Septuagint could serve to close the gap between the Christian Old Testament and New Testament, and the gap between the Jewish Scriptures and writers such as Demetrius, Aristeas, Josephus, and Philo. One could object that such a gap does not exist because we have so many writings from the last three centuries BCE, which are now enhanced by the scrolls found at Qumran. But generally speaking, these writings are not Bible or Holy Writings, because they held a lower level of authority. For early Jewish and Christian authors the books of the LXX were their Scripture, therefore scholars have to determine the theology of that Scripture.¹¹

---

8. Aejmelaeus and Quast, 2000; Zenger 2001; Hiebert, Cox, and Gentry 2001; Schaper 1995. See the following, more negative reviews: Pietersma 1997; Bons 1997. But see also the positive statements by Siegert 1997; van der Horst 1997; and Gzella 2002.

9. A first attempt can be found in Rösel 1998.

10. See Joosten 2000, 33, who speaks of an "approche compareé."

11. Müller 1996. See also Hengel 2002, which is simply a translation of Hengel's

(2) A theology of the Septuagint would, therefore, form an important part of the history of religion (German: *Religionsgeschichte*) of the Hebrew Bible and of a biblical theology as well. In the LXX one can see certain theological developments that later shape the understanding of the whole Bible. It may suffice to mention the growing David tradition in Psalms, the "Solomonization" of Proverbs, or the extended νόμος-theology in both of the aforementioned books.[12] The LXX is an indispensable part of the history of reception of the Hebrew Bible, therefore it should be discussed when dealing with the theology of those Scriptures. If—to mention but one example—Brevard Childs is writing a biblical theology of the Old and New Testament and hardly ever makes mention of the LXX, it is obvious that his results are at the very least incomplete; one could also say that neglecting the LXX is a somewhat unhistorical approach.[13] But on the other side it should also be stated that LXX scholarship itself is part of the problem, because only recently have we begun to offer "invitations to the Septuagint" in order to ease the access for other scholars.[14]

This leads to the next question: Who needs such a theology of the Septuagint, or what purpose should it serve? The answer to this question is very simple: all scholars who are interested in the meaning of the Hebrew Bible/Old Testament in Hellenistic times need such a book and will use it, as they are using Hengel's *Judentum und Hellenismus*, or Schürer-Vermes, or Bousset-Gressmann.[15] As I said earlier, a theology of the Septuagint should serve to give an impression of where, in which texts, how, and why the Greek Scriptures differ from the Hebrew, and on what topics it makes a difference whether the LXX or the Hebrew Bible were used. Well-known

---

contribution to Hengel and Schwemer 1994. I use the singular "Scripture" here to emphasize the meaning of a holy writing or canon. I am fully aware of the problems of this use, but I have the impression that the plural makes things even more complicated.

12. See Kleer 1996; D'Hamonville 2000, 34, and 78–85.
13. Childs 1993. Note the subtitle "Theological Reflections on the Christian Bible," which makes Child's approach even more problematic, because until the time of the Reformation the Christian Bible was almost never the Hebrew Bible. But see, e.g., Barr 1999, 576: "The Septuagint has paramount importance for our purpose, since, at least in many places, it was the form of the ancient Jewish scriptures that lay before the early Christians."
14. See Jobes and Silva 2000. The harsh critique of this book by Barr (2002) is too concentrated on text-critical issues and seems not to be justified in my view.
15. Hengel 1973; Schürer 1986; and Bousset and Gressmann 1966.

examples are the actualization of prophecies in the LXX of Isaiah and the question of resurrection in Job.

I am fully aware of the problems associated with these premises, because scholars are still in the process of detecting those changes, of assigning them to either the *Vorlage*, the translator, or later transmitters, or to readers. Nevertheless, I think that at least some outlines of a theology of the Septuagint can be drawn, and therefore I turn to the next section.

2. Theological and Anthropological Differences between the Hebrew and the Jewish Greek Scriptures

First, it is important to note that the translators of the Hebrew-Aramaic texts were fully aware that they were translating Scriptures in the sense of authoritative religious writings. This led to significant consequences, namely, harmonizations of the text, the avoidance of contradictions, and explanations of one text by another.[16] Numerous examples can be given for these observations; it may suffice to refer to the additions and harmonizations in the account of the creation in Gen 1, or the flood story in Gen 6–8, or to the theological solution of the Cain and Abel problem in Gen 4.[17]

Moreover, even the translation technique used by the translators can express a characteristic view of Scripture, as Joosten has rightly pointed out. It is a commonplace in LXX scholarship that the translation of the Pentateuch is less literal than most of the subsequent books, although even these five translations differ to some extent among themselves. The later translations that follow their *Vorlage* more closely are the result of a more highly developed theology of Scripture or theology of the word of God. To state it another way, the translators' opinions that the texts they were producing were comprehensible—even if the Greek they were writing was hardly understandable—reveals a specific dynamic theology of Scripture that distinguishes these translators or revisers from translators, authors, or rewriters like the translator of Job into Greek, or from Demetrius, Aristobulus, or later writers like Josephus and Philo.[18]

Although further comparative examinations are needed, I would roughly distinguish two major groups of translators and their hermeneu-

---

16. On harmonizations, see Joosten, 2000, 44–46.
17. See Rösel 1994, 100–114; and Jobes and Silva 2000, 212.
18. This argument is based on Joosten 2000, 42–44.

tics: those who relied on their belief that the word of God was effective even if readers could not understand it; and those who believed that the human intellect has a dignity of its own, so that corrections might be in order, if they served to improve the persuasiveness of the Scriptures. The first position led the textual history of the LXX to the different stages of revisions and retranslations—and the Hebrew Text to its pre-Masoretic standardization—the second can be seen in attempts at rewriting the Scriptures, for example, the book of Jubilees, the reworked Pentateuch from Qumran, or the Genesis Apocryphon.[19]

Another important aspect of an implicit theology is the use of κύριος "Lord," for the Tetragram.[20] Scholars generally agree on the point that this equivalent was used beginning with the earliest known Greek translations. By using κύριος in an absolute way—without a depending genitive—the translations were stating that the God of Israel is the Lord of everything, not one θεοί among many θεοί, but ὁ θεός, "God."[21] Moreover, there are certain instances where distinctions are made between the real God and the foreign gods. Numbers 25:2, where אלהים, "God," was translated by εἴδωλον, "idol," serves as an example, because it clearly refers to the gods of the Moabites; in Gen 31:19–35 Rachel's תרפים, "household gods," are again labeled as εἴδωλα. Thus the LXX shows that monotheism had developed, and by means of the Greek language the translators were able to avoid the ambiguity of the form אלהים by distinguishing singular and plural forms or by using different equivalents.

Interestingly enough, one can also see that there is a tendency toward a more systematic understanding of what κύριος means, because as early as in Genesis we can see that κύριος is used for the friendly, merciful portrayals of God, while θεός is used for the powerful actions. This can be seen in Gen 13:10 where יהוה destroyed Sodom, while the Greek version states that ὁ θεός did it. In Gen 38:7 it was ὁ θεός who killed Er, the firstborn of Judah, and in Gen 6:6–7 it was ὁ θεός who decided to bring the flood; but

---

19. See Fernández Marcos 2000, 109–54, for an excellent treatment of the problem of the revisions. Very comprehensive overviews of the Qumran materials can be found in VanderKam 1994, 34–70, and in the articles in VanderKam and Schiffman 2000.

20. "Implicit theology" means the theology of the community that formed the belief of the translator and that person's own overall theological framework as well.

21. Hanhart 1999b, 75; and see Rösel 2000, 5–7.

the Hebrew text has the Tetragram in all these instances.²² Thus we can conclude that a tradition later on attested by Philo and even later by the rabbis is already shaping in the third century belief that the use of κύριος and θεός has a theological significance of its own.²³

Moreover, we can see that the theological consciousness about the names and designations of God developed over time. In the earlier translations, such as in Genesis, the name שדי was translated by ὁ θεός σου/μου, "your/my God" (17:1; 28:3).²⁴ In Exod 6:3 its translation with θεὸς ὢν αὐτῶν, "being their God," was derived from the famous ἐγώ εἰμι ὁ ὤν, "I am the one who is," in Exod 3:14. But in later books the pentateuchal pattern was not followed. Instead we can find translations such as παντοκράτωρ "Almighty" (Job 5:17; 33:4); ἐπουράνιος, "heavenly" (Ps 68:15); θεὸς τοῦ οὐρανοῦ, "God of the heaven" (Ps 91:1); or ὁ ἱκανός, "Mighty One" (Ruth 1:20–21; Job 21:15).²⁵ All these equivalents serve to emphasize the power of the God of Israel, who was no longer called by a name that could make this God comparable to pagan gods; שדי became the universal ruler.

The same is true for the translation of יהוה צבאות by the "Lord of hosts." Again, one can see different attempts to deal with this designation: in 1 Kingdoms and Isaiah the transcription σαβαωθ is predominant; in 2 and 3 Kingdoms as well as Psalms we find κύριος τῶν δυνάμεων, "Lord of the powers."²⁶ In 2 Kingdoms, in the Greek 1 and 2 Chronicles, and in the Dodekapropheton one can also find παντοκράτωρ, "Almighty."²⁷ I would fully subscribe to the results of Cécile Dogniez, who has stated that we can see an evolution of the conception of God from a more mythic imagery to the universalistic idea of a παντοκράτωρ or κοσμοκράτωρ.²⁸

From a methodological perspective it should be stated that these results come from a twofold comparative approach to the task of Septuagint theology: the comparison between the Hebrew and the Greek text, on the one hand, and the comparison of the individual translations, on the

---

22. Similar phenomena can be seen in Exod 3:18; 10:11; 16:7–9. See Rösel 2007; 1991, 376.

23. On the different positions of Philo and the Rabbis, see Dahl and Segal 1978.

24. Rösel 1991, 373.

25. See Bertram 1959 on the LXX; Reiss 1975 on the rabbinic literature.

26. For σαβαωθ see 1 Kgdms 1:3, 11; Isa 1:9, 24. For κύριος τῶν δυνάμεων, see 2 Kgdms 5:10; 6:2; 3 Kgdms 2:5; 18:15; Pss 24:10; 46:8.

27. 2 Kgdms 5:10; 7:27; 1 Chr 11:9; 17:7; Hos 12:6; Amos 3:13; Nah 2:14. On the translation of יהוה צבאות see Dogniez 1997.

28. Dogniez 1997.

other. Thus one can easily see that it does not suffice to confine the work to individual books of the Greek Scriptures.

This view is supported by the evidence of the increasing importance of the "name-of-God theology" in the LXX. There are several instances where we can see a specific reverencing of the divine name: according to Exod 34:14 the Lord is a jealous God and "Jealous" is his name. In the Greek version "Jealous" is not the name of the Lord, but the unspeakable name is in itself jealous. This is confirmed by the famous text Lev 24:16, because here in the Hebrew Bible "One who blasphemes the name of the LORD shall be put to death," in the LXX even the "one who is *naming* the Holy name should die the death."

The distance between God and the world was increasing, and this can also be seen in the so-called antianthropomorphisms of the Greek Scriptures. Since Charles Fritsch's theory from 1943 this problem has often been discussed, and there are a number of studies contradicting and supporting Fritsch.[29] The truth is somewhere in the middle, as often is the case. One cannot say that the translators have generally avoided every notion that could be understood as anthropomorphism. As an example: in Numbers the expression על־פי יהוה, "by the mouth of God," was avoided, and instead διὰ φωνῆς κυρίου, "by the voice/sound of God," was used as a translation (cf. 3:16, 39). That this is clearly the result of a theological consideration can be seen in cases where על־פי אהרן, "by the mouth of Aaron" (or the like), had to be translated, because there κατὰ στόμα Ααρων was used (4:27). The translator did not avoid the idea of a voice of God only that God had a mouth. Distinctions like these can be seen often, such as at Exod 19:3 where Moses was not going up to God (ומשה עלה אל־האלהים) but rather to the mountain of God (καὶ Μωυσῆς ἀνέβη εἰς τὸ ὄρος τοῦ θεοῦ).[30]

The translators of the Psalms sometimes dealt in a very intelligent way with the problem, such as at 17(16):15 where in the Hebrew version the praying person would be able to see God's face (אני בצדק אחזה פניך) while in the LXX that person would be seen (= judged) by God (ἐγὼ δὲ ἐν δικαιοσύνῃ ὀφθήσομαι τῷ προσώπῳ σου; note also the interesting translation of תמונה with δόξα at the end of the verse). Although a type of anthropomorphism is still present, the meaning of the verse has been changed considerably. On the other side there are clear avoidances of metaphorical

---

29. Fritsch 1943; Hanson 1992; Olofsson 1990, 17–39; Soffer 1957. See the latest collection of arguments concerning this problem in Siegert 2001, 247–50.

30. See also Exod 33:11; Num 12:8.

ideas, such as God being a rock (צוּר; cf. Ps 18:3, 47).³¹ While it is not clear why some designations were avoided and others not, there is definitely a kind of theology of the translators; they had an idea of what could be said about God and what not. This could even include the more expanded angelology and demonology that is found in the LXX, as Adrian Schenker has pointed out for LXX Psalms; something that was already found in Exod 4:24 where it was not the Lord who wanted to kill Moses but an ἄγγελος κυρίου.³²

The partial avoidance of anthropomorphisms has consequences for the anthropology of the LXX, because the distance between God and humans is emphasized. This can also be seen in Num 23:19 where the impression is avoided that God and humans can be compared. Instead of לֹא אִישׁ אֵל, "God is not a human being," in the Greek Scriptures one reads οὐχ ὡς ἄνθρωπος ὁ θεός, "God is not as a human being."

To sum up these observations about references to God: it is obvious that the Greek Bible read as a whole, and in its parts, display an image of God different from its Hebrew counterpart. To exaggerate the depiction: the God of the LXX is the θεὸς τῆς οἰκουμένης, "the God of the inhabited earth" (cf. Ps 23[22]:1), while the God of the Hebrew Bible is the אלהי ישראל, "God of Israel." It is obvious that the translators have strengthened a tendency that was present in the Hebrew Bible from the days of Deutero-Isaiah, but that now affects the majority of the texts, as is the case with the Greek Scriptures.³³

I will now only touch on other topics that have one thing in common, that they are found in more than one book of the LXX. One extremely important focus is the vocabulary of cult and worship; here one can refer to the work of Suzanne Daniel.³⁴ The striking observation is that the translators used neologisms to separate the true cult of Israel from pagan cults. This culminates in the distinction of the newly created θυσιαστήριον, "offering place," from the common βωμός, "altar." Using this specific vocabulary the translators were able to express their own interpretation of details of the biblical texts. For a striking example one could look at Num 23:1 where Balaam is building a (pagan) βωμός, although מזבח is usually translated by θυσιαστήριον in LXX Numbers. The same can be seen in Josh 22:10–

---

31. Olofsson 1990, 35–45.
32. Schenker 2001.
33. Albani 2000.
34. Daniel 1966.

29, where the tribes Reuben, Gad, and Half-Manasseh are also building a (pagan) βωμός. The same distinction is made in the first book of Maccabees (1:47; 5:58) and in prophetic books as well (Hos 10:8; Amos 7:9).[35] Moreover, the positive designation for the altar, θυσιαστήριον, is related to ἱλαστήριον, "atonement place," which translates כפרת, "mercy seat" (Exod 25:17, cf. esp. Ezek 43:20; Amos 9:1), so that even from a linguistic point-of-view the cult is a unit. Again we have to note that already the use or nonuse of standard equivalents can imply a theological point of view.

One could also comment on the problem of messianism as a common feature of several books of the LXX beginning from Gen 49.[36] Special mention should be made to the well-known translation ἐξελεύσεται ἄνθρωπος ἐκ τοῦ σπέρματος αὐτοῦ καὶ κυριεύσει ἐθνῶν πολλῶν, "A man will come from his seed and he will rule over many nations," in Num 24:7 for יזל־מים מדליו וזרעו במים רבים, "Water shall flow from his buckets, and his seed shall have abundant water" (cf. also the use of ἄνθρωπος for שבט in Num 24:17).

Another important topic is the strengthening of eschatology even in books like the Psalms or the Greek Job with its clear references to resurrection and a future life of the just.[37] Furthermore, mention should be made of the Greek Proverbs, because it shows a clear tendency to bring νόμος and wisdom into line (cf. Prov 9:10) and to promote an educational ideal that is based on σύνεσις, "intelligence," and παιδεία, "instruction."[38] Again, this specific theology is not restricted to only one book, because we have very prominent texts in the Psalms revealing very similar ideas, cf. the famous δράξασθε παιδείας in Ps 2:12 for the difficult Hebrew נשקו־בר, "kiss his feet/the son."[39] Another important argument for a more eschatological understanding in Psalms can be derived from the εἰς τὸ τέλος/ εἰς σύνεσιν superscriptions of several psalms [30(31):1; 52(51):1], as I have argued elsewhere.[40] Even if attempts to prove this interpretation wrong

---

35. But, βωμός is used in the usual Greek sense in 2 Macc 2:19; 13:8.

36. Rösel 1995; 2006 [ch. 5 in this volume], and see also Fabry 2006 on messianism in the LXX.

37. For the Psalms, see the detailed analysis of Gzella 2002, especially §§3.3 and 3.4. See also Seiler 2001; Gzella 2001; and Schaper 2001. For Greek Job, see the different positions of Gard 1954; Fernández Marcos 1994.

38. See, e.g., Prov 10:17; 16:17, where παιδεία is used even without a Hebrew equivalent. For an overall estimation see Cook 1997, 328–31 (as a summary of his exegesis), and also d'Hamonville 2000, 84–87.

39. See Craigie 1983, 64, for the text-critical problem of Ps 2:12.

40. Rösel 2001 [ch. 10 in this volume].

were to succeed, the fact that these superscriptions have been understood eschatologically by early readers remains.[41] Moreover, the same concept of eschatological understanding seems to lie behind the well-known translation ἐὰν μὴ πιστεύσητε οὐδὲ μὴ συνῆτε for the Hebrew אם לא תאמינו כי לא תאמנו in Isa 7:9.[42] It is also important to note that the idea of David being a prophet was very prominent at that time. It may suffice to call attention to the famous passage in the "Compositions of David" in 11Q5 XXVII, 1-4: "All these (psalms) he spoke through (the spirit of) prophecy which was given to him from the Most High."[43] Thus the more eschatological translation of the LXX fits perfectly into the hermeneutical framework of that time, and I cannot see why this understanding cannot be attributed to the translator as well.

One could also refer to the different anthropologies of several books, beginning with Gen 1:26 and the translation ποιήσωμεν ἄνθρωπον κατ' εἰκόνα ἡμετέραν καὶ καθ' ὁμοίωσιν, which involves a considerable change in the idea of humans being the image of God.[44] Moreover, it is very obvious

---

41. Albert Pietersma (2006, esp. 40–44) has tried to demonstrate that there was no theological intention behind the εἰς τὸ τέλος/εἰς σύνεσιν superscriptions in the Greek Psalter. Because of the nature of this paper it is not possible to respond in detail, but a brief response may be in order. It is obvious that Prof. Pietersma's approach and mine differ at the very point that Pietersma calls a "linguistic heresy," because he is focusing on the single word as the bearer of the meaning, while I would always include the immediate context of the word in question to determine its meaning. As for his argument concerning the εἰς τὸ τέλος superscriptions, his observation that in nonphilosophical Classical and Hellenistic literature τέλος has no eschatological meaning proves almost nothing, because the LXX of Psalms should be seen within the range of Jewish Hellenism of that time; with Pietersma's argument one could also say that keywords like κύριος, νόμος, or χριστός do not have theological meanings, because such meanings are not attested in that same body of literature. Moreover, Pietersma leaves open the question of what the τέλος is to which the translator is alluding—the characteristic use of the article in these superscriptions is in my view pointing to a certain τέλος. Obviously the translator must have had something specific in mind, otherwise he would not have added εἰς τὸ τέλος to the superscription of Ps 30(29), which is a psalm that is connected with the τοῦ ἐγκαινισμοῦ τοῦ οἴκου, "the dedication of the temple," which in my opinion obviously points to the events of the Maccabean revolt. To be fair, Pietersma confirms that readers could gain the impression that these superscriptions have an eschatological meaning; the point of difference is whether this is a phenomenon of translation or of reception.

42. For a detailed analysis of the whole chapter of Isa 7, see Rösel 1991.

43. Translation from García Martínez and Tigchelaar 1997–1998, 1179.

44. Rösel 1994, 48–50; Gross 2000.

that the Greek text of Gen 1 and 2 can best be understood as reflecting the Platonic account of creation in the dialogue *Timaeus*; ideas like these may also lie behind the contrast of πνεῦμα and σάρξ in Gen 6:3.[45] The examples I have presented in this section can be seen as evidence that the translators had their own theological and hermeneutical ideas, which affected their translations. Many more examples have been noted elsewhere, and in my view it is worthwhile to collect them and to arrange them in a systematic way to give an impression of where there are differences between LXX theology and Hebrew Bible theology. Even if we cannot be sure in every instance whether the translator, the *Vorlage* used, or a later redactor is responsible for these theological characteristics, it has to be stated that they are in the Greek text and therefore belong to the history of reception of the LXX.

3. How Can a Theology of the Septuagint Be Written?

Finally, I would like to briefly sketch some elements of such a theology of the Septuagint. As stated earlier, such a work should be more than a collection of excerpts of separate studies on some or all of the books of the Greek Scriptures. But an important basic part of such a study has to be an overview of the individual books, so that readers can get an impression of the different approaches to the task of translation stemming from different times and milieus. This part could also serve as a kind of *Religionsgeschichte* of the LXX connecting the individual books with what is known about the theological and hermeneutical developments of the specific time and place, when and where the translation took place.

As a second step I would determine several themes and topics that can be traced through the canon, such as "designations and imagery of God," "God and foreign gods," "Israel and the nations," "humanity and its fate," "νόμος and ethics." Here I would not only present the "highlights," as I did in the second section of this paper, but I would also show where the Hebrew text was translated without obvious changes. This serves to meet the criterion of the twofold comparative approach mentioned earlier. Moreover, it is a significant fact of Septuagint theology, because even if it is basically the same concept as in the Hebrew Bible, it sounds different in Greek and it can cause different reactions when read by those who are not

---

45. Rösel 1994, 147–50; for the comparison with the Platonic *Timaeus* §§72–87.

familiar with the Hebrew tradition. This would also be the place to deal with semantic and linguistic definitions of several keywords such as ψυχή, νόμος, δικαιοσύνη and ἀδικία, σύνεσις, and their cognates.

Third, I would also try to comment on the implicit theology of later revisions.[46] For example, if we have New Testament quotations from *kaige-*Theodotion (e.g., from Daniel) it would be necessary to determine whether or not there are specific differences between the OG and later revisions. Discerning those differences could also give us clues to where readers may have had the impression that the older translation was not a valid reproduction of the biblical text—which eventually led to further revisions.

Needless to say, in the end there should be a summary, which could open the view to the history of reception of the LXX by asking how later readers such as Jewish or Christian writers perceived the profile or theology of the Greek Scriptures. Thus the perspectives of "*amont*/upstream," meaning a focus on the ideas of the translators, and "*aval*/downstream," meaning a focus on readers of the translations and the reception history of the translations, would finally come together.[47]

I am fully aware that these considerations are very preliminary and that a project like this cannot be accomplished quickly—perhaps not even by a single scholar. But I am confident that in the near future our knowledge about the LXX will be dramatically expanded because of the three important projects in North America, in France, and in Germany. Maybe after their completion then the time will be ripe for a theology of the Septuagint.

Bibliography

Aejmelaeus, Anneli, and Udo Quast, eds. 2000. *Der Septuaginta-Psalter und seine Tochterübersetzungen*. MSU 24. Göttingen: Vandenhoeck & Ruprecht.

---

46. See, e.g., Bergmann 2006; Ego 2006; and Kreuzer 2006, on the theological relevance of revisions; all these papers were read during the same conference in Bangor, Maine.

47. For a discussion of these perspectives see Utzschneider 2001, 2006. See also Kraus 2006. After having submitted the original version of this paper to the editors, the following articles dealing with the question of a theology of the Septuagint came to my attention: Dafni 2002; Cimosa 2000. Although there are some minor differences concerning assumptions and results, which cannot be discussed here, it is interesting to realize that the topic is obviously *en vogue*.

Albani, Matthias. 2000. *Der eine Gott und die himmlischen Heerscharen: Zur Begründung des Monotheismus bei Deuterojesaja im Horizont der Astralisierung des Gottesverständnisses im Alten Orient.* ABG 1. Leipzig: Evangelische Verlagsanstalt.

Barr, James. 1999. *The Concept of Biblical Theology: An Old Testament Perspective.* London: SCM.

———. 2002. Review of *Invitation to the Septuagint*, by Karen H. Jobes and Moises Silva. *RBL*. Online: https://www.bookreviews.org/bookdetail.asp?TitleId=1341.

Bergmann, Claudia. 2006. "Idol Worship in Bel and the Dragon and Other Jewish Literature from the Second Temple Period." Pages 207–23 in *Septuagint Research: Issues and Challenges in the Study of the Greek Jewish Scriptures.* Edited by Wolfgang Kraus and R. Glenn Wooden. SCS 53. Atlanta: Society of Biblical Literature.

Bertram, Georg. 1957. "Praeparatio evangelica in der Septuaginta." *VT* 7:225–49.

———. 1959. "Zur Prägung der biblischen Gottesvorstellung in der griechischen Übersetzung des Alten Testaments: Die Wiedergabe von *schadad* und *schaddaj* im Griechischen." *WO* 2:502–13.

———. 1961. "Septuaginta-Frömmigkeit." *RGG*[4] 5:1707–9.

———. 1972. "Zur begrifflichen Prägung des Schöpferglaubens im Griechischen Alten Testament." Pages 21–30 in *Wort, Lied und Gottesspruch: Beiträge zur Septuaginta; Festschrift für Joseph Ziegler.* Edited by Josef Schreiner. FB 1. Würzburg: Echter.

———. 1979a. "παιδεύω." *TDNT* 5:596–625.

———. 1979b. "στενός κτλ." *TDNT* 7:604–8.

———. 1979c. "στερεός." *TDNT* 7:609–14

———. 1979d. "ὕβρις." *TDNT* 8:295–307.

Bons, Eberhard. 1997. Review of *Eschatology in the Greek Psalter*, by Joachim Schaper. *RevSR* 71:257–58.

Bousset, Wilhelm, and Hugo Gressmann. 1966. *Die Religion des Judentums im späthellenistischen Zeitalter.* 4th ed. HNT 21. Tübingen: Mohr Siebeck.

Childs, Brevard S. 1993. *Biblical Theology of the Old and New Testaments: Theological Reflection on the Christian Bible.* Minneapolis: Fortress.

Cimosa Mario. 2000. "É possibile scrivere una 'teologia' della Bibbia Greca (LXX)?" Pages 51–64 in *Initium Sapientiae: Scritti in onore di Franco Festorazzi nel suo 70. compleanno.* Edited by Rinaldo Fabris. Supplementi alla Rivista biblica 36. Bologna: EDB.

Cook, Johann. 1997. *The Septuagint of Proverbs: Jewish and/or Hellenistic Proverbs? Concerning the Hellenistic Colouring of LXX Proverbs.* VTSup 69. Leiden: Brill.

———. 2001. "The Ideology of Septuagint Proverbs." Pages 463–79 in *X Congress of the International Organization for Septuagint and Cognate Studies: Oslo, 1998.* Edited by Bernard A. Taylor. SCS 51. Atlanta: Society of Biblical Literature.

Craigie. Peter C. 1983. *Psalms 1–50.* WBC 19. Waco, TX: Word.

Dahl, Nils A., and Alan F. Segal. 1978. "Philo and the Rabbis on the Name of God." *JSJ* 9:1–28.

Dafni, Evangelia G. 2002. "Theologie der Sprache der Septuaginta." *TZ* 58:315–28.

Daniel, Suzanne. 1966. *Recherches sur le Vocabulaire du Culte dans la Septante.* EeC 61. Paris: Klincksieck.

Deissmann, Gustav A. 1903. "Die Hellenisierung des semitischen Monotheismus." *NJahrb*:162–77.

D'Hamonville, David-Marc. 2000. *Les Proverbes.* BdA 17. Paris: Cerf.

Dogniez, Cécile. 1997. "Le Dieu des armées dans le Dodekapropheton: Quelques remarques sur une initiative de traduction." Pages 19–36 in *IX Congress of the International Organization for Septuagint and Cognate Studies.* Edited by Bernard A. Taylor. SCS 45. Atlanta: Scholars Press.

Ego, Beate. 2006. "Textual Variants as a Result of Enculturation: The Banishment of the Demon in Tobit." Pages 371–78 in *Septuagint Research: Issues and Challenges in the Study of the Greek Jewish Scriptures.* Edited by Wolfgang Kraus and R. Glenn Wooden. SCS 53. Atlanta: Society of Biblical Literature.

Fabry, Heinz-Josef. 2006. "Messianism in the Septuagint." Pages 193–205 in *Septuagint Research: Issues and Challenges in the Study of the Greek Jewish Scriptures.* Edited by Wolfgang Kraus and R. Glenn Wooden. SCS 53. Atlanta: Society of Biblical Literature.

Fernández Marcos, Natalio. 1994. "The Septuagint Reading of the Book of Job." Pages 251–66 in *The Book of Job.* Edited by Willem A. M. Beuken. BETL 114. Louvain: Peeters.

———. 2000. *The Septuagint in Context: Introduction to the Greek Version of the Bible.* Leiden: Brill.

Frankel, Zacharias. 1841. *Vorstudien zu der Septuaginta.* Leipzig: Vogel.

———. 1851. *Ueber den Einfluss der palästinischen Exegese auf die alexandrinische Hermeneutik.* Leipzig: Barth.

Fritsch, Charles T. 1943. *The Anti-anthropomorphisms of the Greek Pentateuch*. POT 10. Princeton: Princeton University Press.

García Martínez, Florentino, and Eibert J. C. Tigchelaar, eds. 1997–1998. *The Dead Sea Scrolls: Study Edition*. Leiden: Brill.

Gard, Donald H. 1954. "The Concept of the Future Life according to the Greek Translator of the Book of Job." *JBL* 73:137–43.

Gross, Walter. 2000. "Gen 1:26, 27; 9:6—Statue oder Ebenbild Gottes? Aufgabe und Würde des Menschen nach dem hebräischen und dem griechischen Wortlaut." *JBTh* 15:11–38.

Gzella, Holger. 2001, "Das Kalb und das Einhorn, Endzeittheophanie und Messianismus in der Septuaginta-Fassung von Ps 29(28)." Pages 257–90 in *Der Septuaginta-Psalter: Sprachliche und theologische Aspekte*. Edited by Erich Zenger. HBS 32. Freiburg im Breisgau: Herder.

———. 2002. *Lebenszeit und Ewigkeit: Studien zur Eschatologie und Anthropologie des Septuaginta-Psalters*. BBB 134. Berlin: Philo.

Hanhart, Robert. 1999a. "Paul Anton de Lagarde und seine Kritik an der Theologie." Pages 248–80 in *Studien zur Septuaginta und zum hellenistischen Judentum*. Edited by Robert Hanhart and Reinhard G. Kratz. FAT 24. Tübingen: Mohr Siebeck.

———. 1999b. "Die Bedeutung der Septuaginta für die Definition des 'hellenistischen Judentums.'" Pages 67–97 in *Studien zur Septuaginta und zum hellenistischen Judentum*. Edited by Robert Hanhart and Reinhard G. Kratz. FAT 24. Tübingen: Mohr Siebeck.

Hanson, Anthony T. 1992. "The Treatment in the LXX of the Theme of Seeing God." Pages 557–68 in *Septuagint, Scrolls, and Cognate Writings: Papers Presented to the International Symposium on the Septuagint and its Relations to the Dead Sea Scrolls and Other Writings (Manchester, 1990)*. Edited by George J. Brooke and Barnabas Lindars. SCS 33. Atlanta: Scholars Press.

Harl, Marguerite, Gilles Dorival, and Olivier Munnich. 1994. *La Bible Grecque des Septante: Du Judaisme Hellénistique au Christianisme Ancien*. 2nd ed. Initiations au Christianisme Ancien. Paris: Cerf.

Hengel, Martin. 1973. *Judentum und Hellenismus: Studien zu ihrer Begegnung unter besonderer Berücksichtigung Palästinas bis zur Mitte des 2. Jh. v. Chr.* 2nd ed. WUNT 10. Tübingen: Mohr Siebeck.

———. 2002. *The Septuagint as Christian Scripture: Its Prehistory and the Problem of Its Canon*. OTS. Edinburgh: T&T Clark.

Hengel, Martin, and Anna Maria Schwemer, eds. 1994. *Die Septuaginta zwischen Judentum und Christentum.* WUNT 72. Tübingen: Mohr Siebeck.

Hiebert, Robert J.V., Claude E. Cox, and Peter J. Gentry, eds. 2001. *The Old Greek Psalter: Studies in Honour of Albert Pietersma.* JSOTSup 332. Sheffield: Sheffield Academic.

Horst, Pieter van der. 1997. Review of *Eschatology in the Greek Psalter,* by Joachim Schaper. *JSJ* 28:123–24.

Jobes Karen H., and Moisés Silva. 2000. *Invitation to the Septuagint.* Grand Rapids: Baker Academic.

Joosten, Jan. 2000. "Une théologie de la Septante? Réflexions méthodologique sur l'interpretation de la version greque." *RTP* 132:31–46.

Kleer, Martin. 1996. *'Der liebliche Sänger der Psalmen Israels': Untersuchungen zu David als Dichter und Beter der Psalmen.* BBB 108. Bodenheim: Philo.

Kooij, Arie van der. 1981. *Die alten Textzeugen des Jesajabuches: Ein Beitrag zur Textgeschichte des Alten Testaments.* OBO 35. Göttingen: Vandenhoeck & Ruprecht; Fribourg: Presses Universitaires.

———. 1998. *The Oracle of Tyre: The Septuagint of Isaiah XXIII as Version and Vision.* VTSup 71. Leiden: Brill.

Kraus, Wolfgang. 2006. "Contemporary Translations of the Septuagint: Problems and Perspectives." Pages 63–83 in *Septuagint Research: Issues and Challenges in the Study of the Greek Jewish Scriptures.* Edited by Wolfgang Kraus and R. Glenn Wooden. SCS 53. Atlanta: Society of Biblical Literature.

Kreuzer, Siegfried. 2006. "From 'Old Greek' to the Recensions: Who and What Caused the Change of the Hebrew Reference Text of the Septuagint?" Pages 225–37 in *Septuagint Research: Issues and Challenges in the Study of the Greek Jewish Scriptures.* Edited by Wolfgang Kraus and R. Glenn Wooden. SCS 53. Atlanta: Society of Biblical Literature.

Müller, Mogens. 1996. *The First Bible of the Church: A Plea for the Septuagint.* JSOTSup 206. Copenhagen International Seminar 1. Sheffield: Sheffield Academic.

Olofsson, Staffan. 1990. *God Is My Rock: A Study of Translation Technique and Theological Exegesis in the Septuagint.* ConBOT 31. Stockholm: Almqvist & Wiksell.

Peters, Melvin K. 1997. Review of *Eschatology in the Greek Psalter,* by Joachim Schaper. *JBL* 116:350–52. Online: https://www.bookreviews.org/bookdetail.asp?TitleId=2707.

Pietersma, Albert. 1997. Review of *Eschatology in the Greek Psalter*, by Joachim Schaper. *BO* 54:185–90.

———. 2006. "Exegesis in the Septuagint: Possibilities and Limits (The Psalter as a Case in Point)." Pages 33–45 in *Septuagint Research: Issues and Challenges in the Study of the Greek Jewish Scriptures*. Edited by Wolfgang Kraus and R. G. Wooden. SCS 53. Atlanta: Society of Biblical Literature.

Reiss, Wolfgang. 1975. "Zur Deutung von אֵל שַׁדַּי in der rabbinischen Literatur." *Frankfurter Judaistische Beiträge* 3:65–75.

Rösel, Martin. 1991. "Die Übersetzung der Gottesbezeichnungen in der Genesis-Septuaginta." Pages 357–77 in *Ernten, was man sät: Festschrift für Klaus Koch zu seinem 65. Geburtstag*. Edited by Dwight R. Daniels, Uwe Gleßmer, and Martin Rösel. Neukirchen-Vluyn: Neukirchener,

———. 1994. *Übersetzung als Vollendung der Auslegung: Studien zur Genesis-Septuaginta*. BZAW 223. Berlin: de Gruyter.

———. 1995. "Die Interpretation von Genesis 49 in der Septuaginta." *BN* 79:54–70.

———. 1998, "Theo-logie der griechischen Bibel: Zur Wiedergabe der Gottesaussagen im LXX-Pentateuch." *VT* 48:49–62.

———. 2000. *Adonaj, warum Gott "Herr" genannt wird*. FAT 29. Tübingen: Mohr Siebeck.

———. 2001. "Die Psalmüberschriften des Septuagintapsalters." Pages 125–48 in *Der Septuaginta-Psalter: Sprachliche und theologische Aspekte*. Edited by Erich Zenger. HBS 32. Freiburg im Breisgau: Herder. [ch. 10 in this volume.]

———. 2006. "Jakob, Bileam und der Messias." Pages 151–75 in *The Septuagint and Messianism*. Edited by Michael A. Knibb. BETL 195. Leuven: Peeters.

———. 2007. "The Reading and Translation of the Divine Name in the Masoretic Tradition and the Greek Pentateuch." *JSOT* 31:411–28. [ch. 13 in this volume.]

Schaper, Joachim. 1995. *Eschatology in the Greek Psalter*. WUNT 2/76. Tübingen: Mohr Siebeck.

———. 2001. "Die Renaissance der Mythologie im hellenistischen Judentum und der Septuaginta-Psalter." Pages 171–83 in *Der Septuaginta-Psalter: Sprachliche und theologische Aspekte*. Edited by Erich Zenger. HBS 32. Freiburg im Breisgau: Herder.

Schenker, Adrian. 2001. "Götter und Engel im Septuaginta-Psalter: Text- und religionsgeschichtliche Ergebnisse aus drei textkritischen Untersuchungen." Pages 185–95 in *Der Septuaginta-Psalter: Sprachliche und theologische Aspekte*. Edited by Erich Zenger. HBS 32. Freiburg im Breisgau: Herder.

Schürer, Emil. 1986. *The History of the Jewish People in the Age of Jesus Christ (175 B.C.–A.D. 135)*. Revised and edited by Géza Vermès, Fergus Millar, and Matthew Black. 3 vols. Edinburgh: T&T Clark.

Seeligmann, Isaac Leo. 1948. *The Septuagint Version of Isaiah: A Discussion of Its Problems*. MEOL 9. Leiden: Brill.

———. 1990. "Problems and Perspectives in Modern Septuagint Research." *Text* 15:169–232.

Seiler, Stefan. 2001. "Theologische Konzepte in der Septuaginta: Das theologische Profil von 1 Chr 16,8ff. LXX im Vergleich mit Ps 104; 95; 105 LXX." Pages 197–225 in *Der Septuaginta-Psalter: Sprachliche und theologische Aspekte*. Edited by Erich Zenger. HBS 32. Freiburg im Breisgau: Herder.

Siegert, Folker. 1997. Review of *Eschatology in the Greek Psalter*, by Joachim Schaper. *TLZ* 122:39–41.

———. 2001. *Zwischen Hebräischer Bibel und Altem Testament: Eine Einführung in die Septuaginta*. MJS 9. Munich: LIT.

Soffer, Arthur. 1957. "The Treatment of Anthropomorphisms and Anthropopathisms in the Septuagint of Psalms." *HUCA* 28:85–107.

Utzschneider, Helmut. 2001. "Auf Augenhöhe mit dem Text: Überlegungen zum wissenschaftlichen Standort einer Übersetzung der Septuaginta ins Deutsche." Pages 14–27 in *Im Brennpunkt: Die Septuaginta; Studien zur Entstehung und Bedeutung der Griechischen Bibel*. Edited by Heinz-Josef Fabry und Ulrich Offerhaus. BWANT 153. Stuttgart: Kohlhammer.

———. 2006. "Flourishing Bones: The Minor Prophets in the New Testament." Pages 273–92 in *Septuagint Research: Issues and Challenges in the Study of the Greek Jewish Scriptures*. Edited by Wolfgang Kraus and R. Glenn Wooden. SCS 53. Atlanta: Society of Biblical Literature.

VanderKam, James C. 1994. *The Dead Sea Scrolls Today*. Grand Rapids: Eerdmans.

VanderKam, James C., and Lawrence H. Schiffman, eds. 2000. *Encyclopedia of the Dead Sea Scrolls*. 2 vols. Oxford: Oxford University Press.

Walter, Nikolaus. 2001. "Die griechische Übersetzung der 'Schriften' Israels und die christliche 'Septuaginta' als Forschungs- und Übersetzungsgegenstand." Pages 71–96 in *Im Brennpunkt: Die Septuaginta; Studien zur Entstehung und Bedeutung der Griechischen Bibel*. Edited by Heinz-Josef Fabry und Ulrich Offerhaus. BWANT 153. Stuttgart: Kohlhammer.

Wevers, John W. 1990. *Notes on the Greek Text of Exodus*. SCS 30. Atlanta: Scholars Press.

———. 1993. *Notes on the Greek Text of Genesis*. SCS 35. Atlanta: Scholars Press.

———. 1995. *Notes on the Greek Text of Deuteronomy*. SCS 39. Atlanta: Scholars Press.

———. 1997. *Notes on the Greek Text of Leviticus*. SCS 44. Atlanta: Scholars Press.

———. 1998. *Notes on the Greek Text of Numbers*. SCS 46. Atlanta: Society of Biblical Literature.

Zenger, Erich, ed. 2001. *Der Septuaginta-Psalter: Sprachliche und theologische Aspekte*. HBS 32. Freiburg im Breisgau: Herder.

12
A Theology of the Septuagint?
Clarifications and Definitions

The importance of the Septuagint as witness to the theological developments taking place within Hellenistic Judaism has been recognized since the inception of the discipline. In the early days of modern Septuagint research, scholars such as Zacharias Frankel and Abraham Geiger were already identifying important differences between the Greek and the Hebrew Bible.[1] In 1903, Adolf Deissmann spoke of the "Hellenization of Semitic monotheism."[2] A few decades later, Georg Bertram described the Septuagint as *praeparatio evangelica*, coining the term "Septuagint piety" (in German: LXX-*Frömmigkeit*).[3] It was only a few years later that Joseph Ziegler summarized the "legacy and task" (in German: *Erbe und Auftrag*) of LXX research as "the rewarding and fruitful work of carrying out the preparatory research necessary so that the long awaited theology of the LXX can finally be written."[4] One of the most important preparatory works of this kind was Isaak Leo Seeligmann's "Septuagint Version of Isaiah," in which one can find a long and instructive chapter presenting LXX Isaiah as a "document of Jewish Alexandrian theology."[5]

I would like to thank Jean Maurais, Montreal, for his valuable comments on an earlier version of this paper and for improving my English. Two articles, published recently in commentary on a German version of this article (Cook 2017, 12–15; and Ausloos 2017), will be discussed in another paper.

1. Frankel 1851; Geiger 1928; see also Kaminka 1928.
2. Deissmann 1903.
3. Bertram 1957.
4. Author's translation. See Ziegler 1962, 28.
5. Seeligmann 1948, 95–121. See the development of Seeligmann's observations by Schaper 2010.

Scholarship of previous generations remains a treasure trove of instructive examples of theological exposition. In most cases their work has been concerned with theological statements in the narrow sense, such as the use of *pantokrator* or *hikanos* to designate God.⁶ These examples usually emerge from less literal translations such as Proverbs, Isaiah, or Job. Unfortunately, such statements are then presented side by side as if the LXX formed a unified corpus. Moreover, another tendency can be observed: namely, that such findings often reflect the theological interest of the scholars themselves. Not unlike Deissmann, Ziegler saw the Greek Bible as superior to its Hebrew counterpart. For example, he wrote about the "obscure Hebrew words" ("*dunklen hebräischen Wörter*") against which the Greek equivalents "shine like precious stones" ("*wie Edelsteine leuchten*")⁷. Georg Bertram went even further, uncovering in the Septuagint aspects of Judaism that he did not hesitate to criticize. One such example is found in the article on ἔργον in the *Theological Dictionary of the New Testament* and its merging of word and concept, paving the way for a startling conclusion: The use of ἔργον in the Greek Bible is said to make perfectly plain "that the Hellenistic Jew had a complete aversion for work, which he could not but regard as an imposition, a curse, a matter for slaves."⁸ What a statement to make in 1935 Germany! In light of this, one can easily understand why the project of translating the LXX into German met serious criticism by scholars such as Rolf Rendtorff.⁹

The problems associated with the writing of a "theology of the Septuagint" have been the topic of much discussion in recent research. Already in 1985 Emanuel Tov was collecting evidence of theologically motivated exegesis in the Greek text, although he came to the conclusion that there are less elements of exegesis in the LXX than often assumed.¹⁰ In the last fifteen years, Mario Cimosa, Jan Joosten, and I have all enquired about

---

6. For *pantokrator*, see Ziegler 1962, 27; for *hikanos*, see Bertram 1958, 1978.

7. Ziegler 1962, 28.

8. The original German sentence in Bertram 1935, 641 was: "*die unmittelbar ablehnende Haltung des hellenistischen Juden gegenüber der Arbeit.*" See the reference to this article by Tov 1999, 269.

9. This discussion took place during a meeting of biblical scholars in Frankfurt/Main (Jan 22, 2000). But see already Schoeps 1959, 16–21 on the "piety of the Septuagint" and 224–30, with a negative assessment of the LXX because of its responsibility for Paul's misunderstanding of the Torah (mentioned by Mogens Müller, Copenhagen).

10. Tov 1987, 265.

the possibility of producing a theology of the LXX, answering in the affirmative.[11] This has provoked several reactions, including that of Johann Cook, who applied the "maximalist" label to my approach because of my confidence that it is possible to describe aspects of a theology of the LXX.[12] The opposite end of the spectrum is represented by the more skeptical approach of the "minimalists," which is for the most part associated with the American NETS team and Albert Pietersma. Pietersma has himself declared a "crisis in the discipline" since he considers the methodological discrepancies between our approaches as unbridgeable.[13]

In what follows I would like to respond to some of the issues that have been raised and further clarify my proposal for writing a theology of the LXX.[14] I will start by briefly reviewing my earlier argument and then address the following key questions:

- What does "theology" of the LXX mean?
- How does one identify the theology of the LXX?
- What is the meaning of "Septuagint" in this context?
- Is there only *one* theology of the LXX?

1. "Toward a Theology of the Septuagint" (2002)

Briefly stated, the starting point of the argumentation presented in my 2002 essay was that it is methodologically speaking no longer possible to present data from different parts of the LXX side by side, as if the Greek Bible formed a unit.[15] Rather, modern LXX research has emphasized the necessity to treat each book separately, so that it is only possible to describe the theological profile of individual books, for example, the characteristics of LXX Exodus in comparison to those of LXX Numbers. Only then is it possible, as a subsequent step, to summarize features common to the Greek Pentateuch and compare them to those of the Greek versions of Proverbs or Isaiah. Given the state of research, I still hold to the position that the task of writing a theology of the LXX requires a twofold approach:

---

11. Cimosa 2000; Joosten 2000; Rösel 2006 [ch. 11 in this volume].
12. Cook 2010a; 2010b, 590.
13. Pietersma 2006, 51.
14. See Cook 2010a, 637, for whom my considerations are "helpful ... but somewhat premature."
15. See the argumentation in Rösel 2006. For the sake of brevity the references given in that article will not be repeated here.

The comparison of the Hebrew and Greek texts as a first step, and the comparison of the Greek translations with each other as a second.[16] Such an approach also implies that a theology of the LXX must be conceived as incorporating an important diachronic component. This much becomes obvious when one examines how the hermeneutical situation developed within Hellenistic Judaism between the third and first centuries BCE. Several important events occurred in this period that had a significant impact on biblical hermeneutics. We need only mention the reign of the Seleucids, the Maccabean crisis, or the process that lead to the standardization of the Hebrew text.

This twofold comparative approach enables us to identify the features unique to individual translations as well as those that are common to a group of texts. Summarizing the theological tendencies present in several books implies working somewhat against the current trend to focus on individual books for the sake of methodological soundness.[17] But alongside the characteristics unique to each translation, there are in fact important connections between books, such as the common cultic vocabulary or the similar use of terms like *diatheke*. Although it is not possible in most cases to identify a precise geographical location or date for the translation of each book, one can assume that several translations stem from a common milieu, and that this milieu did influence how the translation work was done.[18] This much would justify, at least as far as the Alexandrian setting is concerned, the claim that the identification of theological interpretation in LXX texts calls for a summary of tendencies across several books. This is also important since readers in antiquity have approached at least some segments of the biblical text as a unit, for example, the Pentateuch or the historical books.[19]

A third step would be to bring the insights gained from this twofold comparison into a more systematic ordering. Under this heading, one

---

16. Similarly Joosten 2000, 33.
17. Cook 2000a, 636: "I think that the individual book should act as a guideline as to how 'LXX theologies' should be formulated." Therefore several scholars concentrate their work on some books only, e.g., L. Perkins on the LXX of Exodus; J. Cook himself mostly on Proverbs or E. Glenny on the Dodekapropheton.
18. See Aejmelaeus 2013, or Joosten 2012a and 2012c.
19. This can only be inferred; because the texts were written on scrolls, in most cases only individual books were preserved. For an overview see Kraft 2003, 2014. Nevertheless, in Qumran some texts were found which attest to larger units, such as 4Q1 (4QGen-Exod^a); 4Q11 (4QpaleoGen-Exod^l); 4Q17 (4QExod-Lev^f).

could find a summary of evidence concerning the image of God, the distancing from foreign cults, the issue of messianism, anthropological and other topics. Since an *overall* picture of the Greek Bible is needed, it would be important to identify how various topics and concepts might be different or similar to those of the Hebrew Bible. Another aspect requiring attention at this point is the analysis of the semantic change introduced through the use of several important Greek terms. Words such as ψυχή, διαθήκη, or δικαιοσύνη may have been understood in accordance with the meaning of their Hebrew counterpart at the time of the translation's production.[20] But later, the Hebrew background was lost and their common Hellenistic meaning became predominant.[21] Thus a diachronic approach is also needed in order to properly analyze the semantic content of specific terms found in the Greek translations.

Finally, it seems appropriate to include the analysis of later revisions. This is especially important in cases such as the books of Daniel and Esther.[22] The differences between the initial translation and its revision(s) can potentially indicate why new translations were produced and which topics were theologically significant to the revisers. Moreover, this final step is also important when we consider the issue of the New Testament authors' use of the Greek Bible. As it is well known, the citations of the Hebrew Bible found in the New Testament often deviate from the oldest stratum of the text of the LXX and may reflect the use of a revision.[23] Identifying the differences between the oldest layer of the Greek text and the revisions employed by New Testament authors, when such revision can be identified, can also shed light on issues that were theologically significant to the revisers.

Building on these former observations, I would now like to elaborate further.

---

20. On the problem of the idea of the soul see Rösel 2009.

21. For this problem see Lee 2010. As an example of the complexity of semantic determinations, see Joosten 2012b and his conclusion that ἔλεος has obviously kept its Hellenistic coinage.

22. A very interesting example is the differences in statements about God between the Old Greek of Daniel and the version of Theodotion, see Rösel 2014. For the problem of the alpha text of Esther, see De Troyer and Doyle 2000. See also the observations by Dines 2013, 72, on revisions of the book of Judges and their differences in content.

23. On this problem see Steyn 2008, or the overview by Law, 2013, 85–98: "The Septuagint behind the New Testament."

2. What Does "Theology" of the Septuagint Mean?

In the current debate, a number of terms are used synonymously to describe the same phenomena. Emanuel Tov is rather hesitant to speak of theologically motivated exegesis. Johann Cook uses terms like ideology, exegesis, and *religionsgeschichtliche* activity.[24] Anneli Aejmelaeus and Evangelia Dafni prefer to speak of the theology *of the language* of the LXX.[25] Since it is not always clear how we are to differentiate between these terms, I will attempt to define how I understand the term "theology" when speaking of a theology of the Septuagint:

Usually the term "theology" is understood in the context of Christian systematic or dogmatic theology.[26] But as we study the Greek Bible, it is obvious that we cannot expect a fully formulated system of beliefs. Nor can we expect to find even a shorter theological treatise, with the possible exception of parts of Wisdom of Solomon. Thus, those investigating the LXX for its theology face the same issues encountered when theorizing on a theology of the Old Testament/Hebrew Bible or even the possibility of "biblical theology."[27] Where can one find sufficient data to fill out the categories implied in such a broad understanding of theology? Those holding to a minimalistic position are correct when they point out the fact that a number of decisions made throughout the translation process are not necessarily theologically motivated. Nevertheless, some parts of the Greek Bible do contain theologically motivated translations, a type of theology that could be understood under the label "implicit theology."[28] Texts of this nature can be found throughout most books of the LXX, albeit in varying number and importance.

Gerhard Ebeling dealt with this issue in his 1955 reflections on biblical theology. He suggested as definition that (inner?) biblical theology is that which "emerges out of the encounter of the biblical testimony to revelation and Greek thought," the product therefore of debate and critical reflec-

---

24. Cook 2010a, 622; 2010b, 590.
25. Aejmelaeus 2006; Dafni 2002.
26. For the use of the term "theology" in antiquity, Kattenbusch 1930 is still very useful.
27. On this problem, see Ebeling 1967; Schmid 2013, 9–13.
28. Schmid 2013, 54–58. Already in my article from 2006 I have used the term "implicit theology" (245 n. 20), although in a slightly different sense to refer to the connections between the translator and his community.

tion.²⁹ The proclamation of the Old Testament prophets would not be considered theology under this definition, despite the many scholarly efforts to marshal it on behalf of the project of a theology of the Old Testament.

Konrad Schmid has recently discussed this problem in the context of a theology of the Hebrew Bible. Pointing to the redactional activity that can be observed in individual books, he argued that the text that was handed down to the scribes required interpretation and explanation and thus motivated additions and expansions. Therefore, Schmid understands the corpus of the Hebrew Bible as a "reflective interpretation of preexisting religious texts."³⁰ A similar definition is also set forth by Folker Siegert: "Theology is the intellectual endeavor toward the word of God."³¹

Understanding the theology of the LXX as a *genitivus subjectivus* would imply that the focus of investigation is the implicit theology that emerges from the intentional decisions of the translators. As the locus of theological inquiry, it is to be distinguished from an understanding of theology as a *genitivus objectivus*, that is, the theological systematization resulting from the translated texts. It can be found, inter alia, in the Jewish Hellenistic writings from Alexandria. As such, this understanding also aligns with the distinction between production and reception recently brought to the forefront by Albert Pietersma.³² It is interesting to note, however, that some books of what we now know as the LXX do exhibit elements of theology in the *genitivus objectivus* sense, as theology that emerges from the text. This can be seen in the Wisdom of Solomon, where theology takes the form of doctrinal exposition or apology. In the book of Judith, theology is presented in a narrative form. The concept of the "Lord who shatters wars" (κύριος συντρίβων πολέμους) found in Exod 15:3 becomes the basic premise of the story, which is developed through a narrative account.³³

According to Schmid, an important feature of implicit theology is its character as intellectual reflection. Going one step further, I would like to

---

29. Ebeling 1967, 86.
30. Schmid 2013, 54. See the similar definition by Barr 1999, 249: "Theology is a reflective activity in which the content of religious expressions is to some extent abstracted, contemplated, subjected to reflection and discussion, and deliberately reformulated." This definition was also accepted by McLay 2010, 610.
31. German: "*Theologie ist denkerisches Bemühen um Gottes Wort*," Siegert 1998, 11.
32. Pietersma 2008, 487–89.
33. Schmitz 2014. That also applies if Exod 15:3 LXX means that the Lord will prevail violently in the wars, as Perkins 2007 sees it.

introduce another element which stems from more traditional scholastic theology: namely, the systematization of terms and ideas.³⁴ Perhaps this can be best demonstrated when we consider the terminology of the altar. It is well known that in the Hebrew Bible the word מזבח could be used to designate legitimate Israelite altars as well as pagan ones. The translators of the LXX introduced a distinction through the use of two lexemes, θυσιαστήριον and βωμός. By identifying altars with one term or the other, they were able to signal whether or not an altar or offering was legitimate (e.g., in the Balaam story). They even went a step further and introduced the neologism ἱλαστήριον in order to translate כפרת. Linguistically, this new word corresponds to θυσιαστήριον, the place of offering and atonement. Phenomena such as these can be categorized as a form of systematization. Ongoing reflection on the Hebrew text and its meaning lead to more systematic categorization through the use of distinct and at times more uniform vocabulary. One could add under this category the frequent harmonizations found in the Greek translation, since they aim to achieve a level of textual consistency that goes far beyond that of the Hebrew text.³⁵

3. How Does One Identify the Theology of the Septuagint?

Even those holding to a minimalist approach would not deny the presence of the phenomena that I have labeled as "implicit theology" in the translation.³⁶ The disagreement concerns instead the frequency with which one can expect to find such theology. Moreover, another area of disagreement is the choice to limit the theological investigation to specific decisions made by the translators in the course of their work, and whether the development of terminological equivalents within the Jewish-Hellenistic communities should also be included. Examples of the latter include the

---

34. This does not only apply to translations but also to the Hebrew Bible. See Barr 1999, 249, and more recently Jeremias 2015, vi: "*Es gibt im späten Alten Testament selber eine Tendenz zur Systematik*" ("In the later parts of the Old Testament there is a tendency toward systematization").

35. For an instructive example see Perkins 2013, 26–29 on Exod 4, where the translation is obviously influenced by Gen 17.

36. Aejmelaeus 2006, 35, points to Exod 29:45; Tov 1987, 257–58 believes it most likely that Num 24:7, 17 was understood as a reference to the messiah by the translator; and for Pietersma 2008, 492, the translation of אלהים by ἀγγέλους in Ps 8:6 is "likely exegetical."

common translation of Sheol to "Hades," or *calque*-translations like תורה-νόμος or ברית-διαθήκη.

Another important debated aspect is the problem of the variants found in the *Vorlage*. In many cases, the peculiar readings found in the LXX can be the result of a Hebrew text that is different from the one printed in our modern editions. Thus Alex Douglas, who has recently written "Limitations to Writing a Theology of the Septuagint," considers it important to exclude differences that can be traced back to a different *Vorlage*.[37] He proceeds to demonstrate this point via an analysis of Exod 15:3 (κύριος συντρίβων πολέμους), attempting to reconstruct a different *Vorlage* for the LXX source text. Unfortunately there is not one single textual witness to support this reconstruction. Therefore the more fundamental methodological issue has to do with determining who should bear the burden of proof in such cases. A maximalist approach would posit that the existence of a diverging *Vorlage* has to be proven or must at least be likely.[38] This is especially important since the task of reconstructing Hebrew readings from the Greek text has its own set of methodological problems.[39]

But even if a specific reading is to be traced back to a different Hebrew text and not to an interpretation or expansion of the translator, this does not mean that it is theologically insignificant. The same is also true of the standard equivalents that have been coined within Jewish communities. The custom to denote God as a helper and not as a rock or to call pagan gods not "God" but "idol" (εἴδωλον), is of paramount importance for the understanding of God in the Greek Bible and therefore for its theology in the narrow sense.[40]

This leads me to plead that our inquiry move away from a focus on the translator as a lone creative personality. It seems more appropriate to see the theology of the LXX as the process of reflection and systematization of Jewish Hellenistic communities whose religious beliefs influenced to various degrees the translation of the biblical texts.[41] Whether this creative and reflective interpretation took place at the level of the transmission of the Hebrew text or during the switch to the Greek language is

---

37. Douglas 2012. Similarly Aejmelaeus 1993, 111–12, or Ulrich 1999, 210.
38. Rösel 1998.
39. Tov, 1997, 213–32.
40. See Rösel 2015 on the question of how references to other gods are translated.
41. Also Aejmelaeus 2013 points to the important influence of the communities.

therefore of secondary importance only; it is decisive that it can be found in the Greek Bible.[42]

Two more areas of disagreement will be briefly mentioned. The first objection states that it is nearly impossible to gather theological data seeing that the translators did not usually compose their texts freely. Instead, they felt bound to their *Vorlage*—albeit in different ways—severely limiting the possibilities for theological interpretation. In many cases, only very few deviations were acceptable, for example, when choosing Greek lexical equivalents. But as Ziegert and Aitken have demonstrated from Ruth and Qohelet, even translations that demonstrate close correspondence to their *Vorlage* can contain theologically significant emphases.[43] Therefore it seems appropriate to allow for a kind of cumulative evidence so that every instance should not have to bear the burden of proof. In fact, the most convincing cases of theological interpretation are those that occur in patterns.[44] For example, the differentiating translation of *waw* by *kai* and *de* in the Greek version of the story of Cain and Abel in Gen 4 provides a different structure to the narrative.[45] While a single variation of this type can appear insignificant, the broader picture of the translation of the copulative *waw* in this narrative shows how some aspects of the text were transformed.

The second objection concerns the decision to find evidence for theological emphases specific to the LXX in the differences between the Hebrew and the Greek texts. This evidence can be additions or omissions, but also cases of unusual translation where the stock lexical pairings are abandoned.[46] The decision to proceed in this fashion fits to the "twofold comparative approach" that has been sketched earlier. The methodological consensus of scholars on this point is important because it provides a kind of protection against arbitrariness when interpreting the translation. However, this view was challenged by Tim McLay in a recent paper.[47] McLay argues that this methodological approach should be laid aside so

---

42. The same position is held by Perkins 2013, 18.
43. Ziegert 2008; Aitken 2005.
44. See Aejmelaeus 2006, 31–32; Dafni 2002, 325–26.
45. Rösel 1994, 100–114; Jobes and Silva 2000, 206–14.
46. It should be added that in many cases the use of standard equivalents can also have theological significance, as I have demonstrated in my study on the use of *nomos* and cognates [ch. 15 in this volume].
47. McLay 2010.

that even agreements between both texts be taken into consideration. Since the Greek translations have been read without constant reference to their Hebrew source, it would be appropriate that a theology of the LXX be based on the Greek text as a whole. This approach is in keeping with the thesis set forth by Mogens Müller, who argued that as "the first Bible of the Church," the Septuagint should be given central importance in contemporary theological inquiry.[48]

I would not fully subscribe to this point of view because of the more historical approach of my project. Nevertheless, it does provide an important reminder that concentrating solely on the differences between the Greek and Hebrew texts may not suffice to describe the rich theological implications of the LXX. In a reception-oriented perspective such as that of the French Bible d'Alexandrie project, this overall picture becomes more important than in a production-oriented perspective. A theology of the LXX could be written in such a way that this aspect would receive more emphasis, but ultimately, it would be a different project than the one described here.

4. What Is the Meaning of the "Septuagint" in This Context?

Another important objection to the project of writing a theology of the LXX centers on the problem of the boundaries of the canon and the multiplicity of textual traditions.[49] How can a theology of a collection be written when this collection was constantly evolving? Further, how can one consider the LXX a unity when it consists partly of books translated from Hebrew, others originally composed in Greek, and some eventually abridged (2 Maccabees)?

A pragmatic solution would be to accept the contents of one given collection, for example, one codex or one modern edition.[50] But again, as with the issue of identifying the translator's intention, I would opt for

---

48. Müller 1996, 20–24, 102–12.

49. Douglas 2012, 106–11, and from a different perspective, McLay 2010, 614–16.

50. See the approach of the "Septuagint Commentary Series." The commentary on every book is theoretically based on one manuscript, e.g., on Codex Vaticanus for the book of Joshua; see Auld 2005. See Fabry 2012 for the characteristics of the individual manuscripts. One modern edition is the approach of NETS, LXX Deutsch, and La Bible d'Alexandrie. See Karrer and Kraus 2008 for basic considerations about content and the textual basis of the German translation.

a more open concept. The "Septuagint" or Greek Bible that is the subject of investigation would be that specific text that was regarded as authoritative in a particular community at a certain time. One outcome of this approach is that the LXX of the third century BCE differs from that of the second or first. This corresponds to the twofold comparative and diachronic approach described earlier. Another consequence of this approach is that the revisions could not be excluded, especially if they are the product of the period under investigation. It must be noted that this is somewhat problematic: more research is needed regarding when and where each translation was done.

5. Is There Only One Theology of the Septuagint?

After all that has been said, it may have become obvious that a work entitled "Theology of the Septuagint" can take various forms depending on the perspective that is brought into focus. A Hebrew Bible scholar will be interested in those topics that indicate a modification or prolongation of specific theological trends, such as the strengthening of monotheistic tendencies and the development of angelology or the idea of evil spirits.[51] For scholars working in the field of Hellenistic Judaism, important themes would include the modification of the concept of *nomos*, the view on the temple in Jerusalem, and the life in the diaspora, or the influence of Hellenistic thought on texts like Gen 1–2 and the book of Proverbs.[52] New Testament scholars may find the issue of messianism or the anthropological terminology of the LXX to be of interest. A precise separation of these topics is not always possible. For example, an investigation of the concept of creation in the LXX will prove useful for all of the areas of research that have just been mentioned.[53]

The fundamental issue at stake, however, is that the LXX and the theological developments found within it should be seen as a process that can provide insight into the complex hermeneutics of Hellenistic Judaism. One important consequence of this approach is that Christian biblical theology should no longer be performed without taking the LXX into

---

51. For angelology, see, e.g., Cimosa and Bonney 2010 on the book of Job, and Rösel 2016 on Daniel. For the idea of evil spirits, see Martin 2010.
52. Schmid 2013, 111.
53. Bons 2011.

account.[54] Thus writing a theology of the LXX should also be seen as an important means of communicating the importance of the Greek Bible beyond the narrow field of LXX scholarship. I do have the impression that this would be a goal worthy of all the debates concerning whether or how such a theology should be written.

Bibliography

Aejmelaeus, Anneli. 1993. *On the Trail of the Septuagint Translators*. CBET 50. Kampen: Kok Pharos.

———. 2006. "Von Sprache zur Theologie: Methodologische Überlegungen zur Theologie der Septuaginta." Pages 21–48 in *The Septuagint and Messianism*. Edited by Michael A. Knibb. BETL 195. Leuven: Peeters.

———. 2013. "The Septuagint and Oral Translation." Pages 5–14 in *XIV Congress of the International Organization for Septuagint and Cognate Studies, Helsinki 2010*. Edited by Melvin K. H. Peters. SCS 59. Atlanta: Society of Biblical Literature.

Aitken, James K. 2005. "Rhetoric and Poetry in Greek Ecclesiastes." *BIOSCS* 38:55–77.

Auld, A. Graeme. 2005. *Joshua: Jesus, son of Nauē in Codex Vaticanus*. Septuagint Commentary Series. Leiden: Brill.

Ausloos, Hans. 2017. "Sept défis posés à une théologie de la Septante." Pages 228–50 in *Congress Volume Stellenbosch 2016*. Edited by Louis C. Jonker, Gideon R. Kotzé, and Christl Maier. VTSup 177. Leiden: Brill.

Barr, James. 1999. *The Concept of Biblical Theology*. London: SCM Press.

Bertram, Georg. 1935. "ἔργον κτλ." *ThWNT* 2:631–53.

———. 1957. "Praeparatio Evangelica in der Septuaginta." *VT* 7:225–49.

———. 1958. "ἱκανός in den griechischen Übersetzungen des ATs als Wiedergabe von *schaddaj*." *ZAW* 70:20–31.

———. 1978. "Theologische Aussagen im griechischen Alten Testament: Gottesnamen." *ZNW* 69:239–46.

Bons, Eberhard. 2011."Beobachtungen zu den Schöpfungskonzepten der griechischen Bibel und zu ihrem Einfluss auf das Neue Testament und die Schriften des Urchristentums." Pages 205–16 in *Die Septuaginta*

---

54. See Kraus 2014 for the hermeneutical relevance of the LXX for biblical theology. See also Meiser 2012 for the importance of the history of reception.

und das frühe Christentum: The Septuagint and Christian Origins. Edited by Thomas Scott Caulley and Hermann Lichtenberger. WUNT 1/277. Tübingen: Mohr Siebeck.

Cimosa, Mario. 2000. "È possibile scrivere una 'teologia' della Bibbia Greca (LXX)?" Pages 51–64 in *Initium sapientiae: Scritti in onore di Franco Festorazzi nel suo 70° compleanno*. Edited by Rinaldo Fabris and Franco Festorazzi. Supplementi alla Rivista biblica 36. Bologna: EDB.

Cimosa, Mario and Gillian Bonney. 2010. "Angels, Demons and the Devil in the Book of Job (LXX)." Pages 543–61 in *Die Septuaginta: Texte, Theologien, Einflüsse*. Edited by Wolfgang Kraus, Martin Karrer, and Martin Meiser. WUNT 1/252. Tübingen: Mohr Siebeck.

Cook, Johann. 2010a. "Towards the Formulation of a Theology of the Septuagint." Pages 621–40 in *Congress Volume: Ljubljana 2007*. Edited by André Lemaire. VTSup 133. Leiden: Brill.

———. 2010b. "Interpreting the Septuagint–Exegesis, Theology and/or Religionsgeschichte?" Pages 590–606 in *Die Septuaginta: Texte, Theologien, Einflüsse*. Edited by Wolfgang Kraus, Martin Karrer, and Martin Meiser. WUNT 1/252. Tübingen: Mohr Siebeck.

———. 2017. "Interpreting the Septuagint." Pages 1–22 in *Congress Volume Stellenbosch 2016*. Edited by Louis C. Jonker, Gideon R. Kotzé, and Christl Maier. VTSup 177. Leiden: Brill.

Dafni, Evangelia G. 2002. "Theologie der Sprache der Septuaginta." *TZ* 58:315–28.

Deissmann, Adolf. 1903. "Die Hellenisierung des semitischen Monotheismus." *NJahrb*:162–77.

De Troyer, Kristin, and Brian Doyle. 2000. *The End of the Alpha Text of Esther: Translation and Narrative Technique in MT 8:1–17, LXX 8:1–17, and AT 7:14–41*. SCS 48. Atlanta: Society of Biblical Literature.

Dines, Jennifer. 2013. "What If the Reader Is a She? Biblical Women and their Translators." Pages 56–82 in *The Reception of the Hebrew Bible in the Septuagint and the New Testament: Essays in Memory of Aileen Guilding*. Edited by David J. A. Clines and J. Cheryl Exum. HBM 55. Sheffield: Sheffield Phoenix.

Douglas, Alex. 2012. "Limitations to Writing a Theology of the Septuagint." *JSCS* 45:104–17.

Ebeling, Gerhard. 1967. "Was heißt 'Biblische Theologie?'" Pages 69–89 in *Wort und Glaube*. 3rd ed. Tübingen: Mohr Siebeck.

Fabry, Heinz-Josef. 2012. "The Biblical Canon and Beyond: Theological and Historical Context of Codices of Alexandria." Pages 21–34 in *Text-Critical and Hermeneutical Studies in the Septuagint*. Edited by Johann Cook and Hermann-Josef Stipp. VTSup 157. Leiden: Brill.

Frankel, Zacharias. 1851. *Ueber den Einfluss der palästinischen Exegese auf die alexandrinische Hermeneutik*. Leipzig: Barth.

Geiger, Abraham. 1928. *Urschrift und Übersetzung der Bibel in ihrer Abhängigkeit von der innern Entwickelung des Judentums*. 2nd ed. Frankfurt am Main: Madda.

Jeremias, Jörg. 2015. *Theologie des Alten Testaments*. GAT 6. Göttingen: Vandenhoeck & Ruprecht.

Jobes Karen H., and Moisés Silva. 2000. *Invitation to the Septuagint*. Grand Rapids: Baker Academic.

Joosten, Jan. 2000. "Une théologie de la Septante? Réflecions méthologiques sur l´interprétation de la version greque." *RTP* 132:31–46.

———. 2012a. "On Aramaizing Renderings in the Septuagint." Pages 53–66 in *Collected Studies on the Septuagint: From Language to Interpretation and Beyond*. FAT 1/83. Tübingen: Mohr Siebeck.

———. 2012b. "חסד, 'Benevolence', and ἔλεος, 'Pity': Reflections on Their Lexical Equivalence in the Septuagint." Pages 97–111 in *Collected Studies on the Septuagint: From Language to Interpretation and Beyond*. FAT 1/83. Tübingen: Mohr Siebeck.

———. 2012c. "Language as a Symptom: Linguistical Clues to the Social Background of the Seventy." Pages 185–94 in *Collected Studies on the Septuagint: From Language to Interpretation and Beyond*. FAT 1/83. Tübingen: Mohr Siebeck.

Kaminka, Armand. 1928. "Studien zur Septuaginta." *MGWJ* 72:49–60, 242–73.

Karrer, Martin, and Wolfgang Kraus. 2008. "Umfang und Text der Septuaginta: Erwägungen nach dem Abschluß der deutschen Übersetzung." Pages 8–63 in *Die Septuaginta: Texte, Kontexte, Lebenswelten*. Edited by Martin Karrer, Wolfgang Kraus, and Martin Meiser. WUNT 1/219. Tübingen: Mohr Siebeck.

Kattenbusch, Ferdinand. 1930. "Die Entstehung einer christlichen Theologie." *ZTK* 38:161–205.

Kraft, Robert A. 2003. "The 'Textual Mechanics' of Early Jewish LXX/OG Papyri and Fragments." Pages 51–72 in *The Bible as Book: The Transmission of the Greek Text*. Edited by Scott McKendrick and Orlaith O'Sullivan. London: British Library; Newcastle: Oak Knoll.

———. 2014. "Seeking 'the Septuagint' in a Scroll Dependent World." Pages 573–82 in *In the Footsteps of Sherlock Holmes: Studies in the Biblical Text in Honour of Anneli Aejmelaeus*. Edited by Kristin de Troyer, Timothy M. Law, and Marketta Liljeström. CBET 72. Leuven: Peeters.

Kraus, Wolfgang. 2014. "Die hermeneutische Relevanz der Septuaginta für eine Biblische Theologie." Pages 3–25 in *Die Septuaginta: Text, Wirkung, Rezeption*. Edited by Wolfgang Kraus and Siegfried Kreuzer. WUNT 1/325. Tübingen: Mohr Siebeck.

Law, Timothy M. 2013. *When God Spoke Greek: The Septuagint and the Making of the Christian Bible*. Oxford: Oxford University Press.

Lee, John A. 2010. Review of *A Greek-English Lexicon of the Septuagint*, by Takamitsu Muraoka. BIOSCS 43:115–25.

Martin, Dale Basil. 2010. "When Did Angels Become Demons?" *JBL* 129:657–77.

McLay, Timothy. 2010. "Why Not a Theology of the Septuagint?" Pages 607–20 in *Die Septuaginta: Texte, Theologien, Einflüsse*. Edited by Wolfgang Kraus, Martin Karrer, and Martin Meiser. WUNT 1/252. Tübingen: Mohr Siebeck.

Meiser, Martin. 2012. "Die Bedeutung der Rezeptionsgeschichte für die Septuagintaforschung." Pages 425–43 in *Die Septuaginta: Entstehung, Sprache, Geschichte*. Edited by Siegfried Kreuzer, Martin Meiser, and Marcus Sigismund. WUNT 1/286. Tübingen: Mohr Siebeck.

Müller, Mogens. 1996. *The First Bible of the Church: A Plea for the Septuagint*. JSOTSup 206. Copenhagen International Seminar 1. Sheffield: Sheffield Academic.

Perkins, Larry. 2007. "'The Lord is a Warrior'—'The Lord Who Shatters Wars:' Exod 15:3 and Jdt 9:7; 16:2." BIOSCS 40:121–38.

———. 2013. "The Greek Translator of Exodus, Interpres (translator) and Expositor (interpreter): His Treatment of Theophanies." *JSJ* 44:16–56.

Pietersma, Albert, 2006. "Messianism and the Greek Psalter: In Search of the Messiah." Pages 49–75 in *The Septuagint and Messianism*. Edited by Michael A. Knibb. BETL 195. Leuven: Peeters.

———. 2008. "Text-Production and Text-Reception: Psalm 8 in Greek." Pages 487–501 in *Die Septuaginta: Texte, Kontexte, Lebenswelten*. Edited by Martin Karrer, Wolfgang Kraus, and Martin Meiser. WUNT 1/219. Tübingen: Mohr Siebeck.

Rösel, Martin. 1994. *Übersetzung als Vollendung der Auslegung: Studien zur Genesis-Septuaginta*. BZAW 223. Berlin: de Gruyter.

———. 1998. "The Text-Critical Value of the Genesis-Septuagint." *BIOSCS* 34:62–70.

———. 2006. "Towards a 'Theology of the Septuagint'." Pages 239–52 in *Septuagint Research: Issues and Challenges in the Study of the Greek Jewish Scriptures*. Edited by Wolfgang Kraus and R. Glenn Wooden. SCS 53. Atlanta: Society of Biblical Literature. [ch. 11 in this volume.]

———. 2009. "Die Geburt der Seele in der Übersetzung: Von der hebräischen *näfäsch* über die *psyche* der LXX zur deutschen Seele." Pages 151–70 in *Anthropologische Aufbrüche: Alttestamentliche und interdisziplinäre Zugänge zur historischen Anthropologie*. Edited by Andreas Wagner. FRLANT 232. Göttingen: Vandenhoeck & Ruprecht.

———. 2014. "Der Herr des Daniel: Zur Übersetzung der Gottesnamen in der Daniel-LXX." Pages 399–411 in *Text—Textgeschichte—Textwirkung: Festschrift zum 65. Geburtstag von Siegfried Kreuzer*. Edited by Thomas Wagner, Jonathan M. Robker, and Frank Ueberschaer. AOAT 419. Münster: Ugarit-Verlag.

———. 2015. "'Du sollst die Götter nicht schmähen!' (LXX Ex 22, 28[27]): Die Übersetzung Gottes und der Götter in der Septuaginta." Pages 54–68 in *Der übersetzte Gott*. Edited by Melanie Lange and Martin Rösel. Leipzig: Evangelische Verlagsanstalt.

———. 2016. "Die himmlische Welt der Septuaginta: Angelologische Akzentuierungen am Beispiel des Danielbuches." Pages 232–43 in *Die Septuaginta: Orte und Intentionen*. Edited by Siegfried Kreuzer, Martin Meiser, and Marcus Sigismund. WUNT 1/361. Tübingen: Mohr Siebeck.

Schaper, Joachim. 2010. "God and the Gods: Pagan Deities and Religious Concepts in the Old Greek of Isaiah." Pages 135–52 in *Genesis, Isaiah, and Psalms: A Festschrift to Honour Professor John Emerton for His Eightieth Birthday*. Edited by Katharine J. Dell, Graham Davies, and Yee Von Koh. VTSup 135. Leiden: Brill.

Schmid, Konrad. 2013. *Gibt es Theologie im Alten Testament? Zum Theologiebegriff in der alttestamentlichen Wissenschaft*. ThSt.NF 7. Zürich: TVZ.

Schmitz, Barbara. 2014. "κύριος συντρίβων πολέμους 'The Lord Who Crushes Wars' (Exod 15:3 LXX): The Formative Importance of the Song of the Sea (Exod 15:1–18 LXX) for the Book of Judith." *JSCS* 47:5–16.

Schoeps, Hans-Joachim. 1959. *Paulus: Die Theologie des Apostels im Lichte der jüdischen Religionsgeschichte*. Tübingen: Mohr Siebeck.

Seeligmann, Isaac Leo. 1948. *The Septuagint Version of Isaiah: A Discussion of Its Problems*. MEOL 9. Leiden: Brill.

Siegert, Folker. 1998. "Die hellenistisch-jüdische Theologie als Forschungsaufgabe." Pages 9–30 in *Internationales Josephus-Kolloquium. Münster 1997: Vorträge aus dem Institutum Judaicum Delitzschianum*. Edited by Folker Siegert and Jürgen U. Kalms. MJS 2. Münster: LIT.

Steyn, Gert J. 2008. "Which 'LXX' Are We Talking about in NT Scholarship? Two Examples from Hebrews." Pages 297–307 in *Die Septuaginta: Texte, Kontexte, Lebenswelten*. Edited by Martin Karrer, Wolfgang Kraus, and Martin Meiser. WUNT 1/219. Tübingen: Mohr Siebeck.

Tov, Emanuel. 1987. "Die Septuaginta in ihrem theologischen und traditionsgeschichtlichen Verhältnis zur hebräischen Bibel." Pages 237–68 in *Mitte der Schrift? Ein jüdisch-christliches Gespräch. Texte des Berner Symposions vom 6.–12. Jan. 1985*. Edited by Martin A. Klopfenstein. Judaica et Christiana 11. Bern: Lang.

———. 1997. *The Text-Critical Use of the Septuagint in Biblical Research*. Rev. and enlarged 2nd ed. JBS 8. Jerusalem: Simor.

———. 1999. "Theologically Motivated Exegesis Embedded in the Septuagint." Pages 257–69 in *The Greek and Hebrew Bible: Collected essays on the Septuagint*. Edited by Emanuel Tov. VTSup 72. Leiden: Brill.

Ulrich, Eugene. 1999. *The Dead Sea Scrolls and the Origins of the Bible*. Studies in the Dead Sea Scrolls and Related Literature. Grand Rapids: Eerdmans.

Ziegert, Carsten, 2008. "Das Buch Ruth in der Septuaginta als Modell für eine integrative Übersetzungstechnik." *Bib* 89:221–51.

Ziegler, Joseph. 1962. *Die Septuaginta: Erbe und Auftrag*. Würzburger Universitätsreden 33. Würzburg: Julius-Maximilians-Universität.

13
The Reading and Translation of the Divine Name in the Masoretic Tradition and the Greek Pentateuch— with an Appendix: Frank Shaw's Book on ΙΑΩ

One of the most important topics in biblical theology and in Jewish-Christian relations is the fact that both Jews and Christians believe in the same God whom they call "Lord." This common nomenclature is the result of a long and complex development. In the Jewish tradition, the Tetragrammaton, יהוה, the four letter name of the God of Israel, is no longer spoken but is replaced by the reading *adonai* (אֲדֹנָי). In the New Testament, there are several places where God himself is called "Lord" (κύριος, in Matt 1:22; Luke 2:39; Rom 11:34), but Jesus Christ is also called κύριος (e.g., Rom 1:4), or Aramaic מָרֵא (also meaning "Lord"; see the famous μαράνα θά in 1 Cor 16:22; cf. Rev 22:20). Moreover, Christians could cite the Bible to prove that already the scriptures of Israel were announcing that Jesus Christ is the Lord, thus moving their Messiah closer to God the Father. The most important text in this respect was Ps 110:1, which is cited and discussed in Matt 22:41-46 and 1 Cor 15:25.[1]

1. The Masoretic and Qumranic Traditions

The first of the problems arising is the question whether the Masoretes vocalized the Tetragrammaton as *adonai* (אֲדֹנָי) or as *shema* (שְׁמָא), an Aramaic word meaning "the Name." If the second assumption is correct, the reading "Lord" is to be regarded as a later tradition. The question occurs because some of the oldest and most important Masoretic manuscripts including the Leningrad and Aleppo codices do in fact have the reading

---

1. See Rösel 2000a, 222-30.

יְהוָה. This seems to be the *qere* of *shema* (שְׁמָא), not of *adonai* (אֲדֹנָי).² Only younger manuscripts attest to the reading. On the basis of these observations, one could conclude that this does not represent the original custom of the Masoretes and earlier scribes.

Importantly, however, the testimony of the Leningrad codex is ambiguous. Upon further investigation, one can see that the *qere*-tradition concerning the divine name is very complex. The first observation is that the Tetragrammaton is obviously vocalized as *elohim*, "God," when standing together with אדני (as, e.g., in Gen 15:2; see also Deut 3:24 which reads אֲדֹנָי יְהֹוִה—here we find a simple *shewa* instead of the *khatef*-vowel, because *yod* is not a guttural).³ This use only makes sense when intended to avoid the repetition of *adonai*. The Tetragrammaton read as "the Name" would not cause problems.⁴ Again, one has to note that the *holem*-dot is not written, although *elohim* should be read. But there are a number of verses in the Leningrad codex where the *holem*-dot is written when a Tetragrammaton is standing in contact with אדני.⁵ Moreover, there are several instances where, even in cases when it is standing alone, a Tetragrammaton is written with the *holem*-dot.⁶ Finally, all occurrences of the Tetragrammaton with the particle *le* are vocalized as לַיהוָה (or once in Deut 32:6 as לְיהוָה). There is no other explanation for this use of the *patakh* than the fact that the following word must have begun with a *khatef-patakh* and a guttural.⁷ If the scribe had read שְׁמָא, a *hireq* would have to be expected as a proper vocalization of the particle.⁸

Thus, the conclusion is inevitable that even in the Ben Asher manuscripts mentioned earlier, the *qere* of יְהוָה is אֲדֹנָי, not שְׁמָא. It is likely that the *holem* was omitted deliberately because the Masoretes wanted to make

---

2. Joüon and Muraoka 1996, §16f. n. 2.
3. In Judg 16:28 (אֲדֹנָי יְהֹוִה) there is one single occurrence of a Tetragrammaton with the full vocalization of אֱלֹהִים.
4. Katz 1948.
5. 1 Kgs 2:26; Ps 73:28; 140:8; Isa 50:4; Jer 1:6; 7:20; Ezek 2:4; 3:11, 27; 5:5; 8:1; 12:10; 13:16; 14:21, 23; 16:36; 17:9; 20:39; 21:33; 22:31; 23:32; 24:6, 14; 26:21; 28:2; 30:22; 33:25; 39:17; 43:27; 46:16; Zech 9:14.
6. Gen 3:14; 9:26; Exod 3:2; 13:3, 9, 12, 15; 14:1, 8; Lev 23:34; 25:17; Deut 31:27; 32:9; 33:12, 13; 1 Kgs 3:5; 16:33; Ps 15:1; 40:5; 47:6; 100:5; 116:5, 6; Prov 1:29; Jer 2:37; 3:1, 13, 21, 22, 25; 4:3, 4, 8; 5:2, 3, 9, 15, 18, 19, 22, 29; 6:9; 8:13; 30:10; 36:8; Ezek 44:5; 46:13; Nah 1:3.
7. Joüon and Muraoka 1996, §21, see 16–17.
8. Joüon and Muraoka 1996, §103b.

the pronunciation of the Tetragrammaton impossible.⁹ If this analysis is correct, a typical Masoretic pun would come into play: the unpronounceable name has the same vocalization as *shema*, the holy name.¹⁰ Be that as it may, it is obvious that the Masoretic Text (MT) substitutes "Lord" for the ineffable name of God.

Going further back in the history of the biblical text, I will briefly touch upon the testimony of the Dead Sea Scrolls.¹¹ In the Qumran texts we find some very interesting evidence for the special treatment of the Tetragrammaton. It could be written in Paleo-Hebrew script when the surrounding text was written in square script (11Q5 [11QPsª]). Another solution was chosen by the corrector of the Isaiah scroll from Cave 1, who did not write the divine name but marked its place with four dots.¹² Unfortunately, we do not know how the Qumran people read or pronounced the name. Because of the predominance of the designation אל for God in extrabiblical texts and free compositions (e.g., in Pesher Habakkuk), and because only this word has been written in Paleo-Hebrew characters like the Tetragrammaton (e.g., 6Q15 [6QDamascus Document] 3; 4Q57 [4QIsaᶜ] is an exception, because here all designations for God are written in Paleo-Hebrew letters), one can assume that reading "God" for the Tetragrammaton was the normal custom at Qumran.¹³ In any case, there are also instances where אדוני is used for God in nonbiblical texts (see, e.g., CD XV, 1, the Hodayot, and 4Q507-509). Thus one has to conclude that reading "Lord" was not the only custom employed to avoid the pronunciation of the Tetragrammaton in pre-Christian times. Already in Neh 13 we find אלהים where one would have expected the Tetragrammaton (see Neh 13:14 in reference to the temple, or 13:29 in a prayer).

2. Early Manuscripts of the Septuagint

From the perspective of the New Testament, mentioned above, one has the impression that κύριος is the name of the God of Israel.¹⁴ It was obviously this title that early Christians read in their Greek Bible, the Septuagint

---

9. Rösel 2000a, 2–3.
10. See Marcus 1999 for similar phenomena in the *Masora magna*.
11. See Parry 1997 and Rösel 2000b for a more detailed discussion.
12. Tov 1992, 216.
13. Stegemann 1978, 195–96, 202.
14. McDonough 1999, 6.

(LXX). Here one can find κύριος, "Lord," besides θεός, "God," as the most frequently used designations for God. As a rule of thumb, θεός can be found where the MT has אלהים, and κύριος obviously serves as a translation of the actual name of God, the Tetragrammaton. But the problem of this seemingly unambiguous evidence is that all the complete manuscripts of the Greek Bible that read κύριος (or an abbreviation thereof)[15] were written and transmitted by Christians.

Alongside this mainstream of LXX transmission a different tradition can also be observed. In Jewish versions of the Greek Bible, including Aquila and Symmachus as well as a few LXX manuscripts, one finds a Tetragrammaton in Hebrew characters used instead of κύριος, or else the strange form ΠΙΠΙ, a combination of Greek characters that echoes the Hebrew form יהוה.[16] The church father Origen observed that "in the most exact copies the name can be found in Hebrew characters, not in today's but in older characters."[17] Similarly, in Jerome one reads: "The name of God, the Tetragrammaton, we find in particular Greek scrolls still today in old characters."[18]

These witnesses received only passing attention until, in 1944, W. G. Waddell published a tiny fragment from the LXX version of Deuteronomy. Dating to the first century BCE, this fragment is one of the three separate manuscripts that are collectively known as P.Fouad 266.[19] This papyrus attests the Tetragrammaton in Hebrew square script where other LXX manuscripts have κύριος. Waddell concluded that in the Greek Bible the divine name was never translated by κύριος but was only represented by Hebrew consonants. In his article it remained open whether and how the name was pronounced. Waddell's theory subsequently found support in the discoveries made in and around Qumran. In particular, the Greek

---

15. See Hurtado 199.

16. In Dan 9:2 (LXX) this custom has produced an interesting mistake in the text. While the MT has דבר־יהוה, the LXX, following MS 88, has πρόσταγμα τῇ γῇ, while the older P. 967 has the correct κυρίου.

17. Origen on Ps 2:1, Migne PG 12.1104. See also Jerome, *Ep. 25 ad Marcellum*, CSEL 54.219: "[The name of God] the Tetragrammaton, which is regarded as ἀνεκφώνετον, i.e., inexpressible, is written in these letters: *yod, he, waw, he*, which leads certain people who do not understand it to read it as PIPI because of the similarity of its elements, when they find it in Greek letters."

18. *Prologus galeatus*, Migne PL 28.594-5.

19. Waddell, 1944, 266b. The text is published in Aly and Koenen 1980. See also Kraft 2003, 57. The number in Rahlfs 2004 is given as 848.

13. The Reading and Translation of the Divine Name 295

Dodekapropheton Scroll from Naḥal Ḥever (8Ḥev1 [8ḤevXIIgr]), a text dating from between 50 BCE and 50 CE, is especially noteworthy.[20] This scroll preserves the Tetragrammaton in Paleo-Hebrew characters, rather than using the Greek κύριος. The same phenomenon can also be noted in P.Oxy. 3522 from the first century CE,[21] where in Job 42 the Tetragrammaton is written in Paleo-Hebrew letters by the same scribe who wrote the Greek text.

An interesting phenomenon can be seen in P.Rylands Greek 458.[22] Here we find a gap in Deut 26:18 where one would expect either κύριος or the Tetragrammaton. This gap is large enough to accommodate both words, and it seems likely that the scribe of the Greek text left the space free for someone else to insert the Hebrew characters of the Tetragrammaton.[23]

Another important text is 4Q120 [4QLXXLev^b]. This document, written sometime in the first century BCE, in two places (Lev 3:12; 4:7) attests a Greek transcription, IAΩ, instead of the Hebrew Tetragrammaton or the Greek translation κύριος.[24] Obviously, the text preserves the divine name as it was spoken, rather than a translation of it.

The scholarly consensus changed drastically in the light of this pre-Christian evidence. The prevailing assumption is now that it is self-evident that the original translators of the LXX never rendered the divine name with κύριος, but kept the Tetragrammaton in Hebrew or Paleo-Hebrew characters, or that they used the transcription IAΩ.[25]

---

20. See especially Barthélemy 1963. The critical edition appears in Tov 1990; for details, see also Rahlfs 2004, 943.

21. Rahlfs 2004, 304, no. 3522.

22. Rahlfs 2004, 241, no. 957.

23. A similar phenomenon can be seen in P.Oxy. 656. There are gaps in four instances, three of them having been filled by a later scribe with κύριος (Rahlfs 2004, 292). Note, however, that this papyrus is to be dated in the second/third century CE; see also Kraft 2003, 60-61. Nevertheless, Tov (1990, 12) quotes this papyrus as if it were a pre-Christian manuscript.

24. Skehan 1957, 157-60.

25. For Paleo-Hebrew characters, see Kahle 1962, 232-62; Schulz 1962, 128-30; Howard 1977, 63-66; Fitzmyer 1975, 281. For the transcription IAΩ, see Skehan 1957, 157-58; Stegemann 1978, 205. Skehan (1980) initially repeats his thesis from 1957 that IAΩ is the earliest phase of the development in the LXX; significantly, however, when referring to the translations of the prophetic books, he assumes that here κύριος was originally used to translate both יהוה and אדני, possibly based on an oral tradition to pronounce *adonai* for the Tetragrammaton (28-29).

This theory has, however, been challenged on the basis that the use of the Hebrew Tetragrammaton can be attributed to a pre-Christian revision of the Greek biblical manuscripts.[26] The manuscripts in question also show other traces of revisions of the Hebrew text.[27] Moreover, Albert Pietersma was able to offer explanations for the peculiarities of the texts in question, mostly based on the observation that the size of the gaps in the manuscripts perfectly fits into the space required by the word κύριος.[28] Obviously the scribes had κύριος in mind, even if they wrote the Tetragrammaton into their text.[29] Moreover, from the characteristic use and nonuse of the article in connection with κύριος, Pietersma came to the conclusion that κύριος must be the original translation of the Tetragrammaton.[30]

Others still hold the view that the transliterated name ΙΑΩ is the most likely candidate for the original reading of the LXX. Emanuel Tov came to the conclusion that it is more plausible that the early translators did not translate the divine name with κύριος but represented it as if it were a personal name in its transliteration.[31] As an important argument to support this view, Tov notes the fact that there are other instances in which 4Q120—the only pre-Christian manuscript attesting ΙΑΩ—has some other readings that have to be regarded as more original than the majority of LXX manuscripts.[32]

---

26. Hanhart 1978; Pietersma 1984. Furuli (1999, 166-68) completely neglects this problem when he argues against the originality of κύριος as a translation for the Hebrew Tetragrammaton. The same is true for Trobisch (2000, 13-15). (I am grateful to Otto E. Nordgreen from Oslo for bringing these books to my attention.)

27. Most recently, Emanuel Tov has concluded that, "all the texts transcribing the Tetragrammaton in Hebrew characters reflect early revisions" (Tov 2003, 112). But it should be stated that this argument alone is not convincing, since there are other recensions that show different ways of using/avoiding the Tetragrammaton (see P. 967 in Lust 1996; McGregor 1985). Further research is needed on this problem. (I thank Kristin De Troyer for pointing out this problem to me in a private communication.)

28. Pietersma 1984.

29. This explanation may also be applied to 4Q121 [4QLXXNum], a text Pietersma (1984) did not comment on. There is a gap at Num 3:41 into which κύριος would fit perfectly. In my opinion, the length of the lines strongly supports this reading.

30. Several scholars have followed this argumentation; see, e.g., McDonough 1999, 58-65; Sollamo 2003, 507.

31. Tov 2003, 112-14, following Skehan 1957, 1980, and Stegemann 1978.

32. It is worth mentioning that only one more biblical text is known that has ΙΑΩ as a marginal reading, i.e., Codex Marchalianus from sixth-century CE Egypt; see Rahlfs 2004, 346-50, siglum Q.

13. The Reading and Translation of the Divine Name

Among those scholarly works that also regard the reading IAΩ as the original representation of the Tetragrammaton in the LXX, the unpublished dissertation of Frank Shaw deserves to be mentioned here.[33] In this important contribution Shaw has been able to show that there was an ongoing custom of pronouncing the name IAΩ within some (perhaps lower class?[34]) groups of Hellenistic Judaism, and that there was knowledge outside Jewish circles that IAΩ was the name of the God of the Jews. Thus the use of IAΩ was not restricted to magical practices. Obviously, there had been different traditions regarding how to deal with the divine name, and we have already seen this in the Qumranic use of אל and אדני. The older view of a single term being employed in order to avoid the use of the divine name should therefore be abandoned. One could also add that the use of IAΩ as the shortened form of the divine name, a phenomenon which is well known from the Elephantine papyri that read יהו, points to Jewish circles in Egypt as bearers of this tradition.[35]

But there are also weaknesses in Shaw's argumentation. A major part of the dissertation deals with onomastica. Based on the use of IAΩ-type elements in Jewish names, he concludes that this version of the divine name was already in use at the time when the Bible was read or translated—a conclusion that is hardly convincing. If people wanted to use biblical names for their children, there was no way to avoid the use of IAΩ and similar forms for the theophoric elements of Hebrew names. In connection with this consideration, the Samaria papyri from Wadi Daliyeh could also be mentioned, because also in these Aramaic texts from the fourth century BCE several names with the element יהו (e.g., יהושפט and יהוטב) are preserved.[36] But again, these texts only prove that the shortened name of God was still in use at that time. They give no new evidence for the problem of the original representation in the LXX. So, neither the Samaria papyri nor Shaw's dissertation offer new arguments to support

---

33. Shaw 2002. The dissertation has in the meantime been reworked and published: Shaw 2014. Since it is not possible here to refute his attacks against my position and the "κύριος-as-original-camp" (159), which go far beyond what is common in academic discourse, I have attached an appendix to this article in which I will discuss his arguments.

34. Shaw 2014, 201–2.

35. This assumption fits the observation of Skehan (1980, 29) that the script of 4Q120 is very similar to P.Fouad 266, a papyrus that was found in Egypt. See also on Codex Marchalianus above n. 32.

36. Gropp 2001.

the use of ΙΑΩ as the original representation of the Tetragrammaton in biblical texts.[37]

In my opinion, there is one compelling argument *against* the assumption that ΙΑΩ is the original representation of the Tetragrammaton in the LXX version of Leviticus. It is in this book that we find the strictest prohibition against pronouncing the name of the Lord. The Hebrew of 24:16, which may be translated as "and he that blasphemes/curses [נקב] the name of the Lord [יהוה], he shall surely be put to death," in the LXX is subjected to a characteristic deviation: "But he that names [ὀνομάζων] the name of the Lord, let him die the death."[38] It seems extremely unlikely to me that someone who has translated the verse in this way should have used ΙΑΩ as a representation of the Hebrew Tetragrammaton. Leviticus 24:16 would have read: "He who names the name ΙΑΩ shall surely die." To my mind, this translation would be a self-contradiction. Unfortunately, while this particular verse is not preserved in the extant Qumran manuscripts, the assumption just mentioned would tally nicely with the observation by Johan Lust that the name ΙΑΩ has been inserted into the text of 4Q120 by a second scribe.[39] This would make the originality of ΙΑΩ highly improbable, even if we do not know how ancient readers may have dealt with this verse and its ΙΑΩ-reading.

However, based on the photographic reproductions of 4Q120, it is not clear to me that ΙΑΩ does in fact derive from a different scribe. Be that as it may, it should be added that there are other deviations in the LXX version of the Pentateuch that demonstrate the high esteem in which the divine *name* was held. It may suffice here to refer to Lev 18:21 where the MT has "you shall not profane the name of your God" (שם אלהיך), and where the LXX translates "you shall not profane the holy name" (τὸ ὄνομα τὸ ἅγιον).[40] Thus, I would speculate that the strange reading of ΙΑΩ is a

---

37. It should be added that on p. 162 of his 2002 dissertation Shaw considers whether there may have been several traditions for representing the divine name in the Greek translation. Even if this general assumption is correct, I can see only ΙΑΩ and κύριος as likely candidates "for some sort of uniform original representation of the name" (citation from Shaw 2014, 159-60), not the Hebrew Tetragrammaton.

38. Even if the translator was not reading נקב but יקב, as McDonough 1999, 62-63, assumes, so that he was not deliberately changing the meaning of the verse, it has to be stated that the result of this translation was a prohibition to utter God's name.

39. Lust 1997, 74-75.

40. For more details, see Rösel 1998, 57-58.

secondary replacement that comes from a community (in Egypt?) that still pronounced the name of God in this way.

3. An Exegetical Approach

In what follows I would like to propose a new solution to the problem, since previous analyses of the external manuscript evidence have proved inconclusive. In my opinion, there is important *internal* LXX evidence to support the view that κύριος is the original representation of the first translators.[41] Moreover, it is my contention that one can also glimpse the translator's theological thinking in his use of the names of God in the Greek Pentateuch.[42] I will restrict myself here to texts from the Pentateuch, due to the fact that in these earliest translations the standards have been set for later translations. A broader examination would have to touch upon such related phenomena as the early replacements of the Tetragrammaton in the Hebrew Bible itself or in the various Hebrew texts of Ben Sira.

The basis for the following argumentation is the fact that there are standardized equivalents for the translation of divine names and titles. As mentioned earlier, the translators regularly chose κύριος without the article as an equivalent for the Tetragrammaton, and not infrequently used θεός for אלהים.[43] What is striking is that there are several instances in which these standard equivalents have not been used. There are cases where one reads θεός in texts where the Hebrew text has the Tetragrammaton, as well as renderings of אלהים with κύριος. In most of these cases there is no reason to assume a different *Vorlage*, nor is the transmission of the Greek reading insecure.[44] Some examples may suffice to illustrate the phenomenon.

There is an obvious tendency to avoid the impression that κύριος is acting in an unjust way. This can be seen, for example, in the Greek rendering of

---

41. See Rösel 1991 for an earlier version of this argumentation in German.

42. Tov (2003, 112) is possibly commenting on an earlier version of the present study when he writes: "all the irregularities to the anarthrous use of κύριος can also be explained as having been created by a mechanical replacement of ΙΑΩ with κύριος by Christian scribes."

43. See the statistics by Wevers 2001, 20-25. The interesting result of his survey is that the translators of the Pentateuch have followed the pattern more strictly than the one who worked on the Psalter.

44. In the book of Genesis, there are only a few cases where the editions of Wevers (1990) and Rahlfs differ; see 16:7 where Wevers reads κυρίου τοῦ θεοῦ, while Rahlfs has only κυρίου, and 19:29 where Wevers has τὸν θεόν, while Rahlfs has κύριον.

Gen 38:7, 10—"And Er, the firstborn of Judah, was wicked before the Lord [κύριος] … and God [θεός] killed him"—the Hebrew version of which makes use of the Tetragrammaton twice. This cannot be mere coincidence, because in verse 10 also the second son, Onan, is killed by ὁ θεός, not by κύριος, as the Hebrew יהוה would have suggested.

The same tendency can be seen in Gen 12:17. In the Hebrew text, it is the Lord (יהוה) who strikes Pharaoh and his house with plagues. In the Greek version, it is again God (ὁ θεός). Again, in Gen 4 a deliberate principle in the rendering of the divine name can be observed. Here, in place of the Hebrew text's consistent use of the Tetragrammaton, the LXX makes use of two distinct forms: ὁ θεός does not look upon Abel and his offering (v. 5); κύριος ὁ θεός speaks to Cain (v. 6); and ὁ θεός accuses the murderer (v. 9, 10), who in v. 16 is going forth from the presence of God (τοῦ θεοῦ for MT יהוה). It is interesting to note in addition that there are two verses in Gen 4 in which the regular use of κύριος for the Tetragrammaton can be seen, in v. 3 and 13. These verses speak of Cain's offering (v. 3) and Cain's prayer to the Lord (v. 13). On the basis of such usage, I would conclude that κύριος is avoided whenever the text speaks of the punishing or judging aspects of God. This view gains confirmation in the flood story, since, according to Gen 6:6, 7, it is ὁ θεός rather than κύριος (ὁ θεός), who decides to kill humankind with the flood. In the MT this was the decision of יהוה.

A similar tendency can be seen in other books of the Pentateuch. In the MT version of Deut 2:14, for example, it is יהוה who swears that the wilderness generation will die; according to the Greek version, the swearing is done by ὁ θεός. In Num 16:5, 11, יהוה is speaking against Korah and all his company; the LXX uses ὁ θεός. Exodus 16:7 is also interesting, since here κύριος is used in reference to God's δόξα, whereas ὁ θεός is used when referring to the focus of the murmuring of the people. In both cases the Hebrew text makes use of the Tetragrammaton. Given that the same differentiation can be found in Exod 16:9, the conclusion must be that this is not mere coincidence.

This is not, however, the only theological consideration that can be seen in the use or nonuse of κύριος. In Gen 13:13, one can read that the men of Sodom were exceedingly sinful before God (ἐναντίον τοῦ θεοῦ). The Hebrew text records that the Sodomite men were sinners ליהוה ("before the Lord"). A similar phenomenon can be found in Gen 30:27 and 31:49. According to the Hebrew text, Laban is hoping to be blessed by the Lord, or he is hoping that the Lord is looking after Laban and Jacob (יהוה is used in both instances). In both verses the LXX version has not κύριος but ὁ θεός. Again, I would explain these deviations from the regular practice of translation as theologically motivated. The use of κύριος is avoided since all these men are foreigners, not Israelites. In the case of Gen 31:49, this seemingly deliberate choice of divine name in the Greek may have arisen as a result of the immediate context—in 31:53 mention is made of the אלהי אברהם (LXX ὁ θεὸς Αβρααμ); 32:2 refers to the מלאכי אלהים (LXX ἄγγελοι τοῦ θεοῦ).

A similar consideration may lie behind Exod 3:18. Here Moses is ordered to go to Pharaoh and tell him that the Lord God (יהוה אלהים) has met with Moses and the Hebrew elders, and that Moses and the Israelites are to make a three-day journey in order to make offerings to the Lord God (again יהוה אלהים). The Greek text lacks an equivalent for the Tetragrammaton in both cases. Obviously, the God of the Hebrews should not be identified as "Lord" to a non-Israelite (in this case Pharaoh). The same omission of the Tetragrammaton or its translation appears in Exod 5:2–3. In the discussion between Pharaoh, Moses, and Aaron, Pharaoh does not mention the name of the God of the Israelites at first: "Who is he that I should heed him?" The MT has מי יהוה. In the next verse, Moses and Aaron respond that they want to go and offer to the Lord, their God (ליהוה אלהינו). The Greek version reads only τῷ θεῷ ἡμῶν. Later, in 10:11, Pharaoh allows the Israelites to "go and serve God" (τῷ θεῷ); the Hebrew text has יהוה.[45]

A very similar phenomenon can be seen in the Balaam story in Num 22–24. As John William Wevers has pointed out, the translator clearly had a negative attitude toward Balaam, the foreign seer.[46] As such, all the occurrences of מלאך יהוה ("angel of the Lord") were translated as ἄγγελος τοῦ θεοῦ ("angel of God"). There is only one exception where κύριος is used in Num 22:34, in Balaam's confession of sin. Moreover, in 23:5, 12 it is not the Lord (κύριος, MT יהוה) who puts his word into the mouth of Balaam,

---

45. The situation in Exod 10 is very difficult to explain. It is obvious that the translator saw problems with using the word λατρεύω together with κύριος in the mouth of Pharaoh. In 10:7 it is clear from the MT that κύριος is ὁ θεὸς αὐτῶν. In 10:8, the Tetragrammaton is not translated, so that the Israelites shall serve only their God. In Moses's response to Pharaoh in 10:9, ὁ θεός is added over against the MT, and in 10:11 יהוה is translated as θεός (in Pharaoh's words). In 10:24 again, ὁ θεός is added over against the MT. But one can also see κύριος is used in Pharaoh's speech (see 10:10, 16, 17). Yet, these verses can be understood as a kind of prayer, therefore κύριος may have been appropriate.

46. Wevers 1999.

but ὁ θεός. The same phenomenon can also be seen in Num 23:26 and 24:13. Notably, the Greek version of the Balaam story offers no mention of the Lord (κύριος) speaking to the foreign prophet, although this is what we find in the Hebrew account. Significantly, there are numerous cases in the surrounding context of the Tetragrammaton being rendered by the Greek translator with κύριος.[47]

4. Conclusions

The examples mentioned above will suffice for the purposes of the present article. In my opinion, it is possible to explain nearly all the deviations from the standard equivalents in similar ways. There are also instances in which one has to state that the translators were harmonizing the varying usage of the designations of God. There is also a tendency to use ὁ θεός in statements concerning God's power, as, for example, in Gen 18:13-4, where the Lord himself is asking Abraham whether anything should be impossible with God (θεός, MT יהוה). In Exod 13:21, "God [ὁ θεός] led them by a pillar of cloud and fire." The Hebrew text has יהוה. In the immediate context of this verse, the opposite phenomenon can also be seen. In Exod 13:19 κύριος is used (MT has אלהים; see also the MT and LXX versions of Gen 50:25) because it is about the promise that God will visit the children of Israel (Wevers 1990, 206). Finally, in the important depiction of God's theophany in Exod 19, the translator has very often used ὁ θεός when the MT has יהוה. According to Wevers, "there must be a tendency here to prefer a reference to deity rather than to the personal name in the description of this theophany."[48]

Admittedly, there are also some texts where a sound explanation seems impossible. Moreover, these interventions of the translators only occurred selectively—there was no extensive rewriting of the biblical text. But the result of this short overview is surprisingly clear: the texts of the Greek Pentateuch show a theological tendency to make distinctions between the powerful and mighty aspects of God, expressed by ὁ θεός, and

---

47. There is even one important verse in which this prejudice of the translator becomes explicit. In Num 22:18, the Hebrew text records that Balaam will not transgress the word of יהוה אלהי ("the Lord my God"). The LXX has τὸ ῥῆμα κυρίου τοῦ θεοῦ ("the word of the Lord God")—the Lord is not Balaam's God.

48. Wevers 1990, 305. I wish to thank Professor L. Perkins for directing my attention to this text.

the compassionate aspects of his deeds for Israel (κύριος). In most cases, these deviations can be found in the LXX only, therefore it is unlikely to judge them as textual in origin.[49]

It is important to note that a very similar theological concept can be seen in the differences in the use of the Tetragrammaton and אל or אלהים in 4Q51 [4QSamᵃ], the MT, and the LXX. As Donald W. Parry has pointed out, the scribe of the Qumran scroll not only used the Tetragrammaton more frequently than the MT, he also expressed by this increased use the conviction that it is יהוה who takes an active role in the life of the Israelites.[50] Moreover, the Qumran text also avoids the use of the Tetragrammaton in a context that speaks against the picture of יהוה as the merciful God, a point Parry has not seen. Second Samuel 12:15 relates that the Lord (MT יהוה) killed the first son of Bathsheba and David. Surprisingly, the scroll from Cave 4 at Qumran has אלהים. Obviously, the early translators of the LXX were not alone in following the principle, discussed above, according to which יהוה/κύριος stands for the merciful aspects of God while אלהים/ θεός is used for his powerful and punishing deeds.

In later times, we can find comparable distinctions in Philo, although in his view it is the κύριος title that refers to the powerful side of God, while ὁ θεός reflects his merciful aspects. In the rabbinic literature, we find an outlook that is closer to what we have seen in the LXX. The rabbis saw the Tetragrammaton as a designation of the compassionate God, while אלהים is used for God the Judge.[51] It is obvious that not only the translators of the LXX, but also other writers, reflected upon possible reasons for the appearance of two different designations for God, although they clearly arrived at different conclusions.

Who was responsible for this theological exposition in the Greek Pentateuch? Here one should recall another aspect of Pietersma's argument concerning κύριος as the original translation. Pietersma was able to show that the distinctive use and nonuse of the article serves to distinguish human κύριοι from the one divine κύριος. His conclusion is that this refined concept cannot be attributed to a mechanically working redaction but to the translators themselves. The evidence presented in this article strongly supports this theory and gives sufficient internal evidence to assume that the earliest stages of the LXX read κύριος, not ΙΑΩ. This kind

---

49. See Wevers 1990, 206 on the LXX version of Exodus.
50. Parry 1996.
51. Dahl and Segal 1978.

of unarticulated use of κύριος without a pending genitive was an innovation in Hellenistic times, which served perfectly to express the claim and conviction that the God of Israel was the Lord of the earth (see Exod 8:6).[52]

Shaw uses one interesting argument against Pietersma's theory, an argument that Shaw derived from the work of Royse.[53] There is a noticeable inconsistency in the manuscript tradition about the oblique cases of κύριος, especially between the dative and the genitive. Shaw explains that the scribes saw a Tetragrammaton and translated it into an appropriate form of κύριος. During this process, the errors occurred. But this argument is not sufficient to defend the originality of the Hebrew Tetragrammaton in the Greek text, because these mistakes could have been introduced into the text during a secondary stage when cases of the recensional Tetragrammaton were retranslated into forms of κύριος.[54] Moreover, this argument does not affect the conclusions drawn above. In most cases θεός has been found to be used for יהוה in order to avoid the usual translation, κύριος, and the textual tradition in the verses commented upon is without these inconsistencies concerning the oblique cases. I agree with Pietersma that it is hardly conceivable that later scribes should have changed a Hebrew Tetragrammaton or Greek ΙΑΩ into a form of ὁ θεός.

One should also add that κύριος is not only attested in the LXX but also in the work of Jewish Hellenistic writers such as Aristobulus, who cites Exod 9:3. It seems clear that he read κύριος in his biblical text.[55] One can also mention the citation of Deut 7:18-9 in the *Letter of Aristeas* §155.[56] Moreover, κύριος is also present in those scriptures of the Greek canon that were not translated from a Hebrew *Vorlage*, as was the case with the Wisdom of Solomon (4:17, 18; 9:13) and 2 Maccabees (2:8; 3:33; etc.), and also in the works of Philo.[57] Thus it is apparent that the use of κύριος as a

---

52. Hanhart 1988, 75-76.
53. Shaw 2002, 157-59; Royse 1991, 180-82.
54. Note again the mistake in Dan 9:2 (above, n. 16), which, according to the testimony of P. 967, must have occurred during the transmission of the text. Codex Marchalianus (Rahlfs 2004, 346-50) is also interesting, since there are several instances where a secondary ΠΙΠΙ has been added to κύριος. Shaw (2002, 159) himself points to the possible multiplicity of revisional activities in the process of the transmission of biblical texts.
55. Walter 2001, 86-87 with n. 38; Stegemann 1978, 205 n. 35.
56. Kahle 1962, 222-23.
57. For 2 Maccabees, see Hanhart 1994, 8-9. As mentioned above, Royse (1991) argues that Philo must have read the Hebrew Tetragrammaton in his scriptures but

representation of יהוה must be pre-Christian in origin. Moreover, the citations in the New Testament require at least that κύριος or אדני had been uttered when the Scriptures of Israel were read aloud and studied.

As a result of the foregoing, it seems clear to me that from the very beginnings of the translation of the Pentateuch, the translators were using κύριος as an/the equivalent for the Hebrew name of God, following a principle of replacing the sacred name with the word אדני.[58] In a Jewish monotheistic milieu, this development is easily understandable, since the use of a name as a means of identifying (and distinguishing) one god from others was now no longer needed—there was but one God. And yet obviously this practice was not generally accepted in Judaism, as the later replacement by the Hebrew Tetragrammaton shows. From even later sources we also know that there were circles that pronounced the name of God as ΙΑΩ, and that not merely for magical reasons. This custom must have been considered extremely unusual, if not heretical, in the eyes of those Jews and Christians who were used to calling upon God using the title "Lord" (κύριος or אדני). Therefore, the ΙΑΩ readings in the biblical manuscript 4Q120 are a mystery still awaiting sound explanation. What can be said is that such readings cannot be claimed to be original.

Appendix: Frank Shaw's book on ΙΑΩ

As mentioned above, Shaw's dissertation on ΙΑΩ has in the meantime been published in an expanded and reworked version,[59] including harsh criticism against several scholars who hold the position that κύριος is either the first representation of the Hebrew Tetragrammaton or one of its earliest representations; he calls them "κύριος-is-original camp." Shaw's book has been discussed in a panel during the Society of Biblical Literature's Annual Meeting in Atlanta (November, 2015), and in the following I will reproduce my argumentation, which I presented there:

---

probably pronounced such cases as κύριος. The interesting fact is that, as far as I know, there is no place in Philo's works where he makes reference to the existence of anything resembling a Hebrew Tetragrammaton. Royse wonders how else Philo could have known that the (Hebrew) name of God is written with four letters if not from his biblical texts (180-81). But this is hardly an argument if one considers that Philo had been on a pilgrimage to Jerusalem (*Prov.* 2.64).

58. See Rösel 2000a, for a thorough refutation of Baudissin 1929.
59. Shaw 2014. See n. 19.

In his book Shaw has written in several instances resumés like the following: "The simplistic explanation offered by the κύριος-is-original camp are so easy to criticize because its proponents fail to account, in practice, for this much larger picture."⁶⁰ The much larger picture mostly consists of the details Shaw has gathered in this dissertation. As I have written already in the article, which is reprinted above, this dissertation is an important contribution. Shaw has been able to show that there was an ongoing custom of pronouncing the name ΙΑΩ within some groups of Hellenistic Judaism. And I went on: "The older view of a single term being employed in order to avoid the use of the divine name should therefore be abandoned."⁶¹ It may be that I am a bit stubborn, but I cannot see that this position is simplistic. Moreover, all colleagues who have dealt with the problem in recent years have seen the complexity of the question and added aspects to this multiplicity—even if the result of their studies led them to pitch their tents in the κύριος-is-original camp.

In what follows I will proceed in three steps. First I will try to add another detail to the complex problem of the nonmystical use of ΙΑΩ. In a second step I will renew my exegetical approach toward the question, because unfortunately Shaw has not put forward valid arguments against it. And finally I will present some evidence in favor of my position that most of the translators of the Old Greek have in fact used κύριος as an equivalent for the Tetragrammaton.

(1) It is well known, and Shaw has commented on this fact, that the Jewish community in Elephantine has used the form *yhw/yhh* (Aramaic) as the name of their god.⁶² This form then has later been transcribed into the Greek reading ΙΑΩ. Moreover Frank refers to an article by Jan Joosten, who has pointed to another reference for "Yaho, our bull" in one papyrus from the Amherst collection (no. 63).⁶³ This papyrus poses its own questions, because it is written in Aramaic language but in Demotic script. It is usually dated to the fourth century; its provenance is not completely clear but obviously it stems from Thebes.

The interesting fact is that much more can be derived from this witness than Joosten has written: in columns 12 and 13 it has poems that can

---

60. Shaw 2014, 245.
61. Rösel 2007, 417 [see above p. 297].
62. E.g., Shaw 2014, xii; 250; 254–56.
63. Joosten 2011, 115.

be seen as versions of Pss 20 and 75 and parallels to Exod 15 and Ps 19.[64] In this section there is a specific Demotic word reading 'ḥr^G or 'ḥrw, either written with a determinative for gods or with a *waw* as final character. Since it often stands in parallelism to Hebrew of Phoenician '*dny* or to Aramaic *mr* (both meaning "Lord"), it is clear that it must refer to a god. It is highly disputed how the Demotic characters are to be transcribed into Aramaic. The most convincing proposal comes from the German Egyptologist Zauzich who has offered strong arguments for the reading *yahw*.[65] I myself would prefer the reading *yah* with a determinative for God.[66]

As noted earlier, *yahw* or *yah* stands in parallelism to '*dny* (always with the suffix: "my Lord"); this is otherwise witnessed in biblical literature or texts influenced by the Bible only. Moreover, in a synopsis with Pss 20 and 75 it is obvious that *yahw* or *yah* stands exactly at that position where the Hebrew psalm has the Tetragrammaton, while *adonay* is not mentioned in the Hebrew parallels. Obviously the Tetragrammaton is replaced in P.Amh. 63 by *adonay* and the shortened version *yahu/yah*. Thus the papyrus should be seen as another early witness for the use of the *yahw* or *yah* in a nonmystical use. It bridges the gap between the texts from Elephantine and the references to the Greek IAΩ that Shaw has collected.

(2) "All need to face the facts: the quest for comprehending 'the original' form of the Name in the LXX is, in the current state of our available knowledge, not achievable. Those who claim otherwise, especially with some supposed confidence, are simply not confronting reality."[67] "This position (i.e., suspending a judgment about the quest) is the informed, mature, wise one."[68]

Despite these judgments by Shaw I am inclined not to suspend my asking for *the* or, perhaps better, *one* original form of the divine name in the LXX. In several articles I have gathered observations, mostly from the Pentateuch, which are serving as an exegetical argument (see above, §3). This argument works as follows: There is an enormous discrepancy between the majority of textual witnesses for κύριος as a translation of the Tetragrammaton and the few earlier, pre-Christian witnesses which have either the Tetragrammaton in Hebrew letters or IAΩ. This means that

---

64. Rösel 2000c.
65. Zauzich 1985.
66. See Rösel 2000c, 90–91, for other attempts to explain this reading.
67. Shaw 2014, 271.
68. Shaw 2014, 272.

there must have been a—presumably Christian—revision that changed the earlier readings, so that we now have κύριος in cases where the earlier Greek version and the Hebrew *Vorlage* have the divine name. But the evidence from the texts in the book of Genesis is different. In a large number of instances the Greek translation does not have κύριος but θεός or the combined name κύριος ὁ θεός. Moreover, a significant pattern occurred, namely that κύριος was avoided when the acts of the Lord could be seen as unjust.

These observations are speaking against the assumption of a mechanical representation of the Tetragram by ΙΑΩ and a secondary recension toward the Christian use of κύριος. Moreover, they perfectly fit into the picture of what is known about the theological tendencies of these translators. Shaw did not enter into a discussion of these observations. He confined himself to cite the following judgment by Tov: "all the irregularities pertaining to the anarthrous use of κύριος can also be explained as having been created by mechanical replacement of ΙΑΩ with κύριος by Christian Scribes."[69] Based on this "principle," Shaw merely states that the phenomenon I have described may have also been the work of later scribes.[70]

In the meantime Tov has come back to the problem in an article on the translation of the divine names that will be published in the German series LXX.*Handbuch*. Here Tov renews his theory that presumably ΙΑΩ was the original representation of the divine name, the first choice of the translators, that was "in a later layer of the LXX transmission," "around the turn of the era" replaced by κύριος.[71] So Tov obviously no longer thinks of Christian scribes being responsible for this replacement, which is an interesting detail.

In the later part of his paper Tov deals with the complex problem posed by the inconsistent translation of the Tetragrammaton by θεός, not by κύριος. His result is no longer the assumption of a mechanical replacement but "of harmonizing tendencies within the Greek translation," which were "inconsistently executed."[72] One should have in mind that—according to Tov himself—one of the most important characteristics of the Greek Genesis is its tendency toward harmonization.[73] If we follow Tov, we have

---

69. Shaw 2014, 149; Tov 2003, 112. It should be mentioned that I did not deal at all with the problem of the anarthrous use of κύριος in my articles.
70. Shaw 2014, 150.
71. Tov, p. 5 in the manuscript.
72. Tov, p. 13 in the manuscript.
73. Tov 2014.

to assume two layers of extensive harmonization in the Greek Genesis: at first the translator in the third century and then the replacer-harmonizer around the turn of the era. It should be added that this later harmonizer has not left any other trace of his activity in the textual history of the Greek Genesis. Therefore I still think that my model of the translator being responsible for this deliberate use of the equivalents κύριος and θεός is the more appropriate solution.

It should be added that also scholars who were dealing mainly with textual matters have recently come to the result that the Hebrew Tetragrammata are a secondary phenomenon, replacing κύριος.[74]

(3) In the last section I would like to point to some of the textual phenomena that lead me to the assumption that the translators have chosen κύριος as an equivalent for the Tetragrammaton. First, I would like to recall the results of the investigation in the Balaam narrative in Num 22-24, above §3. The translator obviously had a negative attitude toward Balaam, the foreign seer.[75] There is not one text in the Greek story of Balaam saying that κύριος is speaking to the foreign prophet, although this is what we find in the Hebrew story. Moreover, there are enough verses in which the Tetragrammaton is rendered in the usual way by κύριος. Thus this distinctive use of κύριος cannot be attributed to a mechanical revision. Also the theory of a harmonization fails because the problem of the changing use of *'elohim* and the Tetragrammaton in Num 22-24 has not been solved by the translator.

My second example comes from the Old Greek of the book of Daniel. Again, this is a rather free translation. In several instances the translator strengthened monotheistic statements and differentiated between the Lord of Daniel and the gods of the foreign rulers.[76] In the Hebrew book the Tetragrammaton is used only in the prayer in Dan 9. It is interesting to notice that the translator has used κύριος not only in these instances but also in cases where the Hebrew has אלהים denoting the God of Israel. Moreover, even in parts translated from the Aramaic, κύριος is used, for example, παρὰ τοῦ κυρίου τοῦ ὑψίστου for מן־קדם אלה שמיא in 2:18 or in 2:20: τὸ ὄνομα τοῦ κυρίου τοῦ μεγάλου for שמה די־אלהא. Especially striking is 4:20, where according to the Aramaic text a watcher has come down

---

74. See Gunnar Magnus Eidsvåg on the Greek Dodekapropheton from Naḥal Ḥever (Eidsvåg 2013) and Jannes Smith on P.Oxy 5101 (Smith 2012).
75. Wevers 1999.
76. Rösel 2014.

from heaven (מן־שמיא), while in the Greek he has come from the Lord (παρὰ τοῦ κυρίου). I cannot imagine how in those instances a later revision could have inserted κύριος. Moreover, in the special case of Daniel we have a second edition, Pseudo-Theodotion, obviously an early revision of the Old Greek. Here we can see in all the instances mentioned earlier that Theodotion has the literal translation with θεός or οὐρανός (4:20).

To sum up; I still think that there are good reasons for dwelling in the "κύριος-is-original camp." Nevertheless, as I have stated years ago, the label "original" does not mean "exclusive." As we can see in P.Amh. 63 and in 4Q120 the name Yao/Yahu was used also in biblical texts. Unfortunately the evidence is so sparse that we can only speculate about the amount of this usage. Further, as I have demonstrated, there are still important arguments that in the majority of the texts κύριος was used.

I would like to end with a personal note. I was a bit relieved when I realized that Shaw's prize for "uninformed, immature, and unwise scholarship" does not go to me. Even worse rated is Pietersma's article on κύριος.[77] I quote: "As evidence of this, and as much as Pietersma claims proof, his arguments are quite often sprinkled with provisos such as 'presumably,' 'evidently,' 'in our view,' 'at times' and 'it would seem.'"[78] To the critical reader all this hardly inspires any real notion of "proof." A critical reader of Shaw's book, however, will quickly find out that he himself uses the same language quite often, at times replenished by rhetorical questions.[79]

More important is in my eyes that in his presentation of Pietersma's paper Shaw did not mention one important argument Pietersma has put forward, namely, that the blank spaces in the texts, in which the Hebrew *Tetragrammata* were inserted, have exactly the size to fit κύριος in the handwriting of the first scribe. But more than one hundred pages later, in his synthesis on the LXX, Shaw mentions this observation without referring to Pietersma, but with the remark: "This textual phenomenon has not played the role in the overall discussion … that it should."[80] While I think that Dr. Shaw's book is a stimulating and learned contribution, there are obviously some lessons in academic fairness that he could learn.

---

77. Pietersma 1984.
78. Shaw 2014, 141.
79. See only his use of "likely," "perhaps" or "might not?" in Shaw 2014, 245–63.
80. Shaw 2014, 265.

Bibliography

Aly, Zaki, and Ludwig Koenen. 1980. *Three Rolls of the Early Septuagint: Genesis and Deuteronomy*. Papyrologische Texte und Abhandlungen 27. Bonn: Habelt.

Barthélemy, Dominique. 1963. *Les Devanciers d'Aquila*. VTSup 10. Leiden: Brill.

Baudissin, Wolf Wilhelm Graf. 1929. *Kyrios als Gottesname im Judentum und seine Stelle in der Religionsgeschichte*. Edited by O. Eissfeldt. 4 vols. Giessen: Töpelmann.

Dahl, Nils A., and Alan F. Segal. 1978. "Philo and the Rabbis on the Name of God." *JSJ* 9:1–28.

Eidsvåg, Gunnar Magnus. 2013. "The Paleo-Hebrew Tetragram in 8ḤevXIIgr." *JSCS* 46:86–100.

Fitzmyer, Joseph A. 1975. "Der semitische Hintergrund des neutestamentlichen Kyriostitels." Pages 267–98 in *Jesus Christus in Historie und Theologie: Neutestamentliche Festschrift für Hans Conzelmann zum 60. Geburtstag*. Edited by Georg Strecker and Hans Conzelmann. Tübingen: Mohr Siebeck. [Published in English: 1979. "The Semitic Background of the New Testament Kyrios-Title." Pages 115–42 in *A Wandering Aramean: Collected Aramaic Essays*. Edited by Joseph A. Fitzmyer. SBLMS 25. Missoula: Scholars Press]

Furuli, Rolf. 1999. *The Role of Theology and Bias in Bible Translations: With a Special Look at the New World Translation of Jehovah's Witnesses*. Huntington Beach: Elihu Books.

Gropp, Douglas M. 2001. *Wadi Daliyeh II: The Samaria Papyri for Wadi Daliyeh; Qumran Cave 4.XXVIII; Miscellanea, Part 2*. Edited by Eileen Schuller et al. DJD 28. Oxford: Clarendon.

Hanhart, Robert. 1978. Review of *Papyrus Grecs Biblique (Papyrus F. Inv. 266) Volumina de la Genèse et du Deutéronome*, by F. Dunand. *OLZ* 73:39–45.

———. 1988. "Die Bedeutung der Septuaginta für die Definition des 'Hellenistischen Judentums.' " Pages 67–80 in *Congress Volume: Jerusalem, 1986*. Edited by J. A. Emerton. VTSup 40. Leiden: Brill.

———. 1994. "Textgeschichtliche Probleme der Septuaginta von ihrer Entstehung bis Origenes." Pages 1–19 in *Die Septuaginta zwischen Judentum und Christentum*. Edited by Martin Hengel and Anna Maria Schwemer. WUNT 1/72. Tübingen: Mohr Siebeck.

Howard, George. 1977. "The Tetragram and the New Testament." *JBL* 96:63–83.
Hurtado, Larry W. 1998. "The Origin of the *Nomina Sacra*: A Proposal." *JBL* 117:655–73.
Joosten, Jan. 2011. "Le Dieu Iaô et le tréfonds araméen des Septante." Pages 115–24 in *Eukarpa: Études sur la Bible et ses exégètes; en hommage à Gilles Dorival*. Edited by Mireille Loubet and Didier Pralon. Paris: Cerf.
Joüon, Paul, and Takamitsu Muraoka. 1996. *A Grammar of Biblical Hebrew*. 2 vols. SubBi 14. Rome: Pontifical Biblical Institute.
Kahle, Paul E. 1962. *Die Kairoer Genisa: Untersuchungen zur Geschichte des hebräischen Bibeltextes und seiner Übersetzungen*. Berlin: Akademie.
Katz, Paul. 1948. "Zur Aussprache von יְהוָה." *TZ* 4:467–69.
Kraft, Robert A. 2003. "The 'Textual Mechanics' of Early Jewish LXX/OG Papyri and Fragments." Pages 51-72 in *The Bible as Book: The Transmission of the Greek Text*. Edited by Scot McKendrick and Orlaith O'Sullivan. London: British Library; Newcastle: Oak Knoll.
Lust, Johan. 1996. "The Septuagint of Ezekiel according to Papyrus 967 and the Pentateuch." *ETL* 72:131-37.
———. 1997. "Mic 5,1-3 in Qumran and in the New Testament and Messianism in the Septuagint." Pages 65–88 in *The Scriptures in the Gospels*. Edited by Christopher M. Tuckett. BETL 131. Leuven: Peeters.
MacDonough, Sean M. 1999. *YHWH at Patmos: Rev. 1:4 in Its Hellenistic and Early Jewish Setting*. WUNT 2/107. Tübingen: Mohr Siebeck.
Marcus, David. 1999. "Aramaic Mnemonics in Codex Leningradensis." *TC* 4. https://tinyurl.com/SBL0468c.
McGregor, Leslie J. 1985. *The Greek Text of Ezekiel: An Examination of Its Homogeneity*. SCS 18. Atlanta: Scholars Press.
Parry, Donald W. 1996. "4QSam^a and the Tetragrammaton." Pages 106-25 in *Current Research and Technological Developments on the Dead Sea Scrolls*. Edited by Donald W. Parry and Stephen D. Ricks. STDJ 20. Leiden: Brill.
———. 1997. "Notes on Divine Name Avoidance in Scriptural Units of the Legal Texts of Qumran." Pages 437-49 in *Legal Texts and Legal Issues: Proceedings of the Second Meeting of the International Organization for Qumran Studies, Cambridge 1995*. Edited by Moshe Bernstein, Florentino García Martínez, and John Kampen. STDJ 23. Leiden: Brill.
Pietersma, Albert. 1984. "Kyrios or Tetragramm: A Renewed Quest for the Original Septuagint." Pages 85-101 in *De Septuaginta: Studies in*

Honour of John William Wevers on his Sixty-Fifth Birthday. Edited by Albert Pietersma and Claude E. Cox. Mississauga: Benben Publications.

Rahlfs, Alfred. 2004. *Verzeichnis der griechischen Handschriften des Alten Testaments: Bd. I,1. Die Überlieferung bis zum VIII. Jahrhundert.* Edited by Detlef Fraenkel. SVTGSup1.1. Göttingen: Vandenhoeck & Ruprecht.

Rösel, Martin. 1991. "Die Übersetzung der Gottesnamen in der Genesis-Septuaginta." Pages 357–77 in *Ernten, was man sät: Festschrift für Klaus Koch*. Edited by D. R. Daniels, U. Glessmer, and Martin Rösel. Neukirchen–Vluyn: Neukirchener Verlag.

———. 1998. "Theo-Logie der griechischen Bibel. Zur Wiedergabe der Gottesaussagen im LXX-Pentateuch." *VT* 48:49-62.

———. 2000a. *Adonaj—warum Gott "Herr" genannt wird*. FAT 29. Tübingen: Mohr Siebeck.

———. 2000b. "Names of God." Pages 600–602 in *Encyclopedia of the Dead Sea Scrolls*. Edited by L. H. Schiffman and J. C. VanderKam. New York: Oxford University Press.

———. 2000c. "Israels Psalmen in Ägypten? Papyrus Amherst 63 und die Psalmen XX und LXXV." *VT* 50:81–99.

———. 2014. "Der Herr des Daniel: Zur Übersetzung der Gottesnamen in der Daniel-LXX." Pages 399–411 in *Text—Textgeschichte—Textwirkung: Festschrift zum 65. Geburtstag von Siegfried Kreuzer*. Edited by Jonathan M. Robker, Frank Ueberschaer, and Thomas Wagner. AOAT 419. Münster: Ugarit-Verlag.

Royse, James R. 1991. "Philo, ΚΥΡΙΟΣ, and the Tetragrammaton." *SPhiloA* 3:167–82.

Schulz, Siegfried. 1962. "Maranatha und Kyrios Jesus." *ZNW* 53:125–44.

Shaw, Frank E. 2002. "The Earliest Non-Mystical Jewish Use of ΙΑΩ." PhD diss., University of Cincinnati.

———. 2014. *The Earliest Non-mystical Jewish Use of* Ιαω. CBET 70. Leuven: Peeters.

Skehan, Patrick W. 1957. "The Qumran Manuscripts and Textual Criticism." Pages 148–60 in *Volume du Congrès International pour l'étude de l'Ancien Testament, Strasbourg 1956*. Edited by G. W. Anderson et al. VTSup 4. Leiden: Brill.

———. 1980. "The Divine Name at Qumran, in the Masada-Scroll, and in the Septuagint." *BIOSCS* 13:14–44.

Smith, Jannes. 2012. "The Text-Critical Significance of Oxyrhynchus Papyrus 5101 (Ra 2227) for the Old Greek Psalter." *JSCS* 45:5–22.
Sollamo, Raija. 2003. "The Significance of Septuagint Studies." Pages 487-512 in *Emanuel: Studies in Hebrew Bible, Septuagint, and Dead Sea Scrolls in Honor of Emanuel Tov*. Edited by Shalom M. Paul, Robert A. Kraft, Lawrence H. Schiffman, and Weston W. Fields. VTSup 94. Leiden: Brill.
Stegemann, Hartmut. 1978. "Religionsgeschichtliche Erwägungen zu den Gottesbezeichnungen in den Qumrantexten." Pages 195-217 in *Qumrân: Sa piété, sa théologie et son milieu*. Edited by Mathias Delcor. BETL 46. Leuven: Peeters.
Tov, Emanuel. 1990. *The Greek Minor Prophets Scroll from Naḥal Ḥever (8ḤevXIIgr)*. The Seiyal Collection I. DJD 8. Oxford: Clarendon.
———. 1992. *Textual Criticism of the Hebrew Bible*. Minneapolis: Fortress.
———. 2003. "The Greek Biblical Texts from the Judean Desert." Pages 97-122 in *The Bible as Book: The Transmission of the Greek Text*. Edited by Scot McKendrick and Orlaith O'Sullivan. London: British Library; Newcastle: Oak Knoll.
———. 2014. "The Harmonizing Character of the Septuagint of Genesis 1–11." Pages 315-32 in *Die Septuaginta: Text, Wirkung, Rezeption*. Edited by Wolfgang Kraus and Siegfried Kreuzer. WUNT 1/325. Tübingen: Mohr Siebeck.
Trobisch, David. 2000. *The First Edition of the New Testament*. Oxford: Oxford University Press.
Waddell, W.G. 1944 "The Tetragrammaton in the LXX." *JTS* 45:158-61.
Walter, Nikolaus. 2001. "Die griechische Übersetzung der Schriften Israels." Pages 71-96 Band 1 in *Im Brennpunkt: Die Septuaginta; Studien zur Entstehung und Bedeutung der griechischen Bibel*. Edited by Heinz-Josef Fabry und Ulrich Offerhaus. BWANT 153. Stuttgart: Kohlhammer.
Wevers, John William. 1990. *Notes on the Greek Text of Exodus*. SCS 30. Atlanta: Scholars Press.
———. 1999. "The Balaam Narrative according to the Septuagint." Pages 133-44 in *Lectures et Relectures de la Bible: Festschrift P.-M. Bogaert*. Edited by Jean-Marie Auwers and André Wénin. BETL 144. Leuven: Peeters.
———. 2001. "The Rendering of the Tetragram in the Psalter and Pentateuch: A Comparative Study." Pages 21-35 in *The Old Greek Psalter: Studies in Honor of Albert Pietersma*. Edited by Robert J. V. Hiebert,

Claude E. Cox, and Peter J. Gentry. JSOTSup 332. Sheffield: Sheffield Academic.

Zauzich, Karl-Theodor. 1985. "Der Gott des aramäisch-demotischen Papyrus Amherst 63." *Göttinger Miszellen* 85:89–90.

14
Der hebräische Mensch im griechischen Gewand.
Anthropologische Akzentsetzungen in der Septuaginta

1. Das Problem

Um den hebräischen Menschen ist es eher still geworden.[1] Seit den wichtigen Veröffentlichungen von Ludwig Köhler, Werner H. Schmidt und vor allem Hans Walter Wolff scheint im Prinzip das Wesentliche gesagt zu sein. Neuere Lexikonartikel fassen diese Ergebnisse in der Regel nur zusammen oder modifizieren Details;[2] daneben hat noch das Thema der Gottebenbildlichkeit im Zusammenhang der Frage nach Menschenrecht und Menschenwürde eine gewisse Aufmerksamkeit erfahren.[3] Die wichtigsten Charakteristika hebräischer Anthropologie sind jedoch weitgehend unstrittig—wenn sie überhaupt verhandelt werden—sie lassen sich wie folgt zusammenfassen: Eine wesentliche Gemeinsamkeit alttestamentlicher Aussagen über den Menschen ist, dass ein ganzheitliches Ver-

---

1. Dieser Abschnitt des ursprünglichen Vortrages aus dem Jahr 2002 ist inzwischen nicht mehr gültig. Der erste Satz müsste nun lauten: „Der hebräische Mensch steht wieder im Rampenlicht." Dennoch ist der Abschnitt stehen geblieben, um zu dokumentieren, in wie kurzer Zeit sich das Interesse der Forschung geändert hat, s. auch Janowski 2005, 143, zur veränderten Lage. Zwischenzeitlich ist nicht nur Janowski 2006 erschienen, das aufgrund seiner differenzierten Darstellung weit über die Psalmen hinaus (so der Untertitel) als Standardwerk alttestamentlicher Anthropologie zu begreifen ist. Zu verweisen ist darüber hinaus auch auf Janowski 2005 und Wagner 2009. Die im Folgenden gegebene knappe Darstellung der Charakteristika alttestamentlicher Anthropologie ist dennoch nicht überholt.

2. Köhler 1953; Schmidt 1964; Wolff 1977. Zu nennen sind weiterhin Albertz 1993; Schroer/Staubli 1998, und die einschlägigen Artikel im ThWAT und THAT. Noch nicht zugänglich war zum Zeitpunkt der Erarbeitung der ursprünglichen Publikation im Jahr 2002: Janowski 2006.

3. Koch 2000; Groß 2000 (jeweils mit weiterführender Literatur).

ständnis vorausgesetzt wird. Eine Dichotomie, also die Trennung in Leib und Seele, oder gar eine weitergehende Trichotomie von Leib, Seele und Geist lässt sich nicht feststellen. Der Mensch wurde als Einheit gedacht, was aber beinhaltet, dass es einzelne Schichten des Personseins gibt, etwa die körperlich-vegetative, die emotionale, noetische und voluntative.[4] Alle diese Schichten können mit einem einzigen Lexem, לֵב, benannt werden. Mit ‚Herz' können folglich sowohl Emotionen, Wunsch und Wille, Denken, wie auch die Brust oder das konkrete Organ bezeichnet werden. Gleiches gilt auch für andere Lexeme: Organe, ihre Funktionen und deren psychosomatische Auswirkungen werden mit ein und demselben Begriff benannt; erinnert sei nur an Lexeme wie אַף; Nase (Gen 2,7), das zugleich für das Zornesschnauben (Gen 44,18) stehen kann, oder נפש, das sowohl für die Kehle/den Hals (Ps 69,2; Spr 23,2), die Atmung und die beseelte Personalität des Menschen stehen kann.[5]

Schon mit diesen knappen Beispielen wird deutlich, dass anthropologische Vorstellung einerseits und Sprache andererseits nicht zu trennen sind. Um im Bilde zu bleiben: Wer den hebräischen Menschen beschreiben will, muss sich in das hebräische Denken einfinden.[6]

Der Mensch ist nach der hebräischen Bibel nicht allein über seine Organe und deren Funktionen zu beschreiben, sondern zu seinem Wesen gehört die Gottesbeziehung untrennbar hinzu. Auch wenn er das Ebenbild Gottes ist—so Genesis 1,26–27—ist er nicht anders denn als Geschöpf zu verstehen. Wenn nun Gottes Schöpfung sehr gut ist, dann ist auch der Mensch so zu bewerten. Das bedeutet, dass etwa Begierden nicht als Ausdruck einer gottfeindlichen ἐπιθυμία zu verstehen sind, sondern zum Schöpfungswerk Gottes gehören. Zum Menschsein gehört damit auch die Freiheit zum Handeln innerhalb des von Gott gesetzten Lebensraumes. Zum angemessenen Umgang mit dieser Freiheit leiten in älterer Zeit die weisheitlichen Lebensregeln an, die in späterer Zeit zunehmend theologisiert werden: Weisheit und Gottesfurcht fallen nun ineinander; die Tora wird zur Leitlinie der Bewährung.

---

4. Dies im Anschluss an Fabry 1984, 425.

5. Die in deutschen Bibeln übliche Übersetzung „Seele" ist dem hebräischen Lexem unangemessen, vgl. dazu Seebass 1986, 543–45.

6. Dazu sind noch immer wichtige Anregungen zu finden bei Bomann 1983. Es ist bedauerlich, dass dieser Ansatz besonders in der Septuaginta-Forschung kaum aufgenommen und erweitert wurde.

In zeitlicher Hinsicht ist der Lebensraum des Menschen begrenzt auf das irdische Leben. Der Tod gilt in der Regel als unüberwindliche Grenze, hier endet auch die Gottesbeziehung. Erst in ganz später Zeit, als der stets vorausgesetzte Zusammenhang von Tun und Ergehen innerhalb des einzelnen Lebens kaum noch sichtbar erscheint,[7] verstärkt sich die Perspektive, dass es auch eine Lebensdimension nach der Todesschwelle geben kann (Dan 12; 2.Makk 7).[8] Der hebräische Mensch macht sich auf den Weg in die jenseitige Welt.

So etwa lassen sich die anthropologischen Grundlinien des Alten Testaments in drastischer Verkürzung zusammenfassen. Dies wird in der Regel auch als Basis des neutestamentlichen Menschenbildes formuliert. So liest man etwa in der TRE: „Das Neue Testament steht auf dem Boden der uneingeschränkten Bejahung des irdisch-leibhaftigen Menschen im Schöpfungsglauben der hebräischen Bibel. Deren anthropologische Sprache ... hält sich im NT weitgehend durch."[9] Hier nun setzen die Überlegungen dieser Skizze an: Ist es wirklich so, dass die anthropologische Sprache, derer sich das hellenistische Judentum und die frühe Christenheit bedienten, die gleiche ist wie die des AT? Sind hebräische Aussagen und ihre griechischen Übersetzungen wirklich deckungsgleich?[10]

Die Frage ist natürlich eine rhetorische, denn die moderne Übersetzungswissenschaft hat eindeutig bestätigt,[11] was schon der Enkel des Jesus

---

7. Vgl. dazu zusammenfassend Rösel 2001a, 931–33; Grund 2005, 654–56.

8. Die oben wiedergegebene Mehrheitsmeinung, dass die Jenseitserwartung eine späte Entwicklung in Israel ist, wird in jüngster Zeit unter Hinweis auf religionsgeschichtliche Parallelen und Texte wie 1.Sam 2,6 oder Ps 68,21 zunehmend kritisiert, vgl. dazu Albani 2001. Die Diskussion darüber kann hier nicht geführt werden, doch es ist m.E. einleuchtend, wenn die starre Perspektive des Nacheinanders der Erwartungen künftig durch die Annahme abgelöst wird, dass es in unterschiedlichen Kreisen der israelitischen Gesellschaft unterschiedliche Jenseitsvorstellungen gegeben hat. Dafür sprechen auch Texte wie Ps 73 oder 49, in denen mit dem Stichwort לקח eine postmortale Erwartung signalisiert wird. Zur Problematik s. auch Janowski 2006, 338–39.

9. Hegermann 1993, 481. Anders die Pointierung von Frevel 2003, 122, der trotz der „Kontinuität im Menschenverständnis" auf „erhebliche Unterschiede" verweist.

10. Zu nennen wären außerdem mögliche aramäische Zwischenstufen, die etwa in den alten Targumim greifbar sind. Diese bleiben hier aus Gründen der Übersichtlichkeit ausgeblendet, doch vgl. zum Problem Koch 2003 (mit Literatur).

11. Die Literatur zu diesem Problemfeld ist nahezu unübersehbar. Zum Problem der modernen Bibelübersetzungen vgl. etwa Nida und Tabor 1969; zur Übersetzungswissenschaft Albrecht 1998; Stolze 2001.

Sirach seufzend feststellte, als er das Buch seines Großvaters ins Griechische übersetzte: „Es ist ja nicht das gleiche, ob man etwas im hebräischen Text liest oder ob es in eine andere Sprache übertragen wurde" (Prolog zu Sirach 21–22). Einige erste Stichproben aus der Septuaginta mögen das belegen: Das bereits angesprochene Lexem לב ‚Herz' kann mit einer ganzen Reihe von griechischen Äquivalenten wiedergegeben werden, da das griechische καρδία ‚Herz' und dessen Bedeutungsumfang den Übersetzern nicht immer passend erschien. So finden sich etwa διάνοια ‚Gesinnung' Gen 8,21, νοῦς ‚Verstand' Ex 7,23, ψυχή ‚Seele / Lebenskraft' Ps 21(20),3, oder φρόνησις ‚Denken' Prov 9,16; 19,8 als weitere Äquivalente. Im Gegenzug kann καρδία auch für Wörter wie נפש ‚Vitalität' Ps 131(130),1, קרב ‚Inneres' Ps 93(94),19 und בטן ‚Leib / Inneres' Hab 3,16 (MSS SC) stehen; für קרב ‚Inneres' wurde im Gegenzug in Jer 38(31),33 διάνοια ‚Gesinnung' verwendet. Für נפש ‚Vitalität' konnten so unterschiedliche Übersetzungen wie σῶμα ‚Leib / Körper' Gen 36,6, πνεῦμα ‚Geist' Sir 39,28, ζωή ‚Leben' Sir 11,14, ὑγίεια ‚Gesundheit' Est 9,31 oder ψυχή ‚Seele' (Standard-Äquivalent) gewählt werden. Und ψυχή ‚Seele' konnte wiederum in Hi 27,4 für לָשׁוֹן ‚Sprache' stehen, weil an der konkreten Stelle das Denken gemeint ist.[12] Das Bedeutungsspektrum der hebräischen Wörter *kann* also an solchen Stellen gar nicht unverändert in die griechische Bibel übernommen worden sein.

Das Problem verschärft sich, wenn man linguistische Fragen stärker berücksichtigt. Denn selbst wenn jeweils die Standard-Äquivalente verwendet wurden (נפש – ψυχή; לב – καρδία, etc.), bedeutet das ja nicht, dass die Konnotationen notwendig deckungsgleich wären. Das mag vielleicht für den jeweiligen Übersetzer noch zutreffen, speziell dann, wenn das Hebräische seine Muttersprache gewesen ist. Doch sofern er in einem griechischen Sprachumfeld aufgewachsen ist und das Hebräische erst später gelernt hat—dies ist für Alexandrien zumindest wahrscheinlich und bei einigen Übersetzern angesichts ihrer geringen Kompetenz im Hebräischen durchaus sicher[13]—muss man davon ausgehen, dass Konnotationen vorherrschend werden, die vom Sprachgebrauch der

---

12. Vgl. Siegert 2001, 71.

13. Das gilt umso mehr, wenn man die m.E. sehr plausible Annahme berücksichtigt, dass in Alexandrien das Hebräische mittels der LXX-Übersetzung etwa des Pentateuch gelehrt und gelernt wurde, so Gzella 2002, 33. Auf diese Weise würden sogar die Konnotationen der griechischen Übersetzung das Verständnis der später übersetzten hebräischen Schriften beeinflusst haben. Es sei aber angemerkt, dass die

griechisch-hellenistischen Umwelt her zu bestimmen sind. Es ist folglich einsichtig, dass die griechische und hebräische anthropologische Sprache nicht vollständig deckungsgleich sein können.

Damit wird aber die Forschung vor die Aufgabe gestellt, die wesentlichen Differenzen zwischen den beiden Textzeugnissen—hebräischer Text einerseits, Septuaginta andererseits—ordnend zusammenzustellen. Dabei sei nur am Rande auf das bekannte, aber m.E. unzureichend beachtete Faktum verwiesen, dass ja vor allem die griechische Bibel die Bezugsgröße der meisten neutestamentlichen und altkirchlichen Autoren gewesen ist.[14] Die Erhellung der theologischen und anthropologischen Leitgedanken der Septuaginta könnte folglich ein wichtiger Gesprächsanstoß zwischen den theologischen Disziplinen sein.[15]

2. Der Stand der Forschung

Seit dem Beginn einer eigenständigen Septuagintaforschung hat es auf christlicher und jüdischer Seite verschiedene Versuche gegeben, die exegetischen und inhaltlich-theologischen Charakteristika der Septuaginta zu erhellen.[16] Einen gewissen Höhepunkt hat dies im deutschsprachigen Raum mit der Arbeit von Georg Bertram erreicht, der in einer Vielzahl von Artikeln für das ThWNT nachzuweisen versuchte, dass die wesentliche Prägung neutestamentlicher Zentralbegriffe in der LXX vollzogen wurde. Daher sei die griechische Bibel als *praeparatio evangelica* zu sehen. Im Hintergrund dieser Thesen Bertrams—der zu den Deutschen Christen zu zählen ist—steht wohl ein neo-marcionitisches Konzept der Entsemitisierung der Bibel. So ist auch verständlich, dass seinen Bemühungen um

---

Septuaginta-Forschung an diesem Punkt noch nicht über Vermutungen hinausgekommen ist.

14. Dazu programmatisch Müller 1996; Hengel 1994.

15. Leider fehlt die LXX vollständig in der gesamtbiblisch orientierten anthropologischen Skizze von Frevel und Wischmeyer 2003. Im Teil „Neues Testament" hätte es sich z.B. im Abschnitt „Sprachliche Herkunft" (S. 68) angeboten, auf die LXX als Übersetzungsinstanz hebräischer Denkkategorien hinzuweisen. Ebenso wenig wird bei den Ausführungen zum anthropologischen Vokabular des Paulus (S. 93–95) oder unter der Überschrift „Von der Kehle zur Seele" im Bereich AT (S. 29–30) auf die Problematik verwiesen. Möglicherweise ist das einer der Gründe für das Unbehagen, das Frevel 2003, 121–22 hinsichtlich des eigenen Werks formuliert.

16. Vgl. Frankel 1851; Deissmann 1903, 162; Geiger 1928.

die Theologie der griechischen Bibel, die er „Septuaginta-Frömmigkeit"[17] nannte, kaum Forscher gefolgt sind; zumindest in Deutschland beschäftigte man sich zudem nach dem Kriege fast nur bei textkritischen Fragestellungen mit der LXX.

Die älteren Arbeiten zur Geisteswelt der LXX sind aber auch aus methodischen Gründen problematisch. In ihnen wird nämlich viel zu pauschal davon ausgegangen, dass die Septuaginta eine Einheit ist. Die neuere Forschung hat dagegen erwiesen, dass die einzelnen Bücher über einen Zeitraum von nahezu 300 Jahren hinweg übersetzt wurden, nicht nur in Alexandrien, sondern auch in Palästina und Leontopolis.[18] Hinzu kommen interessante Näherbestimmungen, etwa in welcher Reihenfolge die Bücher mutmaßlich übersetzt wurden—was Aufschluss über die Bedeutung der Bücher zur jeweiligen Zeit in der jeweiligen Region geben kann.

Am wichtigsten ist jedoch die Erkenntnis, dass die einzelnen Bücher nach unterschiedlichen hermeneutischen Kriterien übersetzt worden sind. So finden sich nahezu sklavische Übersetzungen des hebräischen Textes, die für griechische Ohren gewiss barbarisch geklungen haben.[19] Daneben stehen aber auch Bücher wie der griechische Hiob, die man streckenweise als griechisches *re-writing* der Vorlage verstehen kann; die Bindung an den Text ist hier deutlich lockerer. Aus all dem wird deutlich, dass man nur noch in einem sehr eingeschränkten Sinne von „der" Septuaginta reden kann. Methodische Exaktheit verlangt daher, dass zunächst die Schriften

---

17. Vgl. etwa Bertram 1961, 1707–9; ders. 1957. Zu Bertram vgl. auch die wichtigen Bemerkungen von Walter 2001, 83–84.

18. Hier hat sich besonders die Studie von Seeligmann 1948, als wegweisend erwiesen, vgl. auch ders. 1990. Hilfreiche Übersichten zur aktuellen Datierung und Lokalisierung der einzelnen LXX-Übersetzungen finden sich bei Harl/Dorival/Munnich 1994, 92.

19. Das betrifft etwa die im Vergleich mit dem Griechischen sehr einfache Syntax, die in der Regel diejenige des hebräischen Textes nachahmt und folglich im Griechischen ungebräuchliche Nominalsätze oder Häufungen von Parataxen aufweist. Schwierigkeiten bereitet auch die Neigung der Übersetzer, Kompositverben und Neologismen zu verwenden, vgl. dazu etwa Siegert 2001, 149, und jetzt Usener 2004, 89. Einen einsamen Höhepunkt erreicht dies in der Übersetzungstechnik des Aquila, vgl. dazu zusammenfassend Fernández Marcos 1994, 115–17; eindrucksvolle Beispiele für dessen Übersetzungsweise (und Hinweise auf Inkonsequenzen) finden sich bei Barr 1979, 37. Zu unterscheiden ist davon das Phänomen der bewusst uneindeutigen Übersetzungen, auf das Schenker 1994 hingewiesen hat.

je für sich untersucht werden, ihr textkritisches, sprachliches und hermeneutisch-theologisches Profil erstellt wird. Erst danach lässt sich fragen, ob es tatsächlich Gemeinsamkeiten gibt, die als spezifische Septuaginta-Theologie gelten können.[20]

Mit diesen methodischen Überlegungen ist zugleich die Situation angesprochen, in der sich die gegenwärtige Septuaginta-Forschung befindet. In den letzten fünfzehn Jahren haben sich die Studien zu einzelnen Übersetzungen nahezu explosionsartig vermehrt, weltweit gibt es Projekte zur Übersetzung der LXX in die jeweilige Landessprache.[21] Nur wenige Bereiche der alttestamentlichen Wissenschaft haben zur Zeit eine solche Dynamik und einen vergleichbar hohen Innovationsgrad. Gleichzeitig— und das ist auch typisch für solche Aufbruchssituationen—gibt es eine große Methodenvielfalt, die bei denselben Büchern zu völlig divergenten Ergebnissen führen können.[22]

Dabei sind zwei große Themenbereiche strittig, die kurz umrissen seien: Die erste Frage ist die nach dem Verhältnis von Vorlage und Übersetzung. Eine Reihe von Forschern geht davon aus, dass man nur in Ausnahmefällen einen eigenen Aussagewillen der Übersetzer erkennen könne. Die große Mehrheit der Abweichungen sei auf eine abweichende hebräische Vorlage zurückzuführen, die uns zwar nicht erhalten ist, die man aber nach den Funden von Qumran als prinzipielle Möglichkeit anzunehmen habe.[23] Nun haben die gründlichen Untersuchungen zu einzelnen Büchern—paradigmatisch sei hier der am besten erforschte Pentateuch angeführt—gezeigt, dass man durchaus mit einer großen Zahl absichtlicher Neuinterpretationen der Texte im Vorgang der Übersetzung rechnen muss, verwiesen sei hier etwa auf messianische Interpretationen in Gen 49 oder im 4. Bileam-Orakel.[24]

---

20. Dazu programmatisch Rösel 2006a.

21. Zu nennen sind vor allem die groß angelegte „Bible d'Alexandrie" von der seit 1986 insgesamt 12 Bände erschienen sind, die „New English Translation of the Septuagint" (2007, vgl. die Darstellung der Prinzipien durch Pietersma 2007) und das Projekt „Septuaginta-Deutsch" (2009); einen Eindruck davon gibt Utzschneider 2001.

22. Vgl. etwa zu Gen 1 und 2: Rösel 1998a, und die Entgegnungen von Hendel 1999; Brown, 1999. Zu den Psalmen vgl. etwa Austermann 2000, mit Schaper 1995.

23. Dieser Grunddissens steht hinter der von der Society of Biblical Literature unter http://www.tinyurl.com/SBL0468b publizierten äußerst ausführlichen (und m.E. weit überzogenen) Kritik von James Barr an Jobes und Silva 2000.

24. Eine ausführliche Exegese der entsprechenden Texte jetzt bei Rösel 2006b [Kapitel 5 in diesem Band].

Der zweite prinzipielle Einwand besteht darin, dass behauptet wird, dass die Übersetzungsäquivalente der LXX die gleichen semantischen Konnotationen wie die hebräische Vorlage aufweisen würden. Daher dürften sie nicht als Zeichen für eine Eigenaussage des griechischen Textes gewertet werden. Diese Position—hier ist v.a. auf James Barr zu verweisen[25]—rechnet folglich mit einer jüdisch-hellenistischen Sondersprache. Dafür lassen sich zwar bei einzelnen Begriffen Anhaltspunkte finden, doch interessanterweise handelt es sich dabei vor allem um Neologismen der Kultsprache wie θυσιαστήριον (Opferstätte) oder ἱλαστήριον (Sühnestätte).[26] Hinzu kommt, dass sich die Konnotationen eines Lexems nicht einfach aus isolierender Lexikographie ableiten lassen, sondern von der konkreten Satzsemantik, also vom jeweiligen Kontext her zu bestimmen sind.

Was im Folgenden als anthropologische Akzentsetzungen der LXX skizziert werden soll, versucht, die vorgetragenen methodischen Probleme zu berücksichtigen. Angesichts der dargestellten Forschungslage ist allerdings nicht mit einer ausgearbeiteten Anthropologie zu rechnen, sondern es geht darum, einige besonders augenfällige und wirkungsgeschichtlich interessante Phänomene vorzuführen. Dabei werden in einem ersten Schritt wichtige Einzelübersetzungen vorgeführt. Danach wird der Blick auf umfassendere Denkkonzepte ausgeweitet. Wegen der nötigen Differenzierung stammen die Beispiele in der Regel aus dem Pentateuch, den Psalmen und den griechischen Proverbien.

3. Beispiele

3.1. Der Mensch als Ebenbild Gottes

Zu den anthropologischen Schlüsseltexten der Bibel gehört vor allem die Urgeschichte Gen 1–11, die auch in ihrer griechischen Fassung aufschlussreich ist.[27] Hier ist zunächst von höchstem Interesse, dass die beiden Schöpfungsberichte in Gen 1 und 2 nach dem Muster des platonischen Dialogs Timaios zu einer größeren Einheit zusammengefasst wurden: Gen 1 beschreibt nun die Erschaffung der unsichtbaren Ideenwelt, Gen 2 die

---

25. Vgl. Barr 1965.
26. Dazu die grundlegende Arbeit von Daniel 1966, 26–30.
27. Die hier verwendeten Beispieltexte habe ich ausführlich bearbeitet in Rösel 1994; diese Studie wird im Folgenden ohne weitere Seitenreferenzen vorausgesetzt; die Argumentationen sind leicht über die Versangaben zu finden.

14. Der hebräische Mensch im griechischen Gewand 325

der materialen Welt. Dies lässt sich an einer Fülle von Details nachweisen, als Signalgeber dient bereits die Übersetzung von Gen 1,2: Nach dem hebräischen Text ist die Erde תהו ובהו , wüst und leer. Nach der griechischen Fassung aber ist sie ἀόρατος καὶ ἀκατασκεύαστος; *unsichtbar* in Hinsicht auf ihr Urbild und noch *unbearbeitet* in Bezug auf das Material.

Diese Bezugnahme auf Plato hatte offenbar weitreichende Folgen für die Vorstellung von der Gottebenbildlichkeit des Menschen: Im hebräischen Text Gen 1,26 steht als Selbstaufforderung Gottes: „Lasst uns eine Menschheit machen als unser (Repräsentations-) Bild gemäß einer Entsprechung zu uns selbst" (נעשה אדם בצלמנו כדמותנו).[28] Dies ist als funktionale Aussage zu betrachten; der Mensch soll stellvertretend die Herrschaft Gottes über die Welt—angesprochen sind die Tiere—ausüben.[29] In der griechischen Version hat sich die Perspektive verschoben: Die Menschheit wird geschaffen κατ' εἰκόνα ἡμετέραν καὶ καθ' ὁμοίωσιν, „gemäß unserem Urbild und gemäß Übereinstimmung." Die beiden Begriffe εἰκών und ὁμοίωσις werden durch Verwendung der gleichen Präposition κατά gleichgeordnet; der Mensch wird nun nicht mehr *als* (Repräsentations-) Bild, sondern *nach* einem Urbild geschaffen.[30] Dabei sei nur kurz daran erinnert, dass die Vorstellung von der sichtbaren Welt als εἰκών eine Zentralvorstellung platonischer Philosophie ist. So ist schon in Gen 1 ein folgenreicher Perspektivenwechsel zu beobachten: Es geht nicht mehr um die Funktion des Menschen hinsichtlich der Herrschaft über die Welt, sondern um seine Qualität als Abbild und damit um Gott als das Urbild. Die spätere Auslegung hat dann den λόγος als εἰκών verstanden, dem im Menschen die Vernunft νοῦς entspricht. Die griechische Bibel hat hier also die Tür zu einem dichotomischen Menschenverständnis geöffnet, durch die schon die Weisheit Salomonis,[31] dann Philo, aber auch Texte wie Kol 3,10; Eph 4,24 und später die patristisch-mittelalterliche Exegese gegangen sind.

Im Horizont von Gen 1 drängt sich dann auch in 2,7 ein entsprechendes Verständnis auf, wenn der Körper des Menschen aus Staub geschaf-

---

28. Übersetzung nach Koch 2000, 10.
29. Zur Interpretation s. auch Groß 2000, 18–20.
30. Dieses Verständnis wird auch durch die Aufnahme der Formulierung—gegen den hebräischen Text—in Gen 5,1 unterstützt; dem Übersetzer lag ganz offensichtlich an der Qualifikation des Menschen als Abbild.
31. SapSal 2,23; zur Auslegung vgl. Groß 2000, 36–37, der sich der in meiner Dissertation vorgetragenen Deutung von Gen 1,26LXX anschließt.

fen wird und der Mensch durch Anblasen mit dem Lebensatem zu einer lebendigen Seele wird. Hier jedoch kann man eine dichotomische Vorstellung als vom hebräischen Text vorgegeben verstehen, so dass in der LXX nur die Standard-Äquivalente verwendet wurden. Auffällig ist zudem, dass der Zusammenhang von אדמה und אדם nicht wiedergegeben wird; damit fällt m.E. ein wesentlicher Verfremdungseffekt der hebräischen anthropologischen Aussage weg. Dem entspricht, dass in 3,19 der Zusammenhang vom Staub, aus dem der Mensch genommen wurde, und dem, zu dem er zurückkehrt, vermieden wird. Ebenso bleibt in 2,23 der sprachliche Zusammenhang von איש und אשה unübersetzt. Man kann folgern, dass im Griechischen fremd klingende Aussagen vermieden wurden— ob bewusst oder unbewusst, ist kaum sicher zu entscheiden. Wichtig ist jedenfalls, dass durch solche Differenzen auf der Ebene der Rezeption völlig neue Verstehensmuster möglich werden.[32]

3.2. Die Erkenntnisfähigkeit des Menschen

Eine weitere entscheidende Differenzierung wird im zweiten Schöpfungsbericht vollzogen, wo es in 2,9 um den Baum der Erkenntnis geht. Nach dem hebräischen Text pflanzt Gott einen Baum der Erkenntnis des Guten und Bösen (עץ הדעת טוב ורע). Auch hier bietet die LXX durch Zufügung eines Wortes eine charakteristisch verschiedene Aussage, denn ihr zufolge wird ein Baum gepflanzt, der das Wissen vermittelt, was von Gut und Böse *erkennbar* ist (τὸ ξύλον τοῦ εἰδέναι γνωστὸν καλοῦ καὶ πονηροῦ). Es gibt demnach Dimensionen der Erkenntnis, die den Menschen nicht zugänglich sind;[33] später wird noch deutlicher werden, wie wichtig das Thema der Erkenntnis den LXX-Übersetzern gewesen sein muss.

3.3. Geist und Fleisch

Ein wesentlicher Einschnitt für die Menschheit ist nach der hebräischen Bibel die Sintflut. Auch hier hat die griechische Version ihre eigenen Akzente gesetzt, dies schon in der kurzen Notiz über die Engelehen. Der hebräische Text von Gen 6,3 ist nicht völlig klar und bereitet der Exegese

---

32. Dazu etwa Loader 2004, 126–28.
33. Vgl. auch die differenzierende Übersetzung in 3,5, wo durch die seltene Verwendung des Plural ὡς θεοί, für כאלהים zwischen Gott (Sg. θεός in V.5a) und den Menschen unterschieden wird.

bis heute Schwierigkeiten.³⁴ Für unseren Zusammenhang wichtig ist die Tatsache, dass die LXX auch hier wieder zwei Bestandteile des menschlichen Wesens gesehen hat: Gottes Geist soll nicht für die Ewigkeit in den Menschen bleiben, weil sie Fleisch sind (οὐ μὴ καταμείνῃ τὸ πνεῦμά μου ἐν τοῖς ἀνθρώποις τούτοις εἰς τὸν αἰῶνα διὰ τὸ εἶναι αὐτοὺς σάρκας). πνεῦμα und σάρξ stehen sich hier in einer Ausschließlichkeit gegenüber,³⁵ die dem hebräischen Denken unbekannt ist.³⁶ Sie passt allerdings gut in die zeitgenössische stoische Philosophie, in der πνεῦμα als beseelender Lebenshauch, als die gottgegebene Vernunft gilt, die den Menschen leitet.

Auch bei der Beschreibung der Schuld der Menschen, mit der die Sintflut begründet wird, lässt sich Einblick in das Verständnis des Übersetzers gewinnen: Nach 6,5 ist der Grund der Flut nicht eine allgemeine Bosheit aller Menschen, sondern konkrete schlechte Handlungen; jeder Mensch richtet sein Denken auf Übeltaten. Ausgenommen ist Noah, der sich—im Unterschied zu den anderen Menschen—vor Gott bewährt hat. Diese Interpretation wird durch Gen 8,21 gestützt: Die Erde wird hinfort nicht mehr wegen der Menschheit (MT: בעבור האדם) verflucht werden, sondern wegen der *schlechten Taten* der Menschen (διὰ τὰ ἔργα τῶν ἀνθρώπων).³⁷ Doch nun wird die Qualifikation des Menschen grundsätzlicher: Seine Gesinnung—hier steht διάνοια für לב—ist grundsätzlich auf böse Taten gerichtet; daher wären weitere Strafen sinnlos. Die LXX ist zwar skeptisch, was den Menschen betrifft, doch zur Vorstellung einer prinzipiellen Schlechtigkeit hält sie Abstand. Ob das mit der *Eikon*-Vorstellung des Übersetzers zu tun hat, muss dahingestellt bleiben; denkbar ist es zumindest.

Im Zusammenhang der Gegenüberstellung von πνεῦμα und σάρξ ist nun von besonderem Interesse, dass der Übersetzer bei der Wiedergabe von רוח offenbar bewusst differenzierend vorgegangen ist. Denn er hat nur dann πνεῦμα als Äquivalent gewählt, wenn es um eine positive,

---

34. Vgl. nur als neuesten deutschsprachigen Kommentar Seebass 1996, 187.
35. So auch Harl 1986, 126.
36. In der biblischen Tradition ist einzig Jes 31,3 zu nennen (ומצרים אדם ולא־ אל וסוסיהם בשר ולא־רוח), hier sind allerdings die Konnotationen deutlich anders. Immerhin lässt sich in einer schwierigen Passage in 4Q417 (4QInstructionᶜ), Frag. 1, I, 14–18 ebenfalls die Gegenüberstellung von Fleisch und Geist finden, die mit der Differenzierung von Gut und Böse verbunden ist (Hinweis von Klaus Koch). Vgl. auch die Übersicht über dualistische Anthropologien bei Gzella 2002, 104–6.
37. Eine vergleichbare Betonung der konkreten Einzeltaten des Menschen ist schon in der Verfluchung in Gen 3,17 (LXX) zu sehen.

belebende Kraft geht. An Stellen, an denen es etwa um eine bedrückte Gemütsverfassung geht (Gen 41,8; 26,35) oder um den Abendwind (Gen 3,8), wird πνεῦμα nicht verwendet; ein klarer Hinweis darauf, dass zumindest der Genesis-Übersetzer eine klare Vorstellung von dem hat, was πνεῦμα bedeutet.[38]

3.4. Die Seele[39]

Trotz dieser in der Genesis festgestellten Differenzen zwischen den beiden Textfassungen soll nicht der Eindruck entstehen, als hätte man es mit einer Art *re-written Bible* zu tun, wie man sie etwa aus Qumran oder vom Jubiläenbuch her kennt. Im Zuge der Übersetzung wusste man sich immer eng an das Original gebunden und hat daher in der Regel keine konsequente Uminterpretation vorgenommen.[40] Das lässt sich etwa am Umgang mit נפש sehen, das fast durchgängig mit ψυχή übersetzt wurde. Doch das Bedeutungsspektrum des hebräischen Lexems ist so weit, dass nicht immer das Standard-Äquivalent verwendet werden konnte. So steht in der Genesis einmal für ואת־הנפש אשר־עשו בחרן „alle Leute, die sie in Haran gewonnen hatten" (12,5) καὶ πᾶσαν ψυχήν ἣν ἐκτήσαντο ἐν Χαρραν „jede Seele…". Dann kann aber auch כל־נפשות ביתו „alle Leute seines Hauses" mit πάντα τὰ σώματα τοῦ οἴκου αὐτοῦ „alle Körper" übersetzt werden (36,6), was für griechische Ohren gewiss eindeutiger geklungen hat.

Andere Übersetzer haben sich aber meist eng an die Standard-Äquivalente gehalten. Doch oft kommt es gerade wegen des wörtlichen Festhaltens an der Gleichung נֶפֶשׁ–ψυχή zu einem ganz anderen Sinn, vgl. Lev 21,1: die Priester dürfen sich nicht an der an einer Leiche noch haftenden Lebenskraft verunreinigen: לנפש לא־יטמא. In der LXX wird daraus durch Verwendung des Plurals: ἐν ταῖς ψυχαῖς οὐ μιανθήσονται; die Priester dürfen sich nicht *seelisch* verunreinigen.[41] Auch wenn also im Sinne einer

---

38. Dies mit Scharbert 1972, 124. Besonders interessant sind auch zwei Stellen im Numeribuch, an denen offenbar von himmlischen Geistern im Umkreis Gottes die Rede ist (ὁ θεὸς τῶν πνευμάτων; 16,22; 27,16); dies passt dazu, dass πνεῦμα deutlich positiv konnotiert ist.

39. Vgl. zu diesem Thema ausführlicher Rösel 2009.

40. Eine Ausnahme ist allerdings der differenzierte Gebrauch der Gottesnamen in der Genesis, s. dazu Rösel 1991b, aber auch die—wenn auch nicht immer durchgehaltene—Tendenz zur Vermeidung anthropomorpher Aussagen über Gott, vgl. dazu die Studie von Fritsch 1943, zusammenfassend jetzt Siegert 2001, 247–49.

41. So Scharbert 1972, 131, anders übersetzen Wevers 1997, 331, und Harlé und

14. Der hebräische Mensch im griechischen Gewand 329

Wort-für-Wort Entsprechung übersetzt wird, muss der Sinn nicht der gleiche bleiben.[42] Generell kann jedoch im Falle von ψυχή tatsächlich gesagt werden, dass die weiten Konnotationen des hebräischen Ausgangslexems offenbar auf die griechische Übersetzung übertragen werden konnten. Das liegt darin begründet, dass es einen vorplatonischen Gebrauch von ψυχή gegeben hat, der dem von נפש sehr nahe kommt.[43] Offen bleibt jedoch die Frage, wie ein einsprachig-griechischer Leser diese Stellen verstanden hat; ob er hier nicht nahezu notwendig den späteren, philosophischen *Psyche*-Begriff sehen musste.[44]

Das legt sich etwa in der Schöpfungsgeschichte nahe, wo in Gen 1,20–21 und 1,30 anders als im MT davon gesprochen wird, dass die Erde Lebewesen *mit lebenden Seelen* (1,20; Plural gegen MT) hervorgehen lassen soll, dass Gott *jede Seele* der Kriechtiere geschaffen habe (1,21), und dass die Tiere in sich die *Seele des Lebens* haben (1,30). Die Seele gilt also in besonderer Weise als von Gott geschaffen; hier ließ sich von späteren Lesern leicht die philosophisch geprägte Vorstellung von der *psyche* finden und als biblisch begründet verstehen.[45]

Ebenso ist festzuhalten, dass an einer Vielzahl von Stellen ganz typische griechische Begriffe wie ἐπιθυμία oder διάνοια verwendet wurden,[46] die v.a. für לב stehen; καρδία steht dementsprechend seltener. Hier wird die Sprach- und Denkwelt der Umwelt so weit aufgenommen, dass nun zwischen dem Organ und der geistigen Gegebenheit oder Verfassung getrennt wird. Damit wird aber buchübergreifend ein wichtiger Aspekt des einheitlichen Menschenbildes der hebräischen Bibel aufgegeben.[47]

Pralon 1988, 177. Auffällig ist die Verwendung des Plurals ψυχαῖς für den hebräischen Singular; dies scheint mir für Scharberts Auslegung zu sprechen.

42. Dies auch als notwendige Ergänzung zu der Vorstellung der Interlinearität, die sich zunehmend in der US-amerikanischen und kanadischen LXX-Forschung verbreitet, vgl. dazu jetzt Pietersma 2002.

43. So die Ergebnisse von Bratsiotis 1966; Lys 1966.

44. Das zeigt sich etwa im später übersetzten Proverbienbuch an einer ganzen Reihe von Stellen, an denen ψυχή auch ohne hebräisches Äquivalent in Zusammenhängen steht, in denen das weite Verständnis von נפש kaum passend erscheint, vgl. auch d'Hamonville 2000, 114.

45. Vgl. Thümmel 1998, 246.

46. Dazu Siegert 2001, 258–60.

47. Hierzu findet sich auch eine Fülle von Beispielen im griechischen Proverbienbuch, vgl. d'Hamonville 2000, 113–15.

Als Ergebnis dieser ersten Musterung einzelner Begriffe ist damit ein uneinheitliches Bild festzuhalten: Neben Stellen, an denen der Übersetzer den Text deutlich und offenbar bewusst für griechische anthropologische Vorstellungen geöffnet hat, stehen Verse, in denen man griechische Einflüsse nicht feststellen kann. Damit entsteht eine gewisse Misch-Anthropologie, die heute methodisch kaum sicher zu fassen ist. Daher das im Titel dieser Studie verwendete Bild: Der Mensch wird auch in der LXX in manchen Hinsichten auf hebräische Weise beschrieben, doch zugleich erhält seine Beschreibung einzelne sprachliche Kleidungsstücke, die ihn als Griechen ausweisen. Damit wird verständlich, warum der griechischen Bibel sowohl das klassische hebräische Menschenbild entnommen werden kann, wie man es oft für neutestamentliche Schriftsteller voraussetzt, wie auch das typisch hellenistische, wie man es prototypisch bei Philo greifen kann.

Da Philo wohl nur griechischsprachig aufgewachsen ist, kann vermutet werden, dass er die LXX notwendig mit den klassischen griechischen Konnotationen der Lexeme verstehen musste. Für die neutestamentlichen Schriftsteller kann dagegen ein stärkerer aramäisch-hebräischer Einfluss im Umfeld ihres Aufwachsens angenommen werden, weshalb die griechischen Wörter eher die Konnotationen der hebräischen Bibel tragen konnten. Hier bietet sich m.E. der Exegese ein interessantes Feld für disziplinübergreifendes Arbeiten an.

4. Übergreifende Vorstellungskomplexe

4.1. Gott und Mensch

Im nächsten Schritt soll nun der Blick von einzelnen semantischen Differenzen zu größeren Vorstellungskomplexen geweitet werden. Eine wichtige Fragestellung im Grenzgebiet zwischen Theologie[48] und Anthropologie ist etwa die Beschreibung Gottes mit anthropomorpher Termi-

---

48. An dieser Stelle könnte auch dargestellt werden, dass bereits die Verwendung von κύριος zur Wiedergabe des Tetragramms unmittelbare Auswirkungen auf das Gottesverhältnis hat. Zum einen kann absolut gebrauchtes κύριος geradezu als Differenzbegriff zu den Religionen im Umfeld verstanden werden, da hier „Herr" immer mit abhängigem Genitiv verwendet wird. Zum anderen aber wird seit der Genesis κύριος mit den Konnotationen des freundlichen, den Menschen zugewandten Gottes verwendet, dies auch über die hebräische Vorlage hinaus. Dazu umfassend Rösel 1998b, 55–56.

nologie. Hier lässt sich in vielen Büchern der LXX die Tendenz feststellen, Anthropomorphismen zu meiden oder doch abzumindern.[49] Einige bekannte Beispiele dazu: Nach Gen 6,6 reut es Gott (יהוה), den Menschen geschaffen zu haben (נחם), während er (ὁ θεός) es in der griechischen Version überdenkt (ἐνθυμέομαι). In Ex 16,3 wird die Aussage von der Hand Gottes vermieden, statt dessen steht einfach ὑπὸ κυρίου, in 24,11 sehen die Israeliten nicht wie im hebräischen Text Gott selbst, sondern nur den Ort, an dem er stand (καὶ ὤφθησαν ἐν τῷ τόπῳ τοῦ θεου). Num 28,2 vermeidet die Vorstellung von einer Speisung der Gottheit und benutzt statt „Brot" Opfertermini. Diese neuen Akzentsetzungen sind eine Konsequenz des in der Spätzeit immer transzendenter werdenden Gottesbildes, doch zugleich wird die Distanz zwischen Mensch und Gott stärker als bisher betont. So wird in Num 23,19 sogar der Eindruck der Vergleichbarkeit zwischen Mensch und Gott vermieden, wenn aus לא איש אל „Gott ist kein Mensch" οὐχ ὡς ἄνθρωπος ὁ θεός „Nicht *wie* ein Mensch ist Gott" wird. Die Distanz Gott-Mensch wird so betont, dass Menschen nicht einmal gegen Gott sündigen können, sondern nur vor ihm, vgl. Ex 10,16.

4.2. Gottes Gesetz

Zur Beschreibung dessen, was menschliche Sünde ist, wird zum einen ἁμαρτία verwendet, zum anderen aber, und das ist besonders aufschlussreich, werden sehr häufig Bildungen von ἀνομία o.ä. benutzt. Der Begriff νόμος und seine Derivate, auch mit a-privativum, stehen für eine Vielzahl hebräischer Lexeme wie דבר, חק, דת, תורה oder און, חטא, פשע, שוא, שקר; der Nomos wird damit stärker noch als in der hebräischen Bibel zur Bezugsgröße menschlichen Verhaltens. Zu beachten sind zusätzlich die unterschiedlichen Konnotationen: Während *Tora* stärker auf Scheidungen von rein und unrein zielt, hat *Nomos* auch die Dimension der willentlichen Setzung von Verhältnissen und Institutionen;[50] schon in Ex 24,12 kann daher νομοθετέω verwendet werden; in Ps 9,21 wird Gott ausdrücklich als νομοθέτης bezeichnet.[51]

---

49. Vgl. über die oben genannten Hinweise auf Fritsch 1943 hinaus: Hanson 1992; Olofsson 1990, bes. 17–19; Soffer 1957.

50. Material dazu (wenngleich mit sehr zurückhaltender Auswertung) findet sich jetzt bei Austermann 2003, 171–73, vgl. auch Rösel 2007 [Kapitel 15 in diesem Band].

51. Hier steht im hebräischen Text מוֹרָה, das im Konsonantentext offenbar nicht als „Furcht," sondern als „Lehrer" verstanden wurde.

Bei dieser Thematik ist nun besonders auf die griechischen Proverbien und den Psalter hinzuweisen, die in der letzten Zeit ein besonderes Forschungsinteresse erfahren haben. Hier gibt es interessante Berührungen, obgleich die griechischen Sprüche in der Regel als eher freie Übersetzungen mit ausgeprägtem eigenen exegetischen Interesse gewertet werden;⁵² die Psalmen dagegen gelten als deutlich vorlagengetreuer.⁵³ In den Proverbien etwa ist auffällig, dass παράνομος außerordentlich häufig zur Kennzeichnung der Frevler und ihres Verhaltens verwendet wurde; es kann für eine Fülle von hebräischen Lexemen wie רעה, לוז, עון oder חמס stehen. Umgekehrt wird νόμος dort eingetragen, wo es um die positive Orientierung geht, vgl. etwa Spr 13,15: שכל־טוב יתן־חן ודרך בגדים איתן „Gute Einsicht verschafft Gunst, aber der Weg der Treulosen ist ihr Unglück." Daraus wird in der griechischen Version: σύνεσις ἀγαθὴ δίδωσιν χάριν τὸ δὲ γνῶναι νόμον διανοίας ἐστὶν ἀγαθῆς ὁδοὶ δὲ καταφρονούντων ἐν ἀπωλείᾳ: „Gute Einsicht bringt Gunst, aber das Gesetz zu kennen bedeutet guten Verstand; die Wege der Verächter aber führen ins Verderben."

Dies ist nun keine einmalige Eintragung des Übersetzers, sondern dieser Gedanke findet sich ähnlich auch an der bekannten Stelle Spr 9,10: תחלת חכמה יראת יהוה ודעת קדשים בינה „Der Weisheit Anfang ist die Furcht JHWHs; und Erkenntnis der heiligen Dinge ist Einsicht." Im griechischen Text wurde wieder der Gesetzesbezug hinzugefügt: ἀρχὴ σοφίας φόβος κυρίου καὶ βουλὴ ἁγίων σύνεσις τὸ γὰρ γνῶναι νόμον διανοίας ἐστὶν ἀγαθῆς „...das Gesetz zu kennen bedeutet gute Einsicht."⁵⁴ Über das gesamte Proverbienbuch hinweg werden Weisheit und *Nomos* miteinander verknüpft und an die menschliche Erkenntniskategorie der Einsicht gebunden. Auch dies entspricht dem erweiterten Tora-Verständnis der hellenistischen Zeit. Das aber bedeutet, dass es zwischen *Tora* und *Nomos* nicht allein semantische Differenzen gibt, sondern dass die Verwendung von *Nomos* zugleich eine deutlich erweiterte soteriologische Konzeption des Gesetzes impliziert. Diese steht wiederum im Hintergrund neutestamentlicher Auseinandersetzungen mit dem Gesetz.

---

52. Vgl. Cook 2001.
53. Zur Charakterisierung vgl. d'Hamonville 2000, 21–23; Gzella 2002, 23.
54. Dieser Zusatz steht zwar unter dem Verdacht der späteren Einfügung, vgl. d'Hamonville 2000, 53, doch ändert dies nichts am Gesamtphänomen.

4.3. Weisheit, Einsicht und Bildung

Der *Nomos* wird nun interessanterweise mit einem zweiten Thema verknüpft, mit dem von Weisheit, Einsicht und Erziehung. Parallel zur *Paranomia* der Frevler, die pauschal zu Gesetzesübertretern werden, steht ihre Qualifikation als ἄφρων „unvernünftig;" auch dieses Lexem erfährt in der Proverbien-LXX eine besondere Hochschätzung.[55] Wie in 9,10 zu sehen war, fallen für den Übersetzer σοφία und νόμος nahezu ineinander. Damit wird zum einen die Weisheit enger an Gott gebunden (vgl. die Pointierung in 8,22: κύριος ἔκτισέν με ἀρχὴν ὁδῶν αὐτοῦ εἰς ἔργα αὐτοῦ „der Herr hat mich als Anfang seiner Wege für seine Werke geschaffen"),[56] zum anderen wird vor fremder Weisheit gewarnt.

Als wesentliche weitere Komponente kommt nun in gewisser Folgerichtigkeit hinzu, dass der Begriff der Erziehung und Bildung in der Bibel prononciert wird. So steht für hebr. מוסר nun griech. παιδεία, ein Begriff, der das griechische Bildungsideal schlechthin bezeichnet.[57] Interessant ist, dass das Wort an einigen Stellen ohne hebräisches Äquivalent eingetragen wird.[58] Besonders auffällig ist dabei 25,1, wo alle Sprüche Salomos als παιδεῖαι (für משל) gelten.[59] Nun ist aber von besonderem Interesse, dass ausgerechnet der παιδεία-Begriff an einer sehr prominenten Stelle im Psalter begegnet, nämlich in dem schwierigen Text Ps 2,12. Dort heißt es—der hebräische Text (נשקו־בר) ist unsicher und hat zu einer Fülle von Konjekturen Anlass gegeben—δράξασθε παιδείας μήποτε ὀργισθῇ κύριος „nehmt Bildung an, damit der Herr nicht erzürne." Auch in Ps 18(17),36 wird παιδεία ohne Veranlassung durch den hebräischen Text eingetragen: καὶ ἡ παιδεία σου ἀνώρθωσέν με εἰς τέλος καὶ ἡ παιδεία σου αὐτή με διδάξει „und deine Bildung / Erziehung hat mich stark gemacht bis zum Ende / Ziel— und deine Bildung, sie wird mich lehren." Im Torapsalm Ps 119(118),66

---

55. Vgl. 6,12 für בליעל; 9,4 für פתי; 9,13 für כסילות; 11,29 für אויל, s. auch d'Hamonville 2000, 85–87.

56. Dazu Cook 1997, 245–46.

57. Vgl. etwa Bertram 1954, 597.

58. 10,17; 16,17.

59. Die Proverbien-LXX hat eine „Salomonisierung" der Sprüche durchgeführt, indem sie Verweise auf andere Autoren getilgt und (auch durch Umstellungen) Salomo besonders herausgestellt hat, vgl. d'Hamonville 2000, 34 u.ö. Dieser Vorgang ist der Davidisierung des Psalters direkt vergleichbar, vgl. dazu zusammenfassend Kleer 1996.

wird dann παιδεία (hier als ergänzende Übersetzung für דעת!) noch mit der Gebotserfüllung in Zusammenhang gebracht.

Nun stimmen die griechischen Psalmen mit den Proverbien darin überein, dass *Nomos*, Weisheit und Erkenntnis in einen prinzipiellen Zusammenhang gebracht werden; der Mensch wird nun ganz im Licht des *Nomos* gesehen.[60] Den *Nomos* wiederum gilt es zu verstehen, vgl. 16(15),7: Statt: „Ich preise JHWH, der mich beraten hat" (יעץ), liest man: „Ich preise den Herrn, der mich verständig gemacht hat" (εὐλογήσω τὸν κύριον τὸν συνετίσαντά με). Die häufige Verwendung von σύνεσις und Derivaten im Zusammenhang mit νόμος unterstreicht nun allerdings nicht nur die schon festgestellte Nomozentrik dieser griechischen Bücher, sondern auch ein Verständnis des Menschen, das stärker an Vernunft und Einsicht orientiert ist. Das führt so weit, dass eine ganze Reihe von Psalmen nun Überschriften tragen, die den Psalm ausdrücklich auf die Einsicht συνέσεως beziehen. Im Zusammenhang mit anderen Stellen ist zu folgern, dass wahres Verstehen der Tora den Weg zum Heil bedeutet.[61]

Eine letzte, außerordentlich interessante Wendung erhält das Thema des Verstehens nun noch dadurch, dass es in der etwa gleich alten Jesaja-LXX in interessanter Pointierung begegnet. Dort wurde nämlich in 7,9 aus dem bekannten Vers „Glaubt ihr nicht, so bleibt ihr nicht" (אם לא תאמינו כי לא תאמנו) das etwas überraschende „Glaubt ihr nicht, so versteht ihr nicht" (καὶ ἐὰν μὴ πιστεύσητε οὐδὲ μὴ συνῆτε).[62] In Auseinandersetzung mit den Verstehensbemühungen der zeitgenössischen Philosophie—so ist m.E. zu folgern—wurde in der griechischen Bibel das Thema des Verstehens über die hebräische Vorlage hinaus aufgenommen und pointiert: Der Mensch wird stärker intellektuell dargestellt, doch die Herkunft dieser Weisheit bleibt strikt an Gott gebunden.[63] Damit wird wohl eine Mittel-

---

60. Sprachlich wird das auch hier durch eine Häufung von Bildungen wie ἄνομος κτλ. oder παράνομος κτλ. für verschiedene hebräische Wörter deutlich, vgl. dazu Gzella 2002, 43 u.ö.

61. Ein detaillierter Einzelnachweis findet sich bei Rösel 2001b, 136–37 [Kapitel 10 in diesem Band].

62. Eine ausführliche Exegese des Kapitels Jes 7 habe ich vorgelegt in Rösel 1991a [Kapitel 9 in diesem Band].

63. Vgl. auch Hos 5,2, wo es von Gott heißt: ἐγὼ δὲ παιδευτὴς ὑμῶν, für ואני מוסר לכלם. „ich strafe sie allesamt" (vgl. auch Hos 7,12–14 [LXX]). Zum Text von Hos 5 LXX vgl. Muraoka 1986, der jedoch auf inhaltliche Exegesen weitgehend verzichtet, und zum Inhalt Bons, Joosten und Kessler 2002, 97–98 und 116–18.

stellung zwischen dem Einfließen griechischen Denkens in die Bibel und der Abwehr des Hellenismus eingenommen.

4.4. Tod und Auferstehung

Ein letzter Aspekt sei noch skizzenhaft angeschlossen, der ebenfalls weitreichende Folgen hat: Die Frage nach dem Tod des Menschen. Hier ist zunächst in einer ganzen Reihe von Büchern zu notieren, dass hebräisches ‚Scheol' (שאול) mit dem griechischen ‚Hades' (ᾅδης) übersetzt wurde, was notwendig den Einfluss griechischer Ideenwelt impliziert.[64] In den griechischen Proverbien lässt sich sogar die Vorstellung vom Styx wie ein reichhaltigeres Höllenvokabular nachweisen.[65] Interessanter ist noch, dass sich sowohl in den Psalmen, als auch im griechischen Hiob die Vorstellung von der Auferstehung belegen lässt. Nach dem Psalter führt ein toragetreues Leben zur Hoffnung auf Auferstehung; Gerechte und Frevler haben nicht mehr die gleiche Todesperspektive, wie Holger Gzellas Exegese von Ps 1,5 und 16(15),9–11 ergeben hat.[66] Dabei ist aber von Interesse, dass ganz offensichtlich die leibliche Auferstehung vorausgesetzt wird; Leib und Seele werden nach Ps 15LXX nicht getrennt.[67]

Der Übersetzer des Hiobbuches schließlich formuliert explizit, „es stehe geschrieben, dass Hiob auferstehen wird mit denen, die der Herr auferweckt" (γέγραπται δὲ αὐτὸν πάλιν ἀναστήσεσθαι μεθ' ὧν ὁ κύριος ἀνίστησιν 42,17, vgl. auch 19,25–26).[68] Damit wird nicht nur das Hiobproblem auf eine Weise gelöst, die dem hebräischen Hiobbuch noch unbekannt war; es wird auch das Bild vom Menschen und seinem Geschick entscheidend erweitert.

---

64. Vgl. etwa Gen 37,35; Ps 9,18; Spr 5,5; Jes 28,18; Hab 2,5, dazu auch Rösel 1994, 246–47.
65. Spr 9,18, s. dazu d'Hamonville 2000, 127; Cook 1997, 291–92.
66. Gzella 2002, bes. die Abschnitte 3.3 und 3.4.
67. Doch vgl. die eschatologische Vorstellung in Ps 21,30LXX: „Meine Seele lebt auf ihn hin", die durchaus dichotomisch zu verstehen ist, s. Schaper 1995, 52.
68. Weitere Hinweise auf die besondere Auferstehungserwartung des Hiobbuches finden sich bei: Gard 1954. Anders aber Fernández Marcos 1994, der das Buch ganz aus der israelitischen Weisheitstradition versteht und S. 264 die These ablehnt, dass der Übersetzer die Auferstehungshoffnung in den griechischen Hiob eingeführt habe. Das aber widerspricht m.E. dem eindeutigen Wortlaut von 42,17, vgl. jetzt auch Schnocks 2006, und van der Kooij 2007.

5. Schluss

Schon die wenigen vorgeführten Beispiele reichen für die Feststellung aus, dass sich das Menschenbild der Septuaginta an einigen entscheidenden Stellen von dem der hebräischen Bibel unterscheidet. Die Verwendung der griechischen Sprache, der Kontakt mit hellenistischer Kultur und die weiterentwickelte jüdische Gottesvorstellung haben ihre Spuren hinterlassen. Hier wie dort gibt es jedoch keine systematisch ausgeführte Anthropologie. Stattdessen ist an konkreten Textaussagen zu erschließen, wo es Gemeinsamkeiten und Differenzen gibt. Diese Perspektive des Vergleichs ist jedoch eine moderne; den nur noch griechisch sprechenden Lesern in Alexandria und anderswo war sie wohl kaum zugänglich, allenfalls mag es den oben vom Enkel des Jesus Sirach wiedergegebenen allgemeinen Eindruck gegeben haben, dass die Texte nicht ganz aussagegleich sind.

Hinzu kommt folgender Gedanke: Die festgestellten Modifikationen des Menschenbildes lassen sich auch bei jüdisch-hellenistischen Schriftstellern feststellen; die Torazentrierung ist auch in Qumran breit belegt; die Auferstehungshoffnung findet sich auch im Danielbuch. Doch dies sind Schriften, die an den Rändern oder außerhalb des Kanons stehen, deren Autorität wahrscheinlich deutlich geringer war. Die besondere Bedeutung der anthropologischen Akzentsetzungen der Septuaginta liegt demgegenüber darin, dass es sich bei ihr um die Bibel handelte, deren Autorität zumindest in weiten Teilen des Judentums nicht in Frage gestellt wurde. Damit aber hat die LXX für die Religionsgeschichte der hellenistischen Zeit, für die Rezeptionsgeschichte der hebräischen Bibel und die Frage einer gesamtbiblischen Theologie bzw. Anthropologie eine Bedeutung, die man kaum unterschätzen kann. Es ist gut, dass diese Dimension der griechischen Bibel auch in der alttestamentlichen Wissenschaft zunehmend berücksichtigt wird.

Literatur

Albani, Matthias. 2001. „,,Der Herr tötet und macht lebendig; er führt in die Unterwelt hinab und wieder herauf.' Zur Problematik der Auferstehungshoffnung im AT am Beispiel von 1 Sam 2,6." *Leqach* 1:22–55.

Albertz, Rainer. 1993. „Mensch II. (Altes Testament)." *TRE* 22:464–74.

Albrecht, Jörn. 1998. *Literarische Übersetzung. Geschichte, Theorie, kulturelle Wirkung.* Darmstadt: Wissenschaftliche Buchgesellschaft.

Austermann, Frank. 2000. „Thesen zur Septuaginta-Exegese am Beispiel der Untersuchung des Septuaginta-Psalters." Seiten 380–86 in *Der Septuaginta-Psalter und seine Tochterübersetzungen*. Hrsg. von Anneli Aejmelaeus und Udo Quast. NAWG Phil-Hist Klasse 3, 230. MSU 24. Göttingen: Vandenhoeck & Ruprecht.

———. 2003. *Von der Tora zum Nomos. Untersuchungen zur Übersetzungsweise und Interpretation im Septuaginta-Psalter*. NAWG Phil-Hist Klasse 3, 257. MSU 27. Göttingen: Vandenhoeck & Ruprecht.

Barr, James. 1965. *Bibelexegese und moderne Semantik. Theologische und linguistische Methode in der Bibelwissenschaft*. München: Kaiser.

———. 1979. *The Typology of Literalism in Ancient Biblical Translations*. NAWG Phil-Hist Klasse 11. MSU 15. Göttingen: Vandenhoeck & Ruprecht.

Bertram, Georg. 1954. „παιδεύω κτλ." *ThWNT* 5:596–624.

———. 1957. „Praeparatio evangelica in der Septuaginta." *VT* 7:225–49.

———. 1961. „Septuaginta-Frömmigkeit." *RGG*^{3} 5:1707–9.

Bomann, Thorleif. 1983. *Das hebräische Denken im Vergleich mit dem Griechischen*. 7. Auflage. Göttingen: Vandenhoeck & Ruprecht.

Bons, Eberhard, Jan Joosten, und Stephan Kessler. 2002. *Les Douze prophètes. Osée*. BdA 23.1. Paris: Cerf.

Bratsiotis, N.P. 1966. „נֶפֶשׁ–ψυχή. Ein Beitrag zur Erforschung der Sprache und der Theologie der Septuaginta." Seiten 58–89 in *Volume du Congrès Genève 1965*. Hrsg. von G. W. Anderson. VTSup 15. Leiden: Brill.

Brown, William. 1999. „Reassessing the Text-critical Value of Septuagint-Genesis 1. A Response to Martin Rösel." *BIOSCS* 32:35–39.

Cook, Johann. 1997. *The Septuagint of Proverbs. Jewish and/or Hellenistic Proverbs? Concerning the Hellenistic Colouring of LXX Proverbs*. VTSup 69. Leiden: Brill.

———. 2001. „The Ideology of Septuagint Proverbs." Seiten 463–79 in *X. Congress of the International Organization for Septuagint and Cognate Studies. Oslo 1998*. Hrsg. von Bernard A. Taylor. SCS 51. Atlanta: Society of Biblical Literature.

Daniel, Suzanne. 1966. *Recherches sur le Vocabulaire du Culte dans la Septante*. Etudes et Commentaires 61. Paris: Klincksieek.

Deissmann, Adolf. 1903. *Die Hellenisierung des semitischen Monotheismus*. Neue Jahrbücher für das klassische Altertum, Geschichte und deutsche Literatur. Leipzig: Teubner.

D'Hamonville, David-Marc. 2000. *Les Proverbes*. BdA 17. Paris: Cerf.

Fabry, Heinz-Josef. 1984. „לֵב." *ThWAT* 4:413–51.

Fernández Marcos, Natalio. 1994. „The Septuagint Reading of the Book of Job." Seiten 251–66 in *The Book of Job*. Hrsg. von Willem A. M. Beuken. BETL 114. Leuven: Peeters.

Frankel, Zacharias. 1851 *Ueber den Einfluss der palästinischen Exegese auf die alexandrinische Hermeneutik*. Leipzig: Barth.

Frevel, Christian, und Oda Wischmeyer. 2003. *Menschsein. Perspektiven des Alten und Neuen Testaments*. NEB Themen 11. Würzburg: Echter.

Fritsch, Charles T. 1943. *The Anti-Anthropomorphisms of the Greek Pentateuch*. POT 10. Princeton: Princeton University Press.

Gard, D. H. 1954. „The Concept of the Future Life According to the Greek Translator of the Book of Job." *JBL* 73:137–43.

Geiger, Abraham. 1928. *Urschrift und Übersetzung der Bibel in ihrer Abhängigkeit von der innern Entwickelung des Judentums*. 2. Auflage. Frankfurt a.M: Madda.

Groß, Walter. 2000. „Gen 1,26.27; 9,6. Statue oder Ebenbild Gottes? Aufgabe und Würde des Menschen nach dem hebräischen und dem griechischen Wortlaut." *JBTh* 15:11–38.

Grund, Alexandra. 2005. „Tun-Ergehen-Zusammenhang I. (Biblisch)." *RGG*[4] 8: 654–56.

Gzella, Holger. 2002. *Lebenszeit und Ewigkeit. Studien zur Eschatologie und Anthropologie des Septuaginta-Psalters*. BBB 134. Berlin: Philo.

Hanson, Anthony. 1992. „The Treatment in the LXX of the Theme of Seeing God." Seiten 557–68 in *Septuagint, Scrolls and Cognate Writings*. Hrsg. von George J. Brooke und Barnabas Lindars. SCS 33. Atlanta: Scholars Press.

Harl, Marguerite. 1986. *La Genèse*. BdA 1. Paris: Cerf.

Harl, Marguerite, Gilles Dorival, und Olivier Munnich. 1994. *La Bible Grecque des Septante. Du judaïsme hellénistique au christianisme ancien*. 2me édition. Paris: Cerf.

Harlé, Paul, und Didier Pralon. 1988. *Le Lévitique*. BdA 3. Paris: Cerf.

Hegermann, Hans. 1993. „Mensch, IV. (Neues Testament)." *TRE* 22:481–93.

Hendel, Ronald S. 1999. „On the Text-Critical value of Septuagint Genesis. A Reply to Rösel." *BIOSCS* 32:31–34.

Hengel, Martin. 1994. „Die Septuaginta als ‚christliche Schriftensammlung,' ihre Vorgeschichte und das Problem ihres Kanons." Seiten 182–284 in *Die Septuaginta zwischen Judentum und Christentum*. Hrsg. von Martin Hengel und Anna-Maria Schwemer. WUNT 1/72. Tübingen: Mohr Siebeck.

Janowski, Bernd. 2005. „Der Mensch im Alten Israel. Grundfragen alttestamentlicher Anthropologie." *ZTK* 102:143–75.

———. 2006. *Konfliktgespräche mit Gott. Eine Anthropologie der Psalmen.* 2. Auflage. Neukirchen-Vluyn: Neukirchner Verlag.

Jobes, Karen H., und Moisés Silva. 2000. *Invitation to the Septuagint.* Grand Rapids: Baker Academic.

Kleer, Martin. 1996. *Der liebliche Sänger der Psalmen Israels. Untersuchungen zu David als Dichter und Beter der Psalmen.* BBB 108. Bodenheim: Philo.

Koch, Klaus. 2000. *Imago Dei—Die Würde des Menschen im biblischen Text.* Berichte aus den Sitzungen der Joachim Jungius-Gesellschaft der Wissenschaften 18.4. Göttingen: Vandenhoeck & Ruprecht.

———. 2003. „Das Neue Testament und seine aramäische Bibel." Seiten 1–20 in *Die aramäische Rezeption der hebräischen Bibel. Studien zur Targumik und Apokalyptik.* Hrsg. von Martin Rösel. Neukirchen-Vluyn: Neukirchener Verlag.

Köhler, Ludwig. 1953. *Der hebräische Mensch. Eine Skizze, mit einem Anhang. Die hebräische Rechtsgemeinde.* Tübingen: Mohr Siebeck.

Kooij, Arie van der. 2007. „Ideas About Afterlife in the Septuagint." Seiten 87–102 in *Lebendige Hoffnung—ewiger Tod?! Jenseitsvorstellungen im Hellenismus, Judentum und Christentum.* Hrsg. von Michael Labahn und Manfred Lang. ABG 24. Leipzig: Evangelische Verlagsanstalt.

Loader, William R. 2004. *The Septuagint, Sexuality and the New Testament. Case Studies on the Impact of the LXX in Philo and the New Testament.* Grand Rapids: Eerdmans.

Lys, Daniel. 1966. „The Israelite Soul according to the LXX." *VT* 16:181–228.

Müller, Mogens. 1996. *The First Bible of the Church. A Plea for the Septuagint.* JSOTSup 206. Copenhagen International Seminar 1. Sheffield: Sheffield Academic.

Muraoka, Takamitsu. 1986. „Hosea V in the Septuagint Version." *AbrN* 24:120–38.

Nida, Eugene A., und Charles R. Tabor. 1969. *Theorie und Praxis des Übersetzens unter besonderer Berücksichtigung der Bibelübersetzung.* Stuttgart: Weltbund der Bibelgesellschaften.

Olofsson, Staffan. 1990. *God Is My Rock. A Study of Translation Technique and Theological Exegesis in the Septuagint.* ConBOT 31. Stockholm: Almqvist & Wiksell.

Pietersma, Albert. 2002. „A New Paradigm for Addressing Old Questions. The Relevance of the Interlinear Model for the Study of the Septuagint." Seiten 337–64 in *Bible and Computer. The Stellenbosch AIBI-6 Conference. Proceedings of the Association internationale Bible et informatique ‚From Alpha to Byte.'* Hrsg. von Johann Cook. Leiden: Brill.

———. 2007. *A New English Translation of the Septuagint and the Other Greek Translations Traditionally Included under That Title. The Psalms.* Oxford: Oxford University Press.

Rösel, Martin. 1991a. „Die Jungfrauengeburt des endzeitlichen Immanuel. Jesaja 7 in der Übersetzung der Septuaginta." *JBTh* 6:135–51. [Kapitel 9 in diesem Band.]

———. 1991b. „Die Übersetzung der Gottesnamen in der Genesis-Septuaginta." Seiten 357–77 in *Ernten, was man sät. Festschrift für Klaus Koch zu seinem 65. Geburtstag.* Hrsg. von Dwight R. Daniels, Uwe Gleßmer, und Martin Rösel. Neukirchen-Vluyn: Neukirchener Verlag.

———. 1994. *Übersetzung als Vollendung der Auslegung. Studien zur Genesis-Septuaginta.* BZAW 223. Berlin: de Gruyter.

———. 1998a. „The Text-Critical Value of Septuagint-Genesis." *BIOSCS* 31:62–70.

———. 1998b. „Theo-Logie der griechischen Bibel. Zur Wiedergabe der Gottesaussagen im LXX-Pentateuch." *VT* 48:49–62.

———. 2001a. „Tun-Ergehen-Zusammenhang." *NBL* 3:931–34.

———. 2001b „Die Psalmüberschriften des Septuagintapsalters." Seiten 125–48 in *Der Septuaginta-Psalter. Sprachliche und theologische Aspekte.* Hrsg. von Erich Zenger. HBS 32. Freiburg: Herder. [Kapitel 10 in diesem Band.]

———. 2006a. „Der griechische Bibelkanon und seine Theologie." Seiten 60–80 in *Kanon. Bibelens tilblivelse og normative status. Festskrift til Mogens Müller i anledning af 60-års-fødselsdagen den 25. januar 2006.* Hrsg. von Troels Engberg-Petersen, Nils Peter Lemche, und Henrik Tronier. Forum for Bibelsk Eksegese 15. Kopenhagen: Museum Tusculanum.

———. 2006b. „Jakob, Bileam und der Messias. Messianische Erwartungen in Gen 49 und Num 22–24." Seiten 151–76 in *The Septuagint and Messianism.* Hrsg. von Michael A. Knibb. BETL 195. Leuven: Peeters. [Kapitel 5 in diesem Band.]

———. 2007. „Nomothesie. Zum Gesetzesverständnis der Septuaginta." Seiten 132–50 in Band 3 *Im Brennpunkt. Die Septuaginta. Studien zur Theologie, Anthropologie, Ekklesiologie, Eschatologie und Liturgie der griechischen Bibel*. Hrsg. von Heinz-Josef Fabry und Dieter Böhler. BWANT 174. Stuttgart: Kohlhammer. [Englische Übersetzung Kapitel 15 in diesem Band.]

———. 2009. „Die Geburt der Seele in der Übersetzung. Von der hebräischen *näfäsch* über die *psyche* der LXX zur deutschen Seele." Seiten 151–70 in *Anthropologische Aufbrüche. Alttestamentliche und interdisziplinäre Zugänge zur historischen Anthropologie*. Hrsg. von Andreas Wagner. FRLANT 232. Göttingen: Vandenhoeck & Ruprecht.

Schaper, Joachim. 1995. *Eschatology in the Greek Psalter*. WUNT 2/76. Tübingen: Mohr Siebeck.

Scharbert, Josef. 1972. „Fleisch, Geist und Seele in der Pentateuch-Septuaginta." Seiten 121–43 in *Wort, Lied und Gottesspruch. Beiträge zur Septuaginta. Festschrift für Joseph Ziegler*. Hrsg. von Josef Schreiner. Würzburg: Echter.

Schenker, Adrian. 1994. „Gewollt dunkle Wiedergaben in LXX? Am Beispiel von Ps 28 (29),6." *Bib* 75:546–55.

Schmidt, Werner H. 1964. „Anthropologische Begriffe im Alten Testament. Anmerkungen zum hebräischen Denken." *EvT* 24:374–88.

Schnocks, Johannes. 2006. „The Hope for Resurrection in the Book of Job." Seiten 291–99 in *The Septuagint and Messianism*. Hrsg. von Michael A. Knibb. BETL 195. Leuven: Peeters.

Schroer, Silvia, und Thomas Staubli. 1998. *Die Körpersymbolik der Bibel*. Darmstadt: Wissenschaftliche Buchgesellschaft.

Seebass, Horst. 1986. „נֶפֶשׁ." *ThWAT* 5:531–55.

———. 1996. *Genesis I. Urgeschichte (1,1–11,26)*. Neukirchen-Vluyn: Neukirchner Verlag.

Seeligmann, Isaac Leo. 1948. *The Septuagint Version of Isaiah. A Discussion of its Problems*. MEOL 9. Leiden: Brill.

———. 1990. „Problems and Perspectives in Modern Septuagint Research." *Text* 15:169–232. (= „Problemen en Perspectieven in het Moderne Septuaginta Onderzoek." *EOL* 7 (1940): 359–90).

Siegert, Folker. 2001. *Zwischen Hebräischer Bibel und Altem Testament. Eine Einführung in die Septuaginta*. MJS 9. Münster: LIT.

Soffer, Arthur. 1957. „The Treatment of Anthropomorphisms and Anthropopathisms in the Septuagint of Psalms." *HUCA* 28:85–107.

Stolze, Radegundis. 2001. *Übersetzungstheorien. Eine Einführung*. 3. Auflage. Tübingen: Narr.

Thümmel, Hans Georg. 1998. „Die Seele im Platonismus und bei den Kirchenvätern." Seiten 242–54 in ψυχή-*Seele-anima. Festschrift für*

Karin Alt. Hrsg. von Jens Holzhausen. Beiträge zur Altertumskunde 109. Leipzig: Teubner.

Usener, Knut. 2004. „Die Septuaginta im Horizont des Hellenismus. Ihre Entwicklung, ihr Charakter und ihre sprachlich-kulturelle Position." Seiten 78–118 in Band 2 *Im Brennpunkt. Die Septuaginta. Studien zur Entstehung und Bedeutung der Griechischen Bibel*. Hrsg. von Siegfried Kreuzer und Jürgen Peter Lesch. BWANT 161. Stuttgart: Kohlhammer.

Utzschneider, Helmut. 2001. „Das griechische Michabuch—Zur Probe übersetzt und erläutert im Rahmen des Projekts. Septuaginta-Deutsch—Das Griechische Alte Testament in Übersetzung." Seiten 213–50 in *Im Brennpunkt. Die Septuaginta. Studien zur Entstehung und Bedeutung der Griechischen Bibel*. Hrsg. von Heinz-Josef Fabry und Ulrich Offerhaus. BWANT 153. Stuttgart: Kohlhammer.

Wagner, Andreas, Hrsg. 2009. *Anthropologische Aufbrüche. Alttestamentliche und interdisziplinäre Zugänge zur historischen Anthropologie*. FRLANT 232. Göttingen: Vandenhoeck & Ruprecht.

Walter, Nikolaus. 2001. „Die griechische Übersetzung der ‚Schriften' Israels und die christliche ‚Septuaginta' als Forschungs- und Übersetzungsgegenstand." Seiten 71–96 in *Im Brennpunkt. Die Septuaginta. Studien zur Entstehung und Bedeutung der Griechischen Bibel*. Hrsg. von Heinz-Josef Fabry und Ulrich Offerhaus. BWANT 153. Stuttgart: Kohlhammer.

Wevers, John W. 1997. *Notes on the Greek Text of Leviticus*. SCS 44. Atlanta: Scholars Press.

Wolff, Hans Walter. 1977. *Anthropologie des Alten Testaments*. 3. Auflage. München: Kaiser.

15
Nomothesis:
The Understanding of the Law in the Septuagint

The discourse about the "law" is one of the fundamental problems of the message of the New Testament. Νόμος, almost always in the singular, refers in most cases to the torah of Moses.[1] One must differentiate between various usages of the word: it can designate the sum of God's commandments (see Luke 2:22 κατὰ τὸν νόμον Μωϋσέως), it can refer to the five books of Moses (1 Cor 9:9 ἐν γὰρ τῷ Μωϋσέως νόμῳ γέγραπται), or it can indicate the Decalogue only (Rom 7:7). Occasionally, νόμος evidently refers to the whole Bible of Israel (1 Cor 14:21, John 10:34), but this euphemism often indicates an abbreviation of the fuller term "law and prophets" (see the classic formulation in Matt 5:17: τὸν νόμον ἢ τοὺς προφήτας).[2]

Besides these, there are biblical texts in which the meaning of νόμος is exemplified by the immediate context. Thus, according to Rom 2:20, a Jew has the embodiment of knowledge and truth in the law (ἔχοντα τὴν μόρφωσιν τῆς γνώσεως καὶ τῆς ἀληθείας ἐν τῷ νόμῳ); those who live by the law and fulfill its commandments will live by it (ὁ ποιήσας αὐτὰ ἄνθρωπος ζήσεται ἐν αὐτοῖς).[3] This claim, rejected by Paul in Rom 10:5 and Gal 3:12, is a fragmentary quotation from Lev 18:5, omitting the first portions of the verse in which Israel is called to keep all the statutes and ordinances of God (πάντα τὰ προστάγματά μου καὶ πάντα τὰ κρίματά μου).[4] It is significant that the individual laws (pl.) mentioned here are summarized in the

---

1. Only in Heb 8:10 and 10:16 is the plural νόμους used, because here Jer 31:33 (38:33 LXX) is quoted.
2. As an introduction into the topic cf. Smend and Zmijewski 1991; Hübner 1992.
3. Betz 1988, 267–68; Bergmeier 2000, 79.
4. For the interpretation of Lev 18:5c in Rom 10:5 see D.-A. Koch 1986, 290–96.

later reception by Paul to one *nomos* (sg.). The developments leading to this phenomenon will be examined in the following.

It is assumed that in these texts from the New Testament νόμος refers to Hebrew תורה. This corresponds to the contemporary Hebrew language, as it is documented, inter alia, in Qumran, and to the use of Greek in Hellenistic Judaism as well.[5] Torah/*nomos* is the identification-creating key concept of the central traditions of Judaism at the turn of the eras. There is a high amount of scholarly papers dealing with several aspects of the topic, for example, trying to shed light on Jesus's and individual New Testament writers' understanding of the law, or exploring the concept of law in Hellenistic Judaism, or working on the development of the meaning of torah in the Hebrew Bible.[6] In contrast, there are few studies on the issue of the equation תורה-νόμος, its semantics, and its consequences for a project of biblical theology. If one is interested in this question, then the LXX, the oldest available translation of the Hebrew Bible into Greek, receives the most focused interest.[7] Moreover, one can safely assume that the terminology of the LXX in turn was influenced by the usage in Hellenistic-Jewish communities, especially in Egypt.[8]

In the following, I will begin to trace patterns of how *nomos* was understood in the Greek translation of Israel's scriptures. In order to do this, I will first collect data from translations of individual books. This procedure is in accordance with the more recent methodology of LXX research, because contrary to earlier approaches, the LXX cannot be seen as a unit, but as a collection of different translations stemming from different ages, and perhaps also from different places. Second, I will interpret the results and conclude whether they converge into an overall picture.[9]

---

5. See Lichtenberger 1996.

6. It is not possible to provide an exhaustive list; I am only referring to some important works from German scholarly discussions: Deines 2005 (on Matt 5); Berger 1972 (on the understanding of "law" in Mark and parallels); von der Osten-Sacken 1989 (on Paul). For the concept of law in Hellenistic Judaism, see the two volumes by Weber 2000, 2001; Lichtenberger 1996; neither author has a chapter on the LXX, but both see the LXX as a presupposition of Hellenistic thinking. For development of torah in the Hebrew Bible, see Finsterbusch 2005; Crüsemann 2005; cf. the summaries by Achenbach 2005; and K. Koch 1984.

7. Still basic is Monsengwo Pasinya 1973. Helpful is also Blank 1930, who has assembled potential translations of the specific Hebrew lexemes.

8. As for helpful introductions, see Dines 2004; Siegert 2001 (264–66 on νόμος).

9. For methodology, see Rösel 2006 with further literature [ch. 11 in this volume].

1. The Pentateuch

Regardless of the debates about the controversial testimony of the Letter of Aristeas, it is undisputed in the scholarly community that the Greek Pentateuch is the oldest part of the collection of writings called "Septuagint."[10] It is also generally assumed that the translation took place around 250 BCE. Genesis was probably translated first, and the other books followed shortly afterward, although the order in which they were translated is under discussion.[11] It is likely that these early translations reflect the Greek theological terminology coined in the Jewish community to which the translator belonged—probably Alexandria—and whose usage he mirrors in his translation.[12]

1.1. Genesis

The first study ends with a negative result: νόμος is not used in the Greek Genesis. The usual Hebrew equivalent תורה can be found once in Gen 26:5: וישמר משמרתי מצותי חקותי ותורתי—"(because Abraham obeyed my voice) and kept my charge, my commandments, my statutes, and my laws" (NRSV). The LXX translates: καὶ ἐφύλαξεν τὰ προστάγματά μου καὶ τὰς ἐντολάς μου καὶ τὰ δικαιώματά μου καὶ τὰ νόμιμά μου. תורה has been translated with νόμιμος, which is nowhere else used in the Greek Genesis. This translation is notable since from the book of Exodus on νόμιμος is used for חקה/חק but nowhere else for תורה.[13] Also the antonym ἀνομία can be found only once in LXX Genesis in 19:15.[14] One can assume that νόμος was not used in this book because in the course of the narrative God's specific commandments were not yet given, a conclusion supported by LXX Exodus, where νόμος is used only from 12:43 on. Here, a divine command installs the Passover, translating זאת חקת הפסח: Οὗτος ὁ νόμος τοῦ πασχα. One can therefore conclude that *nomos* is reserved for the commandments given by God. Also in the preceding verses 12:14 + 24 חק had

---

10. See Honigman 2003; Rösel 2007 [ch. 1 in this volume].
11. See the overview in Tilly 2005, 50–51.
12. For the methodology of this investigation cf. Rösel 1994, 11–24.
13. See Wevers 1993, 400; Harl 1986, 54.
14. Translating עון; here it is about the behavior of Sodom's inhabitants, which violates any sense of decorum.

to be translated, but here the translator has chosen νόμιμος; thus, νόμος was apparently used with a specific intention.[15]

1.2. Exodus

Turning now to an overview of the book of Exodus, one notes the following: from 12:49 on, all occurrences of תורה were translated with νόμος.[16] Some specifics are noteworthy. First, in every instance the singular is used, even if the *Vorlage* has a clearly recognizable plural and refers to single instructions.[17] This is striking because in each of the verses in question other laws are mentioned, and here the lexemes were translated with Greek words in the plural.[18] On the other hand, in 18:20 it is clarified by adding αὐτοῦ over the Hebrew text that this is about God's law.[19]

Furthermore, in 13:10 νόμος has been used once more to translate חקה. This verse concludes the regulations for the Passover, a comprehensible variation since 12:43 and 13:10 form an *inclusio*.[20] Thus, at the beginning and the end of the passage the instructions for the Passover are qualified as *nomos*. Besides νόμος, the translator of the Greek book of Exodus has used νόμιμος to represent Hebrew חוה or חק. He obviously wanted to differentiate between individual commandments (νόμιμος) and the superordinate term, which refers back to God's revelation and the covenant.[21]

Again in 24:12, another interesting translation can be found: The verb ירה II "instruct" is translated with νομοθετέομαι. The text is about the law as such and the Ten Commandments in particular; God had written them (התורה והמצוה) for their (= Israel's) instruction.[22] The equation ירה II-νομοθετέομαι is used consistently from Exod 24 on in the LXX. This leads

---

15. See Rösel 1994, 228–30.
16. 12:49; 13:9; 16:4, 28; 18:16, 20; 24:1.
17. E.g., in 18:16 + 20; in 16:28 the plural is not clearly recognizable in the unpointed text.
18. 16:28 + 24:12: τάς ἐντολάς; 18:16, 20: τὰ προστάγματα; cf. also Le Boulluec and Sandevoir 1989, 42–43.
19. This is can be seen as a harmonization with v. 16; Wevers 1990, 284.
20. Monsengwo Pasinya 1973, 105, sees a shorter textual unit and assumes the inclusion only in the range of 12:43–49.
21. With Le Boulluec and Sandevoir 1989, 43. So the results of Monsengwo Pasinya 1973, 114.
22. See similarly Wevers 1990, 386: "The Ten Words are not really an instruction in Exod's view but rather give a moral framework for law."

to some interesting translations, as I will show below.[23] The background of this translation is a linguistic parallelization of ירה with תורה, and thus the theme of *nomos* is introduced. Simple instruction evolved to legislation.

Again, the phenomenon of the antonym is worth consideration: ἀνομία "lawless act" (NETS), found in Exod 34 only, the passage about the renewal of the covenant.[24] In three instances in verses 7 + 9 it has been used to translate עון, which in other texts of this book has been translated with ἁμαρτία.[25] Since there is a narrative connection between the giving of the laws in Exod 24 and the renewal of the covenant in chapter 34, it is understandable that the translator deviated from his regular usage and qualifies the transgression explicitly as being directed against the *nomos*. This occurs again at the beginning of the section on the broken covenant and its renewal: in 32:7 God reminds Moses that his people have transgressed the law (ἀνομέω). The Hebrew text is less specific; God told Moses that they have acted perversely; here שחת is used. In summary, in LXX Exodus, the people's relationship to God is intricately related to the *nomos* and on keeping it.

1.3. Leviticus

The picture that emerges in Greek Leviticus is quite uniform: תורה has been rendered by νόμος in all instances. In 26:46, for example, the plural התורת is once again translated with a singular, although the other terms for statutes and ordinances used in this verse are correctly rendered by a plural. Moreover, because the plural חקתי in 19:19 + 37 is translated with the singular νόμος, one can assume this rendering represents a deliberate decision to deviate from a grammatically exact translation.[26] In 6:15(22) νόμος also stands for חק, which is usually rendered by νόμιμος; because this equivalent was used immediately before in 6:11(18), it is possible the

---

23. See below on Ps 9:21.
24. For ἀνομία ee Davison 1985, who examines the usage of ἀνομία in the LXX, but does not differentiate between the individual books. Moreover, he assumes that the meaning of the Greek word can be derived from the Hebrew.
25. 20:5; 28:38, 43.
26. Monsengwo Pasinya 1973, 117–20, assumes that the translator wanted to emphasize the dimension of covenant in this passage. In any case, the translations in 19:19 + 37 create a new bracket of *nomos*-references around a certain content, in this case qualifying the regulations on interpersonal ethics.

translator simply wished to vary. In 15:3 νόμος is added over the Hebrew text. This can be seen as a harmonization with other commandments in this context (especially ch. 14), or with similar headings of sections on specific topics, compare 6:7; 7:1, 11.[27]

Again, the antonym ἀνομία is occasionally used to translate עון, usually translated with ἁμαρτία "sin."[28] In addition, it has also been used twice for זמה "depravity."[29] For the first time the rare ἀνόμημα "transgression of the law" can be found, which also translates זמה (20:14) or עון (17:16).

For Leviticus, the theological significance is again noteworthy: namely, in the completion of legislation in Lev 26:46, we find a reference to the unity of the *nomos* (sg.) closely connected to the idea of the covenant in the immediate (vv. 43–46).

1.4. Numbers

The results of the book of Numbers largely correspond to those from Leviticus: תורה is consistently translated with νόμος; חק/חקה is almost always translated with νόμιμος. Again, the exceptions are of interest, especially in Num 9 in the section on the laws for Passover.[30] In 9:3 νόμος stands for הק (pl.), and in 9:12 and twice in 9:14 also the singular of הק is translated with νόμος. According to L. Monsengwo Pasinya, here in Num 9 as in Exod 12, special emphasis is laid on the theme of observing the Passover as a sign of belonging to the covenant of God. Because also in 15:15 νόμος is used for חק (probably a harmonization with v. 16), another parallel to Exod 12 occurs exemplifying the same phenomenon (v. 49): the texts focus on the proselytes, for which the *nomos* also applies. Both books emphasize the rank of the proselytes; moreover, by naming its regulations *nomos*, they also enhance the status of the celebration of Passover. Since in the texts in question the ceremony is not located in the central sanctuary as in Deut 16, one can easily imagine that the texts are adapted to the special needs of the communities in the Alexandrian diaspora.[31]

---

27. Wevers 1997, 224–25. According to Blank 1930, 276, תהיה was misread to תורה, but this is rather unlikely.
28. 16:21; 22:16; 26:43.
29. 19:29; 20:14. In 18:17 ἀσέβημα is used for זמה.
30. Blank 1930, 269, also hints to the frequent usage of νόμος in the context of regulations for Passover.
31. This consideration follows Monsengwo Pasinya 1973, 121–22.

An interesting problem for the translator was the rendering of the formula חקת התורה, found exclusively in Numbers. Numbers 19:2 uses διαστολὴ τοῦ νόμου "section of the law," and in 31:21 τὸ δικαίωμα τοῦ νόμου "statute/regulation of the law." These two translations demonstrate the reflected way in which the translator carried out his task. In his perception תורה/νόμος is the all-embracing law of God consisting of various sections and requiring different labels.

In contrast to other books, the term ἀνομία is rare in Numbers, occurring only in 14:18 for עון. This is the formulaic proclamation of God's mercy and grace (German: *Gnadenformel*), and the translator obviously oriented himself on the Greek text of Exod 34:6–7. This conclusion is obvious since the third part of the formula has been taken from Exod 14:7 and added to LXX Num 14:18 over the Hebrew; ἀφαιρῶν ἀνομίας καὶ ἀδικίας καὶ ἁμαρτίας stands for נשא עון ופשע. Moreover, τὸν ἔνοχον has also been inserted, which also stems from Exod 34:7. But unlike Exod 34:7, the second occurrence of עון was not translated with ἀνομία but with the ἁμαρτία, the standard equivalent.

Finally, a particularly interesting translation can be found in 32:15: according to the Hebrew text, God swears that the Transjordanian tribes will destroy (שחת) all this people (עם) if they turn away from following God. But in the LXX they threaten the entire synagogue/congregation (συναγωγή), because they act lawlessly against them (ἀνομήσετε). The translation of עם with συναγωγή is remarkable (only once more in Lev 10:3): obviously the Transjordanian tribes are no longer considered part of the community because they live outside the promised land. This is supported by the use of ἀνομέω: they place themselves outside of the covenant, which is qualified by the torah.

1.5. Deuteronomy

In Deuteronomy תורה appears often, and in the Greek translation νόμος is the standard equivalent throughout. In some cases νόμος is added in the Greek version, an obvious attempt to harmonize or clarify the text, as can be seen in 24:8; 29:19 (20), 26 (27); and 32:44.[32] The latter verse has been reformulated in the LXX by repeating 31:22 and thus serves as a signature

---

32. See the overview in Monsengwo Pasinya 1973, 131.

of both the song of Moses as well as of the entire law.³³ Therefore the addition of νόμος is easily understandable. Also of interest is 24:8, where Israel is gathered for instruction (ירה) by the priests and levites. Obviously in the Greek the verb has been translated twice, leading to the phrase: τὸν νόμον ὃν ἐὰν ἀναγγείλωσιν "the law that they will proclaim."

In 17:10, 11 the verb ירה "instruct" had to be translated twice. In the first case, LXX has chosen—as in Exod 24:12—the verb νομοθετέομαι as a translation: everything given as legislation shall be obeyed. In the following verse the verb is related to תורה "the law that they teach you"; here, the unspecific εἴπωσίν σοι was used as a translation for יורוך, but by the insertion of κατὰ τὴν κρίσιν another reference to the legislation has been added: "You shall act according to the law and according to the judgment that they tell you" (NETS).³⁴

In one single instance one can observe that νόμος has not been used for תורה. In 17:19 τὰς ἐντολὰς ταύτας is written for את־כל־דברי התורה הזאת, which has been translated literally in 27:3. One might conclude that *nomos* was not used in this instance because the text describes a copy only (v. 18: δευτερονόμιον) read by the king, but this is speculative.³⁵

The antonym ἀνομία has only been used in 31:29. Here, the *figura etymologica* השחת תשחתון had to be translated, which was done with ἀνομίᾳ ἀνομήσετε. This is in accordance with usual rendering of שחת. A peculiarity can be found in 15:9, where בליעל "worthlessness, malice" is translated with ἀνόμημα (see above on Lev 20:14). In 13:14 בני בליעל is translated with ἄνδρες παράνομοι. This equation בליעל-παράνομος in later translations becomes the standard, as in the historical books, in the Greek Psalms and Proverbs.

Reviewing this short sketch of the Greek Pentateuch, it is apparent that in the LXX law/*nomos* is much more frequently mentioned than torah in the Hebrew text. *Nomos* is exclusively used in the singular.³⁶ The term refers to the one law of God, revealed at Mount Sinai and consisting of sections of individual commandments.³⁷ This theologically weighted transla-

---

33. Wevers 1995, 535.
34. See Monsengwo Pasinya 1973, 131–35, who assumes a more juridical meaning.
35. Similar Wevers 1995, 290.
36. See Siegert 2001, 264.
37. Similar is the result of Monsengwo Pasinya 1973, 139–40, who comes close to an identification of *nomos* and "covenant." However, his study did not deal with the term *anomia*.

tion choice is reflected by a differentiated terminology, in which the singular is used for the *nomos* and the plural for other juridical terms.[38] In turn, negative deeds are seen as a transgression of the *nomos*. In addition, ἀδικία κτλ. have also been used for a variety of Hebrew terms for injustice.[39] Moreover, certain elements of the law are emphasized, particularly the Passover, and the inclusion of proselytes in the *nomos*. The result is a greater uniformity in content and terminology.[40] Thus, *nomos* in the Greek Bible, even more than torah in the Hebrew, is a summary expression of God's will and an integrating element of Israelite religion.[41] With this high esteem of תורה/νόμος in the LXX, the translators continued a development already begun in the Hebrew canon, therefore participating in a lively process of tradition.[42]

The translation of the Pentateuch has a special significance, because usually the standard equivalents established in these first translations continued to be used in books translated later on. Therefore it is not necessary to explore the whole collection "Septuagint," but it may suffice to have a closer look at two particularly instructive translations: the book of Psalms and the Greek Proverbs. Because both writings display a significantly different understanding of the task of translating scripture, they are worth considering. Texts from prophetic books, however, will be treated separately in another paper.[43]

---

38. Other terms for commandments are usually translated in plural, even if the Hebrew *Vorlage* has a singular. See Exod 24:12 τὰς ἐντολάς for והמצוה (parallel to *nomos* in sg.), similarly Deut 5:31; instructive is also Exod 15:21: δικαιώματα καὶ κρίσεις for חק ומשפט; see Blank 1930, 262–63, 269, and the overview in Monsengwo Pasinya 1973, 140–57.

39. Siegert 2001, 236–37, 268; Rösel 1994, 234–35.

40. A similar phenomenon can be found in the cultic terminology of the Greek Pentateuch, here the uniformity is created by neologisms like ἱλαστήριον and θυσιαστήριον, see Rösel 2006, 248–49. [ch. 11 in this volume.]

41. Similar results come from the study of texts found in Qumran; see Fabry and García López 1995, 635–37.

42. See summarizing the development in the Hebrew Bible: K. Koch 1984; Crüsemann 2005; Limbeck 1997 (who inexplicably completely blurs the problem of translation).

43. But see interesting texts such as Isa 8:20; 24:16; 33:5–6, which Sonntag 2000, 137–38 has examined: the *nomos* is presented as support and protection for the people.

2. The Psalms

The Psalms are particularly instructive for the purposes of this paper, because in the later parts of the Psalter the enhancement of the torah concept is already visible even within the Hebrew text.[44] Evidence for this can be seen in the division of the Psalter in five books, comparable to the Torah, or in the fact that torah psalms were inserted to give a structure to the subcollections of the Psalter, such as Pss 1 and 119 (118).[45] This investigation is facilitated by an important study on the translation of LXX Ps 118, entitled "From Torah to Nomos" (German: Von der Tora zum Nomos).[46] The results of this dissertation are important for the entire Greek Psalter.

In the LXX Psalter תורה is translated with νόμος in all instances. Only in Ps 105(104):45 does תורה appear in the plural, recognizable even in the unpointed text due to its parallelism with חקיו. Like the Pentateuch, *nomos* here appears in the singular.[47] In Ps 119 (118):57 νόμος (sg.) is used in a unique, but in the context appropriate, translation for דבר (pl.): God's word is identified with the *nomos*. In Ps 130:4 (129:5) νόμος has been used to translate a verb: תִּוָּרֵא "you may be revered"; the translator obviously corrected תורא to תורה.[48] This translation creates an interesting reference to verse 3, where the question is asked, who can stand if God marks the iniquities/lawlessness (עונות/ἀνομίας)? Facing this threat, the one praying in verse 5 appeals to God for the sake of the law. In verse 8 the psalm ends with the hope that Israel will be redeemed from all its acts of lawlessness (עונתיו/ἀνομιῶν). While in the Hebrew text of the psalm the torah is not mentioned at all, its Greek version is a good example of how the idea of the *nomos* was inserted by translators.[49]

While the mere use of νόμος is not particularly meaningful, it has long been noticed that a large number of other *nomos*-related terms appear in

---

44. See the fundamental study by Olofsson 2001.
45. See Kratz 1996.
46. Austermann 2003.
47. חקיו is translated with the plural δικαιώματα; this is the standard equivalent in the Psalms; see Austermann 2003, 120.
48. *BHS* suggests that the Vorlage had תורתך.
49. Similar considerations are valid for the use of ἐντολή and δικαίωμα, which are not in focus here. More than one Hebrew equivalent was used respectively, thus "the focus is more on the laws and legislation as carrier of the messages expressing God's will than it is in the original" (Austermann 2003, 170; all translations of Austermann are mine).

the Greek Psalter to denote illegal behavior or even the wrongdoers themselves.[50] So ἀνομία was used as a translation in 5:5 for רשע "wickedness," in 5:6 for און "evil," in 7:15 for שקר "falsehood, lie," in 18(17):5 for בליעל "worthlessness," in 18(17):24 for עון "guilt," in 25(24):10 for זמה "wickedness," 30(29):19 for עתק "pride," and in 32(31):1 for פשע "transgression."[51] Since the lexeme is often used for different words within the same Psalm (see Pss 32 [31] or 36 [35]), one must conclude that the translator had a special inclination to use this term.

This also applies to ἄνομος, with which the wicked are designated: in 51(50):15 it stands for פשע "being sinful," in 73(72):3 for הלל "be boastful," and in 104(103):35 for רשע "wicked." In addition, frequently translators chose παράνομος, comparably rare in other books: cf. 5:6 for הלל; in 36(35):2 for פשע "sin," in 37(35):7 for מזמה "mischief," and in 41(40):9 for בליעל.[52] Similar results appear in a study of ἀνομέω: see in 25(24):3 for בגד, and παρανομέω, see in 26(25):4 for עלם.

Another interesting phenomenon is the frequent use of νομοθέτης "lawgiver" and the associated verb νομοθετέομαι. As already observed in the book of Exodus (see above on Exod 24:12), these words were usually used to translate an actual or assumed derivation of the root ירה. This translation choice has led to surprising changes in the meaning of a verse: Well-known is the new interpretation of Ps 9:21. While the Hebrew text reads שיתה יהוה מורה להם "Put, O Lord, fear onto them," the Greek translation reads κατάστησον κύριε νομοθέτην ἐπ᾽αὐτούς "Set a lawgiver over them, O Lord." Obviously the translator read מוֹרֶה "teacher" in the consonantal text.[53] In a second step of interpretation he then made a connection between the teacher and the right doctrine, the *nomos*: thus a teacher became a lawgiver. The same interpretation can be seen in 84(83):7, where מוֹרֶה II "early rain" had to be translated. Instead of an image of the end of a

---

50. See Flashar 1912; of particular interest is the second part of the study pp. 161–89. See also the appendix in Olofsson 2001, 320–28.

51. See the overview in Austermann 2003, 180–92.

52. It should at least be noted that in the context of this short paper the examination of the semantics of παρανομία and ἀνομία cannot be carried out, although it would actually be necessary. It would be interesting to know whether one can find reasons for the translator's choice of one or the other lexeme.

53. According to Siegert 2001, 125, this is the original meaning of the text. He assumes that the position of a torah-instructor was unknown to the Masoretes of the ninth century, so that they vocalized מוֹרָה "fear."

drought by the early rain in the Hebrew psalm, one can now read a confession in the Greek psalm: "because the lawgiver gives blessings."

Other derivations of the root ירה were translated similarly in Ps 25(24):8, 12; 27(26):11; 119(118):33, 102, 104; in these verses, God is always the subject of the verb νομοθετέομαι. As a result, the translation is—as Frank Austermann rightly suggests—a reasoned interpretation of the Hebrew text. The translator has established on the one hand a connection to the language of the Pentateuch. On the other, he shows that he understands "God explicitly as the one who gives his law, teaches his law and therefore interprets his law by himself."[54] This fits well to another characteristic of the Greek Psalms, because the idea of divine education is introduced into the texts of several psalms, see 2:12; 90(89):10.

Summarizing the results of this brief investigation of the use of νόμος κτλ. in the Greek Psalter, my conclusion confirms that of earlier studies. The topic torah/*nomos* is one of the focal points of the translator's theological thinking.[55] The divine law is all-embracing and leads to salvation. Therefore all kinds of violation and improper behavior are ultimately directed against this comprehensive divine law. This broad understanding of *nomos* is even more developed in the Psalms than in the Pentateuch itself, which is probably an effect of the fact that they were translated later. In the second century BCE the development of centralizing the idea of the torah became more important, a development also discernable in the Qumran texts and in writings from Jewish-Hellenistic authors.[56] Also apparent in the frequent use of negative terms such as παρανομία and ἀνομία κτλ. is another dimension of *nomos* developed especially in Greek-speaking communities: now the entire life is determined by references to the *nomos*, and every transgression is now qualified according to God's law.[57] To say it another way: obedience to the law becomes now the precondition for a successful life. This may have been implied when תורה or דת were used in Hebrew or Aramaic-speaking circles, but only in the Greek text does

---

54. Austermann 2003, 178.
55. See Flashar 1912, 169–70; Prijs 1948, 62. Similarly the results of Olofsson 2001, and Austermann 2003, 208. In my opinion, however, Austermann underestimates the active role of the translator in this process.
56. Weber 2000, 37–153, who underrates the importance of the LXX for the developments he is describing.
57. The consideration of Cordes 2004, 235, that the ἄνομοι in the Psalms refer to the non-Jewish majority in the diaspora, is interesting, but needs further support.

this conclusion become overt. This was probably an important step toward the paramount importance of the *nomos*, so influential for New Testament writers.[58] In this process the importance of the Psalms cannot be underestimated, because they belong to those scriptures that were most frequently quoted (or alluded to) in the New Testament, as is apparent in the charts in the appendix of the *Novum Testamentum Graece* by Nestle-Aland.

3. Proverbs and Other Books

These results are confirmed by data gathered from other books. In the collection of Proverbs, for example, the translators were faced with the problem that תורה could refer to divine commandments but also to the instructions of the parents as well.[59] This problem led to interesting solutions: For example, in 1:8 θεσμός "precepts" (in plural) is used for the instruction of the mother (תורת אמך), a translation choice rarely used in translated books. The same translation appears in 6:20, where νόμους (pl.) has been used for the commandment (מצות אביך) of the father.[60] In 7:2, when תורה is translated with λόγους (pl.), again human instructions are meant. In 4:2 and 13:14 νόμος (sg.) stands for human laws, while in other texts (6:23; 28:4–9, 29:18) νόμος often refers to the divine law. Interesting are two adverbs in 31:26–28, a passage describing maternal instructions. Here תורת חסד "teaching of kindness" was translated with ἐννόμως "according to the law" (only to be found in Sirach prologue, 36) and a second time with νομοθέσμως "lawful"; it is obvious that this instruction is related to the νόμος.[61]

In some instances νόμος has furthermore been added without an equivalent in the *Vorlage*. The famous "The fear of the Lord is the beginning of wisdom. And knowledge of the Holy One is insight" (NRSV) in Prov 9:10 appears in expanded form in the Greek: τό γάρ γνῶναι νόμον διανοίας ἐστὶν ἀγαθῆς "for to know the law is the sign of a sound mind" (NETS). Similar additions can also be found in 13:15 and 3:16, therefore disqualifying a possibility that they stem from a coincidence of textual

---

58. See, e.g., Dunn 1996, 312.
59. See also the excursus by Jüngling 2007, 214–16, who unfortunately deals with *nomos* only, not with the antonyms.
60. See the similar interpretation by Cook 1997, 66.
61. νομοθέσμως, a *hapax legomenon*, is probably a neologism by the translator, see d'Hamonville 2000, 341.

transmission.⁶² In turn, in 3:1 תורה (sg.) is translated with the plural ἐμῶν νομίμων, apparently because it does not refer to God's commandments.⁶³

As in the other books investigated above, παράνομος has also been used strikingly often in the book of Proverbs. According to 1:18–19 lawlessness can destroy one's own life (without direct equivalent in the MT); in 2:22 παράνομος stands for בגד "to act faithlessly." In 4:14 the "way of the evildoers" (דרך רעים) becomes ὁδοὺς παρανόμων "ways of transgressors." In 4:17 the lexeme is used for חמס "violence," in 5:22 for עון "sin," and in 6:12 once again for בליעל "worthlessness." This result corresponds to the Psalms, especially since ἄνομος stands in the same way for different Hebrew words (see above in 1:19). Thus, even this brief survey can confirm the impression of J. Cook that the idea of the law is so integral to the thinking of the translator that its importance is more heightened than in the Hebrew text.⁶⁴

Remarkably, the Greek book of Job also displays a preference for ἄνομος and ἀνομία, although the idea of the law plays no significant role in this writing. The lexemes occur twenty times, often without a direct equivalent in the Hebrew text. The same phenomenon can be seen in LXX Isaiah (about fifty times) or in Ezekiel (about fifty times). Finally, the frequent use of νόμος in Ben Sira, Wisdom of Solomon, or the books of Maccabees is striking. In contrast, in the historical books (Joshua–2 Kings, Ezra, Nehemiah, Chronicles) no specific usage can be determined: νόμος is used as the standard equivalent for תורה (or דת in Aramaic) throughout, while ἄνομος κτλ. and παράνομος are rare. This is not surprising: the translations of these books closely cling to their *Vorlage* and show only a little willingness for free renderings or expositions in comparison to other translations.

Even if this overview is quite general, it confirms the previous impressions: the idea of the divine law has a higher priority in the Greek Bible than in the Hebrew. This emphasis becomes especially obvious when considering derivations with α-privative and παρα-. One should note that the phenomenon occurs especially in books used for instruction. If according

---

62. Verse 3:16 is borrowed from 31:26, but translated differently; see d'Hamonville 2000, 177. D'Hamonville 2000, 53, sees 9:10a and 13:15b as later additions by a "scribe 'legaliste.'" If this assumption is correct, the additions would make the original sense even clearer. According to Cook 1997, 260–65, the verse has been formulated by the translator, moreover, he has transferred it from 13:16 also to 9:10. Jüngling 2007, 212–14 leaves the question without decision.

63. In accordance with Siegert 2001, 265.

64. Cook 1997, 331.

to these writings even minor misdeeds not only threaten personal well-being but also signify a transgression of the divine law, it is obvious that *nomos* has become a "comprehensive perspective of the entire order of life and faith."[65] Thus the idea of *nomos* began to play a key role in the life of Hellenistic Jews, who became familiarized with the traditions of Israel in the apparel of the LXX. The "ethicization of the Torah" has begun.[66]

4. Outlook

Even if this survey could shed some light on the use of *nomos* and its derivatives in the LXX, some important questions remain unanswered. One of them would be whether there are specifics or differences in the meaning of νόμος in individual books. Some observations have already been made, for example, the avoidance of νόμος when the text indicates human commandments (Prov 3:1), but it would also be promising to look at the relationship of law (νόμος and derivatives) and justice (δίκη and derivatives). Again, the antonyms could be of particular importance, as ἀνομία and ἀδικία are often used in parallelisms.[67] Moreover, it would be worth investigating whether the idea expressed in 4 Macc 5:20–21 also applies to previous translations, that small and great transgressions (παρανομέω) are of equal seriousness, for in either case the law (νόμος) is equally despised.[68] As for the sapiential writings, the question of the relationship between *nomos* and *sophia* arises. Preliminary results indicate that the answer to this question will probably be different for the book of Proverbs on the one hand and Ben Sira on the other.[69] This further raises the question of whether there is already in the LXX a tendency to understand the torah as the world order, a paradigm apparent in later writings.[70]

---

65. Weber 2000, 23; in German: "eine umfassende Perspektive der gesamten Lebens- und Glaubensordnung."
66. See Weber 2001, 337–39.
67. See Dodd 1954, 76–81.
68. See K. Koch 1984, 51, although his focus is on the book of Jubilees.
69. According to Cook 1997, 331. See also Hoffmann 1999, 321–22, with detailed investigations in 4 Ezra. He summarizes (217–20) that in parts of the apocalyptic literature torah and wisdom are seen almost identical. Unfortunately he does not deal with the Greek terms.
70. Lichtenberger 1996, 16; See also Nickelsburg 2006, 222–35, who differentiates between Mosaic and sapiential approaches in the apocrypha and pseudepigrapha.

Even more important is the question whether and to what extent a shift in meaning from תורה to νόμος is caused only by the fact that the semantic connotations of the Greek word in its Hellenistic usage differ from those of the Hebrew term. Here one should also examine the semantics of Aramaic דת, because in second and first century Palestine Aramaic was the language predominantly spoken.

When dealing with questions like these, besides the seminal work of Charles Dodd, often the German scholar Klaus Berger is cited.[71] According to him: "the translation of תורה with νόμος … was as consequential as misleading" and the תורה-passages of the OT were leveled to "fit into the popular Jewish-Hellenistic understanding of *nomos*," which led to the confusion between the meanings of "instruction" and "law."[72]

Both in Classical Greek and in later Hellenistic usage, νόμος was a clearly defined term that denoted a set of normative of rules, given by a deity and connected with the *polis*, later also the *ethnos*.[73] From the fifth century BCE on, *nomos* denotes a written law given by a human or divine legislator (νομοθέτης), identified with this lawgiver but ultimately credited to Zeus as the actual author of the laws. Therefore the choice of *nomos* as a translation for Biblical תורה is immediately evident.[74] However, in the Greek sphere *nomos* loses its cultic dimensions and thus its connection to holiness. In turn, in philosophical writings the term becomes parallelized with *logos* and *nous*. Having this development in mind, the extension of the meaning of *nomos* toward the idea of a general, all-embracing order of the world can easily be explained.

In sum, it is clear that the differentiations that could be observed in the preceding chapters between individual laws formulated in the plural (νόμιμα, ἐντολαί, κρίματα, etc.), and the universal νόμος in the singular fits well into the usage of the term in the Hellenistic world. For Jews living in the diaspora, it furthermore became possible to minimize the importance

---

71. Dodd 1935, 25; the passage on the differing conceptions of law can be found in pp. 25–41. It is still worth reading if one is interested in the history of research.

72. Berger 1972, 32; in German: "die Übersetzung von תורה durch νόμος … ebenso folgenreich wie irreführend gewesen." Contrary to this is the recently published position of Cordes 2004, 234, who assumes that the meaning of the term *nomos* has largely adopted the meaning of the Hebrew term.

73. Still instructive is Kleinknecht 1942; Heinimann 1945. The current status of research can be found in Gehrke 1995.

74. See Schwemer 1996, 71. But see also Berger 1972, 36, who is more skeptical. See also the nuanced judgment by Segal 1987, who is mostly concerned with Philo.

of single cultic instructions without calling into question the validity of the *nomos*. Thus it seems hardly appropriate to formulate that the translation of torah with *nomos* has leveled out the Hebrew concept of torah, as Klaus Berger has done (above, n. 72).

These brief comments may suffice for this short survey. In my view it is apparent that additional, interdisciplinary research is needed. But already one can conclude that the development of the Jewish-Hellenistic conception of *nomos* cannot be described adequately without considering the LXX and its differentiated treatment of the theme. Greek translators presuppose the understanding of torah as attested in late books of the Hebrew Bible but expand this meaning by emphasizing the dimensions of lawlessness (ἀνομία) and transgression of the law (παρανομία). Thus the characteristic of the *nomos* as an order of salvation is amplified, so that one can almost speak of a *nomos*-soteriology of the LXX. At the same time, for the Jewish communities an orientation is offered within the Hellenistic environment of diverse ethnic and religious groups: their own *nomos* is characterized as superior and of unsurpassable age due to the seniority of Moses, the legislator. Thus it is not surprising that in the second century the well-known statement could be formulated by Aristobulus (frag. 3) "It is clear that Plato followed the tradition of the law that we use [νομοθεσία]."[75]

Bibliography

Achenbach, Reinhard. 2005. "Tora: I. AT." *RGG*[4] 8:476–77.
Austermann, Frank. 2003. *Von der Tora zum Nomos: Untersuchungen zur Übersetzungsweise und Interpretation im Septuaginta-Psalter*. NAWG Phil-Hist Klasse 3, 257. MSU 27. Göttingen: Vandenhoeck & Ruprecht.
Berger, Klaus. 1972. *Die Gesetzesauslegung Jesu: Ihr historischer Hintergrund im Judentum und im Alten Testament, Teil 1; Markus und Parallelen*. WMANT 40. Neukirchen-Vluyn: Neukirchener Verlag.
Bergmeier, Roland. 2000. *Das Gesetz im Römerbrief und andere Studien zum Neuen Testament*. WUNT 1/121. Tübingen: Mohr Siebeck.
Betz, Hans Dieter. 1988. *Der Galaterbrief: Ein Kommentar zum Brief des Apostels Paulus an die Gemeinden in Galatien*. Hermeneia. Munich: Kaiser.

---

75. See Weber 2000, 98–108.

Blank, Sheldon H. 1930. "The LXX Renderings of Old Testament Terms for Law." *HUCA* 7:259–83.

Cook, Johann. 1997. *The Septuagint of Proverbs: Jewish and/or Hellenistic Proverbs? Concerning the Hellenistic Colouring of LXX Proverbs.* VTSup 69. Leiden: Brill.

Cordes, Ariane. 2004. *Die Asafpsalmen in der Septuaginta: Der griechische Psalter als Übersetzung und theologisches Zeugnis.* HBS 41. Freiburg im Briesgau: Herder.

Crüsemann, Frank. 2005. *Die Tora: Theologie und Sozialgeschichte des alttestamentlichen Gesetzes.* 3rd ed. Gütersloh: Gütersloher Verlagshaus.

Davison, James E. 1985. "Anomia and the Question of an Antinomian Polemic in Matthew." *JBL* 104:617–35.

Deines, Roland. 2005. *Die Gerechtigkeit der Tora im Reich des Messias: Mt 5,13–20 als Schlüsseltext der matthäischen Theologie.* WUNT 1/177. Tübingen: Mohr Siebeck.

D'Hamonville, David-Marc. 2000. *Les Proverbes.* BdA 17. Paris: Cerf.

Dines, Jennifer M. 2004. *The Septuagint.* Edinburgh: T&T Clark.

Dodd, Charles H. 1954. *The Bible and the Greeks.* London: Hodder & Stoughton.

Dunn, James D. G. 1996. "In Search of Common Ground." Pages 309–34 in *Paul and the Mosaic Law: The Third Durham Tübingen Research Symposium on Earliest Christianity and Judaism (Durham, September, 1994).* Edited by James D. G. Dunn. WUNT 1/89. Tübingen: Mohr Siebeck.

Fabry, Heinz-Josef, and F. M. García López. 1995. "תורה." *ThWAT* 8:597–637.

Flashar, Martin. 1912. "Exegetische Studien zum Septuagintapsalter." *ZAW* 32:81–116; 161–89; 241–68.

Gehrke, Hans-Joachim. 1995. "Der Nomosbegriff der Polis." Pages 13–35 in *Nomos und Gesetz: Ursprünge und Wirkungen des griechischen Gesetzesdenkens.* Edited by Okko Behrends and Wolfgang Sellert. Abhandlung der Akademie der Wissenschaften zu Göttingen, Philologisch-Historische Klasse 3, 209. Göttingen: Vandenhoeck & Ruprecht.

Harl, Marguerite. 1986. *La Genèse.* BdA 1. Paris: Cerf.

Heinimann, Felix. 1945. *Nomos und Physis: Herkunft und Bedeutung einer Antithese im griechischen Denken des 5. Jahrhunderts.* SBA 1. Basel: Reinhardt.

Hoffmann, Heinrich. 1999. *Das Gesetz in der frühjüdischen Apokalyptik.* SUNT 23. Göttingen: Vandenhoeck & Ruprecht.

Honigman, Sylvie. 2003. *The Septuagint and Homeric Scholarship in Alexandria: A Study in the Narrative of the "Letter of Aristeas."* London: Routledge.
Hübner, Hans. 1992. "νόμος." *ExWNT* 2:1158–72.
Finsterbusch, Karin. 2005. *Weisung für Israel: Studien zum religiösen Lehren und Lernen im Deuteronomium und in seinem Umfeld.* FAT 1/44. Tübingen: Mohr Siebeck.
Jüngling, Hans-Winfried. 2007. "Der Mensch in Schöpfung und Zeit. Gedanken zur Anthropologie der Sprichwörter[LXX]." Pages 203–25 in vol. 3 of *Im Brennpunkt: Die Septuaginta; Studien zur Theologie, Anthropologie, Ekklesiologie, Eschatologie und Liturgie der Griechischen Bibel.* Edited by Heinz-Josef Fabry and Dieter Böhler. BWANT 174. Stuttgart: Kohlhammer.
Kleinknecht, Hermann. 1942. "νόμος A. Der νόμος in Griechentum und Hellenismus." *ThWNT* 4:1016–29.
Koch, Dietrich-Alex. 1986. *Die Schrift als Zeuge des Evangeliums: Untersuchungen zur Verwendung und zum Verständnis der Schrift bei Paulus.* BHT 69. Tübingen: Mohr Siebeck.
Koch, Klaus. 1984. "Gesetz I. AT." *TRE* 13:40–52.
Kratz, Reinhard G. 1996. "Die Tora Davids: Psalm 1 und die doxologische Fünfteilung des Psalters." *ZTK* 93:1–34.
Le Boulluec, Alain, and Pierre Sandevoir. 1989. *L'Exode.* BdA 2. Paris: Cerf.
Lichtenberger, Hermann. 1996. "Das Tora-Verständnis im Judentum zur Zeit des Paulus." Pages 7–23 in *Paul and the Mosaic Law.* Edited by James D. G. Dunn. WUNT 1/89. Tübingen: Mohr Siebeck.
Limbeck, Meinrad. 1997. *Das Gesetz im Alten und Neuen Testament.* Darmstadt: Wissenschaftliche Buchgesellschaft.
Monsengwo Pasinya, Laurent. 1973. *La notion de Nomos dans le Pentateuque grec.* AnBib 52. Rome: Biblical Institute Press.
Nickelsburg, George W. E. 2006. "Torah and the Deuteronomic Scheme in the Apocrypha and Pseudepigrapha." Pages 222–35 in *Das Gesetz im frühen Judentum und im Neuen Testament: Festschrift für Christoph Burchard zum 75. Geburtstag.* Edited by Dieter Sänger and Matthias Konradt. NTOA 57. Göttingen: Vandenhoeck & Ruprecht; Fribourg: Presses Universitaires.
Olofsson, Staffan. 2001. "Law and Lawbreaking in the LXX Psalms: A Case of Theological Exegesis." Pages 291–330 in *Der Septuaginta-Psalter: Sprachliche und theologische Aspekte.* Edited by Erich Zenger. HBS 32. Freiburg im Breisgau: Herder.

Osten-Sacken, Peter von der. 1989. *Die Heiligkeit der Tora: Studien zum Gesetz bei Paulus*. Munich: Kaiser.

Prijs, Leo. 1948. *Jüdische Tradition in der Septuaginta*. Leiden: Brill.

Rösel, Martin. 1994. *Übersetzung als Vollendung der Auslegung: Studien zur Genesis-Septuaginta*. BZAW 223. Berlin: de Gruyter.

———. 2006. "Towards a 'Theology of the Septuagint.'" Pages 239–52 in *Septuagint Research: Issues and Challenges in the Study of the Greek Jewish Scriptures*. Edited by Wolfgang Kraus and R. Glenn Wooden. SCS 53. Atlanta: Society of Biblical Literature. [ch. 11 in this volume.]

———. 2007. "Der Brief des Aristeas an Philokrates, der Tempel in Leontopolis und die Bedeutung der Religionsgeschichte Israels in hellenistischer Zeit." Pages 327–44 in *"Sieben Augen auf einem Stein" (Sach 3,9). Festschrift Ina Willi-Plein*. Edited by Friedhelm Hartenstein and Michael Pietsch. Neukirchen-Vluyn: Neukirchener Verlag. [English translation ch. 1 in this volume.]

Schwemer, Anna M. 1996. "Zum Verhältnis von Diatheke und Nomos in den Schriften der jüdischen Diaspora Ägyptens in hellenistisch-römischer Zeit." Pages 67–109 in *Bund und Tora: Zur theologischen Begriffsgeschichte in altestamentlicher, frühjüdischer und urchristlicher Tradition*. Edited by Friedrich Avemarie and Hermann Lichtenberger. WUNT 1/92. Tübingen: Mohr Siebeck.

Segal, Alan F. 1987. "Torah and Nomos in Recent Scholarly Discussions." Pages 19–28 in *The Other Judaisms of Late Antiquity*. Edited by Alan F. Segal. BJS 127. Atlanta: Scholars Press.

Siegert, Folkert. 2001. *Zwischen Hebräischer Bibel und Altem Testament: Eine Einführung in die Septuaginta*. MJS 9. Münster: LIT.

Smend, Rudolf, and Josef Zmijewski. 1991. "Gesetz." *NBL* 1:825–29.

Sonntag, Holger. 2000. Νομος σωτηρ: *Zur politischen Theologie des Gesetzes bei Paulus und im antiken Kontext*. Texte und Arbeiten zum neutestamentlichen Zeitalter 34. Tübingen: Francke.

Tilly, Michael. 2005. *Einführung in die Septuaginta*. Darmstadt: Wissenschaftliche Buchgesellschaft.

Weber, Reinhard. 2000. *Das Gesetz im hellenistischen Judentum: Studien zum Verständnis und zur Funktion der Tora von Demetrios bis Pseudo-Phokylides*. Arbeiten zur Religion und Geschichte des Urchristentums 10. New York: Lang.

———. 2001. *Das "Gesetz" bei Philon von Alexandrien und Flavius Josephus: Studien zum Verständnis und zur Funktion der Tora bei den beiden Hauptzeugen des hellenistischen Judentums.* Arbeiten zur Religion und Geschichte des Urchristentums 11. New York: Lang.

Wevers, John William. 1990. *Notes on the Greek Text of Exodus.* SCS 30. Atlanta: Scholars Press

———. 1993. *Notes on the Greek Text of Genesis.* SCS 35. Atlanta: Scholars Press

———. 1995. *Notes on the Greek Text of Deuteronomy.* SCS 39. Atlanta: Scholars Press.

———. 1997. *Notes on the Greek Text of Leviticus.* SCS 44. Atlanta: Scholars Press.

Original Publications

Part 1: On the LXX in General

1. "The Letter of Aristeas to Philocrates, the Temple in Leontopolis and the Importance of the History of Israelite Religion in the Hellenistic Period." Translation of "Der Brief des Aristeas an Philokrates, der Tempel in Leontopolis und die Bedeutung der Religionsgeschichte Israels in hellenistischer Zeit." Pages 327–44 in *Sieben Augen auf einem Stein (Sach 3,9): Studien zur Literatur des Zweiten Tempels; Festschrift für Ina Willi-Plein zum 65. Geburtstag*. Edited by Friedhelm Hartenstein and Michael Pietsch. Neukirchen-Vluyn: Neukirchener Verlag.

2. "Schreiber, Übersetzer, Theologen. Die Septuaginta als Dokument der Schrift-, Lese- und Übersetzungskultur des Judentums." Pages 83–102 in *Die Septuaginta: Texte, Kontexte, Lebenswelten*. Edited by Martin Karrer and Wolfgang Kraus. WUNT 1/219. Tübingen: Mohr Siebeck, 2008.

3. "Translators as Interpreters: Scriptural Interpretation in the Septuagint." Pages 64–91 in *A Companion to Biblical Interpretation in Early Judaism*. Edited by Matthias Henze. Grand Rapids: Eerdmans, 2011.

Part 2: On Specific Texts

4. "The Chronological System of Genesis-Septuagint (Genesis 5 and 11)." Translated and abbreviated from pages 129–44 in *Übersetzung als Vollendung der Auslegung: Studien zur Genesis-Septuaginta*. BZAW 223. Berlin: de Gruyter, 1994.

5. "Jakob, Bileam und der Messias. Messianische Erwartungen in Gen 49 und Num 22–24." Pages 151–75 in *The Septuagint and Messianism*. Edited by Michael A. Knibb. BETL 195. Leuven: Peeters, 2006.

6. "The Septuagint-Version of the Book of Joshua." *Scandinavian Journal of the Old Testament* 16 (2002): 5–23.

7. "Salomo und die Sonne: Zur Rekonstruktion des Tempelweihspruchs 1.Kön 8,12–13." *ZAW* 121 (2009): 402–17.

8. "Deuteronomists in the Septuagint of the Historical Books?" Previously unpublished paper presented at the Annual Meeting of the Society of Biblical Literature. New Orleans, 23 November 2009.

9. "Die Jungfrauengeburt des endzeitlichen Immanuel. Jesaja 7 in der Übersetzung der Septuaginta." *Jahrbuch Biblische Theologie* 6 (1991): 135–51.

10. "Die Psalmüberschriften des Septuagintapsalters." Pages 125–48 in *Der Septuaginta-Psalter: Sprachliche und theologische Aspekte*. Edited by Erich Zenger. HBS 32. Freiburg im Breisgau: Herder, 2001.

Part 3: Theology and Anthropology

11. "Towards a 'Theology of the Septuagint.'" Pages 239–52 in *Septuagint Research: Issues and Challenges in the Study of the Greek Jewish Scriptures*. Edited by Wolfgang Kraus and R. Glenn Wooden. SCS 53. Atlanta: Society of Biblical Literature, 2006.

12. "A Theology of the Septuagint? Clarifications and Definitions." Previously unpublished paper presented at the Annual Meeting of the Society of Biblical Literature. Atlanta. 23 November 2015.

13. "The Reading and Translation of the Divine Name in the Masoretic Tradition and the Greek Pentateuch—with an Appendix: Frank Shaw's Book on ΙΑΩ." *JSOT* 31 (2007): 411–28.

14. "Der hebräische Mensch im griechischen Gewand. Anthropologische Akzentsetzungen in der Septuaginta." Pages 69–92 in *Der Mensch im alten Israel: Neue Forschungen zur alttestamentlichen Anthropologie*. Edited by Bernd Janowski and Kathrin Liess. HBS 59. Freiburg im Breisgau: Herder, 2009.

15. "Nomothesis: The Understanding of the Law in the Septuagint." Translation of "Nomothesie: Zum Gesetzesverständnis der Septuaginta." Pages 132–50 in vol. 3 of *Im Brennpunkt: Die Septuaginta; Studien zur Theologie, Anthropologie, Ekklesiologie, Eschatologie und Liturgie der Griechischen Bibel*. Edited by Heinz-Josef Fabry and Dieter Böhler. BWANT 174. Stuttgart: Kohlhammer, 2001.

Ancient Sources Index

Old Testament/Septuagint

Genesis

1:2	66, 325	6–8			66
1:9	47	6:3			264, 326
1:20–21	329	6:5			327
1:26	263, 318, 325	6:5–6			73
1:30	329	6:6			331
2:2–3	77–78	6:6–7			258, 300
2:3	72	6:14			68
2:7	325	6:19–20			47
2:9	72, 112, 326	7:3			73
2:14	75	7:6			76, 89, 91, 93
2:16	74	7:11			98
2:19	72, 112	8:20			152
2:23	326	8:21			320, 327
3:1	73	8:22			76
3:3	73	10:6			104
3:5	326	10:22			94
3:17	73, 327	11:1			68
3:19	326	11:1–9			29
3:23–24	120	11:3			74
4:1	73	11:10			93, 95
4:5	73	11:10–32			93
4:7	78	11:12			93
4:24	91	11:13			93
5:3–6	89	11:22			93
5:3–32	91	11:24			93, 98
5:11	94	11:31			72
5:18	90	12:3			13
5:23	90	12:4			100
5:25–27	90	12:5			328
5:28	98	12:10–20			29
5:28–31	91	12:17			300
5:32	93	13:10			258
		13:13			300
		13:16			122
		15:10			79

Genesis (cont.)

17:1	69, 97
17:17	94, 97
18:13–14	302
19:15	345
21:5	96, 100
22:9–10	73
22:14	74
24:43	208
25:26	96, 100
26:5	345
27:29	74
28:5	75
28:10	72
28:14	122
30:27	300
31:19–35	258
31:49	300–301
31:53	301
32:2	301
32:16	119
36:6	320, 328
37:16	75
38:7	258, 300
41:45	75
42:23	30, 38
46:26	117
47:9	96, 100
48:3	69
49:1	114
49:8	115
49:8–12	114
49:9	115, 126–27
49:10	73, 109–10, 116, 118, 131
49:11	115, 119
49:16	116
49:20	120
49:27	115
49:28	116
50:2	76
50:23	117

Exodus

2:8	208
2:11	125
3:14	259
3:18	301
4:24	261
5:2–3	301
6:3	259
7:23	320
8:6	48
9:3	304
10:11	301
10:16	331
11:6	76
11:17	76
12:40	96, 100, 102–3
12:43	345–46
12:49	346
13:10	346
13:19	302
13:21	302
14:7	349
15:1	171
15:3	79, 279, 281
15:17	169, 171
16:3	331
16:7	300
16:9	300
18:8	125
18:20	346
19:3	260
20:21	169, 171
24:10	80
24:11	331
24:12	48, 61, 331, 346, 350
25:9	169
32:7	347
32:15	349
34:6–7	349
34:10	125
34:14	260

Leviticus

6:11 (18)	347
6:15 (22)	347
15:3	348
18:5	343
18:21	298

19:19	347	24:7	70, 73, 109–10, 120, 127, 129–32, 262
19:37	347		
21:1	328	24:8	126, 131–32
23:23–25	37	24:9	126, 130
24:7	230	24:13	302
24:16	80, 260, 298	24:14	130
25:10	104	24:17	70, 109–10, 120, 128, 131
26:1	121	25:2	258
26:30	121	26:65	149
26:46	347–48	27:17	75
27:23	236	28:2	331
		31:1–8	123
Numbers		31:21	349
1	73	31:37–40	236
1:20	76		
4:11	66	Deuteronomy	
8:9	74	2:14	79, 300
9:3	348	6:16	204
10:10	230	7:18–19	304
10:11	150	11:17	187
14:3	74	12	19
14:18	349	12:5	183
15:15	348	12:14	183
16:2	76	13:14	350
16:5	79, 300	14:7	76
16:11	300	15:9	350
16:15	70–71	17:10	48, 61, 350
19:1–10	37	17:18	183
19:2	349	17:19	350
19:14	76	24:8	349
20:14	125	26:5	71, 75
22:18	121	26:5–6	183
22:34	121, 301	26:18	295
22:41	121	27:2–5	141
23:1	120, 261	27:3	350
23:3	66	27:5–6	183
23:5	301	28:49	29
23:10	122	29:3	188
23:12	301	29:19	349
23:19	123, 261, 331	30:6	149
23:21	124, 126	31:11	188
23:22	126, 131	31:28	188
23:24	126, 130	31:29	350
23:26	302	32:23	75
24:5–6	131	32:44	349

Joshua		10:6	185
1:7–8	154, 186	17:5	189
1:15	186	18:14–20	189
3:17	153		
4:1	153	Ruth	
4:10–11	153	1:20	70
4:24	153		
5:2	149	1 Samuel	
5:4–5	148	7:4	185
5:6	149		
6:7	144	2 Samuel	
6:26	140, 143–45, 154, 183	1:18	162
8:12–13	140	1:23	162
8:30–35	140, 183	7:10	171
9:2	140, 183	7:14–21	160
9:27	183	12:15	303
10:13	162, 165	21:3	129
15:59	140, 145	22:10	171
16:10	140, 146		
19:47–48	140	1 Kings	
19:49–50	147	7:19	231
20:4–6	140	8:12–13	159, 161–74
21:35	140	6:1	96, 100, 102–3
21:42	140, 146	6:11–14	187
22:10	152	9:9	188
22:10–29	261	9:16–17	146
22:10–34	185	10:2	29
22:28	152	16:34	145, 184
22:33–34	140		
22:34	152	2 Kings	
23:5	140	17:7	188
23:7	153, 185	17:15	188
23:16	187	18:17–28	30
24:4	140, 183		
24:5	148	1 Chronicles	
24:14	153, 185	5:27–34 (6:1–8)	102
24:17	186		
24:19	153	2 Chronicles	
24:25	152	6:1–2	170
24:27	152		
24:31	140, 147	Ezra	
24:33	140, 150, 184–85	3:8	96, 100, 102–3
		4:7	29, 38
Judges			
3:12–30	185		

Nehemiah		56(55):1	232
8:8	30	60(59):1	230, 232
13:24	29	62(61):1	231
		68(67):13	231
Esther		68(67):23	240
1:22	29	68(67):25	208
3:12	29	69(68):1	231
4:17	204	70(69):1	230
8:9	29	75(74):1	233
9:31	320	76(75):1	239
		77(76):1	231
Psalms		78(77):35	80
1:5	335	78(77):72	234
2:12	61, 262, 333	80(79):1	231, 239
5:1	229	83(82):9	239
6:1	229	84(83):7	60, 353
7:1	229	84(83):12	80
8:1	229	86(85):1	227
8:3	240	88(87):1	232
9:1	230	90(89):1	227
9:21	47, 58–63, 331, 353	90(89):2–3	71
12(11):12	29	90(89):10	61
15:9	164	91(90):3	69
16(15):7	234, 334	93(94):19	320
16(15):9–11	335	104	30
17(16):12	27	105(104):45	352
17(16):15	260	110(109):1	240, 291
18(17):36	333	111(110):10	234
19:2–7	172	119(118):57	352
19(18):5	240	119(118):66	333
21(20):3	320	130:4(129:5)	352
22(21):1	230	131(130):1	320
27(26):1	243	147(146):2	239
29(28):1	243	147(146):5	234
29(28):6	68	151:1	242
31(30):1	240		
37(36):11	229	Job	
38(37):1	230, 243	5:17	70
39(38):1	231	18:15	162
44(43):23	240	27:4	320
48(47):15	230	42:17	335
49(48):10	240		
49(48):13	234	Proverbs	
49(48):16	240	1:8	355
53(52):1	232	1:18–9	356

Proverbs (cont.)		7:13	205
2:22	356	7:14	197, 207, 215
3:1	356	7:14–17	205
3:16	355	7:18–25	206
4:2	355	7:25	207
4:14	356	9:1–7 (8:23–9:6)	198
4:17	356	9:6 (4)	213
5:22	356	9:12 (11)	199
6:12	356	9:21 (20)	199
6:20	355	10:21	199
7:2	355	11:1	115, 129
8:22	333	11:10	118
9:10	332–33, 355	11:11	199
9:16	320	14:2	199
13:14	355	14:12	213–14
13:15	332, 355	17:3	199
19:8	320	19:18	29
25:1	333	19:19	19
31:26–28	355	19:22	201
		24:14	199
Wisdom of Solomon		28:1	199
2:23	325	30:11	199
4:2	204	30:26	201
10:12	204	31:3	327
		33:16	201
Sirach		36:9	199
Prol 1:20	38	42:6	118
Prol 1:21–26	57	43:10	202
11:14	320	45:8	129
39:28	320	49:7	201
42:15	160	52:15	118, 202
42:15–6	172	55:3	201
47:17	38	59:15	202
		60:19	199
Isaiah		61:1	201
1:3	202	65:11	213–14
4:2	199		
4:3	199	*Jeremiah*	
6:9	202	2:22	227
6:10	201	5:15	29
7	197–216	23:5	116
7:3	200	31:31–34	213
7:4	200	33:15	116
7:9	155, 203, 234, 263, 334	38(31):33	320
7:12	205		

Ancient Sources Index

Ezekiel
- 3:5–6 — 29
- 11:19–20 — 213
- 17:8 — 115
- 17:23 — 115
- 19:10 — 115
- 47:12 — 162, 164

Daniel
- 1–6 — 11
- 1:4 — 30
- 1:17 — 203
- 1:20 — 203
- 2:18 — 309
- 2:20 — 309
- 2:21 — 203
- 3:29 — 29
- 4:20 — 309
- 5:1 — 38
- 6:4 — 203
- 7:13 — 129, 214
- 7:18 — 132
- 8:16 — 203
- 9 — 13
- 9:3 — 214
- 9:22 — 94, 304
- 10:2–3 — 214
- 11:33 — 203
- 12:3 — 154, 203

Amos
- 1:13–2:6 — 66

Habakkuk
- 2:13 — 70
- 3:5 — 69
- 3:16 — 320

Zechariah
- 1:12 — 99
- 10:3 — 162
- 13:7 — 129

New Testament

Matthew
- 1:23 — 215
- 21:16 — 240
- 22:40 — 240
- 22:41–46 — 291

Romans
- 2:20 — 343
- 8:36 — 240
- 10:5 — 343
- 10:18 — 240
- 11:9 — 240

1 Corinthians
- 15:25 — 291

Galatians
- 3:8 — 13
- 3:12 — 343

Ephesians
- 4:24 — 320

Colossians
- 3:10 — 325

1 Thessalonians
- 2:16 — 236

Qumran and Judean Desert

- CD — 141, 293, 327
- 1QM — 202
- 1QpHab — 13
- 1QS — 154, 202
- 4Q1 (4QGen–Exod^a) — 276
- 4Q11 (4QpaleoGen–Exod^l) — 276
- 4Q17 (4QExod^f) — 276
- 4Q27 (4QNum^b) — 127
- 4Q47–48 (4QJosh^{a+b}) — 141
- 4Q51 (4QSam^a) — 303
- 4Q57 (4QIsa^c) — 293
- 4Q92 (4QPs^k) — 225

4Q120 (4QpapLXXLev^b)	295–96, 298, 310	Philo	
4Q158	181	De providentia 2.64	305
4Q171	241	De specialibus legibus 2.62–63	43
4Q174	171	De vita Mosis 2.215–216	43
4Q175	141	In Flaccum 43	8
4Q252	116	Pseudo-Eupolemus	19
4Q364–367	181		
4Q378–379	141	Rabbinic Works	
4Q417	327		
4Q507–509	293	m. Menaḥ. 13:10	19
6Q15 (CD)	327	Sifre to Deut 70	19
11Q5 (11QPs^a)	241, 293	y. Sukkah 5:1, 55a–b	18
8ḤevXIIgr	295, 301		

Papyri

P 967	294
P.Amherst 63	32, 306–7, 310
P.Fouad 266	328
P.Oxy 3522	295
P.Oxy 5101	309
P.Polit. Iud. 4	45
P.Ryl Greek 458	295

Jewish Hellenistic Literature

Aristeas, Letter of	3–20, 35–36, 45, 114, 345
§9	3
§16	4, 14
§31	4, 10, 17
§37	4
§155	304
§311	17
§314–316	40
Aristobulus	11
Artapanus	4–5, 11
Josephus	
Antiquitates judaicae 7.429	172
Antiquitates judaicae 13.64–70	19
Bellum judaicum 7.426–432	19

Ancient Persons and Authors Index

Aesop	40	Rabshakeh (Rabschake)	30
Akhenaten/Echnaton	30	Solomon	29, 159
Alexander the Great	7, 33	Vergil	40, 64, 65
Aristeas	3, 14		
Aristobulus	112		
Berossus	15, 44, 100		
Callimachus. *See* Kallimachos			
Cicero	38–40, 65		
Darius I	32		
Demetrius	10, 44, 101, 112		
Demetrius of Phalerum	4, 16		
Erathostenes from Cyrene	100		
Eudoxos from Knidos	77		
Eupolemus	10, 44		
Haremhab	31		
Hieronymus. *See* Jerome			
Homer	40, 65, 111		
Herodotus	31, 44		
Hesiod	40		
Imhotep	34		
Jerome	111, 219, 294		
Kallimachos	40		
Lucian	4		
Manetho	15, 44, 100, 104		
Melitto von Sardes	37		
Onias III	19		
Onias IV	19		
Origen	294		
Plato	12, 38, 44, 45, 77, 264, 324–25		
Psammetich I	32		
Pseudo-Eupolemus	101		
Pseudo-Longinus	36		
Ptolemy I	4, 76, 172		
Ptolemy II	3, 14, 44, 99		
Ptolemy IV	101		

Modern Authors Index

Achenbach, Reinhard 180, 344
Adler, William 101
Aejmelaeus, Anneli 222, 255, 276, 278, 280–82
Aitken, James K. 282
Albani, Matthias 261, 319
Albertz, Rainer 6, 317
Albrecht, Jörn 31, 38, 319
Alexander, Philipp S. 40
Aly, Zaki 294
Amir, Yehoshua 20
Assmann, Jan 13
Auld, A. Graeme 141, 149, 182, 186, 283
Ausloos, Hans 181, 189
Austermann, Frank 48, 60, 61, 222–23, 240, 323, 331, 352–54
Baer, David A. 19
Barr, James 59, 61, 68, 111, 256, 279–80, 322–24
Barthélemy, Dominique 15, 35, 145, 152, 167, 295
Baudissin, Wolf 305
Baumgarten, Albert I. 35
Beck, John 74, 222
Becker, Uwe 182
Berger, Klaus 358
Bergmann, Jan 211
Bergmeier, Roland 343
Bertram, Georg 253–54, 259, 273–74, 322, 333
Betz, Hans Dieter 343
Bickerman, Elias 37, 38, 44–46, 100
Bieberstein, Klaus 140
Blank, Sheldon 344, 348, 351
Blasberg, Monika 34
Bonney, Gillian 284
Bomann, Thorleif 318
Bons, Eberhard 123, 284, 334
Born, A. van den 163
Bösenecker, Jobst 160, 162, 165, 167–71, 187–88
Bosse, Alfred 98
Bousset, Wilhelm 43, 256
Bratsiotis, N.P. 329
Brayford, Susan 78
Brock, Sebastian 34
Brooke, George J. 12, 241
Brown, Raymond E. 209
Brownlee, William H. 133
Brunner, Hellmut 210
Brunner-Traut, Emma 210
Burney, Charles F. 161, 166
Butler, Trent C. 146, 148, 154, 184
Carr, David 181
Cavenaile, Robert 41, 64
Cavigneaux, Antoine 33
Childs, Brevard S. 256
Cimosa, Mario 275, 284
Clancy, Frank 35, 37
Claussen, Carsten 18, 37
Clements, Ronald E. 205
Collins, John J. 16, 114, 117, 118, 130, 133
Collins, Nina L. 16, 36, 37
Conzelmann, Hans 202
Cook, Johann 67, 77, 262, 275, 276, 278, 332–33, 335, 355–57
Cordes, Ariane 354
Cowey, James M. S. 16, 45
Cox, Claude 81

Craigie, Peter C.	262	Frankel, Zacharias	19, 46, 72, 112, 113, 117, 253, 273, 321
Crenshaw, James L.	43		
Cribiore, Raffaella	40, 43, 65	Fraser, Peter M.	4, 40, 101, 210, 213
Crüsemann, Frank	344, 351	Frevel, Christian	319, 321
Dafni, Evangelia	278, 282	Freund, Richard A.	132
Dahl, Nils A.	259, 303	Frey, Jörg	19
Daniel, Suzanne	121, 152, 261, 324	Fritsch, Charles T.	80, 222, 260, 328
Daumas, François	210	Fröhlich, Ida	12
Davies, Philip R.	43	Gaebel, Peter M.	41, 42, 65
Davies, William	209	García Martínez, Florentino	116, 351
De Troyer, Kristin	183, 187	Gard, Donald H.	262, 335
Dehandschutter	205	Gatz, Bodo	211
Deissmann, Gustav A.	253, 273, 321	Gehrke, Hans-Joachim	358
Delekat, Ludwig	235	Geiger, Abraham	273, 321
Delling, Gerhard	197, 208, 209, 212	Geraty, L.T.	34
Dibelius, Martin	197, 209, 212	Gese, Hartmut	197, 216
Dietrich, Walter	167	Görg, Manfred	76, 161
Dines, Jennifer	37, 39, 41, 44, 57, 66, 277, 344	Gooding, David W.	161
		Greenspoon, Leonard	140
D'Hamonville	256, 262, 329, 332–33, 335, 355–56	Grelot, Pierre	203
		Greßmann, Hugo	210, 256
Dodd, Charles	357, 359	Gropp, Douglas M.	297
Dogniez, Cécile	259	Groß, Heinrich	211
Donner, Herbert	6–7, 10	Gross, Walter	263, 317, 325
Dorival, Gilles	35, 37, 47, 61, 73, 112, 120–28, 143, 237	Gruen, Erich S.	9, 19, 43
		Grund, Alexandra	319
Douglas, Alex	281, 283	Grundmann, Walter	197
Dupont-Roc, Roselyne	69	Guéraud, Octave	40
Dunn, James	355	Gundel, Wilhelm	211
Dus, Jan	164	Guthknecht, Gottfried	212
Ebeling, Gerhard	278–79	Gzella, Holger	113, 126, 262, 327, 332, 334
Eco, Umberto	57		
Eidsvåg, Gunnar M.	309	Haag, Herbert	7, 208
Fabry, Heinz-Josef	133, 225, 262, 283, 318, 351	Hacham, Noah	18
		Hanhart, Robert	8, 13–15, 198, 203–4, 213, 254, 258, 296, 304
Fauth, Wolfgang	210		
Fehrle, Eugen	209, 212, 214	Hanson, Anthony T.	260, 331
Fernández Marcos, Natalio	5, 17, 20, 59, 168, 181, 188, 258, 262, 322, 335	Harl, Marguerite	35, 37, 38, 69, 90, 114, 117, 143, 327, 345
Fischer, Johannes	207	Harlé, Paul	328
Fitzmyer, Joseph A.	295	Hartenstein, Friedhelm	160, 162–63, 165
Flashar, Martin	223, 225, 240, 353–54		
Flint, Peter	225	Hayward, Robert C. T.	120, 127, 172
Fögen, Thorsten	39	Hedley, P. L.	237
Franke, Peter Robert	32–34	Hegermann, Hans	9, 319

Helck, Wolfgang 30
Hendel, Ronald S. 11, 91, 96, 102, 142
Hengel, Martin 6, 18, 57, 199, 214, 255–56, 321
Hertog, Cornelis den 16, 140, 143, 149, 151, 153, 183, 185
Höffken, Peter 205
Hoffmann, Heinrich 357
Hognesius, Kjell 170
Hölbl, Günther 172
Holladay, Carl R. 19, 101
Holmes, Samuel 140
Honigman, Sylvie 3, 14–15, 17, 36, 37, 345
Horbury, William 115, 128
Hossfeld, Frank Lothar 9–10, 227, 229–32, 235
Howard, George 295
Hübner, Hans 343
Huehnergard, John 33
Hughes, Jeremy 91, 93, 96–99, 102
Hugo, Philippe 36, 189
Hurtado, Larry W. 294
Huss, Werner 16
Ilan, Tal 35
Irsigler, Hubert 164
Isserlin, Benedikt 15
Janowski, Bernd 167, 317, 319
Jellicoe, Sidney 18
Jenni, Ernst 165
Jepsen, Alfred 91, 96, 97
Jeremias, Jörg 280
Jobes, Karen 59, 78, 256–57, 282
Joosten, Jan 47, 69, 70, 114, 172, 222, 255, 257, 276–77, 306, 334
Jüngling, Hans-Winfried 355
Kahle, Paul E. 18, 40, 295, 304
Kaiser, Otto 6–7, 11, 198, 200–201, 205–6, 212
Kamesar, Adam 216
Karrer, Martin 116, 283
Kattenbusch, Ferdinand 278
Katz, Paul 292
Kasher, Aryeh 18–20
Keel, Othmar 6, 159, 163–65, 167

Keulen, Percy S. F. van 159, 161, 162, 165, 168, 189
Kilian, Rudolf 197
Kittel, Gerhard 210
Kleer, Martin 242, 256, 333
Klein, Ralph 92, 95
Klijn, A.F.J. 18
Knauf, Ernst Axel 9, 160, 165–66, 180
Knibb, Michael A. 133
Koch, Dietrich-Alex 343
Koch, Klaus 6, 8, 9, 30, 32, 96, 97, 102, 117, 130, 167, 172, 197, 317, 319, 325, 344, 351, 357
Köckert, Mathias 30
Koenen, Ludwig 172, 294
Kofoed, Jens B. 10
Köhler, Ludwig 317
Kooij, Arie van der 19, 30, 38, 40, 44, 46, 66, 67, 113, 121, 130, 131, 143, 186, 197, 199, 201, 203, 209, 222, 242, 335
Kraft, Robert A. 276, 294–95
Kramer, Johannes 41, 64
Kratz, Reinhard G. 6, 352
Kraus, Hans Joachim 229, 233, 235
Kraus, Wolfgang 265, 283, 285
Kreuzer, Siegfried 17, 36, 44, 67, 72, 102, 188
Lange, Armin 181
Lange, Nicholas de 42
Larsson, Gerhard 102
Law, Timothy 277
Le Boulluec, Alan 346
Le Deaut, Roger 80
Lee, James A.L. 44
Lee, John A. 277
Leipoldt, Johannes 39
Levin, Christoph 10
Lichtenberger, Hermann 344, 357
Limbeck, Meinrad 351
Loader, William 326
Lohfink, Norbert 180, 182, 188
Loretz, Oswald 166
Louw, Theo A. W. van der 80
Lust, Johan 109, 117, 118, 125, 128, 130, 132, 297–98

Luz, Ulrich	215	Orth, Wolfgang	15–16, 36, 44
Lys, Daniel	329	Ottley, Richard R.	200
Macchi, Jean-Daniel	114	Parry, Donald W.	293, 303
MacDonough, Sean M.	290, 296, 298	Perkins, Larry	279, 280, 282
MacLeod, Roy	40	Person, Raymond F.	179
Maehler, Herwig	43	Peterca, Vladimir	161
Maier, Johann	243	Petkov, Julian	104
Marcus, David	293	Pettazoni, Raffaele	211
Maresch, Klaus	16	Pfeiffer, Rudolf	40
Margolis, Max L.	139, 140	Pietersma, Albert	5, 41–43, 47, 64–66, 110, 111, 114, 222, 226–27, 232, 238–39, 241–25, 263, 275, 279–80, 296, 310, 323, 329
Martin, Dale B.	284		
Martin, Geoffrey T.	31		
Mazor, Lea	140, 141, 145, 184		
McLay, Timothy	279, 282–83	Pietsch, Michael	168, 170, 189
Meer, Michael van der	182, 186	Pilhofer, Peter	12
Meiser, Martin	285	Pisano, Stephen	189
Mekawi Ouda, Nasser	31	Pralon, Didier	329
Merkelbach, Reinhold	211	Prijs, Leo	112, 117, 354
Meyer, Rudolf	8	Pury, Albert de	179, 182
Moatti-Fine, Jaqueline	140, 144, 147–51	Quack, Joachim Friedrich	31
Modrzejewski, Joseph Mélèze	16, 18, 37, 45	Quast, Udo	255
		Rabin, Chaim	37, 38, 44
Momigliano, Arnaldo	37	Rahlfs, Alfred	230, 238, 244, 294–96
Monsengwo Pasinya, Laurent	60, 117, 118, 344, 346–51	Reade, Julian	33
		Rehm, Martin	166, 168, 170
Morenz, Siegfried	76, 213	Reiss, Wolfgang	259
Mozley, Francis W.	232	Ringe, Sharon	104
Müller, Mogens	57, 255, 274, 283, 321	Ringgren, Helmer	202
Munnich, Olivier	35, 37, 102, 143	Rocati, Alessandro	31
Murtonen, A.	96	Rofé, Alexander	142, 147, 148, 150, 151, 185, 187
Mussies, Gerard	35		
Nachtergael, Georges	40	Römer, Thomas	179, 182
Naoumides, Mark	39	Rösel, Hartmut N.	150, 188
Nickelsburg, George W.	357	Rost, Leonhard	15
Nida, Eugene	319	Roth, Cecil	7
Niehr, Herbert	13	Rowley, Harold H.	214
Niemann, Hermann M.	146	Royse, James R.	304
Nilsson, Martin P.	210	Rüsen-Weinhold, Ulrich	242
Noort, Edward	141	Sacchi, Paolo	7
Norden, Eduard	209–11	Safrai, Shmuel	43
Northcote, Jeremy	89, 99	Sandevoir, Pierre	346
Noth, Martin	166, 179, 184, 188	Sasse, Markus	7
Olofsson, Staffan	70, 80, 222, 235, 245, 260, 261, 331, 352–53	Schaper, Joachim	65, 126, 128, 132, 222, 236, 240 242–43, 255, 261, 273, 323, 335
Orlinski, Harry M.	141		

Scharbert, Josef	328	Soffer, Arthur	222, 224, 260, 331
Schearing, Linda	181	Sollamo, Raija	10, 15, 17, 74, 296
Schenkel, Wolfgang	31	Sonntag, Holger	351
Schenker, Adrian	36, 68–69, 159, 162–63, 168, 171, 173, 186, 261, 322	Staubli, Thomas	317
		Steck, Odil Hannes	180
Schipper, Bernd U.	30	Stegemann, Hartmut	293, 295, 304
Schmid, Konrad	182, 278, 279, 284	Sterling, Gregory E.	9
Schmidt, Werner	17	Stern, Menahem	16
Schmidt, Werner H.	179, 317, 327	Steudel, Annette	115, 133
Schmitt, Armin	76	Steyn, Gert	277
Schmitt, Hans-Christoph	118	Stipp, Hermann-Josef	190
Schmitz, Barbara	279	Stolz, Fritz	160
Schniedewind, William M.	171	Stolze, Radegundis	319
Schnocks, Johannes	335	Stricker, Bruno H.	15
Schoeps, Hans-Joachim	274	Swete, Henry B.	3
Schroer, Silvia	317	Tauberschmidt, Gerhard	75
Schwienhorst, Ludger	180, 182	Tate, Marvin A.	229, 232
Schüle, Andreas	132, 134	Taylor, J. Glen	167
Schulz, Siegfried	295	Tcherikover, Victor	11, 14
Schürer, Emil	13, 19, 256	Thackeray, Henry, St. J.	37, 164, 171
Schunck, Klaus	30	Thiel, Winfried	179, 180
Schwartz, Daniel R.	8	Thompson, Thomas	10
Schwemer, Anna M.	358	Thümmel, Hans Georg	329
Schwiderski, Dirk	30, 33	Tilly, Michael	45, 345
Segal, Alan F.	259, 303, 358	Tov, Emanuel	17, 40, 59, 61, 70, 71, 74, 77, 140, 142–44, 150, 163, 168, 181–84, 186, 190, 198, 274, 280–81, 293, 295–96, 299, 308
Seebass, Horst	117, 120, 121, 125, 318		
Seele, Astrid	39, 111		
Seeligmann, Isaac Leo	197–99, 203–4, 208, 210, 213, 254, 273, 322		
		Trebolle Barrera, Julio	173
Seiler, Stefan	244, 262	Trobisch, David	296
Seminara, Stefano	34	Turkanik, Andrzej	189
Seybold, Klaus	227, 229–31	Uehlinger, Christoph	6
Shaw, Frank E.	297–98, 304–10	Ulrich, Eugene	141, 281
Shenkel, James D.	102	Ulshöfer, Andrea M.	32, 33
Siegert, Folker	36, 59, 68, 70, 109, 260, 279, 320, 322, 328, 329, 344, 350–51, 353, 356	Usener, Knut	43
		Utzschneider, Helmut	265, 323
		VanderKam, James C.	80, 258
Silva, Moises	59, 78, 256–57, 282	Veldhuis, Niek	33, 34
Sipilä, Seppo	140	Veltri, Guiseppe	38
Sjöberg, Åke	34	Vermès, Géza	110, 128, 133
Skehan, Patrick W.	295, 297	Visser, A. J.	224
Skinner, John	98	Vries, Simon J. de	92, 95, 102
Smend, Rudolf	179, 186	Waddel, W.G.	294
Smith, Jannes	309	Wade, Martha L.	62, 113
Smith, Morton	9	Wagner, Andreas	317

Walter, Nikolaus   7, 11, 14, 19, 45, 101, 253, 304, 322
Weber, Reinhard   344, 354, 356, 359
Weinfeld, Moshe   180
Weinreich, Otto   210
Weiss, Hans-Friedrich   8, 20
Wellhausen, Julius   159, 163, 166
Werner, J.   34
Westermann, Claus   30, 93
Wevers, John W.   57, 64, 78, 79, 91, 93, 114, 121–25, 128, 131, 149, 222, 254, 299, 301, 302-3, 309, 328, 345–46, 348, 350
Wildberger, Hans   197, 198, 200–201, 205–6, 208, 213
Willi-Plein, Ina   9
Wischmeyer, Oda   321
Wolff, Hans Walter   317
Wright, Benjamin   3, 4–5, 18, 38, 39, 65
Würthwein, Ernst   145, 161, 184
Zauzich, Karl-Theodor   307
Zenger, Erich   9–10, 227, 229–32, 235
Zepf, Max   210
Ziegert, Carsten   282
Ziegler, Joseph   197, 199–200, 273–74
Ziemer, Benjamin   97, 98
Zimmermann, Johannes   133

www.ingramcontent.com/pod-product-compliance
Lightning Source LLC
Chambersburg PA
CBHW021930290426

44108CB00012B/786